W9-DDI-361

Advance Praise for *The Hand and the Road*

"A marvelous tribute to a great Church leader by his grandson. This long-awaited biography of John A. Mackay—missionary, evangelist, ecumenical statesman, and theological educator— speaks eloquently to the present issues of the Church. Current polarities are challenged by Mackay's vision of such dialectical realities as 'dynamic centrality,' 'evangelical catholicity,' 'personal religion,' 'Christo-centrism,' and the 'Balcony and the Road.' A must-read for all who care about the mission of the Church in the twenty-first century."
—Thomas G. Gillespie, President and Professor of New Testament
Emeritus, Princeton Theological Seminary

"The life, mission, and message of the great educationalist John Alexander Mackay should be known by all new generations of Christians: Protestant, Evangelical, Pentecostal, Independent, and Roman Catholic, not only in Latin America but worldwide. The task undertaken by John Mackay Metzger, the fruit of which is seen in this biography, is worthy of the highest praise. The spirituality of the theologian of mission and statesman of the Kingdom is clearly set out as the firm foundation for his intellectual, missionary, and teaching achievements, always within an incarnational framework. We owe the author a debt of gratitude for providing us with this biographical account, so radically Christ-centered and inspiring, of one who forged an ecumenism that was biblical, evangelical, and challenging."
—Pedro Arana-Quiroz, Presbyterian Minister and Former Executive
Director of the Peruvian Bible Society

"Known in the North Atlantic as a seminary president and a leader of the modern ecumenical movement, from first to last John A. Mackay was a missionary to cultures. John Metzger presents a carefully researched and engaging study of an important ecumenical scholar that will initiate fresh discussions about missionary engagement for the twenty-first century."
—Scott W. Sunquist, Professor of World Christianity,
Pittsburgh Theological Seminary, coauthor with Dale T. Irvin,
History of the World Christian Movement

"*The Hand and the Road* is a meticulous and lovingly produced work of scholarship about the life and thought of a major twentieth-century Christian public intellectual, whose witness and example are very much worth recalling as Christians face the challenges of a new era."
—Robert P. George, McCormick Professor of Jurisprudence
and Director of the James Madison Program in American
Ideals and Institutions, Princeton University

The Hand and the Road

For Dan,

    With best wishes,

       John

2-23-10

The Hand and the Road

The Life and Times of John A. Mackay

JOHN MACKAY METZGER

WESTMINSTER
JOHN KNOX PRESS
LOUISVILLE · KENTUCKY

© 2010 John Mackay Metzger

First edition
Published by Westminster John Knox Press
Louisville, Kentucky

10 11 12 13 14 15 16 17 18 19—10 9 8 7 6 5 4 3 2 1

Book design by Sharon Adams
Cover design by Lisa Buckley
Cover photo: John Alexander Mackay, 1936

Library of Congress Cataloging-in-Publication Data

Metzger, John Mackay.
   The hand and the road : the life and times of John A. Mackay / John Mackay Metzger.
      p. cm.
   Includes index.
   ISBN 978-0-664-23524-6 (alk. paper)
   1. Mackay, John Alexander, 1889–1983.   2. Christian biography.   3. Princeton Theological Seminary—Biography.   4. Theological seminary presidents—New Jersey—Biography.   I. Title.
   BR1725.M24M48 2009
   230'.5092——dc22
   [B]
                                                                                          2009011997

PRINTED IN THE UNITED STATES OF AMERICA

∞ The paper used in this publication meets the minimum requirements
of the American National Standard for Information Sciences—Permanence
of Paper for Printed Library Materials, ANSI Z39.48-1992.

Westminster John Knox Press advocates the responsible use of our natural resources.
The text paper of this book is made from 30% post-consumer waste.

Contents

Sources and Acknowledgments

*J*ohn A. Mackay was a prolific writer, and two bibliographies are helpful starting points for Mackay research. One is *John Mackay: Bibliographical Resources for the Period 1914–1992*, by Stanton R. Wilson in collaboration with William O. Harris (*Studies in Reformed Theology and History*, vol. 1, no. 4 [Fall 1993], 1–58). Samuel Escobar's *Protestantismo en el Peru Guía Bibliográfica y de Fuentes* (Lima, Peru: Sociedad Biblica Peruana, 2001) contains additional Spanish writings and references. The present volume also takes into account published and unpublished materials that are not listed in these resources.

The John A. Mackay Collection at Princeton Theological Seminary (Mackay Collection) is located at the Princeton Seminary Library. To conserve space and because changes may occur when the collection has been fully processed, detailed references to the location of letters and other materials from this collection have been eliminated. Mackay carefully retained copies of memoranda and correspondence sent to others; therefore references to letters from Mackay are generally references to copies of those items, not the originals. Personal materials, documents, and family letters (Mackay Archives) preserved by Mackay's daughter, Isobel Mackay Metzger, have also been useful in the preparation of this volume. Unless otherwise specified, unpublished materials as well as Latin American material cited herein are found in these private collections. Documents released to the author by the U.S. Department of Justice, Federal Bureau of Investigation, under a Freedom of Information Act request, are also cited.

The first letter of the words *Church* and *Order* are sometimes capitalized to denote particular theological meaning.

This volume would not have been completed in its present form without the aid of certain persons. To them I offer my sincere thanks and gratitude for their kindnesses. First, Dr. Raúl Alessandri, a relative of the former president of Chile Arturo Alessandri, skillfully made translations of Mackay's Spanish essays, several Spanish newspaper articles, and two essays by Luis Alberto Sánchez. His friendship, understanding, and kindness in sharing his knowledge of Latin American affairs were invaluable.

Representatives of the Free Church of Scotland, in Edinburgh, particularly Dr. William M. Mackay, the fourth headmaster of Colegio San Andrés, provided me copies of several reports of the General Assembly of the Free Church of Scotland.

During a trip to Lima, Peru, the Rev. Pedro Araña Quiroz of the Peruvian Bible Society kindly guided me around the city and helped me to begin to understand that country. He introduced me to José Belaúnde, the son of Mackay's friend Víctor Andrés Belaúnde, and historian Jeffrey Klaiber, SJ, who answered questions about the religious and cultural life of Peru. Mr. Donald John Macaulay, the director general of the Colegio San Andrés at that time, guided me through the school and introduced me to the educational system of Peru.

Princeton Seminary Library archivists William O. Harris, Robert Benedetto, and Kenneth Henke provided encouragement, many helpful conversations, insights, and research aid in the course of the project. The staff of the Presbyterian Historical Society in Philadelphia helped me in locating letters and articles in these archives.

Helpful and enjoyable discussions on a wide range of topics with Dr. Samuel H. Moffett and Eileen Moffett contributed to my understanding of the missionary enterprise. Their friendship and dedicated spirit are an inspiration. Professor Scott Sunquist provided helpful encouragement and advice. Dr. David Taylor read through an early draft of the whole manuscript and offered encouragement.

Others also provided memories of Mackay or thoughts about Christian missionary work. Thanks are due to Dr. Daniel Migliore, the late Richard Schaull, the Rev. Ben Sheldon, the Rev. David B. Watermulder, Dr. Samuel Escobar, Dr. Charles West, and Dr. Ruth West. Correspondence with Sir John Templeton and Avery Cardinal Dulles, S.J., added helpful details.

The encouragement of family members was a crucial element in the creation of this work. In particular my uncle, the Rev. Robert M. Russell III, prompted my attention and interest to launch the project, and he provided thoughts and comments along the way, always with his characteristic good humor and warmth. Mackay's children, Duncan A. D. Mackay, Elena Mackay Reisner, and Ruth Mackay Russell, contributed memories of their lives with their father. Mackay's niece, Irene Mackay, of London, England, supplied useful insights about Scotland. Mackay's grandson Norman Mackay and granddaughter Ruth R. Brock furnished references to articles, and grandson Dr. Timothy Russell offered his memories of J. A. Mackay.

Above all, the work could not have been accomplished without the consistent, patient love and penetrating wisdom and understanding of my parents, Bruce M. Metzger, now deceased, and Isobel Mackay Metzger, the Mackays' eldest daughter. Their faithful Christian service over many decades is an example and inspiration to many generations of students at Princeton Theological Seminary and to Christians around the world. My mother, Isobel Mackay Metzger, has been an invaluable source of spiritual insights and memories from even her early childhood in Peru. I owe the greatest debt to my wife, Sandra Kay Metzger, whose love and kindness are a great blessing to me. Without her patience, unselfish love, and encouragement this work would not have been completed. It is to her that this book is dedicated.

Introduction

One October day I walked into the back door of Speer Library to begin work on a biography of John A. Mackay. As I quickly discovered, the task was substantially larger than I had anticipated. Although I had been close to my grandfather, visiting him often in my boyhood until he left Princeton, New Jersey, in 1959 and later after he settled in Hightstown, near Princeton, in 1967, I had no idea of the scope and adventure of his life and contribution to the Christian Church. He was not one to reminisce and look backward; there was too much to accomplish in the present moment.

As my project progressed, I read his books, articles, editorials, letters, and addresses as well as some writings of his coworkers. His versatility was striking, and he accomplished a great deal in a great many areas of life. As a promoter, he was astute and persuasive; as an institutional founder, bold and inspiring; as an administrator, decisive; as a platform speaker, articulate and charismatic; as a meeting chairman or discussion leader, fair and encouraging; as an author, lucid and poetic; as a theologian, orthodox but creative; as a philosopher, practical and understandable; as a father, loving; as a pastor, discerning and interested; as a companion, friendly and *simpático*; as a personality, passionate and kind. But above all, as a Christian witness and evangelist he was strong, effective, and faithful.

Following his conversion experience at Rogart and his education in Inverness, Aberdeen, Princeton, and Madrid, Mackay at age twenty-seven began his early career as a missionary educator in Latin America. He was well prepared to enter, identify with, and relate himself to Hispanic culture. In Scotland before departing for Peru, he was compared to the nineteenth-century Scottish missionary educator Alexander Duff of India. Like Duff, Mackay believed education was a modality of mission, and his philosophy of education was biblical: train up a child in the way he should go, and when he is old he will not depart from it. During a period of educational reform in

Latin America, Mackay's philosophy of secondary education planted fruitful seeds in Peruvian culture. The school that Mackay founded contributed
new directions at a time of great change, and his addresses at San Marcos
University and cities in Peru challenged the religious and ethical assumptions
prevailing in the culture.

When the work of the school had been institutionalized, and it was strong
enough to continue without him, Mackay joined the YMCA as a continental
evangelist in Montevideo, Uruguay. In this role he taught, traveled, and gave
public addresses in Spanish in many Latin American cities and towns. Mackay understood the seriousness of the Christian message and studied how to
present it clearly to those who either did not know it or who had a distorted
understanding of it. As part of the task he wrote evangelical and evangelistic
literature in Spanish for publication.

During a journey to the Conference in Jerusalem in 1928 and a furlough trip
to Europe in 1930, Mackay and others met together and thought deeply about
the most effective way to deliver the Christian message in a changing world.
Ideas and religions from the East and West were coming into contact with each
other. To present the Christian message in its uniqueness became an urgent
task. At this time Mackay also began to understand that his role as an evangelist could be carried out more effectively within the Church. He accepted
an offer to join the Presbyterian Board of Foreign Missions, where he worked
directly with Robert E. Speer. As mission board administrators Mackay and
Speer agreed that the role of the missionary movement was to establish church
congregations through individual conversions. The missionary movement provided the scaffolding for the later indigenization of missions.

Twenty years after founding the school in Lima, Mackay faced another
challenging educational task when he assumed the presidency of Princeton
Theological Seminary. He steadily reorganized the institution, which had been
split by the secession of faculty members in a theological controversy, and
began to heal the wounds from the modernist/fundamentalist debate by shifting the emphasis of theological studies. The reorganized institution challenged
the prevailing empiricism and secularism of American culture and displayed
within American culture the practice of a functioning Christian institution. He
believed that Princeton Seminary should be a community and that the ministers it produced should not doubt their task or lack confidence in it.

Mackay's primary legacy will likely be understood as his effort to build
a world Christian movement. In this his missionary efforts were comparable
to those of John R. Mott and his ecclesiastical efforts to those of William
Temple of England. Mackay sought answers to several practical questions
about the Church: How does a denomination relate itself to other churches in

mission when they are all equal? More profoundly, what is the place of the Church in relation to God and God's will? For Mackay ecumenism meant authentic Christian spiritual unity as well as institutional unity. Missionaries had paved the way for the ecumenical church era when a global Christian consciousness and spirituality could emerge. Later Christian church members became witnesses to the world as they worked together across denominational or national boundaries.

In his book *Ecumenics* Mackay referred to the needed theological approach as "dynamic centrality." The term itself is not as evocative as some of Mackay's other metaphors. Describing the phrase he wrote, "It is not a compromise between two extreme positions, to Right and Left. It is devotion to a reality called the Gospel, the center and core of the Christian faith, which is inseparably related to the living Lord Jesus Christ."[1] Mackay's skill in implementing this approach and his creativity as a theologian are manifested in the way he selected theological points of concentration and emphasis and in how he used them over many years to maintain a dynamic centrism: to keep the fellowship on the road and not to allow it to fall off the way into the ditch. Often this involved taking the difficult or hard path. The genius of Mackay's leadership was how dynamic centralism manifested itself in countless concrete situations and the way he discerned the center at any given historical moment as he balanced what he called "the changing and the changeless." Mackay was aware of both the personal and collective goal of following the road of life to Christ himself.

Conferences were the building blocks of world Christianity during much of the twentieth century, and Mackay's philosophy and theology developed on a practical basis as he both guided developments and reacted to new situations faced by and in conferences and councils. Some of his important ideas and insights developed when he was called on to perform administrative work, to organize conferences, to give keynote addresses, to visit mission churches, or to exhort lay and clerical leaders. Accordingly, a large part of Mackay's written theology was created in response to specific historical situations, challenges, or opportunities within the Church and first appeared in the form of addresses and essays. To appreciate fully his work and thought, one must trace his activities and objectives and examine the context of essays or editorials in relation to the spiritual task faced at the particular moment. While performing his work, Mackay was guided by spiritual insights through prayer and interactions with fellow Christians, both laypeople and clergy. Thus, his prolific writings represent the theology of a shepherd: creative yet orthodox and functional, grounded in the Bible and the practice of Christianity. His theology was not developed as an abstract academic exercise.

Mackay developed and held a high and balanced doctrine of the Church and its worshiping, prophetic, redemptive, and unitive functions under the purposes of God. At the level of institutional ecumenism Mackay played an active role in the formation of the World Council of Churches, making a key address at its First World Council Assembly at Amsterdam. As chairman of the International Missionary Council, he advocated that mission should be at the heart of the church universal. At the same time, his role in the World Alliance of Reformed Churches and the Presbyterian Board of Foreign Missions reinforced these efforts by grounding the ecumenical movement in a confessional, denominational framework. Mackay could write that Presbyterianism was "ecumenical in a double sense . . . *naturally* and *natively ecumenical* . . . not to be an end in itself, but to serve the church universal," and also it is *"ecumenical in its world outreach and dimensions."*[2] Paradoxically, he felt both more Presbyterian in appreciation of the heritage and less Presbyterian because its "highest glory . . . consists in having a vision of the Church Universal, and in contributing our part to its visible unity upon earth."[3]

One of Mackay's evangelistic and ecumenical goals was "evangelical catholicity," a term he carefully defined as "that form of Christian universality which is centered in the Gospel, which proclaims Jesus Christ as the World Saviour, and which is ready to welcome as fellow Christians all those who give their whole-hearted allegiance to Christ and whose lives bear the marks of the spirit of Christ."[4] As evidence of the fruit of his efforts and the efforts of others, by the end of Mackay's life denominational boundaries were being transcended by personal spiritual relationships between and among laypeople and some clergy of diverse Christian traditions who associated with one another in a common faith in the same Lord and Master.

At the level of spiritual and institutional ecumenism Mackay's vision was to build the Church and lead members to conscious spiritual unity, a bottom-up process. For Mackay the Church was a spiritual body, a functional spiritual organism, God's instrument in the world. Theology was a tool to serve the Lord and his Church. Conscious of the delicacy of spiritual relationships, Mackay was reflective about actions he took as a Church leader, evaluating their potential ramifications, cautious in taking steps that would be counterproductive to goals he discerned, and aware that a leader must be representative as well as prophetic.

As a public intellectual working in the media of public thought, essays, and addresses, Mackay led a debate in both North and South America about the meaning of true religious liberty. He vigorously championed personal religion in Latin America that allowed parallel development of institutional Roman Catholicism and Protestant Christianity. He understood his Latin

American mission as a spiritual contest. In North America Mackay studied the different interpretations of the principle of religious liberty and strongly resisted Roman Catholic efforts to advance controversial social policy in the United States. His efforts and those of others ultimately culminated with new understandings of the Church. Pope Paul VI pressed for a vote on September 21, 1965, and the Declaration of Religious Liberty was overwhelmingly adopted by the Second Vatican Council. The principle of religious establishment passed away, giving way to the sixteenth-century Reformation idea of the conscientious liberty of the Christian individual.

A German scholar of the biblical text once wrote, "Apply yourself totally to the text; apply the text totally to yourself."[5] From his earliest years Mackay studied and meditated on the books of the Bible as the source of revelation of spiritual truth. The authority of his later preaching was rooted in his dedicated application of scriptural truth in his personal life: he practiced what he preached. Since Christianity is "caught as well as taught," Mackay never underestimated the power of a single Christian spiritual life as an example for others to emulate. Mackay's devotional diary shows that as a youth he asked God in prayer for spiritual gifts. Those gifts were granted to him, and Mackay used them for the benefit and the upbuilding of the Church. By putting biblical principles first, he also enjoyed a happy and stable family life. God granted him a dedicated wife and companion who aided him in his vocation and was a Christian leader herself. All three of Mackay's daughters married Presbyterian ministers, and his son served as a Presbyterian elder.

Mackay was an orthodox, biblical Christian deeply interested in social welfare and development, and his theological approach defies glib labels and does not fit the categories that some historians have used. The term *neo-orthodox* does not apply to Mackay because that movement was primarily an intellectual movement rather than a spiritual and intellectual one. Similarly, while Mackay was eminently practical and realistic, he was not a part of the movement called "Christian realism." He had the humility and wisdom to realize the unintended consequences of purposive social action. Following the wisdom of his friend William Temple, he realized the delicacy of advocating particular social programs as a risk to the unity of God's people in the Church. In accordance with the dominical precepts in Mark 12:29–31, Mackay followed the two great commandments together in the priority that Jesus endorsed: Love God with all your heart, soul, mind, and strength, and, second, love your neighbor as yourself. When steadfast commitment to God is present, it overflows, enabling the church to serve its neighbors as it ought.

As a Princeton Seminary student Mackay preached a sermon on the verse "My times are in thy hand" (Ps. 31:15). The verse had struck him deeply and personally. He was a Christian, not a "Christophile" or a "Christian idealist," and one of his books later articulated the difference between Christian appearance and reality. In retirement years Mackay intended to write his memoirs with the title *The Hand and the Road*, a title appropriate on both a spiritual and literal level. His travels were an integral part of his work and accomplishments that required unusual strength and energy, and his addresses to Christians around the world were designed to develop a consciousness of the global, spiritual, transnational Church. Mackay's evangelistic efforts, and those of others, built up the Church spiritually and materially in many regions of the world. Accordingly, an attempt has been made to document Mackay's travels in some detail.

This study falls into three segments. The first segment, chapters 1, 2, 3, and 4, presents the spiritual formation and the educational, social, and psychological preparation and development of a man destined to become an influential leader in the Church. Chapter 1 deals with his home, boyhood, and secondary schooling, a time during which Mackay's calling and conversion experience occurred, an experience that motivated his entire life and work. Chapters 2 and 3 treat Mackay's higher education at the University of Aberdeen and Princeton Theological Seminary, respectively. Chapter 4 recounts his first journey to Latin America, where he made numerous contacts, and his final training in Madrid, Spain.

The second segment, chapters 5, 6, 7, 8, and 9, focuses on Mackay's career as a missionary. In chapter 5 he establishes a mission and founds a mission school in Lima, Peru, on behalf of the Free Church of Scotland. He earns an academic degree and gains respect as a member of the educational reform movement. In chapter 6 Mackay begins his affiliation with the YMCA, nurtures the mission school to the point where it could continue without his leadership, and is appointed to the chair of metaphysics at San Marcos University. In chapter 7, called to a broader work, Mackay relocates his family to Montevideo, Uruguay, and embarks on a mission as a continental evangelist under the auspices of the YMCA, making his first trip to Brazil. In chapter 8 the travels continue. First, Mackay journeys to Jerusalem for the meeting of the International Missionary Council, where Latin America is recognized as a mission field. After his return and further work in Latin America, he and his family next travel to Europe on furlough where he becomes acquainted with Karl Barth in Bonn and studies with him. After the furlough the family returns to North America, this time based in Mexico City. In chapter 9 Mackay's continued reflection on the Church leads him to accept an invitation from Robert E. Speer to join the Presbyterian Board of Foreign Missions as a secretary based in New York. He chose to evangelize under the auspices of the Church rather than outside it.

The third segment, chapters 10, 11, 12, and 13, presents Mackay's work in North America and beyond. Chapter 10 describes Mackay's presidency at Princeton Theological Seminary during the economic Depression and after the secession of several professors. In those twenty-three years he taught, wrote, and lectured; reorganized the faculty; revitalized the academic program; and expanded the physical plant of the institution. Chapter 11 deals primarily with the social and political dimensions of his theological activities and his increasing focus on the nature and vocation of the ecumenical Church as he worked within the Federal Council of Churches and its successor, the National Council of Churches. As a public intellectual Mackay helped brace the culture and the Church during the crisis of World War II, advocated the principle of religious liberty, and supported a model of the Church free of clerical dominance. As the author of *Letter to Presbyterians*, he and the Presbyterian Church stood firmly against fierce onslaughts of McCarthyism.

Chapter 12 deals primarily with spiritual and evangelistic dimensions of Mackay's theological efforts in the Presbyterian Board of Foreign Missions, the International Missionary Council, the World Council of Churches, and the World Alliance of Reformed Churches. His leadership in these groups advanced both spiritual and institutional ecumenism. Travels for these institutions took him to Asia and Africa as well as to Europe and Latin America. Finally, chapter 13 describes Mackay's retirement years and considers his final writings, travels, thoughts, and reflections as he observed and challenged the radical changes within the churches and the culture beginning during the turbulent 1960s. Excerpts of Mackay's writings are included throughout to allow the reader to hear Mackay speak with his own voice.

The story of the Christian movement of Mackay's time is the story of a collective effort. Accordingly, this volume also pays tribute to many men and women who worked with him to preserve, interpret, and transmit the true faith and to bring about the spiritual and institutional unity of the Christian Church. They bequeathed to the next generation a clear and vital understanding of Christ's gifts that are given and available to all people. Scholars have noted the important spiritual revival in Latin America at the end of the twentieth century, but years of sowing and ploughing in earlier decades helped bring it about. The men and women that worked with the Mackays in the Protestant evangelization of South America included Gonzalo Báez-Camargo, Webster Browning, Charles Ewald, Samuel Guy Inman, J. H. Maclean, W. Stanley Rycroft, Anne Soper, Robert E. Speer, and many others. The ecumenical movement was also a collective effort, including such men as Samuel Cavert, Walter Freytag, Norman Goodall, Hendrik Kraemer, Rajah Manikam, Pit Van Dusen, W. A. Visser 't Hooft, Max Warren, Luther A. Weigle, and many,

many others. The history of Mackay's times is the context for these movements, showing how their work has been a catalyst for social change, human growth, and improvement in countries that had been socially stagnant.

To claim, as some who write from a humanistic background do, that the missionary movement was "conflated with colonialism" or that missionaries "sublimated their imperialist motives" is to create misleading and false generalizations. Broadly imputing psychological states subverts factual historical accounts. Moreover, the financial and spiritual benefits of the missionary movement and of European economic colonialism flowed in opposite directions to and from the developing world. A study of Free Church missions that were carried on through private, nongovernmental support clearly illustrates this fact. Though it may have coincided chronologically with colonialism, the missionary movement was a discrete, spiritually motivated venture embodying self-sacrifice and self-denial with risks of cholera, typhoid, tuberculosis, and malaria that sometimes resulted in premature death. Missionaries gave literal meaning to the expression "spending your life."

Mackay lived a full life between two worlds, the spiritual and the material. What is unusual for a man of thought and prayer was that his external actions and activities were as significant in their impact as his inner life and thoughts. This introduction to Mackay's life, work, and thought makes no pretense to finality or complete coverage of its subject. As a study of effective Christian leadership, it is an attempt to remember and document a significant human life, to evaluate and describe a career, to suggest principles of successful Christian leadership, and to show the effect of the man on those who knew him and on the world in which he lived. It is hoped that this introductory work may stimulate further study by others and document the contours of a life worthy of emulation.

Chapter 1

Boyhood (1889–1907)

"Enter ye in at the strait gate." (Matt. 7:13 KJV)

"*N*ation Greets Mission Societies" trumpeted the *New York Times* in a front-page headline on Sunday, April 22, 1900. The next day, under the front-page headline "Missions of the World in Review," the paper carried the schedule of speakers for that day at the conference, and page 2 printed abstracts of addresses by some of the missionary speakers.

The occasion that caused this excitement was the Ecumenical Conference on Foreign Missions held in New York from April 21 to May 1, 1900. It was organized and intended as the direct successor to earlier mission conferences held in London in 1888 and in 1878. Two thousand U.S. delegates and four hundred delegates from abroad were expected to attend the New York conference. In the prior January the president of Columbia University, Seth Low, had presided at a meeting to organize the scope of the conference.

National political leaders attended and participated in the gathering at New York. Former president of the United States Benjamin Harrison presided over the body itself and delivered a prepared address on Saturday afternoon emphasizing the importance of the conference. On Saturday evening, the incumbent president, William McKinley, and a future president, Theodore Roosevelt, governor of New York, welcomed the missionary group at Carnegie Hall. President McKinley was welcomed with a long-standing ovation when he gave the opening address. Governor Roosevelt followed, welcoming the delegates with "heartiest admiration and good will."[1] Next, General Harrison, the presiding officer of the conference, welcomed the group. By any standard, the conference began with an extraordinary start!

President and Mrs. McKinley had arrived at the Hotel Manhattan by carriage, passing over the Hudson River by ferry at midday Saturday. Groups of bystanders doffed their hats to the president along the way, and he responded in kind, to the delight of those watching the procession. An unsettling incident occurred on Saturday afternoon as the president was returning to the hotel:

1

"One of the horses slipped just as the carriage drew up near the entrance and fell, while the other horse reared and plunged so that the driver was nearly flung from his seat, and the President stood up in some alarm. A policeman caught the plunging horse by the bridle and the other immediately jumped to his feet."[2] The excitement soon passed, and the president gave the opening address of the conference that evening. The next morning President McKinley attended Sunday services at Brick Presbyterian Church, where he heard a talk by the Rev. J. H. Laughlin of Ching Chow, China, on missionary work in China. Meanwhile, at Madison Avenue Presbyterian Church, seven speakers presented the general view of the state of Christianity in South America.[3]

The conference got under way in earnest on Monday at Carnegie Hall, where speakers addressed the purpose and authority of missions. The Reverend Augustus H. Strong, president of the Rochester Theological Seminary and a Baptist, delivered a rousing speech developing the idea that both the authority and purpose of missions was Christ himself. Next, J. Hudson Taylor, founder of the China Inland Mission, spoke on God as the source of the power in foreign missions and gave examples of answered prayer for missionaries and financial resources: "The church is not a number of isolated organizations, but an organized body. The Church as a whole must recognize its responsibility to go forward."[4]

Finally that morning a Princeton University graduate, Robert E. Speer, a layman in his early thirties originally from Pennsylvania, took the platform to speak on the "Supreme and Determining Aim." The aim of missions is not social reorganization, he said

> [and] we must not confuse the aim of missions with the methods of missions.
>
> Our work is not a philanthropic, political, secular movement. I would rather plant one seed of the life of Christ beneath the crust of the heathen life than cover the whole crust over with the social influences of Western civilization.
>
> The aim of foreign missions is to make Jesus Christ known to the world with a view to the salvation of men. . . . This supreme and determining aim must rule our methods by an iron hand.[5]

To generate enthusiasm for its goals, Speer articulated the objective of the conference that gathered in New York. It was not a secular, socializing movement but rather a spiritual movement whose goal was to bring spiritual light to the hearts, minds, and souls of people who had not yet received it. That selfless goal characterized a generation of men and women who could have gained success in virtually any walk of life.

Later in the week two other important speakers took the platform at Carnegie Hall to present addresses: John R. Mott, general secretary of the World's Student Christian Federation, New York; and the Reverend J. Ross Stevenson, vice-chairman of the executive committee of the Student Volunteer Movement, U.S.A., Chicago.[6] Benjamin Harrison noted that the missionary conference maintained its intensity and enthusiasm for a longer time than any political convention that he had ever known or experienced.[7]

Scotland

Far from the busy city of New York and thousands of miles to the northeast across the Atlantic Ocean, spring was arriving in Scotland, the home of John A. Mackay. Mackay, the eldest of five children, was born on May 17, 1889, in a house on Hill Street in the ancient city of Inverness, the capital of northern Scotland. Both Mackay's mother and father were "Macs," of Celtic ancestry. Duncan, John's father, had come to Inverness from a place called Kishorn, Loch Carron, in western Ross, Scotland, where he had been raised using the Gaelic language. He had come to settle in Inverness, a place of opportunity where he worked hard to establish a business as "Tailor & Outfitter" at 52 High Street. In time the business prospered and became fashionable—a kind of Brooks Brothers—and Duncan's success as a merchant could be measured by his employment of fourteen tailors in the enterprise.

Duncan and his wife, Isabella, were very gracious people, active in entertaining and helping others. A pious and conscientious man attentive to John's education, Duncan frequently kept young John in his clothing shop to keep an eye on the boy so he would not come under negative influences. John's mother, Isabella MacDonald Mackay, had grown up on a farm in Strathnairn. Some members of her family had begun to emigrate when John was very young. They had gone to South America to settle and farm sheep in southern Chile and on the island of Tierra del Fuego, beyond the Magellan Strait. When John showed an interest in their going, they told him they would take him along. John took them seriously and was greatly disappointed when he was left behind.

John Mackay had two sisters and two brothers. His brother Duncan, younger by seven years, emigrated to South America as his cousins had done and later became a proprietor of a large sheep farm in southern Argentina near Tierra del Fuego. His sister Isabella (Ella), who never married, became a nurse, and sister Helen (Nellie) married a dedicated Christian layman, Alexander (Alec) Fraser. The couple lived to celebrate their fiftieth wedding anniversary. William Roderick, the youngest of the family, was nineteen years younger than John. Willie, as he was called, followed his older brother and became a clergyman and served as a moderator of the Free Church of Scotland in 1958.

The region where John grew up has an ancient heritage. The Celts, whose history extends back 2500 years, have been a challenge to historians and anthropologists. The Celtic people had no country of their own and were found in parts of Scotland, especially in the northern region, and in Ireland, Wales, France, and Spain. Some Celtics mingled with Anglo-Saxons and Danes to form the British people while others mingled with the Iberians to form the Spanish-speaking people.

The Gaelic language is found in Scotland's western islands, the Inverness area, and to the north of it. Paradoxically, in Caithness, the most northerly region that was influenced by Norwegians and by Danes, pure English and not Gaelic is spoken. As one enters Inverness from the south, one crosses the Grampian Mountains, and near Inverness is one of the chief Scottish mountains, Ben Nevis.

Young John absorbed the rich atmosphere of history and legend in the gateway of the Highlands and the formidable history of the clan. It is said that after St. Columba, the missionary, landed in Iona about 563, he visited the Pictish King Brude, ruler of the North, at his residence at the hill known as Craig Phadrig. A half a millennium later the Scottish King Macbeth (1040–1057) lived in a castle thought to be nearby.

Within the city itself Inverness Castle sits on a hill overlooking the river Ness, which connects the Moray Firth (a bay) on the west with Loch Ness. Although the present castle built of red sandstone dates only to 1834, and court sessions and council meetings occur there, the original Inverness Castle dated back to 1427. It was captured by the Jacobites in 1715 and was razed in 1745. Robert Burns, the greatest Scottish poet, wrote in 1787 a poem called "The Lovely Lass o' Inverness" to commemorate a visit he made to the town.

The last battle on British soil was fought about five miles from Inverness at Culloden Moor on April 16, 1746.[8] Loyalists tried to return Charles Edward Stuart, known as Bonnie Prince Charlie, to the throne. The Jacobites were quickly slaughtered, and the British army was permitted to commit terrible atrocities. The Scots' loss in battle, and, later, the Highland clearances of the eighteenth and nineteenth centuries, resulted in the destruction of the Highland way of life. A statue and monument of Flora MacDonald, the prince's sweetheart, stands in Inverness today. In 1652, after Oliver Cromwell's campaign against Scottish rebels had resulted in control of Inverness, his forces began construction of a fortress there to accommodate a thousand men. This relocation had cultural consequences for Inverness. The classical English that Cromwell's men used from that time became the model for that region and may partly explain why Invernesians do not have a strong Scottish brogue.

Highland society was organized in an ancient system of clans, septs, and families, a system of "cousinship," and the Mackay clan came from the most northern parts of the Highlands. The name "Mackay" is said to mean "son of a fire brand," and its crest is a hand with a sword above the words *manu forte*, "with a strong hand." The clan had a dark tartan, similar to one originally worn by the Black Watch, and it included many formidable warriors. According to some philologists the original Mackays were said to be the Aedui who supported Julius Cæsar in the war with the Teutons. Much later, Donald Mackay of Strathnaver is mentioned as the chief who headed his clan that fought under the banners of Robert Bruce, at Bannockburn, 1314. In 1427 when James I of Scotland summoned chieftains to Inverness, one that he called was the Mackay chieftain Angus Dhu (or Dow) Mackay, *dux quatuor millium de Strathnaver*, leader of four thousand Strathnaver men.

In the seventeenth century two important military leaders emerged from the clan. Sir Donald Mackay (1591–1649), a supporter of Charles I, raised three thousand men to serve in Germany, where they intended to aid and support Charles's brother-in-law, Frederick V, elector of the Palatinate. Later in gratitude King Charles raised Sir Donald Mackay to a peerage with the hereditary title Lord Reay. The Scots were among the best troops that served in the Thirty Years' War.[9] William Mackay, a lieutenant colonel in the service of Gustavus Adolphus, was killed at Lutzen in 1632, at the same battle where Gustavus Adolphus of Sweden died. The military prowess of the Scots is reflected in historical literature through *A Legend of Montrose* by Sir Walter Scot, which drew upon the annals of Sir Donald's regiment, recorded in an unusual book known as *Monro's Expedition* (1637). Daniel Defoe wrote about the fictional cavalier Colonel Andrew Newport in *Memoirs of a Cavalier* (1720), and used as background the Thirty Years' War, including the Scottish regiment of Lord Reay.

After the monarchy had been restored in England, the second leader emerged. Young Hugh Mackay of Scoury (1640?–1692) served Charles II in France and returned to receive commendation from the king in 1664. A brave and devout man, Mackay of Scoury was described by Bishop Burnet as "the most pious man that [he] ever knew in a military way." Later in the general's career he served King William III as commander in chief of the forces in Scotland, during 1689 and 1690, and as colonel commandant of the Scotch Brigade in the service of Holland and a privy counsellor in Scotland.[10] A branch of the Mackay clan also settled into prominence in the Netherlands, and by the eighteenth century several clansmen immigrated to North America. Colonel Aeneas Mackay, who had traveled with Colonel George Washington from Virginia to the Ohio country in 1754, served as commandant of Fort Pitt. James Mackay, an explorer and surveyor, became one of the first English-speaking settlers of Upper Louisiana.

John inherited the strength, courage, and dignity of the Highland Scots. In his adult life the hardy strength of his ancestors of the Mackay clan enabled him to carry out an extremely demanding physical schedule of travel and public speaking on behalf of the Church. Having a passionate spirit, he never shied away from a debate if an important principle was at stake.

Duncan Mackay, John's father, was extremely conservative. A man of devotion and intellectual curiosity, he owned a great many books, acquiring volumes he thought would be of interest and significance for one's religious life, including works by David Brainerd and Jonathan Edwards. He encouraged his son to read. When John was a lad of ten or twelve, he was given a large edition of John Bunyan's *Pilgrim's Progress* with fascinating pictures, and it became a great influence in his life. In raising his son, Duncan was interested in keeping the boy from becoming involved with youths or any activities that would make him into a "young rascal." The family practice was to have devotions and Scripture reading twice a day, in the morning and in the evening. The devotions were led by John's father, who read the lesson, then the family knelt in prayer. Grace was said at the table at the beginning and at the end of the meal. In the Mackay household the Sabbath was a holy day, and work was forbidden. John's father shaved before midnight on Saturday, and John's mother would do the major part of the cooking for Sunday on Saturday.

The religious history of Scotland is long and complicated, and the Reformation there formed the environment in which John Mackay came of age as a Christian. In later years he reviewed books on this history for the public. The most important leader of the Scottish Reformation, John Knox, set the direction and distinctive tone. Knox had been ordained in 1536; during the 1540s he was converted to Protestantism and inspired to a sense of prophetic calling. In 1547 after traveling to St. Andrews, Knox received a call to preach. His vocation was therefore as a preacher, not as an academic theologian, ecclesiastical organizer, or political theorist. His goal was purification of worship and the return to the ideal of spiritual Israel for Scottish corporate religion. For this inspiration he relied heavily on the Bible, especially the Old Testament, as an influence.[11]

In 1560 the reformed Church of Scotland had originally been established as a Presbyterian church, but this form of church polity or organization was not finally and firmly rooted in the society until the revolution in 1690. In the interim the Stuart kings tried to establish an Episcopal form of church structure. For more than a century the authorized form of worship was unsettled, and it was during this period of history that the famous National Covenant was signed in Glasgow. The Scottish Covenanters and the Long Parliament tried unsuccessfully to create Presbyterian uniformity for the British Isles in 1643.[12]

Later, in 1843, a major split and schism known as the "Disruption" occurred in the Church of Scotland, when about one-third of the ministers left the established church over an issue of religious freedom: whether a congregation had the right to object to a new minister that was being imposed on the congregation. Thomas Chalmers, a hero to John Mackay, was the first moderator of the new group, called "The Free Church of Scotland," and he organized the new denomination skillfully. This schism was not finally healed until 1929.

In Inverness, however, Duncan Mackay's family did not attend either of the major denominations, the established Church of Scotland or the Free Church of Scotland. Rather, they attended a church of the smallest Scottish denomination, the Free Presbyterian Church, located about a mile away from the home where they lived. It was "wee'er" than the "Wee Free," as the Free Church was called. Founded in late 1893 with two ordained ministers and several divinity students ready to be ordained, the group had broken away from the Free Church of Scotland in opposition to what was called the "Declaratory Act." One author has referred to this as the Second Disruption.[13]

John Mackay later described the denomination:

> The total constituency of this church, including members, adherents, and children, was never more than some 5,000. Its leaders believed, however, that the Free Presbyterian Church, which rejected relations with any other Christian denomination, was the one true church of Christ in Scotland and in the world. Worship was most austere. Easter services were associated with the Roman Catholic Church, which was regarded as Antichrist. The Westminster Confession of Faith was given the same sanctity as the Bible, and the church refused to sanction the changing of a single word or phrase, or accept any fresh interpretation of its traditional standards. But the church's leaders, both clergy and laity, believed in their denomination's destiny. Said a layman to me in my early youth, "Our church may be despised today, but when the Millennium comes it will be recognized as the one true church!"[14]

In the Mackays' congregation three preaching services were held on Sunday, and young John was taken to all of them. The church services alternated between two in Gaelic and one in English, then two in English and one in Gaelic. Even though John did not know Gaelic and never learned it, his parents insisted that he be there in church and listen to the Gaelic services. Each of the services would take about an hour and a half: the tradition was that a sermon would last about an hour, and the singing of psalms would follow for half an hour. The denomination did not permit hymns and only sang the metrical version of the psalms. When John was eleven the family heartily enjoyed the visit each Sunday afternoon of a black student from South Africa, who was studying for the Christian ministry in Inverness.[15]

The schedule of the three services John attended was rigorous. The first service started at eleven o'clock in the morning and lasted until twelve-thirty. Since it would have taken him about a half hour to return home, he would visit the home of some friends before attending the afternoon service beginning at two o'clock. The third service followed later at six-thirty in the evening.

The governing concept of this denomination was to avoid involvement in anything that was strongly secular. Dancing was considered to be in very bad taste; theater was absolutely forbidden; and sports were generally ruled out.

Young John played soccer with companions at school but did not mention it to his parents at home. Since the games were scheduled during school time, when he returned home he would tell his parents he was in school but would say nothing about soccer, and his parents would be none the wiser. He also enjoyed walking, and would walk to Culloden Moor with his friend, a boy who lived on the other side of the road. Once they left at ten in the evening to watch the sun rise from the top of a mountain.

But there was time for other recreation, too. John was given a bicycle, and it became one of his great loves in early youth. He pedaled on it several times to Kishorn, a seashore valley beyond the place where his father had been born. While there he met his grandparents for the first

Duncan Mackay and Isabella McDonald Mackay with their infant son, John.

Duncan and Isabella's four eldest children, Helen (Nellie), Duncan (with kilt), Isabella (Ella), and John.

and only time. A great deal of his time was spent amusing himself on his own, and in Kishorn, he would roam in the hills and row a boat. He became self-reliant, taking the initiative to find suitable activities. In early years he had little companionship from his own peer group, but, of course, when he went to school there was soccer to play with other boys.

Mackay reflected on his youth in later writing:

> My summer vacations were usually spent by the shores of a sea loch in Western Scotland. The local fishermen taught me where the best haddock banks lay, and how to find my way thither by observing certain landmarks in the hills behind the shore. For the banks were not marked by floating buoys by which one could guide one's course towards them. On an early morning I would sit down at the oars and head my boat for the deep water. When, after a time, the roof of the Laird's house became just visible above a clump of trees, and the white foam of a mountain torrent peered over a great boulder of rock, I knew that, at the point where those two lines of vision crossed, lay the bank, and that it was time to ship my oars and drop anchor for the fishing. I had moved forward to my destination, guided by landmarks on the receding shore.[16]

Rogart—A Commission of Grace

The central event of Mackay's life occurred when he was fourteen years old. Mackay's spiritual encounter came during the summer of 1903. He had been pleading with God in prayer, and God answered him with a profound gift of grace when Mackay encountered the risen Christ at Dornoch. The experience was awe inspiring, ecstatic, and profound in a deep, life-changing way. It came during the Scottish Communion season, within the context of sacramental worship of the Free Presbyterian Church. For three centuries the Communion season was the high point of church life in the Highlands, organized once or twice a year and lasting for five days. The season commenced on Thursday, the "Fast Day" when regular church services were held as on Sunday. By tradition, businesses were closed on Thursday as a holy day even in areas where churches did not have the five-day sequence of services. Friday was the "Men's Day" when laymen, usually having the status of elders would "speak to the Question." The Question was some spiritual issue, usually involving Christian experience and the characteristics of the true believer, particularly how a person became a Christian. The issue would be offered for discussion by one of the speakers, and a large number of other leaders would join the discussion while the congregation listened. The minister would always summarize the discussion and add his own comments in closing. Saturday was "Preparation Day." At the close of the morning service, Communion tokens were distributed to prospective communicants, as evidence of their qualification to be admitted to Communion. Those who might wish to become communicant members and receive Communion for the first time had an opportunity to appear before the session.

"Communion Sunday" began with a seven o'clock prayer meeting led by the elders. The regular worship service in the Highlands would be held outdoors and attended by hundreds, even thousands, of people and could last all day, from eleven in the morning until about five o'clock in the afternoon. The sermon lasted an hour, followed by the "fencing of the tables," when the presiding minister would make plain who had a right to sit down at the "Lord's Table" and who did not. Then the tables would begin to be served, at least three at a time. Covered with white cloths with seats on both sides for communicants, the tables were located in front of the "tent" or wooden pulpit. Communicants would file into their places while verses of Psalm 103 were being sung. After the tokens were collected, the presiding minister gave a brief address and then administered the sacrament. The elders distributed the elements. The "Table Service" ended with a brief admonition to those communicating, who then returned to their places as the psalm was sung.

Table after table followed the same way, each lasting for about an hour, as different groups came to the tables. Instead of enlarging the table or increasing their number, the number was limited so that the rite involved service after service.

Originally the Sunday service ended the Communion season liturgy. In later years, however, Monday was added as a day of Thanksgiving to commemorate the famous Kirk of Shotts Communion in Lanarkshire where, on a Monday morning in the seventeenth century, five hundred people were converted as a result of one sermon preached by a young minister, John Livingstone.[17]

For the Mackay family the Communion season of 1903 was a special time. In the spring of that year a young man from Dornoch, who needed medical care, lived in the Mackay home for several weeks. Warm feelings grew between him and the Mackay family. His parents were so grateful that they wanted John and his mother to spend some time in their home on the Dornoch Firth north of Inverness. The summer was Communion season, and the Mackays' visit came at the time when the traditional first-day Communion services were held in Highland parishes. In some churches Communion services were held twice a year, but because of a lack of ministers, Communion services were usually held just once a year during a five-day period. Hundreds of people came from all over the region to attend the services. Many were held outdoors, and wine, not grape juice, was used for the sacrament. Some people spent the whole month of their summer vacation just going to Communion services. That was advantageous for them, because for five days of the week they would be supported, ministered to, and live in the homes of other members of the congregation. The Mackay home, too, would be packed with people in the Communion season. These visits bound the community together.

John's mother and he were warmly received by the boy's family in Dornoch. The group attended the parish of Rogart, and the daily gatherings were held on a hillside because the local congregation had no building large enough to hold all the people attending the services. John's spiritual encounter took place at the Saturday service. During the nights while staying in Dornoch, John felt gripped by his need of God and repeated, "Lord, help me. Lord, help me. Lord, help me." Then on that hillside God spoke to his soul at that Saturday service. The reality of God's presence and God's approach to John's life overwhelmed him. His soul heard the words, "You too, will be a preacher, and you will occupy that pulpit." After supper that evening John walked along a rugged road in the hills in an ecstatic mood. He spoke to God, looking at the stars. God had suddenly become real to him. He had a mission in life. He thought himself to be in another world with a divine relationship.

Mackay wrote and preached about his conversion experience more than once, sometimes emphasizing a different nuance or element of his understanding of the experience. The most complete description was published in 1953:

> I was a lad of only fourteen years of age when, in the pages of the Ephesian Letter, I saw a new world. I found a world there which had features similar to a world that had been formed within me. After a period of anguished yearning, during which I prayed to God each night the simple words "Lord, help me," something happened. After passionately desiring that I might cross the frontier into a new order of life which I had read about, which I had seen in others whom I admired, I was admitted in an inexplicable way, but to my unutterable joy, into a new dimension of existence. What had happened to me? Everything was new. Someone had come to my soul. I had a new outlook, new experiences, new attitudes to other people. I loved God. Jesus Christ became the center of everything. The only explanation I could have to myself and to others was in the words of the Ephesian Letter, whose cadences began to sound within me, and whose truth my own new thoughts and feelings seemed to validate. My life began to be set to the music of that passage which begins, "And you hath he quickened, who were dead in trespasses and sins" (2:1).
>
> I had been "quickened"; I was really alive. The quickening came on this wise. It was a Saturday, towards noon, in the month of July of 1903. The "preparation" service of an old-time Scottish Communion season was being held in the open air among the hills, in the Highland parish of Rogart, in Sutherlandshire. A minister was preaching from a wooden pulpit, traditionally called "the tent," to some hundreds of people seated on benches and on the ground, in the shade of some large trees, in the glen. I cannot recall anything that the minister said. But something, someone, said within me with overwhelming power that I, too, must preach, that I must stand where that man stood. The thought amazed me, for I had other plans.
>
> For the rest of the summer I literally lived in the pages of a little New Testament which I had bought for a British penny. Strangely enough, it was the Letters of Paul, rather than the Gospels, which I read and marked most. It was perhaps because the Gospels had been very familiar to me, whereas Paul's Letters, which had never particularly interested me, had for me now in my new outlook all the novelty and freshness of a romance. This was particularly true of the Epistle to the Ephesians which became then, and has continued to be since, my favorite book in the Bible. From the first my imagination began to glow with the cosmic significance of Jesus Christ. It was the cosmic Christ that fascinated me, the living Lord Jesus Christ who was the center of a great drama of unity, in which everything in Heaven and on earth was to become one in him. I did not understand what it all meant, but the tendency to think everything in terms of Jesus Christ

and a longing to contribute to a unity in Christ became the passion of my life. It became natural then, and it has remained natural ever since, to say "Lord Jesus," to a personal Presence.[18]

The depth and authenticity of the experience is seen in Mackay's subsequent references to it in his speeches and writings. First, he absorbed the experience in his private devotional diary as a student in Aberdeen, and the existential aspects of his calling powered his life as a foreign missionary. He also reflected on its mystical, biblical, theological, and social implications throughout his life. In public life in 1934 he interpreted it with the Pauline mystical phrase "in Christ Jesus":

> The dividing gulf was bridged. God became a living, loving reality in my life. I talked to Him naturally. Everything became new to me. The woods and hills looked different and the ground had a fresh smell. . . . The center of my new life and faith and outlook was Jesus Christ. I was intoxicated of love for Him. My heart, thought, and imagination were gripped by the phrase "in Christ Jesus"—the Christ in whom history and eternity, man and God, the Crucified and the Living One, were blended. I felt called to the service of Christ, with a sense of vocation which at times in my life since then has been the only thing I could be absolutely sure of. My religious life from that time to this has been Christo-centric.[19]

In 1942 he elaborated on the Cosmic Christ:

> That was my encounter with the Cosmic Christ. The Christ who was and is became the passion of my life. I have to admit, without shame or reserve, that, as a result of that encounter, I have been unable to think of my own life or the life of mankind or the life of the cosmos apart from Jesus Christ. He came to me and challenged me in the writings of St. Paul. I responded. The years that have followed have been but a footnote to that encounter.[20]

The event was still vivid and real to him in old age. In his eightieth year Mackay wrote of Christ as not bound by church structure.[21] He used the word "ecstatic" at a gathering three years later[22] and again in a later interview.[23] In an article titled "What Jesus Means to Me?" he wrote, "[This] boyhood experience made me certain of the spiritual world and convinced me of the reality and power of God's initiative. It bound me to Him by a sense of loving gratitude and gave me a mission in life."[24] And at the age of eighty-five he referred to being "gripped by the hand of God"[25] as a teenager.

Mackay never referred to his own encounter in a divisive manner that could make it a stumbling block to others. He talked and wrote about the experience using a vocabulary designed to help his listeners understand and comprehend. Sometimes he used the phrase "God's grip" rather than the term "mystic," which could have alienated some listeners, especially in North America. Mackay's communion with God was God's action on him, not his own action. In later years he preached about the Christ-mysticism of Paul, the existential reality of being "in Christ" described by Adolf Deissmann as Paul's religion: "It is God Who brings about communion with Christ. He has the initiative at the mystic initiation."[26] Mackay refers to Deissmann's emphasis on "being in Christ" in his book about the Church, *God's Order*.[27] Mackay's calling occurred in the context of the Highland Communion season, and his piety thereafter reflected a high view of the mystery of the sacrament of Communion.[28]

As a speaker and evangelist Mackay used the living encounter as a basic theme of his ministry in Latin America. The living Christ in the soul of man became "the Other Spanish Christ," the alternative to the dead Christ of Latin America grotesquely twisted on a crucifix. He used his understanding of the Spanish mystics, especially Saint Teresa of Avila and St. John of the Cross, as a bridge to connect with Hispanic listeners.

The nature and quality of his calling gave authority to his important essay "Personal Religion," published in 1943.[29] Here Mackay does not speak in the first person but writes how evangelical commitment can lead to the highest level of knowledge of God. He wrote, "This highest level is *spiritual union with God*."[30]

In a missionary sermon in 1934 Mackay drew on his own experience when he spoke of the "pleasing pain":

> This is the goal and this is the spirit of true missionary effort. The goal is to lead men to God in Jesus Christ, that they may give themselves to one another. The spirit of this work is to be so possessed by God, with the "pleasing pain" of his Spirit in our hearts, that we shall lovingly incarnate ourselves in other lives. As they, too, through God's grace, experience this same pain, they will learn in turn that satisfaction and relief are only found in the service of God, and will re-echo the refrain,
>
> "O for more of God in my soul!
> O this pleasing pain!"
>
> May we, fathers and brethren, as members of a fellowship which has been called to a world task, enjoy this paradoxical pain as we face our obligations. Through the power of Christ's resurrection may we be equipped to share the fellowship of his sufferings. And through his holy agony for us and in us, may this "world" for which we are responsible be saved from sin unto holiness, from selfishness unto fellowship, from hate unto love.[31]

In later years the effect of Mackay's spirituality became manifested to others in his demeanor and countenance. He appropriated a deeper understanding of a remarkable Old Testament incident. In his student diary Mackay wrote and prayed boldly about the spiritual glow described in Exod. 34:29ff. He wrote,

> ... the shining of Moses face. This is that solar look the possibility of which materialists have never been able to deny, but the significance of which they have sought to explain away.
>
> Lord may I have this look, indicating a mind at perfect peace with God, and the existence of a union between me and the divine Saviour. Sanctify me thus O Lord, keep me in all my ways.[32]

Later several witnesses discerned something distinctive about his countenance. During his mission to Peru, Luis Alberto Sánchez referred to him as "the seraphic Mackay" (*el seráfico Mackay*),[33] and Víctor Andrés Belaúnde referred to him as "El Seráfico."[34]

In summary, the encounter at Rogart had the criteria of a classic Christian mystical experience of union of the soul with God, and it introduced Mackay to an unforgettable lifelong sense of companionship. The signs pointing to mystic union include his many references to it in his college diary in the context of the Song of Songs, his lifelong memories of the experience, and the authority that it gave him in his ministry. It did not take him away from the world but allowed him to be immersed in the world more effectively. At times during his ministry Mackay was reticent about the gift. Rather than focusing attention on it and on himself, he used the gift as an invitation and illustration to others to come to faith and to life in its fullness.

In a convocation address at Princeton Seminary, Mackay discussed his understanding of "personal religion as the most basic expression of Christian faith and life." As distinguished from conventional religion, personal religion in a general sense "is a religion in which divine reality . . . exercises an overmastering influence upon life. It becomes the fountain-head of emotion, the master light of thought, the source of moral energy." Personal religion in the Christian sense "might be defined as acquaintance with oneself and with God. There is in it self-knowledge and the knowledge of God."[35]

Personal religion, Mackay taught, is an authentic relationship with God available to all people. "If you take God seriously, he will take you seriously," he told the present writer in the 1960s. A relationship with God is the fruit of committed, sincere effort: in the vocabulary of Spanish mysticism, *determinación* and in the biblical teaching of Jesus, ardent and eager seekers enter it by force.[36]

Early Education

Later that summer of 1903, when young John and his mother returned to Eve-lix, where they were living outside of Dornoch, John's life had been changed. He would go trout fishing on a brook or "burn," which he loved to do: it was his favorite sport. He would lay the fishing rod on the bank with the fishhook in the water. He would lie on his face reading a small New Testament that he kept all his life as one of his treasures. Paul's Letter to the Ephesians became especially dear and meaningful to him, especially the words that in the King James Version read, "And you hath he quickened," that is, made alive, "who were dead" (2:1). The Revised Standard Version renders this passage as "And you he made alive, when you were dead." John was a new being. He hoped to give expression to the thought in an autobiography that he intended but did not write. In later years reflections on the Rogart experience and its consequences in his life became the source of his thought of "the Hand," which became a strong theme in his devotional life. In words, he felt he was "in a Hand." He was also gripped by the words of the psalmist, "O LORD: I said, thou *art* my God. My times *are* in thy hand" (Ps. 31:14–15 KJV).

As a result of his conversion and call, John's life changed in other ways. Always a vigorous reader, he now became a devotee of the works of Jonathan Edwards. There were periods of spiritual devotion, and he began to visit old Christian people and listen to their experiences. He wrote that when he was fifteen he

> made a pilgrimage to the grave of the most famous of our Highland preach-ers, Dr. John MacDonald of Ferintosh. There I consecrated myself afresh to the service of the *Beloved*. MacDonald's evangelistic ministry in the Highland glens had caught my imagination. The passage in his biography that I liked most to read told of an occasion in which hundreds of hearers were moved to seek Christ by a sermon he preached on the text: "I will betroth thee to Myself for ever."[37]

Mackay's experience with the church denomination took longer to develop. He attended prayer meetings on Wednesdays. He wanted to attend the Com-munion services but "was twice refused church membership because the evi-dence was not sufficiently clear that I was a subject of divine grace. The third time I applied I was admitted into full communion" at the age of sixteen.[38]

But young John's life soon changed in another way also. Although Dun-can looked forward to his son joining him in business, when John returned to Inverness from Rogart and Dornoch, he learned that he had been awarded a scholarship for secondary education, making it possible for him to attend a private school, the Inverness Royal Academy, which served a large part of the Highlands of Scotland. He entered the academy in autumn of 1903 and, after completing his studies in four years, was graduated in the summer of 1907.

The Inverness Royal Academy has a continuous history of over seven hundred years. The current school was founded by Royal Charter in 1792, when the academy took over some staff, pupils, and assets from the town grammar school. The grammar school had been located in a building called the Dunbar Center since 1668, and it, in turn, developed directly from an earlier school that began with the founding of a Dominican Priory in the Friars Street area of Inverness in 1223. The school's

John Mackay as youth.

motto, *labore et vertute*, means *work and excellence*. The school had 801 pupils in 1955 when Mackay returned to speak at the academy's traditional prize-giving ceremony.[39]

Two exceptional teachers, William J. Watson, the rector who taught classics, and Thomas Cockburn, who taught English and history, strongly influenced Mackay and helped form his cultural identity as an educated Scotsman. A well-rounded individual, Watson was a graduate of Aberdeen and Oxford, where he studied with Sir William Ramsay and Sir John Rhys, and won a double blue at Oxford. At the age of twenty-nine and at a difficult moment after the directors had dismissed his predecessor, Watson was appointed rector of the school. He quickly won the respect of parents, students, and directors. For financial reasons separate facilities for boys and girls could no longer be maintained, and Watson persuaded the directors to allow the boys and girls to be taught together in the same classes. He remained rector of the academy for fifteen years from 1894 to 1909. During that time he increased its academic standing and its managerial efficiency. In 1914 Watson moved to the University of Edinburgh, where he occupied the chair of Celtic Languages, Literature, History, and Antiquities from 1914 to 1938. A native Gaelic speaker, he became an expert on Celtic history, languages, literature, and antiquities and later published a leading work, *Celtic Place-Names of Scotland* (1926).[40]

The second powerful influence was Thomas Cockburn, who taught English and history. As a student at Edinburgh University, Cockburn heard Thomas Carlyle give his famous address at his installation as rector of the university. Cockburn's approach to literature fascinated and inspired Mackay and the other students. His lasting educational influence on Mackay was evident in his student's lifelong appreciation of the work and cultural significance of men of letters and his Merrick Lectures in 1932 in particular.

John had good friends among students at the academy, including John and Donald Baillie. The Baillies' parents had come from western Scotland, and both boys were older than Mackay. John Baillie remembered John Mackay "coming as a 'new boy,' very modest and quiet, to our school in the Scottish Highlands."[41] One of the most stimulating experiences for Mackay was the students' Friday Debating Society, whose president was John Baillie. Mackay enjoyed these meetings, where any topic or problem could be brought up, because of the friendships and responses to issues, and he made his debut in public debate in the society. A large proportion of the group entered the ministry. In addition to John and Donald Baillie, J. Y. Campbell became professor of New Testament in Westminster College, Cambridge, and Donald Ross became minister of the Mayfield Church in Edinburgh. Mackay progressed very well academically and gained his "leaving certificate" from the academy in 1907 with passes at higher level in math, English, Greek, and Latin; he was also named dux in classics and won other academic prizes.

By 1907 the Mackay family had moved successively to 36 Academy Street, then to a home called Birchdale, Culduthel Road. During these early years Mackay continued to grow spiritually, later noting, "Joseph Cook and his Boston Monday Lectures played a very decisive part in shaping my thought on the eve of entering University."[42] From the Inverness Royal Academy, John went to Glasgow University to begin his university education.

Chapter 2

Scottish Education (1907–1913)

"Ask, and it shall be given you." (Luke 11:9 KJV)

Mackay's education in Scotland challenged him as he continued to grow intellectually, spiritually, and emotionally. At Aberdeen, his academic focus became philosophy. After attending services and listening to sermons at several local churches and at the university, he joined a Baptist church where through active participation in its life, he continued to grow spiritually. Since Presbyterianism is the national religion and the established church of Scotland, his membership in a church independent of government control was consistent with later advocacy of the independence of church from state influence.

Mackay's pastor at Gilcomston Baptist Church, Aberdeen, guided Mackay's spiritual growth and appreciation of the church as a collective experience of believers. When Mackay decided to begin his studies for the Free Presbyterian ministry, the theological tutor for his synod was an outstanding exemplar of a Scottish theologian. This professor of theology entered Mackay's life at an important stage and touched him both as a scholar and theologian. The professor's prayers were an unveiling of his own soul and a valuable influence on his students. During these years Mackay kept a devotional diary that gives concrete expression to his daily thoughts and choices, which slowly and steadily brought him toward fuller spiritual maturity.

To Aberdeen

In 1907 Glasgow University was the institution of choice of Free Presbyterian students seeking advanced education because in Glasgow there was a Free Presbyterian congregation. One did not exist in Edinburgh. So in the autumn 1907 Mackay began his university studies at Glasgow University, where he lodged with a friend, Tom Cameron, whom he had met at Rogart and Dornoch. Cameron, a few years older, was also preparing for the ministry. After three weeks of study Mackay learned that he had been awarded a scholarship in the University of Aberdeen. Since there was no Free Presbyterian congregation in Aberdeen, this created a dilemma for him, but he nevertheless decided to accept the scholarship. His decision may also have been affected by Aberdeen's larger proportion of Highland students compared to the other three Scottish universities.

The city of Aberdeen, on the east coast of Scotland, is nearer to Inverness than is Edinburgh, and it is known as the Granite City because most of the buildings there had been erected of granite found in abundance in the hills around the city. Mackay's parents approved the change of universities and were proud that their son had received a scholarship, which through a fund paid all fees for his studies. As a result, his only cost for college was for lodgings. Thus it came about that a few weeks after having begun at Glasgow, Mackay traveled to Aberdeen and entered King's College, where he continued his studies during the 1907–1908 term in Latin and in Greek.

The University of Aberdeen had been formed in 1860 by the union of two colleges. King's College, the older, was the classical center, and the studies at King's were focused on classical culture, languages, philosophy, and history. The other college, Marischal, founded in 1563, was a larger structure, located about a mile from King's. A greater variety of studies was available in Marischal, including many courses on science, and Mackay took courses there in psychology and sociology.

A Czechoslovakian student named Joseph L. Hromádka arrived in Aberdeen in the autumn of 1911, and after the two world wars recorded his memories of his life and studies there, noting that the "British Empire . . . nurtured in its citizens the pride of being citizens of the world."[1] Studying in the United Free Church College at Aberdeen, Hromádka felt the close ties between the church and his theological studies and in later years became Mackay's close friend and colleague. Hromádka experienced "the cosmopolitanism of British political thought and especially the missionary zeal of the ordinary member of the Scottish Church."[2] He noted also that social questions took on an urgent character: "David Cairns certainly also had in the fervent core of his faith a fine sense for the social poverty of the so-called lowest classes, and in his theological lectures he was able to show how the Gospel brings help to the poor and to the most miserable."[3] To the present time Aberdeen University has a reputation for both rigorous scholarship and warm piety. Mackay found life there liberating as he experienced new horizons opening before him, new friendships beginning, and new fellowship in religion and in secular culture.

Student Diary

In the tradition of some of the men that had most influenced him, Mackay began a diary to give expression to his thoughts, feelings, and experiences, and particularly his Bible readings. This diary is valuable in showing the developing mind and feelings of a young man who later rose to a position of importance in the Church. It comprises five handwritten notebooks containing over one-hundred-thousand words. Mackay began making entries in 1907 when he entered Aberdeen at age eighteen and continued it intermittently to age twenty-five. The student devotional diary contains a wealth of cultural, theological, psychological, devotional, and biographical material. Sometimes Mackay made entries two or three times a day, and sometimes days passed without any entries at all if he did not have time to write during periods of travel or changes in his life. For example, when he went home on vacation, he never did any "diary work" as he called it. He used his diary only when he was active in some kind of ministry.

On a Sunday in October 1911, after his first week back at Aberdeen, Mackay was studying a memoir of the life of Henry Martyn, a missionary to India. He read and copied into his own diary a comment of Martyn, making Martyn's purpose his own. "My object in making this journal is to accustom myself to self-examination, and to give my experience a visible form, so as to leave a stronger impression on the memory, and thus to improve my soul in holiness; for the review of such a lasting testimony will serve the double purpose of conviction and consolation." Mackay then noted that he, like Martyn, had "found that nothing is more helpful to me than to give my expression such a printed form." But, realizing the possibility of self-deception, he pleaded with God, "may I be a faithful observer and recorder of my status."[4]

The diary is integral to a clear appreciation of the nature and quality of Mackay's devotional life, the core of authenticity for any religious leader. Its passages illuminate crucial periods in his spiritual formation, his aspirations, and his soul's response to the conversion experience at Rogart. His soul cries out to God, often in biblical language, and excerpts show piety understood as an intimate relationship to God and a devoted obedience to God. A reader glimpses Mackay's yearning and seeking for God's guidance in forming human relationships, his confessions of sin and pride, his Highland passion and intensity, and praise and thankfulness expressed in heartfelt poetic form. Mackay sensed the burden of his future potential, and the diary shows the influence of the Psalms on his devotional life and worldview.

In his prayers Mackay asked God to purge him of his sins and grant him enlightenment and wisdom. He recalled the sweet memory of the Rogart conversion experience and asked God to sweep idols from the land. Mackay sought theological understanding and glimpses of Christ as redeemer. He envisioned a unity of multitudes as one in Christ and sought for himself the ability to hand down the word of life faithfully to posterity. On one occasion Mackay asked God for the mantles of Paul the apostle and Samuel Rutherford. He noted the Christian movement in the student world and prayed about his own relationship with the Christian Union of Aberdeen. He prayed for a united Church. He found and experienced the fellowship of kindred minds in reading the Psalms. He prayed for guidance, for the ability to emulate the apostle Paul, and for a female friend, identified only as C., that he viewed as a possible marriage partner. He grieved for the unbelief of the generation and the shortcomings of the church and clergy, and referred to the union of Christ and his people.

Aristotle said that the unexamined life is not worth living. The diary excerpts included here from Mackay's first term allow him to speak in his own voice, and they provide a window into his inner life and thoughts. Excerpts of prayers and self-examination flow together, beginning with reflections on Psalm 26: "Examine me, O LORD, and prove me; try my reins and my heart" (Ps. 26:2 KJV). Viewed in retrospect these excerpts of his meditations take on both a personal prophetic note and a quality of universality. Though his language and expressions may sound somewhat quaint, the heartfelt sincerity in unmistakable.

But still, Lord, I would indeed pray Thee to weaken more and more the selfish motives and desires which enter into my every service. And now in the solemn silence of this hour I would lay bare my heart before Thee. Is it altogether a bond of selfishness that unites me to a new found friend? Is Thy glory to have but a second place? O forbid, Lord, that it should be so. But sanctify our friendship and bless it, adorn it with unfading Godliness— that like the Corinthians we might first give ourselves to Thee, and then to each other, but only in Jesus. . . .

But "Thou shall arise, and have mercy upon Zion: for the time to favour her, yea, the set time, is come" [Ps. 102:13]. O let me see this day; and if Thy will so be, give my hands strength and power to raise her ruined walls again. Teach my fingers forever for the contests that are looming.[5]

O Lord, what at all is my hope if it be not this, that thou will manifest Thy goodness to me, that while I abide and tabernacle with men? "Thou wilt guide me by Thy counsel and afterwards receive me to glory" [Ps. 73:24]. Otherwise is not my life meaningless—and my present position vain? But, O my God, I trust I will not live in vain; but that Thou wilt make of me a vessel of honour to bear about the sweet incense of the name of Christ. O give me power day by day to die unto Sin and live unto Righteousness; and may I be enabled to face the greatest trials with these words on my lips,

"I can do all things through Christ that strengtheneth me" [Phil. 4:13].[6]

And now this day is almost at an end—another Sabbath day. . . . But all is in Thy hand "who didst separate me from my mother's womb and called me by Thy grace, and revealed Thy Son in me" [Gal. 1:15–16a]. O that I may know more but Christ and Him crucified.[7]

Search me and try me, and know my ways, and see if there be wicked way in me [Ps. 139:23–24]. My darling sins and idols of my heart—purge and destroy them all. O refine me, the gold is being dimmed. Sanctify me through the truth. Enlighten me by Thy teaching. Guide me by Thy counsel. Fulfill the holy benediction to me—"that the grace of the Lord Jesus Christ and the love of God, and the communion of the Holy Ghost be with me for ever" [2 Cor. 13:14]—Amen.[8]

O Rogart, my heart yearns for that sweetness again, which it did enjoy with its saviour in thy dear Highland hills. Never, never, can I forget thee. And to that I will yet sound thy glens with the word of salvation—O for a hire of souls in Rogart. But what is it I hear of thee, dear Lord of my birth? That thou art altogether given to vanity. Yet I know my Lord wilt not leave thee. Thy very stones to me are dear. Rogart, Rogart. Christ shall have thee yet.[9]

Oh for life and reality in our public worship. And oh, for that iconoclastic power, which imbued with grace and holiest zeal, would sweep all idols from our land. A perverted aesthetic taste—the baneful ruin of personal godliness.[10]

It is thine eyes alone, Lord that canst sweep through times to come, that canst scan every winding of futurity as being present to Thy omniscience. Dear Lord, bring closer to Thy bosom Thy wayward child. Palls of darkness enshroud my coming years. Thy promise alone pierces as a ray of hope and comfort through this gloom. "But my times are in Thine hand" [Ps. 31:15]. Be thine everlasting arms around, O Jeshurun's God [cf. Deut. 33:26].[11]

Oh is there not in this promise all that I could desire, if only I had grace to lay hold upon it? And so, Lord, I cast myself helplessly upon Thee, and upon Thy word. If my God fails me, my life is meaningless and vain.[12]

Blessed Jesus, give me deep glimpses of Thy personality, deep glances of faith into thy office as Redeemer.[13]

Oh, I am a deep mystery, a dark inscrutable enigma, a strange compound of seriousness and levity. What am I?—What I was not. What shall I be?—What I am not now. True, true. A corpse, wrapped in the confines of the tomb. Chill unbelief, thou wouldst enshroud me now in thy unhallowed gloom.

Yet soon thou'lt hear my farewell, at the dawn of everlastingness—a long adieu sink, sink, my enemy unhand me, thou art doomed. My Redeemer lives, and so shall I.[14]

"While I was musing the fire did burn" [Ps. 39:3], *exclaims the psalmist on another occasion. The flame of grace cannot be hid, nor lie dormant in the soul. But leaving the metaphor, how is it that grace in a believer's soul is peculiarly enlivened?—By association with those of kindred mind. Iron sharpeneth iron* [Ps. 27:17]. *There is a spiritual magnetism attracting and uniting souls like circumstanced, whose sorrows and whose joys are the same. And then from their united hearts aspirations arise in heavenly fusion. Nor is it possible for only two souls to be thus united, it is gloriously possible for multitudes to be as the one in Christ Jesus.*[15]

Lord, I am withered like the very grass. My mind wanders and is distracted. My soul knows not the heavenly dew, nor through it flow streams of heavenly love. How barren do I find all duties and exercises of mind. But, O Lord, do thou hang me again upon that nail which Thou hast set in a sure place.[16]

Lord, do Thou vindicate all the mysteries of Thy word. In due season teach me how apparently contrary principles can be reconciled. And this I would ask that I may be enabled at all times to glorify Thy name, and to hand down to posterity the pure undiluted word of life.[17]

"God dwelleth not in temples made with hands" [Acts 7:48]. *How deep the need to have inculcated upon our minds that the first great principle in Christian worship is godliness. Godliness! Whoever hears the name nowadays. It is but sneeringly associated with airy mysticism or speculation. Ah there is none now to warn the rich not to "trust in uncertain riches, but in the living God"* [1 Tim. 6:17]. *They hold the chief offices in the church, and so build for themselves hopes of carnal security. O Lord, make me faithful to their souls.*[18]

How various and how many are the streams that flow through this vast creation at which it is lawful for man on occasion to drink, yet let them remember that however full and copious the waters of these minor streams may be, this but approaches the great fountain as streaks of sunlight do the Ball of Light.

Another parallel thought. The inspired word has ceased to be in men's estimation as it was. They are loth, even professed Christians, to take it as an absolute and infallible guide in all things. We see the outcome of this baneful tendency. Deep spiritual life has become warped. We have not now those who sound the depths of human nature, as so the depths of the divine fullness are left unfathomed too. A full reaction is necessary. Let us lay aside all save the one essential word of truth and with that alone achieve our conquests, and then will the streams of grace flow anew throughout the whole world.[19]

Paul the aged in fettered chains raising his heart to heaven on behalf of the youthful Timothy. What a deep heart of love he had, that prisoner of Christ! From this very city, too, went up the breathings of another prisoner of Christ, Samuel Rutherford. His prison here was "Christ's Palace." Oh may I catch their holy zeal. May their mantle fall upon me. May I be willing to suffer all reproach yea to be accounted as the off-scouring of all things for the name of Jesus. "Thy name is as ointment poured forth, therefore do the virgins love thee" [Song 1:3].[20]

Lord, help me. Thou didst hear that prayer once when the lips of child-hood hoped it. Hear it now again, when renewed fears assail me.[21]

O my saviour. Will time and eternity brand me with foul ingratitude? Will Heaven and earth and Hell point at me the finger of scorn as a type of unparalleled baseness? Lord, let me start anew. Enable me to surrender my all to Thee again.[22]

There is a wonderful movement throughout the student world at present. Lord, is Thy kingdom to be ushered in shortly? Though fire and sword lie between? Dear Lord, keep me ever in Thy own service.[23]

Sin indeed doth weigh down my soul. . . . What, Lord, are to be my exact relations to the Christian Union here? Thou knowest how heavily the matter tells upon me. My difficulties are well known to Thee. O if it were but Thy will, Lord Jesus, willingly should I embark upon the work heart and soul. But there is much, much in the Union that grieves me bitterly, and Thou mayst have me to stand by and prepare until Thou Thyself callest me forth to witness. This night Lord, I cast it all upon Thee. Thou hast never failed me, and canst not now.[24]

Lord, give me grace to "sound the trumpet in Zion" [Joel 2:1, 15], *to call the world to hear Thy voice. Give me grace to herald the glories of Christ and of His kingdom. And O grant that I might willingly be submerged in nothingness, while Christ leads on in triumph his gospel car.*[25]

I remember the first time that these words were brought to my mind. It was Rosie Boyden that pointed them out to me at the Communion in Laing. She had received them as a sweet portion from the Lord. And she wished to share them with me. Dear Rosie, my dearest friend on earth. And truly these words have often comforted me amid disquieting fears and unbeliefs. Is not my present position and profession vain and meaningless, unless Thou hast wrought a work in me? A disquietude has seized my mind regarding my call to thy service. Lord, but in thy word and promise do I trust, my God. "Thou wilt ordain peace for me . . ." [Isa. 26:12].[26]

Are not all Christians still members of one great family? Are they not all "one in Christ Jesus" [Gal. 3:28]? *It must be so. But wherefore, then, this disunited Christendom? A deep purpose of grace doubtless runs through this severed unity. Still must that prayer of Christ be fulfilled "that all may be one"* [John 17:21]. *Lord, purge the Churches as a refiner and from their ruined dissolution raise for thyself a spiritual, united Church.*[27]

'Tis not enough to have a sound creed, encased in some remote corner of our brains, we must have sound conduct that can never be condemned. "Faith without works is vain" [Jas. 2:17, 20, 26], *says the apostle James.*

Lord, consecrate my life to Thee. "Give me neither poverty nor riches" [Prov. 30:8], *as thy saint prayed of old. But give me grace, devotion, and a burning zeal for Thy glory.*[28]

Speak evil of no man; be no brawler, but gentle, shewing all meekness unto all men. For we ourselves also were sometimes foolish, disobedient, deceived, serving divers lusts and pleasures, living in malice and envy, hateful, and hating one another [Tit. 3:2–3]. . . .

Truly it is all of sovereign grace that I am what I am—else would I be a sensualist of the deepest water.[29]

How universal in sentiment and experience these blessed songs are. What a link they serve to bind together the faith of God's heritage through all time. The Christian meets in the psalms to the fellowship of kindred minds. However wide the range of his spiritual experience he finds it in every stage marked out and embodied by some who went before. How the church of God should cling to the psalter. Lord, wilt Thou not cause a reaction back to these inspired utterances. Such if it be Thy will would do much to bind up and heal again our disunited Christendom.[30]

O my covenant God, what means this turmoil of varying religious sentiment? I stand solitary and alone in the place wrapped up in the seclusion of my own thoughts. O may Thy gracious spirit direct me in that path that wilt best serve thy glory's ends. O dark lowering future, let thy gathering gloom dispel as hope beams me onward to meet the dawning, the sunrise of my Redeemer's glory.[31]

Lord, is it pessimism or is it sober thought and contemplation that makes me set in close proximity the crisis of the cause? Guide me every step. But better perish now, than I should cause one inglorious stain upon Thy name.[32]

It is the morning of Thy holy day, a season when above all others I ought to seek Thy communion. Yet have I been seeking and reveling in communion with my pride. O did they know who love me, and look up to me, how very inconsistent I am when in secret with my God, their thoughts would stand aghast. But so it is I am inconsistent, very, very.

Lord, root out this gnawing pride, else it will open in my soul great gaping wounds.[33]

Wondrously, Lord, hast thou guided me in the way, and wondrously Thou guidest me still. So 'tis not Thy will that I should at present share actively in piloting the Christian Union. Thou seest otherwise for me. I bless Thee Lord, Thy will be done. 'Tis best.[34]

Oh, if my heart longs for the sweetness and sympathy of human love, how much more ought it yearn for conscious communion with Christ Jesus. . . .

And now I bring before Thee her case with whom I had so interesting a conversation last night. How like my own were many phases of her experience. Give her thy grace dear Lord, to testify for Thy name among her fellows. Give her boldness and strength to bear Thy reproach, considering thy reproach more ennobling than the praises of her fellows.[35]

It were well if this were ever before the mind of ministers now. No wonder the Christian ministry has fallen into such disrepute where ministers mix so promiscuously in all the world's carnal services.[36]

It is with expectation that I look forward to contemplate anew the conversion of the greatest of apostles. O Lord, lay it upon my heart to strive with a holy emulation to serve Thee with the same zeal and glowing ardour that characterized Thy Apostle Paul. O enable me to deny myself as he did, and to take up my cross and follow Jesus.[37]

Lord, Thy Sabbaths are little esteemed in this city.[38]

My soul, cast back the eyes of thy memory, and let thy doubts be dissolved forever by the testimony light of ages. Oh, what is thy hope, thou trembling inmate of my being, if it be not upon the word of God? What is thy hope to ever animate an ambassador of the cross, if not that thou hast a saviour's promise. I remember the day. Will eternity efface it from my memory? It was amid the lovely hills of Rogart which by day reechoed with the voice of praise of an assembled congregation, and by night with my lord heard that Christ chose me for his own. He chose me to be His own child: he chose me and appointed me to be His servant. O my blessed Jesus. "This word of thine my comfort is." It buoys up my spirit in all its gloomy forebodings. For "Thou wilt guide me by Thy counsel and afterwards receive me to glory" [Ps. 73:24].

The word of my God shall stand forever.

But O my unworthiness, Lord Jesus, my brutishness, my loathsomeness. Change me; renew me. Sink me in nothingness that Christ may be exalted.[39]

Lord, keep me from melancholy. Oh, could I but with certain mend appropriate Thy promises in this chapter. One thing I can take to myself and that is Thy complainings against Thy people—"thou hast not called upon me, O Jacob: thou hast been weary of me, O Israel" [Isa. 43:22]. *Oh, whence this weariness of Thee, Lord? How unsuited for serious application does this melancholy make my mind. It infuses within me a yearning for seclusion, for freedom from all conventional trammels.*[40]

It is worthy of note, also, that many great figures in profane history also carried on an arduous life's work buoyed up by the conviction that heaven had decreed a certain destiny for them which must come to pass.[41]

"If any man," says the Lord himself, "would be my disciple, let him take up his cross and follow me" [Matt. 16:24, Mark 8:34; Luke 9:23]. *How many of us are more prone to mourn over our crosses rather than to bear up under them, and follow Jesus even if it be with faltering steps.*[42]

"And the elephant's knees that will not bend, God must break," said godly Rutherford.[43]

I am all a chaos tonight. Holy Spirit, break Thou upon the heaving disquietude of my thoughts that peace and calmness may reign within me once more.[44]

O Lord, make me earnest about my salvation. Make me earnest for the salvation of others. Lord I am a selfish being. My prayers are narrow. It is but a small circle that they embrace. But oh, if only the sun of Righteousness would arise, my prayers would more easily take wing and soar from this chill wintry air into the presence of God himself, pleading for dear precious sinners throughout the world. "If Thou shouldst mark, O Lord, who could stand before Thee?" [Ps. 130:3].[45]

O Lord, break the neck of my pride. Of this cruel murderer within me. How can I ever preach Jesus only, when pride and self demand so much flattering and attention and their tastes pandered to?[46]

But it is not its variegated garment that we ought most to consider but the great truth embodied in these gorgeous hues. Christ is made the center of all God's ways to man. God hath ordained Him, and by Him will He bring the world into judgement. How significant, therefore, that Christ should have the most conspicuous place in every scheme of religious thought. How estimable in the Father's eyes is this Jesus. How we, too, ought to prize Him. Yet, oh, how manifest that essentially Christ is receiving a secondary place in the ministrations of the pulpit. How otherwise can we consider it when the great doctrines of grace and of God's plan of Salvation are observed and not presented to the hearts or understanding in their glorious essence? Surely evidence of the waning of Christ's glory in his professed Church is the scant reference to the blessed union that exists between Him and His people. When the spiritual horizon of the Church was brightest, this mystical union was the theme of the deepest thoughts of Christendom. But alas, alas, for this age. Yet brighter days are coming, though the bleakness of darkness lie between—"Even so, come, Lord Jesus" [Rev. 22:20].[47]

How can I ever forget Thee or that place where my Redeemer did tryst with my soul.[48]

This whole generation have lost their anchor and are tossed upon the heaving deep of unbelief.[49]

Paul at Ephesus. How dear an association to me! For was it not to the Ephesian believers that Paul afterwards wrote that wondrous chapter which opens, "And you hath he quickened, who were dead in trespasses and sins" [Eph. 2:1]. And was not this chapter made peculiarly precious to me? Was it not my constant companion when my eyes were opened to see my lost condition in the light of God's salvation? O precious remembrance, when with the eyes of a newborn child I viewed with wonderment my new creation. All things were new and strange to me, and myself the strangest enigma of all.[50]

O wretched professor, you have neglected your midday devotion. O Lord, pardon me. Thou knowest what it was that distracted my mind, and still distracts it. So here is my trust and faith in Thee, a trust which ever I expressed ever in this matter. How I dread to be found a hypocrite! O heart-searching God, purge away my hypocritical dross.

"Who is among you that feareth the Lord, that obeyeth the voice of his servant, that walketh in darkness and hath no light? Let him trust in the name of the Lord, and stay upon his God" [Isa. 50:10].

Lord, my ways are indeed darkness, and I have no light. But do I stay upon my God? Is this step that I have taken a rash [one], or hast Thou Thyself directed it, and so art answering my prayer? O dear Lord Jesus, grant that no evil may ensue from it. Do thou thyself put words in dear C.'s mouth that a perfect understanding may presently be come to. We are wholly in thy hands. Do with us united or individually as seemeth good in Thy sight.[51]

"For they shall see eye to eye, when the Lord shall bring back Zion" [Isa. 52:8]. *All faithful ministers shall yet have their hearts moulded into one under blending rays of the Sun of Righteousness. All hardness and self shall flow away, and pure love shall have the victory alone.*[52]

Thou knowest too it is my impulsive nature that has brought it upon me. Yet would I fain hope Thy own guide has been guiding me even in this. Thou knowest my prayers Lord, for such a friend as C. is. Have her feelings been awakened as mine have? I believe so, O Lord. Mould our love and friendship for thy glory. Blend or dissever as seems best to Thee. Our all is in Thy hands.[53]

Generally He makes their path clear by directing their mind to a portion of his truth, but often by impressing upon their mind in some inexplicable way a truth concerning the future. Some may have felt as if God spoke to their hearts out of heaven, so real was the voice they heard. This is no mystic fancy, else is my life one great delusion, and my future empty and inane—"Remember the word unto thy servant, upon which thou hast caused me to hope. This is my comfort in my affliction: for thy word hath quickened me" [Ps. 119:49–50].

Again is the hour of midnight drawing near when another week of my being will be clipped wholly into the past. It has been an eventful week this, that now draws towards an end. In it may have been determined the bounds of my earthly relations. But again my thoughts may all pass as a fleeting dream and never be embodied in reality. Lord, Thou knowest my case. 'Tis well Thou dost. O guide me, let me not slip from thy hand. And now as the day of rest is being ushered in, I commit me to Thy care and keeping. Welcome, day of God![54]

And now, Lord, at the close of this Sabbath day before I retire to rest, I would seek to render to thee my thankfulness for all Thy kindness to me.

And not least would I praise Thy name that I have this evening heard a true gospel minister. Oh that I could hear more of this kind! Grant it be in thy glory's cause that he be settled permanently in this city. . . . Ever be my guide in all things, in things humble and lowly as well as in things high and lofty. Strengthen my mind for the arduous study of this week.[55]

Oh to be rid of all the hypocritical drolling of this age. A formal ritual seems to have sapped the marrow of the gospel. But it shall not always be so. Pure righteousness must again assert its dominion when the Lord shall restore Zion. Oh for simplicity in the service of God. The more simple the less open are we for the temptation of the natural self.[56]

The cause is thine. Mine is the duty and the task. Aid me, O Lord of my strength, my right hand covenant God, that I may cleave these powerful billows and bring Thy storm tossed church to port at last. Thou art the rock of ages, the rock of hope in a troubled sea.[57]

My first University Session is now ended. How many strange experiences have I had since I left home for Glasgow University in October. A month in Glasgow and then to come here! How strange. Yet I feel thine hand, Lord, did guide me. So here in Aberdeen my future destinies are to be shaped. For what shall I praise Thee most? Thy goodness to me has been wonderful.[58]

Spiritual Influences

Initially upon his arrival in Aberdeen Mackay regularly attended the Free Church of Scotland, which was most similar to his own denomination, the Free Presbyterian Church. Though Mackay occasionally attended the university chapel, students were free to attend services at various churches led by theologians and ministers who were skilled and knowledgeable preachers. By January of 1909, exercising choice in this atmosphere of freedom at Aberdeen, Mackay decided to affiliate himself closely with Gilcomston Baptist Church. That congregation became his church home, where he met Jane Logan Wells, a petite young woman five-feet-four-inches tall who would later become his wife and life's companion. In Aberdeen a banquet of preaching was available to him, and Mackay's diary summarizes and evaluates many sermons and preachers. This environment stimulated the development of his own distinctive preaching style.

A typical Sabbath for Mackay was filled with attendance at public worship and religious study. For example, he generally attended a church study group at 9:30 a.m. followed by a morning service at 11:00 a.m., an afternoon lecture at 2:30 or 3:00 p.m., and an evening service at 6:00 or 6:30 p.m., often followed by another talk or study group. On the Sabbath of October 18, 1908, theologian P. T. Forsyth, an Aberdeen graduate and principal of Hackney College, Hampstead, preached at the chapel of King's College on an Old Testament text. Mackay's comment was that "the matter of his discourse was good, but too compressed and intellectual. Signs of general restlessness were manifest before he concluded."[59]

On November 1, 1908, Mackay heard Sir W. Robertson Nicoll, the journalist and editor, preach in the chapel on the text "I stand at the door and knock" [Rev. 3:20] combined with a text from Deuteronomy. In Mackay's description, "He dwelt on love, human and divine. I felt my heart on fire, first as I thought on one whom I now believed had an awakened love towards me and then of this earthly love mingling with and being lost in the love of Christ to us both. Dr. N. has a peculiar delivery, but on this occasion I think it added impressiveness to his theme."[60] Nicoll also lectured in the afternoon.

On November 8, Mackay went to Communion in the Free Church where Professor Macleod preached from the text Rom. 8:3. The method of partaking of Communion was different here from what Mackay was accustomed to: "Communicants sat at the tables when they entered the Church first in the modern fashion. It was the first time I had seen it thus. The preacher seemed to express that he would have desired they had come forward in the old style. How differently did I feel from times when at Communion in the Highlands."[61] As part of his participation in a study group, three weeks later Mackay was scheduled to deliver a paper at the 10:00 a.m. meeting on "the Mystical Union."

After another morning chapel service Mackay recorded his response to the

Lord Bishop of Carlisle, who preached from the words, "Ye that love the Lord, hate evil" [Ps. 97:10]. A grand evangelical discourse. The Bishop is a very little man, with, however, a finely shaped head, and a beautifully expressive face. He preached forcibly from Scripture and reason that true love must have in it a negative and a positive element—a perfect hatred of sin, and a perfect love of holiness.[62]

One Sunday in late October 1908, after Mackay attended a morning service at the Free Church, a friend brought him to attend the 6 p.m. service at the Gilcomston chapel, a Baptist church located not far from Marischal College but independent from the university. He found the meeting "extraordinary" and commented, "Such true pleading with souls I think I never heard before."[63] This congregation meant the very most to him in those years. It was the place he felt most at home, and he joined it. He found that in the Gilcomston Church it was possible not only to attend and be edified by church services and to hear sermons but also to participate in meetings. This was a church that did not devote itself merely to the official routine church services but had many group meetings and missionary circles. As time passed, Mackay came to know the pastor, the Rev. Alexander Grant Gibb.

At this time Mr. Gibbs was becoming more and more interested in the missionary movement. He invited a group to meet in his home once a week to consider the missionary situation, and they studied missions in India. It was an extraordinary and moving experience for Mackay. Although John was the youngest member of the group, the others invited him to be its chairman. Jane Logan Wells also attended that meeting, and John accompanied her home to her lodging. Jane was also a student, not at the university but at the Aberdeen Training Center for Teachers, and she took courses at Marischal. The school trained teachers, and Jane later taught at the Demonstration School of the Training Center. From time to time John and Jane Wells met and talked and walked together.

Mackay described the presentation and responses to his paper on mystical union that he had faithfully prepared for the study group:

> Today has been an eventful one. I did not fall asleep until about 3 o'clock this morning. I awakened about three hours afterwards and rose about seven to finish and revise my paper on the "Mystical Union." It was no wonder that while reading it at the meeting my eyes seemed to swim in my head, obliterating almost my whole vision, this because of my dilatoriness. Let this experience teach me a lesson. I was told also that my voice was indistinct. This statement came as a surprise to me. I could not account for the truth of it at all. But I believe now it was owning to my nerves being so shattered at the time of delivering the paper that I failed to measure the tone of my voice. The criticisms passed upon the paper itself were all very favourable, but such criticisms are very cheap nowadays.[64]

In January 1909 Mackay joined a Bible circle studying the "Desire of India" and in early February attended a tea at the home of Grant Gibb, Pastor of Gilcomston. He wrote, "At tea at Grant Gibb's tonight. Several other Baptist students there. Enjoyed myself very much. I am being more and more attracted to Mr. Gibb. Oh, use him, Lord, to feed my soul."[65]

Mackay was established enough within the congregation to speak briefly at the evening service on February 14 at the Baker Street mission on the words "Grieve not the Holy Spirit of God" (Eph. 4:30). This well-attended meeting was the first time he publicly addressed "sinners and saved." He walked home with Miss Wells, and they had an interesting conversation. Mackay compared her to his friend C.: "She feels as I do in regard to the popular religions in this city. She is a very fine type of a Christian. In many ways she is quite a contrast to C. She is free in expressing herself whereas C. is very reticent."[66] The following week he heard "Miss Wells pray for the first time. A beautiful prayer she had," he wrote. "Gushing up from the depths of her heart. Dear girl. She is a bright adornment of her profession."[67]

Life continued to become richer for him as Mackay became acquainted with movements of Christians that he had not known about earlier. In February, a few days after hearing Miss Wells pray, Mackay learned that he had been elected to the Committee on the Christian Union, even though he had deliberately stayed away from the meeting. As he felt more and more at home in Gilcomston Church, one of the leaders asked Mackay to take a class at Baker Street and deliver the quarterly class to seventy-five or one hundred children. It was a privilege that met "a deep desire" of his to speak to children.

The Sabbath school class went well. Mackay wrote,

4:30 p.m. Baker Street Sabbath School. I delivered the quarterly address to the children upon "Jesus"—his person, character, and work. Spoke for half an hour with a good measure of freedom. Children seemed deeply attentive. Was congratulated at the close. I must say I enjoyed the theme myself. Speaking to children is one of the fine arts worth cultivating. Three things in particular I would desire to cultivate—the ability to preach the gospel fully and faithfully to children, illiterate or degraded persons, and the most cultured audience. Give me thy grace, Lord, to attain to these, if by so doing I might the better win souls."[68]

Toward the end of March 1909 as he was about to leave Aberdeen for a term break, he recorded a note of bitter sadness in his diary. The fact that it was a common experience did not make it less unpleasant for young Mackay. Mackay's friend C. told him that

he could never be her friend in the closest sense. She showed not the least sympathy for my feelings. I was as composed as possible, but ever since almost resentment has been boiling in my heart. But I am calmer now, and will never charge her with leading me on, though I can never hold her guiltless in this respect. But it is all for the best. I bear her no ill will. . . . I believe, Lord, that when my feet are on the track which I should tread onward to the grave, Thou wilt then, if thou seest good, give me a dearly earthly companion.—I have done.[69]

Mackay took his disappointment philosophically, expressing the belief that a marriage is to be formed by mature individuals who know their place in the world.

The summer session at Aberdeen began at the end of April and continued to July. During this new session the trends that had begun in Mackay's life deepened and intensified. He continued in the Christian Union and the Student Volunteer Movement. In the latter there were various discussions about India, including a discussion on caste. A professor from William Carey's college, Serampore, spoke at a Sunday morning meeting. The example of Carey remained with Mackay into his own ministry in South America. Carey, apprenticed to a shoemaker as a boy, had become a convinced Baptist. After his conversion he continued as a shoemaker at night while serving as a pastor and running a school by day. Gifted at languages at a ministers' conference in 1792, he had coined the slogan "Expect great things from God and attempt great things for God." The modern Protestant missionary era dates from Carey's mission to India, 1793, when Carey traveled to Bengal. Later he became a professor of Sanskrit, Bengali, and Marathi at Fort William College, Calcutta, and translated the whole Bible into Bengali in 1809. His activism was instrumental in the banning in 1829 of suttee, the custom of the burning to death of a widow at her husband's funeral. Years later as a missionary in Peru, Mackay followed the "Carey Principle" of turning his outside earnings over to the mission for its use.

The summer period in 1909 was also a time of increasing spiritual insight for Mackay. Among his spiritual readings at this time were George Mueller's *Life* and John Pulsford's *Quiet Hours*. His work at the Baker Street mission made him feel humble. He became aware of how ill adapted he was at that time in leading sinners to Christ. He felt ignorance of the working of the Holy Spirit in a clearly defined conversion. Mackay even feared that because of the "peculiar nature" of his own conversion, he would "never be successful in personal dealings with souls." In response he threw himself into God's hands completely: "Do with me and use me as Thou seest fit."[70] His later pastoral exhortations and dealing with individuals show that this prayer was answered abundantly.

One Monday evening young Mackay walked home with Mr. Gibb after a fellowship meeting at Gilcomston Church. They had an illuminating conversation about the causes of the superficiality of religious experience around them at that time. They traced it to several sources: the hustle, bustle, and hurry of the times, even among Christians; the tendency to lose sight of sin and the doctrine of the atonement; and a tendency to look on Christ merely as an example. The conversation is historically and spiritually illuminating. In Britain during the reign of Edward VII, son of Queen Victoria, at a time of unprecedented missionary expansion, two Christian men lamented the lack of religious experience among their fellows.[71] Despite the apparent closeness of the church and the world in some historical periods, the conversation shows the truth of von Ranke's observation that in every historical period an individual soul is equally distant from God.

At the university Mackay was active in advancing the Christian cause. On Friday, May 21, 1909, Mackay gave a paper at the Christian Union on the need of conversion before any service of God is possible. With the group from Gilcomston he sought more converts and prayed for increased strength and personal quickening and for the coming Baslow conference that he attended. On June 11, 1909, he heard Professor David Cairns speak at the Christian Union on "The Heart of Religion," which consisted in communion with God. "Enjoyed his spirit and intensity very much. Oh, that I heard more like him, declaring that this communion is the only thing in life worth

The Rev. Grant Gibb, Pastor of Gilcomston Baptist Church, Aberdeen, Scotland. Mackay's friend and pastor during his college years.

seeking after," thought Mackay.[72] Afterwards at the Student Volunteer meeting, papers were delivered dealing with the Indian Church.

The next day life intensified for Mackay on a personal level as well when Mackay's relationship with Miss Wells deepened. The Gilcomston congregation scheduled a picnic in Pitmedden Park in Aberdeen, and John and Jane were both invited. While the picnic was going on, the couple strolled through the hills and woods, and they felt something happening between them. They had been moving towards a love experience, and that afternoon they fell in love, told each other how they felt about each other, and prayed together. He wrote explicitly about it in his diary ten days later: "J. W. is mine in Christ united with me in the bonds of a most solemn compact. . . . Christ was never more precious to me. . . . We have both consecrated ourselves anew to Christ's service in the Gospel."[73]

Academic Life and Studies

During his first session in Aberdeen from 1907 to 1908 Mackay studied Latin and Greek. When he returned to Aberdeen in October 1908, his course work was in English, logic, education, and geology, and during the fall of 1908 Mackay's social horizons began to expand. Instead of a predominantly interior focus, Mackay's diary records an increasing number of activities and experiences at the university and elsewhere. He thought of getting some copies of Mott's addresses and considered starting a prayer circle especially for the spiritual life of the university.

During the 1909–1910 session Mackay's courses in moral philosophy, logic, and advanced and comparative psychology were particularly stimulating. In Aberdeen University there were also opportunities for the students to become friendly with faculty members. On a Thursday evening in January, Mackay attended a formal dinner of seventeen people at Prof. William Leslie Davidson's home. After dinner the group played whist with Miss Davidson sitting in for Mackay, who did not play whist or other card games because of his religious upbringing. Mackay felt awkward in this setting and thought, somewhat sentimentally, how none of the "brilliant company of ladies [was] . . . so sweet, gentle, and winsome as . . . [his] own beloved."[74]

Professor of philosophy James Black Baillie (not related to theologians Donald or John Baillie) keenly stimulated and challenged Mackay at Aberdeen and was central to his cultural experience, especially during his study for his honors degree. J. B. Baillie was a southern Scot, a very distinguished scholar who had studied in Oxford. He translated both Georg Wilhelm Friedrich Hegel's *Logic* and his *Phenomenology of Spirit*.[75] Though he was agnostic and occasionally cynical, one day Baillie said, "In my opinion, there is a book that is unique in human literature, without any kind of peer, and that book is the Book of Psalms. Because there you have the unique fact of man speaking to man, and man speaking to God in a way and in a dimension that you will not find in any other book in human literature." This evaluation by a worldly professor greatly impressed Mackay because at that time he belonged to a denomination that sang only from the book of Psalms, and also because the Psalms were a central reality in his own devotional life that he read morning and evening. Mackay reacted to Baillie's agnosticism in a positive way—against it—and it did not rub off on him.[76]

A notable period of Mackay's spiritual insight occurred in December 1909 as he meditated on 1 Corinthians 15 after a lecture on moral philosophy. He prayed to be "guarded from the subtle meshes of idealism," and he noted that "Paul was by no means an Idealist. He says, what advantage it me if the dead rise not? Let us eat and drink; for tomorrow we die" [1 Cor. 15:33 KJV].[77] This conscious development at an early age was a key to his spirituality. During his later life Mackay could recognize those that were "Christian Idealists."

Although he did not establish personal contact with the American speaker at that time, during the first week of February 1910 Mackay attended the Duff Lectures, sponsored by William Pirie Duff, the son of Alexander Duff, missionary to India. That year the lecturer was a young man from the United States, Robert E. Speer, and the lectures were later published. Mackay found Speer's lecture on missions and the native churches a "most masterly treatment."[78] The next evening at the Christian Union, with Professor David S. Cairns presiding, Speer gave a fine address on finding and following God's plan for our lives, and gave reasons why men and women should seriously consider the foreign mission field. Mackay concluded, "Speer was the greatest personality I have ever known."[79] That meeting influenced Mackay on his life work. When he learned that Speer had been a student at Princeton Seminary, Mackay found a significant basis, among several others, for becoming interested in studying there himself. A few months later in July 1910, Speer attended the world missionary conference held in Edinburgh.

One evening after a warm introduction from Sir William Ramsay, Mackay's Latin professor, the principal of the college gave an apologetic defense of religion to a packed hall. But the pressures of work during the winter term had taken a toll on Mackay's health. On the Friday in March before he was scheduled to return home to Inverness, he spat up some blood. The attending doctor in Aberdeen diagnosed it as having come from his left lung. Mackay remained in bed for four days and went home with his father on the following Tuesday. The family doctor at Inverness advised Mackay to take another week in bed. He consoled the youth by saying that it was "just a little vein that had been ruptured owing to the excessive strain of the previous months."[80] About six weeks later after a good recovery, he was back at work in Aberdeen with the doctor's permission. The summer term, April to July in Aberdeen, included special programs at the local church in support of the Edinburgh Missionary Conference that was scheduled for June. During that term Mackay took up an interest in Hegel, reading parts of Edward Caird's *Hegel* (1883).

After his return in May 1910 Mackay noted several events and mileposts in his diary. On May 7 King Edward VII died during the night, and shortly before that Professor Caird's wife, Helen, had died of Bright's disease. Mackay also celebrated his twenty-first birthday, adapting a little verse from John Milton as his own. The Christian Union and the Sociological Club sponsored a debate on "Shall Religion Be Taught in Public Elementary Schools?"[81] and the affirmative won. Another night at the debating hall the speaker impressed on the students the need for retaining principle at any cost. And finally on the last weekend in May Mackay took a two-day trip away from Aberdeen to give his first sermon. About eighty persons were present, and Mackay spoke on "joy in general and the highest joy." In the evening he gave a clear talk on "two methods of Gospel ministry, as exemplified by St. Paul at Athens and at Corinth."[82]

Continuing to expand his social contacts, Mackay had an afternoon out at Professor J. B. Baillie's and the next day enjoyed tea at Mr. Gibb's, where he met a number of missionaries from China. After tea he greatly enjoyed his first opportunity to play croquet. On several mornings Mackay rose early to play golf with his friend Ewen.

On June 14, Mackay led a Student Volunteer devotional meeting in preparation for the Edinburgh Missionary Conference. D. S. Cairns played an active role in presenting the report on the missionary message.[83] On the Sabbath, June 19, Mr. Gibb returned from three days at the Conference and spoke on his impressions. Mackay evidently did not attend but supported it through church meetings and prayer.

Towards the Ministry

Despite his many activities Mackay felt spiritually dead in the college environment. During the summer of 1910 he decided to leave Aberdeen and begin studies toward ordination in the Northern Presbytery of the Free Presbyterian Church. He wrote,

> I felt a strong reaction against mere worldly wisdom, and began to consider what were the great issues at stake in the ecclesiastical world. These, I believed . . . to be, the absolute infallibility and authority of Holy Scripture, and the fundamental principles of Protestant Doctrine. As both these were defended in theory and practice in the Free Presbyterian Church, I could not see my way to abandon it on minor considerations. So I resolved to sacrifice next years Honours and begin studying for its ministry now.[84]

On October 3, 1910, John Mackay appeared before the Northern Presbytery of the Free Presbyterian Church to seek acceptance to study for the ministry under Mr. J. R. Mackay in January 1911. The request was granted.

In the winter months that followed, young Mackay became a theological student in Inverness under John Robertson Mackay, the theological tutor who also happened to be the family's minister. Though also named Mackay, J. R. Mackay was not a close relative but was a very able man and a good theologian. Young John was one of three students who studied under his auspices, first with courses in Hebrew and theology. The Reverend Mackay meant a great deal to his student. A man of massive figure and massive mind the elder Mackay went on in 1918 to become a minister of the Free Church and a professor of New Testament exegesis in the Free Church College, Edinburgh. In those later years his old denomination treated him almost as a heretic.[85]

Mackay's diary records an illuminating incident related to a sermon he gave for Prof. Mackay at the afternoon service on February 3, 1911. The student spoke on the subject of Phil. 3:10 (KJV), "That I may know . . . the fellowship of his sufferings." At class on Monday, his teacher told Mackay that he disagreed with the central point of the sermon, thought the exegesis was wrong, and thought Mackay "made too much of the Christian's sufferings."[86] In response, the student suggested several related passages to support his point of view, and that night he studied the matter from all points of view.

After class the next day Prof. Mackay asked young John to wait afterwards, and he apologized to his student. As authority, the professor took out Calvin's *Commentary* and read the appropriate portion that supported what Mackay had preached in his Sunday sermon. Young John's spiritual sensitivity and reaction to this situation is illuminating:

> My mind was greatly relieved, but I soon found the uprising of pride and indignation within my heart, which, given utterance to such lofty sentiments as I had done. . . . Oh, I am an excellent talker but a very bad doer, an excellent framer of high ideals for myself and others but a miserable realiser of the same.[87]

Later for his studies Mackay preached at churches in Strathnach, Beauly, and Tain.

During the summer the local church invited Mackay to become a student minister for thirteen weeks in the town of Tain, Rosshire, about fifty miles west of Inverness. This change of environment and experience had a great influence on his life, and he was given important ministerial responsibilities there. Mackay spoke to a congregation, and generally had to prepare for three services each Sunday: morning, afternoon, and evening. The congregation usually had one service in Gaelic, but Mackay was not a Gaelic speaker, and he gave that service in English. He lived in beautiful woodland surroundings in the lovely home of a widow, Mrs. Ross, and her two daughters, in the countryside about a mile and a quarter from Tain. As far as he could, John tried to be just a member of the family. His health improved greatly as a result of the concern of the mother and two daughters, who gave him lots of milk and allowed him to rest.

In Tain, Mackay prepared himself carefully for preaching and for visitations. The congregation was about seventy or eighty persons, and in the course of exercising his pastoral responsibility Mackay visited each household four times, except one that was located outside town that he visited three times. That summer Mackay got around by walking, since he had no car or bicycle. He enjoyed walking in Tain, as he had done in Inverness and Aberdeen. The habit became ingrained, and he continued to enjoy walking for exercise his whole life.

Mackay also got to know a Free Church minister living nearby who invited Mackay to meet him. He also became acquainted with a Free Church elder, Walter Sinclair. Both men courted Mackay and tried to influence him to leave the Free Presbyterian Church and become a member of the Free Church. They told him, "You can be sure, we will use all our influence to see that you are accepted as a minister."[88] This influence was in the background as he evaluated and considered his future path, which finally led to the Free Church sponsoring him as a missionary. They assured Mackay unofficially that when he left for Princeton, they would back him up in South America.

Return to Aberdeen

John had done enough work in three years at Aberdeen to get his degree, but he now wished to study for honors in philosophy and postponed the degree for a year. After studying at Inverness with the Rev. Mackay, in the fall of 1911 he resumed his student life in Aberdeen where he had left it, with academic and social engagements. He heard the dean of Westminster give a lecture on the six days of creation in Genesis 1 on November 5, 1911. Mackay thought that the dean did not do full justice to all the historical material he might have used but presented a well-worked-out paper, though Mackay did not agree with the conclusions. The next week Mackay made his first appearance on the platform of the debating society and was congratulated on his performance. He took the negative side on the question, "Has war been the most efficient instrument in the promotion of human progress?"[89]

By now in good health again, he studied hard in Moral Philosophy Honours, Logic Honours, and Comparative Psychology Honours and won his degree of first-class honors in philosophy with important prizes: the Bain Gold Medal and the Hutton Prize. From July to October he was in Tain except for one weekend when he went to Liverpool to see his younger brother, Duncan, sail for a new life in South America. At the end of October 1912 he went to Wick in Caithness-shire to attend theological classes in New Testament and church history under Mr. Braton. His fellow students, D. MacFarlaine and D. Macdonald, and he all lodged together in one large room. After a fortnight in Wick,

Mackay returned to Aberdeen to study for the Fullerton Scholarship, which he won and which made it possible for him to study at Princeton Seminary. After the examination he returned to Wick where he studied until the end of March. In April 1913 Mackay returned for the summer term in Aberdeen with separate classes in zoology and German. At church he led a mission study circle on South America, choosing Speer's *South American Problems* (1912) as the textbook over Bishop Thomas B. Neely's *South America: Its Missionary Problems* (1909). He also continued speaking, giving three addresses, one for Mr. Gibb at Gilcomston, one to children in the Old Town Mission, and another in the open air on the Old Bridge o'Dee.[90] An academic opportunity presented itself to Mackay when the professor of logic invited John to become his assistant with the possibility of a career in the academic world. Mackay decided against the opportunity since he had other goals.

Many years later when reviewing his diary, Mackay found evidence of quiet moments and the direction of providence, unexpected on his part, when the "Hand" of God led him forward on the "road" of life. He heard Speer present an address; he became a part of the Student Volunteer Movement that focused on missions and established some very good friends in the group. The great motto of the Student Volunteer Movement was to capture the world for Christ in this generation. One summer Mackay went south to Baslow, England, for a conference sponsored by the Student Movement, a more general movement of Christian Students than the SVM, and heard Samuel Zwemer, the missionary to Muslims, speak. Zwemer was then affiliated with Princeton Seminary, and this connection to Princeton also registered in Mackay's thinking and influenced him.

Central to Mackay's philosophical reading were the works of Plato, Aristotle, F. H. Bradley, and others, as well as Hegel, whose works he came to know quite deeply. But apart from study and purely academic life, Mackay had many other personal contacts and involvements. He tried to be part of the community in both its academic and its human dimension. As a student he lived a balanced life and made strong efforts to become aware of events in Aberdeen in both secular and religious groups. Some groups met for prayer and discussion, and others considered a wide variety of secular issues and extended invitations to eminent scholars and writers. On Sundays, in particular, he devoted time to visiting people who were aged or sick. This pastoral sense came out naturally as being what a Christian should do, not because Mackay theorized or speculated about it.

Though the Bible constituted his daily readings, at the heart of Mackay's religious experience was, of course, Jesus Christ. In talks he gave, and in personal meditations and thought, Christ was central. Mackay had a sense of the "holy and loving union between Christ and His people."[91] His diary shows that Mackay encouraged conversions to Christ as he came in contact with students and others. He did not impose on them but endeavored to come to the point in conversation and friendship when he would be free and inspired to say something about Jesus Christ: to move beyond formalities and to find in Christ a refuge. This sense of refuge was illustrated by the words that meant so much to him prior to the Rogart experience: "Lord, help me."

In particular, and in both a religious and theological sense, the sense of Christian unity became meaningful to Mackay as he sought in Aberdeen to move beyond denominational connection. Promptings came into his mind and concerns arose as to how Christian unity could be formed in the world, in the churches, and in student groups. But he realized that before there could be real Christian unity or church unity, there would have to be a real communion with Christ. He wrote,

> Are not all Christians still members of one great family? Are they not all "one in Christ Jesus"? [Gal. 3:28]. It must be so. But wherefore, then this disunited Christendom? A deep purpose of grace doubtless runs through this severed unity. Still must that prayer of Christ be fulfilled "that all may be one" [John 17:21]. Lord, purge the Churches as a refiner and from their ruined dissolution raise for thyself a spiritual, united Church.[92]

In meditating on John 17 he saw how Jesus "pleaded for the unity of His church, a unity based on the oneness between Himself and the Father."[93]

Then Mackay went on to write on the text "That all may be one." He thought that "all may be one in Christ," undergirded by his personal experience with Christ in which he said "guided by my beloved, my blessed Jesus. This word, my comfort is, it buoys up my spirit in its gloomy foreboding. Our unworthiness, Lord Jesus, all my unworthiness, . . . Lord Jesus, my brutishness, my loathsomeness. How I dread to be found a hypocrite." And sometimes a melancholy mood came into his feelings: "It imposes within me a yearning for secularism, for freedom from all conventional trammels." It seemed then that the secular world offered more freedom than the religious world did. "The Church of Christ is true to its nature when it represents a mystical union. . . . When the spiritual horizon of the Church was brightened, this mystical union was the theme of the deepest thoughts of Christendom. But alas, alas, for this age, yet enlightened, yet brighter days are coming."[94]

The authors that appealed to Mackay the most were not merely intellectual but were also spiritual. The mystic reality of communion with God—conversing with God and listening to God—were realities for Mackay. The experiences of Robert Murray M'Cheyne, for example, a brilliant young man who died in his late twenties, enthralled him. The life and example of Samuel Rutherford also made a strong impression on Mackay. Rutherford appealed to him because he was a man of very, very deep religious experience. Samuel Rutherford had called his prison house in Aberdeen "Christ's palace," and as a master theologian spoke about other subjects also. He combined heart and mind and Christian outlook, a balanced combination that was important to Mackay's later theological approach. In his studies in Spain, for example, Mackay learned about Santa Teresa, but he did not know of her at this time. Like M'Cheyne she was a symbol of the combination of heart and mind, of intellect and feeling, piety and theology, both centering on Christ. To become truly a Christian, he thought, and to have a mystic personal relationship with Christ does not detach the individual from the world, either in thinking or in living. It gives light and strength to move into human reality and to fulfill obligations as a Christian in a Christ-like manner.

Thus, a confluence of influences led him to become a student at Princeton Seminary. Reverend Mackay admired the Princeton theologians, and Pastor Macleod of the Free Church of Inverness had a link with Benjamin Breckinridge Warfield in Princeton and had traveled there to see him. Zwemer was linked to Princeton, and Robert E. Speer had studied there and was the mission board secretary. Mackay wished to get away from the Free Presbyterian Church, and by going to Princeton under the auspices of the Free Church he could also make contact with people there from Latin America. A new era in his life was about to open before him.

Gradually, Mackay had become increasingly linked through friendships with members of the Free Church of Scotland. They wanted him to become a member of their church, and he was willing, wishing to get away from the Free Presbyterian Church because he did not believe that he had any real future in that denomination. During the summer of 1913 Mackay came into contact more than ever before with members of the Free Church. He was led to understand that the Free Church was now intensely interested in South America as a mission field and required only a man to offer himself for the work in order to take up operations there. Mackay was further led to understand "that it would give the greatest joy to those interested"[95] if he would offer himself for the mission. Representatives of the Free Church told him, "You are interested in mission work, and we would be willing to sponsor your missionary service in South America, if you would become a missionary of the Free Church." After long deliberation and prayer for guidance, Mackay intimated to his Free Church friends just before sailing for America his intention of offering, and at the same time he tendered his resignation from his position as a student studying for the ministry of the Free Presbyterian

Church. On the Sabbath afternoon before he departed for the United States, John spoke for Prof. Macleod to the congregation in the Free North Church in Inverness from the verse "Now then we are ambassadors for Christ" [2 Cor. 5:20]. This address in the Free North Church was a pivotal event not only for Mackay but also for his family. The pastor of the Free Presbyterian Church was angry when he heard that Mackay had spoken at the Free North, and the Mackay family soon thereafter left the Free Presbyterian Church and became members of the Free North Church.

Mackay remembered that summer of 1913 most of all because of the time he was able to spend with his beloved Jane. As he wrote in his diary, "How many rambles did we have through the woods and fields around Pitmedden. How many times did we there read the Word together, softly lift up our voices in praise, and together approach the mercy seat, surrounded by the song of birds. For ever will Pitmedden remain in our memories as a Bethel."[96]

In early September John and his father, Duncan, set sail to New York so that John could continue his studies at Princeton Theological Seminary in North America.

Chapter 3

Student Days at Princeton (1913–1915)

"Study to show thyself approved." (2 Tim. 2:15 KJV)

When Mackay came to Princeton Seminary to study, he had already committed his future life to a Christian religious vocation. He was not simply seeking an external credential for social purposes but was committed to prepare himself spiritually for lifelong service on the foreign mission field, and he used the opportunities at Princeton toward that end. He never expected to return permanently to North America and even less to be called later to the presidency of Princeton Theological Seminary, but his experiences, impressions, and ideas as a student there were of great use to him later when he returned to create an agenda for reforming and strengthening the academic life and program of the seminary. His mature thoughts and writings on the nature and purposes of a theological education and on a Christian seminary community were rooted in his early student experiences in Scotland but especially as a student at Princeton.

Princeton Theological Seminary

John's parents agreed that it could be a very good thing for him to study at Princeton. The pastor, the Rev. Macleod, was a great friend and admirer of Dr. Benjamin B. Warfield, a prominent professor there. When John's parents realized that the minister had been to Princeton, they got a great deal of information about the seminary, its name, and its orthodoxy before John became a student.[1] John's parents were fully supportive and not chagrined or disappointed at the change in denominations.

John, now a man of twenty-four, set sail for New York on September 6, 1913, from Greenock on the *Cameronia* and arrived in North America a week later. His father was so interested in his coming to Princeton that Duncan traveled with him and spent a few days on the seminary campus with his son. They arrived about a week before classes started. John met a fellow student on the campus, Peter Emmons, who had two rooms in Hodge Hall. Pete, as he was called, very graciously gave those rooms to Duncan and John Mackay to use until the seminary opened, and thus the two students began a friendship that lasted for the rest of their lives. During his first year John lived on the fourth floor in Hodge Hall, and in his second year he lived on the third floor of Alexander Hall.

Duncan thoroughly enjoyed visiting Princeton and after a week left for Montreal, from which he sailed for Glasgow on the *Athenia*. He had hoped to see Nova Scotia, but there were some difficulties for ship travel in the year before the First World War began.

Princeton Seminary's physical plant was more modest in 1913 than it became later. At the time there were two old library buildings that students and faculty used, Lenox Library and "the Brewery." The students could sit and study in the downstairs of Lenox, a dark and dismal place with poor lighting. There was a gymnasium located in what later became the administration building. Intramural soccer games were played outside Brown Hall. Clubs played football against each other, but since Mackay had not been brought up on that sport, he did not get involved.

Because he had already had two years of study for the ministry in Scotland—theology with his pastor in Inverness, and church history and New Testament studies in Wick—John entered the seminary as a "middler" or second-year student. Gradually this new world opened up to him. He made new friends, including William Miller, a junior, and Pete Emmons, who was also a middler. There was no student center, and new students became aware of the club system soon after their arrival on campus because the club representatives began to recruit the new students for membership. When John learned that Emmons was a member of the Adelphia Club, he became interested in it. The Benham Club was considered the club of the elite, and it customarily postponed inviting anyone to membership because it considered that the club had such dignity that all students aspired to become members. By the time John was approached to become a member of Benham Club, he was already a member of the Adelphia Club.

Adelphia Club was located on Alexander Street opposite the entrance to Brown Hall. The Calvin Club and Warfield Club were two separate clubs that later were combined. A fifth club, the Friars' Club, was used by older students. Few women were around the campus in those days. The Adelphia Club was the most diversified, having a larger number of foreign students and non-Presbyterians than any of the other clubs. Before the end of his first year, John was elected club vice president, which was unusual for a foreign student. In 1914–1915 he was elected the club president.

Mackay liked the courses at the seminary and took them seriously. As time passed he did well in his studies, but his mind was absorbed in reflection on the purpose of theological education and his own future ministry. His main interest was a missionary one, both on the campus and beyond it. He was less interested in Princeton as an institution than he was excited about Princeton as an instrumentality or community whereby a person lived in a Christian manner with fellow students and prepared, through relationships with fellow students, for life beyond its walls.

As a mature young man, Mackay's objective was academic preparation for something beyond the merely academic world. In the seminary at the time, he found an "absolutization" of mere learning to be able to pass examinations and to get the needed knowledge for the next stage. A professor might give the same lectures over and over again for fifteen years, and some academic courses were so rigid that a professor's lectures had actually been printed. Students could purchase lecture notes before they went to class and know what the professor was going to speak about. Mackay found attendance in the classroom a less than exciting experience, but attendance was required. Of the faculty at that time, Mackay found Drs. Machen and Erdman to be good preachers, but Dr. Warfield and the other men were primarily scholars.[2]

One of Mackay's friends and fellow students, William McElwee Miller, later a missionary to Persia, also noted a missing dimension in the education at the Princeton Seminary of that era: "It seemed to me that the seminary lacked a warmth of spiritual life which such an institution should have." Miller recounted a class prayer meeting where one classmate "prayed with fervor, 'O Lord, revive this cemetery!'"[3]

During Mackay's first year at Princeton, Benjamin Warfield was the acting president. The former seminary president, Dr. Francis Landey Patton, had resigned effective the prior August 1 due to age and failing eyesight. Patton was a graduate of Princeton Seminary who worked as a pastor, editor, and professor and then returned in 1881 to Princeton Seminary, where he served for a continuous period of thirty-two years in various capacities, including serving as its first president beginning in 1902 following retirement from the presidency of Princeton University. A man of important background in the Presbyterian Church, he was highly esteemed and was selected for the post to give distinction to the seminary, but he was not expected to make any special contribution. Prior to the time of Patton's election as president, the senior faculty member took on the functions of the office of president as the chief administrator, and that system continued during Patton's tenure. Patton was an exceptionally able preacher and a fine orator, and John heard him give his famous sermon on fundamentals. Coming from Scotland, however, Mackay was not sensitive to the background and context: that fundamentalism in the United States was a kind of solidification of nineteenth-century American theology.[4]

Mackay had contacts with various faculty members while at Princeton. B. B. Warfield, John D. Davis, John De Witt, and William Park Armstrong were older, and they administered the seminary primarily as a faculty without a president. William Park Armstrong's teaching assistant was Gresham Machen, assistant professor of New Testament literature and exegesis, whom Mackay found to be a wonderful teacher who was responsive to students.[5] He lived in a room in Alexander Hall, the only room he could get anywhere, and ate in the Benham Club. He became a controversial force in the Presbyterian Church a decade later.

Robert Dick Wilson, a very friendly and quite genial person, taught Old Testament. When students met him, the conversation would never center on personal matters but on something that had to do with the Old Testament, on learning and erudition, and on some kind of story or joke he would tell about those things. William Benton Greene lived on Alexander Street. Oswald Allis was one of the younger men teaching Old Testament at that time.

During his two years at Princeton Seminary Mackay continued occasionally to make notes in his diary, a task he usually performed on Sunday evenings. As in Scotland he recorded his impressions of the seminary and of its students and professors, jotted down summaries of sermons and lectures and his reactions to them, and also wrote his own prayers, thoughts, and spiritual self-examinations. The diary is a valuable source of contemporaneous social history of Princeton, its spiritual atmosphere, and the nature and content of the theological education there at the time. Perhaps more importantly, the diary documents Mackay's responses and spiritual growth. Course lectures were a routine aspect of the formal education, but sermons, conferences, special events, role models, and examples were an especially valuable part of the educational process for all students, including Mackay.

Sundays were a time of both personal spiritual growth and vocational development for aspiring young ministers. Mackay described his Sunday thoughts and activities in some detail. As in Aberdeen, the quality of the preaching was robust and centered on the deity. On the first Sunday after arriving in Princeton, Mackay heard a sermon by Benjamin Warfield on John 3:16, "God so loved the world," and the following week a sermon by William Benton Greene who preached on 2 Cor. 9:15, "Thanks be unto God for his unspeakable gift" or "the gift that cannot be told." Mackay found this latter sermon "a profound and devotional discourse." He was

> helped by it to some new thoughts on the Divine majesty, the heinousness and demerit of sin, and the love of God in giving His Son. He [Greene] set forth the greatness of the gift from three points of view, in particular: (1) we had no claims upon God for it, (2) of what it secures, (3) of what it cost. Made the striking remark that in Christ who had life in Himself becoming obedient unto death, we had the nearest possible approach to a logical contradiction, an indication we here approach one of the great mysteries and realities of our faith.[6]

Within a month after his arrival Mackay took an active role in worship at the seminary by leading a Wednesday prayer on the verses in 1 John 1. The next Sunday morning he attended a Communion service at Princeton's Second Presbyterian Church, but the worship style of North America differed from that of the Scottish Highlands to which Mackay was accustomed. He recorded in his diary, "Did not enjoy the service very much. My mind wandered a great deal. The service had too many frills for my taste. They all served to distract concentration."[7] A conference followed that afternoon led by Dr. Greene, who "gave a helpful address upon the meaning of the confession made by sitting at the Lord's Table." Mackay added that he "was asked, to my surprise, to lead in prayer. Did so with some little measure of liberty."[8] After the conference Mackay's friend, William Miller, invited him to the Canterbury Club for dinner, where he received a hearty welcome, joining the men in prayer after dinner.

Afterwards Mackay went to hear Robert E. Speer speak in Princeton's First Presbyterian Church. He was

> little changed from the time when I heard him in Aberdeen nearly four years ago. Gave a powerful address from the words, "Then there came again and touched me one like the appearance of a man, and he strengthened me" [Dan. 10:18 KJV]. He spoke of the power of the touch of a living personality . . . that friendship should be lived on a higher level. That the bonds of friendship should be not merely external or meretricious.[9]

The following Sunday evening, Mackay was in a more reflective mood, having just laid aside *Life of Henry Martyn*: "When I feel lonely and dejected, I find in dear Martyn a kindred soul, one who can understand me and whom I can understand. There are some truly earnest souls in this Seminary here, but in deeper moments I get closer to Brainerd and Martyn than to them."[10] Public worship that morning was led by Dr. Davis, who, wrote Mackay, preached in Chapel from Psalm 37 [v. 5 KJV], "I have not seen the righteous forsaken, nor his seed begging bread." At the afternoon conference Dr. [Geerhardus] Vos gave a rich and full exposition of the words in Mark 10—"The Son of man came not to be ministered unto, but to minister, and to give his life a ransom for many." Dr. Vos is my favorite among all the members of the faculty.[11]

Mackay's personal plans were developing, and that week he had received a letter from a friend in Dingwall, Scotland, telling him that it appeared certain that he would be accepted if he offered himself to the Free Church for service in South America. The congregation would heartily support the mission. This good news prompted Mackay to make a prayer of thanksgiving and for continued guidance.

Mackay attended a special fall conference on October 14.[12] It began on Monday night with an address by Dr. J. R. Davies, Philadelphia, on Robert Murray M'Cheyne, one of Mackay's own favorite clergymen. "The speaker spoke of the M'Cheyne type of minister as the great need of the age," Mackay wrote. "I was surprised to find that scarcely any of the American students had ever heard of M'Cheyne. I hope the address may stimulate interest in that life which has meant so much to me."[13] At the conference addresses were delivered on the subjects of the Minister as Prophet by Dr. J. O. Boyd; as Teacher by J. H. Raven; as Preacher by Dr. D. J. Burrell; as Pastor by Dr. C. Robinson; and as Missionary by Sherwood Eddy. Mackay found Eddy, a missionary from India, particularly impressive. The next morning Eddy led an early morning prayer meeting where he stressed "the need of spending much time in the reading of the word and prayer in the early hours of each morning." This struck a chord with Mackay who recognized in himself his own weakness in morning prayer, and he resolved to make greater efforts, praying that God's strength be perfected in his weakness.

The Sunday morning service was led by Dr. Robert M. Russell, Moderator of the General Assembly of the United Presbyterian Church and president of Westminster College, who preached a searching sermon on the gift of the Holy Ghost from John 7:39. "What do I know of the Holy Spirit in my life?" Mackay asked himself. At the afternoon conference Dr. Russell also made a strong impression speaking on pastoral evangelization. "The Minister," Russell said, "should always work for a verdict." Mackay took this lesson to heart and wrote, "I have been prone to rest satisfied when my words made a certain impression upon the minds of men. I have been unskilled in bringing souls to the valley of decision. Temperaments do differ, but herein I hold myself inexcusable before God for neglected opportunities, and for not having made the utmost of opportunities I did seek to turn to profit."[14] The goal and focus of a minister or evangelist always working for a verdict in the minds and hearts of listeners made a strong impression on Mackay.

The following week offered the young Scot an opportunity and privilege of attending a dedication ceremony. On October 22, 1913, Dean Andrew Fleming West opened the Princeton University graduate college that was located adjacent to the seminary campus. Mackay heard former president of the United States, William Howard Taft, now a professor of law and legal history at Yale Law School, deliver the main address. President Woodrow Wilson, who had not succeeded in locating the graduate college on the university campus, refused to attend the event. Taft's speech praised Grover Cleveland.[15] Francis Landey Patton had also been invited to attend the dedication, and because of his background and eminence as a former president of Princeton University, he thought he would be invited to give an address. Instead he was asked to give the opening prayer. Mackay was present and was amazed that Dr. Patton prayed for twenty minutes—the longest prayer he had ever heard. In his prayer Patton crystallized the thoughts that he had expected to put into an address.[16]

The following Friday evening Mackay heard his former professor from Aberdeen, Sir William Mitchell Ramsay, lecture in Miller Chapel on the subject of Paul's relation to the pagan mysteries.[17] Mackay spoke to Sir William at the close and received a warm greeting. Another speaker presented an illustrated address on Saturday evening and preached and conducted the conference on Sunday. He struck Mackay as appearing to live "in a region of high spiritual communion with God. Told some almost incredible stories of his experiences. But all to the Glory of God's grace. Spoke of the comparative paganism of life in America and Britain."[18]

In chapel and conference Mackay heard Dr. Roger Macmillan present an address, basing his thoughts on the words in 1 Cor. 16:19, the churches of Asia greet you. In the afternoon, speaking on the call to and relation of missionary service, Macmillan used the analogy of military service, but only about a dozen students and one faculty member, Dr. Greene, were present. "One thing impresses me most unfavorably," Mackay wrote in his diary. "It is the very bad examples the members of the Faculty set the students in the matters of attendance at the regular Seminary services."[19] Recalling this impression, as seminary president Mackay used his influence to increase faculty attendance at chapel services.

That evening Mackay "had a look through" *Life of Joseph Addison Alexander*. A few days later Mackay received a letter from Inverness telling him that the members of his family had all joined the Free North Church from the Free Presbyterian Church! The denominational change had been triggered by the Free Presbyterian Church's disapproval when John had spoken at the

Free North Church the previous summer. "The dye has now been cast," Mackay wrote in his diary, anticipating his future calling as a missionary within the Free Church.[20]

On Sunday, November 9, Mackay heard Dr. D. S. Kennedy of Philadelphia, editor of *The Presbyterian*, preach a highly illustrated sermon in a style that reminded Mackay of Dr. Russell. Other speakers he heard that week were Frank Higgins, the famous sky pilot; Dr. Vos; and Prof. Armstrong. He found the latter's address "pretty much a dry exegesis."[21]

Toward the end of November Mackay received an invitation to travel to a church in Ontario and to preach at Christmas time as a candidate for the pulpit of the congregation. Mackay accepted the invitation to preach but in declining the candidacy to be the church's pastor, he explained his sense of call to the mission field. He thanked God, nonetheless, for providing him with a place of retreat during the vacation.

Mackay also had the opportunity of hearing a professor speak personally of his "late experience of affliction and bereavement" when Dick Wilson preached in chapel from John 14:2: "'If it were not so, would I have told you?'" Mackay wrote,

> At points he was very affected. He told us how those words had stayed his soul when struggling with doubt. At conference in the afternoon he gave one of the finest practical addresses I ever listened to. He dealt with several matters in the student's life in a most direct way. He bubbled over with sanctified humour time and again![22]

Mackay continued his reading in the lives of missionaries with Samuel Zwemer's *Life of Raymond Lull*. He wrote in his diary, reflecting perhaps the comforts and temptations of academic theology, "I am realizing that very special grace is required to keep one spiritually alert in a Theological Seminary. 'Lord, quicken me, for I am weak.' Before next Sabbath I hope to hear the result of the [Free Church Foreign Mission] Committee's decision."[23]

Mackay's training was not restricted to the vicinity of Princeton, New Jersey, and he traveled the last weekend of November to New York for extension work. There he heard J. H. Jowett, an Englishman trained at Edinburgh and Oxford, pastor of the Fifth Avenue Presbyterian Church, preach twice, and Dr. Russell once. Jowett's subjects were both on Paul: "The Persecutor Turned Preacher" and "Whose I Am, and Whom I Serve." Dr. Russell spoke on "The Sword of Gideon." Mackay "rather enjoyed Jowett, but Russell," it seemed to him, was "the more definitely evangelical."[24]

At the end of November Mackay wrote that he had received

a letter from Walter Sinclair, Edinburgh, announcing the [Free Church Foreign Mission] Committee's decision. They unanimously agreed to accept my application, and to recommend the starting of a mission in South America to the General Assembly. It was also agreed that I should go home in May to go throughout the Church awaking interest in the project. . . . Today it was much upon my mind to abandon the idea of returning here for a second year, and to take my closing year in the F. C. College, Edinburgh, where I should be in close touch with the students and the church, where I could better promote the interests of the mission. But, O Lord, "My times are in Thy hand." Do with me as Thou wilt. Only save me from self-will and from mistaking the promptings of my carnal ambitious heart for the promptings of Thy Spirit.[25]

On the first Sunday of December Mackay again attended Communion in the Second Presbyterian Church. That afternoon Dr. Greene presided at the conference, and Dr. John Fox of New York spoke from 3 John 1. Mackay and two others were asked to lead in prayer. Continuing his reading of the lives of missionaries, that afternoon he dipped with great enjoyment into the lives of John Livingstone Nevius and Walter M. Lowrie, both missionaries to China and graduates of Princeton Seminary. "How different were the conditions here in those days," he wrote. "The spiritual life of the students appears to have been much more vital, and the outlook upon life much more serious. I also did some discussion reading in a missionary volume entitled *The Evangelization of the World*, a volume in memory of the 'Cambridge Seven.'"[26]

After spending Christmas in Canada, Mackay had a great experience attending the Student Volunteer Convention in Kansas City, Missouri, from December 31 to January 4, 1914. Professor Erdman and twelve students from Princeton attended.[27] The event occurred every four years, and this particular convention was particularly impressive. There were 3,984 students and professors present from 755 institutions. Speakers at the main session included William Jennings Bryan, Secretary of State of the United States, and leaders were R. F. Horton of Great Britain, John Mott, Robert E. Speer, and Sherwood Eddy. The Rev. Robert F. Horton of London described a moment in the convention and the force motivating the volunteers:

On Sunday morning after public session, the Volunteers who have definitely pledged themselves to missionary service assembled, 1500 strong, on the floor of the Convention Hall, and then a hundred and more who expect to sail during 1914 were called to the platform. It was one of the most thrilling moments of my life to look down on that sea of radiant faces; . . .

In the Middle Ages the Crusades were undertaken for a poor object and prosecuted by very questionable means. Very properly they failed; for even if it was desirable to possess the Sepulchre where our Lord lay, it was hatred of the Saracen rather than love of souls that prompted the attempts, and in no case could swords, siege, and massacre be supposed to honour Christ. But this crusade of the twentieth century aims at a very different object and is carried on by very different means. The object is to carry to all mankind the Gospel which is meant for all, and the weapons of the warfare are not carnal but spiritual, the living Word, the Spirit of God, the consecrated lives of those who, being redeemed by the love of Christ, cannot but love and seek their fellows.[28]

"The Convention meant very much to me," wrote Mackay, "in giving me a view of the immensity of the task before the Church of God, and in awakening in me a new spirit of sympathy towards all who earnestly seek to follow Christ."[29] In the springtime Mackay visited Maryland and Washington, DC. Then, on May 1, 1914, after successfully passing his seminary examinations, he left Princeton, sailing home to Britain on the *Caledonia*.

During the spring and summer of 1914 in Scotland, Mackay's relationship with the Free Church crystallized. At the assembly held at the end of May, he was unanimously accepted into the Free Church as their prospective missionary to South America. Thereafter, Mackay visited the congregations of the Free Church, trying to awaken and promote interest in the new mission. From towns in northern Scotland to Campbelltown in the south of Scotland, he spoke to about thirty congregations that summer.

Duncan Mackay and family in front of their home at Inverness. At right sits youngest son, William Roderick, who became Moderator of the Free Church of Scotland in 1958.

During the summer of 1914, Mackay visited the Keswick Convention, which was a "great blessing" to him. He wrote, "I was in need of spiritual refreshing and quickening, for my 'body of death' was making its influence felt." This retreat to Keswick was the fourth in a progressive pattern of spiritually meaningful religious assemblies that Mackay traced in his diary. First had been the Communion season in Rogart, where his "soul was quickened to by God's grace and clinched towards the ministry while a lad of fourteen" and, second, Baslow, six years later where he was led to dedicate himself to the mission field. Third, at Kansas City his "vision of the world's need was enlarged and . . . sympathy towards all true Christians quickened."[30]

Mackay also made three trips to his beloved Aberdeen, where he visited Jane Logan Wells. He reflected that it had been five years since they had first walked together in Pitmedden Park and that it could be a long time until they wandered there again. He wrote, "God spoke to our hearts giving us the confidence that He would protect us both during the long months of separation in troublous times"[31] of war. They dined together in the Carlton and walked together towards the demonstration school where Jane taught. "Our words were few, for we could not trust our ownselves to speak much, and at a busy street corner we bade one another farewell."[32] A fortnight later Mackay sailed for New York from Liverpool aboard the *Baltic*.

When he returned he found Princeton Seminary in an administrative transition. At its May 1914 meeting, the board of directors elected J. Ross Stevenson, a former professor at McCormick Seminary and pastor of Fifth Avenue Presbyterian Church in New York City, as president of the seminary. Because the General Assembly of the Presbyterian Church had the power to veto elections of professors and presidents of the seminary, Stevenson's inauguration was postponed until after the next General Assembly meeting. President Stevenson's inauguration actually occurred in October 1915 after Mackay had left Princeton.[33]

During his second year Mackay emerged as a student leader, though he had been willing to discontinue his education at Princeton Seminary if another avenue toward his goal of missionary service was more expedient. A selection of Mackay's diary allows him to reflect in his own words about his decision to return to Princeton for a second year of study and about the changed atmosphere that a new president and new administrative structure brought about at Princeton:

I have now returned to Princeton because it was the feeling of the members of the Foreign Mission Committee of the Church that it would be most to my advantage to complete my course in Princeton. Personally, I had been led to the point of willingness to abandon the thought of Princeton if it should appear to the Committee desirable in the interests of the new enterprise that I should spend my last session in Scotland in the F. C. College, Edinburgh. Since my return to the Seminary, the conviction has grown upon me that my presence here is of God, and that he has a work for me to do here, and that He has provided for me here influences that will contribute to preparing me for my life's work in the southern continent.

In many ways Princeton is a changed place this year. There appears to be a much more serious tone pervading the whole student body. God has now set over us as our new President, Dr. Stevenson, a man of spiritual power who is in intense sympathy with the life, difficulties, and aspirations of the students. Two new features at least are to mark life in the Seminary this year. The Sabbath afternoon conference is to become a real Conference, and occasionally the Y.M.C.A. meetings on Tuesday evenings are to be turned into discussion conferences conducted by the students themselves. For the latter I am chiefly responsible, and have been entrusted with preparing a programme of subjects to be discussed. I have resolved to limit subjects to such as have a bearing upon the advancement of the Kingdom of God in thought or practice. It has pleased God indeed to raise me to a wonderful position of influence among my fellow students here. Since my return I have been elected president of the senior class. Oh, how I desire that I may be enabled to set a true standard of piety before the eyes of all: not that men may say that I am Christ-like, but that they may say that it is necessary and comely to be Christ-like. Oh, Lord Jesus, may Thy lineaments appear more and more in me.

As to classroom work, I am concentrating on Theology, in which department I am doing the work of a Fellowship. The thesis is on "The Idea of Revelation." I get credit for Church History and in its place I am taking a three-hour course in Spanish at the University.

Tomorrow, [October 26, 1914] I hope to go to New York to attend a Conference of Theological Students to discuss Immigration and Industrial Problems."[34]

Thirty men from the seminary attended the Conference,[35] and on this trip, which Mackay recalled fifty years later, he heard J. H. Jowett preach, and he sang a hymn for the first time which became a favorite, "Come, Thou Fount of Every Blessing."[36]

During the fall term of his final year Mackay continued to emerge as a student leader, including taking a leadership role in a discussion conference, speaking with Professor Erdman on "Experimental Religion." In November Mackay preached in Pennsylvania for Dr. Workman, who was recovering from an operation. Mackay found him "a most interesting man, of the robust old Evangelical sort. His ancestors hailed from the Shetlands."[37]

Mackay described a highlight of the term, the annual Easter convention of Student Volunteers in Lancaster, Pennsylvania, which was attended by 320 delegates representing 52 institutions:

Our delegation, of which I was leader, numbered 15. I was disappointed in the fact that Mr. Taylor, an evangelistic missionary from S. America, whom I was looking forward to meeting, was unable to come at the last moment. The conference seemed to lack the leadership of a dominating spiritual personality. Consequently the devotional life of the conference suffered. Nevertheless, I carried away from Lancaster some things which I hope will be valuable, especially matters that relate to increasing the interest in missions. After the last meeting on Sabbath night, our delegation met and drew out a programme for a report meeting on our return to the Seminary and also discussed afterward some practical suggestions, which I had drawn up.

These suggestions related particularly to the buying of a new missionary map of the world, and of having the names of Seminary alumni on the field written on gummed tags over their service states; the securing of a volunteers book; the issuing of a monthly missionary bulletin. When all was over, we found the main doors of the Y.M.C.A. building had closed, and we had to go out a side door. I brought the suggestion before the Volunteer Board on Wed. morning. All was approved, and I was appointed Editor of the Bulletin. On the following Wednesday, again at the time of the mission prayer meeting to which an extra half hour was added, the conference report was delivered. Six of us took part. I closed with an appeal for South America. Dr. Stevenson and Erdman were both present.

This morning I had the privilege of speaking to the Volunteer Board in the [Princeton] University. I spoke as usual on South America, which apparently they had never been addressed on before. The novelty of the subject was doubtless largely responsible for the large attendance. At the close I was heartily thanked. One at least in the Board hopes to go as a missionary to S. America. May some of the others be led to go, too.

I had suggested to the Foreign Mission Committee of the Free Church to consider the taking on of Mr. José Osuna, a very dear friend of mine in the Seminary, as another prospective missionary for Peru. But the Committee, while treating the matter very sympathetically, resolved that until I reported concerning the needs and prospects of mission work in Peru, it would be unwise to take on any other prospective agent. I feel that this attitude is very sensible, although I feel disappointed somewhat that José and I cannot go to the field together. He is eminently qualified for undertaking the kind of work contemplated in Peru, but God "reigneth."

For devotional reading I am going through 1 Corinthians in Greek with the help of Godet's Commentary. I am getting a good deal more reading done, devotional and otherwise, than I did last year.

As to my mind and spirit I am still oppressed with dilatoriness. I need to be more judicious and abstemious in eating, in order that I may be as fit and able to use up every hour of each day for the highest ends. I try to remain active every afternoon by kicking football which I have not done much for ten years, and I find the exercise beneficial for mind and body. Football is not a sin nor a temptation to me as it used to be when, as a boy of 14, I felt that, in the interests of my spiritual life, I had to abjure it wholly. Yet as temperamentally I am able to do only one thing at a time, and as I find it most difficult to delete myself in thought or memory from anything I have engaged in with interest, I feel that my recreation is beginning to play a larger part in my thought life than it ought. Lord, enable me to be truly spiritual. Bodily exercise profiteth a little, and I know it, but give me more of that godliness which is profitable for all things.[38]

Mackay perceived the absence of a "dominating spiritual personality" at the Lancaster Conference. The observation may have strengthened his own resolve to become just such a strong spiritual presence at future conferences and assemblies during his own ministry. In his second year Mackay was elected chairman of a new student organization, the student body. Unlike the social experience for students in Aberdeen, there was little informal mixing between students and professors at Princeton Seminary. Concern arose over relations between students and faculty, and Mackay was asked to see Dr. Stevenson, the new president, to discuss with him the whole question of student-faculty relations. While sympathetic with the students' perspectives, Stevenson's sympathy had limits, and he showed little interest in becoming a member of the student community. Within his philosophy of campus relationships, the students were completely subordinate to the faculty and were under the jurisdiction and control of the faculty, and Stevenson believed students should recognize this fact and take it seriously.[39] The impressions Mackay formed through his experiences as a student leader on major issues of the status of students, student-faculty relations, and the function and role of a theological seminary in relation to the church, the world, and the missionary movement, provided a practical basis for his own writings on the role of seminary education when he returned as president.

There were, however, several important exceptions to the general aloofness of the faculty. Charles Rosenbury Erdman was the only professor on the campus at that time who showed a social and personal interest in the students. He invited student groups into his home, and one of John's own great experiences as a student was to be invited to the home of Dr. Erdman with a few other students and to be served tea and to get to know him personally. Visits to the homes of professors were also possible for special reasons: if the student had a problem, for example, or if any kind of relationship or mutual friend existed between the particular faculty member and student. In this way he also visited and had dinner with Professor and Mrs. Frederick Loetscher at their home.

The speech professor also made a strong impression on Mackay. Students gave sermons under his auspices in Miller Chapel. It happened by a coincidence—not quite what Mackay later would term "an undesigned coincidence"[40]—that the last student in class to preach and give a sermon was John Mackay, whose subject was "My Times Are in Thy Hand." Revelation of God's personal care implicit in the verse had special meaning for Mackay throughout his life. Mackay assumed the sermon was well received, for neither the professor nor the other students criticized the sermon afterwards.[41]

During his second year in the United States Mackay's missionary focus was strong. He sought out professors at Princeton University who shared the interest in Latin America and attended meetings where South America was being considered, even taking some Spanish classes at the university. The son of John R. Mott was one of the liberal arts students at Princeton University that he contacted, and a Latin American student, José Osuna from Puerto Rico, was on the roster of Mackay's senior class at Princeton Seminary. He and Mackay often talked together, and John tried to learn as much as he could from José about the language and culture of Latin America.

On Sunday evenings in a large room along the first-floor corridor of Hodge Hall, young Mackay met with a group of students for discussion and for prayer to support the missionary movement. The eating clubs played a more important part at that time than did the seminary itself in sponsoring meetings and missionary visitors who came to stay and speak. Occasionally lectures would be held in the chapel, but generally there were few seminary-wide events.

Mackay majored in theology and won the theological fellowship[42] with his mature and perceptive thesis titled "The Idea of Revelation." When Dr. Warfield told him that he had won the fellowship and a stipend to go with it, Mackay asked him, "Where could I go or where should I study and make use of it?" World War I was being fought, and it was impossible for students to go for study in Germany. Study in Britain was also ruled out because the theological faculties had been broken up to allow students to respond to the call for military service. Dr. Warfield then made the suggestion that Mackay should consider going to Spain to study the Hispanic religious tradition. "If you really want to be prepared in the fullest way for your work as an educational missionary in South America," Warfield said, "you should prepare yourself for it. If you plan to go to South America, wouldn't it be good to go to Spain and prepare yourself linguistically and culturally for that vocation?

Spain is not involved in the war." This significant recommendation led to Mackay's studies in Madrid, and the fellowship prize money made it possible for him to live there.[43]

At this stage Mackay was leaning toward serving in an educational mission capacity rather than an evangelistic preaching one. His sense of vocation and motivation was to introduce evangelical thought into the cultural fabric and to develop an individual relationship with Hispanic culture in order to emphasize and introduce the evangelical dimension into it. At this time the Board of Foreign Missions of the Presbyterian Church in the U.S.A. conducted missionary work in Brazil, but, in contrast, these missionaries did not become closely related to Latin American culture. Mackay was successful in his evangelical efforts and over time was invited to speak in thirty-five Latin American universities. It was known in cultural circles that he had been professor of metaphysics in San Marcos University in Lima and had been head of a school that, unlike most mission schools, made Spanish rather than English the language of instruction.

The future path still lay ahead, but it originated and grew from Dr. Warfield's suggestion. Thus, while studying at Princeton Seminary Mackay was consciously developing missionary principles that he could apply and that led him to identify himself with the people in his mission field, to become one with them, and to win the right to be heard by them. In his later writings Mackay gave expression to these principles as the "incarnational missionary approach."

The Foreign Missions Committee of the Free Church of Scotland had arranged for Mackay to make a fact-finding trip to Latin America after his graduation. On the eve of leaving for South America as his plans were developing, Mackay went to New York to meet Robert E. Speer at his office at 156 Fifth Avenue. Speer, a difficult person to get to see, was not able to have an interview with him, but Mackay did meet his assistant. Mackay recalled in later years that when Speer received a visitor, one had all the opportunity one wanted to talk to him and expound one's ideas, but that Speer would remain silent, creating an embarrassing vacuum. Although Speer would not suggest that his visitor go or that the time was up, the visitor would nevertheless realize it. Before departing Mackay also visited John R. Mott and talked with him at his downtown office at the YMCA. Mott would give his visitor a number of minutes when one had an engagement with him, and he would also indicate how long you could be with him.[44]

After the arrangements for the exploratory trip to Latin America had all been made, Mackay prepared to embark.

Chapter 4

Final Preparations (1915–1916)

"Go, view the land." (Josh. 2:1)

*T*he seventeen-month period between Mackay's graduation from Princeton and his departure for Lima, Peru, to begin a mission was an immersion for him in the Spanish language and in Hispanic history, geography, culture, and religion. He began with a four-month exploratory tour to Latin America under the auspices of the Free Church, and the trip introduced him to the countries, institutions, and terrain of the vast continent. In Argentina Mackay met experienced YMCA workers who acquainted him with the challenges that would lie ahead, and he discussed strategies to accomplish his planned mission. He realized and evaluated the severity of the task and the spiritual and material needs of the region. During the sojourn Mackay kept a travel diary to recall details of the trip and to help in preparing his report on the trip to Free Church officials in Scotland.

After returning to Scotland Mackay soon departed again, this time to begin academic studies at the university in Madrid for the solid background of thought and learning that would make him well prepared to work among the student class and enter intellectual circles in Peruvian and Latin American culture. The continent as a whole and these educated groups in particular were experiencing a spiritual vacuum that Mackay was being prepared to fill with the gospel. In Spain he met philosopher Unamuno, the secular writer that influenced his life more than any other. The Panama Congress of 1916, prepared by Robert E. Speer and others, signaled the coordinated evangelization of South America, a continent that had been neglected by the Edinburgh Missionary Conference of 1910.

A Missionary Tour

Before sailing from New York on the *Cristobal* on May 14, 1915, Mackay secured letters of introduction from four men deeply interested in his trip who supported the prospect of a Free Church mission in South America: Robert E. Speer, secretary of the American Presbyterian Board of Foreign Missions; Ethan Theodore Colton, associate general secretary of the International YMCA; Samuel Guy Inman, executive secretary of the Panama Conference; and A. Stuart McNairn, general secretary of the Evangelical Union of South America (EUSA). These letters enabled Mackay to receive a cordial welcome from evangelical workers wherever he went. The committee preparing the upcoming Panama Congress took advantage of his trip to enlist Mackay to publicize the upcoming congress and to distribute conference materials.

Shortly before departure, however, Mackay discovered that he had to be recommended for a passport by some well-known British subject in New York. To finalize his travel document, Mr. Scott, Speer's assistant at the Board of Foreign Missions, provided a letter of introduction to Dr. Jowett, the well-known and respected pastor of Fifth Avenue Presbyterian Church, who was glad to sign the document.[1]

On May 23 the *Cristobal* docked in Colón on the Isthmus of Panama. Mackay's "Diary and Notes of the Trip" records contacts with fellow travelers that he made on the *Cristobal*, which had been the first steamer through the Panama Canal.[2] For its size Colón was one of the most cosmopolitan cities in the world. As a result of the careful sanitary supervision of the United States government, the former notorious death trap had become a comparatively healthy city. For Mackay every moment of the three days spent in the muggy heat of Colón seemed like living in a Turkish bath. But once again on his way, passing through the Panama Canal to the Pacific Ocean, Mackay was struck by the great triumph of engineering. Its majestic motto, "The Land Divided; the World United," contrasted sharply to the zone around the waterway, which he saw was far from being a section of the "Way of Holiness." The few evening hours he spent in Panama City, a beautiful city on the Pacific, shocked Mackay for its open, unself-conscious vice. Since practically nothing was being done for the native population on the isthmus, Mackay hoped that the Latin American conference, scheduled to meet there in February 1916, would lead to the initiation of practical policies to address the moral and religious conditions on the Isthmus of Panama.

After passing over the equator and steaming up the Guayas River, the ship anchored opposite the city of Guayaquil, Ecuador, the center of the Panama hat industry and a "hotbed of yellow fever and bubonic plague." No passengers for Peru or Chile were allowed ashore. The ship touched several ports in northern Peru before landing at Callao. Mackay enjoyed the cooler weather on this part of the passage from Colón, which lasted a week and passed from nine degrees north of the equator to nine degrees south of it. The unexpected

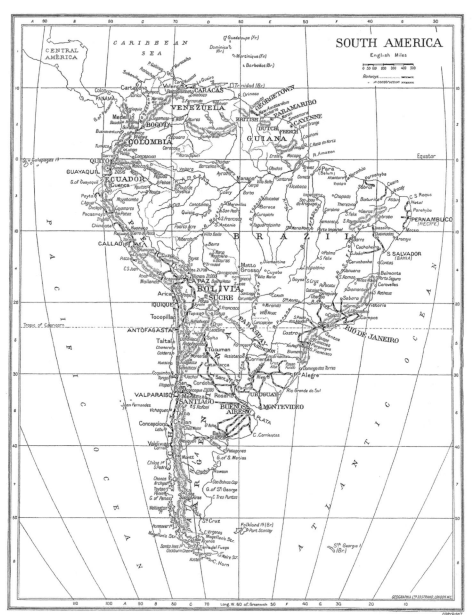

Latin America, 1913

coolness of the tropical region was due to the Humboldt current flowing north-wards along the west coast of South America from the Antarctic Ocean.

When the ship docked at Callao, John Ritchie, a man in his late thirties working with the Evangelical Union of South America, came aboard the ship from a little motor launch to meet Mackay. The old town of Callao was entirely destroyed by an earthquake and tidal wave around 1860. The modern town, though commercially important, appeared dull and filthy to the new-comer. Cases of smallpox were relatively common, and church influence was evident through imposing processions with the occasional sight of barefooted little girls carrying large crucifixes draped in green, gauze veils.

Mackay spent five happy and profitable days at Ritchie's home in Callao. Ritchie's path to the foreign mission field had been different from Mackay's and had begun with the South American and Indian Council of the Regions Beyond Missionary Union, which unanimously accepted him for service in Peru in 1905.[3] He left for Peru the next year and spent his first five months in Arequipa. During that period he made a three-week trip through south-ern Peru with a colporteur, and from it realized the value of evangelization through the printed word. By 1908 Ritchie had set up a permanent office in Lima, and in December 1909 he married Sofia Maria Schulz of Callao, a delightful lady who had been born in Peru, educated in Germany, and spoke English, Spanish, German, French, and Italian. The year before going home on furlough in 1912, Ritchie had begun publication of *El Heraldo*.

Sitting with Ritchie in his little study, Mackay told him that the purpose of his tour and visit to Lima was to supplement the educational work of the EUSA and to work among the student classes. Ritchie was passionate about the work in Peru, but he was overburdened and seemed to be on the verge of a breakdown. They discussed Protestantism in Peru, which was making absolutely no headway. Ritchie thought that Protestant schools should be of the very highest character to train youth from earliest years in an evangeli-cal atmosphere. The people of South America did not think that religion had a bearing on life, and it was hard to convince them that it did. Ritchie did not think highly of the two Methodist schools at that time, which Mackay visited during his time in Callao. In the evening Mackay and Ritchie went to Ritchie's printing office and the bookstore where Ritchie sold Spanish evangelical literature, the best Spanish pedagogical books, and Everyman's Library. Later Mackay attended a prayer meeting at a little church with about twenty persons present.

The port of Callao was linked to Lima by an excellent system of electric trams, which climbed the ten-mile gradient from port to capital in twenty-five minutes. Mackay's initial impression of the city of Lima was that it bore a striking resemblance to Edinburgh. It had landmarks similar to Arthur Seat and the Salisbury Crags, and he found the atmosphere somewhat aristocratic, romantic, and historic, like that of Edinburgh. After conquering the Incas' Andean kingdom, Pizarro and the Spaniards needed a port to maintain contact with Spain. Pizarro founded Lima on January 6, 1535, the Feast of the Epiphany. Its first name therefore was "The City of the Kings," and in the colonial period Lima was the seat of the viceroys. In the years that followed, Lima became the traditional center of Spanish culture in South America. When Mackay arrived, its size was somewhat smaller than Aberdeen, and it had quite a modern city life. The city experienced explosive population growth during the twentieth century, growing from 173,000 in 1919 (the population tripled by 1940) to over seven million by 2007.

Mackay's first impulse after being comfortably settled was to explore the churches and to get a sense of the religious life of the city. Lima's cathedral, the largest in South America, was originally built by Pizarro himself, and his mummified remains lay in a glass case in a mosaic-covered chapel to the right of the main door. One afternoon Mackay wandered into the cathedral while an imposing ceremony was in progress. Priests and friars of different ranks and orders, decked in magnificent attire, sat opposite one another in two long rows on either side of the high altar. They rose and sat repeatedly as they read, chanted, and sang. Then a procession was formed, and whoever wished to join it was given a lighted candle. In the center of the procession walked the archbishop, canopied above by a cloth of brilliant colors, held up by poles in the hands of four young priests. He held the Host before his face in a golden casket. As the procession moved around the cathedral, boys swung censers to and fro, causing sweet-smelling incense to rise. Periodically the procession would stop, and several very elderly priests preceding the Host would turn round and bow. A crowd of women followed at the rear, their heads covered with mantas—heavy black veils or shawls—or mantillas—light gauze veils of black color—required for women in place of a hat. Some broken-down men in tattered clothes were a part of the procession. Preceding the procession were the only two men that Mackay saw in the cathedral that appeared to be of the upper class, and they seemed to be government officials. Each carried a long pole with a small cross on the end of it. At each elevation of the Host the old, great bell of the cathedral sounded. In colonial times this would have been a sign for business to stop outside in the Plaza Mayor and men to uncover their heads and genuflect, but now when the old bell sounded, the hum of business outside never ceased.[4]

Mackay also visited other churches in Lima, which totaled about seventy in number. He found the outside of the majority of them to be plain and unattractive while the inside displayed a profusion of gaudy and fantastic images. In every case the image of the Virgin had the place of honor, and he saw nothing in painting or sculpture that suggested the truth of the resurrection. Mackay was present when different types of services were in progress and was struck with the absence of men. On one occasion, though, he did see a large number of young men at a church service, but they were university students who clustered around the inner doors laughing and grimacing at what the students thought were the farcical antics of the deluded worshipers and their spiritual fathers. On another occasion when Mackay was struck with the number of people in a certain church, he discovered posted on the door outside a notice granting a special indulgence from the Pope to whoever entered that building at any time within a certain period. The frequency of religious processions, the sight of barefooted friars, and the almost constant ringing of church bells were other features of the religious life of Lima that struck Mackay. He learned that in the years prior to his arrival an influx of foreign priests had aroused new enthusiasm for the ceremonies of the church but that their relations with native priests were strained.

The Scottish visitor was also particularly interested to visit the city's educational institutions. A law student who had studied for many years in the United States and who sympathized with evangelical work took him through the university. San Marcos had been founded in 1551, well before Harvard, Yale, or Princeton, in the United States. They attended some classes in literature and philosophy, and Mackay's guide introduced him to the rector of the university, Dr. Jose Pardo y Barreda, who was the President-elect of the Republic of Peru.[5]

Mackay also was introduced to Mr. MacKnight, an American and the head of the Men's Normal School in Lima. He gave Mackay some valuable information about intellectual and educational conditions. In addition to taking Mackay through his own institution, MacKnight accompanied him on a visit to Guadalupe College—the leading boys' high school in the republic. Here they spent two hours together. Although it had magnificent buildings and equipment, it produced poor educational results. Mr. MacKnight told Mackay that young men had frequently come to the normal school who were supposed to have had four years in a high school in Peru but were not able to do the multiplication table! MacKnight was one of four American educators hired by the Peruvian government to reorganize the educational system of Peru.[6]

During this initial journey Mackay also contacted and visited evangelical churches and workers. The EUSA and the Methodist Episcopal Church of North America were represented in Lima, as were representatives of the Salvation Army and the Seventh-Day Adventists. Mackay was initially critical of the Adventists, who he thought did incalculable harm on the South

American mission field. Its missionaries never entered unoccupied territory but only places where evangelical work had already been begun. They visited persons who had been won by the gospel and disturbed their minds with fine points of their doctrine.

John Ritchie was the head of the Evangelical Union Mission in Lima. The activities of this mission consisted of a preaching hall, a small elementary school, a printing office and bookstore, and a monthly magazine in Spanish, *El Heraldo*, edited by Ritchie. The mission staff consisted of five workers, including two wives of missionaries. The Methodist Episcopal Church had two preaching stations and a monthly magazine. While in the city, Mackay spoke on two occasions, once at a weekly meeting of all the evangelical workers in Callao and Lima, and once at a Sabbath service in Mr. Ritchie's hall. On both occasions, Mackay spoke and preached, and Mr. Ritchie interpreted him in Spanish.

In his diary Mackay recorded his reaction to Mr. Ritchie's hard-pressed school:

> Yesterday morning I accompanied Mr. Ritchie to his school. It has been only two years in existence, and already there are sixty-five children on the roll. But Mr. Ritchie fears that unless the E.U.S.A. directors give him support, he will have to shut the school down very shortly, as it is in debt. I was impressed very much by many of the children. As bright "bairns" some of them seemed as any in a school at home. Three mornings in the week Mr. Ritchie teaches the Bible lesson which lasts half an hour. I should like very much to see this school taken over by the Free Church and built up with a high school and college.[7]

Mackay left Lima on June 11 and sailed on board the *Ortega* for Mollendo, the port for Southern Peru, arriving there two days later. After spending the night in Mollendo, Mackay took a train for Arequipa, located in the mountainous desert of the Western Andes, a city of forty-thousand inhabitants situated at the foot of an extinct volcano, El Misti, that had a snow-capped, conical peak over 19,000 feet above sea level. The city was popularly known as the most religiously fanatical city in South America. Mackay saw more men at a service in the cathedral of Arequipa than in any church building in South America. In addition to a large number of churches, the city had a university, a famous observatory, and a hospital, undoubtedly the finest in Peru, but where, nevertheless, an average of 50 percent of the patients died! All nurses were nuns lacking true medical qualifications for their work. Mackay felt pity for all those who must pass under their care, but especially for those patients who were known to sympathize with Protestantism.[8]

It was a great joy for Mackay to meet the staff of the Evangelical Union, the only mission in Arequipa aside for the Adventists, and especially their leader the Rev. Mr. Foster, who had a preaching hall, where he often had large audiences, and an interesting club for young men. The nursing work of Miss Pritchard, another of the staff, had done more than anything else to break down prejudice among the people against the gospel and the missionaries. Miss Pritchard had access to some of the best homes of the city and was constantly asked by the leading doctors to assist them at operations and other serious cases. Mackay was led to understand that the Arequipa doctors would welcome the establishment of a good hospital, and some of the best families in the city would welcome the opening of a high school by the mission and would raise no objection to religious instruction being made a compulsory part of the curriculum. Mackay realized that the way was being prepared for the gospel in this most religiously fanatical city in South America.

Cuzco

Leaving Arequipa after a stay of four days, Mackay began a two-day, four-hundred-mile train trip to Cuzco. The night was spent on the high Sierra at a place called Juliaca because no passenger trains passed over Peruvian railways during the night. It would be far too dangerous in view of the many windings and steep gradients on the line. On the first day of the trip the train reached a height of 14,666 feet. At this altitude a great many of the passengers were sick with the dreaded *soroche*, mountain sickness, but Mackay did not suffer much from it though he had dreaded this ascent. It was dangerous for any person with a weak heart to attempt the journey across the Andes. On the second day the travelers crossed the watershed of the Andes, one of the sources of the Amazon River. Then the train descended towards Cuzco, which lay at the head of a beautiful valley 11,500 feet above sea level. The grassy *pampas* and *punas* on the high uplands of Peru, with their flocks of sheep and herds of llamas and alpacas, reminded Mackay of the mountain pasture lands in his native Highlands. In fact, he noted that the physical features of Scotland and Peru have much in common.

Cuzco is the old capital of the Incan empire and is still the center for the great indigenous population of Peru. The whole region for hundreds of miles around is ancient with history and romance. Some of the most wonderful archaeological ruins in the world are found here. Mackay stayed in Cuzco for several days as the guest of Dr. and Mrs. Fenn of the Evangelical Union Mission, the only mission in the city. Cuzco had one of the four universities of Peru. Mackay met Dr. Geisecke, the American rector of Cuzco University and a teacher of political economy who had introduced many educational reforms. He assigned students to prepare summaries of books and lectures and did not let them know in advance when to expect an examination. Mackay was favorably impressed by the work there. Dr. Geisecke told him the government of Peru was highly centralized, but among people in the province of Cuzco and Southern Peru there was a strong desire for separation from the control of Lima. Many wished to see Cuzco made the capital of the republic for all those who had a large proportion of indigenous blood. Mackay thought that if the government gave the region more autonomy it would be favorable for the cause of evangelical missions, since public opinion would be increasingly open to outside influences.[9]

Cuzco's hospital seemed squalid, although it had a better nursing staff than the hospital of Arequipa. Written above the door of one of its many churches, Mackay noted a reference to Mary rather than Christ, where the invitation of Matt. 11:28 was "blasphemously rendered, 'Come unto Mary all ye who labor and are burdened with your sins and she will relieve you.'"[10] Mackay was very interested in the evangelical and medical work of the Evangelical Union Mission, and greatly appreciated the kindness and hospitality of Dr. Fenn and his cultured wife. On two occasions he spoke in the hall of the mission. He also visited the grave of William Hewett Newell, a Protestant missionary who died there at age thirty-two of typhoid fever.[11]

On June 25, in the company of Mr. and Mrs. Thomas E. Payne, a newly married missionary couple, Mackay rode out to the Urco Mission Farm. This large farm, or more accurately a good-sized estate, was the property of the Evangelical Union and was situated in a beautiful valley about twenty-four miles from Cuzco. Mr. Payne was in charge of the farm and was assisted by Mr. Ganton, a Canadian; an American lady, Miss Stockwell, who conducted a school; and a nurse. He also had a native helper who could preach in Spanish and Quechua, the indigenous language, and operated a *botíca* or druggist's shop in the township of Calca, two miles away. When Mr. Payne first appeared in Calca from Cuzco eight years before, he was driven away by stoning and fled for his life. The year before Mackay's visit, he was asked to stand for election to the town council in Calca, which he did, and although he did absolutely no campaigning, Payne came in first in the poll. The parish priest was also a candidate but failed to get a seat. Mr. Payne's first motion in council was to have future council meetings held on a weekday and not on a Sunday, the day on which they had been held for generations. Much to the surprise of the missionary, the motion was carried unanimously. When Mackay visited, Mr. Payne had already been asked to become mayor of Calca, and the next year he intended to accept the office. The missionary's standing in the district was such that the parish priest dared not now say a word against the evangelical work carried on at the farm. The happiest memories of Mackay's tour of South America centered in the Urco Valley and in the signs of promise he saw there for the triumph of the gospel in that region of Peru. Mackay realized that the farm was known and its positive influence felt over a wide surrounding area.[12]

Mackay and Mr. Payne also discussed the opportunities for a medical mission in the region of the farm. Payne told Mackay that such a mission was exactly what the region needed. It would attract thousands of the dwellers in the upland grasslands, *punas*, and tropical valleys. Since Mackay knew of the Free Church mission committee's wish to find a location for a medical mission, he undertook a tour of investigation in order to advise the committee of the details as completely as possible. The trip covered seventeen days and over three hundred miles. Mr. Ganton accompanied Mackay along with a young Peruvian, Julio Richarte, an excellent woodsman, who acted as their guide and carried a revolver. The occasionally difficult and uncomfortable conditions of the trip gave Mackay new insights into his own nature. The group set out to the valley on mule back with their supplies. They travelled along the Urubamba River, passing through the towns of Urubamba and Ollantaytambo. On six nights they slept under the stars, among the trees, or on the soft sand beside the river—a tributary of the Amazon. Other nights they spent in large haciendas or farms in the valleys. At one stop they held the first evangelical service in the valley near Maranura for about thirty men, women, and children.[13] At noon another day they crossed the head of the valley among the eternal snows, and that evening they ate a meal of toasted maize and barley far below among tropical undergrowth. They traveled downwards through the country of orange and banana groves; through plantations of coffee, rice, and cotton; and through great sugar estates that reach from the snows to tropical heat. Mackay doubted if there was another region in the world outside Peru where it was possible to drink snow water in the morning, to eat the apples and peaches of the temperate zone before midday, and at the evening meal for dessert to have oranges, mangoes, bananas, and all the fruits of the tropics.

On the way back to Urco the travelers reached the foot of the path leading up to Machu Picchu and, after a steep ascent, reached the ancient Inca city. Mackay found the surrounding view magnificent. He noted that although Professor Bingham was the first to conduct excavations in Machu Picchu, he was not actually the discoverer of the city, as he claimed. It had been known of for years and was mentioned in old Peruvian geography books, Julio told Mackay.

In these productive and beautiful valleys on the eastern slope of the Andes, the group found a great deal of misery, sickness, and spiritual destitution. Often the travelers were hailed in pleading voices from the doors of huts that they rode past, the voices asking them to enter if they were able to render medical aid. Mackay arrived back in Urco after an absence of sixteen days with a throbbing heart and a mind made up on the need of a medical mission.

Bolivia and Chile

Mackay's mission was chiefly to visit Peru, but the Free Church committee had also given him permission to tour the other mission fields in South America with a view to gaining all the experience he could. Accordingly, he left Cuzco on July 25 by the weekly train to La Paz, Bolivia. That night he spent on a steamer that crossed Lake Titicaca, the highest lake in the world at 12,000 feet above sea level. He noted that the steamers that sailed on its waters were built by Denny's, Dumbarton, Scotland. On reaching La Paz the following day, Mackay was the guest of the Rev. Baker of the Canadian Baptist Mission, whom Mackay found to be an all-round missionary and a keen student who possessed a fine library.[14] Here he spent five enjoyable and profitable days visiting, in particular, the university and the "American Institute," a school of the Methodist Episcopal Church that was subsidized by the Bolivian government.

Saying goodbye to his new friends in the highest capital in the world, Mackay took the weekly night train for Arica, a beautiful port with tree-lined streets in the north of Chile, where he boarded the *Limari* for Valparaiso. Mackay reached Valparaiso on the fourth of August and soon discovered that it would be impossible for him to cross the Andes to Buenos Aires by train because the tunnel was entirely blocked. There was no alternative but to make arrangements for the voyage to Buenos Aires via the Magellan Straits.

While in Valparaiso Mackay found the first and only YMCA on the west coast of South America, with a large building equipped with a restaurant, gymnasium, billiard room, and bowling alleys. Mackay had a letter of introduction to Mr. Ewing, who was absent on a trip to Buenos Aires. In his place Mr. Turner gave him a warm welcome, and Mackay made the YMCA his headquarters while staying at the Royal Hotel. During the three days of his stay in this port city, Mackay visited Union Church, founded by David Trumbull,[15] whose then-current pastor, Mr. Inglis, was a Scotchman. He also learned that a Methodist church had been split by the Holiness people, who became known as Pentecostals, and that Holiness churches had more

Webster Browning, Latin American missionary and educator in Chile, and John Mackay's friend and colleague.

adherents than any other evangelical church.[16] Mackay also visited the headquarters of the Bible Society, one of the Presbyterian mission schools and a state commercial school.

The weekend from August 6 to August 9 Mackay spent in Santiago, where he was the guest of Webster Browning, head of the Instituto Ingles, a large mission high school of the Presbyterian Church of America and undoubtedly the finest school of the kind in South America. Its diploma was accepted in the leading North American universities.[17] Browning's educational philosophy included always eating *almuerzo*, luncheon, in the dining hall with the boys, eating the same food they ate. Browning provided Mackay valuable ideas about the educational work of evangelical missions.

Mackay and Browning later became lifelong friends and colleagues working together in the Presbyterian Board of Foreign Missions. Several years after this first meeting Browning baptized Mackay's first child, Isobel.

On Saturday after they had seen the classes at the school, one of the teachers took Mackay on a hike around Santiago. They walked up St. Lucia Hill where years before the Spaniard Valdivia had fortified himself against the Araucanians. As they ascended, Mackay noticed a small monument by the side of the path. The mayor of Santiago had put up the monument some forty years before to commemorate the spot where Protestants had once been buried, and Mackay thought it expressed the true Catholic attitude toward Protestants. The inscription read, "To the Memory of those Exiles from Heaven and Earth Who in this Place Lay Buried For Half a Century. 1820–1870." On Sunday morning Mackay spoke to the boys at school and later in the day preached in Union Church.

Returning to Valparaiso on Monday, Mackay addressed a special meeting in the YMCA, making the first distinctly religious address given in the institution during its three-year history. That night he stayed with Mr. Stark, head of the British and Foreign Bible Society and a Scot from Kilmarnock. The next day Stark and Turner took Mackay down to the port, and Mackay boarded the *Orita*, a 12,000-ton coal-powered ship, for the voyage through the Magellan Straits to Montevideo. Despite the short stay, Mackay had become attached to these men and looked forward to the day he would call them fellow workers. The *Orita* coaled at Coronel, the Chilean naval base from which British ships sailed before the naval battle less than a year earlier in which Germans sank both the *Good Hope* and *Monmouth*. The British officers knew they were lost before they went to sea.[18]

Mackay was struck by the snow-covered mountains that rose on each side of the narrow channel as the ship sailed into the straits. If Mackay had known earlier that he would be forced by snows to take the sea route to Buenos Aires, and if he had had time in Valparaiso, he could have arranged to meet his brother, Duncan, at Punta Arenas where the ship stopped. Mackay went ashore on a steam launch, only to learn that because of the steamer schedule, if he were to visit his brother, he would be forced to add a month to the length of his trip. Duty did not allow him to do that, and at 10:00 p.m. the ship sailed with Mackay aboard. It stopped briefly at Port Stanley in the Falkland Islands where, Mackay recalled, less than a year before German ships had fired at a wireless station. British ships immediately set out from the harbor, chased the German ships, and eliminated the German squadron. The *Dresden* escaped only to be blown up at Juan Fernández off the Chilean coast three months later.

Montevideo and Buenos Aires

Mackay arrived on Sunday morning in Montevideo, Uruguay, a modern city where most of the large shops were open on Sunday. He spent the afternoon with Mr. Conard, the YMCA secretary whom Mackay had met formally at the Student Volunteer conference in Kansas City, and Mackay gave an informal talk to some of the members in the afternoon. The YMCA in Montevideo had a fine building and five hundred members, but the young Scot noted that the only religious work undertaken was informal conversation around the tea table on Sunday afternoons. Mackay was particularly interested to meet Professor Eduardo Monteverde, a professor of mathematics at the university, an earnest Christian worker, and Mr. Conard's assistant secretary. That evening Mackay attended a Methodist church, which was the most magnificent that he had seen on the South American continent.

At this time and when they met again on a second visit, Monteverde described and discussed the student problem in South America as it had never been opened up to Mackay before, and Mackay was greatly impressed by his ideas. Although the cultural, intellectual, and scientific standards in

Latin America were high, the spiritual and moral aspects of education were not. Religion and science were opposed to each other; agnosticism prevailed in the universities; and authentic Christianity was not understood because the Gospels were not studied. Monteverde realized the importance of reaching the student class through special lectures in a secular hall and through the establishment of secondary schools that would prepare students for achieving secular educational standards and also provide sound religious instruction. The YMCA program could reach university students; the basis of pure religion could be presented at student camps; and Christian literature could also be distributed.[19]

In his first visit to Buenos Aires, Argentina, Mackay was chiefly interested in becoming familiar with the work of the YMCA, which had a large students' department, about six hundred members, a fine gymnasium, and the finest swimming pool in Buenos Aires. A graduate of the University of Buenos Aires was one of the secretaries. Mackay learned all he could about the intellectual and religious interests of the students and visited the university faculties of philosophy and letters, which were located in separate buildings since there was no central university building. Mackay was disappointed not to be able to meet the YMCA continental secretary, Mr. Ewald, who was away on a visit to Porto Alegre in Brazil. In future years the two became good friends and worked very closely. On this occasion, however, Mackay met Mr. Ewing of the YMCA and Mr. Hercus, a New Zealander, formerly of the Evangelical Union Mission, both of whom were especially helpful.

On Sunday morning Mackay conducted a Bible class in St. Andrew's Scotch Church, addressed a widely advertised meeting in the YMCA in the afternoon, and gave an address in the Methodist church in the evening. The afternoon address was translated into Spanish by the British and Foreign Bible Society for distribution in pamphlet form in South America.[20] During the last two days of his stay in Buenos Aires, Mackay was the guest of Dr. Fleming, pastor of St. Andrew's Scotch Church, the largest and wealthiest Protestant church in South America. Mackay also met Don Pablo Besson, pastor of an evangelical church and a favorite pupil of the famous French exegete Godet. Besson was an enthusiastic textual critic, standing valiantly for the *Textus Receptus*, who had written pamphlets on points in the Westcott and Hort text. The pastor was interested in dogmatic questions as well as textual ones. Mackay had a discussion with him about the kenotic theories of the incarnation, which Besson upheld; on the *Ordo Salutis*, he put justification before regeneration, and Mackay held the reverse.

Mackay liked the city of Buenos Aires. The newspaper *La Prensa* was probably the greatest in the world. A red light glowed at the top of its office building to announce major events, and a siren was also sounded for the most important events. Ewing and Mackay visited the Chamber of Deputies, a magnificent edifice. The university was decentralized, and Mackay visited the faculties of medicine and letters. He attended a lecture on philosophy at which about fifteen men and women were present. The *Biblioteca Nacional* was a library with over 800,000 volumes.

But the climax of Mackay's tour were candid discussions with the experienced Christian workers Hercus, Ewing, and Monteverde about his plans for his own future work and the circumstances that he would face. These experienced men encouraged Mackay. Mr. Hercus greatly encouraged him to press forward and prepare to present "a Christian apologetic to the cultured minds of South America." Hercus believed that up to now "missions in South America have been too narrow in their outlook. . . . The educated classes have been practically neglected."[21]

Ewing, the YMCA secretary and an earnest fellow, and Caminria, a full-time Argentine worker, both encouraged Mackay to carry out his program plan to go to Madrid and then to enter a South American university as a student. Ewing initially thought it would be a mistake for Mackay to go to Lima but changed his mind after Mackay told him frankly that he did not believe he could immediately make any contributions to the work in Buenos Aires or Montevideo. Mackay felt that if he settled in either place where Christian work was more progressive than in Lima, it would mean that he would not have time to do the study he needed. On the other hand, by going to Lima Mackay thought he would have much time to study quietly and equip himself for whatever opened up for him to do ultimately. Ewing was personally very interested in the students of South America. Before Mackay left Ewing suggested that they should pray together, which they did. Mackay wrote in his diary that Ewing

> then opened a little leather-covered book on one page of which he had the signatures of men who were especially interested in the student problem of Latin America. There were five or six names in all, including Inman's, James Smith of Brazil, and McLean of Santiago. He asked me to sign mine. I am thus more than ever dedicated to the students of Latin America. I have not had hidden from me the extreme difficulty of the method I propose: to enter the University of San Marcos as a student, but all agreed that it was worth trying.[22]

After returning to Montevideo Mackay visited the university with Prof. Monteverde, and, as at Buenos Aires, he got literature about the various faculties. Monteverde encouraged Mackay to go forward with his plans for Christian work and read Mackay an article that he had written on the idea of a students' church. Mackay disapproved "entirely of the idea for the present [since] [t]he forms of a church service are meaningless and ridiculous to the students." Then Mackay noted an irony: "And yet strangely enough he himself had gone to an evangelical service as a mocker and had 'remained to pray.' He was won by the lives of the worshippers."[23]

On September 3 Mackay sailed on the *Ruahine* for Plymouth and arrived there almost three weeks later. Time pressure did not allow a short visit to Brazil. Mackay stepped once more on the soil of England with a profound thankfulness to God for preserving him by his loving care from many dangers on mountain, plain, and sea.

Analysis of the Missionary Situation

Mackay returned to Scotland and prepared a sophisticated analysis of the spiritual needs of Latin America, and Peru in particular, to present to the Free Church Foreign Mission Committee, and he developed a well-thought-out plan of action on how the church could meet those needs. Mackay's report identified and analyzed six themes for the committee to consider that stood out in the missionary situation in Latin America. It is a useful religious and cultural benchmark of Latin American society for the time during World War I when Mackay began his ministry.

First, while the social and political influence of the Roman Catholic Church was still a power to be reckoned with in the region, particularly in Peru and Chile, and least in Uruguay, religiously the Roman Catholic Church's influence was rapidly declining. There was a serious lack of candidates for the priesthood. For example, in 1914 there were only six students in the Roman Catholic Seminary in La Paz, the chief and probably only seminary in Bolivia. Rarely did a young man of social standing or ability study for Holy Orders. The ranks of the priesthood had to be recruited from the lowest social classes and from among the children of orphanages and foundling asylums. Mackay found the immorality of the clergy to be a consistent theme throughout the continent, and often there was an angry wail in the public press about their illiteracy and general inefficiency. His report quoted from a recent article appearing in a leading newspaper of La Paz: "We have no prophets in the land who will point us out the way; our priests are ignorant and are given to sordid pursuits, and there is no one who can and will consider public questions from a disinterested platform."[24]

In the great sierras and valleys of Peru and Bolivia the Church was practically pagan. Incredible rites and superstitions abounded. The feast days were the occasion for fireworks, rioting, drunkenness, buffoonery, and sensuality, but by degrees the eyes of the people were opening. Even in Peru, which had so far refused religious toleration, clubs of young men had been founded in many of the cities to challenge the Roman Catholic Church and the priesthood. The mayors of several townships in southern Peru sent invitations to the Protestant missionaries to come and address public meetings on religion at which the mayors themselves would take the chair.

Second, there was a rising tide of infidelity and immorality. Practically the whole of the student class and the greater proportion of the educated and thoughtful people were infidel or agnostic. Astounding though it might appear, half the graduates in the Jesuit College in La Paz were avowed infidels. Those people who had discarded Catholicism but still had spiritual wishes and impulses became spiritualists or Christian Scientists. The men of South America seldom attended church, and when they did, it was only on some great occasion or for purposes of political expediency or domestic concord.

Morally, South America was in a serious condition. Mackay noted there was a complete breach between religion and morality. Male chastity was utterly unknown. Fornication was not considered a sin. There was no such thing as civic religiousness and little public spiritedness. Politics was utterly corrupt. The word "unselfishness" was not found in the everyday speech of South America.[25] The reality that the word signified was viewed as an illusion that had never been realized in a human being, and, in the words of a leading Chilean, it was "one of the traits of insanity in the Anglo-Saxon temperament."[26] In other words, one of the most deplorable symptoms of moral and spiritual degeneracy in South America was not only that there was no such thing as disinterested conduct but also that such conduct was believed to be impossible. Mackay met missionaries who told him that they had been asked over and over again by intelligent South Americans, "Now, tell us exactly what you get out of this business." When the virtue of unselfishness is coveted, and when men can believe in each other's motives, that will signal the dawn of a new era in South America, Mackay believed.

Third, Protestant missions had gained some prestige but had not caused even a ripple in the current of national life. Mackay observed that prejudice against evangelical missions was gradually breaking down. For example, Mr. Payne of the Urco Farm was now an influential councilor in the village where eight years ago he was stoned. Dr. Browning, head of the Instituto Ingles in Santiago, was asked some years earlier by the government of Bolivia to reorganize the educational system in that country. A leading Argentine statesman had publicly commended the activities of the YMCA in Buenos Aires. The advantages of an education in a Protestant mission school were also widely recognized and appreciated. Despite these advances, the evangelical cause had made comparatively little headway in South America, and some of the leading missionaries were despondent because they seemed to be having relatively little impact on a typical South American's ideals.

Of course, Protestant missions in South America had not been operating as long as had missions in India and China, for example, but there was no denying that Protestant missions in South America had been pitifully ineffective. For one thing, the missions working on the field had no common missionary policy. Efforts at evangelization had generally been small and spasmodic. Important missions had often been handicapped by the lack of continuity in their personnel. Up to that time mission boards had not grasped the real magnitude and difficulty of the churches' task in South America and too often had sent missionaries to South America who were not suited for more favored fields. Moreover, while many missionaries arrived on the field with little vision and inadequate preparation, others with a vision and adequate preparation were not given time to study and equip themselves for increased efficiency. Many workers with vision, zeal, and ability had until then been tied down to routine work and were unknown to one another. They did not have the inspiration that would come from the knowledge that others, too, had seen a vision and were striving hard to realize it.

Fourth, Protestant missions in South America had especially suffered from the lack of good literature in Spanish. Only a small quantity and a mediocre quality of evangelical literature existed in Spanish and Portuguese. Mackay believed that it was imperative to provide strong Christian apologetic literature to Protestant workers in South America. Clearly the time had come when missionaries having the ability would be allowed time and opportunity to do the necessary reading and writing in order to produce works in Christian apologetics that would challenge the attention of the educated classes.

Fifth, the crux of the missionary problem in South America was the educated classes. The immediate ideal that should be kept before Protestant missions in South America was that of well-equipped mission schools in various centers and of a great Christian university that would realize the ideal of Alexander Duff to have "religion as its foundation and animating soul."[27] That ideal was at that time actually being cherished on the South American mission field. The realization was dawning that in the past the educated, and especially the student classes that would have the destinies of their countries in their hands, had been horribly neglected.

Sixth and finally, the Panama and sectional conferences that had been scheduled to meet in the early part of the next year, 1916, were expected to have a significant impact. In the main conference the problems of Latin

America would be treated as a unity, and in the sectional conferences to be held later in Lima, Santiago, Buenos Aires, and Rio de Janeiro, specific local problems would be discussed. These conferences, Mackay hoped, would produce an enlarged vision of the field and its needs, a common and adequate missionary policy, and increased cooperation on the part of missions working in the field.

Recommendation to Found a Mission

One of Mackay's greatest joys during his tour was to learn how cherished the missionary traditions of Scotland were. The Free Church would not enter the field as intruders but as a welcome participant. It gave him great pleasure to report that missionaries everywhere were glad that Scotland would at last enter the mission field of South America. The sentiment was that the land of John Knox had a real contribution to make to the advance of Christ's Kingdom in South America, and a mission from the Free Church of Scotland was eagerly anticipated. A leading missionary told Mackay, "It ought to be in accordance with the very genius of the Free Church to have a Mission in South America."[28]

But beyond the good wishes and sentiments of missionaries, Mackay formulated a specific plan to recommend to the Free Church Mission Committee. He concluded that there was a significant zone of opportunity in Lima, the capital of Peru, for a Free Church educational mission, and an equally great opportunity in the sierra or mountain region of Peru for a Free Church medical mission. He provided reasons and analysis supporting these conclusions.

First, Mackay believed that a first-class educational mission in Lima was needed that should be conducted along strictly Christian lines. A good school was always welcomed in South America, and parents were generally quite agreeable that the Scriptures would be taught, as long as their children received a good preparation for life, and especially a good moral education.

Second, a first-class educational institution working for supreme spiritual ends would have the opportunity of forming the country's youth so that, with God's blessing, they would become good Christians and good citizens. As an illustration he noted that the work of the Instituto Ingles in Santiago had made an indelible impression on the native life of Chile.

Third, after a few years such an institution would pay its own expenses if it were successful, especially after it began to accommodate boarding students. For the last twenty years the American Presbyterian Mission Board had not been required to pay anything to support the Instituto Ingles.

Fourth, Lima would be the best location for such a school since Peru had no great Christian institutions comparable to Instituto Ingles, which was then engaged in molding life and thought in the country. It would not be difficult to compete with the national schools in Peru. Moreover, Lima was the great stronghold of Rome in South America, the center of Spanish culture in South America, as well as the center of Peruvian life and thought. An onward movement in Peru could be expected to arouse the conscience of the Free Church and the evangelical conscience of all Scotland, Mackay believed.

Fifth, a small, three-year-old elementary school belonging to Mr. Ritchie of the Evangelical Union could become the basis of a larger institution. Without more financial support from his board, Ritchie would be forced to close it down. But rather than close the school, he would prefer to hand it over to the Free Church if the church would be willing to accept it. Mackay was prepared to meet objections to his plan—for example, that this work would be slow in coming to maturity and devoid of romance—with references to the experiences and precedent of Dr. Alexander Duff's work in India.

As a second venture, using his experience at Urco as a basis, Mackay recommended a medical mission in the sierra region of Peru for several reasons. First, there were no doctors outside the larger towns of Peru, a country that like India was largely made up of villages. To reach the nearest doctor often meant a journey of hundreds of miles. While Mackay had been staying at the Urco Farm, a young man had arrived carrying his sick wife and a large bundle. A friend who had been cured of dysentery by Mr. Payne's native assistant had recommended the farm to him. To get there he had traveled six days over the mountains.

Second, Peruvian doctors would not and could not raise any objections to foreign doctors being established in a sierra region that was far from the sphere of their own practice and would not compete with them.

Third, Mackay identified and recommended Calca, the large village adjoining the Urco Farm, as an ideal center for a mission hospital for many reasons: (1) In the district the people were already friendly because of the work at the Farm. (2) Calca lay at the head of several large valleys, and a hospital there would tap a region in its immediate neighborhood with a population of 78,000. (3) After the initial expenditure, a hospital in Calca could potentially pay for itself. Patients would come to it even from Cuzco, which lay twenty-two miles away. (4) A good hospital in Calca would soon become known throughout southern Peru and would be a great contribution to the progress of the evangelical cause. (5) The climate of Calca and the district around was ideal. A wide variety of fruits would be abundant, and farm and dairy produce could be obtained from Urco Farm. (6) Mr. Payne had a practical knowledge of building, and he had promised to give all the advice and help he could if the Committee agreed on the erection of a hospital.

The Free Church Foreign Missions Committee was greatly pleased with the report and presentation and decided to move forward. The committee encouraged Mackay to pursue his studies in Spain, which he did after a visit with his family.

Studies in Spain

After several weeks in Scotland, Mackay left by train from Waverly Station, Edinburgh, for Madrid to take up the fellowship he had won and study Spanish civilization.[29] As he wrote later one purpose of his year in Spain was to "get the Scotchness out"[30] in preparation for his mission in Latin America, so that he could more fully enter into the life of the culture where he would minister. Mackay studied in Spain during the reign of King Alfonso XIII, a period of Spanish liberalism. Francisco Giner de los Ríos, who had held the chair of law at the University of Madrid, had died in February, a few months before Mackay arrived in the country, but his strong, liberal influence continued to be felt by a new generation of students, teachers, writers, and statesmen. "For nearly a year, I lived in the intellectual atmosphere Don Francisco had created, and in close friendship with his disciples,"[31] wrote Mackay. He noted that Giner's love of freedom clashed with the ideas of the Spanish church hierarchy. Although Giner wished to remain in the Catholic tradition, he was excommunicated, and in 1915 when he died, his body could not be buried in a Church cemetery. Fifteen years later Giner's disciples founded the Spanish republic. Mackay's studies in Spain influenced him to support the Spanish republic strongly in the 1930s.

In Madrid Mackay studied in what was then called the Institute of Historical Studies and lived in a unique hall, *La Residencia de Estudiantes*, that housed able students from all over Spain who engaged in work or attended courses in different parts of the university. At *La Residencia* Mackay established contacts with important Spanish personalities, including Federico de Onís, who was his teacher,[32] and Miguel de Unamuno y Jugo. De Onís was descended from a distinguished family; his great-great-grandfather, Don Luis, had been ambassador from Spain to the United States in the years of Thomas Jefferson. His father, Don José, was librarian of the University of Salamanca in the early 1900s. Later Federico became a distinguished professor at Columbia University in New York. His wife, Harriet de Onís, was a highly skilled literary translator.[33]

In 1915 Protestants in Spain were permitted to hold religious meetings freely. For spiritual companionship in Madrid Mackay attended a fellowship of Plymouth Brethren.[34] In the spiritual life of the city, Mackay noted two intellectually distinguished Spanish clergy: an Anglican bishop and a Presbyterian pastor. "Both of them had left the Roman priesthood. . . . and dedicated their lives to reviving the evangelical tradition in their country."[35] Mackay recalled that the first time he "gave a religious talk in Spanish was at a cottage meeting in the workmen's district of Tetuan, on the outskirts of Madrid."[36]

Miguel de Unamuno, who was not then widely known, was a major intellectual influence on Mackay's development and on his ministry in Latin America. From 1901 to 1914 Unamuno had been the rector, or president, of the University of Salamanca, one of the world's four oldest universities— sometimes called "Oxford in the sun"—but he was relieved of his duties after supporting the Allied cause in 1914. Mackay first made contact with the poet-philosopher when Unamuno attended a lecture given at *La Residencia*.[37] Though he did not like large cities, Unamuno was in the habit of staying there during visits to Madrid.[38] After their initial contacts in Madrid, Mackay visited Unamuno for the first time at his home in Salamanca during Christmas week 1915.[39] Don Miguel showed Mackay his library, which had books in fifteen languages. If a writer interested him, Unamuno learned the language in order to avoid translations. He showed Mackay the *Poems of Leopardi*, *Obermann* of Senancour, and the New Testament, three favorite volumes that were always on his desk.[40] Mackay found Unamuno to be an intellectual in the best sense: opposed to the "deification or absolutization of ideas."[41] He was also a Christian in the profoundest sense: he became committed to Christ but did not belong to the Roman Catholic or to the Protestant church, which did not exist there. He never studied for the priesthood or studied theology formally or ecclesiastically. Unamuno stood for personal relations between God and with one's fellows. He was a man of high moral character, the purest type of man, and a family man. Mackay remembered that unlike most intellectuals of Spain, Unamuno never engaged in fornication or in sexual relations outside marriage.[42] He also never smoked.[43]

Unamuno had a profound influence on Mackay's ministry and message, and Mackay brought and interpreted his insights and ideas to Latin America. Don Miguel was instrumental in leading Mackay to the Spanish mystics and also to the great book *Don Quixote*. He opened up to Mackay the meaning of being truly Hispanic and helped him see Hispanic culture and tradition in its fullness, including those elements scorned at that time by other Spanish intellectuals.[44] Mackay referred to Unamuno as a modern-day Spanish mystic and drew attention to his ethical teaching.[45] In his mature years Mackay in turn contributed a number of essays and writings that helped North Americans become better acquainted with Unamuno.[46]

In years after meeting Mackay, Unamuno's career continued to be turbulent and unpopular in some quarters. During the administration of Primo de Rivera he was forced into exile, but later he returned to Spain and was reelected rector of Salamanca in 1931. Unamuno became influential in the establishment of the republic. Franco took over, and the republic, that Unamuno had strongly supported, ceased to exist. In October 1936 he denounced Franco's Falangists and was put under house arrest. He died the last day of the year. During the winter of 1929 on a furlough from South America to the Scottish Highlands, Mackay had another opportunity to visit Unamuno when he spent two days with him during his exile in the frontier town of Hendaye, across the border in France.[47]

Portrait of Miguel de Unamuno that hung on the wall of Mackay's study in Princeton, NJ.

Mackay recorded his impressions of his journey to Salamanca to visit Unamuno during Christmas vacation 1915, and he also visited the city of Avila on the way. The notes he made on his trip to Old Castile show his state of mind and attitude to Roman Catholicism during his year of studies in Spain. On December 21 he left Madrid's Estacion del Norte at 9 a.m. in a third-class compartment that he found quite comfortable, and arrived via a three-horse omnibus at the Hotel Ingles, where he took a front room with steam heating. His room's window overlooked the door of the cathedral on the other side of the little plaza. That afternoon with his friend Herso Mackay visited the grand romanesque cathedral, where he felt a "tremendous impression." After noting the perfect *murallas* (walls) around the city with thirteen gates and eighty-six towers, he felt "transported back hundreds of years." He visited the Convento de Santa Teresa and the adjoining Carmelite monastery built on the site where the saint was born and baptized. An elderly monk with spectacles guided him through the building. In conversation Mackay told him that he was just reading the works of Saint Teresa and Saint John of the Cross. The chapel held an exquisite statue of St. Teresa that on certain occasions was carried at the head of processions. Mackay also saw other relics, including the saint's forefinger, her large rosary, a sandal, and a handwriting sample in a firm, bold style.

The next morning Mackay visited the Basilica of Saint Vicente. In the nave were the tombs of a number of Spaniards martyred by the Moors. At another location Mackay saw the tomb of the inquisitor general of Spain, "the man whose hands at death were stained with the blood of thousands of the noblest men and women of Spain." Next, he visited the Church of Saint Thomas, where Prince Juan, the only son of the *Reges Catolicos*, was buried, and the Monastario de Santo Tomas, founded by Ferdinand and Isabella. The Inquisitor Torquemada was buried in the sacristy.

In the afternoon he visited the Convent of the Incarnation, where Saint Teresa spent about thirty years of her life and where St. John of the Cross spent five years as confessor. A little girl showed Mackay through the chapel. He heard a choir of nuns singing behind a large screened *rajas*. At the other end of the convent Mackay ascended a stair and found himself in a small chapel with four chairs. He sat in the large one belonging to John of the Cross and observed several other relics.

"I believe they now sing before the throne," thought Mackay. Then, inspired by their fervent example, he prayed silently, adding a self-rebuke:

> But turn, my soul, from the errors which they cherished. Thou doest not need a virgin, nor a patron saint, nor a crucifix. In thy Lord alone thou hast enough. Though thou hast to say with shame that those two, despite all their errors, loved Him more than Thou, Arise, for shame. Love Him more and prove that no helps are needed to love Him deeply and to feel His love. Remember Paul, remember Rutherford.[48]

During this year in Spain Mackay began to absorb an understanding of the Spanish mystics and reformers, a group that challenged the traditional Roman Catholic ideas or procedures. While he remained a loyal Protestant, he admired Teresa of Avila, and if he had a saint, it would be Teresa: "She combined two unique traits. She was a mystic in the truest sense and enjoyed a personal relationship with Jesus Christ. But she was also active. She traveled all over Spain."[49] In an article published in 1929 he referred to her as the "most extraordinary woman who has lived on earth" ("*la mujer más extraordinaria que ha vivido en la tierra*").[50]

In light of his own calling and conversion Mackay took great interest in the religious experiences of other devout Christians. He noted that the Spanish mystics formed no school of followers: "The Spanish mystics are great individual, solitary souls, each of whom feels he 'has a king within him,' whom he has obliged to descend into his heart."[51] He also later noted that in the language of mysticism the Spaniards were *acting* mystics; the Puritans were *reacting* mystics.[52] Because of the unique cultural conditions of sixteenth-century Spain, it is difficult to draw psychological and spiritual comparisons between Mackay's experiences and those of Spanish mystics such as Teresa. Mackay retained interest in her work, however, acquiring various editions of her writings, in which she used figurative language to describe her experiences. For example, in her *Vida*, Teresa included a famous metaphorical description of prayer when she described the convent garden. To make the flowers grow, there are four ways to water the garden, and each successive method requires less labor from the gardener: water can be brought from a well; water can come from a water wheel; water can come from a stream; or, finally, water can come from a heavy rain. This fourth way is by far the best since the garden is soaked by God with no effort from the human gardener.[53]

The Panama Congress

While several events within Peru prepared the way for Mackay's work there, forces outside of Peru were creating a structure to support and coordinate Protestant missions in Peru and around South America. The most important was the Committee on Cooperation in Latin America, which had its genesis at the Edinburgh Conference.

When the Edinburgh Mission Conference was held in 1910, one element of the Anglican Church had exerted its influence to exclude South America from the conference agenda. That element strongly emphasized the importance of formal sacramental rituals and deemphasized evangelicalism. Some other traditional churches opposed the establishment of missions in Latin America because they thought they would be an imposition and that Latin America, like Canada, was not a true mission field.[54] The American participants at Edinburgh did not share the view and believed that Roman Catholicism, as practiced in Latin America at that time, should not preclude Protestant endeavors on that continent. Until that time Protestant missions in Latin America generally provided spiritual care for fellow Americans, Britains, or other Protestants in the business community who went there. They did not directly confront Hispanic reality or the Roman Catholic Church, which did not follow the traditions represented by Saint Teresa and Saint John of the Cross. After the Panama Congress the impositional nature of Latin American Catholicism was seen more clearly.

Due to the skills and efforts of Robert E. Speer, who began organizing support at two luncheon meetings in Edinburgh during the Conference, the continent of South America was not forgotten.[55] In the words of one Latin American writer, they were not to "become permanent outcasts from the ecumenical movement . . . rejected by their brother-Protestants in other countries as something like bastards, with little or no right to exist and breathe the ecumenical air."[56] As part of the ongoing work of the Edinburgh Conference twenty-two regional meetings were scheduled for follow-up attention. The participants from Speer's two luncheon meetings prepared a statement to address the issue of missions in countries "nominally Christian" but not included in the Edinburgh Conference and whose residents were being deprived of the "full pure Gospel."[57] Later, the Foreign Missions Conference of North America also sponsored a meeting dealing with Latin America. The organizing committee chose to call itself the "Committee on Cooperation in Latin America," and it was to be chaired, appropriately, by Robert E. Speer.

The years of preparation for the Panama Congress were a time of sifting, balancing, and weighing competing emphases. In the process Robert E. Speer was successful in synthesizing and imprinting his own understanding of Protestant Christianity upon it. It was a delicate task to organize extremely divergent interests of those churches and the field workers and to reconcile political, theological, and social emphases. Furthermore, underlying historical and cultural tensions between North and South America had recently erupted in the Spanish American War in 1898. There were tensions between those of different denominations that rigidly held to certain theological and doctrinal positions. There was conflict over what posture to take regarding the Roman Catholic Church and anticlerical sentiment. There were also disagreements over the level of social involvement that should be endorsed.

Samuel Guy Inman, a Disciples of Christ missionary from Mexico, became the organizing secretary for the Conference. During 1914 he traveled throughout South America to try to make clear that the Conference was for missionaries and national leaders themselves and was not designed as a congress or federation of missionary boards. Panama was chosen as the location over Rio de Janeiro and Buenos Aires because of its central location and the improved health standards that accompanied the construction and recent opening of the Panama Canal. The Conference date coincided with the 370th anniversary of the birth of Martin Luther.

As noted, the Edinburgh Conference had avoided confronting comprehensive issues of Christian unity by excluding South America from its scope. The Panama Congress is significant for Christian history because it led directly to Protestant parallel development and challenges to Roman Catholic theology and practice in the mission field. Preparation for the Panama Congress posed unique issues for the Episcopal Church of North America, where forces of

ritualism and evangelicalism opposed each other at the mission board conference. The Episcopal Church of North America confronted a choice. Should
it endorse directing missionary attention to a continent that had already been
nominally evangelized in the name of Christ by the Roman Church? If it did,
what would be the reaction by the Church of Rome to Anglican initiatives of
union with Rome? That question was tentatively answered in May of 1915
when the Protestant Episcopal Board of Missions voted to send delegates to
the Panama Congress.

The vote, however, produced sharp dissention within the Episcopal Church
between the "High" and "Low" parties as to whether that support should be
rescinded, and these disputes take on added interest in light of other efforts for
unity among churches later in the century. At a meeting of the board of missions of the Protestant Episcopal Church at the end of October 1915 in New
York, the ritualistic wing of the church demanded that the Episcopal Church
not send delegates on the grounds that to do so would be a direct insult to the
Roman Catholic Church. On the day before the meeting was scheduled, Guy
Inman published a letter in the *New York Times* refuting the criticisms lev-
eled at the Congress.[58] The next day at the Episcopal mission board meeting
partisans nevertheless had a bruising debate. Attempting to put matters in proportion, George Wharton Pepper, a Philadelphia lawyer, wondered whether
"the Pope in the Vatican would tear his robes and his hair when he heard that
the Episcopalians were about to send delegates to the conference."[59] Bishop
Weller of Fond du Lac, Wisconsin, failed to see the humor in the remark and
resigning from the board, went on to charge that supporting the Panama Congress was defiance of the Episcopal House of Bishops.

The debate continued within the Episcopal Church until the end of the
year.[60] Broad churchmen ultimately prevailed when efforts to organize a special meeting of the house of bishops were dropped. Ostensibly the meeting
was to elect a successor for the deceased bishop of South Dakota, but it could
also have conducted "other business," namely, to consider participation in
the Panama Congress and to override the decision of the mission board. The
issue of Episcopalian participation was abandoned when Presiding Bishop
Tuttle, of St. Louis, recalled his order for a special session in Philadelphia on
January 12 because he did not receive favorable responses from fifty-eight
bishops; only fifty-two replied.[61]

Bishop Anderson of Chicago, the head of the Episcopalian Commission
on the World Conference on Faith and Order, was to have led a group to
the Vatican to request that the pope consider a plan to unite Christian
churches. He harshly criticized the Panama Congress in a pamphlet about
the "Panama Spider." The Congress, he wrote, would not bring unity within

the Episcopal Church, between Roman Catholics and Protestants, or within Protestant churches themselves.[62]

The controversy of the Episcopal mission board in the United States is an example of dissention that may confront church leaders attempting to bring about structural, institutional, and spiritual unity within one denomination. Good faith and creative humility are prerequisites for those working together toward church unity. The conflict illustrates strong differences at that time about the nature of church unity being sought and highlights tensions between advocates of institutionalism and evangelism. The series of informal discussions of the 1920s known as the Malines Conversations, which explored possible reunion between the Roman Catholic Church and the Church of England, were unsuccessful in light of the Bull *Apostolicae Curae* of 1896, which had denied that Anglican orders were valid.[63]

The Congress itself augured a new era for Latin America. The president of Panama, Dr. Belisario Porras, planned to speak at the Congress despite the opposition of the Roman Catholic Bishop for the Diocese of Panama, William Rojas.[64] The report of the Commission on Survey and Occupation declared the woeful condition of the Christian faith in Latin America.[65] But because the reports were written in English, there was some misinterpretation among Latin American delegates as to the scope of future work in Latin America. Several of the leading delegates, however, worked successfully to resolve these misunderstandings.[66] As the Congress came to an end, Guy Inman was elected General Secretary of an enlarged committee for cooperation, and Dr. Speer summarized the work that the Congress had accomplished.[67]

Those with a true vocation as leaders do not seek or maneuver for power; they step forward to meet a need and in the process create new structures and guide movements to respond to that need. Speer, Mott, Brown, Inman, and others did just that at the Panama Congress. Like the Edinburgh Conference, Panama established a continuation committee to follow and organize the work of Protestant missions on an ongoing basis after the Congress ended. In seeking Christian spiritual unity, however, the Panama Congress went a step beyond Edinburgh because it confronted the issue that Edinburgh had deliberately avoided. The Panama Congress necessarily focused thought and attention on Roman Catholic theology and its practice in its Spanish American embodiment.

In the historical setting and to human logic what the leaders of the Panama Congress envisioned and were attempting to accomplish seemed "impossible."[68] To one Presbyterian the Continuation Committee of the Panama Congress seemed an imperium in imperio, a wonderfully constructed piece of quasi-ecclesiasticism erected in the very midst of the ordinary ecclesiastical machinery which is supposed to control Missions and Missionary-made Churches. . . . Its final effect, if consistently carried out, is the reshaping and reorganizing of all Missions which accept its spirit and method based on one comprehensive general principle, namely interdenominational co-operation leading toward and in many cases distinctly aiming at the attainment of Church unity as distinguished from the more general concept of Christian unity in the older usage of that term.[69]

To achieve their goal, the leaders would be required to steer a peaceful course in the mission field between Roman Catholicism and rationalism, and gain cooperation between Protestant groups whose theological emphases and points of view were frequently at odds. A commentator characterized the goal of the committee as one that "begins with Co-operation, continues with Federation, and ends with Unification."[70] As a catalyst the committee began a process that is continuing today. The thrust of the movement was not to arouse old conflicts or controversies between different church groups, thus it was necessary to downplay some nonessential theological differences and still find common ground through joint evangelistic effort. In that process conducted in good faith and over time, Christian missionary leaders discover common viewpoints to achieve spiritual unity in evangelization.

After the Panama Congress ended, delegates dispersed in four regional deputations to regional conferences held in the Latin countries themselves. These conferences were intended to carry and interpret the spirit and results of the Panama Congress, to study the problems firsthand, to test the findings of the Congress, and to encourage the workers in the field.[71] The Conference at Lima, Peru, was held March 1–5, 1916. Among those present were Francisco Penzotti and Ruth Rouse. Among other things the conference in Lima noted that as of November 1915 the constitutional ban on the practice of religions other than Catholicism had been lifted, and Scriptures could be sold publicly. This was accomplished a year before Mackay left on his mission.

Marriage and Farewell

When his studies ended in Spain, Mackay returned to Scotland through France. He was commissioned by the Free Church of Scotland to be a missionary to Peru, and Jane Logan Wells and John Alexander Mackay were married on

August 16, 1916 at the Imperial Hotel in Aberdeen. The Reverends Macleod of Inverness and Grant Gibb of Aberdeen presided at the ceremony.

The Free Church held a farewell meeting for the couple in Edinburgh on Tuesday, September 26, 1916. After some introductory remarks by others, Mackay stepped to the platform and began to speak about his call and the opportunity of missionary work. God's hand had led them to the place where they had come, he told the gathering. He explained why he was ordained a foreign missionary and not a home pastor. Several people had told him he was a fool "to leave . . . [his] drunken landlord-ridden Scotland to work in Peru."[72] He had not hurried this decision. He had considered the opportunities for study and literature and history that were available at home. Scotland placed claims for his service because less than half the population attended church. The claim of Scotland was strong, but the claim of Peru was stronger.

Mackay told the group that he found that it was as difficult to analyze his missionary call as it was to analyze his call in grace. But he assuredly felt the call and must answer to God and not men. The time was ripe because of the interest in Latin America outside that continent, including the Panama Congress, and because the time was right to initiate a new mission on behalf of the church as a spiritual institution and tell the people of Latin America of the principles of righteousness.

Mr. Archibald MacNeilage spoke next and paid Mackay a high compliment. He said that he had heard Mackay preach twice on the previous Sabbath and was then reminded of the question that "the old Cameronian asked when listening to the youthful Alexander Duff in Dr. Symington's church in Stranraer: 'Where got the Establishment that man?' Mr. Mackay was a gift to them, as Duff had been to the Scottish Church when the night of Moderatism was passing away."[73] MacNeilage then presented the couple a traveling tea basket—which he noted with humor was a very useful part of a missionary's equipment—a gold signet ring for Mrs. Mackay, and a check for £75. When Mackay thanked MacNeilage for the gift, his words were greeted with applause as he noted that MacNeilage had come from the Free Presbyterian Church and that when Mackay returned to Scotland for his furlough, he hoped to find the two churches had become one!

On the following Sunday, October 1, Mackay preached in Glasgow and on the 8th he preached in Edinburgh. Then the young couple left Europe to start a new life. They sailed for Peru on Friday the 13th from London on the SS *Kanuta* via the Panama Canal.

Chapter 5

Earning the Right to Be Heard (1916–1922)

"You need someone to teach you." (Heb. 5:12)

*I*n 1916, the devastating Battles of Verdun and the Somme were being fought, and the outcome of World War I was uncertain. In mid-October of that year the Mackays sailed from London for South America. They were the only passengers on the coal-powered cargo freighter *SS Kanuta*, and Jane L. Mackay recorded details of the five-week trip in a notebook. Steaming down the Thames past Woolwich Arsenal, they heard guns being tested, and passing an aerodrome, they saw aeroplanes flying, looping the loop, and alighting.

The steamer passed the chalk cliffs and Margate, Ramsgate, Deal, and Dover. At Deal the *Kanuta* dropped its pilot, who went over the side of the freighter by ladder and got into a small boat. As the ship entered the busy channel, a patrol boat hailed it, and a bag was thrown on board. The bag contained private papers from the Admiralty Office indicating to the captain which route to follow. The freighter passed the Isle of Wight and later Eddystone Lighthouse. That evening after looking at her native land for one last time, Mrs. Mackay "felt queer inside." Once at sea the travelers sighted two other vessels, one a large steamer and the other a fully rigged sailing ship. On Sunday the captain did not suggest a religious service, so the Mackays held private devotions by themselves, and the captain joined them in the evening. The officers played biffs, a croquet-like game, just as though it were not the Sabbath.

On November 2, after seventeen days spent crossing the Atlantic, Cape Hatteras was sighted, and the freighter made its way to Hampton Roads, Virginia, anchoring for the night between two large American battleships. The next day the freighter was towed to the coaling jetty, and the Mackays climbed down a rope ladder onto Virginia soil. The coaling operations began in the evening and created a deafening noise. The Mackays explored Newport News and Norfolk, returning just in time before the *Kanuta* departed for Colón. They were thankful to God when they learned later that crossing the Atlantic they "had been in the same longitude and within some fifty miles of an enemy submarine, which had gone three miles round a Norwegian vessel to ascertain the nationality."[1]

On arriving in Lima, Mackay contacted John Ritchie and again visited the school that Ritchie operated. Mackay was present for an examination of the pupils and was impressed by the fifty or sixty students in attendance and the three Peruvian teachers. Lacking sufficient students and financial support, the school was nearing collapse. Mackay made arrangements to take it over in the name of the Free Church and to reorganize and relocate it. Mrs. Mackay, a fully qualified and experienced teacher who had taught in the Demonstration School of the Aberdeen Teachers Training Centre, planned to take charge of the English department. John would provide instruction in the Bible.[2]

The Mackays' mission to Peru began at a decisive period in Peru's history. Political and social liberalism were emerging as part of the modernization process, and political initiatives toward religious freedom reflected social liberalism. Mackay's contributions to the country were religious, educational, and cultural: the establishment of a Presbyterian congregation and a Protestant school in Lima and the introduction of Reformation ethical values into the country's culture. His work began at the precise moment that forces within Peru were manifesting strong interest in educational reform. Attracting progressive students and teachers to the school, Mackay was at the heart of the change.

Peru was known as a difficult field for Protestant missionaries, who had made little progress in the previous ninety years, and the number of foreign religious workers there was small. In May of 1917 there were only twenty-nine foreign workers and eight Peruvian ministers. Of the foreign workers, six men were ordained ministers and three were professors while five women were teachers, four were nurses, and ten were wives of missionaries.[3]

The political, religious, and social power of the Roman Catholic Church was embedded in the Peruvian culture, and the Roman Catholic hierarchy responded to the challenge that Protestant missions were making to its preferred position. The Spanish form of Catholicism that Francisco Pizarro brought to Peru was a politicized religion radically different from and opposed to principles of Protestantism. The early Protestant missionaries of the twentieth century intended to bring sixteenth-century Reformation principles to the Peruvian people.[4]

Early Protestant Mission Work

One of the first Protestant workers in Peru was James Thomson, a Baptist affiliated with the British and Foreign Bible Society who had set out to establish schools there. These schools were based on Lancasterian theories of education under which advanced students acted as monitors and helped new or slower students. Thomson had introduced such schools in Argentina and Chile, and from 1822 to 1824 he attempted to introduce them in Peru. Despite adversities, three schools were founded, and later thirty more were organized through a variety of supporters. Thomson collaborated with Roman Catholic priests who supported his efforts, and he did not attempt to start a separate Evangelical Church. He hoped instead to stimulate reformation through the Catholic Church by education and biblical study. By 1852, however, when it became clear that his methods did not have the desired result, he tied his reform efforts to the establishment of Protestant missions.

Later in the nineteenth century a number of English-speaking Protestant congregations were organized in Peru, including an Anglican congregation for the benefit of the British diplomatic legation. The Anglican Church had been established with the provisional consent of the Peruvian government, and the first chaplain was appointed in 1849. The congregation suffered a setback in 1879, however, when the congregation's fifth chaplain became a convert to Roman Catholicism. Afterwards the congregation was held together by efforts of the laity until the position was filled by a new chaplain in 1885.

From 1859 through the mid-1880s a number of efforts were made to organize Protestant worship in the Port of Callao where a steamship company had set up a workshop. Those efforts were not systematic and were not directed toward the indigenous population. Rather they gave spiritual and religious support to the European commercial class at the port.

During the twenty-five or thirty years before Mackay's arrival, two incidents occurred, one near Lima and one in southern Peru, that paved the way for his ministry and shifted public opinion towards religious freedom. Francisco G. Penzotti was a young Italian whose family moved to Uruguay while the boy was in his early teens. He had become a Christian believer in 1876 under the influence of a Methodist missionary. Penzotti worked as a pastor before the American Bible Society hired him, and between 1883 and 1886 he made three trips across South America distributing Bibles. His spiritual gifts suited him for his work as did his fluency in Spanish, his preaching and pastoral skills, his training as a colporteur, a pleasing personality, and a supportive wife. In July 1888 Penzotti, in his midthirties, with his wife and children and an assistant, J. B. Arancet, arrived in Callao to start an American Bible Society agency in Peru, and also to work in Ecuador, Bolivia, and Chile.

Penzotti distributed Scriptures in the neighborhoods, and the religious meetings held in his home grew so large that a warehouse had to be rented to accommodate the expanding congregation. Penzotti trained his congregants to go out two by two to evangelize on Sunday afternoons. When Arancet and a new convert left to take the Scriptures to Southern Peru, news reached Penzotti that they had been stoned by a mob. He quickly set out to help. Soon all three were jailed for selling Bibles in Arequipa, a conservative stronghold in the south, but they were released on orders of the president of Peru.

By 1890 when the Methodist superintendent visited Callao, the congregation became a recognized Methodist Episcopal congregation, but it continued to experience resistance. Article IV of the Peruvian constitution provided that "the nation professes the Apostolic Roman Catholic religion. The state protects it and does not permit the public exercise of any other." To accommodate Penzotti's Protestant worship services, an arrangement was created whereby the congregants would enter the building by presenting a ticket, and the doors to the service would be kept closed. The congregation was harassed when a priest put a lock on the single closed door during the service. A worshiper who arrived late for the service luckily had a key in his pocket that fit the lock and freed the congregation. Later when another priest accused Penzotti of violating Article IV of the Constitution, he was arrested and imprisoned.

Penzotti refused to compromise, declining to be freed and deported since to do that would be to admit that Protestant services violated the Constitution of Peru. Penzotti's wife remained with him and brought food each day, but their daughters went to Chile for their safety. As time passed, his imprisonment aroused sympathy and liberal feelings among the citizens. At last, the matter came to trial, and Penzotti was acquitted by the local court on the basis that if someone could lock the door from the outside during the service without the congregation noticing, the door must have been properly closed. But his accusers appealed to an intermediate court, where Penzotti was again acquitted, but they persisted, appealing finally to the Supreme Court. After a delay the court was recalled from a recess and its ruling found him innocent. He was released March 28, 1891, Holy Saturday. Penzotti's health deteriorated during his imprisonment, but he gained attention and sympathy for his cause, and two thousand liberal anticlericals petitioned for broader freedom of religion.[5]

The second incident, one that led to an amendment to the Peruvian constitution, also eased the way for Mackay's work and occurred in the southern region of Peru where two Seventh-Day Adventists had arrived in 1898. They were arrested in Arequipa and deported for distributing tracts in the city square. Some years later mission work began on the southern shores of Lake Titicaca, where the indigenous people spoke Amara not Quechua. A campesino named Manuel Camacho attended a Protestant school and after serving in the army started a school in 1904 to improve the lives of his people. He was socially active and led a protest group to the president of Peru asking the government to protect local people from large landowners and asking for schools, but without success. Although the school was not a religious one, the bishop of Puno sent friars to preach against the school. In the words of one sermon reported in a newspaper of Puno, "God never intended them [the campesinos] to go to school and get learning. Their business was to attend to their sheep and crops, and that if they persisted in attending school, their crops would be blighted and disease would kill their flocks."[6] The bishop then accused Camacho of fomenting unrest among the locals, and he closed the school. Camacho believed that with the support of foreign missionaries, he would be protected, and he sought support from John Ritchie or another missionary in 1907, but neither could go to help at that time. The Adventists, who had been working in southern Peru, took up the opportunity, and the school opened in 1910. After a number of contacts, a Protestant missionary, named F. A. Stahl, along with a nurse and Stahl's wife, Ana, who was a teacher, moved to Plateria in 1910, where Stahl was assigned to full-time work the following year.

Stahl was not a sectarian Adventist but realized that he must meet the social needs of his hearers, and he preached the gospel of salvation by grace.[7] The people were open to the grace that was offered, and the Stahls taught them principles of personal hygiene, brought smallpox vaccine, and taught from the Bible. Soon up to eight hundred persons were attending Sunday services. The work advanced so well that mission buildings were erected in 1913.

But the bishop of Puno continued to try to wipe out the mission. In an effort to make these local people submissive once more to the landowners and to the church, he attacked the buildings on March 3, 1913, with several governmental officials and two hundred campesinos from Chucuito, destroying school materials and mixing up the medicines. A priest beat Camacho with a whip, while his eleven-year-old son pleaded with the bishop to save his father's life. The campesinos were sent to jail in Puno and then released by the local judge, who forwarded the case to the Supreme Court in Lima because a bishop was involved in the matter. The judgment releasing the campesinos was confirmed by the Supreme Court.

This incident set off both progressive and reactionary consequences. In order to satisfy the liberal belief that if a crime had been committed by the local people, the secular authorities, not the church, should have addressed the problem, a senator from Puno introduced legislation to amend Article IV of the Constitution dealing with religion. As amended it read, "The nation professes the Roman Catholic Apostolic religion; the State protects it." The final clause, "and does not permit the public exercise of any other," was deleted. John Ritchie and other Protestant missionaries publicized the bill, urging support for it in the Congress.

For his part the bishop of Puno accused the Stahls of encouraging the campesinos to rebel against proper authority. The president of Peru set up a commission to investigate the charges that produced a report favoring the Stahls and disputing the bishop's claim. By September 1913 the change to the constitution had been passed, and after receiving final ratification, it became law on October 20, 1915,[8] a year before the Mackays' arrival.

The persecution of Penzotti in Callao and of the Stahls in southern Peru were catalysts in the transformation and development of twentieth-century Peruvian life. These incidents shifted public sentiment in favor of change in the restrictive article of the Peruvian constitution that gave legal and constitutional exclusivity to the Roman Catholic religion in Peru prior to 1915.

The Free Church Mission, *Escuela Anglo-Peruana*, Established

In late November 1916 the Mackays arrived at Lima, just as summer was beginning in the southern hemisphere. During the next three and one half years the mission work took hold, culminating in the establishment of a congregation of the Free Church of Scotland. The missionaries described those first days in Lima through letters to the Foreign Mission Committee, contributions to the *Monthly Record of the Free Church of Scotland*, and to *The Instructor*, a magazine for children. Before submitting his first transmittal for publication Mackay waited "to catch a glimmer of light in the darkness and see a few yards of the path."[9]

Mackay realized his arrival in Peru came at a dynamic historical moment. He later wrote of the period, "History teaches us that there are divine, providential moments in the life of men and nations, when they are particularly susceptible to a new religious message. Such a moment has come in the Latin lands of America."[10] His initial work in founding and building the new school into a going concern required special organizational skills. He had to attract pupils, deal with families, obtain equipment, organize staff, and communicate with the mission board in Edinburgh during wartime. As time passed his Christian influence extended beyond the school to the city and to the country and continent at large.[11]

By the beginning of January 1917 Mackay contracted for the transfer of the EUSA school and leased a new building for it in a populous district on a street having mainline transportation by street car. The school's old name, *Escuela Diego Thomson*, after the first Protestant missionary to Peru, was changed. Its new name, *Escuela Anglo-Peruana*, was painted on a sign above the door. Mackay applied for a license, had prospectuses printed and dis-

Jane and John Mackay when they commenced their mission to Peru in 1916.

tributed, and published occasional notices in two of the leading papers. By early February the Mackays were busy with carpentry, painting, and window cleaning to get the facility ready for the new school year. Several teachers had resigned from the Normal School and were establishing private schools in various parts of the city that would compete for students with *Escuela Anglo-Peruana.* On February 15 the Free Church school opened for matriculation, and Mackay met parents during the remainder of the month. On March 1 the school opened with about forty pupils. Exactly eight weeks later the school had eighty-five students on its rolls.

The students came from many racial ethnic backgrounds: Spanish, English, Chinese, Quechua, and African. Mackay was encouraged by the interest shown at the morning Bible lessons that all pupils attended. The school was not a center of religious indoctrination, but an environment of confessional freedom, lacking clerical prejudices.[12] The staff consisted of three Peruvian teachers, John and Jane Mackay, and John had full charge of the two highest grades for some weeks. As he wrote to the Free Church, "Our aim is threefold—first, to meet the educational needs of the Protestant cause in Peru; second, to prepare teachers and preachers for direct missionary service; and, third to influence the community through the children who pass through our hands."[13]

The biblical motto that Mackay chose for the school was "The fear of the Lord is the beginning of wisdom." It reflected the Christian realization that faith, knowledge, reason, and wisdom are directly linked. A student's belief in and relationship to God are the basis and foundation for education. They control what the student will know about the world and how he or she will know it. Wisdom, derived from a relationship with God, will enable a student to know the right course in situations that are not governed by moral law. The students' personalities developed from their understanding and appreciation of the talents God had given them and their efforts to bring those talents to full fruition. The school was an avenue for these qualities to enter Peruvian life and culture.

Highlights of the First Year

During 1917, the Mackays' first year in Peru, four events stand as highlights and indications of the direction of Mackay's future work on the continent. These were his association with the Committee on Cooperation in Latin America, a two-week travel vacation, a celebration of the Reformation in Lima, and Mackay's incorporation into San Marcos University.

The first of these events occurred on May 16, 1917, when the Rev. Samuel Guy Inman, secretary of the Committee on Cooperation in Latin America, visited Lima and spent a week at the Mackays' home, the first houseguest of their married life. Two long meetings of the local Committee on Cooperation were held during his visit. At the second meeting the participants agreed that the region of northern Peru, with Trujillo as center, would be recognized as the mission field of the Free Church of Scotland, subject to the approval of the Free Church. Lima was regarded as common ground and the natural focus of all missions working in the country.[14]

The only issue remaining to be settled was whether the Free Church should occupy another center by the coast or turn north into its allocated territory in the sierras. Without having yet visited the region, Mackay was distressed that two million people who lived in the sierra and forested regions of the country and in the north two territorial divisions, Ancash and Cajamarca, were still untouched by the gospel. The field offered an opportunity for all branches of missionary work, awaiting only the workers.[15]

In a letter to Alexander Stewart, the convener of the Foreign Mission Committee, Mackay discussed his meeting with Inman.[16] The Free Church had been allocated northern Peru, and there was a choice between Trujillo on the coast or Cajamarca inland as the center of the work. Stewart suggested Mackay take one step at a time and keep the issues of the school before the church through his writing home.[17] Mr. Bell, clerk of the Foreign Mission Committee, reported in the committee minutes with pleasure the Northern

A friend, Miss Lovejoy, and Jane Mackay stand near a donkey at the market in Huancayo, Peru.

opportunity and approved the hiring of Rodriguez, a new teacher.[18]

Inman, who also reported the meeting, was impressed by the missionaries' thorough mastery of Spanish. The Great Commission would not be interpreted as "Go ye into all the world, and teach the English language to every creature." Missionaries were needed "who will make themselves Brazilians, or Chileans, or Peruvians for Christ's sake."[19] When Inman stopped in the Cuzco district, he read a novel *Birds without Nests*, written by a local woman in which two young people fall in love. When they are about to get married, however, they find out they are both the children of the same priest. Moral conditions had deteriorated since the Spanish conquest.[20]

Mackay's familiarity and understanding of Peru expanded in July 1917 when John and Jane Mackay closed the school for the regular two-week vacation and traveled by train to Huancayo in the highlands. On the journey via the highest railway in the world passing over 15,800 feet to their destination, the travelers suffered *soroche* or mountain sickness on the way to their destination at 10,600 feet. Local people gathered in the town, traveling four, or five, or even fifteen days to come to the market in Huancayo. Poverty and hunger were so severe that children were often sold or given away into slavery. A twenty-five year-old woman, who said she had eight children, offered Mrs. Mackay her baby as a present.[21]

The third highlight of Mackay's first year in Peru occurred in the fall 1917 when the evangelical community supported a celebration of the four-hundredth anniversary of the Reformation. A series of meetings was held in churches to discuss and present various aspects of the Reformation, and then public meetings were offered in Lima and Callao. Over two thousand people were present at a meeting in one of Lima's largest theaters. Dr. Gonzalez Prada, a literary figure, was the chairman. Shortly after Mr. Ritchie began his address, "The Reformation in the Development of Civilisation," leaflets scurrilously attacking Luther's character were thrown down from the upper galleries like confetti. Most of the audience protested loudly. This provoked Ritchie to launch out into controversial subjects, and the excited crowd greeted his speech with outbursts of applause. Towards the end a hired gang tried to enter the hall, but police stopped them, preventing serious consequences. Nevertheless, there were scuffles in the streets, and revolver shots could be heard. Mr. and Mrs. Ritchie slipped out of the hall by one door, and Mr. and Mrs. Mackay left by another. On his way home Mackay met a boy whose head was bloodied and bandaged. A follower of the priests had battered his head with stones when the boy refused an order to shout "Long live the Religion."[22]

A member of congress for the city presided over the meeting in Callao. In his address he "eulogized the Reformation, and said that Peru could never come to her own until some other religion than Romanism moved the hearts of the people." Mackay believed that

> these meetings have served to show that the Protestant movement in Peru has the sympathy of many of the best thinking men in the country, and that the time is ripening for a great onward movement. Until this year public Protestant meetings have been unknown in Peru, but now we intend to have them frequently, and upon vital and constructive themes.[23]

The fourth important event, and perhaps the most important for the mission's future, was Mackay's formal entrance into the intellectual life of Peru on November 6, 1917, when he was voted to be incorporated into the University of San Marcos.[24] His thesis, "Don Miguel de Unamuno: Su Personalidad, Obra e Influencia," the first to be written on Unamuno, was published in the university journal.[25] Opportunities grew, and Mackay was soon invited to give a course of lectures on English literature. At the end of August 1918, he presented his inaugural lecture at the faculty of letters, "The Cultural Value of Studying English Literature."[26] The first year made strenuous demands on John and Jane Mackay, but within a year their efforts transformed a small elementary school into a recognized and sought after educational center.[27]

Colegio Anglo-Peruano Takes Root

To generate support for the school within the Free Church in Scotland, Jane and John Mackay both wrote letters and reports for publication in church periodicals. Jane's letters dealt with the setting of the work in Peru, describing the Carnival, a visit to one of the churches, and the religious custom of saying the *Santa Marias*. She also described the life of the school, the children of Peru, the Bible lesson at the school, the pupils, the infant department, and some of the challenges of the work.[28]

When the school's first year came to an end in December 1917, it was judged a success, and Mackay's evaluation and annual report were published in the *Monthly Record*.[29] Two Peruvians monitored the examinations that were held on two successive afternoons. On the closing day the children went through an assembly, and an exhibition of their work was held. A distinguished Peruvian gentleman who edited an educational review presented prizes and awards at a large gathering of families and friends. Then Mackay made a speech on the aims and prospects of the school. Two of the leading city newspapers published favorable paragraphs about the ideals and work of the school two or three days later. This notoriety caused the head of a large French business concern to arrange an interview with Mackay and to take his son out of the Roman Catholic school and put him in Anglo-Peruano, "offering at the same time to pay double [the] fee for the education of his son."[30]

Mackay realized from conversations with Peruvian citizens that "a first-class institution inspired by British ideals in teaching and morality" would prosper in competition with the Catholic schools. In the wealthy city of Lima where Roman Catholic schools charged exorbitant fees, the Free Church school could charge a fair fee for the education offered and could soon support itself with a small subvention.[31]

While Mackay never believed himself to be fitted or called to be a pedagogue, he believed that he was situated at the school as "the most strategic vantage-ground from which to begin a bombardment of the enemy's positions." He added, "By God's grace I will stand fast until more capable hands relieve me to rush onward to the assault. I burn to be able to give myself with abandon to the active and positive work of the Gospel."[32]

Some members of the Free Church in Scotland wanted more attention given to evangelism, and Mackay met objections directly about whether evangelistic work was contemplated. In addition to the daily place of the gospel in the school, Mackay vowed never to rest until forces were mustered to carry the Word of Life up the northern coast and across the mountains to the east:

> This must be our great missionary objective—to proclaim to all and sundry the message of the gospel—but the only means to realize such an objective is to develop some such institution as I have suggested. But if it be objected that such an establishment was not a condition of missionary success in the early apostolic age, it is answered that the first disciples attended the Master's peripatetic school by the Sea of Galilee, and were "capped" when the spirit, like tongues of fire, descended miraculously on their heads. In the present age of missionary effort, God has left it to His Church to provide the "tongues," while He Himself provides the "fire." And therefore

we believe that the success of the gospel in Peru will ultimately depend upon the equipment given to sons of the soil whose hearts the Lord has touched. . . .

With her school, the Free Church holds the key to the present missionary situation in Peru. Let her provide men and women of outstanding Christian character and gifts who will develop it, with funds to enable them to work, and abounding prayer to make their work successful, and a people will one day arise from among these mountains "to call her blessed." The call of the present situation is for spiritual preparation on the part of the Church, that she may enter in and possess her inheritance. The field is ripe, and, according to every indication, God's hour has struck; may He not have to send us back into the wilderness for forty years more from the very borders of the waiving harvest.[33]

Mackay maintained the school's finances scrupulously. The first school year began on March 1 and closed on December 20, 1917. The total enrollment was 128 children ranging in age from three to sixteen. Of that number 45 were withdrawn at various times and for various reasons. As one student left another filled his place, and the year closed on a successful note.[34] The finances of the school were supported by the fees charged. They started with a grant from the Free Church Mission Committee and a gift from the Inverness Free North Church Sunday School, which when converted to local currency produced £105, 9s. 7d. Start-up expenses were heavy. Salaries, rent, and taxes averaged £22, 10s. Expenditures for the year were £378, 13s. 1d., and monthly fees brought in £238, 10s. 7d. Total income for the year was £370, 7s. 8d., producing a first-year deficit of £8, 5s. 5d. Thus Mackay pointed out in his yearly report that the mission work in Peru should not be considered purely a charity. A school not charging a fee or charging a low fee is a school that would not be given respect in Peru. Mackay's goal for tuition was to steer a middle course between the government schools, where there was no charge, and the Jesuit and German schools, where the tuition was exorbitant.

Administration and management of the school required action on many fronts. Organizationally Mackay's point of contact with the Free Church was the convener of the Foreign Mission Committee, Alexander Stewart. During the first years of the school's existence a primary need was teachers. Near the end of the school's first year, Mackay learned that Free Church clergyman Calvin Mackay was interested in coming to Peru.[35] Mackay, however, was not interested in another potential missionary who did not seem completely open to work that was most needed but instead had preconceived ideas as to what role he would play.[36]

The beginning of 1918 was a desperate time for Britain in the course of the World War. By April 1918 the convener wrote Mackay that as far as aid for the school was concerned the church's hands were tied. He also noted that a bill in parliament had a clause for calling up to service ministers under fifty years of age: "Our back is to the wall and we are fighting for our very life." Stewart promised to send reinforcements to the school as soon as possible.[37] The Russian revolution freed the German military from the eastern front, and they were focusing their attention to the west, but it was only in late 1918 that the western front broke under General Pershing and the American expeditionary force. In early October the Germans sought peace based on Wilson's "Fourteen Points," and the war ended with an armistice on November 11, 1918. The Free Church Assembly voted to dedicate Calvin Mackay for work in Peru. He was approved unanimously but could not travel to Peru immediately because of the war.[38]

In the meantime the staffing needs of the school were providentially met. After a number of false starts to secure new premises for the school, Mackay decided in February 1918, before the start of the second year, there was no choice but to dig themselves in at the old premises. March 5 was the first day of class, and the outlook was bleak. Mrs. Mackay, awaiting the birth of their first child in May, would soon have to retire from the work indefinitely. A letter arrived from the mission committee that no help could possibly reach the school so long as the war lasted.

At this point providence intervened, "raising up those who were bowed down." On the very week that Mrs. Mackay was forced to relinquish her duties, a young New Zealander arrived in Lima, Vere Rochelle Browne. From a Methodist friend Mackay discovered Browne was a Presbyterian—in fact a member of the Presbyterian church of Auckland who was acquainted with Mackay's old friend Tom Cameron, whom Browne regarded as a spiritual father. Since Browne had a BSc and MSc with first-class honors in chemistry and had worked two years on a scientific scholarship from the New Zealand government, he could easily have secured a lucrative position as an analyst with any of the large mining companies in Peru. Instead, he chose to work for the school. Mackay saw this addition to the staff as "the Lord's doing."[39]

God also answered the school's need for a female teacher. Mackay had been told that no women were being allowed to leave Britain. Discouraged over the possibility of preserving the school's gains, Mackay received a letter from a young lady in southern Peru, Elsie E. O. Yeats. She had seen an ad in the weekly paper and was attracted by the fact that Mackay was a graduate of Aberdeen. Yeats sent her references. She had been a pupil in Banff Academy, graduated from Aberdeen Teachers Training Centre the year after Mrs. Mackay, and had

Mackay stands in front of the Internado, the Colegio's boarding department, at Miraflores, Peru.

taught in Scotland and northern England. She had come to Peru as a governess but found that the high altitude where she lived undermined her health, and she wished to move to the coast. She arranged to arrive in Lima on June 10 to take up her duties. Mackay's anxieties were relieved by the assurance that God was prospering the work and by the new forces coming into line.[40]

Mackay viewed his mission as a spiritual contest. To illustrate the challenge, he described a fire at a church in Ica, a provincial center south of Lima, where the "Lord of Luren," a venerated image, was destroyed. A few days after the fire, the burned image was buried with tears and honors. Polytheism and idol worship characterized popular religion in Peru.[41] Critical of religious carnivals, fiestas, and images, Mackay correctly recognized, however, that a Good Friday preaching liturgy that originated in Peru and centered on the seven last words of Christ, could be adopted for broad devotional use.[42]

During the school's third year, some students would be ready to advance to secondary school level, and Mackay aimed to provide secondary education by the beginning of 1919. In October 1918 when a building at Calle Corcovado, one of the most central parts of Lima, became vacant, Mackay rented it from the landlord, the postmaster general of Peru, who had the reputation of being one of the most bigoted Catholics in Lima. Since the school would now have students in primary and high school sections, its name was changed to Colegio Anglo-Peruano. Since Mackay had received a Doctor of Literature

Leslie Cutbill supervises students in physical education behind the Internado.

degree from the University of San Marcos, he believed the school would have no difficulty in obtaining a secondary school license. Mackay did anticipate difficulties at the end of the year, however, because to receive a certificate of promotion at year end, each student was required to pass an exam in Roman Catholic dogma. Anglo Peruano would protest the requirement, but the outcome was unpredictable. Some public opinion was expected to support the school despite the power of the Church.[43] For a change of pace before the third year began in January 1919, Mackay and Browne took an exploratory trip to the highlands, where they visited a Methodist mission in Tarma.[44]

Administrative management of the Lima mission was challenging for several reasons. Communications with the Foreign Mission Committee headquarters in Edinburgh by mail took up to two months. When decisions or guidance was needed, the committee could act on some issues, but due to its limited authority, General Assembly approval was required for major actions such as the purchase of property. Stewart sent Mackay both formal and informal letters; the former described the official actions of the committee, and the latter contained candid exchanges of opinions on external and internal management issues. The Rev. Macleod of the Inverness Free North Church served as the convener of the committee for the year 1918–1919, but when he would not take another year of it, Stewart returned and replaced him. Stewart stressed to Mackay the "imperative duty" to have something about the mission in every issue of the *Record*.[45] Despite the heavy load of teaching Mackay did his part as an evangelist, writing for an evangelical magazine, teaching a class for Sabbath school teachers and local pastors, and preaching frequently on Sabbaths.[46]

By 1919 the war had ended, and new mission personnel arrived from Scotland, presenting sensitive and delicate new administrative challenges. For a little less than a year Mackay's efforts to build the mission were undermined by the presence of an individual unsuited for the foreign mission calling. Difficulties began soon after her arrival in August 1919, when she claimed she had no contract and her duties were unspecified. When Mackay wrote to Scotland to verify this with Stewart, he refuted the claim in detail.[47] The four-month closure of San Marcos University made it difficult for the new worker, a doctor, to get her Peruvian qualification, but rather than work as a nurse pending accreditation, she hoped for a position at the university. Instead of living with the Calvin Mackays in central Lima, she chose to live at the boarding department of the school, located in Miraflores a few miles away, which was then the extended home of Dr. and Mrs. Mackay. The doctor formed a pattern of missing some appointments as she attempted to advance a friendship with Mr. Browne, Mackay's right hand at the school for two years. If his loyalty and enthusiasm for the school had been weakened, the home could have been disrupted and the school brought to disaster. After a particular incident, Mackay, fearing potential scandal, forbade Browne and the doctor from remaining together after the others in the mission had retired to bed. The doctor then moved to the boarding department of the school for nurses.

Slander followed, causing some of the Mackays' close friends to become cold and reserved towards them. Instead of aiding a missionary nurse, the doctor moved among the English community, who were not missionary enthusiasts, and treated patients despite a specific warning from the British chargé d'affaires. A negative impression of the Free Church Mission began to be formed, since the church seemed to have sent the doctor to Peru for missionary service against her will. One lady familiar with the situation told Calvin Mackay's wife that the doctor "should never have been in the Mission: she is too fond of life."[48]

Money also became a source of friction. When her salary failed to arrive from Scotland and she made charges that she lacked money, Mackay provided a loan from school funds. The loan was later repaid, but reports still reached the school administration that Mackay was treating the doctor unjustly. When the Free Church sent money to pay for her medical examination, Mackay banked it until it would be needed, but the doctor claimed "that Mackay was wrongfully refusing to pay over the money that was actually hers." Mackay challenged her. The doctor then attempted to laugh off her claim. Mackay gave her the fee money as an advance of salary after showing her a letter written by the Free Church treasurer in Edinburgh stipulating how the funds were to be used. Later she declined to sign a contract required by the Foreign Mission Committee connected with receipt of the fee for the exam, and decided not to use the money for the exam at that time. In frustration, Mackay prepared a resignation statement to read at a special staff meeting, but the doctor did not appear for the meeting. Mackay's fellow workers believed that he had erred on the side of leniency over and over again.[49]

Another important issue of philosophy and management was the delicate balance between the mission's evangelistic and educational work. Mackay wrote a lengthy letter to Stewart before the beginning of the 1920 school year discussing and analyzing the relation between the school and other forms of missionary effort. Mackay had proposed to purchase land for the school that would have been a sound investment on its own terms but realized that the proposal would have to go before the General Assembly, where it was likely to be defeated. The suggestion itself could ignite smoldering criticism in Scotland that too much attention was being given to the educational work of the mission and that it was being overdeveloped. Mackay sent Stewart a comprehensive statement explaining and advocating his education policy in Peru. Showing his skill as an advocate in the letter, Mackay touched on the type of institution to be developed, the aim of the institution, the conditions of its success, and its relation with other forms of missionary effort.[50]

The letter began by pointing out that in 1916 when the General Assembly had granted authority for the school, the pressing issue became what kind of school to develop. Instead of simply forming a "good elementary school to meet the demands of the evangelical community," Mackay advocated development of "an institution which would have first class primary and secondary departments, whose sphere of influence would be the whole nation." In Mackay's estimation Peru needed a school "permeated with the highest moral principles, where the Scriptures shall be taught in their purity, and whose educational standards" were "worthy of the best Scottish traditions." It was Mackay's ambition to give the youth of Peru the same "chance to serve God and their country as . . . John Knox and Reformed Truth has given to the youth of Scotland." If the committee were in agreement, then no artificial limit could be set on the school's growth.

To accomplish this Mackay's aim was to divert to the school's classrooms some of the youth that otherwise would flow into Roman Catholic schools, where they become enemies of Protestantism. Mackay's success in this goal was steadily growing. The school also served evangelical children and their families since it was the only school in the country to give evangelical children a chance to enter professional careers such as teachers, doctors, lawyers, and engineers, rather than commercial ones. They were eligible for a 33 to 50 percent rebate on the fees. Without this opportunity the evangelical students would not have a future in national life. The school also aimed to make an evangelical impression on all the pupils. In addition to conversions among older boys, the school was awakening interest in the Scriptures, which boys sometimes read even during playtime. Finally, he wrote that the successful development of the school offered a "valuable point of contact with the community and will constitute a prominent platform for the public proclamation of the Gospel." Having taught native workers at a Bible institute and preached the gospel in mission halls, Mackay felt he had gained by now the linguistic ability and skill to launch out to preach the gospel to the country itself.

Next, he refuted the charge that the educational work was overdeveloped by noting that the Free Church had yet to send a single professionally trained teacher specifically for the use of the school. A quality school was needed since the prestige of British Protestant education was at stake before the Peruvians, and the prestige of the Free Church of Scotland was at stake before the mission societies of the Western Hemisphere. There was no limit to what a skilled young teacher from Scotland could accomplish in Peru even by giving a five-year commitment to the school. Mackay backed away from his suggestion to purchase property and agreed to remain in rental property. He foresaw that the school would be able to pay its own working expenses without subsidy from the church. By supplementing these funds with private subscriptions that Mackay would solicit, critics in the church would be free to support whatever missionary activity in other parts of the country that they deemed best.

Finally, Mackay set forth his view of the relation between the school and other forms of missionary effort. The school in itself was never the ultimate end of Mackay's mission policy, but he had kept it before the church because a successful school was the key to the "conquest of the land for our Lord." The ultimate goal was "an evangelical mission with an educational aspect." Calvin Mackay, Miss MacDougall, and the doctor were brought to Peru not for the school but for evangelistic and medical work in Peru, but they had not yet learned the language thoroughly enough to proceed. Mackay concluded the letter by asking for a competent commission to visit Peru by the following July to examine the work firsthand so that any misunderstandings would not undermine the work.

The beginning of the school year in 1920 was particularly difficult. Vere Browne had been in a serious canoe accident on the River Huallaga, an Amazon tributary; Miss Yeats was getting married; the newly arrived doctor had a hemorrhage; a five-year lease was taken on a new building for the school; and Mackay's second child, Duncan Alexander Duff Mackay, was born that February.[51] During this trying period Calvin Mackay wrote to Stewart explaining why he (John Mackay) had resigned the superintendency.[52] At this point, when Stewart wrote seeking contributions for the periodicals at home, a discouraged John Mackay wrote, "I have little heart to write articles about the mission. It took me all my time to keep the mission in existence."[53] "When will you send us teachers?" Mackay pleaded with Stewart.

Nevertheless, its reports and financial statements show that the school grew steadily. Mackay's missionary approach followed the Carey principle. William Carey, the pioneer missionary to India, believed that missionary work should be self-financing and that when possible the missionaries themselves should contribute to the work. Knowing that it would take time for the work to be self-financing, Mackay contributed to the school the fees he received from translations, from teaching English at the university, and later from holding chairs of history of modern philosophy and metaphysics at the university. The boarding department also was run at a profit to help the mission.

The General Assembly of the Free Church in May, 1920, approved John Mackay's request and decided that a deputation would travel to Peru that summer to visit the school.[54] At first Stewart thought he would make the journey, but the final selection for the deputation was the Rev. Finlay MacRae, Minister at Plockton, and the Rev. Prof. J. Kennedy Cameron. Mackay wanted the Church at home to take part in making significant decisions affecting the future of the mission. Some continued to be concerned that secular education was absorbing too much of the mission's efforts and evangelization should be the focus. At the same time church officials did not want to impede the remarkable success that the school was experiencing. Cameron recounted the details of the mission and the work in Peru in a mission study book published the following year.[55]

The study book, containing nine chapters and fifteen illustrations, ably described and defended the mission's work. It systematically treated the social, religious, cultural, and political obstacles that were being met and overcome, and it made plain what would be expected from the church at home to support the continued efforts. The evangelical teaching in the school would have a long-term impact on the many social problems that Peru was confronting. As Mackay noted after the ringing endorsement by the church's visiting deputies, he no longer needed to concentrate on apologetics for the educational side of the work: "The way has been opened for the study and practice of missionary dynamics."[56]

The five-week visit of the deputation was a decisive moment. It marked with approval the first stage of the Free Church mission, its work in the school.

After careful discussion a decision was made to begin work in northern Peru in the beginning of 1921. A congregation was organized in Lima, having a fully constituted Kirk Session. Mr. Browne was ordained to the office of elder. Every Sunday meetings were held in the school building, and a prayer meeting in English was held on Thursday afternoons. Twice during 1920 the congregation celebrated the Sacrament of the Lord's Supper.[57] The deputation also resolved personnel issues with the doctor, who resigned from the mission.[58]

The *Protervia*

In his 1915 report to the mission board Mackay evaluated the needs of the region. His own analysis of the religious problem of Latin America was confirmed independently of any missionary purpose by James Bryce—constitutional scholar, British ambassador to Washington, and, later, Viscount Bryce, who recorded his own impressions of South America from a four-month trip at the end of 1910. One of the features of South America he noted was the disinterest of men in religion and the persistence in South America even into the twentieth century of anti-Catholic ideas of late eighteenth-century Europe, in contrast to the greater vitality of Catholicism of that time in France, Germany, and Italy. Bryce noted that the "absence of a religious foundation for thought and conduct is a grave misfortune for Latin America."[59]

God's providence began leading Mackay into this vacuum. Through contacts at San Marcos University his connections expanded, producing increased influence within the intellectual circles of Peru. He was exhilarated to enter this world that was so different from academic life of Britain. There was little school spirit; the school buildings were not conspicuous because of the distinctive Spanish architectural designs; education was utilitarian, in particular preparing lawyers for careers; the area of the arts was neglected; and there was no understanding of a classic liberal education in the British sense. Mackay recorded his impressions in an article published in *Student World*, the official publication of the World's Student Christian Federation, July 1920.[60]

At this time a student movement for education reform that had started in Córdoba, Argentina, was sweeping into Peru. As a Protestant intellectual during Peru's process of national development Mackay encouraged the country's national cultural reform. He extended his influence by contributing articles for publication in various journals and newspapers and by encouraging his companions to do the same.

Mackay's 1921 article in *Biblical Review* both drew attention to the role of Christian thought in the intellectual development of Peru and documented particular historical events marking his specific intellectual contributions.[61] In due course his expanding contacts led to his inclusion in a literary group of intellectuals nicknamed the *Protervia*, a name that came from Rubén Darío's 1896 poem, *coloquio de los centauros* (conversation of the centaurs).[62] Like many Latin American intellectual groups the meetings were composed of lawyers, diplomats, philosophers, and editors. At least one member, Dr. Antonio Sagarna, *Enviado Extraordinario y Ministro Plenipotenciario de la Republic Argentine*, had enrolled his son in the Colegio Anglo-Peruano.[63]

The *Protervia*, an influential group, was formed by Víctor Andrés Belaúnde, a Professor of Philosophy at the University of San Marcos who founded a new literary review called *El Mercurio Peruano*. Five members of this group were corresponding members of the Spanish Academy. The European correspondents were brothers: diplomat Francisco García Calderón, whose volume *Les Démocraties Latines de l'Amerique* had been issued in Paris in 1912 and translated and published in English the next year, and his brother Ventura. After service at the Paris peace conference, García Calderón was appointed Peruvian ambassador to Belgium.[64]

Mackay's connection with the *Protervia* began after he was incorporated as a doctor of literature and asked to give several lectures. His inaugural lecture was about the cultural value of studying English literature and was presented in the *Salón de Actuaciones*. Belaúnde then asked Mackay to contribute three articles on English literature to the *Mercurio* that were to appear in alternate months.[65] Mackay's participation in the group won him further respect. In other articles he introduced the lives of Woodrow Wilson and Lloyd George to his audience and called for a Peruvian Wordsworth.[66]

The visit of the Uruguayan Embassy to Lima in October 1918 produced a good deal of material for the literary review. The student federation organized a *velada literaria* (literary evening) as the chief public meeting for Baltasar Brum, the chancellor from Montevideo, who got a wonderful reception. The event of the evening was a speech by the "arch *protervo*, Belaúnde," Mackay wrote. "It was a marvelous effort, the finest thing I ever listened to in the Spanish tongue. Belaúnde is undoubtedly a man of the future."[67]

Belaúnde's responsibility took him to Montevideo, Uruguay, as the Peruvian minister, and Mackay's friend Webster Browning called on him there.[68] After establishing contact, Browning wrote Mackay that the esteem Mackay held for Belaúnde was mutual: "I see Belaúnde frequently, and we never fail to speak of '*El Seráfico*,' as he calls you. I am wondering if Leguia will continue him in his position."[69] Browning was referring to political developments in Peru. The news had traveled quickly. At 3:00 a.m. on July 4, 1919, a police force and two military regiments took President Jose Pardo y Barreda prisoner in the palace and proclaimed Augusto B. Leguía the new president of the Republic of Peru. By October Belaúnde was no longer minister in Uruguay. "Changing conditions in Peru made him ashamed to remain longer as minister," wrote Browning.[70] By the end of the year Belaúnde had returned to Lima.

Philosophy and theology were subjects for discussion within the literary circle. In mid-December 1919 Belaúnde gave a lecture on Pascal, in which he treated the Frenchman's religious philosophy in sympathetic terms. The lecture was delivered before an enormous audience in the largest theater in Lima. The subject matter marked a new era in the public utterances of the *nuestros intelectuales*, and it convinced Mackay that the time was ripe to deliver public lectures on similar grand themes from an evangelical viewpoint. He even speculated to Browning whether in Lima they would be able to inaugurate Webster Browning's cherished ideal of a university church.[71]

During 1920 Mackay continued to enjoy fine Tuesday evening meetings with the *Protervia*. On one occasion Mackay raised the question of definite discussions or debates, and it was taken up enthusiastically. The following week Iberico spoke on Rousseau. The next evening offered a debate on Plato and Kant as philosophers. Mackay maintained the claims of Plato, and Iberico, those of Kant. Seventeen were present, and quite a number took part in the discussion that followed. It was one of the most enthusiastic meetings the group had ever had. The interest in the subject was so great that on another Tuesday evening the debate was continued. Mackay's goal of introducing theological ideas into the discussion was about to be achieved, for the next Tuesday evening the subject for discussion was Hellenism and Christianity! Manuel Beltroy, the poet, was to speak in favor of Christianity, and Honorio Delgado, the psychiatrist, on the claims of Hellenism. Mackay saw that the situation was full of possibilities. His young friend Edwin Elmore wished to prepare some kind of manifesto to the "Intelectuales de la República," but the idea required further study. Mackay hoped that "some definite intellectual orientation would be the outcome of the meetings and that the Mercurio Group may become a dynamic power for truth in the Republic of Peru."[72]

During the school year of 1921 in a lecture in the patio of San Marcos, Professor Belaúnde addressed the students about government abuses. During the address, government secret agents provoked a disturbance that escalated into a student riot, complete with gunfire. Most of the faculty resigned in protest of the government invasion of the university. The government could not find qualified replacements for those that had resigned, and declared the university in *"estado de reorganización,"* and it remained closed.[73]

As time passed the situation in Peru became more drastic, and the closure of the university presented delicate choices to Mackay:

The situation in Peru is becoming more abnormal and complicated every day. The University is still closed, and the professors, including the rector, who took a stand after Belaunde's conferencia, have been removed from their posts. A revolutionary committee—the protégé of the Government— made its appearance about a month ago. As a result of this new revolutionary movement the University is to be opened this week, the old professors being replaced by *catedraticos libres*. As I did not sign the now famous document of protest, my own position has remained unaltered; but I do not feel that I can accept any University position now under the present circumstances, and so as soon as I am called to arms I intend resigning too, stating that as a foreigner I should prefer that the University were functioning normally before I take any part. The present situation has meant a tremendous loss to Belaunde, but I feel it is making a new man of him. He is throwing all his strength into the *Mercurio*, and I think that the latter is on the eve of a new and prosperous era. There is the greatest enthusiasm among most of the members of the group, and it has been agreed to initiate a course of popular lectures after the Centenary. Belaunde, José Galvez, and I were appointed a committee to draw up a programme, which we did last Saturday. The proposal is to give fortnightly lectures, probably in the Geographical Society, with a view to the propagation of new civic and spiritual ideals. If all goes well I shall probably have to give the second, which will be on the subject of Representative Men or Nationalism and Internationalism. This new movement is full of hope, and I do feel that we are on the eve of something. Galvez, who has charge of the Centenary number of "Mundial," the most popular weekly published in Lima, has asked me for an article on "El sentimiento religioso en el Peru" or "La falta del sentimiento religioso en el Peru." I intend making an effort to prepare such an article, and hope to be able to get into it the most direct religious message that I have yet put into print. I have now become associated in the minds of all the members of the *Mercurio* with definite religious interests, and can get published anything whatsoever along that line. Belaunde has also told me that he intends making reference in one of the coming numbers to the present movements towards unity throughout Christendom.[74]

Mackay's literary efforts bore fruit elsewhere as well. After his article appeared in the *Biblical Review* of New York, two colleagues from Lima also contributed to its pages, probably as a result of Mackay's influence. In 1923 Belaúnde himself published an article titled "The Alienation of the Latin-American Mind from Christianity,"[75] which continued along the line of the observation and analysis Lord Bryce had initiated a decade before in his volume on South America. Belaúnde explored the theme in more detail, distinguishing the religious sentiments of various social groupings of society and evaluating the receptivity in South America of a nuanced rather than rigid and dogmatic liturgical Christianity.

Mackay's missionary colleague John Ritchie also contributed an article to the *Biblical Review* titled "The Rise and Growth of Evangelical Congregations in South America."[76] Based on his sixteen years as a missionary in Peru, the article evaluated the effectiveness of mission schools and foreign missionaries. Although he did not mention it by name, Ritchie's references to the Methodist mission school in Peru produced bad feeling in the Methodist camp.[77] Implicit was an idea that certain techniques of foreign missionaries do not achieve the goal of organizing self-supporting, indigenous congregations in Peru.[78]

Having established himself with credibility and having earned the right to be heard, Mackay broadened his evangelistic work. The first public address, or *conferencia*, delivered to a Peruvian audience was given at the provincial council of Tarma, a town located in the central highlands to the east of Lima. The *conferencia* on the evening of February 16, 1921, inaugurated a series of popular cultural extensions, held monthly, initiated by Mackay's friend Dr. José Galvez, the mayor of Tarma, who presided. The lecture, titled "La Profesión de Hombre" (The Profession of Being a Man), is an example of Mackay's skill as a public intellectual and evangelist commending and advocating Christian moral and ethical values and the new life in Christ.[79] The lecture awakened great interest in the town. According to a report his audience found him an appealing speaker who presented his ideas with logic and whose interest in poetry was very acceptable. A newspaper described him as a young, tall man with penetrating eyes and the appearance of a writer, whose energy, poise, and life were an example to others. He presented his ideas with knowledge and charisma.[80] In retirement years Mackay remembered this *conferencia*, whose "title is difficult to render in English but may be phrased 'The Profession—the vocation—of being a real human being.' One can become truly human, . . . only when Jesus Christ becomes a reality in one's life."[81]

After seeing a printed copy of the speech, an enthusiastic reader sent a memorandum to John R. Mott about the address:

> Reflecting a wealth of Spanish and South-American culture and tradition and at the same time drawing upon the finest sources of Anglo-Saxon literary inspiration, this address, which fixes and defines the special appeal of Christianity to the present day Latin-American student, seems to me easily the most effective piece of literature I have seen for the promotion of Student Movement activities in Spanish America.[82]

By 1921 Mackay's attention was becoming more widely directed. He used the centennial of Peruvian independence to advocate social change in Peru.[83] The literary figure Luis Alberto Sánchez observed that Mackay had around him at the school the vanguard of Peruvian thinking:

John and Jane Mackay with fellow believers at Tarma, in the Highlands of Peru.

In the Anglo-Peruvian School, Mackay had a delicate sense of what was happening in Peru in relation to what was happening in the world. He realized that the transforming force was in a youth, but a youth that loved culture by its own sake, and life by the same culture, and instead of calling to the school those that we could call educational professionals who know a lot about systems but not as much about the matter to be applied with the system, called restless youngsters, capable of shaking the environment, of getting in touch with the students, of discussing with them one on one and, for good measure, to learn with them what every good teacher does when he has dignity and loves his profession. He learns every day and for that reason he is a student of himself and of his students. In that group of teachers, all of them young, were Haya de la Torre, Raúl Porras Barrenechea, Jorge Guillermo Leguía, and if I am not wrong, a little later Jorge Basadre, who was too young, also Vega y Luque, a group of youngsters who were students and teachers at the same time, not yet graduates, but already University students. In the end, Mackay had participating in the school all those at the vanguard, without quotation marks, this vanguard, truly the vanguard for the renewal of Peruvian thinking.[84]

Mackay realized that at the end of 1922 the school would reach its limits in terms of the number of classes. Careful management rather than pioneering work would be required. Since the critical early years were over, Mackay no longer regarded himself as indispensable to the school. By October 1921 the evangelistic side of the mission was meeting with success in Cajamarca. Mackay saw northern Peru as the principal mission field and the school in Lima as a "buttress" to prepare future leaders for the evangelical cause. Mackay yearned to work as an evangelist "with absolute freedom of action and a continent for [his] parish. . . ." He wrote Stewart that "the prospect of being called to do the work of an evangelist kindles into a flame the longing that was aroused within me seventeen years ago as I stood by Dr. Macdonald's grave in the church-yard of Ferintosh."[85]

The terms of a call to evangelism came in November 1921 when John Mott approached the Free Church about the possibility of loaning Mackay's services to the YMCA for two years. He noted the spiritual unrest that was occurring among educated men who had a responsibility for the moral and spiritual guidance of the country. Since the YMCA was in contact with these social classes, evangelical missionaries and native pastors urged the organization to start a special spiritual work within and among this class through its auspices and for a man to travel among the universities "giving his whole time directly to an apologetic and evangelistic effort through the Y.M.C.A. amongst the students and related classes."[86] Because of his spiritual and intellectual qualities Mott believed Mackay was the man for the task. Mackay would greatly help in the development of Spanish-language religious literature that was so greatly needed. Mott asked the Free Church to loan Mackay's services to the YMCA for a period of two years, at which point an evaluation would be made as to whether Mackay's future service would be better with the Free Church or the YMCA.

The Cajamarca Mission

John Mackay's intention as superintendent of the Free Church of Scotland Mission was to establish a work that would have lasting impact. He did not wish to commence a northern mission prematurely. After Calvin Mackay had learned Spanish sufficiently, he sailed north from Lima on April 14, 1921, to make definite arrangements to establish a mission station in the Cajamarca region in accordance with the wishes of the Foreign Mission Committee. After this exploratory trip Calvin Mackay and his family left Lima in mid-June 1921 to found the Free Church Mission in Cajamarca.[87] The committee's wish was to establish a direct evangelistic effort with the local people. Calvin Mackay held services on Sabbaths and weekdays and started a Bible class at a national college (boys' high school), and a reading room was opened for the boys. Bibles and tracts were sold and distributed. By December 1921 serious opposition arose, and the mission asked the government to aid in its protection. Calvin Mackay's landlord, who feared further violence, began eviction proceedings. In early 1922 Calvin Mackay purchased a property to continue the work.[88] In January 1922 Sarah MacDougall of the mission began her medical work in Cajamarca.

The mission work of the Free Church contrasted dramatically with the Spaniard's methods of propagating Christianity. On July 26, 1533, conquistador Francisco Pizarro, the former Estremaduran swineherd, along with his Dominican Friar Vincente de Valverde and about one hundred sixty men, chanted the creed as they garrotted Atahualpa, the Inca, in Cajamarca.[89] The spiritual significance of establishing a Protestant mission in the region of Cajamarca almost four hundred years after Pizarro's entry must have thrilled and inspired Free Church members. It fulfilled the prospect of Cameron's mission report.[90] John Mackay visited the Cajamarca mission in November 1921.[91] During a visit he delivered his address, "Los Intelectuales y los Nuevos Tiempos" (The Intellectuals and the New Times) in the theater at Cajamarca. It was an inspirational address to the intellectuals and students of Peru, challenging and calling them to a new sense of duty and renewal. Mackay was injecting ideas from outside of Peru into the revolutionary mix developing in the life of the republic.[92]

In his address Mackay set forth his conception of the role of intellectuals. In the new, emerging epoch he saw the destructive forces (disputes over frontiers, racial hatred, class strife) balanced against new constructive forces, such as international associations aimed at world peace, student and women's associations, and the norm of public opinion. At this moment intellectuals enjoyed an unparalleled opportunity to guide the thought of the masses. At this time they should not search for mere esthetics, bookish erudition, or historicism. Mackay developed his arguments using many historical and literary allusions and flowery language. Just as when the Renaissance Humanists replaced the Scholastics, modern intellectuals must "open the original text of true life, and study man and his vital problems, not with the old goal of doing literature, but with that of finding solutions." The nation has taken a great step forward by recognizing "the value of the anonymous people, when they sacrifice themselves for the nation in a war." A new sense of humanity is represented by the new cult of the "unknown soldier." Intellectuals have a "duty to cast the light of truth and remove the obstacles from the road of progress." They must champion popular education and social justice. Secondly, they must cultivate a new sense of God, through the Bible, and the total interpenetration of our spirit with Jesus Christ. The Bible is the epic poem of God's love for man. That is the historical movement in which, through the centuries, God revealed himself to humanity. In the Bible we find the discovery of man by God, and the discovery of God by man. . . . When the teachings of Jesus Christ will be seriously applied to the solution of individual, national, and international problems, the life of man will issue such a sweet and harmonious music as the legendary one of the spheres.[93]

He closed the address by rallying his listeners to a sense of resolve, optimism, and constancy as they set out to change the world.

Furlough

The Mackays left Peru for Scotland in 1921 for their furlough from the foreign mission field. Near the beginning of his furlough, Mackay met with the Free Church Foreign Mission Committee to discuss and explore a possible change of direction. The committee noted the success of the work in Peru, which was still in the initial stages, and also observed that the confidence the community had in the school was largely due to Mackay as a key person. The Free Church wanted to encourage the development of the new mission and suggested that the YMCA work could be done for six months because Mackay's presence as superintendent of the Free Church Mission was still needed. Continued contact with the school and the Free Church Mission would enable the committee to endorse the arrangement before the Free Church General Assembly. This arrangement would allow Mackay to carry out the evangelistic commission and conserve the mission interests of the Free Church at the same time. At this point Mackay would be relieved from teaching duties at the school, and his role would be primarily advisory and directive.[94] Mackay addressed the Free Church General Assembly when it met at Inverness in May 1922, and the assembly approved his six-month arrangement with the YMCA.[95] In order to stimulate interest in Scotland in Free Church missions, an itinerary was arranged for Mackay to visit the church's congregations.[96] During August and September 1922 Mackay visited congregations in the presbyteries of Glasgow, Inveraray, and Lorne, addressing over thirty meetings.[97] In October Mackay addressed a missionary congress held in Milton Free Church, Glasgow, on how to deepen interest in missions in church congregations.[98]

In Scotland during the spring of 1922 Mackay helped to build the staff of the school in Lima by recruiting two British Methodists. In May 1922 the Free

John and Jane Mackay and family leave Peru for furlough in Scotland, December 21, 1921.

Church of Scotland had run a short advertisement in *The Christian Herald* saying that it immediately needed two teachers for its boys' school in Lima, Peru. Stanley Rycroft responded to the advertisement in early June 1922 before he was graduated from Liverpool University. At the request of the Foreign Mission Committee, he met Mackay in Edinburgh, hardly realizing the lasting impact that Mackay would have on his life. When they met, he identified Mackay by his clerical collar, one of the few times Mackay wore one.[99] Mackay asked Rycroft, who was going to attend a Student Christian Movement conference, to look out for a man who was a graduate in science. Rycroft, in turn, recruited Leslie J. Cutbill, from the SCM in Liverpool. Rycroft later wrote, "I was greatly impressed by Dr. Mackay, his personality, his manner and his dedication to the missionary cause. He inspired great confidence in me and I felt I wanted to serve in the school he had founded."[100] W. Stanley Rycroft, BCom., and Leslie Cutbill, BSc, left for Peru on the SS *Orita* on September 17, 1922. They arrived in time to replace Browne, who had decided to take a furlough, and to move on to other forms of missionary work.

Mackay was a strong advocate within the Free Church of Scotland on behalf of missions participating in the autumn of 1922 in the Scottish Churches' Missionary Campaign. Twelve entities including ten churches cooperated in it. The Rev. Donald Fraser, DD, chairman, led the campaign, which lasted from Monday, November 20, to Sunday, December 3, 1922. Through their shared cooperation Mackay and Fraser developed a lasting friendship. The kindly man with a wonderful smile inspired Mackay's own missionary approach. On Wednesday of the campaign week, he and Mackay were scheduled to address a mass meeting at Caird Hall. The chairman of that meeting was Sir William Henderson, and a massed choir of 450 voices led the singing. The eager crowd filled the hall early, and the police closed the doors, as was their custom. A policeman summoned Dr. Fraser from the platform room when "a man outside refused to go away quietly."[101] Dr. Fraser went to the door and found Dr. John A. Mackay of Lima, Peru, who was to share the program with him that evening. Fraser had been active in the Student Volunteer Movement in the early 1890s, had been ordained in 1896, and later became a United Free Church missionary to Nyasaland, now Malawi. In 1922 he became moderator of the United Free Church General Assembly. Mackay nurtured this new connection and continued to correspond with Fraser after Mackay returned to Latin America.

The furlough to Scotland had allowed the family to visit John's parents, Duncan and Isabella Mackay, in Inverness, and Mrs. Mackay's widowed mother, Elizabeth Wells, whom they saw for the last time. Elena, the missionary family's third child, was born in Scotland. When the furlough ended, the Mackays sailed again for Latin America, this time from Liverpool, with three young children, and reached Callao on January 19, 1923.[102] They were more established in their lives in Peru than when they arrived for their mission six years earlier. When they landed this time, the novelty of the new surroundings was gone, and they wished immediately to learn the news from the six members of the mission staff that met them at the ship when it docked. The coming school year proved to be a very eventful one.

Chapter 6

Evangelist to Students (1923–1926)

"And he gave some . . . evangelists." (Eph. 4:11 KJV)

*B*efore Mackay left Lima for his furlough, he had befriended a student, Haya de la Torre, from an aristocratic family in Trujillo province in northern Peru. Haya's mother's family was descended from a president of Peru, and his father was the publisher of a newspaper. Haya had come to Lima to study law at San Marcos, became the president of the Students Federation of Peru, and after he became acquainted with Mackay, agreed to teach Spanish and other subjects at the Colegio Anglo-Peruano.

As Mackay walked with his new friend one afternoon along the seaside at Herradura, beyond the Lima suburb of Chorrillos, Haya told Mackay, "You don't know what it takes out of me to say 'God.' Why, that name is associated in my mind with people and attitudes and institutions that I feel I must give my life to combat; for me to say 'God' is to experience a sensation of nausea in my mouth."[1] Mackay later wrote, "It was Haya de la Torre's discovery of the ethic of Jesus and of the Hebrew prophets that gave him his first start back towards Christianity."[2]

Haya, the twenty-seven-year-old student, taught at the school while Mackay was in Scotland on furlough in 1922, and Vere Browne served as acting director. Although Browne was skeptical of his contribution to the school,[3] Mackay's judgment about Haya and confidence in him was well justified. God had brought this future leader into Mackay's view as a subject for personal evangelism. In February 1923 Mackay had the "unspeakable joy of listening to his profession of faith in Christ." Haya, Mackay wrote, "has identified himself whole-heartedly with our school and cause."[4]

An incident described in Mackay's report to the Free Church General Assembly illustrates the effectiveness of Haya's teaching role. The school at the time had a license only to teach boys, so Isabel Rodriguez had to be examined at the National College of Guadalupe, the main government school in Lima. A priest was on the board of examiners, and when the time came for the part of the examination on Roman Catholic doctrine, Isabel Rodriguez said she had not studied it but would stand for examination on the contents of the Bible. When the priest realized that she was a Protestant, he asked all the other pupils to leave the room. He then began with a tirade against Protestant belief, especially Luther, but the sixteen-year-old girl gave a strong defense of Luther, which further infuriated the priest. When Isabel was failed in her examination, one of the other examiners protested. The incident became the talk of the National College, and the great majority sympathized with the Protestant girl. Finally, the State Department of Education charged the priest with indiscretion. The girl had based her answers on information that Haya de la Torre had taught her in his general history class.[5]

Haya was also an ardent supporter of the Young Men's Christian Association in Lima, and during the Easter week 1923, Mackay and Haya shared a tent while they attended a four-night camp sponsored by the YMCA. The camp was held in Chosica in the foothills of the Andes. The two men shared the speaking duties at the "morning watch" and at the evening campfire. "It was a great joy," wrote Mackay, "to speak to them around the camp fire on the night of Easter Friday about the greatest things in life, and tell them what the Association signified in the life of youth on the continent, and why the name 'Christian' was enshrined in its official title. I know of no activity of the Association in South America which is so productive of good as the Camp."[6] At that time Haya was also an important social leader of Peru and guided a student-workman association that joined in a movement having a strong cultural and ethical character, the Gonzalez Prada People's University. Students mentored campesinos and artisans "in the various branches of knowledge, including hygiene, citizenship and the formation of character." Haya had "passed through a profound moral experience . . . and a sincere love for the common people and resolved to give his life to obtain social justice for the masses."[7] Mackay supported Haya's effort and contributed to *Claridad*.[8] But the presence of de la Torre as a teacher at the school led to a dangerous incident in the life of the Colegio that could have ended both the school and the mission.[9]

Mackay's Return from the South, 1923

In an attempt to reassert the religious and cultural unity of Peru and to tighten the linkage between church and state, President Leguía planned a public ceremony in 1923 that ended in a "fiasco"[10] for the Roman Catholic Church. Leguía announced that the Republic of Peru would be dedicated to

A group of students and teachers c. 1923 (1st row L. to R.: Duncan, Isobel; 2nd row L. to R.: Stanley Rycroft, Isabel Rodriguez, Winnie Browne, John Mackay, Jane Mackay, Victor Raúl Haya de la Torre, Leslie Cutbill).

John Mackay and Haya de la Torre with students at the Colegio.

the Sacred Heart of Jesus, a large bronze image placed beside the cathedral. The ceremony implied closer relations with the Vatican, possibly the signing of a concordat, and special privileges for the Roman Catholic Church, which directly supported certain politicians. This would mean the domination of the country by the clergy, so anticlerical feelings ran high. Haya de la Torre had leaflets printed and organized a large meeting at the university.

Haya de la Torre recuperates under care of John and Jane Mackay in spring 1923.

The government did not prevent the meeting but sent spies to disrupt it. The spies were suppressed, but Haya learned that a warrant had been issued for his arrest. A general strike was called on the eve of the proposed dedication ceremony. As the group was going from the university to the Plaza de Armas, shots were fired from above the crowd, and mounted troops charged the workers and students. A student, a worker, and a policeman were killed in the confusion. Haya persevered and spoke to the crowd at several locations, including the plaza and even from the steps of the cathedral. The students were able to recover the corpses of the dead that the government had intended to bury privately. But the university was now besieged. Students were ready to defend their position in the university by the use of explosives and acids from the laboratories. Twenty government spies were locked in a room. At last, on May 25, a public holiday, the bodies were buried, and Haya made a passionate speech to the crowd from a monument in the cemetery. Later Haya escaped capture by running through the back streets of Lima in the dark and swimming the river. That night the archbishop announced that the dedication would be suspended because of the trouble caused for the government, and the strike ended immediately.[11] The movement Haya organized stopped the proposed consecration, and his pacifism prevented more deaths by deterring the crowd from retaliating against the government.

Because of the strain he had been under as leader of the movement, Haya became ill and was on the verge of bronchial pneumonia. About a week after

the riot, Mackay "risked great danger by hiding Haya."[12] He brought Haya out
to Miraflores, seven miles from central Lima, where he lived at the school's
boarding department. He stayed for about a month as Mrs. Mackay nursed
him back to health.[13] During that time neither the boarding students, Mackays' own children, nor the outside world knew that Haya was there. Soon
Haya had recovered and was back to work at the school where he was a full-
time teacher. The workers supported him strongly, and the government left
him alone. By mid-July Haya was back at the school, and Mackay decided
he could safely proceed on his planned, three-month lecture tour to the south.
Cutbill, Rycroft, and Haya were left in charge of the school. As a precaution
in the event of trouble, a coded message by cable was preestablished in case
Mackay had to return quickly.

Mackay, who had already delayed the journey for three months, finally left
Lima in July for the YMCA evangelistic tour of the southern republics, Chile,
Argentina, and Uruguay. On the trip he spoke often and to diverse audiences
and congregations, ranging from university students and reserved and aus-
tere worshipers in the Scots Presbyterian Church in Buenos Aires to "ragged
newspaper boys" in Valparaiso.[14] In Buenos Aires, where he spent three
weeks, he spoke twenty-four times and was "impressed to note the genuine
spiritual hunger manifested by many young men connected with the YMCA
in that city."[15] After nine days in Montevideo he had spoken sixteen times.
Mackay discovered that as a YMCA representative he enjoyed unequaled
opportunity and was welcomed by members of other churches and missions
without suspicion or jealousy. The YMCA's work helped break down the
prejudice that the educated classes of Latin America had toward religion.

At the school the routine continued smoothly until October 2 when the
secret police seized Haya, who was returning to the boarding department
after teaching at the popular university. Haya was taken and held temporarily
at the island of San Lorenzo and deported shortly thereafter. The next morning when Rycroft arrived at school, he learned that Haya had been arrested.
In "the days which followed, the situation became very tense."[16] Peruvian
workers had agreed previously that if Haya was arrested or deported, they
would call a nationwide general strike. Although Haya was simply a member
of the school staff, the government mistakenly thought the school itself was
a center for political activity. To protect the school facilities, Cutbill and
Rycroft slept at the director's office on alternate nights. Police on horseback
made their presence known in the Plaza Francia nearby. Several days later
a friend told Rycroft that he had overheard two policemen talking. One told
the other that Dr. Mackay would not be permitted to disembark from the ship
when he returned to Peru from the south.

Rycroft and Cutbill reacted quickly. First, the secret coded message was sent to Mackay. Then two further decisions were made. The school would try to carry on its affairs normally, and life proceeded as smoothly as could be expected. Haya and a friend had to be replaced, and Mrs. Mackay assisted by teaching classes in the emergency. Because Mackay had probably contacted some of Haya's friends in Chile and Argentina and might be bringing letters, photographs, or other documents with him for Haya, someone would have to meet Mackay in the south and brief him fully on the situation.

Cutbill, Rycroft, and Mrs. Mackay developed a plan, and Rycroft and Cutbill approached a former secretary of the Colegio for help. They met Margaret Robb in a tea shop across the street from the bank where she was employed in a responsible position. There they outlined the plan and the risks she would face. Robb had been born in Peru and was bilingual, and her father was head accountant for a major American company in Lima. She decided to help.

After getting leave from the bank, she left Callao the next day on a vessel scheduled to arrive at Mollendo shortly before Mackay's boat, coming north, would dock there. To verify that Mackay was actually on board, and in case of a mix-up in transit, Robb sent two radio telegrams to the boat. One addressed to a fictitious person was returned to her as "Not on board"; the other to Dr. Mackay read, "Destroy hay goods." She hoped Mackay would recognize the code: "Hay" meant "Haya." When this radiogram was not returned to her, she assumed that Mackay had received the message and might expect someone would meet him.

When Robb's boat arrived at Mollendo, she made contact with Mackay and briefed him on the situation. When he knew the government would try to stop him from landing at Callao, Mackay destroyed some photographs and papers. Other documents that he wished to keep he handed to Robb, who "stitched them into the lining of her jacket."[17]

On Sunday morning at 9:00 a.m. the boat carrying Mackay and Robb landed in Callao. Cutbill, Rycroft, and Mrs. Mackay went to meet it. Robb disembarked, but immigration officers asked Mackay to step aside and detained him. Since no charges had been filed against Mackay, Cutbill left to get help from the British chargé d'affaires, who was at the time worshiping in an Anglican Church. The chargé intervened with the Peruvian government, and Mackay was finally allowed to set foot on land at Callao in late afternoon just before the boat was ready to depart. Mackay's luggage, however, was held for two weeks before being returned to him.

Mackay realized that the effort to deport him had been instigated by the Roman Catholic Church through the government of Peru in order to destroy the Colegio Anglo-Peruano and thereby limit Protestant influence in the country. Denunciations of the school were "thundered from many pulpits in the city."[18] To deport or imprison teachers and slander the institution maliciously, wrote Mackay, was "simply a clerical intrigue to blot our school out of existence. The satellites of the Archbishop availed themselves of the present Minister of government, who is head of the clerical party, to do the work, but they have been foiled."[19] Later Calvin Mackay met with the United States ambassador in Cajamarca and told him that he had heard through seemingly reliable channels that the "Archbishop of Lima, during his recent visit to Rome, promised the Pope that by 1925 all the Protestants would be expelled from Peru."[20]

Mackay did not write about these events for publication because he did not wish to "prejudice personal opinion abroad regarding the present administration of Peru."[21] He felt duty bound, however, to obtain complete written exoneration so that "at no future time can our friends in the Roman Catholic church serve out recent happenings as an instance of what Protestant missionaries do in these countries."[22] The process of obtaining exoneration was lengthy and complicated. Mackay sent the British chargé a detailed letter protesting his innocence,[23] and a few days later he responded to questions raised by the chargé. Mackay pointed out that the dispute was religious and not political and that the government had never asked him to dismiss Haya from the school.[24] Mackay, therefore, was innocent of any violation of Peruvian law. He next sent a copy of his finished letter with exhibits to the Peruvian Minister of Government.[25] The Peruvian government realized that a "serious diplomatic situation had been created and pleaded to allow the matter to be settled directly between" Mackay and the Minister of Government.[26]

When Mackay finally met face to face with Rada y Gamio, the Minister of Government told him about the charges. Mackay was accused of "supporting a known conspirator,"[27] and his trip to the southern republics had raised further suspicions. Mackay responded that he could prove that he gave Haya nothing but his salary from the school and that his own trip south was exclusively for YMCA work. Rada y Gamio requested supporting documentation, but he subsequently refused to meet Mackay on two occasions.

Because letters of inquiry and responses crossed between the British Foreign Office, the Peruvian government, the British chargé in Lima, and the Free Church Foreign Mission Committee, Mackay wrote another letter to Alexander Stewart in Edinburgh to explain clearly that neither Mackay nor the Anglo Peruvian College had been implicated in politics. The May protest against the consecration of Peru to the image of the Sacred Heart was a purely religious and not a political movement. Mackay was interested in education and social justice, not in politics. At the school Haya was dedicated to his teaching and not the "ventilation of his ideas on political and social problems . . . [or] opinions on the existing Government. . . . He considered it beneath the dignity of a teacher to take advantage of his position to propagate his special ideas on debatable questions." Above all, the government had never objected to Mackay or anyone else at the school about Haya's presence or teaching there. Haya's arrest and deportation were based on an unauthenticated document "purporting to have been written to Haya de la Torre by a deported politician in Guayaquil," [28] mentioning the forwarding of firearms.

Since the Peruvian government wanted the whole affair to drop, Mackay decided to take the matter back to the British government in order to vindicate his "own honour and that of the Institution and all Protestant work in Peru, [and] to receive from the Government a document exonerating [him] of all complicity in political intrigues."[29] With pertinent documents Mackay convinced an individual who was expected shortly to take the office of foreign minister of his complete innocence. This ally assured Mackay that he would receive a statement completely exonerating him, but only after the former minister of government, who was prejudiced against Mackay, had been replaced by a successor.[30] Prime Minister Ramsay MacDonald sent a note to the Peruvian government protesting Mackay's treatment by the immigration authorities.[31] As expected there were personnel changes in the Peruvian cabinet by May 1924, and Mackay received documents from the Ministerio de Relaciones Exteriores saying there was no accusation against him concerning any political matter.[32] To close the matter Mackay sent copies of these documents to Lord Herbert Hervey, the British minister in Peru.[33] The immediate effect of the episode on Mackay was to fortify his confidence and evangelistic resolve.

Turbulence in Peru

During 1924 and 1925 Mackay's ministry in Lima was active, well coordinated, and integrated on several diverse fronts. He served as the superintendent of the Free Church Peruvian mission and headmaster of the Colegio Anglo-Peruano, lectured for the YMCA, was a missionary doing evangelism and outreach at San Marcos University, and performed organizational work and writing for the Committee on Christian Cooperation in Latin America. The attempted deportation by the Leguía regime had simply strengthened his resolve to bring the new life in Christ to the people of Peru. Having established its base in Lima, the Free Church mission extended its work in northern Peru. In a letter to Walter Sinclair, a family friend and very active layman, Mackay described the political situation in Peru that hindered the mission work:

I had arranged to go to Cajamarca a week ago; but a few days before the date of my intended departure, the political horizon became so over-clouded with the outbreak of simultaneous subversive movements in different parts of the country that I was strongly advised not to leave the capital just at that time. The result is that the School reopens again in a few days and I have not been able to fulfil my intention. It is difficult for one in the homeland to understand the present situation in Peru. Political elections have just taken place. The President was the only candidate for the next presidential term, all opposing candidates having been eliminated either by deportation or intimidation. And so the country has the prospect of her destinies being ruled by this gentleman for another period of five years. In a very real sense, one does not know "what a day or an hour may bring forth." There will almost certainly be an upheaval in September when the President of the United States has given his decision on a forty-year old territorial dispute between Peru and Chile. Should the arbiter's decision be unfavourable to Peru, there is no saying what may happen. National sentiment is very much bound up with the two provinces of Tacna and Arica, which have been the course of the dispute referred to. The case is very similar to that of Alsace-Lorraine. Peru lost these provinces after a war with Chile forty years ago, and has been reclaiming them ever since.[34]

Mackay also wrote the Free Church Foreign Mission Board describing the situation:

The political situation in Peru at present is very tense. The press censorship is tremendously strict. The latest achievement of the Government appears to be the purchase of the only surviving opposition daily. The Rector of the University and President of the Committee of the Pan-American Scientific Congress is in hiding, and the General Secretary is on the island of San Lorenzo. If it were not that the Scientific Congress is scheduled to meet here in December, the University would undoubtedly be closed down. As it is it will likely survive the present year.[35]

Mackay took the opportunity to consolidate the position of the mission school by negotiating a merger of the Methodist boys' mission school into the Colegio Anglo-Peruano. Under terms of the merger, Mr. Stanger, a Methodist, became subdirector of the Free Church school, to be paid by the Free Church and not the Methodists, and he would teach four hours a week during 1924.[36] By 1924 Mackay wrote that the Anglo Peruvian College was the largest missionary school of its kind in Spanish-speaking South America, excluding Brazil. Pupils ranged in age from four to twenty. In 1924 a total of 378 pupils were enrolled, and 144 of them were in the secondary department. The effort to banish Mackay had made the work spiritually stronger and had given the school more sympathy and confidence. A Sunday school had been operated for the boarding department for several years, but this year one was also started for day students that about thirty pupils attended. The students came to school each Sunday with the consent of their parents, and some of them were the school's best students.[37]

In early August four British-based naval cruisers visited Peru, part of a squadron that was navigating an around-the-world tour. Conscious of the problem of drunkenness, Mackay noted that "some of the ladies and gentlemen of the British colony in Lima organized a Dry Canteen for the Sailors." The men were served tea, coffee, lemonade, and sandwiches at the mission school since they could not obtain another suitable building for the occasion. Since the school was on vacation for a week, a reception there could conveniently be arranged. In turn, Rycroft and Mackay took about forty students whose families lived near the school aboard one of the ships, the *Dauntless*, a light cruiser of the "D" class.[38]

Sadly, during the year one teacher, Cutbill, contracted tuberculosis, and his severe illness complicated life for the school, putting pressure on the other teachers to perform his responsibilities. Three weeks after his return from Montevideo in 1925, Mackay secured a return passage for Cutbill back to England.[39]

The Cajamarca Mission and Moyobamba

At the end of July 1923, before John Mackay left for the south on his evangelistic tour for the YMCA, Calvin Mackay came to Lima to confer with him about the northern mission. John thought it was in "healthy condition and offers great prospects for the future."[40] Having two geographically separated stations, however, made management of the mission in Peru difficult. Communications were slow between the stations, and the difficulty was compounded because Calvin Mackay communicated directly to the mission committee in Edinburgh and, perhaps disingenuously, told John that he had not been led to understand that a copy of his official reports and recommendations should also go to him as superintendent. John Mackay wrote Stewart about the difficulties of decision making for the mission when he lacked copies of the reports on which Stewart later needed his opinion. Mackay added his strong view that the structure of a missionary superintendent was not a satisfactory one, adding, "I know of no other Presbyterian Mission which still retains it. More satisfactory . . . would be a 'Field Council' and a permanent Secretary."[41] That structure would facilitate collegial decision making.

With regard to a theological point about rebaptism that Stewart raised, John Mackay replied to the mission committee in Edinburgh, "I am entirely in sympathy with Mr. Mackay when he asks for liberty to re-baptize converts from Romans. It seems to me that to deny this Christian privilege to intelligent converts from a system which in that particular region of the country is more pagan than Christian, would be to deny them a fundamental Christian right and rob them of their heritage."[42]

John Mackay's position was "not only very delicate in the sphere of personal relationships, but a very difficult one in the sphere of mission policy."[43] Some friction may have developed between the Lima mission and the Cajamarca mission over the commencement of a school. By 1924 Calvin Mackay attempted to establish a school, but Mackay pointed out that it had not been authorized by the mission committee. Moreover, John Mackay believed that the mission was too small to undertake such a step at that time.[44] Nevertheless, Mrs. Calvin Mackay established a primary school that Christina Mackay (not a close relation) operated in 1924.[45] Calvin wanted a furlough, but scheduling it was delayed because Nurse Sarah MacDougall worried about staying alone in Cajamarca.[46] To resolve the issue, the mission committee accepted John Mackay's idea that Mr. Moohan, a fellow missionary from another denomination, should relieve Calvin Mackay when he went on furlough.[47]

For a time the Free Church of Scotland also sponsored the independent mission work of two single women, Annie Soper and Rhoda Gould. John Mackay referred to their work as "one of the most heroic and purest examples of Christian missionary devotion in modern times."[48] Born about 1883 and brought up in relative poverty, Annie Soper was the youngest of a family of eleven. Her early life was hard and lonely: her father had died when she was three years old, and her mother had died when she was ten. In due course Annie became a member of the Rye Lane Baptist Chapel, Peckham, London, and for two years she had been sister tutor at the Regions Beyond Missionary Union's maternity home for missionaries called Bromley Hall. At the home she met the young widow of William Newell, missionary to Cuzco, who had two small children. The memory of Peru stayed strong in the widow's heart, and it was through conversations with her that God called Annie Soper to the mission field. Soper applied to various missionary societies, but they turned her down because of her ill health. Her sense of vocation was strong, and she persisted, so she traveled to Canada to work as a nurse. In Canada Soper was invited to serve as sister tutor in the hospitals of Lima where the Mackays met her.

In Peru Soper's medical work prospered, making others jealous. Some nuns spent their time in the hospitals arranging flowers at the feet of the images of saints and neglected to wash the ill and suffering patients in the

Anne G. Soper, independent
missionary to northern Peru.

hospital. These nuns resented the innovations and popularity of the Protestant
nurses. One day Soper and an American
colleague were poisoned. The American
had to return home, but Soper recovered
and continued her work. She convalesced
from her severe illness in the Mackays'
home at the end of 1920 and in turn
assisted by taking charge of the school's
boarding department while Mrs. Mackay
recovered in the mountains of Tarma
from the stress of overwork.[49]

A missionary visiting Lima told Soper
about Moyobamba, a remote center east of
the Andes range. When he asked, "Can't
you go there, Miss Soper?" the visitor
planted the seed for her future mission.
During a furlough to Britain Soper tried
again to get the support of a missionary
society to send her to Moyobamba, but the societies were still unwilling to
undertake work in the remote interior of Peru.[50] Still feeling the call strongly,
she decided to go alone to Moyobamba, and a fellow nurse, Rhoda Gould,
agreed to accompany her and work with her. The five-week journey from
Lima began with four hundred miles by steamer to Pacasmayo, then fifty
miles by railroad to Chilete. After visiting Calvin Mackay of the Free Church
mission in Cajamarca on the way, the missionary nurses arrived in Moyobamba, 130 miles to the east, on July 27, 1922. There they worked at the
Hospital San Juan de Dios. The Free Church supported them financially in
the early years. Later John Mackay recommended to the Free Church of Scotland Foreign Mission Committee that Soper and Gould be supported from
Edinburgh with an annual grant and that Calvin Mackay visit to assess the
possibility of incorporating their mission into the work of the Free Church.
But this did not look promising.[51]

The work in Moyobamba prospered, and in 1925 Soper wrote John Mackay of the need for an ordained clergyman, imploring him or another minister
to come to Moyobamba to baptize the new believers and to perform marriage
ceremonies for those needing to be married.[52] Mackay admired her work, but
as the Free Church mission was itself understaffed, he could offer no solution
except to urge Breckenridge, the Bible Society representative, to make the
trip. Mackay agreed to write to Edinburgh, and he gave her encouragement of

the intention that the Free Church's former grant would be continued.[53] One of the difficulties in reaching the local people through evangelism was the Quechua language they spoke. By 1939, however, locals were among those who asked for baptism. Despite physical hardship, disease, and strong clerical opposition, over time this faith mission prospered dramatically. By 1954 it had established twenty-seven congregations in towns and villages.[54]

In retrospect, some of the difficulties of the Free Church mission effort resulted from missionaries holding too closely to Scottish practices brought from their native country and not modified on the mission field. These included resistance to organizing picnics and outings, use of singing psalms with traditional Scottish tunes, and refusal to use musical instruments. The need to change the historic patterns of the church to adapt to another culture is demonstrated by the greater success of the Free Church of Scotland in the Lima school under Mackay and in recent times where the connection with the church was looser.[55]

The Lima YMCA

As early as 1918 there had been great interest in Lima for establishment of YMCA work there. The British government policy was to release men from military service for work in the commercial houses in Latin America to maintain British economic interests in the region, but the International Committee of the YMCA had a fixed policy not to ask for men to be released from military service for YMCA work, even if the work was to be with the military. Due to the shortage of YMCA secretaries, it had decided not to enter new cities during the war.[56] The next year a gentleman named Ricardo Tizón i Bueno returned from Montevideo determined to start a branch of the YMCA in Lima. He gathered over one hundred signatures of supporters, including senators and foreign diplomats.[57] In response, J. C. Field arrived in 1920 to start the operation and his work prospered, although the Catholic Church forbade its members to belong to the YMCA because of its Protestant affiliation.[58]

In 1924 a lecture series by a YMCA secretary, Julio Navarro Monzó, had been scheduled for him, but because Field, who was in charge, was away traveling in the United States,[59] and because Johnson, the physical secretary, was ill, the responsibility for organizing and making arrangements for Navarro Monzó's series of lectures and visit to Lima fell to Mackay. Always the gracious host, Mackay also spent a great deal of time with Monzó during his visit.[60] The time, wrote Mackay, also "served to cement our former casual acquaintanceship into a close friendship."[61]

The group that was the first YMCA in Lima, Peru (L. to R.: Haya de la Torre, Beltroy, Mackay, unkown, Johnson, unknown, Cutbill, Field, Rycroft).

Navarro Monzó arrived in Lima on Saturday, May 17, for six weeks. On Tuesday he gave the first lecture of the series on the "History of Religion."[62] During the course of his lectures Mackay wrote,

> Don Julio is making a tremendous impression in Lima. Tonight he gave his sixth lecture. The interest increases with every lecture and the hall of the Association is packed every evening with a most select audience. I have got closer to our friend this time than ever before. He is certainly a remarkable man and an invaluable acquisition for the work of the Kingdom in which the Association is engaged.[63]

When the series ended and after saying goodbye to Monzó on the *Essequibo*, Mackay wrote a long letter to Ewald evaluating the effect of the program on the work of the YMCA.[64] He noted the possibility of a split in the missionary community as a result of the lectures:

> Navarro Monzó was with us recently for about six weeks. He gave a course of twenty lectures in the YMCA on the "Evolution of Religion in the Ancient World." His ideas on some things were rather radical and we have been threatened with a rift in Evangelical circles as a result of workers having taken sides on the matter. I hope, however, that the whole affair will blow over; but so far our friends in Negreiros have taken a rather uncompromising stand.[65]

Attempting to draw Mackay into controversy, Ritchie asked for Mackay's impressions of the series for the Evangelical Union of South America for publication in *Renacimiento* to show where Mackay stood on Monzó's theology, but Mackay declined.[66] He believed that Ritchie had already sufficiently expressed his views on Monzó.[67] Paulson, a YMCA official, believed that Monzó's thought would become more tolerant the more he associated with Mackay. He referred to Ritchie's article and responded to Mackay's request for more aggressive leadership in the YMCA.[68] Because Mackay's own time and energy were stretched to the limit, he concentrated on helping the YMCA indirectly through his work in the university, and Mackay declined to receive income from the YMCA for 1925.[69]

Montevideo Congresses—Committee on Cooperation

A cooperative movement among missionaries in Latin America had grown out of the Panama Congress held in February 1916 and the local committees formed to follow the conference. A second congress was planned for Montevideo to bring together missionaries and representatives of the evangelical churches that were interested in the movement. Sixty North Americans attended to evaluate how the work could be made most useful in each republic. The Committee on Cooperation in Latin America, the entity established by the Panama Congress to continue its work, had begun to publish a Spanish-language journal titled *La Nueva Democracia*. At first Inman and the other advisors did not wish to put any Anglo-Saxons on the journal's board of advisors, but because of Mackay's place of distinction among writers in South America and because he had already been a helpful advisor to the periodical, they added his name to the board.[70] Mackay thanked Inman and agreed to "serve the best interests of the Magazine and be absolutely frank in the opinions I express."[71] For the next thirty years Mackay contributed articles to *La Nueva Democracia*, which became influential in disseminating progressive ideas in Latin America.

Two major gatherings for Protestant world Christianity occurred in 1925. In Europe in the wake of World War I, the archbishop of Uppsala, Nathan Soderblom, and others organized an Ecumenical Conference on Life and Work held on August 19–30, 1925, in Stockholm. Originating from a call to peace by Christians in neutral countries, it sought to promote Christian influence in the developed world, particularly in the context of the political, economic, and social life. To a Roman Catholic observer sympathetic with the ecumenical movement, this conference seemed to be dominated by common moral attitudes rather than any unity of belief—"human considerations" rather than "supernatural faith."[72] Latin America, in contrast, had been spared the devastation of the war, and in April 1925 the Protestant gathering held in Montevideo focused on the practical work of evangelization of the continent.

Despite agreements of cooperation, friction and denominational rivalries continued in some areas of the mission field. For example, the North Andes Mission Conference of the Methodist Episcopal Church believed that the Evangelical Union was seriously misrepresenting their work both verbally and in writing.[73] Other frictions had to do with differences in approach to narrow or broad missionary work, such as Ritchie's attitude toward the YMCA lecture series. The idea of holding a congress to increase coordination had been discussed early in 1921 and had been tentatively scheduled for 1923. It was postponed until 1925 to allow sufficient time to prepare the reports that were to be considered. The congress was intended as a venue to discuss progress and difficulties, consolidate gains, and continue the forward movement of evangelization. Although the summer vacation would have been more convenient for Mackay, the meeting was scheduled for the beginning of April 1925 in Montevideo after the tourist season when the summer's heat and activities had ended. The delegates would all be able to stay under one roof.

A three-day continental conference on education was held in Montevideo immediately prior to the opening of the larger Congress on Christian Work in South America. Both conferences were under the auspices of the Committee on Cooperation. The educational conference had a personal touch, beginning informally with a reception at the Crandon Institute, a North American school for girls and a leading educational center of Montevideo. The son and daughter of two missionary families provided entertainment at the opening reception as one sang a baritone solo and the other played a violin solo.

The education program included addresses by prominent speakers. Mackay's friend Dr. Webster Browning, a relative of the celebrated poet, was the organizing secretary for Latin America for the Committee on Cooperation. Widely traveled, Browning had served as head of the Instituto Internacional (later renamed the Instituto Ingles) founded by the Presbyterian Church in Santiago, Chile, in 1886. Under his direction the college flourished, and its influence increased. Browning was an authority on the Lancasterian system of education, applied chiefly in primary schools, in which more able or brighter students were used to teach other students under the direction of an adult. Under this monitorial system one adult could teach two hundred or a thousand students. Navarro Monzó was scheduled to address the group on the place of the Christian school in society.

After introductory remarks by Browning, Mackay gave, in fluent Spanish, the initial lecture of the educational conference. The address presented Mackay's philosophy of education that underlay the school that he had founded and a teleological view of history. Titled "Our Ideals," Mackay's address developed three themes demonstrating how the fundamental principles of education are personal and adaptable to different conditions: first he introduced the pedagogic theme: that the school is for the pupil; next, the sociologic theme: that the pupil is educated for life; and finally, the transcendental theme: that life is eternal.[74]

In propounding that the school is for the pupil, Mackay rejected the old idea that a boy is simply a small man. Rather, the child is an original and originating being, and the teacher's task is to develop that potential. The teacher's goal should not be to make the child fit into the ideas of elders and to repress or suppress all natural spontaneity. The true educator must adapt the school to the pupil in order to study the relative capacities of pupils, enabling them to be divided into natural groups in order to bring out their potential. Teachers can then educate them better and study each child's interests as a basis for vocational guidance.

Since personality is formed by contact with personality, the true teacher must devote all of his or her time and energy to the task. Two things will then disappear: the tendency to break up life into segments and to give only part time to teaching.

Mackay continued in a sociological and historical vein. Various societies believed that a pupil should be educated towards an institution or profession. In South America this had brought about the dictatorship of the professions. As other examples he referred to Napoleon's idea that education was purely a function of government when he tried to govern public instruction in France to serve his own ambitious theory. The Bolsheviks introduced what they called "proletariat culture" in the interests of their political theory. Germany had directed its educational efforts to the production of a nationalistic and autocratic sense, and most of the governments in Latin America had attempted to adapt education for their own purposes and party politics. True education, on the other hand, should be for nothing less than citizenship in the widest and most human sense of the term. It should not merely serve the functions of government but be a safety valve to promote enterprise that must inevitably be defined in terms of citizenship for life in a particular country.

Finally, Mackay moved toward his transcendental conclusion. This religious principle, said Mackay, has often been misinterpreted and grossly distorted by making for a religion that is coextensive with a given institution or code of ideas tending to limit thought or chain thought down. Furthermore, the recognition by sociologists and politicians that religious faith is a stabilizing factor in national life had led such men as the dictators of Italy and Spain to make blind faith subsequent and secondary to their political policy.

True education does not limit thought but rather expands and stimulates it. Life for God simply means life for the plan of things, which is continually evolving. When individuals, institutions, or nations do not conform to eternal principles and laws, the inevitable result is decadence. Life must be studied from the point of view of the whole divine plan for humanity. As an example, Mackay cited Gandhi of India, who said that he would sacrifice the liberty of India if it conflicted with truth.

Mackay concluded that only devotion to Christ and the kingdom of God gave men sufficient resolution and the spirit of sacrifice to live and die for great human ends. For this reason religious instruction was a necessity for the production of farseeing and dynamic personalities. "Christ gives the power and the enthusiasm, God controls the world, and the world marches towards progress at his command, and life is for ever."[75]

This speech, presenting the purpose and goals of education as Mackay saw them, no doubt drew on his own experiences at the Inverness Royal Academy. Mackay also modeled the Colegio on the purposes and principles of Thomas Arnold, the English clergyman and educator, and he made this connection in a letter to an English diplomat when he explained that "the ideal of the Institution [the Colegio] is the same as inspired Dr. Arnold of Rugby—the production of educated Christian gentlemen."[76] Students learn and acquire habits of virtue, attaining a supernatural and eternal outlook on life, informed by practical knowledge of the arts and sciences. For Mackay Christian education was a basic means of social transformation. True education was more than learning virtue through repetition so that virtue became second nature; it was taking on the mind of Christ through the study of the Bible, its revelation, and its principles.

After the education congress ended, the much larger Missionary Congress of Montevideo began. Nine years had passed since the Panama Congress had begun to coordinate Protestant evangelization, but more needed to be done: a better understanding was needed between missionary bodies since some tasks could only be accomplished by joint effort. Two years before the conference took place special questionnaires on twelve missionary problems were distributed to all regional committees on cooperation in South America. They were returned in due time, and the results were synthesized into twelve reports by special committees. These reports formed the basis of discussion at Montevideo.

Mackay was active in the conference preparations both in planning and writing. He had solicited and edited questionnaires from the field in the course of compiling reports and written the report of commission eleven, and he also joined in decisions about who should be invited to participate. With Browning, Inman, and Ewald, he discussed whether or not to invite outside intellectuals to meet at Montevideo. Mackay opposed such invitations because he believed the internal issues among Protestant missionaries should be dealt with among themselves privately and because he believed that the outsiders might be a diversion and distraction from the central point of the meeting.[77]

In fact, adverse publicity for the Montevideo Congress resulted when Inman nevertheless invited several intellectuals who were nonbelievers. Mackay wrote Inman to tell him about an article published in the January 10 morning edition of *El Día* of Montevideo, containing a letter from Alfredo Palacios, a professor at the University of La Plata. It was published with a double-column headline: "Categorical Reply to a Suggestive Invitation to the Christian Churches of North America." "It is real audacity to invite people who would not feel comfortable among church people to participate in a congress of this nature," Palacios told the reporter. The editor of the paper was ex-president Brum, a close friend of Palacios. Mackay believed that while Brum "may not endorse all that Palacios says about the missionaries being the advance guard of the flag and commerce, yet he and his party would be in pretty close sympathy with all that has to do with the religious aspect." Voluntary attendees were discouraged since their presence would seem to camouflage the real object of the Congress. Mackay asked Inman for material to publish in the "profane" press, if any was available. He believed that a strong article on the Congress and its goals was needed for the nonreligious press. "It looks like the only thing to do is to keep on smiling and pray for the illumination of all minds as to the real purposes of the Congress," Mackay wrote with irony.[78]

Confusion about the goals of the Montevideo Congress may also have arisen from Inman's article "Imperialistic America" published in the *Atlantic Monthly*, in which he tried, successfully, to "arouse discussion."[79] Inman explained that he was speaking as an individual about the "un-Christian acts in connection with our commercial and political relations with smaller and weaker countries." Not surprisingly, however, Inman found Colombians sensitive when he wrote "that they were not entirely sovereign."[80] A feeling against North America manifested itself also in *La Nación* of Buenos Aires, and some persons attributed part of the hostility to mistakes made by Inman in organizing the Congress.[81]

An important practical point to be resolved in connection with the Congress was the relationship of the Young Men's Christian Associations with the churches. The issue was whether the associations of the YMCA should send full official delegates or fraternal delegates to the Congress. The YMCA

Continental Committee did not want to send delegates at all, believing such participation would undercut the effectiveness of the associations' spiritual service. But the decision not to send delegates was then criticized by others who wanted the YMCA to acknowledge a more open evangelistic purpose. The outcome was that the Committee on Cooperation renewed its invitation to attend the Uruguayan Conference, and the associations sent fraternal or nonofficial delegates. Speer considered that an "Association is the loyal auxiliary and agency of the Churches."[82]

The effective missionary relationship of the YMCA to the churches was, however, complicated and delicate. Any YMCA denial of proselytizing would imply that evangelical churches were proselytizing. Some wondered whether the association would take the place of the church and become a "wall instead of a door." Mackay believed that for the YMCA to present a "vague mysticism [was] not sufficient."[83] The decisions about attendance in turn raised the question of a choice between an evangelical basis or personal basis for membership in the associations, namely, whether a boy or man was required to be a member of an evangelical church to qualify for membership or whether he must simply have a personal relationship with Jesus Christ as a condition for membership. Over time a realization emerged that a personal basis was preferable for YMCA membership.

Montevideo proved to be an ideal location for the Congress. It was easily accessible from the United States and the west and east coasts of South America. At that time Uruguay occupied in international affairs in South America the place that Switzerland occupied in Europe, and Montevideo was the South American Geneva. Its inhabitants also considered it the South American Athens because of the number of eminent writers who resided there. It was a congenial atmosphere for discussing issues involved in the evangelical missionary enterprise as well because Montevideo was a place accustomed to the free expression of thought and the launching of new policies.[84]

The heat of summer was almost over when the delegates arrived at the seaside hotel of Pocitos that had been especially reserved for the Congress. All except the local delegates were lodged in the hotel, and the meetings were held in one of the large dining rooms whose windows looked towards the ocean. The fresh sea air and the gentle sound of waves breaking on the shore stimulated thought.

There were three hundred and fifteen delegates and invited guests who represented thirty-five different Christian organizations and belonged to eighteen different nationalities. The largest number of representatives were from the United States because American missions were the most numerous in South America. One remarkable feature of the gathering was that nationals were equally represented with missionaries and the representatives of mission boards, so that fully half of those present were South Americans. At Panama in 1916, the official language of the Congress had been English, and that was the language most used. At Montevideo, however, the official languages were Spanish and Portuguese, and most of the speaking was done by the South American delegates.

Brazil's delegation was the most interesting group, composed of over fifty members, mostly Brazilian nationals. Those delegates represented some 800,000 evangelical Christians in Brazil, evidence of remarkable progress in that country. Some of the Brazilian pastors were as effective and influential in their demeanor, education, Christian character, and preaching skills as Protestant pastors in any part of the Christian world. One of them, Dr. Alvaro Reis, was the pastor of a large church in Rio de Janeiro having two thousand members, including many community leaders, politicians, and journalists. Several delegates were from Europe: three from Spain, one from France, and one from Switzerland; and the evangelical church in Italy was represented by some Waldensian pastors in Uruguay. The Evangelical Mission of South America was represented by Ritchie of Lima and King of Argentina. Mackay represented the Free Church of Scotland.

The Congress proper opened on Sunday afternoon, March 29. Robert E. Speer, Chairman of the Committee on Cooperation, proposed as President of the Congress Dr. Erasmo Braga, an eminent Brazilian who had acted for several years as national secretary to the Committee on Cooperation in Brazil. Braga was unanimously elected and took the chair. The two opening addresses followed, one given in Portuguese by Braga and the other in Spanish by Mackay.

Mackay set an inspirational tone. In his speech he declared that springtime had come in South American life. Some observers thought Mackay

> struck the keynote of the conference, when he said that we should love the living, loving Christ, we should love one another, and accept the full consequences of such allegiance and love. "Our message is to be prophetic rather than sacerdotal: the living word of the living Christ to living man, the essence of Christianity being not a rite or a creed, but communion with the living God and service of men as our brothers, growing out of the inspiration of fellowship of that communion."[85]

After Mackay spoke, one of the delegates from Spain said, "I never knew that a foreigner could speak with such eloquence in Spanish."[86] The first evening meeting was entirely dedicated to the address in English by Dr. Speer. The ten days that followed were devoted to business, with three main work sessions each day. Evening sessions varied and had less intense content. Between the afternoon and evening sessions special meetings were held in the city hall, the Atheneum, under the auspices of a local committee. Some of the leading figures at the Congress addressed these meetings. Their object was to show the bearing of Christian principles on some of the problems in modern life.

The Congress studied and discussed the following South American issues in a comprehensive and wide-ranging way: unoccupied territory, indigenous peoples, evangelism, education, literature, the relation between national and foreign workers, the Roman Catholic Church in its relation to evangelical Christianity, and missionary cooperation and unity. To facilitate discussion the delegates were divided into six commissions, each dealing with two problems. Groups of five or six members, called "findings committees," gathered up the discussion results in the form of resolutions, which were then submitted to the business committee of the Congress. After revision by that committee they were finally submitted to the Congress on the closing day for its approval. In this way the Congress avoided a charge brought against such gatherings that the findings adopted are cut-and-dry resolutions that are rushed through without sufficient discussion or contributions from rank-and-file delegates. At Montevideo each member had the opportunity to make a constructive contribution to the findings adopted on the closing day and was not obliged to wait until that day in order to know their purport and implications before giving an opinion. Because the findings were handled democratically, they represented a true index of the mind of the Montevideo Congress and had significant value for the direction of missionary policy in South America for the next ten years.

The Congress reports, the findings adopted, and a digest of the discussions were published in two volumes before the end of 1925. From a list of over one hundred findings, the following, in abbreviated form, are of special interest:

1. Evangelical action on the continent should be intensified.
2. To provide the schools with better equipment and better trained teachers, evangelical forces should cooperate in an international effort and unite as far as possible to evangelize the whole continent.
3. The cross of Christ should be presented as a symbol of triumph over the forces of evil and of the truth of his death and resurrection.
4. A course of lectures giving the evangelical interpretation of the great problems of the day should be directed as ministry to the intellectual classes.

In addition to presenting the opening address and contributing to discussions, Mackay made a substantial contribution to the substance of the conference as author of a report for Commission Eleven on special religious problems, comprising seventy printed pages in the volumes of the Congress's Official Report.[87] His report included treatment of the problems of contemporary religious consciousness, the Roman Catholic Church as dominant religious influence, minor religious forces, and the problem of evangelical work and progress. The sophisticated analysis presented certain issues in a new perspective. Mackay noted, for example, quoting Unamuno and Carlos Octavio Bunge, that "Christianity in its Roman Catholic form, never succeeded in awakening a consciousness of sin as moral evil in the Iberian race."[88]

In reviewing the social and political context of missionary strategy for the continent, Mackay highlighted ways Vatican diplomacy was attempting to bring South American governments closer to the papacy. He analyzed aspects of the strong appeal of the church in South America, including appeal to pride, fear, and spiritual indolence. Then Mackay noted the Roman Church had taken cognizance of the Protestant movement, to which it was hostile, and he concluded with examples of how the Roman Church was taking initiatives, such as student camps that had been originated by the evangelicals. Most important, however, were Mackay's conclusion and recommendation of the positive attitude and posture that the evangelical movement should take toward the Roman Catholic Church. It should not be an object of attack. A constructive, independent policy should be pursued:

> Rather with one eye on Christ and His Gospel and the other on human need, they will develop a constructive policy of their own. . . .[89]
>
> To conclude, the best way to combat these systems will be to demonstrate that in the gospel of Christ and in the kind of life it produces are found ideal solutions for the musings of the mind, the agitations of the heart, and for the translation of thought and feeling into noble and constructive activity. There is no cosmic scheme like the scheme of redemption in Christ; no guidance so practical and luminous as the companionship and the guidance of the Spirit of the living Christ; no enthusiasm for humanity like the enthusiasm engendered in the hearts which have become fellow-workers with God in the establishment of His Kingdom; and no faith so potent for attacking evil and suffering everywhere as the faith of those who can do all things through Christ Who strengtheneth them.[90]

The discussion led to six findings presented in eloquent language:

1. The encouragement of the study of South American history, literature, and the Roman Catholic Church
2. The use of the *conferencia sin culto* (the delivery of a religious message without the ordinary trappings of a religious service) as a recognized form

of evangelism to reach people with the gospel for whom the liturgical aspects of Christianity had no interest

3. Specially prepared men to be set apart to work with the educated class, to lead them to a full experience of Christ and gradually to an outward expression of their faith

4. The consciousness of sin to be deepened through the presentation of individual moral and social obligations in light of the principles of Christ

5. The call for a fresh interpretation of Christ's place in all "constructive thought on human problems and of His sufficiency to meet all the yearning of the human heart"

6. A fresh presentation of the cross of Christ, not as a symbol of the Master's fate but as a symbol of triumph[91]

The process of thorough preparation using questionnaires led to a comprehensive conference report on all facets of the missionary problem in South America. The congress report was published in two volumes totaling about one thousand pages and was divided into twelve topics. In addition to his work as chairman of Commission Eleven and the presentation of the report on special religious problems,[92] Mackay focused as a missionary educator on youth and education, contributing to the discussion of the report on unoccupied fields,[93] education in Peru,[94] and discussion of the needs of Christian education.[95] At this congress he also began a lasting friendship with Charles Clayton Morrison of the *Christian Century*.

Two missionary friends from Peru also contributed to the Congress. Although suspicious and skeptical of the movement toward unity on the field,[96] John Ritchie spoke of the need for literature[97] and of the needs of the Urco Farm mission to the Indians.[98] Dr. E. A. MacCornack, a missionary physician from Lima, made useful contributions to the commission dealing with medical missions and health ministry.[99] Dr. and Mrs. MacCornack were visitors to the Montevideo Congress, and it was noted that they were developing a good training school in Lima.[100] At the close of the discussion Dr. MacCornack observed that the medical profession in South America was competent though unwilling to go outside the larger cities. Resistance to the entry of outside physicians occurred and "commercial greed controls the medical societies."[101] The doctor believed the key to medical missions was to set up hospitals around the work of qualified nurses. He thought a future conference bringing together doctors from North and South America would also be desirable.

The Congress provided an opportunity and venue to clarify the relationship between the YMCA and the mission churches in the evangelization of Latin America and to review the impact of fundamentalism and modernism on the Protestant mission field there. Charles J. Ewald, of the Continental Committee of the YMCA, had presented the report of Commission One on unoccupied fields, giving a general introduction to conditions in South America. In a letter to colleagues after the Congress, he reviewed its positive results from the point of view of the YMCA. He believed that both missionaries and church leaders who were nationals of the country had a new understanding of the aims and problems of the YMCA and a new confidence in the movement.[102]

The Continental Committee of the YMCA had named nine fraternal delegates to the Montevideo Congress, and there was also one on behalf of the World's Committee and the National Council of the United States.[103] Other friends and sympathizers of the YMCA were in the Congress as representatives of other institutions. The Rev. Alvaro Reis, Rio de Janeiro, however, criticized the work of the associations.[104] Because of the friction, Dr. Ortz Gonzalez, Editor of *La Nueva Democracia*, moved a resolution. He proposed that the Congress name a committee to investigate so that if relations between the churches and the YMCA were wrong they might be corrected.

Ewald told Speer he had no objection to the formation of a committee, and when it was organized, it was composed of Bishop Oldham as chairman, Dr. Erasmo Braga (who had wanted an official delegation), Rev. Balloch, Elizabeth McFarland of the YWCA, and Ewald. Bishop Oldham then followed Ewald's suggestion of calling together all church leaders who had attended the YMCA secretaries' conference in order to air any concerns. The criticisms proved not to be directed against the YMCA movement itself but against several secretaries. In fact, representatives from Argentina, Brazil, Chile, Peru, and Uruguay voiced such strong support for the YMCA's goals and its capacity to meet those goals that the business committee followed the unanimous recommendation of the special committee and dropped the whole matter.

Mackay later evaluated the significance of the Montevideo Congress in terms of Roman Catholic–evangelical relations, noting that

> this conference marked an epoch not so much in the progress of evangelical work on the continent, as in the organization of the Roman Catholic reaction against evangelical Christianity. On the one hand, Protestant effort on the continent has been violently and systematically attacked, while, on the other, Protestant methods of work have become increasingly adopted.[105]

Although Speer and others wanted Mackay to write the Spanish-language report of the Congress, his pressing duties to the school and to San Marcos in 1925 did not permit him to undertake the work, so Webster Browning wrote the Spanish version.[106] An attack on the Congress was published by the

Juventud Católica del Uruguay (the Association of Catholic Youth in Uruguay) titled *Violando la Clausura* (Violating the Entrance Ban).[107] Mackay thought it "a very weak performance although a lot of time and work has been put into it. Its chief value and interest lies in its symptomatic character. It is an indication of a catholic raise."[108]

In his evaluation Inman was very satisfied with the results at Montevideo and believed that the Congress had been more stimulating as a result of outsiders being invited as guests. He was also pleased that the Protestant missions emerged from the Montevideo Congress with South American public opinion friendly to the movement, since there was a strong nationalistic movement in every foreign mission field at that time, including China, Japan, India, and Africa. The fact that nationalism did not take a more objectionable form in Montevideo was "remarkable."[109] Inman's interpretation of the Congress appeared in his mission study book, *Ventures in Inter-American Friendship*, intended for use in North America. Referring to conclusions of the Committee on Special Religious Problems,[110] it quoted Mackay's view that "our spiritual relationships must be separated from political" ones.[111]

The study book quoted the religious views of Chilean poetess and later Nobel Prize winner Gabriela Mistral, whose works had been encouraged several years before by Dr. Federico de Onís of Columbia University. In a letter to the Congress, Mistral warned against materialism as a norm of conduct and stressed the need for authentic religion to be a factor in individual as well as social education and for Catholicism to address the social movements of the time.[112]

During his trip south to Montevideo Mackay met William Morris, a well-known Anglican clergyman based in Buenos Aires. In the course of thirty years as an educational missionary 140,000 Argentine children had passed through the schools Morris founded.[113] Mackay later recounted an anecdote from his time with Morris. On the roof of a new orphanage, El Alba (The Dawn), a congressman who was a member of a small political party said to Morris, "'We socialists in Argentina have never been able to do anything of this kind. We do not seem able to produce the type of self-sacrificing spirit that incarnates itself in work like this. How is it done?' 'Christ,'" Morris replied.[114] When Morris died in 1932, seven thousand children per day were being educated in thirty-seven buildings.

Mackay's Return to Lima

After the Congress at Montevideo Mackay spent his first three weeks in Lima normalizing affairs at the school and arranging for the departure of a teacher,

Manuel Beltroy, Jane Mackay, and John Mackay, at front left, at the large academic gathering.

Leslie Cutbill, who had contracted tuberculosis. Arrangements proved difficult until Mackay found a place on the *Orita* after some passages from Valparaiso were cancelled at the last minute.[115] Robert E. Speer responded to Mackay's constant search for new teachers when he agreed to help the school and to seek suitable teachers through the Student Volunteer Movement and the Methodists.[116]

Mackay also entertained in Lima "stragglers" from the Montevideo Congress. A party led by Speer and Bishop Francis John McConnell arrived first, then a regional congress party under Guy Inman stayed in Lima for five days. Next, W. E. Vanderbilt and J. L. Jarrett, an early missionary to Cuzco, turned up with plans to stay five days before they settled down again to their tasks.[117]

Changes were occurring in academic and physical education offered at San Marcos. The library of San Marcos was being reorganized, and the university had the only gymnasium at a state university in South America. It was directed by a young Peruvian educated in Springfield, Massachusetts, at the YMCA college.[118] Mackay and his colleague Rycroft had been teaching English in San Marcos University, but in 1925 Mackay's role at the university was greatly expanded. Early in 1925 Mackay was appointed to the chair of modern philosophy to teach the most able students studying for the doctor's degree in *Letras*. Prado y Ugarteche and Belaúnde had held the chair before him, and Mackay considered it the "key position in the Faculty of Letters as regards exercising an influence over the thought of the students."[119]

Because of a plea from students and faculty, Mackay also accepted the chair in metaphysics. It was a golden opportunity to present the Christian worldview to over one hundred students,[120] but it involved hard work, requiring five or six lectures on philosophy per week.[121] Manuel Beltroy, a poet and Mackay's colleague, was awarded a doctoral degree at San Marcos and was elected to fill the vacant chair in Spanish literature.[122]

Mackay heartily enjoyed his work at the university and the goodwill of the students. In early September he planned to give an address in the Salón de Grados on the subject of "Tres Hindús Contemporáneos" (Three Contemporary Hindus), namely, Gandhi, Tagore, and Sundar Singh. His work kept him so busy that Lima became his exclusive focus:[123]

> The last six months of my stay were a wonderful experience. I had to work at top pressure to be able to attend to the duties attached to the two chairs of History and Philosophy and Metaphysics and keep the school going at the same time. Happily, however, I was able to mechanize myself to such an extent as to be able to over take the work, not to my own satisfaction, but in such a way as won the affection of the students.[124]
>
> I was specially pleased with the interest shown by my metaphysic class. During the term I assigned three subjects for essays from which one might choose. Two thirds chose the subject "The Metaphysics of Religious Experience." My last lecture was on the "idea of God" the classroom was packed even to the passages. I spoke for an hour by candle light as the electric light went out at the beginning of the hour. After I had closed, a few moments of profound silence were followed by a burst of applause which continued for several minutes. I appreciate the students' good will but what made my heart leap was the obvious fact that religion had come to occupy a place in the thinking and outlook of the youth of San Marcos. The new light may be no stronger than the flickering of the flame that lit our last encounter as students and teacher, but I hope that it will shine unto the perfect day.[125]

Lima's literary scene experienced a tragedy that touched Mackay and his circle. The poet laureate of Peru was José Santos Chocano, who in one poem wrote of himself, "I am the singer of America, aboriginal and wild."[126] Chocano's opinions strongly differed from those of another Latin American intellectual, José Vasconcelos, the former minister of public instruction in Mexico and an internationalist. Both had published material attacking the other in a variety of periodicals. Some of the university students in Lima openly supported the ideas of Vasconcelos. These included Edwin Elmore Letts, who was one of Mackay's closest friends, a colleague in La Protervia, and a

YMCA member. One day Chocano learned that Elmore had submitted an article to the newspaper, *La Crónica*, that Chocano believed was personally insulting to him, and he demanded an apology from Elmore. Later, when the two men met in the El Comercio building, one thing led to another. Elmore hit Chocano with his fists, then Chocano drew a revolver (later claiming self-defense) and shot Elmore in the abdomen. Elmore died a few days later in early November 1925.[127] Mackay attended his funeral. The Peruvian justice system took action, and the correctional court gave a three-year prison sentence to Chocano and fined him $10,000. Some years later after having been exiled to Chile, Chocano himself met a violent end when he was stabbed to death on a streetcar in Santiago by a man suing him in an alleged swindle.[128]

In Lima the Mackays had also become close friends of a missionary doctor and his family. Dr. Eugene A. MacCornack, of Whitehall, Wisconsin, who was one of the most eminent surgeons in the United States, became the surgeon in the British American Hospital in Lima, under the Methodist Episcopal Church. His original intention had been to give a tithe of his work on the mission field, three years of missionary work out of an expected thirty-year career. But he made such a name for himself that the dictatorship supported him for work in Lima despite opposition from the medical faculty there. "He got his degree after examination, but only when the President threatened that if it were not granted him he would have a special law passed through Congress to allow him to practice legally."[129] Mackay and MacCornack were part of a tennis group that "helped to make Saturday afternoons a time of joy and a source of fresh strength for jaded brains."[130]

In a remarkable career MacCornack significantly influenced social change and development in Peru. In late 1925 Dr. MacCornack was appointed mayor of the port of Callao.[131] He also generated interest in building a modern hospital[132] and was successful in bringing it into being. On return from a trip to North America, he wrote Mackay that the "nation is making great progress in medical treatment and hospital improvement." He had been given land for the erection of a new, private hospital.[133] President Leguía's personal surgeon, MacCornack performed the last operation on him, and MacCornack accompanied Leguía's son, Juan, to Chile after the Supreme Court found him not responsible for defrauding the government and released Juan from prison.[134]

Mackay's Resignation from the Free Church

Early in 1925 Mackay had decided to carry on his work under the auspices of the YMCA and to leave the Free Church mission. In Lima he had the prestige

Walter R. T. Sinclair, at right, a Free Church elder and friend of the Mackay family in Scotland, with his sister Kate

of reputation, a relatively calm life, and tangible accomplishments, so it was a particularly wrenching experience for the family to leave Lima. Mackay was aware of the risks that this step could mean for his established friendships in Scotland. His personal covering note to Kenneth Cameron, now the convener of the Foreign Mission Committee, that accompanied his resignation letter acknowledged that the step risks "being disinherited of the kindly thoughts and prized affections of lifelong friends," but, quoting Luther, Mackay wrote, "Here I stand I can do nought else. God help me." The letter was Mackay's "pint of agony."[135]

Prominent Peruvian Catholics such as Javier Prado y Ugarteche, Víctor Andrés Belaúnde, José Matías Manzanilla, Carlos Ledgard, Luis Fernan Cisneros, Cristóbal Lozada y Puga, and many others held Mackay in the highest esteem.[136] He enjoyed the friendship of Dr. Luis Miró Quesada, publisher of the *Comercio* and mayor of Lima from 1916 to 1918. Mackay's departure in 1926 from the faculty of arts of San Marcos also came at a difficult moment for the university. Mackay and Beltroy left, then Galvez, Bustamante, and Dulanto went to Arica on juridical commissions. There were several candidates for English class, including Steene, Field, Gillot, and Arca. The government also withdrew $35,000 a month from the university's income.[137]

Mackay's resignation from the Free Church mission rested on three grounds: in the crisis of Latin America the opportunity with the YMCA was unique for an evangelist; the school in Lima had reached a point of develop-

Walter R. T. Sinclair
with friends out for a
drive.

ment where Mackay's leadership was no longer irreplaceable; and relations with several colleagues were at a point of "such incompatibility of temperament and missionary outlook" as to put at risk the work of the mission and to be against its best interests.

It would be an understatement to say that the resignation came as a great shock to the offices in the Free Church in Edinburgh. At first Cameron declined to submit Mackay's resignation to the committee for several reasons: because the request from the YMCA had not yet arrived, and it would not be in order to submit it till then; because Cameron wanted Mackay to reconsider for his own sake and for the sake of the church; and finally because he felt that Mackay's last two reasons were not explicitly stated.[138] Mackay replied in some detail, reiterating his point that leaving the "calm, the prestige, the tangible results and future hopes . . . for a pioneer endeavour, ceaseless travel, little home life, and an unknown future" was a difficult step but was impelled by his desire to follow Christ.[139]

Besides the Free Church, Mackay's other correspondents in Scotland were shocked to learn the news. He had sent a letter dated February 14, 1925, to Walter Sinclair, who responded with a cable: "Letter distracting, I should rejoice in your new mission, providing you remain even nominal head of the college, otherwise fear Church friends becoming sport for the Philistines, Sinclair."[140] But it was Alexander Stewart's reaction to the resignation that was most comprehensive. He, too, discouraged Mackay from making a complete severance with the Free Church, appealing to Mackay's conscience and the effect of his change on the Free Church.[141]

Mackay's idea for leadership succession at the school, to be developed from the vantage point of the mission field, differed from the views of the Free Church leaders in Edinburgh. Mackay recommended Rycroft to become head of the institution based on his three years of experience and increased capability.[142] Cameron wrote that the Free Church selected A. M. Renwick to succeed Mackay as superintendent of the mission. Church regulations required that "all responsible teachers and Agents, even unordained men, in the Mission field must be members of the Church."[143] Mackay rebutted these arguments in a pragmatic way, based on the agency relation that Rycroft held and the fact that the church should have made this clear in his contract originally.[144]

The Free Church found it hard to let go of Mackay. To retain contact with him, the church offered Mackay a position to remain a minister of the church without charge, but with a seat in the Presbytery of Inverness. This honor Mackay declined:

> I have come to a point in my life when I can profess but one absolute loyalty, loyalty to God and Truth. As this loyalty would inevitably conflict with the loyalty I should be bound to profess if I accepted the honour that the Committee have wished to confer upon me, I am compelled to decline it.
>
> My loyalty henceforth must be loyalty to a cause rather than to an institution. In the present chaotic condition of the religious world, in which the orthodoxies and the heterodoxies are scattered piecemeal throughout the denominations, and at a time when it is evident that there must be new alignments, I am unwilling to accept any denominational label. I have given my life afresh to the living God for His Cause and His glory, and to belong officially at this moment to the ministry of any given denomination would only tend to embarrassment and misinterpretation.[145]

Mackay reiterated his "undying interest in the Missionary work of the Church"[146] but declined to affiliate himself formally with the Free Church. The Free Church, however, did not remove his name from its rolls. As his formal career changed, and later changed again, Mackay also continued a lifelong connection supporting the school he had founded.

Chapter 7

The YMCA in Montevideo (1926–1929)

"A cottage in a vineyard." (Isa. 1:8 KJV)

From as early as 1924 Mackay had been exploring the possibility of identifying himself definitely with the work of the YMCA. During the exchanges leading to his affiliation with the YMCA, Mackay had reflected deeply about the evangelistic job ahead and how best to perform it.[1] Mott and Jenkins of the YMCA Foreign Department had been very interested in the proposal, but before an offer could be made, Ewald had to take it up with the Continental Committee in Montevideo. Ewald himself was extremely enthusiastic at the prospect.[2] By October 1924 Ewald had been authorized to secure Mackay's full-time service, and he wrote Mackay explaining the procedures to join the association work and the structure of the arrangement. Employment arrangements were made through the YMCA International Committee, but Mackay actually served under the Continental Committee in the same way that the foreign secretaries of the International Committee were "loaned" to the Continental Committee. Ewald wrote Mackay, "I have had few joys since I entered the South American work twenty years ago as great as the joy with which I write this letter, and I look forward with eagerness to our working together."[3]

Mackay decided not to have the YMCA send a request to the Free Church to have him released from his work with the church. To simplify matters he considered an ordinary resignation explaining his reasons for the change to be sufficient. Initially, Ewald suggested that the Mackays would be stationed in Buenos Aires, heading up the work there. Mackay thought of this as, in effect, a "practical apprenticeship before presuming to guide the religious work of other Associations."[4] Both the Young Men's and Young Women's Christian Associations were well rooted in Montevideo, and at the time the Roman Catholic influence in Uruguay was not as strong as it was in other Latin American countries.[5]

Mackay's new focus was set when he left the mission of the Free Church of Scotland and began full-time work with the YMCA: "As I have stated repeatedly, the fundamental principle in my outlook and my work is the solidarity of Evangelical work in Latin America, not in any sectarian or ecclesiastical sense, but in the broad Christian sense of everything that reflects the light of the Master and makes for righteousness."[6]

During the seven and one half years that Mackay worked as an evangelist and spiritual teacher under the auspices of the YMCA, he traveled widely in Latin America and was separated from his family for months at a time. He made two major intercontinental journeys, the first to participate in the Jerusalem Missionary Council in 1928, traveling from South America to Jerusalem via North America. The second one was his furlough to Britain in 1930, sailing from South America via North America to Europe. On both journeys he made many evangelistic addresses advancing the movement, and in doing so he expanded his circle of friends and acquaintances. While Mackay journeyed, the full burden of child rearing for months at a time fell to Jane Mackay.

The Work of the YMCA

After the school year had ended, the Mackay family traveled from Lima to Montevideo, Uruguay, where they were to live. They began by ship from Callao to Valparaiso, Chile, where they stayed for a few days before traveling by train over the Andes Mountains to Buenos Aires, where they spent a few happy days visiting its sights and wonders. A few days later, tired and weary, they embarked for an overnight passage across the La Plata River to Montevideo.

By February 1926 the family was living in a home of their own on the outskirts of Montevideo. It was an old-fashioned house, set back from the street with a large garden surrounding it. In a letter to his friend, Dr. MacCornack, John wrote that it reminded him of the biblical phrase "a cottage in a vineyard" (Isa. 1:8 KJV). At first Jane Mackay was homesick for Lima, but gradually as the fine, pleasant climate gave her new energy and life, she became enthusiastic about Montevideo, and John sensed that she became a different being. The children also became much more robust. Mackay was able to continue his Saturday afternoon tennis with a group that played next door at the home of a neighbor from southern Scotland.[7] Soccer became another interest. The Uruguayan Football Association had been organized in 1900, and the program came to full bloom when Uruguay won Olympic championships in Paris in 1924 and Amsterdam in 1928. While living in Montevideo, Mackay and his son, Duncan, attended memorable soccer matches between teams from Argentina and Uruguay.

During the years Mackay served as an evangelist under the auspices of the YMCA and not under a church, his focus was on personal conversions and building up authentic fellowship. He believed that his work would be more effective outside the turbulence of theological disputes occurring at that time within the churches. By focusing his message on a personal encounter with the person of Christ, he largely avoided the controversies and technical formulations that were distracting many from the evangelistic work that needed to be done. He also found that opportunities to present the message and for it to be heard were greater under the YMCA than would have been the case working under church auspices.

Of course there were operational and organizational differences between the association and a church. A church has a creed that members are required to affirm and believe, but the fundamental element for YMCA membership was known as the "basis." The World's Alliance of Young Men's Christian Associations had been formed in Paris in 1855, and that meeting had formulated the purpose of the organization as a confederation. The World's Alliance, a federation of national movements, had as its motto "That they all may be one—that the world may believe."[8] The "personal work" or personal evangelism of the YMCA was to win others to faith in Christ through friendship. Since 1869 under the so-called Portland basis of participation, members or officers of the YMCA had to be young men in communion with the evangelical churches: "The Young Men's Christian Associations seek to unite those young men who, regarding Jesus Christ as their God and Saviour according to the Holy Scriptures, desire to be His disciples in their doctrine and in their life, and to associate their efforts for the extension of His Kingdom amongst young men."[9]

As early as 1866 a "fourfold program" developed when the New York YMCA defined its purpose as "the improvement of the spiritual, mental, social, and physical condition of young men." A building was constructed in New York to carry out the program, and it became a model for work in North America. A professional staff, called "secretaries," managed the building and its program, and the training of the secretaries was through "literature, summer institutes, and colleges at Springfield and Chicago."[10]

Mackay had been acquainted with the work of the YMCA in South America for more than ten years since his first trip south in the summer of 1915. During his tenure as an evangelist with the YMCA, however, change in the federation focused on the underlying basis of membership in the organization. The issue was whether to accomplish its purposes through an "ecclesiastical basis" of membership, whereby a youth was required to hold membership in an evangelical church as a prerequisite to membership in an association or through a "personal" basis or "unmediated" membership whereby a personal commitment to Christ was required but evangelical church membership was not. In most Latin American countries the YMCA reached out to all young men who were willing to make a personal and individual commitment to Christ regardless of church affiliation, and both Mackay and Ewald were strong advocates of a personal basis. In Brazil, particularly, the question of membership basis became a point of controversy. The institutional shift was finally consummated in 1931 when the international convention declared common loyalty to Jesus Christ the basis rather than membership in an evangelical church.[11]

One theme that crystallized in Mackay's thinking at this time and whose importance continued for him throughout his life was the distinction between an institution and a movement: a movement is alive and dynamic, not static and worldly. A movement goes beyond mere atmospherics. This differentiation was captured in a letter to Ewald in which Mackay expressed the goals and purposes that he saw for himself as a religious secretary. The religious work of the YMCA movement that Mackay attempted to build was a clear forerunner of the ecumenical movement as Mackay understood it, a dynamic concept of the Church as a fellowship of the road, its members moving forward together toward Christ.

An excerpt from a letter to Ewald illustrates the scope and nuance of Mackay's thinking on the association's task of kindling a Christian movement in South America:

> I was greatly interested in your letter of September the 10th, in which you continue the discussion of the religious mission of the Association where we left it. I am quite at one with you in the idea that the supreme end of our work in South America should be the creation of a "movement" rather than the aggrandizement of an Institution. On this matter, however, I feel it is necessary for us to clarify our thoughts. It seems to me that some times when we talk about a "Movement" what we are really thinking about is an "atmosphere." Now, between a "movement" and an "atmosphere" there is a world of difference. An atmosphere can be formed by the diffusion of an influence. It can depress and asphyxiate or it can vivify; but it cannot create. A "movement" on the other hand, has no meaning whatever except as power moving in a definite direction and reaches its full meaning only as power moving in a definite channel. The Renaissance was an atmosphere; the Reformation a movement. Now, what do we conceive our supreme task in South America to be? Is it simply to distil a diffused Christian influence into the continental environment, obtaining thereby a general interest in religion and a completely nebulous attitude towards Christ? Or do we

not rather aspire first and foremost to generate passionate hearts which in virtue of a personal experience of divine power become themselves generators of a new "movement" in thought and life.

Now, do not think for a moment that I mean to minimize the tremendous importance of creating a Christian, or rather a Christianized "atmosphere" in South America, in the sense of distilling throughout the continental environment, Christian view points on all matters of human interest. Two questions, however, occur to me. In the first place, should a Christian organization commit this very important work of distillation to the sole control of any group of South Americans who are only vaguely or coldly loyal to the Christian Lord and his ideals, simply for the sake of being able to affirm that the work was entirely directed by Latin Americans? To my mind, there are principles of much more fundamental and universal validity in work for that Kingdom which has no frontiers nor recognizes racial hierarchies, than the principle of nationality. I am of the opinion that loyalty to Christ is much more fundamental than nationality and that there is, moreover, a spiritual nationalization, as well as political.

My second question would be this. If our objective as an Association is to produce a great Christian Movement, would it not be wise to begin by an intense concentration on the presentation and interpretation of the Christian Lord? Personally, I should feel very sorry if we gave birth to any new committee or organization until we were able to saturate peoples' minds with the fact and claims of Christ. I consider that one of the first things we have to do is to give new life and reality to our Basis. I see the increasing danger of the Association being strangled by the Physical Department. I mean to fight for the rights of the Spiritual and if we fail to give it its own place on the throne of Association activity, we can then think of abdicating and launching a purely spiritual movement. But give the Spiritual Department a square chance for a few years without introducing any radical changes, or delegating to an unknown quantity some of its primary functions.

In a word, let us seek the cooperation in the great task of all well disposed men; let us sink our own personalities out of sight. But let us not abdicate or delegate our functions before we are reasonably certain that a group of capable Latin Americans have caught the full orbed mission and that the ideal of a Christian literature for South America is safe in their hands.[12]

Two considerations were important to Mackay's strategy for evangelization in Latin America: how to work on a continent that was predominantly Roman Catholic and how to present the proper observance of the Sabbath. In analyzing the work of the YMCA he considered what work the YMCA could do, how best to perform it, proven means of accomplishing the work, the qualifications and preparation for workers, problems that would be confronted, and publicizing in North America the opportunities in South America.

Realizing there would be religious opposition to such work in Roman Catholic lands, he wrote,

> The hierarchy opposes the Y.M.C.A.'s because of its religious work. The main reason for this opposition is their claim that the Y.M.C.A's undermines the authority of the church and spreads "religious indifferentism." By "religious indifferentism" is meant indifference to the claim of the Roman Catholic Church to be the only avenue of salvation. They further claim that religious education is exclusively the function of the clergy or specially trained and authorized lay teachers. Doubtless a further reason for opposition is the fear of a growing lay leadership, not under the control of the clergy.
>
> [Since] this opposition is not shared by the majority of the Roman Catholic laymen to whom the Y.M.C.A. addresses itself, and as it does not affect the vitality and growth of the movement, it would be unwise to attempt to meet this opposition by argumentation or organized opposition on the part of the Y.M.C.A. The policy of going ahead and letting the results of the work speak for themselves and the earnest determination to cooperate and not to oppose will in time thoroughly establish the Y.M.C.A. as a lay movement in Roman Catholic lands. We would at the same time recommend that Y.M.C.A. leaders seek personal relations with the clergy and lay helping them to a better understanding of our movement.[13]

The proper use of Sunday had been a concern of Mackay's since his boyhood in the Free Presbyterian Church, and he now recognized that thinking regarding the right use of Sunday had not kept up with life's changing industrial and social demands. He considered how to value Sunday as a day of rest and worship in a positive rather than a negative way. But he also realized that a

> rule for Sabbath observance was exceedingly hard to get and much harder to get it observed. Christ taught that Sabbath observance was not a matter of rules but of principle, namely that the day was for man, and he set the principle forever by basing his usage of the day on unselfish considerations. . . . If men are not observing Sunday correctly, it is because they have not caught the spirit of Jesus. In proportion as they catch that spirit will the day be truly observed. Our countries are not yet Christian. When they are Christian we may expect a Christian Sabbath. Until then we must go forward to work faithfully to improve a rest day now imperfectly observed.

While providing practical and theological principles for consideration, Mackay concluded that in "determining its Sunday program the Associations should be guided by the judgment of those earnest Christian nationals who are its counselors in all other vital matters."[14]

The roots of the YMCA work in Montevideo were comparatively deep, although the founding of its institution was relatively recent. Rather than sending South Americans to North America for training, the idea had developed of founding an institution for training YMCA secretaries in South America. A senior college in Montevideo called the Instituto Técnico had been opened in 1923 for that purpose, and Mackay began his work with the Association based at the Instituto.[15] The director was Philip Conard, who had joined the work of the YMCA in Latin America in 1906, organized a YMCA there in 1909, and was responsible for the success of the Instituto. Because the Montevideo association was responsible for training, it was an influential branch of the organization. The YMCA program made a significant contribution to physical education and athletic programs in Latin America and had a significant role in organizing the first Latin American games held in 1922. James Stewart Summers trained leaders in the Instituto, and his colleague Frederic W. Dickens led the first team from Argentina to the Olympics.[16]

A second part of the YMCA program was to address the spiritual needs of intellectuals through the spiritual work of the organization. Charles Ewald hired Mackay and Julio Navarro Monzó to address that task. Mackay's work at the Instituto was also designed to develop the spiritual strength of the Latin American secretaries. During 1926 Mackay put a great deal of effort into the courses he taught at the Instituto Técnico. The first was on the "Personality and Teachings of Jesus," and the second, to those same students after returning from his first trip to Brazil, was titled "Fundamental Principles of Christianity."[17] In May Mackay gave a *conferencia* to a full house of the student division asking, "Is There a Relationship between the Young Men's Christian Association and Religion?"[18] Mackay argued that while not a church or a sect, the organization had a religious goal, to form Christian men, and it treasured a religious experience that it wished to share with everyone. The lecture delivered on May 15, 1926 precipitated controversy and a discussion of religious authority.

While based primarily at the Instituto, Mackay spent February 8 to March 9, 1927, lecturing in Chile.[19] Knowing Latin America's need for evangelical literature, he relished the thought of an uninterrupted period for writing until the following July, and he hoped to bind together the associations by sending some pages of inspirational material at regular intervals to all the Latin American associations.[20] He also wished to concentrate on training new leaders for the association and to leave written materials on the subjects that he would teach, such as "The Basic Ideas of Christianity," "The Teaching of Jesus," and possibly a course on the "Philosophy of Religion." He intended to devote August 1927 to the Buenos Aires association. Mackay continued

Mackay with his YMCA colleagues at the YMCA camp at Piriapolis, Uruguay
(1st row L. to R.: Malcolm Crew, unknown, unknown, James Stewart Summers, and Galland;
2nd row L. to R.: unknown, unknown, Ewald, Mackay, Navarro Monzó).

to write Christian literature for Latin America, producing *Más Yo es Digo*, which he referred to as his "little book about the parables," a 250-page book published in Montevideo in November 1927.[21]

Pan-Americanism

Mackay began to write also on particular international political issues to create public awareness of the region and to encourage a political environment favorable to the spiritual movement he was advancing. Pan-Americanism had been rooted in part in the idealism in foreign policy that followed World War I. Broadly speaking its demise started with the American decision not to join the League of Nations or the International Court of Justice, and its use of arms to protect investments. The demise reflected the passing away of the concept of equality before international law of large and small nations. Mackay's thought and spirit in international relations reflected this Wilsonian idealism, whose goal was friendship and understanding between nations.

Mackay realized that he could work more effectively as a missionary in Latin America as a British citizen than as a North American, since the currents of Pan-Americanism did not affect him. Though somewhat reluctant to express an opinion, Mackay wrote on this subject with more detachment and objectivity than could a citizen of North, South, or Central America. Mackay believed that the U.S. intervention in Nicaragua, the threats of intervention in Mexico, and the justifications for it by President Coolidge and his secretary of state had "killed Pan-Americanism."[22] Latin Americans needed assurance that national sovereignty would be respected and that the United States government would not adopt "as a permanent policy the defense, by force of arms, of the interests of speculators."[23] To assist young people in other countries to understand political issues in Latin America, he also wrote about the border dispute between Chile and Peru at Tacna and Arica. He used this conflict as a teaching moment, presenting "an account of the origin, history, and present state of this problem."[24]

Argentina

Though based in Uruguay, during March 1926 Mackay made a brief trip to Argentina on behalf of the YMCA. In the previous twenty-five years since the Association had been in Buenos Aires, the city's population had grown from 800,000 to 2,000,000. Mackay travelled there to familiarize himself with the activities, especially the spiritual activities, of the association, and to become acquainted with the program for the coming months. Mackay found a great deal of activity there but also found that the secretaries were concerned with the institutional aspects of the YMCA. Although there was some activity of an ethical and philanthropic character, the association had become timid in doing the explicitly religious work of bringing members to the point of definite surrender to Jesus Christ. The secretaries and members, however, wished that such work would be initiated. Mackay spoke on the subject of the "Mission of the Young Men's Christian Association" at the Sunday lecture at the Buenos Aires headquarters:

> I dealt briefly with the significance of the Association movement in the modern world, from its inception to the present time. I spoke particularly of its creative originality in producing a new type of home for young men, a new integration of human personality, and a new expression of international idealism. I referred to its development in South America, emphasizing particularly cases in which the Association had initiated new currents and forms of activity, such as the Play Ground movement in Uruguay, campaigns for sexual purity, disinterested services to immigrants, the introduction of a new spirit into work for delinquent boys, and last but not least, the introduction of Mothers Day into the life of South American

cities. I mentioned also the wonderful influence of Association camps as creators of character, speaking specially of Piriapolis, our great forge of ideals and friendships. I closed by making a distinction between mere virtue and plenitude. I gave it as my conviction that the greatest problem facing our Association movement was the danger of being satisfied with a purely virtuous type of character moulded by rules and precepts, without creating that quality of inner spiritual life that expresses itself in acts of redemptive passion that crosses the frontiers of convention and does what no law of virtue demands. I tried to interpret the meaning of the Cross and the principle of the "Second Mile."[25]

The response was cordial. In the audience were three men who exemplified three types that were increasing in South America and that naturally gravitated towards the YMCA. One was Mackay's friend from Peru Dr. Sagarna, who after completing his service as Argentine Minister to Peru had become the Minister of Public Instruction in Argentina. Sagarna's early development had been influenced by missionary educator William C. Morris, and Sagarna had now in turn "revolutionized the spirit of education in the country." The second type was represented by Doctor Jimenez, a medical doctor and former member of the National Congress who at that time was a member of the town council of Buenos Aires. He was a socialist who published a steady stream of pamphlets on social reform, temperance, and sexual purity. One of these pamphlets was titled "The Biology of Don Juan" and showed "that the classic libertine of the Spanish poet Zorilla, who has symbolized the attitude of Spanish and Spanish American youth towards sex and woman hood, was a biological monstrosity."[26] Representing the third type was Sr. Fingerman, a journalist and teacher of experimental psychology in the National Training College for Secondary School Teachers, and a friend of Navarro Monzó's when Monzó was the art critic for *La Nación*. Fingerman was not yet a member of the association, but Mackay believed that he was likely to become one soon.

Mackay found the leading secretaries in Buenos Aires unanimous in their wish for a forward spiritual movement. Mackay recounted that he

spoke to a group one afternoon on Paul's words: "Put ye on the Lord Jesus Christ" [Rom. 13:14], and they were with me on the need of an absolute identification of our lives with Christ and his purposes for men. I spoke to a larger group of some thirty secretaries and other employees on three classic sayings of the Master that synthesize his message: "Come unto Me" [Matt. 11:28], "Believe on Me" [John 14:12; 17:20], "Follow Me" [Matt. 4:19], and I have never experienced an intenser silence than that which followed.[27]

Mackay gave the "lightning talk," lasting only six minutes, one afternoon during lunch hour. It was well received, and the men asked for another before the end of the week. Mackay thought his most interesting address was to the "spiritual elite" of the Argentine membership, a talk he closed with a

> reinterpretation of the principle of the Cross, in terms of the conscious and active choice of suffering for the good of others; some of those present opened up their hearts. One told how he had had an experience of Christ and inward renewal in a crisis of his life when he refused to treat a person who had wronged him as he himself had been treated. He forgave the offender and his forgiveness was the pathway to a new discovery of Christ. There was general agreement that only Christ and the application to life of the principle of the Cross could redeem men and solve the problems of human life and society.[28]

Mackay found in the group "spiritual unrest and the desire for a great spiritual movement in the Buenos Aires Association." It was in a "position to touch the spiritual life of this great country as no other institution is."[29]

Brazil

At the end of June 1926 Mackay began his first trip to Brazil, a nine-week visit to Rio de Janeiro, São Paulo, Campinas, and Porto Alegre. Its purpose was to familiarize him with the association's work in Brazil and the nation itself, a Portuguese-speaking country now part of his continental parish.[30] As he traveled he became acquainted with his fellow YMCA secretaries, preached, and gave addresses and conferences. During the trip he kept a thorough diary as he had done during his trip to Spanish South America in 1915, and he made a firsthand study of conditions in Brazil, describing his travels, persons he met and talked to, sights that he witnessed, events he participated in, and impressions of the culture, people, and country. Writing the diary became a tool to clarify his thoughts, interpret the spiritual and religious life of Brazil, and preserve details of the trip for general interest and for future reference in preparation of addresses. The incidents he recorded in his letters and diary, especially his guidance of a leaders' retreat in Rio, provide examples of how a Christian leader can build a movement and conduct an evangelistic campaign at the grassroots level.[31]

To become familiar with the life of youth and young men, Mackay visited schools, colleges, penitentiaries, an observatory, an orphanage, and churches, where he met pastors and teachers. The Independent Presbyterian Church had separated from the United Presbyterian Church about twenty years before Mackay's visit. There were no real doctrinal differences; the separation had been caused by problems created by Free Masonry in the Presbyterian Church of Brazil. Mackay found relations between the denominations were currently good.[32] There had been a plan to combine the seminaries in Campinas and São Paulo, but as Mackay noted, "The scheme broke down owing to the opposition of a number of laymen. It is much easier to cause a breach than to heal it. The clergy open it, and the laity keep it open."[33] Mackay also visited the Union Seminary in Rio de Janeiro where Methodists, Southern Presbyterians, and Congregationalists were united, Presbyterian students making up the majority.[34]

One of his findings was that the youth of Brazil were much more indifferent to the subject of religion than were the youth on the west coast. Mackay's response to this difference was the "need for the concrete presentation of Christ and his teachings without . . . mentioning the name religion, and also of the great need for literature to show that the modern world, so far as thought is concerned, has a place for religion."[35]

One of the churches Mackay visited in Rio was the large Presbyterian church where Alvaro Reis had been the pastor. Reis had died a few months after the Montevideo Congress in 1925. The church had a full-fledged string band in addition to a choir. The preacher, following the tradition of Alvaro Reis, preached for an hour and a half. The sermon ended at 2:00 p.m., and Communion ended at 3:00 p.m. It reminded Mackay of the services of his boyhood in the Scottish Highlands.[36]

While traveling in Rio, Mackay enjoyed sightseeing along the beautiful avenue of royal palms in the botanical gardens and the views from the outskirts of the city. He met Dr. Hugh C. Tucker, the Bible Society agent, and his wife. Tucker had completed forty-one years in Brazil, and his ideas on evangelization of the educated classes coincided exactly with Mackay's thinking.[37] Mackay also used spare time on the trip to build intellectual capital. While traveling to Rio, he found himself developing a passion for things German just as he had done for things Spanish. "I must learn this language thoroughly," he wrote, "in order to avail myself of new fountains of knowledge and inspiration to present Christ more effectively."[38] In addition to German language study, he read Augustine's *Confessions* for the first time.

On arrival at the YMCA headquarters in Rio, Mackay thought that satisfactory work of the spiritual department would be virtually impossible so long as the Rio association was housed in its present building. The lack of space and of quiet was a handicap for student work. The building was "satu-rated with sound" and at some hours "a constant hubbub of voices mingle[d] with the thud on the gymnasium floor, in the upper story."[39]

He also noted that the close relationship with local evangelical churches was both an advantage and disadvantage to the Association. The institutional development and growth of the Association as "much more than a special-ized appendage of any church or group of churches," was impeded by the ecclesiastical basis in which evangelical church membership was a prereq-uisite for YMCA membership. Since the question of membership basis was again being discussed in Rio, Mackay was optimistic that "with a new build-ing and a new basis, there will be no excuse left to this Association to become a great power in the lives of young men and boys in this great city."[40]

Mackay also got to know and understand the human dimension of the Association by leading the staff devotional meeting at 9:00 a.m. for a week, leading an afternoon conversation titled "Life," and presenting a Saturday lecture titled "The Influence of Physical Education on the Formation of Char-acter." He attended weekly meetings of secretaries and directors where he introduced himself to the staff and conveyed to them the Continental Com-mittee's interest in religion and in the personal basis. He expressed his view that the "ecclesiastical basis very seriously trammeled the spiritual liberty of the Association,"[41] and had reason to believe that his presentation influenced the thinking of some directors.

A highlight was a weekend retreat held at Niterói, the capital of the state of Rio, and the location of a large English population. The group of twenty-three left in midafternoon for the twenty-five-minute trip across Guanabara Bay. The travelers found the view of Rio from the opposite shore was superb. Mr. Davidson, a local leader, had organized the retreat, and Mackay was the principal speaker. Mackay's record of the meetings shows his ability to guide discussion and his goal of stimulating a movement from the bottom upward. An examination of the retreat illustrates what Mackay meant by the incarna-tional approach to evangelism and provides a case study in group leadership and inspiration.

After an early dinner together, Mackay spoke about the mission of the Association. For the next two days the group discussed

> the relation of the institution and the movement, religious work in the Association, the inconstancy of members, and the problem of voluntary workers. . . . The question of the personal basis was discussed, and it was brought out how terribly indifferent Brazilian youths are to the whole sub-ject of religion. There is very much more indifference in Brazil than on the West Coast.[42]

After tea on Saturday there was a volleyball match.

Mackay's group discussion facilitated new insights and inspired new levels of commitment:

> Most of those present took part in all the discussions, which at times became very animated. If solutions were not reached on all or many matters, difficulties in the way of progress stood out in a new light, and problems became more clearly visualized and formulated. And, after all, one of the chief benefits accruing from such discussions is not necessarily the solutions that may be proposed, but rather the degree of clear insight attained regarding the character of particular problems and of the conditions that produced them and at the same time the ability to discern a defect in a region where one was complacently unaware of its existence before. To visualise imperfection and receive inspiration, to work for their removal is the first and most important step towards constructive work. And this end, I feel sure, was achieved at the "Retreat."[43]

On Sunday morning Mackay gave an address from a text that he frequently used but this time he based it on a different translation, "rendering into Spanish Moffatt's translation of the phrase, 'I take every project prisoner to make it obey Christ'" [2 Cor. 10:5]. That evening at Davidson's request Mackay presided at the closing session, designed as an "open-heart meeting." Several members took the opportunity to explain what the retreat meant for their own experience. A letter to the Brazilian students studying at the institute was written and signed by all. Before leaving Mackay read the Gospel account of another closing scene, the one recounted in John 21, at the Sea of Galilee on the morning "that the Risen Lord ate with his disciples and elicited the threefold confession of Peter's love."[44] As a commentary on the words "Follow me!" (John 21:19), Mackay read the concluding words of Albert Schweitzer's classic *The Quest of the Historical Jesus* and told the group the story of Schweitzer's missionary work.[45] The group then stood and formed a ring, wrote Mackay, "clasping each other's hands, and bowing our heads, we consecrated ourselves and our Association to the service of our Lord."[46]

As a result of the visit to Rio, Mackay drew a number of conclusions about the religious work of the Association and his own work in particular, and he articulated for Charles Ewald his own incarnational approach to missions. To get a hearing the religious leader must "live in close contact with men, and to arouse in men a sympathetic interest in himself by being able to do or say things which they consider to be interesting or valuable." This will allow him a "sympathetic hearing regarding what he considers to be the deepest and most vital things in life. Being interested in him for his own intrinsic worth, men will give a sympathetic hearing to his message regarding the Christ who has made his life what it is, and can make all life what it should be."[47]

Mackay also realized the need for study books and programs for study circles. During the trip he had talked with Dr. Santos, who was engaged in religious work in the Association, and Mackay evaluated the training school, which had five students, sincere fellows, Mackay thought, but without strong academic preparation. He intended to meet the need for literature through his own writings within his own time constraints. He hoped to redirect the approach to intellectual work, shifting it from being one of classes to being one of ideas. He hoped to help the members face and address life's problems of thought and action.

Finally, the visit to Brazil helped Mackay to reconsider the best allocation of his own time and efforts and the ideal way to carry on continental work. "A continental secretary should do local work with a continental vision in order to be able later to do continental work with a local vision," he wrote. These insights take on particular interest as a foreshadowing of his later ecumenical thinking:

> Speaking for myself and for my own work, I have reached the conclusion, that no great benefit can accrue from my field activities if I simply limit them to "conferencias," to meetings with secretaries, to giving advice, and to stimulating certain kinds of organization, extending over a period of a number of days or weeks.
>
> I am convinced that the present situation is such as to demand that I should spend from three to six months in a given city or country, become during that time, part and parcel of the life of the local community, devote myself to cultivating the friendship and awakening the interest of the elements we are particularly interested in, and endeavour to organize and become responsible for certain activities during sufficient period to guarantee that they take root and have a chance of becoming permanent. After having cultivated different Associations over a period of from three to five years it would then be possible to do continental work as it should be done. One would know intimately the local Associations, and local community conditions. One would be in a position to do much more from Headquarters than is at present possible and at the same time guarantee a much larger audience throughout the continent for one's "conferencias" and publications.
>
> In other words, my proposition is that one part of each year should be devoted to an intense cultivation of selected cities and countries, and the other to the production of literature. Or to crystallize my point of view in another form, I have come to the conclusion that for the present, continental work should consist in doing local work throughout the continent.

A continental secretary should do local work with a continental vision in order to be able later to do continental work with a local vision.[48]

Mackay's visits to educational institutions and churches in São Paulo, Campinas, Santos, and Porto Alegre gave him a broad perspective of Brazil. While in São Paulo he visited MacKenzie College, the largest missionary institution on the continent, with 1,500 students, about 250 of which were in the engineering department.[49] Mackay concluded that Brazil was "a whole world in itself, with cultural and economic conditions utterly distinct from anything else in South America."[50] When he returned to Montevideo at the end of August, he had concluded that work in Brazil required specialized attention for it to progress and keep up with the advances of the country and the country's varied religious forces.

A Nine-Month Journey—Jerusalem Missionary Council

At the end of 1927 Mackay began a long journey that lasted until late August 1928. It carried him the farthest afield for the longest period from home and gave him the most varied experiences that he had yet had in life. During that time Mackay visited parts of the Spanish-speaking mission field located in the Northern Hemisphere. He also addressed English-speaking audiences in North America. On December 21, 1927, Mackay's ship reached New York from Montevideo, and he had soon made three important addresses. First, joining Mott, Speer, and Reinhold Niebuhr, he spoke in Detroit at the Quadrennial Convention of the Student Volunteer Movement, December 28, 1927, to January 1, 1928;[51] second, in New York at the annual meeting and banquet of the Committee on Cooperation in Latin America on January 9; and third, in Atlantic City, New Jersey, at the annual gathering of the Foreign Missions Conference of North America, January 10–13, 1928. Mackay's address to the Conference there contained the first use of the term "ecumenical" in religious context: "Rojas is an ecumenical Christian, the silver mouthpiece of a considerable number of men and women in South America who are unattached to any religious denomination, but who are Christian in the most absolute and ecumenical sense."[52]

From continental North America, Mackay spent fourteen days in Puerto Rico and spoke there on twenty-nine different occasions. Next he visited Cuba while the Pan American Congress was in session. The Young Peoples Societies of the Evangelical Churches of Havana took united action for the first time in their history, and Mackay spoke on the Sermon on the Mount at joint meetings held successively in the Baptist, Methodist, Episcopalian, and

Presbyterian Churches.[53] On returning from the Caribbean, he lectured at the Kennedy School of Missions at Hartford Seminary.

Social, political, and economic changes greatly affected foreign missions between the Edinburgh Conference in 1910 and the Jerusalem Conference in 1928. World War I produced an awakened sense of nationalism outside Europe and a sense that something was wrong within Western civilization itself. Formerly, the missionary's message had been taken for granted. Now, as resistance hardened to the message in some regions and as nationalism began to assert itself, a new stage of mission history began to develop. Missionaries began to realize that all depended on the message as their work moved forward.[54] The message began to be seen to have both individual and social elements, but the individual element of conversion remained primary. The gradual but increasing secularization of mission theology through a focus on economic development decreased the urgency of the task.[55] For Mackay the Conference was personally significant as he became acquainted with English and Continental European mission leaders and rose to new levels of recognition and responsibility within the movement.[56] He looked back at his work to date, formulated his thoughts on the Christian message in an important paper, and called for missionaries to have more theological understanding.

So far as possible the South American delegation to the Jerusalem Conference travelled together and met on the ship *Adriatic* from Naples to discuss questions and issues the Conference would face.[57] During their stop in Cairo Mackay heard Speer speak in the magnificent, new auditorium of the American University.[58] During the stop Mackay also had an opportunity to visit historic locations in Egypt. One afternoon he accompanied Inman's party to Memphis and the Sahara, returning by way of the pyramids, where the group lingered until sunset. Mackay found the pyramids "more wonderful, in fact, than I had expected."

"What may not be buried by sand and time when Memphis was buried!!" he wrote, and he "thought of Moses." "In [the] Sahara," Mackay continued, I "visited the subterranean vaults where the sacred bulls were buried in as many gigantic granite coffins. Got candles at the entrance. One of the most impressive places I have ever been in. What a sense of death the Egyptians had!"[59]

The method for studying non-Christian religions at Jerusalem, unlike at Edinburgh, was to enlist experts to outline the enduring spiritual values of each non-Christian religious system as the expert perceived them: Dr. Nicol Macnicol, for Hinduism in India; Dr. Kenneth Sanders and Dr. August Karl Reischauer, for Buddhism; Dr. Leighton Stuart, for China; and the late Canon William Henry Temple Gairdner, for Islamic lands. In a new but significant departure, Dr. Rufus Jones dealt with secularism. Each religion had its own view of the world.

In mid-March at Cairo, German and other continental European representatives held a meeting where scholars aired and clarified theological issues that were ambiguous or unclear in the papers.[60] Barth's thought had influenced the thinking of continental delegates who stressed the uniqueness of Christ. In reviewing the papers that had been prepared and circulated in advance, some Europeans believed that some papers overemphasized the spiritual "values" of other religions. They felt that Anglo-Saxons were presenting Christ as a fulfillment of truths that other faiths possessed in some measure but incompletely. The use of the term *values*, a term that theology had begun to use but whose original usage had been economic, may have involved suggestions of syncretism, in part because of the continental European's use of English. Part of the confusion arose from Professor William Ernest Hocking's use of the term *syncretism* and his use of psychological ideas in the context of theology.[61] The Cairo meeting reassured the continental delegates that the English-speaking delegates continued strongly to believe in the uniqueness of Jesus Christ. Without such belief Christian mission efforts would have been undermined.

Officially the Jerusalem Conference, meeting the two weeks before Easter, was an enlarged meeting of the International Missionary Council, under the leadership of John Mott. The 240 delegates from 51 countries, including 35 from North America, worshiped together as they considered important issues of the Christian message and the presentation of the Word.[62] At Edinburgh in 1910 only seven or eight of the 1200 delegates had not been American or European.[63] Two laypersons that attended the Jerusalem Conference, Williiam Ernest Hocking of the United States and Hendrik Kraemer, born in Holland, later would publish sharply opposing points of view regarding the missionary movement.

To convene, Doctor Martin Schlunk welcomed the Conference to the hall of the German Sanitarium built by "German missionary donations before the war."[64] A special camp was built on the Mount of Olives to house the delegates, and Russian nuns allowed women delegates to use their convent. Church leaders and internationally known experts on economics and labor brought their experience to the problems the Conference faced. English was the official language, but hymns were translated in English, French, and German. The delegates from around the world wore a variety of styles of clothing ranging from gaiters and vests to flowery flowing garments.[65]

Mott's opening address commented on the location of the meeting: "The Mount of Olives, where the meetings are held, has sacred memories of the frequent visits of Jesus, whose custom it was to come here for quiet communion. Therefore, tents and huts have been erected so that under the olive trees overlooking the Holy City the delegates can walk and talk together." He also introduced the themes of discussion. First, was "an attempt to discover and state the spiritual values of non-Christian systems of religion as well as of secular civilizations"; second, "to reach a more profound understanding of the truer sense of the interdependence between the younger Churches, especially in Asia, and the older Churches"; and third, to deal with the problem of "rapid expansion in Asia and Africa of Western industrialism,"[66] and issues of race relations and education in the context of national secular education.

On Sunday, with Lord and Lady Herbert Charles Onslow Plumer, the British high commissioner and his wife, in attendance, the bishop of Salisbury, chairman of the Missionary Council of the National Assembly of the Church of England, preached, making important points on equality and unity within the church:

> We have to work with God to make out of the present world, with its racial, industrial, social and war problems, a better world. In face of the race problems we must insist on common equality in the family of God. . . . Division among the churches of the West is regarded as a scandal in Asia, and the International Missionary Council meeting affords a practice ground for reunion of the churches. . . . God will, through us, make all things new, to unite all Christians in order to bring peace among races, nations and classes.[67]

On Tuesday, lively statements and creative tensions emerged as delegates discussed spiritual and social elements in Christianity. In the morning program, Robert E. Speer presented the person of Christ as the focal point of the missionary movement. The challenge was to separate him from all that obscured him. During the afternoon the council divided into five sections, and the largest of these focused on secularism. Professor R. H. Tawney, William Temple's lifelong friend, and Harold Grimshaw of the International Labor Office, Geneva, made a vigorous challenge to Speer's theologically dominant conception presented that morning. Born in Calcutta and influenced by the broad-church Anglicanism of the Rugby School, Tawney believed that the industrial problem was a moral problem. Earlier in the 1920s he had written two significant books, *The Acquisitive Society* (1920) and *Religion and the Rise of Capitalism* (1926), the latter extending and shifting some ideas of Max Weber. At the meeting Tawney remarked, "We are trying the impossible in offering to save the individual, yet leaving the social structure pagan. The Common man, the miner, the steel worker, the boilermaker, wants to know what organized Christianity is going to do to better the world he inhabits. If the Christian Church is to lead the way into the future it must enter the field of human society."[68] Grimshaw was critical of the exportation of economic exploitation by "self-called Christian civilizations"[69] in "exporting . . .

precisely those elements in our secular civilization which have produced social injustice and the most widespread suffering."[70]

Representatives of countries receiving missionaries were heard the next day. Siruano Kulubya said that Uganda had avoided difficulties between missionaries and local peoples because of the large majority of locals in church organizations and Christian chiefs in tribal organizations, and a sympathetic British protectorate. Bishop Adolphus Williamson Howells of Nigeria also addressed the issue of relations between the sending and receiving churches. He said that "the relation of the church to the missions should be that of mother and child. If a mother was too careful of a child for too long it was bad for the child. Missionaries should not remain too long among the natives, but withdraw gradually."[71] Miss Helen Kiduk Kim of Korea, Mrs. Ochimi Kurbushirm of Japan, and other women commented on Jesus' recognition of "the value of women in all relationships and for herself" and by contrast that "Buddhism, Shintoism and Confucianism . . . never gave women a place as persons as Christianity did."[72]

Dr. Luther A. Weigle of the Yale Divinity School, later the chairman of the American Standard Bible Committee, presented the key address on Christian religious education. In the afternoon at the discussion meetings all agreed that education and religion belonged together, but how to do so in state-supported schools was an extremely difficult problem. Professor Tawney spoke out again on social development:

> You cannot maintain a double standard of morality. . . . Life is all of one piece, and it is not possible for men and women to accept one standard of social ethics in private life and another in economic life. What we require is to build again a Christian sociology originally adapted to a similar day. The formulation of the principles involved is the work of generations. It is for the churches to prepare the way for a society where man will enjoy material well-being and also spiritual peace.[73]

Several anecdotes demonstrate the difficult issues faced by the Conference relating to the "value" of non-Christian religions. Dr. Reischauer, after drawing some sharp distinctions and nuances, felt that the correct attitude to other religions was "sympathetic insight accepting generously all truth wherever it is found. All the non-Christian systems are reaching out toward the great truths of the Gospel. They are children of God, like the Buddha, whom one may think of as a child of God who did not know his heavenly Father."[74] Sadhu Sundar Singh, a Christian, was reported to have said that if his mother, a saintly Hindu, was not in heaven, he would refuse to enter.[75] William Temple, then Bishop of Manchester, addressed what difference being a Christian would make to Mahatma Gandhi, asserting that in addition to finding God in a fuller sense, his social policy would be affected by moralizing and spiritualizing the results of scientific progress rather than turning his back on them.[76]

When Palm Sunday came, crowds lined the streets of Jerusalem to see Crown Prince Humberto of Italy, a member of a Catholic royal family, who was visiting the Holy City and the Church of the Holy Sepulchre. Dr. McInnes, Anglican bishop of Jerusalem, led members of the Missionary Council on a pilgrimage through the streets, following the likely path taken by Jesus on Palm Sunday. At stages of the walk, including at Bethany, Bethphage, and the slope of the Mount of Olives at Gethsemane, the delegates heard readings from the Gospels, prayed, and sang hymns.

With his address to the assembled dignitaries on the afternoon of Palm Sunday, Mackay emerged as a recognized leader in the world missionary movement. His address on the power of evangelism drew a picture of how he had approached the mission field of Latin America, a region of idealism and modern culture where the majority of all men had repudiated religion. Mackay's formula in this environment was to "win a right to be listened to" and to deliver the message without ritual or ceremony. Thus far he said his work had been "largely ploughing and sowing."[77] One significant result of the Conference was the recognition of Latin America as a mission field, and Mackay's presentation of the case for evangelistic effort in Latin America, he learned later, was a factor that encouraged the Conference to adopt a motion unanimously that representatives of the evangelical movement in Latin America should be elected regular members of the International Missionary Council.[78] As a member of the Commission on the Christian Life and Message, Mackay had a part in framing the report of that commission. He also acted as secretary to the subsection on secularism, of which Dr. Surendra Kumar Datta was chairman.

On Maundy Thursday the council unanimously adopted the report of findings on the Christian message. The unanimous vote was in large part due to the skillful handling by Speer and Temple and especially to Temple's skillful draftsmanship, which he called his "parlour trick of fitting everybody's pet point into a coherent document when they thought they were contradicting one another."[79] All delegates were pleased at the outcome. Traditionalists had feared the Conference might veer towards a modernist position, and modernists feared that the message would prove too traditional.[80] An economic report, principally drafted by Tawney, had been adopted the day before. On the morning of Good Friday, a devotional service was led by Bishop James Linton of Persia, and in the afternoon a three-hour devotional service was held at St. George's Cathedral, with Canon Danby of Jerusalem presiding.[81] On Saturday, the council unanimously passed resolutions critical of racial prejudice and the conditions arising from it.[82] Easter Sunday was dedicated exclusively to devotional services. The delegates thought the statement on the Christian message, which contained a significant shift in missionary emphasis from death to life, was marvelous.[83] Mott found the gathering "one of the most courageous meetings [he had] attended in forty years of national and international gatherings."[84]

Mackay's friend Freytag saw a threefold significance of the Conference: "the discussion about our message confronting the non-Christian religions, the new impetus to take up the social problems in Asia and Africa and the strong representation of those who then were labeled younger churches."[85] Mackay concluded in retrospect,

> The meeting was dominated by the conviction that secularism was the most sinister and potent force which affected the spiritual life of mankind. It, therefore, called upon the non-Christian religions, as well as the Christian churches throughout the world, to combat the sway of the secularistic spirit. Taking place in the heyday of optimism regarding the possibility of a true international order, the Jerusalem Conference lacked somewhat the intensity and the tragic sense of life which its successors were to reflect.[86]

Arthur J. Brown, Secretary of the Presbyterian Board of Foreign Missions, noted that the Protestant missionary enterprise, represented by 20,188 missionaries, now had "a clear mandate, an expanding program and a unified world outlook."[87]

Muslim opposition to the Conference was also evident. Although the delegates were permitted to make an afternoon visit to the Mosque of Omar, which is ordinarily closed to non-Muslims after 11:30 a.m., local Islamic newspapers sharply disapproved of the meeting being held in Jerusalem.[88] After the Conference ended, the Islamic press throughout Palestine, Syria, and Egypt vigorously protested missionary activities in general and the holding of the conference in Jerusalem. An Arab smashed the window in the Foreign Bible Society's new building. The Islamic Supreme Court in Jerusalem ordered shops in the old city closed on April 21 in a sympathetic response to Muslims injured when police had broken up a hostile demonstration in Gaza.[89]

When John R. Mott organized the final documents of the Conference for publication, he asked Mackay "to prepare one of the most important papers," and include his "own constructive treatment of the subject . . . quite apart from what you may have heard in our meeting."[90] Mott transmitted a reprint to Mackay with the following comment:

> I appreciate the fact that you shrink from preparing the special chapter which we have reprinted for you, but you should be reassured when I tell

you that every person to whom I have spoken about our reprint to you—
and I have spoken to many—has received the work with the most lively
satisfaction. If you will trust my judgment, no one can take your place.[91]

Mott found the contribution to be a "valuable paper . . . just what [they]
wanted."[92] Another writer concluded, "The report volume on the Christian
Message will be a notable book that will help to greatly strengthen the missionary purposes of our churches."[93]

Mackay's essay on evangelism appeared as the climactic paper of the first
volume of the Jerusalem Conference message prior to the council's statement.[94] The paper, "The Evangelistic Duty of Christianity," is a powerful
statement of the centrality of the person of Jesus Christ to the work of missions:

> Not His teachings about God and man, not even the uniqueness of His
> religion, but He Himself, in whom we discover "what God is and what
> man through Him may become," is the quintessential element in Christi-
> anity and its unique message to the world. Christ is the religious value of
> intrinsic and absolute worth which Christianity has and which the world
> needs.[95]

Christ is the transformer of character and the incarnate revelation of God.
Mackay urged evangelists in presenting the message to win the right to be
heard: "Represent some human value that the group he proposes to evangelize can appreciate, or he will not be seriously listened to."[96] The missionary
must present that aspect of Christ or of truth that the situation requires. As an
example of this emphasis, Mackay took the prophetic masculinity of Jesus
in clearing the temple courts as an aspect of Christ's character fitted to the
South American situation. In Latin America Christ had long been portrayed
as an object of pity.

Professor David S. Cairns singled out Mackay's paper and the companion
piece by William Temple as highlights of the Conference.[97] He drew attention to one passage where Mackay expressed a central lesson of the entire
volume:

> The missionary movement must become more theological, not primarily
> for those to whom missionaries go, but for the Church herself and the mis-
> sionaries who represent her. The strength and success of these will depend
> to a very great extent on their clear apprehension of the relation between
> the Jesus of history and His teachings and the Living God.[98]

Cairns concluded that the reports of the 1910 and 1928 conferences demonstrate that the "missionary expansion of the Christian Church is in the mid-
stream of human history and human thought."[99]

Robert E. Speer also saw the Conference as a key event. He wrote about it in his major apologetic work, *The Finality of Jesus Christ*, emphasizing the contribution of the continental contingent.[100] Speer also believed that the strong presence of the indigenous churches played a much greater role in Jerusalem than in Edinburgh. The indigenous church leaders still needed the help and support of the established churches of the West, which suggested that the foreign mission enterprise had just begun. Jerusalem made clear that "the world's standards and measurements are fallacious in the work of the Kingdom of God. Here it is not heavy battalions and clever publicity and skilful organization and money which prevail. It is spiritual quality and character."[101] Understanding of the scope and power of the Christian missions was expanding. "The Jerusalem Meeting saw the missionary situation less in geographical terms of East and West than in functional terms of the relation of the world mission of Christianity to industry, to the rural life of the world, to education and to non-Christian systems of thought and faith."[102]

When participants arrived home they reported on the accomplishments of the Conference. Dean-elect Weigle returned to New Haven and gave his conclusions. He saw the Conference as a necessary defense of Western ideas and institutions that had come under attack.[103] Missionary organizations pledged to remain independent of the efforts of government to be diverted from their task.

The missionary leaders at the Jerusalem Conference realized that the missionary purpose was best served and the gospel most effectively communicated by formulating the essential message in terms of Christ himself. In the minds of the receiving peoples, the gospel was thus to be stripped of the accompanying imperfections of Western economic culture with which Christianity was often associated. The method focused attention on the essence of Christianity's uniqueness and universality while distinguishing it and separating it from certain attributes that Christianity shared with other faiths, such as spiritual awakening, the sense of the brotherhood of man, or some forms of mysticism. Implicit in this formulation of Christ, the gospel is also the fully developed religious doctrine. At the same time it afforded the possibility of avoiding controversy over certain historical conceptions that had been superseded through scientific discoveries. Some elements of Protestantism were less ready to accept change from a bibliocentric religion to a christocentric religion.[104] For Mackay an important aspect of this christocentric religion was emphasis on religious experience formulated in terms of friendship with the deity. Other segments of the church came to this understanding and made the change more slowly. For them this emphasis ran the risk of becoming a form of idealism or external imitation of the Savior. For a twentieth-century

theologian like Mackay, the continual challenge was to separate the "changing from the changeless."

Mackay summed up his impressions of the Jerusalem Conference in a letter to his friend, J. J., "Josh," Osuna, who at the time was dean of the College
of Education at the University of Puerto Rico:

> We had a great time in Jerusalem. The conference infused a new meaning
> into the word "missionary," gave unique expression to Christian unity, and
> the Anglican brethren on one occasion taking communion with us Non-
> Anglicans according to our simple rites, and incorporated a new content
> into the purview of missionary statesmanship. I refer, of course, to Latin
> America which finds itself now within the consort of Evangelical organiza-
> tions in virtue of its great indigenous Evangelical churches.[105]

After the Conference was over Mackay lingered a while around the Sea of
Galilee and then, taking a boat in Beirut, coasted around the Mediterranean,
making brief visits to Antioch, Tarsus, Cypress, and Athens.

Return to North America

On his return to North America Mackay continued to travel extensively,
building the YMCA movement and making platform speeches. Mackay
returned to New York on May 9 and spoke at a YMCA in the vicinity. Later
he gave a short course of lectures at the Kennedy School of Missions, Hartford Seminary. He then left for the western United States, doing deputation
work to awaken or deepen interest in the work of the YMCA in Latin America. He spoke at various occasions at hotel luncheons and in YMCA buildings, as well as in several churches in Lansing, Dayton, Detroit, Duluth, Des
Moines, Wichita, Tulsa, Fort Worth, and San Antonio, where he made many
acquaintances.

His annual report for the year 1928 shows Mackay had begun to be disillusioned by certain emphases of the YMCA and its direction.[106] Mackay's
vision for the YMCA was that it should become "above everything else, *a
center of soul-life and energy*" not just a mere sports club. Its leadership in
the area of physical activities had been achieved before the era of spiritual
unrest that was passing over Latin America. It seemed to Mackay that now,
once its sports program had been taken up by governments and private institutions, the physical side must remain strong, but that it should now focus on
spiritual matters and altruistic activity connected with intellectual and religious themes. Mackay felt strongly that if the YMCA could not refocus, a

new movement either independent of or connected with the YMCA ought to be formed to carry out these goals. Other areas of need were for "the preparation and propagation of dynamic literature" and for a first-class magazine to address spiritual issues. Organizationally he thought that those who have been asked to serve a cause and not an institution "should enjoy a great deal of autonomy."[107]

While Mackay was returning from the Jerusalem Council meeting to South America through New York, Speer approached him about joining the Presbyterian Board of Foreign Missions. An offer was extended to Mackay in June 1928.[108] Mackay was interviewed for the position on August 2, 1928, and he accepted the appointment the following month.[109] Some adjustments were considered for the Home and Foreign Departments to bring Mackay on, since he did not wish to take on all of Speer's administrative work (particularly for India, Persia, Syria, and Iraq, though India and Japan were of interest for the future) and to allow him to work four months of the year in Mexico and the Caribbean.[110] But when Mackay read the official minutes of the action by the Board at its first fall meeting September 17, he immediately withdrew. As negotiated, the employment agreement was to include the possibility of spending some months each year doing direct missionary work in Latin America. He believed it was his duty and his call. The time and opportunity were favorable, and his preparation for such work was unique. The meeting's minutes reflecting his call, however, contained the caveat that his evangelistic work would continue, "until such time as other adjustments may become desirable in the interests of the general work."[111] Mackay could not accept such a limitation.

The young missionary had considered the offer carefully, for Speer's friendship was "one of the most stimulating and stabilizing influences in [Mackay's] life."[112] But he was not willing to entertain the possibility of complete severance from the work he was doing at a crucial time.[113] He explained his decision to Speer:

> This region wants me and needs me as no other cause or region can, and I have no authority from God to enter into any relationship which would imply consent to leave it in the future. My present feeling is that only an act of God, such as the closing of doors or a breakdown in health, could justify an alteration of my present programme. I recognize that according to every human standard, a secretaryship in the Presbyterian Board would be more important and influential than the very undefined position which I have. I am equally convinced on the other hand, that the contribution which God may enable me to make in my lonely adventure shall be of greater qualitative importance for the Kingdom of God than anything I could do in

another capacity elsewhere. If my judgement should prove wrong it will be because love and not personal considerations led me astray.[114]

With renewed vigor he formulated a revised methodology for his work in Latin America and explained to Bishop Robert Paddock,

> I have no higher ambition than to give myself entirely, and for life, to these Latin lands. In 1930, after I have had a vacation and spent a winter in study in Germany, I intend putting into operation a new plan. Instead of rotating all over the Continent, as I have been doing for the last year or two, I propose devoting prolonged periods to definite areas. The first of these periods I intend giving to Mexico and the countries of the Caribbean Basin.[115]

The Board's offer was not the only one Mackay received that autumn. President J. Ross Stevenson wrote Mackay on October 17, 1928, urging him to consider the appointment to the chair of apologetics and Christian ethics at Princeton Seminary. He wrote that he believed Mackay would be "an ideal man for the place and as the duties involved keep one here in Princeton only from the first of October to the first of May, some arrangement might be devised whereby you could spend a part of the year with your family here and the other part in carrying on your work in South America."[116] Mackay felt he could hardly accept after so recently turning down the position with the Presbyterian Board of Foreign Missions.[117]

Earlier in 1926 Speer had strongly recommended Mackay for the chair of Systematic Theology at Western Theological Seminary in Pittsburgh, but Mackay declined President Kelso's offer to put his name in nomination.[118] In somewhat eloquent terms Mackay replied,

> I am not my own to make such a decision. My life is thirled to South America. Only God, by as clear guidance as that by which He led me to the Continent, or Death, can free me from my betrothment. But happily you are not dependent upon me. You will not find it difficult, I am certain, to find capable men whose energies are unpledged for life to some specific task to teach theology to your young men at Western.[119]

First Trip to Mexico

Wending his way from Jerusalem home to Uruguay in June 1928, Mackay made an evangelistic stop in Mexico, which near the end of Plutarco Calles's four-year term as president was experiencing a period of intense religious persecution.[120] For twelve days in Monterrey under the auspices of a committee of prominent townspeople, he gave a series of addresses on the Sermon on the Mount at the main hall of a normal school, under the chairmanship of Prof. Andrés Osuna, a prominent evangelical and one of Mexico's leading educators. He also spoke on Unamuno at evangelical churches, to public schoolteachers, and to the bar association at the College of Law. The listeners appreciated it so much that they organized a special luncheon for Mackay several days later. Mackay then traveled on to Mexico City where he spent six weeks. He found the atmosphere there "charged with spiritual interest."[121]

In mid-July he gave an "address at the University . . . to an attendance of over 350 people: the room was filled and a number stood throughout the lecture."[122] At the first lecture the president of the university presided. Later Mackay recalled, "The most momentous academic experience of my life was in Mexico in 1928."[123]

> In the federal capital I spent altogether nearly six weeks. They were, I believe, the most fruitful weeks of my long tour. I found the atmosphere charged with spiritual interest and unrest, which made itself felt in all social classes, from men and women of culture and position to their brothers and sisters in lowly walks of life. The Mexican people, so far from being irreligious or anti-religious, are the most religiously disposed people I have come across in Latin America.
>
> My main series of addresses was given in the lecture hall of the local Association, and consisted of ten lectures on the "Sermon on the Mount." After an introductory lecture on "Jesus among the Laymen," I endeavoured to present Christ's ideal for life, bringing my audience face to face at the close of the series, with the problem of how to obtain the necessary strength to realize that ideal. My plan was to prepare the way for the appreciation of Christ's Gospel by presenting the sublime standards of His Law. I gave myself chiefly therefore to ploughing and sowing. In spite of the fact that during the period in which I gave these lectures, the life of the city was agitated by the death of the aviator, Carranza, followed by the assassination of the president elect, General Obregon, the series was not interrupted nor the attendance greatly affected.[124]

Mackay's friend and YMCA superior Charles Ewald was also in Mexico at the time, and he received a letter signed by several prominent educators requesting that Mackay be stationed for a number of years in Mexico, because Mexico was passing through a critical and decisive period. They also gave Mackay a silk flag of Mexico as both a souvenir of their affection and a pledge that Mackay would return to live and work for Mexican youth.[125] Guy Inman described the impact of Mackay's trip to Mexico in the *International Review of Missions*: "Dr. John Mackay had a most remarkable series of meetings in Mexico in July 1928. Crowded meetings were held, as well as quiet retreats with small groups representing some of the most influential leaders in the intellectual and political life of the country."[126]

The extraordinary need and opportunity for evangelistic work in Mexico that he saw during this trip was a significant factor in Mackay's reversing his decision to join the Presbyterian Board of Foreign Missions as Speer's replacement. One veteran worker told Mackay that unless Mackay moved to Mexico "it may be another twenty years before any one is raised up to do this fundamental work." He then added, "This is no exaggeration. For the past twelve years I have personally been looking forward to the day when some great spiritual leader could win his way into the hearts of our intellectual and moral leaders in Mexico. You have won their hearts and they are ready for you. How I wish you could come!"[127] Another missionary to Mexico visiting New York wrote Mackay that when he "called at the International Headquarters of the Y.M.C.A. in New York to say goodbye to Babcock and Ewald I found them lifting up their voices in protest and metaphorically 'throwing ashes on their heads' because of your cable accepting your appointment with the Presbyterian Board."[128]

At the end of August 1928, Mackay finally arrived home in Uruguay. He then began in September a busy period of writing and teaching at the Instituto Técnico. His courses were the Philosophy of Religion and the Teachings of Jesus. During this teaching period he wrote several articles including one in Spanish for *La Nueva Democracia* titled "The Religious Renaissance in France"; an article called "A Latin Leader Discovers Christ" about *The Invisible Christ* by Argentine writer Ricardo Rojas;[129] and "Cultural Peaks of Contemporary South America," which he delivered at the annual banquet of the Committee on Cooperation in Latin America and which was later reproduced in the *Bulletin of the Pan American Union*. Earlier that year he produced an article already mentioned, "The Evangelistic Duty of Christianity," for volume 1 of the Jerusalem Conference reports. The year 1929 began with addresses in picturesque Camp Piriapolis to the English-speaking secretaries of the YWCA in South America, followed by travel to the Argentine Students' Camp in Sierra de la Ventana.[130] In February he finished two more articles for the *International Review of Missions* and *Student World*.[131]

After the quadrennial convention meeting in Montevideo during Easter week, during the months of April, May, June, and part of July, Mackay began his first English book. Its working title was *The Almond Spray* or *Spiritual Forces in Contemporary South America*, but it was later published as *The Other Spanish Christ*. Within the same period he prepared for publication the course of addresses delivered at the Argentine Students' Camp. At

Inman's request Mackay also submitted a paper for discussion at the Hispanic American Evangelical Congress held at Havana, June 20–30, 1929.[132] The paper was a fine survey and analysis of the reform movement in Latin American education, the "university revolution" Mackay called it, that had begun in Córdoba, Argentina, in 1918 and in which Mackay had played a role by injecting ethical teaching and evangelism into the revolutionary mix of ideas. His general study of education included specific references, because the countries that he knew were representative of the countries that he did not know. Student life in all Spanish America had more than a few generic traits.

As 1930 approached, Mackay prepared again for furlough and a journey that meant additional separation from his family. In June 1929 Mackay saw his family depart by ship from Montevideo on their way home to Inverness, Scotland, via Southampton, England. John Mackay himself remained two months more and left Montevideo in early August 1929 to travel through Argentina, Chile, and the west coast of South America on a lecture tour before rejoining them in Scotland for furlough.

Chapter 8

The Christian Message, Furloughs, and Travels (1929–1932)

"What think ye of Christ?" (Matt. 22:42 KJV)

*A*fter his trip to Jerusalem and while still under the auspices of the YMCA, Mackay made a second intercontinental journey, this time to the British Isles and continental Europe in 1930 for his furlough. Mackay used the time, nevertheless, in personal study, evangelistic addresses, and meetings of evangelistic strategy and tactics with other leaders in the YMCA movement. He became acquainted with people who later led the ecumenical movement, including Visser 't Hooft, Emil Brunner, Karl Barth, and others. At one important meeting a group reflected together about the nature of the Christian message and how to present it in that changing era. Mackay's furlough was designed so that the family could live in Bonn, Germany, while John spent the spring term perfecting his German and studying theology with Karl Barth. This period of work and reflection began to redirect Mackay's creative focus toward the nature of and the role of the Church.

Leaving Montevideo

Since Mackay had speaking engagements in various places in Latin America, he and his family returned separately to Scotland for the family's first furlough since 1922. In June of 1929 Jane Mackay and the four children left by ship from Montevideo bound for England. After a three-week voyage to Southampton, they arrived in England. Jane's sister Nellie Wells met them at the dock in Southampton and traveled with them to London where they all spent a week sightseeing before traveling north to Scotland to visit John's parents in Inverness. Later Jane was able to find a home to rent for the family's temporary sojourn there. That school year the children attended the Inverness Royal Academy.

While the family was settling temporarily in Scotland and the children were getting to know their grandparents, aunts, and uncles, John stayed on in Montevideo to finish his work. He left that city at the end of July 1929 to continue evangelistic travels in other parts of the continent. He journeyed westward from Montevideo then north via the west coast of South America. As the trip was about to begin, he met Count Hermann Keyserling, who was living in the River Plate region for several months. This connection planted the idea later to use the ecumenical concept in the context of the Christian church. An aristocrat from a wealthy German family, Keyserling had lost his estate in Estonia during the Russian Revolution. Married to the granddaughter of Chancellor Bismarck, the count had begun a "school of wisdom" in Darmstadt, Germany, which was inspired by such schools in Northern India. The count gave three lectures in Montevideo, and Mackay had the opportunity for two long talks with him. Mackay saw an opportunity for personal evangelism and to guide public opinion toward Christianity through the influence of this author. Keyserling had "got a terrible idea of Catholicism in these countries" and "received more hostility from the Church than ever he had received in his life from any institution." It appeared that "an attempt" had "been made to prevent his trip to the Pacific countries. However he is going to La Paz, Cuzco, Lima and Chile." Mackay offered to arrange for someone completely reliable to be at his disposal in each city he visited. With a view toward influencing his book on Latin America, Mackay was "very anxious that he should see some of the Evangelical work in the mountains."[1]

Keyserling "had written twice on the United States, [but he had] never been in contact with the Church or Missionary groups of the country. He didn't even know John R. Mott by name!" The States symbolized materialism to Keyserling. Mackay asked him whether he would mind if a group of representative Christian leaders were invited to meet him. The idea seemed to please Keyserling, who told Mackay "that he was well aware that there was in the United States among the minority of the population, a higher grade of spirituality than he had found anywhere." During his visit to Latin America Keyserling felt indebted to Navarro Monzó, who had written several reports for *La Nación* of Buenos Aires interpreting Keyserling's work, and Keyserling had written a public letter to *La Nación* saying "that his lectures had been better interpreted in that paper than ever before by the press in any part of the world." Mackay concluded that Keyserling's "influence will be to the good, although one is bound to say that, so far, I have been able to discover no dynamic in his teaching."[2]

This encounter also helped form aspects of Mackay's thinking. He was stimulated by the discussions with this "brilliant but erratic philosopher." Keyserling had a very early sense of globalism and called the world an "ecumenical organism" brought about by man's technological achievements.[3] Keyserling's book, *The World in the Making*, had been published in 1927, and thus Keyserling first introduced Mackay "to the word 'ecumenical' in a context giving it contemporary relevancy."[4] Later in 1930 after further reflection on Keyserling's observations, Mackay wrote an article in the *Student World* titled "Reflections on the Christian Message in the Present World Drama." There he wrote,

> East and West, so long regarded as impermeable to each other's influence and interests, have reached the point of mutual interpenetration. The symbolic "Chauffeur" has gone East and the Sadhu has come West. With the sweep around the globe of great ecumenical currents, purely local history has come to an end. For weal or for woe, humanity is one; only its newly achieved unity is not that of joy or of love, but rather that of pain and of struggle.[5]

Before turning north for a tour in Peru from September 10 to October 2, Mackay made lecture stops first in Buenos Aires, from August 1 to August 10, and Chile, from August 12 to September 3.[6] In Buenos Aires he had long talks about a literary project with Ricardo Rojas, president of the University of Buenos Aires, and with Sagarna, Mackay's friend from Lima, and he gave a lecture at the University of La Plata on the ecumenical spirit.[7] He also spoke to five hundred boys at the upper school of the Colegio National. A storm in the Cordillera, the Andes mountain range, delayed Mackay's arrival in Santiago by three days. While in Santiago he made six addresses, then four in Concepción, and two in Valparaiso before suddenly coming down with the grippe. Trusted by the Presbyterian Church, Mackay acted on its behalf in Santiago when he looked into some construction overcharge problems that the Instituto Ingles was experiencing.[8]

Peru and Colegio Anglo-Peruano

The Colegio Anglo-Peruano had faced a number of challenges since Mackay had left it for YMCA evangelistic work, and the Free Church General Assembly of 1929 was a turning point for the school. The location at the Plaza Francia was bursting at the seams, and the school was turning away qualified pupils for lack of space. The landlord declined to renew the lease after 1929. Alexander Renwick took up John Mackay's initiative for the church to invest in a school building. Money was available: the Free Church had £32,000 in foreign missions capital and the Peruvian mission was requesting £20,000.

But the proposal met economic and philosophical opposition. Should the money be spent at all, and was a school a valid agency of missionary work or a drain on funds that could support pastoral or directly evangelistic work? In 1928 the issue of expanding the school was sent for consideration to the local presbyteries, which approved the project by a narrow majority. When the issue of authorizing the expenditure went to the General Assembly in 1929, it passed after a warm debate, to the great relief of the mission staff.[9] The amount borrowed by the school was paid back over the years.[10]

In Peru Mackay investigated and addressed an ominous issue of church-state relations that directly affected the work of the Colegio. On June 29, 1929, President Leguía had issued a decree that threatened Protestant missionary education, for it required all private educational institutions to teach Roman Catholic doctrine or be closed. Members of the Adventist Mission told Mackay of a visit from a papal delegate to the Lake Titicaca region, where their work had "been making ... phenomenal progress, and ... as soon as he returned to Rome they began to have trouble." Mackay viewed this as "evidence of the new and overweening policy of the Papal Court." Two members of the Peruvian Cabinet, the minister of public instruction and the minister of foreign affairs, who were sympathetic with the clerical party, advocated the new policy. Mackay believed Leguía had opposed it "as long as he could."[11] American Ambassador Alexander Pollock Moore succeeded in obtaining a sixty-day delay in the enforcement of the decree before he returned to the United States. In Washington, DC, Methodist representatives met with Secretary of State Henry L. Stimson and Assistant Secretary White about the matter.[12] Because of the effect on the Colegio Anglo-Peruano, the matter was also taken up from London under the government of Ramsay MacDonald and by the British minister in Lima, Charles Bentinck, who was "a declared Christian man and a sincere friend of the School."[13] In addition, Inman cabled Mackay on September 12 on behalf of the Committee on Cooperation: "Please investigate for committee school legislation consulting missionaries recommend action."[14]

A month later Mackay wrote Speer about the situation. After referring to the archbishop of Lima, Mackay explained the outcome of his meeting with President Leguía concerning the decree:

> I have had some wonderful experiences in Peru. My chief addresses were given in the University and a theatre. The Archbishop honored me with a special pastoral letter after he had read the report of my University address in which I made the remark that the great problem facing Latin American youth was to rescue the figure of Jesus Christ for life and for thought. You will be interested to know that I had an interview with President Leguía in which we spoke among other things about the now famous decree. I have the

impression that there is nothing to be alarmed about. The President's own interpretation is very different from the one which the decree will stand. I have also discovered that there is not the slightest desire on his part to close evangelical schools. I cannot vouch for his attitude towards the Adventist schools in the south, but he was most emphatic regarding his appreciation of the work done by the others. Moreover, everybody anticipates that when the Cabinet was reorganized on October the 12th the ministry responsible for the decree would go out of office. The man insistently mentioned as his successor is known to be a decided liberal and anti-clerical. Even if the decree is not erased from the statute book it will become a dead letter so far as evangelical schools are concerned. More than that, the most conservative opinion in Peru is agreed that the bishop has been playing a very dangerous game in recent years. There is every probability that when the "deluge" comes, as come it must one of these days, the fate of the old church in Peru may be terribly tragic, not less tragic possibly than it is yet in Mexico.[15]

Mackay maintained interest in the school through correspondence with his friend, Stanley Rycroft, and in March 1927 Mackay had recruited a teacher for the school, a lady from Argyll, Scotland, working in Buenos Aires. She arrived at the school in March 1927.[16] Through Rycroft, Mackay also learned of tensions in the school. One of Mackay's stated reasons for leaving Peru had been incompatibility of temperament and missionary outlook: frictions over issues within the Free Church mission. In 1928 his decision to leave seemed correct as controversy touched Rycroft, who was summoned back to Edinburgh for questioning on his theological beliefs.[17] Rycroft also wrote Mackay expressing his frustration with the Free Church and its educational philosophy. He found that a newly instituted educational emphasis was unsuccessful, the "transmissive form of religious education instead of the life-centered and activist type is getting nowhere."[18]

The frictions in the Lima mission extended to the Moyobamba mission as well. On December 29, 1931, Renwick left Lima to return to Scotland westward through Brazil via Trujillo, Cajamarca, and Moyobamba to Iquitos. From there he planned to travel by boat down the Amazon and to cross the Atlantic to England, arriving in March.[19] On his way home to Scotland Renwick visited Lamas mainly to arrange the transfer of the Moyobamba property. Annie Soper "refused to give her signature whilst Dr. Kenneth was in charge."[20] William Soper, her brother, thought that "we have at last impressed upon the committee something of the real significance of the situation."[21] Despite these internal difficulties, Mackay continued loyally to support and publicize the work of the school, though he found it very difficult to raise funds during the Depression.

Evangelism and Travels during Furlough

Mackay arrived in the United States from Latin America in mid-October and traveled to Chicago for the National Council of YMCA's Spiritual Emphasis Conference at the Edgewater Beach Hotel, October 19 to October 24, 1929. The subject of the Conference was "See God and Share Him with Others." One of Mackay's addresses was titled "God Is in Sight!"[22]

From October 28 to November 10, 1929, Mackay returned briefly to Mexico in order to make contacts there and to prepare for his work in that new mission after his furlough. He then sailed from Mexico to New York, arriving November 18 to begin the final leg of his journey to Europe. On November 30 Mackay landed in Gibraltar; then, by way of Spain, France, Switzerland, and Germany, he finally arrived at Inverness a few days before Christmas.[23] A part of the time spent in Madrid and Barcelona was used to visit Spanish-language publishers and to look into publishing arrangements.[24] From December 15 to December 20 he was in Switzerland.

This trip back to Britain had two personal highlights. In December Mackay made a long-dreamed-of visit to Miguel de Unamuno, who was living in exile at a little hotel in Hendaye, France, some yards away from the Spanish border. During the visit Mackay saw a plaster cast of a bust of Don Miguel. Unamuno had made a cross over his heart in the plaster with his finger. The cross represented an internalized form of Christianity, and Mackay saw this cross as an invitation to Spain and Latin America to study anew this meaning of Jesus and the crucifixion.[25] Later in December Mackay visited Haya de la Torre in the Berlin suburb of Charlottenburg. Mackay found that Haya was continuing the regime of exercise that he had begun in Peru and that "he had greatly matured [and] his spiritual outlook was both calmer and clearer." Haya showed Mackay his well-marked Bible. He then told Mackay about a banquet in Mexico where he and the Soviet minister were both guests. In a speech following one by the minister, Haya disputed the Soviet's suggestion that their social organization would be ideal for Latin America. Haya responded "that mystic sentiment . . . is our greatest asset for the future" and "there are men who propose integrating that sentiment into the coming social revolution in Latin America."[26]

When John finally reached Scotland, the Mackay family spent Christmas and much of the month of January together at Inverness. Mackay's energy and his sense of mission, however, drew him to many speaking engagements and activities during his furlough year. Before leaving Inverness Mackay had preached twice in Aberdeen on January 12, 1930: first at noon for his old friend and mentor Grant Gibb, and then in the evening at the Free Church.[27]

Near the end of January Mackay left Scotland to begin a series of speeches, sermons, and addresses in London, Oxford, and Cambridge. From January 26 to January 28 he spoke at Cambridge at an evangelistic program that included the bishop of Salisbury.[28] One of the students, future missionary leader Lesslie Newbigin, recalled, "[Mackay's] visit to Cambridge during my undergraduate days was one of the factors that made me begin to understand the greatness of the Gospel."[29] Mackay was booked to stay in college rooms at Emmanuel College, and with the permission of the Bishop of Ely, Mackay was scheduled to preach at Holy Trinity Church Sunday evening.[30] Mackay was the speaker at a missionary breakfast at Oxford on February 5,[31] and at Mansfield College, Oxford, where he met author Basil Matthews.

These student evangelistic messages were interrupted by a two-week trip to Geneva in mid-February for planning meetings of the World Alliance of Young Men's Christian Associations. One was a meeting of the Executive of the World Committee from February 17 to February 20. There the group worked to prepare for the Cleveland meeting, the Twentieth World Conference of YMCA's, to be held in August 1931. On February 16 Mackay preached in Geneva at the American Church for the Federation Day of Prayer.[32] Prior to the meeting of the Executive Committee, he was also scheduled to attend the final ten days of the preliminary conference on meeting materials that extended from February 1 to February 16.[33] In Geneva, Visser 't Hooft, W. W. Gethman, Mackay, and other leaders discussed the federation's message, and from those discussions Mackay and Gethman were charged with the responsibility for putting together written material.

After returning to Scotland Mackay posted to Gethman a draft he prepared of the first two sections of a document on "Mission and Message."[34] Gethman circulated the draft and received comments from other committee members. Visser 't Hooft thought the message part was "extraordinarily good" but that the movement portion might be revised to reflect class differences prevalent in some nations where the association was active. He also believed that not all associations were as institutionally oriented as the draft suggested. Visser 't Hooft recognized that as far as message strategy was concerned, they were "now between the Scylla of narrow confessionalism and the Charybdis of a watered down interconfessionalism."[35]

Mott was enthusiastic about Mackay's draft and thought the paper "will do untold good. We have never had, so far as I recall, a paper of such stimulating power in connection with any previous conference of the Association. It deserves to rank with the best papers sent out before Jerusalem."[36] The final document, "Reflections on the Christian Message in the Present World Drama," was published in two formats.[37]

In late February Mackay returned to England where his meetings and speeches continued. Through Canon Tissington Tatlow, he met Cosmo Lang, the Archbishop of Canterbury, on February 25.[38] At the end of February, at the request of veteran Free Church missionary Donald Fraser, Mackay addressed a group of about seventy or eighty missionaries that were home on furlough at the Bridge of Allen Retreat.[39] Sir John Reith, the director general of the BBC, wanted Scottish speakers, and Mackay was tapped to make a missionary talk for BBC radio, broadcast from Edinburgh on March 16, 1930. His experiences with Latin American Catholicism were still vivid to him, and Mackay was asked to omit some parts of his talk that, it was supposed, might offend Catholics.[40]

If Mackay had been interested in becoming simply an academic theologian, he could have done so easily again at this time since he was flooded with proposals for speaking and writing projects. For lack of time he was forced to turn down opportunities, and he believed God was calling him elsewhere. The prior fall he had already declined a renewed offer of a full professorship at Princeton Seminary and deferred a request to give lectures at Princeton.[41] Helen Hill Miller, journalist and wife of Francis P. Miller of the World Student Christian Federation, suggested Mackay make a translation of Unamuno's essays. She thought, "It was a good time to get it out due to renewed activities in Spain."[42] Mackay replied, diplomatically requesting that she should tell Dr. Madariaga of his interest, and he thought the essays "My Religion," "The Christ of Velasquez," and "The Recumbent Christ of Palencia" particularly suited, but Mackay's schedule was then so strenuous he wrote her that "he would have to get back to work in order to rest."[43] About this time Mackay also declined a request to write a book on the Holy Spirit.[44] At the end of 1930 Mackay declined "an invitation from the Presbyterian Board of Foreign Missions, U.S.A. to accept the Joseph Cook Lectureship to the Orient for 1931–32. Acceptance would involve a course of lectures on the Fundamentals of Christianity in the leading cities of Japan, China and India."[45] In 1931 A. L. Warnshuis of the International Missionary Council proposed an evangelistic trip to the Philippines, but Mackay replied he would not be able to consider it before 1935.[46]

Studies at Bonn

Knowing that Karl Barth planned to join the theological faculty at Bonn, Germany, in mid-May 1930, Mackay moved his family to a furnished apartment in Bonn, where they lived from the beginning of April until the end of

July. While living there Mackay became proficient in German and studied firsthand the new theological movement that had recently arisen on the European continent. He became confident enough of his German to accept an invitation to speak at the local YMCA about the work of the association in South America. The address was published later in the official publication of the German associations.[47]

For several years immediately before coming to Bonn, Karl Barth had been a professor *ordinarius* at Münster, where he had published his first attempt at dogmatic theology and a volume of essays.[48] He was forty-four years old when he came to Bonn and remained there during the rise of Adolf Hitler and the imposition of tyranny. In Bonn he began to publish the work for which he is best known, *Kirchliche Dogmatik* (*Church Dogmatics*). In 1935 Barth was forced to leave Germany and took the chair of theology at Basle, Switzerland.[49]

Mackay wrote Speer that two things brought him to Germany. First, he had for some time felt the need to know German for the future of his work, and second, he had "been deeply interested in the Barthian movement and . . . wanted to spend some time close to its fountainhead."[50] Not fully grasping the significance or the details of the movement, when Professor Hocking learned that Mackay had gone to Bonn to study, he said, "Look out lest they spoil him."[51]

In spring 1930 Mackay attended Barth's lectures and started a friendship with him. A few weeks after the course had commenced, Mackay began to go to Barth's house each day to teach Barth English and discuss theology.[52] Barth lectured to overflowing classrooms each morning at 7:00 a.m., four days per week on ethics and one day on the Epistle of James. He also conducted a seminar on the basis of Anselm's *Cur Deus Homo*. Mackay particularly enjoyed the Wednesday evening open meetings at Barth's house that eighty to a hundred students would attend. The German students, who migrated from one university to another, discussed all the important theological ideas of the country, and Barth elaborated on his own ideas.

Mackay found the religious thought in Germany fascinating. A new realism was replacing traditional idealism. Everywhere there was a strong reaction against subjectivity and a search for an objective foundation for life and thought. Schleiermacher was being eclipsed, and Harnack, Otto, and Keyserling had little influence. The thought of Kierkegaard, Dostoyevsky, Luther, and St. Paul lay behind the new movement, and the young Barthians exerted the strongest and most significant influence. Bultmann and Brunner were the most radical with their biblical criticism. A new situation was emerging in European thought.

After Mackay left Europe, he wrote a long letter in Spanish to his friend Navarro Monzó describing his reactions to the movement and giving his impressions of it; he was energized by some of the ideas but declined to call himself a Barthian:

> The revival of the thought of Kierkegaard in German intellectual life is as strong and significant today as was that of Spinoza at the beginning of the romantic age which produced Hegel and Schleiermacher. The realism of Dostoyevsky, with his intense feeling for the paradoxical and the reality of sin, has been combined with the influence of Kierkegaard to stamp a dialectical character upon all human thought, that driven crazy [*el mismo desquiciado*] attempts to build around the ultimate reality. The religious experience of Luther with the rediscovery of the very core of the sense of grace and faith, as well as the writings of the German reformer have left a profound mark on the new school. Undoubtedly the decisive influence has been that of the Apostle Paul. Drifting in a sea of relativity produced by the dissolution of all old values, and at the same time steeped in Kierkegaard and Dostoyevsky, Karl Barth began to study the Epistle of Paul to the Romans. The result was a prophetic and glowing commentary such as there has not been in the history of Biblical criticism. In this new "Sartor Resartus" of theology the reader hears the sounds of the great prophetic phrases of our time. "By religious work no soul will be justified before God." That which Paul called Law, Barth calls Religion. That is to say that religion is a natural phenomenon that follows its proper course over a long evolution. But he flatly denies that this psychological phenomenon sheds a reliable light on the reality of God. He maintains on the other hand that there is something missing "in the beyond of religion." According to Barth this beyond we have in the direct and special revelation of God in Christ: the Word and above all on the Cross. This revelation cannot be reached or rationalized by any philosophy of religion. It constitutes "primary data" which shines in the sky of man, a fact overflowing with paradoxes and unattainable by all principles called rational, a genuine folly to the unilluminated reason, but to the anguished heart that believes, the result is the might and power of God.
>
> Another wide-spread tendency that one encounters involves the de-Hellenization of Christianity. This appears in the sharpest antithesis, "Plato or Christ." It maintains that the Hellenic influence has enervated the pristine strength of the Christian religion. In new studies that are made regarding the New Testament the influence of Greek thought is increasingly discounted. Within this tendency one finds Albert Schweitzer whose basic ideas are fundamentally opposed to those of Barthians. In his latest book, *The Mysticism of Paul, The Apostle*, Schweitzer maintains that the mystic ideas of Paul are clearly within the Hebraic tradition. On the other hand a

growing number of critics accept the well-known thesis of Schweitzer with regard to the basic eschatological thought of Jesus. The ideas of crisis and decision within the synoptic tradition begin to play an important role. With regard to the criticism of the Fourth Gospel, it is refuted with fundamental, critical reasons that it may not be in the purest Hebraic lineage. Even the Greek concept of the Logos, which appears in the Prologue and later disappears, they say has a more Hebraic content than Greek.

This and many other signs make one think that Berdyaev had much reason to affirm in his book, *Un Nouveau Moyen Age* (The End of Our Time), that in the contemporary European spirit the Renaissance is coming to an end. In the new age that is unfolding Judea and not Attica will have the last word.

Now, what is my position with regard to the new situation? That is what you and my other friends will wish to know. I can say that I have returned from Europe without raising the banner of any school or any special personage. However, it would be insincere of me not to say that I feel deep sympathy for certain ideas of the new German theological school. I believe that Karl Barth and his friends are rehabilitating in contemporary thought the concept of God held by the great Hebrew prophets as well as that of Jesus Christ. In the last times the immanence of God has been emphasized at the expense of his transcendence, that is to say from what makes him God. Divinity has been converted into a regulating idea or spiritual principle or cosmic energy or the soul of the universe at the expense of his transcendence. The personality of God as well as his power, his freedom and especially his infinite love, which moved the hearts of Isaiah, Jeremiah, Jesus, and Paul has been emptied of any real sense. There has been an endeavor to sponsor God explaining him to himself in order to point out the sphere and frontier of his action. God is God, at the same time the Creator, Father, and Saviour of mankind. It is necessary for us to come out of the vague sterile religiosity that today substitutes for the robust faith of the first Christians to a new vision of the God of the prophets and of Jesus. As well as calling him, "Father," I also call him, "Lord of the heavens and the earth."

I am also drawn to the way the Barthians transcend modernism and orthodoxy creating a new problem. They say that the real problem of the Scriptures begins where the historical and psychological problems end. What are the words and deeds of God that this human book orders? The only thing that is important is what God has said and is saying. The Bible does not contain theology; it contains the Word, the Logos. The task of theology is to gather, to interpret and systematize the objective facts of the Logos. Theology is thus a human task. Barth says, "I don't have my theology in my pocket." He in his interpretive and systematic effort compares himself to a man who attempts to climb a tower at night looking carefully for the rope-banister in order to guide himself, when suddenly by mistake, he grabbed the bell rope. The bell rang and what a surprise! Everybody began to listen. From my point of view one can escape a sterile and weak relativism on the one hand and on the other the absolutism of an authoritarian hierarchy built on a particular revelation of God whose absolute form we have in Jesus Christ. If God has spoken, he also speaks. In this way particular situations in life are not resolved by simple general rules even if they are taken from the Bible but by a specific word that is relevant since God is not only our ancestor but also our contemporary. Thus, there is a plan from him for all the different moments of life and history. The Lord and Father of Jesus Christ has not abdicated.

There are also certain other tendencies of the dialectic school that arouse my sympathy. They are, for example, the new emphasis that is placed on faith as the means of initiation and progress in spiritual life, the realistic analysis of sin and its implications in human life, and the recognition that the Christian, in his time, must live at the highest level for his time placing on all his actions the stamp of eternity and not to be under the illusion that what he and his contemporaries call progress is not necessarily identified with the kingdom of God. It would be too much now to analyze each tendency in order to explain their diverse ramifications, some very new and novel. In conclusion I will only say that in what is referred to as Barthianism I find some of Barth's thinking very uncongenial. One of them is the lack of importance he seems to attribute to the figure of the historical Jesus. His interest in Christ in accordance with the Spirit is his curious concept of history that causes cutting down confidence in specific deeds in the life of Jesus. The other aspect which I find equally disturbing is Barth's categorical negation that spiritual life can be considered as something in itself or as a possession of the Christian. He, therefore, seems to underrate mysticism and all types of saints, quietist or pietist. Fortunately, as much as the reaction on religious thought is remarkable, I cannot call myself a Barthian. Moreover, I see that I must undertake my own solitary path in the sphere of thought but propelled as never before by a thirst for God. From the living God I will walk confident that he who has placed on my path the luminous North of the Word made flesh, making me a participant in the new life in Christ, will illumine each step of the road and will give me the strength I lack to complete, in his name, my destiny.[53]

During the spring and summer Mackay interrupted his studies at Bonn by traveling to give addresses at other locations. From May 6 to May 10 he participated in the Waldenburg Conference arranged by Prince Günther von Schönburg-Waldenburg at his castle in Waldenburg, Saxony, with Roman Catholics on ecumenism.[54]

From June 17 to June 24 Mackay presented a series of addresses at St. Cergue, Switzerland, on the occasion of the biennial meeting of the World's Committee

Conference of the YWCA. The removal of the World's Committee office from London to Geneva in the spring 1930 gave a special character to the meeting at St. Cergue.[55] Mackay presented thoughtful addresses titled "The Message of Christ" and "Bible Studies," which are included in the volume called *Presenting the Christian Message*: "If Christian organizations do not become vocal on vital matters of faith, they will cease to be, or they will become beached on the banks of the river of life."[56] Mrs. Montague Waldegrave, president of YWCA of Great Britain and president of the World Committee, appreciated his talks. Mackay arranged later in the summer to speak at Swanick on July 12 on "The Man Christ Jesus," and on July 13 on "God in Christ."[57]

Mackay also met other members of the new theological movement: Emil Brunner in Zurich and Eduard Thurneysen in Basle.[58] He concluded that the movement's

> emphasis on the transcendence of God, the reality of sin and the character and significance of faith in Christianity restores a true perspective to Christian thinking. On the other hand there are certain aspects of Barth's thought especially in regard to the Jesus of History, which I am not prepared to follow. I intend, however, with my new knowledge of German to make a thorough study of the movement and its implications.[59]

Speer shared Mackay's perspective on the movement: "It is good to see this swing back from the extreme subjectivism and empiricism of present day theology to the New Testament."[60] A few months later Speer told Mackay by letter that he had quoted Mackay in "a Barthian sermon he preached on May 11 at the Fifth Avenue Church." Continuing to seek Mackay's services on the Presbyterian Board of Missions, he added that he hoped that "within the next three or four or five years you will be led to make this your base of action."[61]

The Christian Message

Thus, during the early 1930s new factors challenged Mackay's philosophy of mission and his thinking about the Church. His time and energy were spent both in theorizing about the Christian message and in delivering that message in as many venues as he was able. Through studies and contacts in Bonn he was being gripped by a new understanding of the meaning and role of the Church.[62] The early 1930s, following the Jerusalem Conference, proved to be a new stimulus for Mackay's thinking. The effects of the Jerusalem Conference reverberated through mission leadership for the next few years. Mackay wrote to Speer about the need to reformulate the presentation of fundamental doctrine:

I was delighted to have your news regarding the last Assembly. The unanimity that was manifested in seconding the proposals for union with other Christian bodies was most inspiring. I come to feel increasingly that a united Evangelical Church is the indispensable condition for a revival of Christian doctrine and a fresh baptism of the Holy Spirit. How glorious it would be if in the coming years we could reach a fresh formulation of fundamental doctrine which should not be the expression of our differences, but the affirmation of our unity. Three things are clear, however, it seems to me, in the present situation: the irrepressible longing for oneness with Christ, the consciousness of the supreme importance for spiritual life and progress of a doctrinal background, and a feeling that the greatest need of our time is to re-discover the Holy Spirit.[63]

In addition to the February meeting in Geneva, a second important gathering on the subject of the Christian message was held during the summer of 1930. Francis Miller and Visser 't Hooft assembled a group of theologians to develop and think about the Federation. One participant, Joseph Oldham, was convinced that the Church did not seem to be able to speak to the modern world with real power. But at the gathering the group could not reduce the issues to a common denominator because of the diverse cultural, theological, and spiritual backgrounds and points of view. They could only listen carefully to the others and remember their close relations through Jesus Christ. This event may have been significant as in later decades members of the group began to reconceptualize the meaning of the term *church*, recovering the idea of close Christian fellowship in the context of a worldwide body.

In his *Memoirs* Visser 't Hooft noted that this gathering at the beginning of August in 1930 at Zuylen near Utrecht, Holland, was the "nursery" of the ecumenical movement.[64] After the war, twelve from the gathering were on committees or staff of the World Council of Churches. They were F. P. Miller, Ambrose Reeves, Pierre Maury, Suzanne de Dietrich, Reinhold Niebuhr, J. H. Oldham, William Paton, H. P. Van Dusen, H. L. Henriod, John A. Mackay, W. Tindal, and W. A. Visser 't Hooft.[65]

Mackay attempted to address a paradoxical problem in his essay "Reflections on the Christian Message in the Present World Drama": "Christian Missions to non-Christian lands have reached their zenith, many of the people of those lands turn a deaf ear to the Christian Message, because of what they know about conditions in the lands from which the Missions have come."[66] Taking Jesus as "our fixed star," Mackay found that it was

of paramount importance to observe and emphasize that for Jesus, the most original thing about God was that His love was of a creative and redemptive quality. . . . For if to be perfect as the Father in Heaven is perfect means, above all else, to share God's creative love-passion, then we cannot rest satisfied with simply being helpful to men and in contributing to the harmonious development of their personality. It is one thing to do good to others; it is quite another thing to turn others into doers of good. Something much higher than ethical decency must be our goal. Our work for others can only be finally successful if we succeed in reproducing in their lives the creative love-passion of God.[67]

It is our conviction that the present world situation offers a greater challenge than any other that has ever existed to be truly and utterly Christian. While fully recognizing that no permanent spiritual advance can be achieved by the reorganization of human society in accordance with the mind of Christ, while man, himself, remains unchanged—and that only God can change man—we consider it to be the sacred duty of every Christian, to apply the principles of Jesus Christ in the sphere of business, of literature, of politics and of the Church. The sternness of the present hour, in which Christianity is considered by many to be a spent force, requires that Christians should scan afresh their temple courts and look into these apocalyptic eyes which blaze as a "flame of fire."[68]

Relocation to Mexico, 1930

When the furlough ended, the Mackay family sailed back to North America to a new mission field. In the bracing sea air aboard the SS *Caledonia*, Mackay felt the thrill of a new beginning and a new understanding of a favorite passage in Ephesians, the passage from death to life and a new oneness in Christ [Eph. 2:1–8]. He wrote Speer:

Here we are off the coast of Nova Scotia on this ship from the mother land. We left the Clyde a week ago and are due in New York on Monday morning. Mrs. Mackay and the children are with me, all longing to get settled down in our new home in the mountains of Mexico. Not long ago our little Ruth, aged six, tired with constant changes of abode and uncertain to where she belonged, said, "Papa, are we going into Mexico forever?"—And Papa replied, "Yes, my dear, *forever*" [emphasis in original].

I feel this time as I have never felt before on returning to the field, something has happened in me. I have returned through labyrinthine ways to a fresh and satisfying view of Ephesians 2, the place of vision which transformed my outlook as a boy. I am conscious of intense coming struggle, and every fibre of my being thrills with joy and awe at the prospect. Life has been with me a constant beginning, but I feel this beginning is going to be different from the others that have been. I am going into my new parish in the heart of the Americas absorbed in the thought of the Living God who works creatively now as ever through Jesus Christ His Son.

It was a great pleasure to receive your two letters. I have been particularly delighted to know that Dr. McAfee has accepted a Secretaryship in the Board. He will be a most wonderful asset with his rich mind and wide experience of conditions at home and abroad.

I greatly appreciate your reference to the door that is still open for me in the Board fellowship. God also sets before me at the moment an open door. Perhaps this door and the other may coincide some day—perhaps not. I cannot tell beforehand what may happen. God Himself will decide the matter for me in the events of the next few years. I am resolved to live in the eternal present, in the tense for-everness of living opportunity.[69]

Mackay's first intention had been to remain in the United States until the end of 1930, but the family was eager to return to Hispanic America and put down roots in Mexico. He realized during "the fifteen months that" he "had lived without an established residence . . . how much" he needed "a plot of ground and a home that" was his, "in order to be able to work in a constant and fruitful way."[70] One of the factors drawing Mackay to Mexico was missionary Walter Taylor's requests and his descriptions of the need for evangelism there.

Social change in Mexico at that time was taking a more violent turn than in other Latin American countries, and the Soviets attempted to bring their form of revolution to that country. The Roman Catholic Church was closely associated in the public mind with authoritarian forces and itself became a target of the revolutionaries. The Mexican Constitution of 1917 was anticlerical, but certain provisions were not enforced during its initial years. Persecution of the Roman Church became strongest from 1924 to 1929. Then U.S. Ambassador to Mexico Dwight Morrow facilitated an understanding that allowed the churches to reopen. But persecution broke out again between 1932 and 1935.[71]

From 1910 to 1936 Mexico was in various levels of turmoil, and because of geography and difficulties of communication, the revolution varied in intensity in different regions of the country. Mackay's evangelistic work took place again in an environment of sharp, violent opposition of church and state. By the mid-1930s even an experienced observer like Kenneth Grubb predicted that the country could become a federation of totalitarian states within an authoritarian federal government.

Mackay served in Mexico during the era that *Jefe Máximo* (Supreme Chief) Plutarco Elías Calles held authority. Calles had served in the cabinet of his predecessor, Álvaro Salido Obregón, before ascending to the presidency of

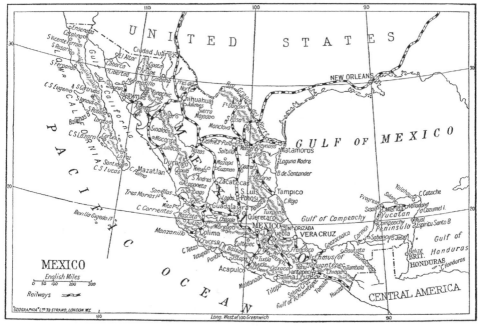

Mexico, 1913

Mexico in 1924. Determined to push the revolution forward, Calles enforced the religious provisions of the Constitution of 1917 against the Catholic and Protestant churches. In 1928 during Mackay's first trip to Mexico, Obregón was reelected to the presidency, but he was assassinated on July 17, 1928, before his inauguration. After the assassination Calles again became Mexico's leader, filling the power vacuum for the next six years. During that time three men held the title of president: Portes Gil, Ortiz Rubio, and Abelardo Rodriguez.

During the period of Mackay's principal evangelistic activity in Mexico between 1928 and 1934, the Mexican Constitution of 1917 applied as the fundamental law. Since the document included detailed and particular provisions, it was more of a political plan than a constitution in the sense in which a North American would understand the term. Article 3 of the Constitution dealt with the relation between religion and the state. A law promulgated in 1926 intensified the antireligious forces, and many priests and religious were imprisoned and put to death. On the last day of July 1926 the Roman clergy suspended every public act of worship that could not take place without a priest.[72] The church property was required to be turned over from ecclesiastical to civil owners. The Bishops of Mexico City protested the outrageous arrest of the Bishops of Huejutla.

The Mexican mission field differed from the other fields in South America where Mackay had worked, but he had gained some acquaintance with it during his first visit in 1928. It had predominantly been occupied by missionaries from the United States and therefore lacked the influence and perspective of missionaries of other nationalities. Cooperation between denominations did not occur in Mexico with the same intensity that it did in South America. The various denominations from the United States reproduced themselves in Mexico without the level of united effort that occurred in Peru, for example. In South America this united front was a decisive factor for the evangelical movement because the Latin mind, accustomed to the unity of the Roman Catholic Church, saw the evangelical movement as a unified one. Because of the geographical proximity some in Mexico saw the missionary movement as the advance guard of North American commercial interests. For these reasons, as a Scot, Mackay's voice had a very favorable opportunity to be heard.

To arrive at their new home in Mexico City, the Mackays traveled for a full day from the port of Veracruz on one of the world's most beautiful scenic railways. Mexico City lay

> seven thousand feet above sea level in an immense valley, which in Aztec times was largely covered with water. Great mountains, some of them pine clad to the summit, surround the city on all sides. Among those mountains stand out side by side the two majestic volcanic peaks of Popocatepetl and Ixtacihuatl, which look down from their snowy heights upon the Mexican capital, almost every afternoon toward sunset.[73]

In a letter to Visser 't Hooft from his new home in Mexico City, Mackay reflected on the personal meaning of his recent travels and his new understanding of faith:

> I am writing this from the mountains of Mexico. At long last, after a year and a half's uprootedness, have I taken earth once more and am able to be myself again. I was never so conscious as during these last eighteen months of homelessness and wandering, that in order to think creatively, I need the solitude of my study walls. And now that I have found a new sanctum, whose walls are beginning to be lined with long lost friends, I feel I don't want ever to leave it save to range through my wide parish. I am convinced that my chief contribution to my own parish and beyond it will be by allowing all the fibers of my being find their nutriment in the everlasting Here and Now

of my concrete situation. The moment I have begun to wander beyond the confines of my parish I lose my sense of eternity, not as quantitative but as qualitative, without which I cannot think or work to purpose.

And yet I know that the multitude of new impressions which I have received in the course of the last months have created a ferment within me which is fast affecting an inner revolution in my ways of thought, especially in my method of approach to the problem of theology. I am reaching intellectually the point to which religious tradition and personal experience led me many years ago. But henceforth my starting point will be neither tradition nor experience but faith, faith in the new light in which I now see it. Something has happened in me. I am beginning life again. But I must have long solitude with my God and my work before I can ever be a helpful companion or guide to others in their work. . . .

John Mackay on the road walking with a friend in Vera Cruz, Mexico.

I have just received the *International Review of Missions* and have read Brunner's article twice through. It raises the whole discussion of Secularism to a new level, the true level, I believe.[74]

The light shed by Brunner's article on secularism as a problem for the church provided illumination to Mackay's path as he continued to reflect on the Christian message in the early 1930s, and it prepared him for his evangelistic calling to North America later in the decade. Brunner's article pointed to the complex forces in the last three hundred years that had led to Western man's autonomy, neither bound to society nor bound to higher powers such as religious belief. Mackay brought the ideas of Brunner to another level and applied them specifically through "indirect preaching," showing modern humans the destructive nature of their thoughts and bringing them to a level where they could hear the message of Christianity and come to a "living insight."[75]

Mackay described the unique historical and social opportunity that he found in Mexico in October 1930 using the metaphor of the volcano. He used the image of an Uruguayan writer, "a rosary of craters in eruption," to describe the political conditions throughout the Latin American continent. Mexico, however, was at rest at that moment, having passed through twenty years of struggle. Mackay went on:

> Mexico has had that which no Latin American country has yet experienced, a social revolution. This is the chief impression which one receives who knows the life of other Latin lands in America. The reality and beneficent results of a great social upheaval force themselves everywhere upon the observer. Twenty years ago Mexico as a land of law and order, ruled by the rod of iron of a famous dictator, Porfirio Diaz. At that time the whole country was in the hands of a small number of great land owners. The Indians, who constitute more than two thirds of the population were serfs uneducated and devoid of rights. Nothing whatever was done for popular education. Little by little the country was passing into the hands of foreigners. Today the land belongs to the people. The great estates have been divided up. The Indians have become Mexicans and are no longer simply Indians. They enjoy the full right of Mexican citizenship. The system of rural education, by means of which the aboriginal race is being incorporated into civilization, has won unstinted admiration from leading educators of other lands as the most remarkable rural education effort in existence. Special normal schools for rural teachers have been established all over the country, while groups of "missionary teachers," young men and women with a great human passion, travel throughout the land conducting educational institutes for local teachers. University students are made to feel before graduation that they are morally bound to devote their professional knowledge to their community's welfare. And most interesting of all in this connection, the great surge of social passion which was born of the Revolution and eddies through the country today, is regarded by many leading members of the party in power as a direct and inseparable expression of the true spirit of Christ. As this may sound strange to those who have regarded Mexico as the Russia of the American continent because of its religious iconoclasm, I am going to give my impressions of the present religious situation in the country.[76]

Mackay then explained how a large number of Mexicans who curbed the power of the Roman Catholic Church as a political system were not irreligious but were themselves Catholic: "Now that the Roman Catholic hierarchy, after several years of an ecclesiastical strike, has accepted the simple principle laid down by the government that all ministers of religion must register before exercising their profession, there is perfect religious peace in the country."[77] The advances of Protestantism as a spiritual power in the country, wrote Mackay, were evident in the consecration of Bishop Pascoe, a Mexican citizen, and by the examples of

> two brothers, Moisés and Aaron Saénz, sons of a Presbyterian father who still lives. Moisés is Mexico's leading educationalist, while Aaron, who is still under forty, has held in turn the portfolios of Foreign Affairs, Education and Commerce and Labor. He has also been a candidate for the presidency, having retired his candidacy in favor of the actual president of the country, Pascual Ortiz Rubio.[78]

Mackay's Ministry in Mexico

Mackay had formed a plan for his work in his new parish and had the "good fortune" to arrive in Mexico City towards the end of the academic year, allowing the family to get settled before his full program began in February. In a letter to his friend William Ewen, he wrote,

> When February comes I propose lecturing on the Fourth Gospel on Sunday mornings for people who attend no church. I intend besides giving one lecture a week on what I call "New Voices in the Wilderness." This course will deal with Kierkegaard, Dostoevsky, Unamuno, Albert Schweitzer and Karl Barth. I feel that by dealing with the personality and thought of these men I shall be coming to grips with some of the most vital questions in Christianity and civilization. I propose in addition to lead a seminar on the Sermon on the Mount and modern life.[79]

Soon after his arrival in Mexico, Mackay addressed the town of Puebla in what he called "one of the most interesting and stimulating experiences" of his life.[80] An evangelical pastor wrote that the mayor of that old historic town wished Mackay to come to Puebla for a one-week course of lectures that were to be of a "strongly ethical character." The lectures would be held in the Chamber of Deputies and were to be sponsored by the state governor and local municipality.

Mackay had not intended to go to Puebla until February, three months later, but because of the unique opportunity, which he considered providential, Mackay arranged the lectures for November. The series of five lectures led to an evangelistic climax in the fifth address. First, Mackay spoke on the Spanish philosopher Unamuno, laying bare his soul and going to the heart of his religious position. Second, Mackay explored the concept of true manhood, rejecting Don Juanism as subhuman and pointing to an ideal of manhood that involved sacrifice. The third night was dedicated to youth, and Mackay discussed the youth movement in Latin America and the places youth respectively succeeded and failed. The fourth lecture addressed the prevalence of pessimism and despair and the joyously exultant song of the communists nearby. The task, Mackay said, was to create a spiritual type "superior to the Russian communist, but as dynamic and incandescent as he."[81] How could that be done?

Mackay answered the question in his final lecture, "Reverence for Life," where he brought his "audience face to face with Jesus Christ, the author of the only saving ethical principle which humanity has ever known . . . reverence for the Divine Life, for the life of nature, for life in oneself and one's neighbour."[82] Mackay closed by applying the principle to the present position and problems of the Mexican nation:

> When I concluded on the last evening, the audience of six hundred seemed glued to their seats. I had spoken for an hour and a quarter and they seemed to want more. The unusual attitude of the audience, which was representative of all classes in the community, from elegantly dressed ladies and gentlemen to workers in their overalls, deeply impressed the Mayor and the platform party.
>
> The following morning I was officially received by the town council as a guest of honour and was handed an inscribed parchment in remembrance of my visit to Puebla.[83]

This lecture trip proved the existence of a great longing in the hearts of all classes in Mexico for a message about the deepest things of life. It also proved that because of the religious situation a person affiliated with the YMCA would have opportunities unavailable to those under the auspices of a Protestant or Catholic Church. Mackay and the other officials of the National YMCA were convinced of the unique opportunity that was opening to them in this field. In January Mackay became acquainted with new friends when he called on Mr. and Mrs. Walter Lowrie at their hotel. Lowrie had brought a letter from Speer, and he impressed Mackay as "an exceedingly interesting and able man." Mackay wrote that he looked forward to future contacts with him.[84]

Mackay brought spiritual strength and cohesion to the YMCA staff in Mexico through a retreat just as he had done in Brazil. In mid-January, 1931, a four-day secretarial retreat was scheduled at a camping ground known as Oaxtepec Wood, *El Bosque de Oaxtepec*, in the state of Morelos where the revolution's struggle was most intense. The campground was located near the foot of the mountain peak Popocatepetl, and they came the final distance with donkeys they had picked up on the grounds of an old Dominican monastery that had been turned into a normal school by the revolution. The donkeys transported the camping gear to the appointed place, where the group erected seven tents. The location was near an *aguahuete* tree that sends all its roots toward water, a useful metaphor. The campfire was kindled next to a large stone that in Aztec times had been used for sacrifices and had many significant marks on its surface.

The motto for the four-day program was "Inspiration, Friendship, and Study." At the retreat the participants tried to discover the will of God for the Association. They talked of the secretary's mission in life, examined the obstacles that were blocking progress, considered the function of volunteers, and looked at conditions for true progress. A prophetic voice that had begun the retreat now said,

> Before we think of expansion we must be sure of the depth and reality of our own spiritual lives. Expansion can only come in the form of an irresistible overflow of spiritual solicitude and power. Our preoccupation must be the creation in ourselves and in our fellow members of such a concern for youth, such a desire to give to youth what we ourselves have found in Christ, that the Mexico City Association will burst its borders in an overflow of enthusiasm. Only thus and not by the cautious engineering of any Committee will progress be possible.[85]

Mackay thought the Aztec stone altar had never witnessed such sacrifices as flowed from the group on the final evening when the participants bared their hearts. A worker for twenty-eight years now felt they had achieved a Christian Association. Friendship was sealed at the campfire after a hymn. The group returned with a new outlook on life.

During all of March and part of April Mackay presented his program as planned for the YMCA in Mexico City, speaking on Kierkegaard, Dostoyevsky, and Nietzsche. In April 1931 Mackay spent a week lecturing every evening in Chihuahua. The state governor and civic and military leaders attended most of the lectures. On May 1, at 11:25 p.m., Mackay addressed a mass labor meeting of over two thousand working men and women in the largest theater in the town. He discerned an intense stillness come over the audience as he spoke on "Reflections of an Intellectual Worker," and at the close he brought the audience face to face with eternal things. In Monterrey his program was somewhat similar but more intense; three of his public addresses were broadcast by the leading local radio station.[86]

By May of 1931 the financial situation of the YMCA was desperate. When the call came to interrupt his evangelistic work, Mackay willingly did his part to help raise funds for the movement. He was called on to speak at a series of venues in the United States. On May 11 Mackay began his deputation work under the income production department.[87] E. J. Simonds drove Mackay by car from Monterrey to San Antonio, arriving May 11, 1931, at noon.[88] After crossing the border, with the goal of raising money for the work, Mackay addressed one or more meetings in San Antonio and Fort Worth, Texas; Tulsa, Oklahoma; Cedar Rapids, Iowa; Chicago, Evanston, Oak Park, and Wheaton, Illinois; Neenah, Wisconsin; and Flint, Michigan.

Sometimes he spoke in churches, as on the 17th when he addressed gatherings in the Fourth and First Presbyterian Churches in Chicago. On the 24th he spoke in the First Presbyterian Church of Flint. Other meetings were held in the homes of community leaders. On May 25 Mackay spoke at a significant "dress occasion, and the group was made up mostly of young millionaires and their wives." He found the attendees, aged thirty to forty, hungry for a religious message and a cause to support, and recommended that the group be cultivated by the association. Mackay believed that this method was along the right lines and would establish a firm basis for the future. Hurried methods would not fit the present constituency and would imperil the future. During the visit Mackay found the atmosphere of the United States had changed.[89]

Also in May Mackay preached at the General Assembly of the Presbyterian Church. His address illustrated his knack at turning a phrase: "If Christianity ceases to be a way of thought, it will soon cease to be a way of life."[90] Spending a few days at Lakeville, Connecticut, in June he delivered a talk titled "The Basic Insight" for the Decennial Conference on Missionary Policies and Methods of the Presbyterian Mission Board: "As we study Jesus Christ two great insights flash from His personality. Ours must be a love such as His was, a love which redeems, crossing every frontier, convention, class and race to do its redeeming work. Our relationship to God must be what His was, a relationship of Will with the Lord of our lives."[91] He apologized to Robert E. Speer for leaving the Conference early to attend and speak at a Methodist gathering in Ohio.

At the ten-day Methodist Conference, where the topic was "The Significance of Jesus Christ in the Modern World," Mackay stepped unexpectedly into the limelight. He presented a controversial message for that time titled "A Preface to the Christian Message," in which he differentiated between Christianity as mere dogmatism with Christianity as a way of life with stress on understanding and insight.[92] His address challenged assumptions of the times that he said were treated as axioms. Mackay advocated a transcendent God, a cosmic Christ, a creative approach to reality that meant passion in the Christian movement, and new meaning to the term "abundant life," which had come to mean a rationalized human personality and realization of values.

Twentieth World's Conference of YMCA's, Cleveland, Ohio, August, 1931. (L. to R.: Henry Lightbody, Scotland; John Mackay; Toyohiko Kagawa, Japan; John R. Mott, U.S.A.; T. Z. Koo, China; Alphons Koechlin, Switzerland.) Mackay addressed the Conference.

This speech provoked a debate two days later with Dean Albert C. Knudson of Boston University School of Theology, who challenged Mackay's Barthian approach. The two probably agreed on more than they disagreed, but the debate proved stimulating to the 350 conference participants.[93]

Mackay spoke at major gatherings of the YMCA and the Student Volunteer Movement. He attended the YMCA World Alliance meetings held July 27 to August 2 and August 4–9, 1931, the first in the organization's seventy-six years to be held in North America. The two sessions were an adventure of faith in God, unity, and fellowship from the beginning to the end. Mackay joined an extraordinarily strong platform of speakers.[94] He delivered a keynote message at the Twentieth World's Conference of YMCA's in Cleveland on August 4, speaking on the theme of the Conference, "Youth's Adventure with God."[95] He inspired the crowd with his words: "Life attains its supreme meaning and achieves its most creative expression when it becomes an adventure with God, with the living God, who is ever on the march."[96] Mackay also supported the adoption of Resolution 5 on international relations and specifically on war guilt, for which he did not wish to burden the German people collectively.[97]

As the new year arrived, Mackay addressed the Eleventh Quadrennial Convention of the Student Volunteer Movement for Foreign Missions, held in Buffalo, New York, December 30, 1931, to January 3, 1932. His topic was

"God's Springtime in Latin America."[98] In January 1932 Mackay delivered lectures on the spiritual condition of Latin America at Chicago Seminary, January 11–15, and later that month at Princeton Seminary.[99]

His friend Webster Browning wrote to Mackay in October 1931, telling him that he seemed to be at the height of his power to "move others by your words and your pen." Browning also sent Mackay a copy of the English edition of Ricardo Rojas's book *The Invisible Christ*. Mackay had helped Browning with the translation. In the letter Browning also remarked on Speer's attitude toward Mackay: "He seems to have a violent fancy for you, and never loses an opportunity to refer to you as the ultimate authority in whatever the matter may be. It is good to have such a friend, yet I have sometimes wondered if it is not just a little embarrassing."[100]

The evangelistic challenge in Mexico became more intense, however, when an edict in April 1932 declared that all grade schools receiving financial aid from religious organizations must be closed.[101] Mackay's Christian evangelism for the YMCA continued unabated, however, during May and early June, when he delivered a course of five lectures on the Spanish mystics. They were held once a week at the association building and repeated the following evening in the Coyoacán Church under the auspices of the Presbyterian Seminary.[102]

Chapter 9

North America and the Mission Board (1932–1936)

"Go ye therefore, and teach all nations." (Matt. 28:19 KJV)

*T*he early 1930s were a bleak and difficult time. Nationalism was a force in some regions of the world, and new ideologies of fascism and communism were taking hold in others. For North American mission societies the times were particularly dismal; critics from both left and right assaulted them. The vitality of the mission movement had been clear at the Jerusalem Conference, which pointed a new theological direction for foreign missions, and a Barthian critique was also being incorporated into the message.[1] Some clergy and laity whose theology emphasized salvation and commitment to rigid doctrinal tenets opposed these theological changes. Moreover, the world financial depression caused the lay financial supporters of missions to examine them more closely. Efficient travel was making the world smaller, bringing greater contact between East and West. The situation offered a new challenge to Mackay, and he joined the Presbyterian Board of Foreign Missions in 1932. His focus was on the Christian Message as it was preached and lived by the Church.

In Protestant thought during the 1930s two differing points of view emerged about the relation of Christianity to other world religions. Mackay wrote about this ongoing contrast much later. On one side was a low view of Christ, or in theological terms, a low Christology, which came to be known as the "liberal" view of the Christian religion. It was exemplified by Professor William Ernest Hocking. For a liberal, wrote Mackay,

religion is defined as "a passion of righteousness and for the spread of righteousness, conceived as a cosmic demand." It is religion's supreme role to establish a civilization and to keep the civilization sound. Thus the real absolute is culture whose servant religion is to be. Rethinking Missions was convinced that events the world around were moving in the direction of the emergence of a common world culture. Religion's task was to provide that coming world culture with a soul.[2]

On the other side, dynamic, orthodox Christianity was alive and well, associated with and exemplified by missionary Hendrik Kraemer, and the meeting of the International Missionary Council that gathered at Madras in 1938. Mackay could not attend this council because of new commitments at Princeton Seminary, but he wrote about the meeting and also reviewed the seven volumes of proceedings for the *International Review of Missions*.[3] Hendrik Kraemer, a missionary in Java whom Mackay had met at the Jerusalem Conference, was asked to prepare a study on the Christian message for the Madras Conference. In response he produced the influential work *The Christian Message in a Non-Christian World*.[4] The views in this book, influenced by Barth and Kierkegaard, took a high Christology and a high view of revelation, stressing the discontinuity between Christianity and the other religions. Mackay's friend Henry P. Van Dusen witnessed and described the power and promise of the missionary movement at Madras, a meeting from which only the Koreans were absent because of Japanese persecution.[5]

Mackay Joins the Presbyterian Board of Foreign Missions

Though Mackay had turned down the Presbyterian Board of Foreign Missions' offer in 1928, Speer and the Board sought Mackay's services again after he returned to North America from his furlough in 1930. They achieved an agreement in the fall of 1931.[6] The Board elected Mackay to a secretaryship on January 18, 1932.[7] Under the rules of the Presbyterian Church, the General Assembly had to approve the election of executive officers of the various boards. Dr. McAfee advised Speer that "since he comes from the most conservative group in Scotland, the Assembly will probably have no hesitation in approving his election."[8] To accomplish the formalities smoothly, Speer believed that it would be advantageous if Mackay's application papers were lodged with the presbytery in advance of General Assembly meeting. Mackay, whose name had not been removed from the church rolls, forwarded his ordination certificate, which his brother-in-law, Alec Fraser, had obtained in Scotland, to the Presbytery of Morris and Orange. When the presbytery met on May 20, 1932, Mackay was received into membership. The approval of the General Assembly also went smoothly. Speer advised Mackay that the "General Assembly unanimously confirmed your election as Secretary of the Board."[9] His election was announced in the *Presbyterian Magazine*.[10]

Having become a member of the Presbytery of Morris and Orange, Mackay moved his family to Summit, New Jersey, a suburb within commuting distance of New York City, where the mission board had its headquarters. He continued to travel and lecture in Latin America and Mexico during those years. As a portfolio Secretary of the Mission Board, Mackay's evangelistic job specifications changed; he was no longer an "entrepreneur" but a "traveling salesman."[11]

In December 1931 Mackay described the reasons for his move to the mission board in a letter to his friend Charles Ewald from the YMCA. Mackay emphasized the decisive nature of the challenge and the need to do lasting work by equipping the churches:

> The Presbyterian Board of Foreign Missions has never ceased to keep before me their appeal of three years ago. After a prolonged and prayerful consideration I have decided to accept their proposal.
>
> I feel there is little use entering into the reasons which have led me to this new decision. I cannot expect that you would see eye to eye with me on this matter. I want to say, however, that my state of mind on this occasion is absolutely calm, whereas three years ago it was a perfect turmoil. I think I see the situation more clearly than I did then. I do not say that I did not do right in my final declination of the Presbyterian appeal at that time. Two things in particular, however, have happened since then. I feel that the kind of situation has been created in the general missionary movement which constitutes the challenge which I have consistently regarded as the one inescapable circumstance which could lead me again into an administrative position. In accepting, however, such a position, I shall continue as now to render direct service to the common cause in Latin America and elsewhere.
>
> The second thing which has happened is that I have felt a growing longing for a closer relationship to the Christian Church. Long reflection on the Latin American situation convinces me that creative and lasting work must be done through the Church, and to the equipping of the Church and church agencies for their task in Latin America and elsewhere, I have resolved to give what remains of my life. I am not interested in what final predominant religious expression Christianity may receive in Latin America, but I am interested in the strongest possible ferment being thrown into the present situation. In the years ahead wherever I get an opportunity to deliver the Christian message which I have been delivering these years, I will deliver it, but my main effort will be directed to stimulating and equipping national churches and agencies for their task. The very fact that the work of the Evangelical churches is in many respects so imperfect and that they have been the object of so many attacks decides me to stand by them.[12]

Mackay made efforts to retain his friendship with Ewald. Sensitive to his correspondent's feelings, Mackay sent a second letter to Ewald so that he would not in any way consider Mackay's resignation as an implicit criticism of the work that Ewald proposed to carry on through his "Fellowship for

Christian Cooperation."[13] This direct but nuanced sensitivity is also evident in Mackay's response to his former colleague Conard regarding comments Mackay made about the Instituto in Montevideo.[14]

Looking back on these years, Mackay saw the hand of God directing his path:

> New horizons began to open. . . . New Issues had to be confronted that challenged my philosophy of mission. I was gripped by a new sense of the Church, its meaning and its role. Responding to what I believed to be God's call to a new type of missionary service, and in obedience to the directive guidance of the "hand," I moved to the United States. . . . I began to play a part in the shaping of mission policy.[15]

Re-Thinking Missions: A Laymen's Inquiry after One Hundred Years

Mackay joined the Mission Board a few months before a controversial report was issued about the missionary enterprise. The idea for *Re-Thinking Missions: A Laymen's Inquiry* (also referred to as the *Laymen's Inquiry* or "the report"), had originated in January 1930. The stock market had crashed at the end of October 1929, and John D. Rockefeller brought a group of Baptist laypeople together to hear an address by Dr. John R. Mott. Rockefeller was concerned that his own sons would not be as interested in foreign missions as he had been. "Would it be possible so to interpret and conduct mission work as to have it appeal to the oncoming generation with the same power that it has to the one now nearing the close of its years of great vigor?" he asked.[16] Establishment of a commission was proposed to evaluate the work of the Baptist Foreign Mission Society, to determine if further financial support to missions was warranted and, if so, to suggest changes to the program in view of changed conditions abroad. Soon six other denominations joined the project. First, fact finders gathered information, including inspections of the missions in India, Burma, China, and Japan, in five volumes. The information was used as the basis for the second stage of the *Laymen's Inquiry*, the Commission of Appraisal.[17]

The report was clearly recognized as a milestone. An editorial in the *Christian Century* correctly assessed its meaning and the emerging strength of modernism within the North American churches' leadership: "The Laymen's report signalizes distinctly the obsolescence of dogmatic orthodoxy and the emergence of an effective and responsible modernism."[18] Another observer concluded, "The publication of this *Report* has moved the battleground into more advanced territory."[19] The fact that the questions about missions were asked at all showed that times had changed radically. Mackay and others realized that true missions are conducted by people with a strong faith for whom doubt is not an issue. To the extent that missionary activity had been one element of expansive outward movement of Western culture in demographic, political, economic, and religious terms, an era was coming to an end. The report, using weak methodology and naïve assumptions, came as a surprise and stirred indignation. Its contents came to represent what Europe thought of the U.S. religious establishment.

Two persons through their writings and speeches tried hard to modify basic principles of the missionary movement in a liberal direction: William Ernest Hocking and Pearl Buck. Buck, the bright but troubled daughter of a Presbyterian missionary in China, publicly criticized the missionary movement a few weeks before the report was issued. Buck had won the 1932 Pulitzer Prize with her novel *The Good Earth* and was employed with her husband as a teacher in the University of Nanking, but she was not an ordained minister or elder of the Presbyterian Church. Her writings and speeches undermined the cause of missions in public opinion, but the controversy kept the author's name before the public. On November 2, 1932, to honor Buck, a committee of Presbyterian Women held a luncheon at New York's Hotel Astor for two thousand persons. Dr. Henry Sloane Coffin gave the invocation, and Dr. Cleland B. McAfee, secretary of the Presbyterian Board of Foreign Missions, was also present. In such a setting Buck's words must have seemed rude to her hosts and hostesses: "In the Orient one finds the same questions as here in regard to whether foreign missions are worthwhile. . . . We must send abroad a better type of missionary from America. We must know better the needs of the people to whom we go."[20]

About two weeks after this luncheon, a conference was scheduled at the Hotel Roosevelt in New York to present the *Laymen's Inquiry* to the public. In advance of the conference a quotation from the report critical of the missionary movement appeared in a *New York Times* editorial on November 6.[21] Naturally, there were questions raised about the publicity methods for the report and the leak. When a person at the conference asked "why the report was released piecemeal in the newspapers before being formally presented to the foreign missions boards of the participating denominations,"[22] Hocking replied that it was too long to summarize in one release. It was "purely a laymen's inquiry and its purpose was to awaken widespread interest in the missions among the laity."[23]

Professor Hocking wrote the first four chapters of *Re-Thinking Missions*. He presented the church as a kind of "foreign service or ambassadorship,"[24] a blend of political and religious ideas. As to God, he wrote, "God works throughout human history bringing men toward unity in a love which is universal in its sweep."[25] Furthermore, he argued, "That final truth, whatever it may be, is the New Testament of every existing faith."[26] Conversion was neglected. The concept behind *Re-Thinking Missions* would have transformed missions into a religious and cultural sharing rather than a preaching venture, and it would have changed the type of person that became a missionary. To increase the quality of the person that would go on the mission field to one that had gone to college and learned history, philosophy, and comparative religion would make the new type of missionary a proto modernist focused on the social gospel, not motivated by a God of salvation for sinners.

At the introductory conference Dr. Woodward of Chicago, the Vice Chairman of the Conference, said there were "too many instances of amateurs undertaking to serve as specialists," but found the work of Professor Buck at Nanking University and the writing of Pearl S. Buck of "tremendous value."[27] Mrs. Buck, who was present, focused on humanitarian relief, saying she "'would like to see the missionary sent to satisfy the special needs of a community,' as a technical expert, research worker, hospital nurse or recreation expert."[28]

Those drafting the report had to find agreement in order to achieve harmony among themselves, and to do so, the appraisal commission discarded theology. The only way to achieve unity of agreement among groups of those expressing loyalty to Jesus Christ, those motivated by altruistic service, and those seeking "a more adequate fulfillment of the divine possibilities of personal and social life"[29] was to accept this latter position as the lowest common denominator because that was the only position shared by all three groups. Theologically, there were serious concerns: "Many of the brethren seemed troubled, because they missed certain familiar terms, such as 'sin,' 'salvation,' and 'redemption.'"[30]

The transcript of the Conference at the Hotel Roosevelt shows that those in attendance were in high spirits indeed as the speakers were interrupted over fifty times for laughter and forty-nine times for applause.[31] Mrs. Harper Sibley, an Episcopal churchwoman, announced, "By this report we have taken missions away from the sentimentalists, we have rescued missions from the dust pile where the colleges tried to put them, and we have placed missions at the forefront of the modern world movements making for world betterment."[32]

Some mission boards and missionaries reacted sharply in the vigorous debate that followed the publication of the report. In his critique of *Re-Thinking Missions*, Visser 't Hooft referred to its liberal naiveté and its unclear and undefined conception of religion.[33] He referred readers seeking a critique of the Report's theology to Mackay's article "The Theology of the Laymen's Foreign Missions Inquiry," published in the *International Review of Missions*.[34] In the article Mackay found the report lacking in three fundamental areas: its description of the contemporary situation, its conception of Christianity, its superficial interpretation of the Christian missionary objective.

In his critique Mackay was dismissive of the report's grasp of theology. From the official transcript, he quoted a "pathetic" exchange that occurred at the meeting:

The Chairman: I have been handed some questions. The first question, which I propose to refer to Dr. Jones, is as follows: "Does the Commission consider it possible to give an adequate interpretation of the trend of theological thinking in the last hundred years without taking account of the fact that in the last decade new and potent ideological currents have appeared which take direct issue with the characteristic thought tendencies from which the Commission has derived the particular philosophy of religion underlying its report?" (Laughter.)

Dr. Jones: I think Dr. Hocking ought to answer this question. (Laughter.) Well, I am quite certain I don't know what the "potent ideological currents" are that have appeared unless it is in interpretations of Christianity in this critical time. I rather assume that is what is intended in the question, but I am not sure, and until I have more light as to exactly what is wanted here, I cannot very well both give the dream and the interpretation thereof. (Laughter and applause.) (P. 37.)[35]

First, using an anecdote from the official report itself, Mackay showed that in venturing beyond their depth, the laymen exposed their ignorance of theological developments of the previous ten years including the Kierkegaard renaissance: "the requiem of a thought day that is dying rather than the trumpet of dawn of a day that is coming, the sunset glow of nineteenth-century romanticism caught and prolonged in the mirrors of *Re-Thinking Missions*."[36] Similarly, its treatment of the modern cultural situation, which assumed a world culture was emerging, did not take into consideration communism, fascism, and various brands of nationalism.

Second, Mackay felt that the report's conception of Christianity was inadequate. The report assumed Christianity to be a general truth and its difference from other religions simply a difference in form. It did not regard Jesus' answers to the problems of religion as being "final." Its presentation of the person and teaching of Jesus were reduced only to certain facets:

The mere "Christophiles" of today who have not found a place for Christ in the eternal order are becoming less and less a power to be reckoned with. Religiously, they are beautiful but uncreative souls. Intellectually, they are unable to answer the humanist's question, "Why Jesus more than anyone else?" They have lost . . . the tremendous missionary urge of Christianity. The religion of Jesus is failing them and they reject the faith of Christ.[37]

Third, in Mackay's view the report interpreted the missionary objective superficially. The motive inspiring the religious philosophy of the report was the "desire for a deeper knowledge and love of God, seeking with men everywhere a more adequate fulfillment of the diverse possibilities of personal and social life."[38] They will engage in a "mutual sharing with people of other faiths, looking forward . . . to a future religious synthesis."[39] The missionary basis thus described was too weak to create or sustain any missionary movement. Rather, Mackay wrote, "a missionary movement of any character involves the consciousness of an absolute certainty which is regarded as valid for everybody."[40]

Mackay's forceful conclusion articulated the missionary objective as an incarnational approach of dynamic Christianity in both word and action unfolding the message—"Jesus Christ":

What is the Christian missionary objective? To make Jesus Christ inescapable for men everywhere. Not acceptable but inescapable, the only possible solution, the only saviour of men who have become deadly in earnest about the problem of living. This will involve the closest and most sympathetic identification of missionaries with the people among whom they work. The foreign word must become indigenous flesh in those who bear it. The missionary will devote himself to unfolding by word and deed the content of this message—"Jesus Christ." All his gifts of mind and heart will be concentrated on making his Lord concrete, meaningful and compelling to men and women. The true missionary, whatever be the class to which he belongs, will be supremely a lay priest, whose objective will be to produce the kind of crisis in other lives which shall lead to the immolation of the old self and the reception into the life of Christ and all He stands for. Christian teachers, doctors and agriculturists will not regard their specific tasks as a bait or a lure, but as the expression of the spirit of Christ, tasks which they are in honour bound to discharge in accordance with the highest professional standards. At the same time, in so far as they are Christian missionaries in a real sense, they cannot avoid being priests and doing priestwork with the Gospel in the deep intimacies of personal friendship with their pupils and patients and fellow-villagers.[41]

Re-Thinking Missions also presented a thoroughly secularized concept of the church radically different from the supernaturally functional concept of the Church that Mackay and others developed in the later 1930s, 1940s and 1950s.[42]

Years later, writing from a historical perspective about the report, Mackay referred with a tinge of irony to the "distinguished professor" and quoted a portion of Hocking's book *Living Religions and a World Faith* (1940), which illustrated his liberalism:

> The idea of a divine plan considered as a dated product of God's wisdom and goodness, wholly unimaginable to man, is I fear, an ingenious invention of St. Paul. To take it up again today is to place a halter around the neck of Christianity for those to tug at who are disposed to work upon the more graven fears of the human heart. It is time for a robust and honest Christianity to have done with all this rattling of ancient moral chains.[43]

Following publication of the report, perhaps with the goal of enhancing her own book sales, Buck fueled the controversy with speeches and articles. Her glowing review of the *Laymen's Inquiry* appeared in the *Christian Century*: "I have read a unique book, a great book. The book presents a masterly statement of religion in its place in life, and of Christianity in its place in religion. . . . I think this is the only book I have ever read which seems to me literally true in its every observation and right in its every conclusion."[44] Her critique of missions, *Is There a Case for Foreign Missions?* was published both as a pamphlet and as an article in *Harper's Magazine*.[45] But Pearl Buck's clash with the Presbyterian Board of Foreign Missions came to a head when she published an article called "Easter, 1933" in *Cosmopolitan Magazine*, where she expressed a number of heretical views.[46] When the Board of Foreign Missions allowed her to resign from the Board instead of firing her, more controversy followed.[47] By the summer Buck had decided to divorce her husband, an agricultural missionary, and in June of 1935 she married her publisher in Reno, Nevada.[48]

While the syncretistic work of his friend Hocking was the "saddest and bitterest moment in [Speer's] career," another group charged the Board of Foreign Missions and its missionaries with heresy.[49] Professor J. Gresham Machen challenged Robert E. Speer and the leadership of the Presbyterian Mission Board in his pamphlet *Modernism and the Board of Foreign Missions of the Presbyterian Church in the U.S.A.*[50] Machen intended to undermine the confidence of donors to the Board of Foreign Missions.[51] The struggle between Speer and Machen has been well documented elsewhere.[52]

Mackay, now a member of the mission board, was drawn into the strife when Machen criticized him in the pamphlet faulting Mackay's articles on the Oxford Group movement in *The Presbyterian Banner* and his presentation at the Lakeville, Connecticut, Conference of 1931.[53]

Webster Browning wrote his friend Mackay and described the Board's difficult situation:

> The Board is certainly in a difficult position, between extreme conservatives and extreme liberals, not being able to satisfy either. A very large section of the church is evidently aggrieved because of the Board's acceptance of the resignation of Mrs. Buck under any condition, feeling that she ought to have been continued in her work in China, while another, possibly equally large section and certainly more belligerent, under the leading of Machen, are extremely vocal and attack the Board because it accepted the above mentioned resignation "with regret," claiming that she should have been summarily dismissed as a heretic and not in any sense a Christian. I have never known Dr. Speer to speak with such a sense of utter discouragement in regard to the general situation. But I am hoping that matters at the Assembly will take a more favorable turn than has been anticipated. At the last moment the Council and Board voted that Dr. McAfee should go also, since he is the one who has had the Buck affair in hand.[54]

After learning the results of the General Assembly of 1933, which were favorable to Speer, Mackay on a mission trip to Brazil wrote to Browning from shipboard:

> The news about the Assembly reached me in B.A. [Buenos Aires]. What a landslide in favour of John McDowell! Dear old Robert E., how my heart has been sore for him! Truly the eighth beatitude and the other marks of the saints are being fulfilled in him! I have been saying to myself, If Machen and his gang do this in the green tree what will they not do in the dry! I am not a controversialist by nature, but one of these days my Celtic blood is going to boil and Dr. Machen is going to know it. He will find that he can't take out a patent on Christianity and then indict for daring to be a Christian a man whom I adore, without a violent clash with me. When the next barrage comes I hope to be on the spot.[55]

The Christian Message

Under the auspices of the Presbyterian Board of Foreign Missions, Mackay continued his evangelistic work. Some of his addresses and writings specifically attempted to reformulate the Christian message, focusing on the gifts of meaning, human fulfillment, and Christian insight. In November 1932 Mackay delivered the Merrick Lectures at Ohio Wesleyan University, ideas he had been developing in Mexico dealing with Kierkegaard, Dostoyevsky, Nietzsche, Unamuno, and Barth under the title "Prophetic Thinkers."

In this 1932 lecture, "Kierkegaard: The Existential Thinker," Mackay noted the distinction between the philosophical questions, "What can I know?" and "What shall I do?" The idea of conscious action as a means of knowing truth also appears in Mackay's image of the balcony with the road. This theme had an evangelistic meaning and a missionary message as Mackay used the image of calling others to join him on the road of life. It became an invitation used to reinvigorate and evangelize those who lived in North America and who believed that they were already Christians. Actually doing the will of God can become a crucial step in moving from nominal to authentic Christian experience. The approach had sound biblical foundation (see John 7:17).

On May 30, 1934, he delivered an address titled "Our World Mission" at the Presbyterian General Assembly held at Cleveland, Ohio. In addition he served as a speaker at quadrennial conventions of the Student Volunteer Movement in 1928, 1932, and 1936.[56] One person influenced through a conversation with an SVM secretary in 1936 was future Presbyterian leader Robert Bilheimer.[57] In addition, Mackay delivered strong evangelistic messages at smaller gatherings[58] and contributed general articles on Latin American affairs to the Board's magazine, *Missionary Review of the World*.[59]

Mackay also contributed an important chapter to the collection *The Christian Message for the World Today: A Joint Statement of the World-Wide Mission of the Christian Church*.[60] Professor Wilhelm Pauck wrote in a review,

> Particularly the chapter by John A. Mackay on "The Gospel in Our Generation" deserves wide reading. It is one of the profoundest and most moving statements of Christian faith given in recent times. For Dr. Mackay is fully aware of the cultural, economic, and political complexity of the modern crisis, and he gives evidence of having passed through all the stages of the modern theological development—and he now comes forward with a positive affirmation of the continued validity of the Christian gospel which must give cheer to all who long for a new positiveness of the Christian message.[61]

Presbyterian Mission in Mexico

The work of the Presbyterian Board of Foreign Missions began in 1872 in Mexico City. The principal boards of missions of the United States working in Mexico entered into a mutual agreement at Cincinnati, Ohio, in 1914, that

provided for a territorial division of the mission field among the denominational missions. The Presbyterian Board became responsible for Mexico City
and the seven states and territories south of the Federal District. Nationalism
was a factor in relations among Presbyterians, and complete autonomy was
granted to the Presbytery of Mexico City on April 1, 1929. The Board of
Foreign Missions, however, retained responsibility for educational work in
central Mexico and had responsibility for evangelism and education in about
one half the area originally allocated to it.

Governmental hostility toward religion was far stronger in Mexico than in
Peru in the 1920s and 1930s, and the Peruvian president urged moderation.
On August 3, 1926, President Leguía wrote and asked the *Jefe Máximo* to
"use his powerful influence in reestablishing harmonious relations with the
Church." Calles replied flatly the next day, "The Constitution of Mexico is
not a special law but a general and fundamental code which I am obliged
and am decided to enforce without fear of interdicts or supernatural punishment."[62] By September 1926 quotas had been established for priests in
the different states. In November 1928 an outstanding member of the Calles
cabinet said that "Protestantism had lost its greatest opportunity through failure, in some way, to seize the exact moment. . . . Protestantism, by its Anglo-
Saxon division into sects, which to the Mexican are largely artificial, is sadly
weakened."[63] The initial phase of religious persecution ended in July, 1929,
and religious services were reinstituted.

The social revolution in Mexico centered on three contentious issues: the
relation of church and state, equitable land distribution, and nationalism.
Hostility to religion played a role in each, and Mackay analyzed this anticlerical attitude in Mexico both broadly and by reference to the educational
cycle. The primary cause was a natural reaction to the religious regime that
had constricted social life in Mexico for three hundred years. Secondarily,
the generation of intellectual leaders in their thirties and forties had not been
exposed to liberal culture. When the revolution of 1910 broke out, those men
were university students, and the dominant philosophy in the country then
was the positivism of August Comte. Their lives passed through two decades
of revolutionary violence, and when it began to decrease, Marxist positivism influenced them. Their antireligious point of view had been reinforced.[64]
Mackay cited many examples of the anticlerical attitudes of Mexico's leaders
at the time.[65]

Protestants found it easier to operate within the anticlerical laws than did
the Roman Catholics. During a period when all foreign Roman Catholic
priests were expelled from the country, Protestant ministers were allowed
to reregister for work in the country as professors. They were allowed to

continue preaching but could not conduct a service or administer the sacraments.[66] Some found original ways to evangelize, such as Norman Taylor, a Presbyterian missionary born in Canada, who distributed Bibles and religious literature among the men and officers in the military camps and patrols situated around the country.[67]

Serious difficulties arose for the Presbyterian mission in connection with its educational efforts. In 1927 the Mexican government expropriated church property, including all the Presbyterian schools as well as churches. There were a number of exceptions, however. The Presbyterian Mission Board believed that the government takeover of two large schools, San Angel and Coyoacan, and other adjacent buildings in Mexico City was improper on the grounds that these two schools were owned by a holding corporation, Sociedad Educadora, which was not a religious body but an educational body.[68] The 1928 report of the Board of Foreign Missions noted that these two schools were the first Protestant schools to receive governmental recognition in Mexico, and recognition aided their educational efforts. Coyoacan had 85 boarders and 61 day pupils, and San Angel had 108 boarders and 44 day pupils.[69]

A period of peace and progress for the schools was short-lived as a second phase of religious hostility began. In 1931 the Roman Catholic Church organized a large commemoration for the 400th anniversary of the appearance of the Virgin of Guadalupe that was attended by hundreds of thousands of people. To deter large ceremonies with many clergy, the government responded with a new law requiring registration of clergy and assignment to a church. A papal encyclical followed.[70] In this climate, difficulties began again for the schools when a hostile politician became minister for public education, and he withheld government recognition of the schools, since from the point of view of the government there was confusion whether the schools were religious or educational. The lay principle was that no religion could be taught in schools and no minister of religion could be a teacher. Government recognition was important to students since it allowed them to receive credit for work done and to enable them to enter professional schools.

Mackay had developed friendships with Presbyterian missionaries in Mexico while serving there with the YMCA and consulted with them about the matter in early 1932, before officially joining the Board of Foreign Missions. The situation was critical for the Presbyterian schools at Coyoacan and San Angel. Parents had been removing children from the schools for fear that the schools would not be recognized by the government. Legal papers had been prepared and were ready to go to the notary, and the new civil society to hold the property had been formed.

Because of the dubious status of the new legal entity, Mackay realized when he reviewed the situation that the best course of action from the legal and ethical points of view was that the mission board should once again appear as proprietor. Although in Lima he had incorporated the Colegio Anglo-Peruano, Mackay thought that incorporation into the state system was not ideal. On the other hand, students of evangelical parents could enter the professions by passing the government exams. Many evangelical students did not attend mission schools.

In early 1932 Mackay reported on the situation to Rex Wheeler of the Presbyterian Board.[71] Mackay considered that the issue of government recognition had been raised providentially to present an opportunity to restudy missionary education in Mexico. He gathered information so that when he came to New York to serve on the Board of Foreign Missions, he would be fully versed on the matter. The national synod in Mexico wanted Mackay to be present for a synod meeting in June or December. Mackay replied that he would have to await guidance from the Board. He personally considered a meeting with the Mexican national church of paramount importance.[72] His visitations to Mexico attempted to bring these denominational strands of missionary and local efforts together in cooperation. By the end of 1932, a new period of cooperation seemed to have begun among the indigenous church and the mission.

Two years later, on behalf of the Board of Foreign Missions, Mackay journeyed to Mexico again from March 7 to April 1, 1934. In addition to preaching in Methodist and Presbyterian churches, his trip was the catalyst for an interdenominational mission conference to focus attention on the common problems of missionary education in Mexico. The Foreign Missions Conference of North America at a recent meeting in Atlantic City had recommended such a joint approach. In Mexico, several boards took steps to accommodate their policy to the new situation. Immediately after the interdenominational conference ended, Presbyterian missionaries held their own denominational conference on the future of the Coyoacan Boys School, located not far from Mexico City. The time of the meeting was accelerated on the calendar because Mackay was present in Mexico and because of the seriousness of the issue. The Board of Foreign Missions in New York had formulated principles of its educational policy at its February 1934 meeting, and these were a basis for discussion. The girls school in the adjoining suburb of San Angel had been closed about a year before. Deliberations were made difficult by a small group from the Mexican Presbyterian Church who believed that progress of evangelical Christianity in Mexico could not be made in relationship with members from an imperialistic country. These disgruntled members carried on a "barrage of vituperation."[73] In the discussions the Board's education principles were applied to the situation, and it was decided that the school should close its doors.[74] Given the choice between preserving its identity as a church or merging into the general community, the Board declined the progressive secularization of schools and closed them instead. To continue the schools would have required economic self-sufficiency, trained staff, and real Christian influence. Thereafter, Christian policy and cooperation between missions and the national church took new lines of action.

By 1936 Báez-Camargo reported that an educational awakening was occurring in rural Mexico and that religion was "becoming a burning question for everybody."[75] Indeed the Protestant churches were less "concerned about theoretical recognition of religious liberties" than "the much more practical issue of how to make the best use of the present opportunities, for the spiritual upbuilding of the nation."[76] During the period of his service on the Board of Foreign Missions, Mackay publicized the issues of the Mexican mission field in a number of articles.[77] He felt a special place in his heart for Mexico. During his visit in 1934 a gathering was held to recognize the retirement of Presbyterian William Wallace, DD, a cultured Christian gentleman who had worked as a missionary for more than thirty-six years. The religious restrictions made missions in Mexico unique, and Mackay wrote, "It was necessary to adopt a Quaker type of service for unchurched people. Among the Mexican mountains, far from any organized meeting of the Society of Friends, I learned the meaning of silence in religious worship."[78] The group of missionaries in Mexico wrote a special tribute to Mackay when he became the President of Princeton Seminary, since they held him in a place of affection.

Peruvian Visitation

In April 1933 Mackay set out on a six-month visitation of the South American mission field on behalf of the Presbyterian Board of Foreign Missions. The trip included Peru, Chile, Brazil, Argentina, and Uruguay. He landed at Callao, Peru, the first stop, on April 21, 1933, and found Lima to be the second most beautiful capital in Latin America, second only to Rio. Events occurred there that illustrated God's guidance and confirmed Mackay's conviction of God's hand intervening in the affairs of human history.

In Lima Mackay had arranged to stay at the British legation with Charles H. Bentinck, the British minister to Peru, an evangelical Christian who took great interest in San Andrés School and had been taught Spanish by one of its teachers.[79] During the first week Mackay gave a number of lectures. Then, on

April 30, in the middle of the visit, President Luis Miguel Sánchez Cerro (Mackay once referred to him as a "little Mussolini") was shot twice and assassinated at the Lima racetrack where he had been reviewing troops. Political opponents wanted to blame the assassination on Haya de la Torre, who was once again in prison, and this threat to his life was a serious one.[80] Sánchez Cerro's funeral was postponed from Wednesday to Thursday, and

> a plot was formed to let the mob loose on the Penitentiary to kill Haya. José Galvez, Raúl Porras, and others phoned John at the British Legation to use his influence with the British minister to prevent this dread happening, and the minister at once lined up the Diplomatic Corps and petitioned the Government to protect the prisoner. It was done, but while Haya's life was spared, he was put back into the dark cell he had been kept in for many months and from which he had recently been released. John's *conferencias* were, of course, interrupted by the imposition of martial law and the prohibiting of all public meetings, so he left.[81]

These channels of communication formed and existing for Christian purposes were now also used for a secular political purpose to protect Haya's life. The information transmitted from Galvez and Porras to Mackay and then to Bentinck and the diplomatic corps thwarted the assassination plot and permitted Haya's influence in Peruvian politics and culture to continue after the threat was averted.

From the perspective of Jane Mackay a second and familial example of God's guidance occurred next. John had written her that he hoped to return to Lima to finish the mission that he had begun there. Jane knew the volatility of Peruvian politics and feared for John's safety, and she fell to her knees to pray that he would be guided away from Peru. The next day the answer came when Webster Browning told her that the Mission Board had changed Mackay's itinerary and that he would proceed to Brazil rather than return to Peru. Jane saw this as an answer to her prayer.[82] To Christian believers these episodes suggested God's providence in human affairs and God's intervention in the details of history, a dimension going beyond purely humanistic understandings of historical processes.

Mackay's moral and spiritual influences on the principles of the Aprista movement through his association with Haya are seen in a book that Haya himself encouraged and helped the author to write. These influences on Haya and the movement include ethical emphasis on education; honesty; separation of church and state; the advocacy of personal transformation; the value of individual conscience, the moral force in his thought; nonviolence in politics; and Haya's later comparison of Christ's sufferings to accomplish his goals with the need for Apristas to suffer to accomplish the moral regeneration of Peru.[83]

Mackay's writings about Haya and Peru also focused on the proper male role in society and the transformative power of conversion: "Haya de la Torre had passed through a profound moral experience. From being an irresponsible, flat-chested dandy, he became changed into a robust young crusader, who because of his social passion had to forfeit the financial support and the good will of his parents, members of an old colonial family of Trujillo."[84]

Brazil: The Interior

Soon after joining the Presbyterian Board of Foreign Missions in the summer of 1932, Mackay traveled to Brazil to speak at the World Sunday School Conference in Rio.[85] Concerned with secular trends, he referred to secularism as having the hopelessly limited perspective of a frog in a puddle ("da perspectiva de uma rã dentro do charco"). He noted the tragic form of secularization in churches. To be a true person rather than an alone individual, the person must open to God.

During a trip the following year, Mackay traveled to the interior of Brazil.[86] After visiting the larger cities, Mackay traveled inland for five weeks, visiting the states of Goyaz and Mato Grosso, which were in an early stage of development. The missionaries there conducted a ministry of reconciliation: God with humans and humans with one another. As an example Mackay recounted a story of two farmers in the eastern part of the state of Goyaz. One had a herd of Brazilian hogs that freely invaded the cultivated land of his neighbor, ruining it. One day the hog owner rode over to his neighbor and instead of pulling a gun from his pocket, pulled out his pocketbook to pay for the damage the hogs had done. The two men embraced in brotherhood. Later, at a small farm in the coffee region of Goyaz, Mackay and several missionaries, Mr. and Mrs. Salley, Mr. Martin, and Mr. Reasoner, celebrated a Communion service with a congregation of small farmers (*fazendeiros*) and their families numbering about 150 persons. The fellowship originated seventeen years before when a colporteur sold several copies of the Scripture, and the fellowship prospered unrelated to any other Christian group.

Mackay's trip in the missionary car ended at Burity, near the river port of Cuyabá, fifteen hundred miles from the coast and two thousand miles up the river from Buenos Aires. A Christian farm school was being operated there. At Cuyabá, the capital of Mato Grosso, Mackay preached to four hundred persons one evening in the open air. They were members of an evangelical congregation with a national pastor. From there Mackay left to go down river to Corumba, near Paraguay, then return home. Modern Brazil was a great testimony to evangelical missions.

Mackay's evangelistic and missionary work also continued through speeches at the spiritual emphasis conference of the YMCA.[87] On May 30, 1934, at the General Assembly in Cleveland, Ohio, Mackay delivered a passionate address on the subject of missions. He closed with the story of the pig farmers of Goyaz and concluded with challenging words on pleasing pain, cited previously in chapter 1.[88]

The Murder of Eliot Speer

Personal tragedy struck Robert E. Speer and his family one evening in September 1934 when his thirty-five-year-old son, Eliot, the headmaster of Mount Hermon School, Northfield, Massachusetts, was shot through a window of his study with a twelve-gauge shotgun. The crime created a great sensation. The district attorney, who had also been the school's counsel until stepping down to avoid a conflict of interest, concluded he did not have enough evidence to indict anyone because the weapon was never found and there were no witnesses to the crime. Instead an inquest was held that lasted more than a month and had fifteen hundred pages of testimony. The case was still open in the late 1970s when a college friend of Eliot's investigated the records himself. His research concluded that Eliot had been shot by Dean Thomas Elder who was under a strain during the inquest and who left the school and never returned to it. The dean believed he had been passed over for the headmaster's job in favor of Eliot as the result of statements made about him by the school's former treasurer to the previous headmaster. In addition, the dean may have disagreed with the direction of educational innovations that Eliot was bringing to the school. The lesson to be learned from the tragedy, however, was how the power of Christian belief enabled Eliot's parents to persevere through the crisis and maintain their grace without becoming resentful.[89]

Mackay's First English Books

The first of Mackay's English books, *The Other Spanish Christ*,[90] represents the new Christology that Mackay's evangelism was bringing to South America. It contains sophisticated discussions of Hispanic art, history, poetry, and literature that manifest the working philosophy and theology of Spanish Catholicism. The book introduced North American readers to an area of the world they knew little about. Reinhold Niebuhr, a reader for Scribner's, was enthusiastic about the manuscript and wrote Mackay that it "must be published for it is rich in both original insights and in erudition in a field of literature still a closed book to most of us."[91]

The title is striking but at first glance difficult to understand.[92] In the title and the book Mackay is creating a dialectic to juxtapose and discuss two contradictory conceptions of Jesus Christ and to examine the personal and social consequences of each. The thesis in its most simple form is that the dominant conception of the Spanish Christ—which Mackay shows actually originated in Tangiers—is a dead Christ. The "other Spanish Christ" is the living Christ of the Spanish mystics. Mackay draws on the lessons of Unamuno, his former teacher, to make these points, and he weaves together art, poetry, history, and philosophy to make his case. It is systematically drawn dialectic between two conceptions of Christ, one dead and one alive.

Mackay is not interested in institutions per se in this book. He is above all interested in a human soul having a living, dynamic experience of Christ. It is also important to make quite clear that Mackay is not "anti-Catholic." In the words of a reviewer in a Dominican periodical, "Dr. Mackay is no bigot. He is not antagonistic to Catholicism as such. On the contrary, he recognizes the expression of 'true Christianity' in many of its manifestations and can speak with warmth and admiration of many of its past and present achievements. But he has a horror of two things: the Society of Jesus and, the 'Virgin cult.'"[93] Writes Mackay in *The Other Spanish Christ*, "Philosophically speaking, Spanish Catholicism has passed straight from aesthetics to religion, clearing ethics at a bound."[94] It is a "catholicism de-Christianized."[95]

The vigor of Mackay's thought and writing is apparent in the following passages:

A Christ known in life as an infant and in death as a corpse, over whose helpless childhood and tragic fate the Virgin Mother presides; a Christ who became man in the interests of eschatology, whose permanent reality resides in a magic wafer bestowing immortality; a Virgin Mother who by not tasting death, became the Queen of Life,—that is the Christ and that the Virgin who came to America! He came as Lord of Death and of the life that is to be; she came as Sovereign Lady of the life that now is.[96]

In Spanish religion Christ has been the center of a cult of death. And yet, paradoxically enough, it was the passion for fleshly life and immortality that created this interest in death. The dead Christ is an expiatory victim. The details of His earthly life are of slight importance and make relatively small appeal. He is regarded as a purely supernatural being, whose humanity, being only apparent, has little ethical bearing upon ours. This docetic Christ died as the victim of human hate, and in order to bestow immortality, that is to say, a continuation of the present earthly, fleshly existence. The contemplation of His passion produces a sort of catharsis, as Aristotle would say, in the soul of the worshipper, just as in the bull-fight, an analogous creation of the Spanish spirit, the Spaniard sees and feels death in all its dread reality in the fate of a victim. The total sensation intensifies his sense of the reality and terribleness of death; it increases his passion for life, and, in the religious realm, makes him cling desperately and tragically to the dead victim that died to give him immortality.

The Spanish religious passion for life has not, however, aimed at life in the qualitative Johannine sense; it has been a craving not for regeneration, but for immortality, for "total immortality in its vilest and sublimest meaning." Its supreme dread has thus been death not sin.[97]

Mackay drives home the distinction by citing two Argentine intellectuals, Dr. Juan B. Terán and Ricardo Rojas:

These two heads of Argentine universities are agreed that South American Catholicism has lacked two constitutive features of the Christian religion. It has lacked inward spiritual experience and it has lacked outward ethical expression. People have possessed religion, but a religion has not possessed them. They have practiced religion, but have not lived it. Religion has been neither a subject of intellectual preoccupation nor an incentive to virtuous living. Souls have not been in agony. There has been indifference and there has been peace; but the latter has been that eerie, aesthetic peace which haunts the graveyard; the peace of death, not the peace of life.[98]

This conception of Christ in death is represented by the recumbent Christ of Palencia, in the *Iglesia de la Cruz*, the dead Christ, "cradled in the arms of Franciscan nuns, He is dead forever."[99]

Mackay contrasts this idea of Christ with the Christ of another religious tradition in Spain, the living Christ of the Spanish mystics. Quoting an anonymous mystic poet viewing the wondrous Cross, and then Raymond Lull, a missionary, Mackay writes,

Henceforth the love of Christ will be the compelling motive of his life and not the hope of reward or the fear of punishment, either in this life or in the life to come. Religion is here a quality of life and not the simple prolongation of existence. It is the passionate response of love and not a sordid appeal for things. . . .[100]

Christ is for him [Lull] our Life, our new, eternal Life. He does not immortalize life as it is, but transforms it into what life should be. The evidence, moreover, that we shall never die is not that we believe in our immortality but that we love.[101]

Mackay's focus is on a personal experience of Christ, and he does not concern himself with institutions but with movements. As one reviewer noted, he ignored the fact that "all the great Spanish mystics were convinced institutionalists and devoted children of the church."[102] But that is not the point; Mackay also is not interested in the institutional structure of Protestant religion. He writes,

Nothing has been more needed, nothing is more needed to-day than a true expression of Protestant Christianity in these countries. This does not mean that what is wanted is a replica of Protestant institutions which have grown up in Anglo-Saxon countries, still less a projection into the Latin world of the sins of Protestant denominationalism. The fact must be emphasized that Protestantism is essentially a movement, a religious attitude, rather than an institutional system or a collection of dogmas.[103]

Mackay explicitly makes clear a "common need presses upon the Spanish and Anglo-Saxon worlds: to 'know' Christ, to 'know' Him for life and thought, to 'know' Him in God and God in Him."[104]

Mackay's next volume, *That Other America*, also received wide attention in church publications and elsewhere.[105] One reviewer, Spanish philosopher, José Ortega y Gasset, whose review was republished in a variety of Latin American newspapers, pointed out that in this book Mackay solves the problems that he has proposed in *The Other Spanish Christ*.[106] The conception of a world Christian fellowship is expressed in comprehensive detail in this second book. It also contained discussion of the situation in Mexico and more examples from Brazil that reflected Mackay's further travels, studies, and contacts after completing *The Other Spanish Christ*.

Mackay writes with clarity about Christian fellowship and community, first discussing different types of friendship and fellowship. The fellowship Mackay is talking about goes beyond "tavern fellowship" (*amistad tabernaria*), associations for amusement or recreation; "library friendship," a friendship born of common interest in ideas; or "star friendship," friendship patterned on good manners, named for the orderly rhythmic relations that the heavenly bodies bear to one another. "The highest form of human association," writes Mackay, "is fellowship on the road. This is a fellowship of people who share a common concern and march together towards the same goal. In 'road friendship' a single loyalty transcending merely individual interests binds the members of the wayfaring fraternity together for common achievement."[107]

A corporate fellowship is Mackay's goal in transnational relations. That fellowship is another name for the church. "The supreme need is that the Christian church be a fellowship. Let the church be the church, let it be true to its inmost self, that is, to the reality of fellowship."[108]

> A fellowship in Christ, a community in which Jesus Christ is believed upon, loved and obeyed, in which Christlikeness is the standard of all relationships, that and only that is the true universal fellowship, and only that fellowship has a future. The realization of the contemporaneousness of Jesus Christ as the everlasting source and standard of life is the one unbreakable bond of fellowship and history's true fulfillment.
>
> It is the basic assumption of this book that what is ultimately real is God's will to fellowship in Jesus Christ. Deriving from this assumption is the other, that the supreme way in which Christians in the United States can serve the lands of the other America, and their own as well, is to lead men and women in the two Americas to serve God's plan for a world fellowship. A missionary urge is an inevitable expression of living Christianity. Those who have experienced fellowship with God in Christ cannot but desire that fellowship to be coextensive with the whole human family. They find themselves impelled to be witnesses to the imperious demands of the Christian faith and the transforming character of the Christian experience in every community and land.[109]

An example of Mackay's interest in social change resulting from basic change at the individual level are his comments on the Road to Fellowship where he discusses "our quest for the ideal form of human relationship":

> What we have in mind is rather the establishment of a corporate fellowship among people belonging to all nations on the continent, of such a quality that it shall express the true meaning and end of life, and, at the same time, fit those who belong to it for the highest form of citizenship in their respective countries. Our concern, in a word, and the chief interest of this book, is the emergence in the Americas of a community that shall contain at once the pattern and the seed of a single new America, very different from the Americas that are. Such a community can come into being and be sustained only through a common loyalty, on the part of those who belong to it, to what is above and commands them all, the eternal and the unconditioned, the living God.[110]

He concludes some pages later that "true fellowship in the Americas, as elsewhere, can be consummated only on the basis of faith in God's revelation of himself and life's meaning in Jesus Christ."[111] He illustrates his argument with two expressions of the "divine will to fellowship" from the Old and New Testaments.[112]

The "supreme aim is to make that fellowship coextensive with human society."[113] In so doing he referred to Ambassador Dwight Morrow and alluded to the importance of Christian believers serving as government officials:

The memory of the Morrows will never die in Mexico. For a man who is a minister of his country to show himself also a minister of Jesus Christ and of the country to which he goes, is to incarnate the highest range of spiritual influence which a human being can express. I have known a foreign diplomat in Latin America who was this kind of man. Were his type more universal, international relations would offer fewer problems and the road would be shorter to the city of God, with its ever radiant light and its ever open gates.[114]

These books and his other Spanish writings clearly established Mackay's academic credentials. When Mackay was approached to become the president of Princeton Seminary he hesitated at first, believing that if he accepted the position "it would deprive" him "of the privilege of [the] responsibility of being in the missionary enterprise." While he was considering the matter, one day he met a Methodist friend outside the Fifth Avenue office, who said to Mackay, "John, don't you know that a seminary campus can be a mission field?"[115] Robert E. Speer attempted to persuade him using a different tact. "John," he said, "if you go to South America you'll do a great deal of good, but if you go to Princeton, you'll triple your work."[116] Speer, a member of the Seminary Board of Trustees, abstained from the vote. Speer's multiplier effect in fact came to pass. As Mackay led the seminary, the missionaries trained and sent out certainly exceeded the work he could have done by himself. This was the idea that Mackay cited in his farewell letter to the members of the West Africa and Latin America missions, June 6, 1936, when he left as secretary from the Board of Foreign Missions.

Chapter 10

Return to Princeton (1936–1959)

"That your way may be known upon earth,
   your saving power among all nations." (Ps. 67:2)

Mackay's influence during his twenty-three-year tenure as president of Princeton Seminary transformed the institution. His steady leadership, recognized by his contemporaries, turned the seminary from a faltering, sick condition to an institution that was a leader in its field. One colleague, the only professor who had been a faculty member both on Mackay's arrival and his retirement, Henry S. Gehman, recognized Mackay's role in "formulation of a definite policy," assumption of "leadership in the life of the Seminary," encouragement of "scholarship both in the faculty and in the students," and the maintenance of "academic standards." Mackay assembled a unified faculty, contributed his own scholarly output, raised funds, constructed and acquired new buildings, added new lands, and formed a seminary that was an authentic Christian Community. Again in the words of Gehman, "In intellectual prestige and leadership Dr. Mackay is in the same rank as the presidents of the leading universities of our land."[1] The task was arduous, requiring a steady, long-term strategy and effort. From this base the influence of Mackay and the seminary radiated in numerous directions nationally and internationally.

Relations with Princeton Seminary before 1936

While Mackay was working in the mission field of Latin America during the 1920s, in North America two competing theological forces contended within the Presbyterian denomination. One group favored older dogmatic formulations of the faith while the other favored a more inclusive church, less rigid in its stated beliefs. These differences were crystallized in several events. A sermon titled "Shall the Fundamentalists Win?" delivered at First Presbyterian Church of New York City in 1922 by the American Baptist

234 The Hand and the Road

champion of liberal Christianity Harry Emerson Fosdick, set off an attempt to require conformity to the Westminster Confession for those preaching in Presbyterian churches. The next year, emerging leader J. Gresham Machen, assistant professor of New Testament at Princeton Seminary, published a strong, well-written defense of orthodox Protestantism titled *Christianity and Liberalism*. When more than one hundred liberal leaders of the church signed the "Auburn Affirmation," the 1924 General Assembly of the Presbyterian Church attempted to censure them, but, even after several years of study, nothing was done.[2]

Mackay became acquainted with the controversy through contacts he maintained with President Ross Stevenson, who during the 1920s favored a more inclusive approach to church membership. In June 1925 Stevenson wrote to Mackay inviting him to give a course of five mission lectures on the campus at Princeton Seminary sometime during the next year or two. In previous years Mackay's friend Webster Browning and Augustus Reischauer had given those lectures. Mackay responded positively, telling Stevenson of his new opportunity with the YMCA and of his expectation that within the next couple of years he would be back in North America, enabling him to deliver the lectures.[3] But the plan did not go smoothly. The following March Stevenson wrote Mackay, advising him of a difficulty. In order for the faculty to issue a unanimous invitation to give the lectures, Mackay would have to provide assurances that he was still a "thorough-going Calvinist" and had not gone over to the "modernists."[4]

Mackay responded with intensity to this challenge to his orthodoxy, and his passionate response shows him as a formidable debater and theologian.

> Your letter of March 26 was a great surprise to me. I had no idea that I had come to figure as a "Modernist," and still less can I imagine with what authority it has been alleged that I am one. It occurs to me, however, that the Scottish informant of the professor to whom you refer in your letter identified the Young Men's Christian Association, to which I now officially belong, with Modernism; the implication being that incorporation into an organization some of whose members are Modernist proved one to be so too. If that was not what he meant, said informant showed himself a very unworthy representative of Scottish Presbyterian tradition which has consistently refused to admit the validity of any accusation regarding the theological opinions of a minister based on mere hearsay or suspicion, and not substantiated by concrete evidence founded on public utterance. That I am not regarded in Scotland as having given expression by word of lip or pen to any opinions out of harmony with the doctrines I subscribed at my ordination the following fact should be convincing testimony. I have

received a letter dated March 3 from the Convener of the Foreign Missions Committee of the Free Church of Scotland in which he states that the Committee would like my permission to recommend to the General Assembly that I should be recognized "as a Minister without charge of the Free Church, but with a seat in the Presbytery of Inverness." Those who are acquainted with Scottish Church life know that the Free Church is one of the most conservative churches in the world.

I take it, however, that the main point at issue with regards to my fitness to give a course of lectures in Princeton Seminary is after all, not so much whether I have given expression to Modernist opinions as whether I sympathise with the modernist position. I want to say, without any mental reservation, that I am not a modernist, understanding by this term one who denies the reality of the supernatural, the Deity of Christ, the reality of His atonement, and His bodily Resurrection. I believe and teach these truths today with more intellectual passion than I have ever done in my life. If you go further and ask me, as you in fact do, whether I am a "thoroughgoing Calvinist" I must ask what precisely is implied by this phrase? Who is the arbiter of its connotation? What is its relation to the Declaratory Acts of Scottish and American Presbyterianism? Does it mean agreement with the main outlines of the Calvinistic System, or agreement with every statement and form of expression in the Confession of Faith? I am not ashamed to call myself a Calvinist, but wherever and whenever I find that the dogmatic symbols of Calvinism are not in accord with Holy Scripture, with demonstrable truth and the witness of God's spirit in my experience I reserve to myself the right of dissenting from and repudiating that phrase. I covet but one absolute loyalty, loyalty to God and Truth.

If the Faculty considers that I am not unfit to give a course of missionary lectures in the Seminary it will give me the greatest pleasure to accede to your original request. If, perchance, I am considered unworthy of that responsibility I shall feel no bitterness in my heart, but pass sadly onwards to other open doors. In any case, I should appreciate an early reply regarding the Faculty's decision in order to be able to plan my programme well in advance.

Thanking you and Dr. Erdman very sincerely for your kindly interest in me personally and with kindest regards to all the other members of the Faculty.

I remain, Yours very sincerely.[5]

In his response to Mackay's protest, Stevenson explained that during the previous summer Dr. Wilson was in Scotland where a Free Church elder had shown him several letters that had pleased the elder and had been written by Mackay. Wilson believed that Mackay would be disqualified from speaking at the seminary due to the part he had played in the Montevideo Conference.

Princeton Seminary Professor
Charles R. Erdman.

Stevenson went on in the letter to explain the situation at Princeton where "a kind of censorship has been established." Stevenson held Dr. Machen largely responsible for the "spirit of suspicion and distrust."[6]

Mackay was not interested in entering the controversy. He wrote Stevenson that he would rather defer giving lectures at Princeton, preferring that any formal invitation be unanimous. In the meantime, he wrote, his ambition was "to prepare books in Spanish on different aspects of Christian Thought in the interests of the Kingdom here. I am more interested, that is to say, for the present, in speaking to South America, than about it."[7] Later Mackay learned that a story circulated by John Ritchie while he had been in Scotland was likely the source of the charges of modernism against him.[8] Six and a half years after the original invitation, Mackay did present the mission lectures at Princeton January 25–29, 1932.[9]

Mackay had opportunities to return to the seminary during the turbulent 1920s as a professor. In 1926 Stevenson wrote to Mackay that Dr. Machen was largely responsible for a growing spirit of suspicion and distrust at the seminary. The "reactionary party" had removed Dr. Erdman as student advisor, opposed his candidacy for moderator of the church, and attempted to bring Dr. Macartney, who had been agitating the church for three years, from Philadelphia to Princeton Seminary. When Erdman and Rev. William Oxley Thompson were elected moderator in successive years, the "reactionary party" suffered strong defeats. Although Machen was elected to succeed Dr. Greene as professor of apologetics and Christian ethics, Stevenson opposed "his election in the board of Directors mainly on the ground of his antagonism to the Church, more particularly the boards and agencies of the Church." Machen's election had to be referred to the General Assembly for confirmation, and because of the strong opposition to his election as professor, the Committee on Theological Seminaries decided to send a committee of visitation to Princeton to investigate the situation further. Meanwhile Machen's professorship was held in abeyance. Stevenson anticipated a strong, thorough committee investigation and hoped the "narrow, exclusive and at times un-Christian spirit may be rebuked and that the Seminary may be brought out into a still larger place of influence and of service."[10]

The committee met with the faculty on November 23, 1926, and found significant differences of opinion about what the seminary's role and relationship with the Presbyterian Church should be. Stevenson framed the issue as whether the seminary should swing to a position emphasizing Bible-school, premillennial-secession fundamentalism. Historically and legally the seminary represented the whole church.

The visitation and inspection committee concluded that management by two boards, one for property and one for education, was inefficient and could produce friction and that the seminary charter needed to be strengthened to ensure the General Assembly's control of the seminary's property. The committee reported this to the General Assembly of 1927, and all faculty appointments, including Machen's, continued in abeyance pending these reorganizations. Machen's appointment to the chair of apologetics was significant to his professional advancement. At the time Machen taught at Princeton, only one full professor served in each department. Park Armstrong, the New Testament professor, was only five or six years older than Machen. Because of their proximity in age, it was unlikely that Machen would succeed him as professor of New Testament.

Joining Dr. Stevenson's assessment of Machen was Princeton University professor Henry van Dyke, a former moderator of the General Assembly, pastor of Brick Presbyterian Church, and formerly Woodrow Wilson's ambassador to the Netherlands. In 1923 when Machen was a supply minister at the First Presbyterian Church, Princeton, van Dyke walked out of the church to publicly protest Machen's sermon. Van Dyke wrote the session to say he had no interest "in listening to such a dismal, bilious travesty of the Gospel. Until he is done, count me out, and give up my pew in the church. We want to worship Christ our Saviour."[11] The men being attacked by Machen were van Dyke's friends and were well known for their exemplary Christian lives.

When in 1928 Machen withdrew his name from candidacy for the chair, Stevenson suggested to Mackay that he would be the "ideal man" for the "important post."[12] Mackay, who had just declined a secretaryship with the Presbyterian Board of Foreign Missions, also declined this offer because he believed his special calling was to Latin America.[13] When the institutional crisis became more acute for Princeton the following September, Stevenson and Erdman jointly telegraphed a renewed "plea" for Mackay to take the full professorship, suggesting the chair of apologetics could be a base for his mission work.[14] Again Mackay gently declined.

The theological conflict reached the breaking point when the General Assembly of 1929, after deferring for a year, settled the Princeton issue by decisively adopting the majority report favoring reorganization. As a commissioner at the assembly Machen argued that the reorganization would remove the seminary's evangelical foundations. When the governance structure of Princeton Seminary was reorganized, a group of professors left to found Westminster Seminary near Philadelphia.[15] Westminster opened its doors in September 1929 with a faculty of eight and a student body of fifty-two. In his address at the opening of Westminster Seminary on September 25 in Witherspoon Hall Machen said, "Though Princeton Seminary is dead, the noble tradition of Princeton Seminary is alive. Westminster Seminary will endeavor by God's grace to continue that tradition unimpaired."[16] Two other new church entities were also formed: the Independent Board of Presbyterian Foreign Missions and the Presbyterian Church of America.

An unsent paragraph from a draft of Mackay's letter to Stevenson in 1926 eloquently and concisely summed up his insights into the conflict between fundamentalism and modernism:

> I have but one thing to add to make my position absolutely clear. As I am not a Modernist, neither am I a Fundamentalist. Modernism I reject because of its unchristian hypothesis regarding God; Fundamentalism because of its unchristian attitude towards men. Modernism is a disease of the mind; Fundamentalism a disease of the heart. Modernism betrays the content of Christianity; Fundamentalism betrays its Spirit. The future of Christianity lies, I believe, with neither one band nor the other but with those who are resolved at whatever cost to seek the Truth and hold it in love, who have sufficient faith in the living God to believe that truth loyally sought will be discovered and that truth loyally proclaimed will be victorious. In this faith I endeavour to live and serve my God.[17]

The deep doctrinal and spiritual fissures in the denomination were clear at the 1935 General Assembly when leaders brushed off a request to go on record that the assembly actually believed the Apostles' Creed after reciting it![18] The Creed was not enforced. Some may have thought back to a period of Calvinist fragmentation and to Matthew Arnold's remark that "Presbyterianism is born to division as the sparks fly upward."[19]

With the benefit of a half-century's hindsight, one of the Westminster participants in the schism expressed regret based on several grounds. Edwin Rian, a vigorous supporter of the Westminster movement and a friend of Machen's, had a change of heart and was reordained in the denomination that he had left. Those who withdrew, he wrote, "were fighting [against] Christians, and not the world, the flesh, and the devil"; their action was "to elevate certain convictions and declare them to be essential to a church" although the views were "non-essential doctrines of the Christian church." In addition, he wrote, "there is a self-righteousness and an intolerance in the attitude of withdrawal," and the group "had a closed system of doctrine." Mackay's success as a reconciler is evident in Rian's conclusion that "Mackay turned out to be a great friend."[20]

Mackay's Presidency Begins

After the schism Princeton Seminary seemed to be a "sick institution" in a period of "theological rigidity."[21] A group of faculty members had seceded to start a new seminary, and their leader, J. Gresham Machen, had proclaimed that Princeton was dead. A new missionary board had begun to compete with the Presbyterian Board of Foreign Missions led by Robert E. Speer. The missionary effort itself had been weakened by the *Laymen's Inquiry* and challenged by contact with non-Christian religions. Theological writers were aware of the crisis of the 1930s but seemed unable to act.[22] Wilhelm Pauck, a church historian, described the elements of the crisis. The "cry for guidance . . . can be provided only by new thought," he wrote.[23] Francis Miller asked, "Can the Protestant churches survive as reliable witnesses to Christian Faith?"[24] Mackay's calling was to offer new thought, to inspire others to follow a new direction in theology, and to rebuild a community at Princeton Seminary.

For several years Mackay had served as a Board Secretary for South America and Africa and was based in New York at the offices of the Presbyterian Board of Foreign Missions. Robert E. Speer had anticipated that Mackay would succeed him on his own retirement in the crucial and highly visible position as leader of the Board. Furthermore, Mackay believed that his own role in the church was to be directly connected with the missionary enterprise. So he turned down the first request that came to him to become president of Princeton Seminary.[25] The committee considering the presidency of Princeton Seminary continued its work, meeting again in Philadelphia on March 30, 1936. In its deliberations it considered a letter from Dr. J. W. Langdale, book editor of Abingdon Press. Langdale was certain that "Christian advance in the near future is conditioned by our ability to outthink secularism. I esteem John Mackay to be our chief hope as the leader of thought in American Protestantism in the next twenty-five years . . . [for] a creative Christian thinker is a rare gift of God."[26] After further discussion the committee decided to ask Mackay again to accept the position. Dr. Lewis Seymour Mudge was directed to meet with Mackay to inform him that his name would be presented to the Board at its May meeting with the unanimous recommendation of the committee that he succeed Dr. Stevenson as president of Princeton Seminary.

When the second invitation came, Mackay pondered whether to take the position. If he accepted the offer, he thought, he would be deprived of the "privilege" and "responsibility of being in the missionary enterprise where . . . [he] had been for sixteen years."[27] The Methodist Mission Board headquarters was located nearby the Presbyterian headquarters on Fifth Avenue, and one day Mackay confided to a friend working there that he had received the offer. The Methodist asked, "John, don't you know that a seminary campus can be a mission field?" Looking at the opportunity in that light, Mackay realized that a seminary was a place to become interested "not in ideas or organizations, but in people, in students."[28] He accepted the offer, and at the trustees meeting in May 1936, Mackay was elected the new seminary president.[29] At the June meeting of the Presbytery of Morris and Orange, Mackay carefully followed the formalities of Presbyterian order by "requesting permission to retire from his secretaryship with the Board of Foreign Missions in New York, and to answer the call to serve as President of the theological seminary at Princeton."[30]

The Mackay family moved from Summit, New Jersey, in 1936 to take up residence in Princeton at "Springdale," the Gothic revival house at 86 Mercer Street, the official private residence of the president of Princeton Theological Seminary. Designed by John Notman, the house had been built on Springdale Farm in 1851 for Richard Stockton, the son of Robert F. Stockton. During the Mackay years at Princeton Seminary, Mrs. Mackay made the house a home. Acting on countless occasions as hostess to entertain students, faculty, and visitors, she personally planned receptions, held regular Sunday afternoon teas for students, and showed a Christian graciousness, hospitality, and charm that is rarely seen.

When an institution takes on new leadership, an institutional officer customarily charges the new leader with the agenda to be carried out. In February, on behalf of the Board of Trustees, Robert E. Speer delivered the "Charge to the President," formally and publically focusing his presidency on the spiritual tasks ahead. In a fourfold spiritual charge, Speer called on Mackay to train the students to think "firmly and courageously," to make the seminary environment a place of "evangelical piety" uniting "doctrine and experience," to continue the seminary as "a fountain of missionaries who will go to the ends of the earth," and preserve the tradition of Christian temper of the gentlemen of Princeton where "consideration and considerateness" are still combined. Finally, Speer added a material task to the agenda, the "small matter" of the revival of the *Princeton Review*.[31]

Portraits of Jane and John Mackay, 1936.

His new position at Princeton Seminary also provided Mackay a visible platform from which to address the larger population and culture of
the United States, and he wasted little time in doing so. Mackay presented
his inaugural address, titled "The Restoration of Theology," in the Gothic
Princeton University chapel on February 2, 1937, and the *New York Times*
reported the event.[32] "The time has come and is long overdue," Mackay told
his audience, "when the presuppositions of culture must give way to theology. We are living in a time when only the emergence and dominance of a
great theology will produce a great philosophy on the one hand and a great
religion on the other." The powerful cultural forces of the times, he pointed
out, were theologies rather than philosophies: "The thesis which I want to
develop on this occasion is that our major intellectual need is theology, theology that brings to a focus the rays of light that streamed from above in Jesus
Christ along the line of the vertical and continue to come to us through Him,
and that transmits these rays as undimmed as possible to every sphere of life
and thought across the wide plane of the horizontal."[33]

Mackay's voice filled the void that Pauck, Miller, and others had also
identified. The address was an eloquent call to restore theology, the queen of
sciences, to its rightful place in the life of the church and in academic circles.
A *New York Times* editorial recognized "evidence that a great thinker has

come . . . into . . . intellectual theological leadership. . . . He gives promise of being one who will speak with authoritative voice to youth and to help set them on the 'luminous road' toward a new cultural era."[34] Later in February Mackay's ideas reached a broad audience when an article about him and his views appeared in the *New York Times Magazine*.[35] In the article Mackay discerned the signs of the times: "Our time is a time between the times, a time of formlessness between an age that is dying and one that is still unborn. But it is nevertheless God's time."[36]

When the school year began at the Autumn Alumni Conference, Mackay gave the first address, a challenging call titled "Concerning Man and His Remaking."[37] By the end of the first year he had charted a new course for the seminary both in the *Seminary Bulletin* and in *The Presbyterian*, a denominational publication designed to reach a broader audience.[38] The seminary must "prepare heralds of the gospel and shepherds of souls." In addition, for Princeton the task was "to match in the sphere of evangelical learning the studies offered by influential graduate colleges in the several branches of secular culture," and to have a "place of decisive leadership in the theological world." What is most needed at the time, he added, was "confessional theology . . . hammered out within the fellowship of the Church and [that] becomes an instrument of the Church Militant at a time when new rivals challenge her claims."[39] At the end of his first year in office Mackay was awarded an honorary Doctor of Divinity degree from Princeton University.[40]

The Faculty and Program

During the economic depression the faculty of Princeton had been depleted by the secession of some key members, but a strong core remained.[41] Mackay realized "that theologically speaking we are in a very real missionary situation at the present moment, so far as our seminary is concerned, and every step that we take must be taken with the same combination of caution and decision that is always necessary on the mission field."[42] He moved firmly and steadily to fill the vacuum of Christian teaching and understanding in North America locally and nationally. For Mackay Protestant Christianity was a matter of both the heart and the mind, and he emphasized these themes as he worked to break the spell of modernism and to encourage devotion to the person of Christ at the individual and corporate levels.

Mackay's key to shifting the focus of academic theology and responding to modernism was the person of Professor Emil Brunner of Switzerland. Mackay had met Brunner in Europe in 1930, and began to discuss with him a move to Princeton at Oxford in 1937, but it took all of Mackay's persuasive ability to convince Brunner to consider leaving Europe to teach in North America.[43] Brunner, with Karl Barth and Karl Heim, was one of the three great continental theologians. Mackay's twin emphasis to the mind was his focus on the heart, the personal relationship of the individual soul with Jesus Christ. This second essential focus on personal religion, the authentic experience of Christ's love, was a return to the Reformation emphasis.[44] Building on the conservative core like Speer, Erdman, and Frederick Loetscher, who remained devoted to Princeton, Mackay gradually replaced faculty members as they retired or died and developed a new faculty that shared a spiritual affinity and unity through their relationship to Christ.

Mackay's efforts to attract Brunner to Princeton required a high level of diplomatic skill and finesse, in part because of the need to subscribe to a confession of faith. In October of 1937 Mackay sent Brunner a copy of the Constitution of the Church, a formula, and requests for certain clarifications of his position. Along with them came an article written by Charles Hodge on the meaning of adopting the Confession of Faith.[45] Brunner was not inclined to respond to clarifications about his beliefs before receiving an offer since to do so would make him a job applicant rather than the recipient of a call from the seminary.[46] Like Mackay on the mission field, Brunner believed that God had placed him in his current task, and only an imperative call could cause him to move. After studying the materials Brunner told Mackay that

> he had no difficulty with either [i.e., the Confession of Faith, chapter 1 in particular, and Princeton's Formula of Subscription] when they were interpreted in terms of the statement of Dr. Charles Hodge regarding the meaning of subscription to the Confession of Faith—namely, that one was committed to the system of doctrine contained therein. [Brunner] found himself in greater harmony [with the Confession of Faith and Form of Government] than any other similar statements that he knew.[47]

Although Brunner ultimately declined a permanent position in Princeton, his role and influence during the academic year 1938–1939 helped Mackay to redefine the direction of Princeton Seminary.[48] Brunner's presence on campus stimulated "eager interest in theological discussion" and a "more constant use of the library" among the students.[49] Brunner's presence contributed to

> healthy theological discussion, carried on in the finest Christian spirit, [which] overflowed the bounds of the classrooms, invading the dormitories and clubs. It was not that we accepted all that Dr. Brunner said by any means. In several matters we differed from him, Faculty and students alike.

But he stirred the campus in a creative way by his effort to refocus and restate the everlasting verities."[50]

The return of a higher percentage of Presbyterian students to Princeton Seminary than had attended during prior years showed that the seminary "belongs more to the Presbyterian Church and enjoys the confidence of the Presbyterian Church to a greater extent than it has done for very many decades."[51] Mackay's influence on the Presbyterian Church was beginning to take hold.

Brunner's residence in the United States jolted the Presbyterian establishment, sparking controversy. Mackay introduced him to the broader church in an article in *The Presbyterian* in February 1938.[52] A difference of opinion on Brunner's thought led to a "constructive and highminded debate" between Dr. Barnhouse and Mackay that appeared in *The Presbyterian*.[53] Debate and discussion appeared also in *Christianity Today*,[54] which reprinted an article critical of Mackay that said, "Today Princeton is virtually a bulwark of dialectical theology," and called Mackay a "vigorous propagandist of this new faith."[55] By February 1939 Brunner had decided to return to Switzerland because of the changed situation in Europe and also because the "experiment" in North America presented formidable difficulties and the "forces of resistance were still so great that a somewhat slower process must be taken into consideration." He "earnestly hoped that Princeton would have the courage to move on" and persist in the new direction.[56]

Mackay's efforts to assemble a distinctive and united faculty continued gradually and steadily, and by the end of Mackay's tenure Dr. Henry Gehman was the only faculty member that he had not hired. Those selected combined both distinguished scholarly and pastoral ability. Several came from foreign countries, providing a diversity of spiritual and academic backgrounds. The group, however, formed a deep and real Christian community joined in a unity of purpose.

Bringing together a new faculty was not a simple task, and it was sometimes necessary to overcome controversy. In September 1937 Elmer G. Homrighausen had been appointed to a position as professor of religious education. A staff correspondent of the *Christian Century*, Homrighausen was also a "successful pastor [and] able theological writer,"[57] but because General Assembly approval was needed, the Standing Committee on Theological Seminaries held a hearing to determine his fitness for service. Mackay and William Pugh spoke on his behalf against concerns presented to the committee by Clarence E. Macartney and Samuel G. Craig. The committee voted to take no action, and the seminary trustees withdrew Homrighausen's name from consideration, intending to resubmit his name the following year at the General Assembly. To strengthen his position, Homrighausen moved to Princeton, wrote an article for *Christianity Today* and was expected to publish another book.[58] At the following General Assembly in 1939, after much of the controversy had diminished, Homrighausen's name was resubmitted and approved.[59]

Otto Piper began lecturing at the seminary in the fall of 1937 with Homrighausen. Born in Thuringia in November 1891, he had studied before the war in Germany and Paris. He was an initiator of the prewar Youth Movement in Germany before entering the army in 1914. As a result of a wound that Piper received in service in World War I, he was blinded in one eye and read with a magnifying glass. After the war he studied further and took a degree at Göttingen. In 1929 he was appointed to the Chair of Systematic Theology in the University of Münster, succeeding Karl Barth. As the result of a series of lectures in 1933 on "State and Church," Piper was dismissed from his chair at the university and prohibited from holding a position in Germany. Thereupon, he moved to Great Britain, where he taught in a Quaker college in Birmingham and at universities in Wales. Piper served on the same committee with Mackay at the Oxford Conference, and Mackay brought him as a guest professor to Princeton Seminary.[60]

Along with Mackay, Joseph Hromádka was a powerful spiritual presence on the campus. In 1939 Czechoslovakia was occupied by the Nazis, and Professor Hromádka and family travelled by way of Geneva and Paris to the United States. Visser 't Hooft greatly assisted their journey from Geneva. The family arrived and settled in Princeton, and Professor Hromádka taught at Princeton Seminary for eight years as guest professor in the Stuart Chair of Apologetics and Christian Ethics. In his first year Hromádka taught a course on "Church and State." From the year 1940 to 1941 until his return to Europe in 1947, he offered a course in "Theology of Crisis,"[61] with a balanced perspective between fundamentalism and more liberal theology. Hromádka had a pastor's heart, lectured enthusiastically, and wanted his students to grasp the basic problem of theology and move beyond the practical outlook of American thinking. When a student at a conservative seminary asked, "what Barth would have chosen if given a choice between fundamentalism and modernism, Hromádka replied: 'He would blow them both up!'"[62] In his theology he emphasized God's "proclamation of sovereignty over all historical and social systems"[63] and also that the "gospel is the 'good news' . . . fundamentally, a positive message, an offer and an invitation."[64]

The composition of the seminary faculty embodied the worldwide nature of the universal church. Several other examples illustrate the geographical diversity and the academic quality of the faculty of the seminary at that period. Two

Senior Faculty of Princeton Theological Seminary, c. 1945 (L to R.: J. Christy Wilson, Howard Kuist, Henry Gehman, Frederick Loetscher, John Mackay, Emile Cailliet, Otto Piper, Andrew Blackwood, Joseph Hromádka).

Frenchmen, Georges Barrois and Emile Cailliet, were added to the faculty. The education and career of Barrois followed a rather complex path from his confirmation in 1909 by Cardinal Luçon, archbishop of Reims. Led to take holy orders, he entered the Dominican Order, whose theological college was in Belgium. While in military service he was sent to Syria, at his request. After graduation in 1925, Barrois took further studies in the French Biblical and Archaeological School in Jerusalem, where one of his leaders was Father Lagrange, the founder of the school and the master of modern Catholic exegesis. In 1934 Barrois was called back to Belgium as professor of Old Testament literature and biblical archaeology in the Dominican College, which was shortly moved to Paris after the French government relaxed its laws against religious congregations. In 1940 he left for a position as visiting professor in the Department of Egyptian and Semitic Languages and Literatures at Catholic University of America in Washington, DC. There he became a Protestant and was received as a member of the Presbytery of Washington. He later obtained a doctor's degree from Princeton Theological Seminary, and became an assistant professor of biblical literature and theology at the seminary in the fall of 1947.[65]

Emile Cailliet, Stuart Professor of Christian Philosophy, was born and educated in France, and served and was wounded in World War I. He held both PhD and ThD degrees. In 1932 he had been elected as a National Fellow of the French Academy of Sciences. A dedicated layman, he was an eminent authority on Blaise Pascal.[66]

Edward J. Jurji, a scholar of world religions, became professor of Islamics and comparative religion. Born in Lebanon where he had been a schoolmate of philosopher and diplomat Charles Malik, Jurji was educated at the American University in Beirut, Princeton University, and Princeton Theological Seminary, and before joining the faculty of the seminary was a member of the Institute for Advanced Study at Princeton. From 1950 to 1980 Jurji also served as a pastor of a Syrian Church in Brooklyn, to which he traveled each Sunday with his wife. When he told the congregation that they should have an English-speaking pastor, the congregation persuaded him to lead the church.[67]

George Hendry, a Scot, arrived in Princeton in 1949 and taught theology. He had studied classics in Aberdeen with first-class honors in 1924 and divinity in Edinburgh, receiving a BD with distinction in systematic theology. Later he studied in Tübingen and Berlin. A very able scholar, Hendry produced works titled *God the Creator*, *The Gospel of the Incarnation*, and *The Holy Spirit in Christian Theology*.[68]

Lefferts A. Loetscher, professor of church history; Charles T. Fritsch, professor of Old Testament; and Bruce M. Metzger, professor of New Testament, each from the United States, balanced the geographical composition of the faculty. Loetscher, author of *The Broadening Church*, focused on American church history and polity. Fritsch's scholarship included a commentary on the book of Genesis and a study published as the *Qumran Community: Its History and Scrolls*. Metzger, the first American member of the European-based Studiorum Novi Testament Societas (SNTS), led work in the fields of New Testament studies, textual criticism, and biblical translation.[69] Under music director David Hugh Jones, the traveling choir steadily expanded the seminary's evangelistic outreach.

Administratively, Mackay placed the seminary on a sound financial footing through his own fund-raising efforts and by assembling a dedicated and capable board of trustees. Mackay's initial fund-raising campaign for a student center and to modernize buildings began in 1937.[70] The Board also expanded. Ray Vance, a dedicated layman, had been a trustee of the seminary for some years. Vance invited John Templeton, who worked with him at the same firm, to a meeting of trustees and told Templeton that Mackay had invited him to join the Board. Templeton accepted and served on the Board for forty-two years, including two six-year terms as chairman. Since Templeton and Vance considered their counsel to the seminary as part of their charitable work, they never billed the seminary for investment advice. At each meeting Templeton presented investment suggestions, and the investment committee of Vance, Templeton, Harry Kuch, John Lenen, and others voted on how to invest the funds.[71]

Mackay also began a teaching-fellow program by which young instructors were given an opportunity to teach at Princeton Seminary, then to remain or move on to other institutions. Mackay believed that there was a need not only to train preachers and pastors but also to develop and recruit able students as teachers in theology and other disciplines. In 1944 the School of Christian Education was started, which opened the door for women to study under the same professors as did the future clergy.

With a strong faculty Mackay was able to improve substantially the relationship of the seminary with its local neighbor, Princeton University, a separate institution. A friend of President Harold Dodds, Mackay maintained a connection with Princeton University's philosophy department, when in 1941 he was nominated by professors and elected by trustees to the Princeton University Advisory Council of Philosophy.[72] Mackay remained on the council, where he served with Laurance S. Rockefeller and others following his retirement from Princeton Seminary in 1959.[73]

Mackay introduced a doctoral studies program: the first ThD degree in the history of the seminary was granted in 1944 in the field of Old Testament under Henry Snyder Gehman. The campus was expanded through the purchase of property and buildings from the Hun School, a local secondary

John A. Mackay and Robert E. Speer at the 1947 Institute of Theology, Princeton Theological Seminary.

Evangelist Billy Graham with John Mackay in front of Princeton Seminary Chapel, 1953.

school, and this expansion enabled a three-year program leading to the master of religious education degree to be introduced in 1944 as the School of Christian Education.

The Institute of Theology was established to meet the clergy's need for continuing education. Mackay believed conferences alone were no longer sufficient because the "contemporary situation in the Church and in the world is so baffling" and many were "confused and disheartened."[74] The Princeton Institute of Theology was set for July 5–15, 1943, to combine the intellectual atmosphere of a school with the inspirational aspects of a conference for Christian workers. Within several years the Institute of Theology was well established, and for July 1947 plans were made to expand it.[75] It proved to be a strong asset of the seminary and the Presbyterian Church over the years.

Mackay believed that within its mission as a seminary, it should provide a platform for notable speakers who had a message regardless of their particular point of view. Albert Einstein, for example, addressed Princeton Seminary in May 1939.[76] In the 1951–1952 academic year campus speakers ranged from Rudolf Bultmann in November to Martin Niemöller in March.[77] Billy Graham visited Princeton Seminary in February 1953 and stayed with the Mackays at Springdale. Mackay answered one Graham critic by saying, "There are unevangelized areas in all our lives." He later defended his fellow evangelist from unwarranted criticism in writing a few years later.[78] Mackay's

John A. Mackay with his neighbor, Albert Einstein, and Einstein's colleague, c. 1938.

friend Visser 't Hooft gave the commencement address in 1958.[79] Diplomats John Foster Dulles and George F. Kennan also spoke at Princeton Seminary during Mackay's tenure.[80]

Mackay exerted significant leadership nationally in the realm of theological education. The Presbyterian General Assembly directed the formation of a Council on Theological Education, which was organized in Philadelphia on October 10, 1943. From 1943 to 1946 Mackay was its first president, working hard to enhance the status of theological education.[81] The goals of the council were to "achieve solidarity among the seminaries of the Presbyterian Church, . . . to make Presbyterian seminaries second to none in educational efficiency, . . . to awaken a sense of ministerial vocation among the youth of the Presbyterian Church, . . . and to make theology missionary again."[82] On the same subject Mackay wrote elsewhere that the role of the seminary was threefold: "to conserve and transmit the full Christian heritage . . . train pastors and teachers and such other full-time servants of the Church as the Church needs for the fulfillment of its spiritual task . . . and do equal justice to the vertical and horizontal reference in all theological education" balancing man and revelation.[83]

In addition to a clear understanding of what theology was, Mackay also advocated high standards for Christian ministers, excluding from the ministry those plagued by doubts. He defined theology as "an intellectual effort to interpret the meaning and apply the implications of God's self-disclosure of himself in history," adding, "there is absolutely no place in a theological sem-inary for a teacher, or in the Christian church for the graduate of a theological seminary, who has any real doubt about the truth and efficacy of the Christian gospel."[84] As a Presbyterian seminary the message of Princeton emphasized the insights derived through scriptural revelation and treated Scripture as the word of God.[85] Failing to do so would have created "a rational bourgeois religion" rather than a religion of supernatural vitality.[86]

His address for the American Association of Theological Schools, which he served as president from 1948 to 1950, was titled "Finality of Theologi-cal Education."[87] He understood the term "finality" in two ways: first, with reference to knowledge as "the crown and central light of all education," and, second, with reference to service, to prepare "servants of God . . . who shall give practical expression in word and in deed to the revelation of God."[88] The address thoroughly developed both these themes. For the goals of a seminary to be accomplished, however, "the community of teachers and students in a theological seminary must be in the fullest sense a Christian community. If a school of theology does not succeed in becoming a Christian community, it will not succeed in the fulfillment of its essential functions."[89]

Scholarly Work at Princeton

During the decade 1940–1950 Mackay also maintained his literary out-put. The first three books he published at the seminary formed in a "certain sense . . . an undesigned trilogy. In *A Preface to Christian Theology*," wrote Mackay, "I tried to say: Leave the Balcony for the Road. *Heritage and Des-tiny* sought to embody the thought: The Road to Tomorrow leads through Yesterday. The burden of . . . [*Christianity on the Frontier*] might be stated . . . : Take the Road to the Frontier."[90]

A Preface to Christian Theology (1942)[91] was published while the Neth-erlands was invaded and France fell to the Nazis. Mackay's intent for the work, described in the author's preface, was not a "manual of theological ideas . . . but a foreword to theological discussion, a glimpse at the borderland between theology and religion."[92] The book brought conservatives and liber-als together based on the rediscovery of the Bible's view of God's sovereign relation to humanity and the world. Henry Sloane Coffin recognized it as the work of a "passionate and robust thinker."[93] The book was not for "a sophis-ticated skeptic seeking . . . apologetics or the advanced scholar [but brings] to the average minister and thoughtful layman . . . simply and beautifully, the best . . . in the attitude and in the insight of a new age."[94] It presented thought on social ethics and the secular order, quoting broadly from Catholic writers like Karl Adam and Jacques Maritain to Protestants such as Woolman and Rutherford. In the context of spiritual freedom, Mackay discussed the Grand Inquisitor story from *The Brothers Karamazov*. In retrospect, Brevard Childs noted that the book "introduced a whole new catalog of virtually new names to the American theological scene."[95] These included Berdyaev, Dostoyevsky, and Pascal. The influence of Kierkegaard's thought is also apparent.

In the second book, *Heritage and Destiny* (1943), a collection of essays,[96] Mackay's thesis was that "there is thus but one answer to the appeal of the Axis powers to national heritage. It is the Judaeo-Christian revelation contained in the Bible and worked out by men and women in terms of living experience."[97] Mackay developed the contrast of our existence as forward-looking "chauffeurs, whose passion has been movement and power and speed," and the "boatman [who] moves intelligently forward by looking backward."[98] In the book he interpreted the revolution and change in light of culture and religion, and paid tribute in the final chapter, "God and the Nation," to the religious heritage of the United States.

Finally, in the collection of essays titled *Christianity on the Frontier* (1950),[99] Mackay's theme is that the church and individual Christians should live on the "frontier" of life. He merged the European and the American understanding of the term "frontier" as a place of tension and the threshold of unoccupied territory, to be "possessed in the name of Christ."[100]

In the two-week vacation at the end of 1950, Mackay worked hard on a chapter for a symposium on "Protestant Thought in the Twentieth Century, Whence and Whither."[101] To write the chapter Mackay reviewed the basic missionary literature from the beginning of the century, especially the records of the IMC world gatherings, and gave special attention to the *Laymen's Inquiry* and Kraemer's *The Christian Message in a Non-Christian World*. Mackay intended "to offer a critique of Protestant, especially missionary, thought in relation to the Non-Christian world during this first half century."[102] His article noted that in the 1870s James Clement Moffat of Princeton Seminary produced the early paper on comparative religions.

In 1942, another important literary and evangelistic project was initiated: the publication of the *Westminster Study Edition of the Holy Bible* (1948). The editors worked with the following belief, which was stated in the preface: "There is no growth in the knowledge of God and no progress in the Christian life without the constant study and restudy of the Holy Scriptures."[103] In this edition the prose sections of the Authorized Version of the Bible were set in paragraphs and the poetic sections as verse. It also contained a concordance, historical maps, and introductory essays providing a clear understanding of

John Mackay writing at his desk in the president's office at Princeton Seminary.

the meaning and message of the Bible, its history, and its interpretation.[104] Mackay was chairman of the project and contributed the preface and a section called "God Has Spoken."

This project was accompanied by the founding of *Theology Today*, a journal embodying Mackay's vision of seeking "to relate what had been revealed through the Scriptures to the needs and problems of the present day."[105] Creation of the periodical responded to Speer's presidential charge to Mackay in 1937 to revive the *Princeton Review* in a new form. Launching a journal during wartime required resourcefulness and ingenuity, and the journal began with a subscription list 50 percent larger than the target for the end of the first year. The initial editorial board of *Theology Today* included Robert E. Speer; Richard Niebuhr; J. Harvey Cotton, president of McCormick Theological Seminary; and John Sutherland Bonnell of the Fifth Avenue Presbyterian Church, New York. The four stated goals of *Theology Today* were (1) to restore theology as the supreme science to renew both religion and culture; (2) to study the central realities of the Christian faith and life, and to set forth their meaning in clear and appropriate language; (3) to explore anew the truths rediscovered by the Protestant Reformation, especially the Reformed tradition, and to show their relevancy to the contemporary problems of the Church and society; and (4) to provide an organ in which Christians from different spheres of intellectual activity "may combine their insights into the life of man in the light of God, with a view to interpreting our human situation and developing a Christian philosophy of life."[106] Mackay served as the editor for the first seven years of the journal, then as "other frontiers" called him, he became chairman of the editorial council in 1951.

From the beginning the practice was to focus each issue on aspects of a basic topic or to group together several related topics that constituted a core theme. The human situation from the perspective of the divine was the theme of the first issue; the first three issues digested three important works: *Romerbrief* of Karl Barth, *Nature and Destiny of Man* by Reinhold Niebuhr from his Gifford Lectures, and *Studies in History* by Toynbee. The first five volumes dealt thematically with the unity of the church through belief and commitment and the centripetal forces that were bringing individual churches together to form a unity. At the end of the first five years of its existence, four issues prepared the way for the World Council of Churches meeting in Amsterdam.[107] Mackay's editorial, "The End Is the Beginning," put the founding of the World Council into the context of church history.[108] By the end of 1952 *Theology Today* was "the most widely distributed religious quarterly in the world."[109] Many early articles have continuing interest for readers today.

In 1937 as a professor, Mackay introduced a first-year required course, "Ecumenics I," which he continued to teach until his retirement in 1959. Ecumenics was progressive and challenging; it was based on what Mackay later termed the "Ecumenical Quadrilateral" encompassing "(1) the history of the missionary movement; (2) non-Christian religions and the rivals of Christianity; (3) inter-church relationships within Christendom; and (4) emergent frontiers of thought and action to which the church should give special attention."[110] When, during 1953–1954 Mackay traveled to perform his moderatorial duties for the Presbyterian Church, Samuel H. Moffett, a missionary who served in Korea, taught the course as a visiting lecturer.[111]

Mackay's teaching skill challenged students to reach deeper for authentic Christian experience. One student related to Mackay how his life was changed from an idealist to a genuine friend of God through Mackay's course:

> I entered Princeton Seminary in the winter of 1944, having been discharged under good conditions from the Navy. My reasons for wishing to enter the Gospel ministry seemed good to me then. Having learned a little of what Godlessness does to a nation, or a man, I sincerely believed the Christian

faith had the answer, and I wished to identify myself with that as my life work. My first semester at Princeton brought me into your course on Ecumenics. . . . But it all came as an immense revelation to me as you held before us the Lordship of Jesus Christ. Here were concepts about Him, and about the world, which is held together in Him which had never entered my mind or heart before. As I continued to attend your classes, you brought me to the place to which you were led at noon at Rogart. With your witness and guidance I beheld Him truly for the first time, and my life was changed.[112]

Finally, Mackay's scholarly influence extended to two less conventional forms. First, his reputation as a Christian leader enabled him to provide helpful introductions or forewords for books by others, including by Bates, Cailliet, Hromádka, Barth, and Zwemer. These introductions amounted to a kind of imprimatur for lay readers. Second, Mackay's formal addresses to the students of the seminary community were highlights of the academic year. At the beginning of each academic year, students crowded the aisles and pews of the chapel to hear Mackay's inspirational convocation addresses, in which he often reported on new developments in the Christian world or aspects of the Christian life. One of these addresses articulated Mackay's core belief on Christian religious experience. Titled "Personal Religion," the address was delivered on September 22, 1943, and contrasted conventional religion with personal religion as "the most basic expression of Christian faith and life."[113] This idea was related to the idea of biblical theology: "The reality of biblical authority could not be proven, only experienced."[114] The convocation address delivered on September 27, 1949, "Basic Christianity," was also noteworthy.[115] These two addresses both reflect Mackay's original understanding of his task at Princeton Seminary as work on a mission field. The dozens of essays that Mackay contributed to *Theology Today* and the *Princeton Seminary Bulletin* during his tenure provide an enduring legacy.

Thus, as a man of letters and through his personal influence, Mackay put his own intellectual stamp on North American Protestantism during the 1940s. Influenced by his early training and education, his writing style appealed to both heart and mind, joining logic with passion and lyric. He often used epigrams and creative images in writings, sermons, and speeches to interpret and analyze the present moment. Examples of his imagery abound, including such expressions as "The Balcony and the Road," "Don Quixote and Robinson Crusoe," "The Road to Tomorrow Leads Through Yesterday," "The Church Must Live on the Frontier," "Ardour and Order," and "The Uplifted Cross of Christ and the Recumbent Buddha of Bangkok." In a speech in Brazil he described a materialist as a "frog in a puddle." His phrase "undesigned coincidences" is a fascinating example of Mackay's creative spiritual ability to describe a phenomenon of the Christian life: "By 'undesigned coincidences' I mean *happenings that occur which one had neither intended nor could have anticipated, but which, when they take place, enable a person to fulfill a commitment he undertook in obedience to what he considered to be God's Will*" [emphasis in original].[116] As Mackay once remarked, "If a man does not believe that God is actually in control of human affairs and at work in human life, he is unprepared to take advantage of undesigned coincidence."[117]

The Campus Expands

In November 1940 the seminary began a campaign for the construction of a student center building. When he described the campaign in 1941, Mackay used the campus center as a unifying theme for Presbyterians. He recognized that theological divisions had caused Presbyterians to shift their donations to support of nondenominational theological institutions, but he now called for a rallying back to Princeton Seminary. Mackay called on the church to support the seminary and used the building of the campus center as a symbol of that support.[118] After spring 1946, when the old gymnasium had been reconfigured as the new administration building,[119] the next project on the agenda was the campus center, a sign of unity providing a common dining room that would maintain the "spirit and comradeship engendered by the traditional clubs."[120]

Students still ate their meals at four older clubs, the Warfield, the Calvin, the Friar, and the Benham, but Mackay was not happy about the club system that had exclusive, undemocratic, and rowdy elements. For example, the so-called "less devout" members of the Benham Club enjoyed playing practical jokes on visiting guests who were not connected with the seminary. Members sometimes placed water in the concave surface of the wooden chairs of their guests and enjoyed the surprised reaction when the guests sat down to dinner. When construction started on the campus center, the students realized the days of the club system were numbered.

In October of 1952 the campus center was dedicated, and Mackay did not want the rowdiness of the Benham Club to persist into the new dining hall with wet napkins or water on the seats. He asked Ben Sheldon, then a student and later a missionary to Korea, to be the steward of the dining room to help enforce order for the common meals. All students now ate together at the same time in the new dining hall. It was one of Sheldon's jobs to close the dining room door at the appointed time, and latecomers were turned away. Table fellowship was an aspect of Mackay's effort to build a sense of community.

In June 1952 after the school year ended, Mackay wrote to a colleague linking the local construction projects to ecumenical efforts:

This has literally been a tremendous year . . . in which the local has absorbed me as I have not been absorbed for years. A great new building has been going up on the campus for the last fifteen months. Structural questions, added to arrangements to furnish and equip it and to organize its life when the building is finished and furnished, have taken up a great deal of time. Concomitantly I have been immersed in another building project of still larger dimensions, a library building to house half a million volumes with some classrooms incorporated into the new structure. . . . But, after all, unless the local is attended to and a firm base laid in individual institutions and denominations, neither the ecumenical ideal nor reality will prosper. So, I feel quite unashamed, looking forward to the time not far hence when we shall be in a position to play the part of hosts to ecumenical gatherings on this campus. Our Student Center building will be quite unique so far as Seminary facilities are concerned. There will be dining room facilities for 450, and an auditorium capable of seating 400, in addition to a number of small lounges and other room.[121]

Peter Emmons, Mackay's longtime friend, presided at the dedication of the campus center. Mackay addressed the gathering and stressed that "this house is designed to serve the household, the community that lives on this campus."[122] The dedication speech expressed Mackay's philosophy for the building, exemplified the heart of community that was being created, and offered a teaching moment:

But we must never make even this household an end in itself. Our Seminary family is now, and I trust will ever be, for Christ and His Church. It is always a temptation for a community whose members enjoy one another to be so enamoured of community and good fellowship that there is no beyond. It is fatal for institutional life, it is fatal for congregational life, it is fatal for the ecumenical movement, when unity and community become ends in themselves. We desire to cultivate our oneness, to get all we can out of each other's fellowship, to experience to the full every spiritual pleasure, both personal and collective. But let everything be a preparation for service, to serve Christ and His Church.[123]

Presenting a passage with extended imagery, and merging attributes of Bunyan's "Palace Beautiful" with it, Mackay saw the campus center as "Interpreter's House" in John Bunyan's allegory "where relations were perfect, where wayfarers rested for the night, where they achieved new insights into things spiritual, leaving it again for the road at the break of day."[124] He hoped that the center would provide comfort for the wayfarer and a place to know Christ better. He noted that "in the days of His flesh [The Pilgrim's Master] was no more than a wayfarer about whom biographers said, 'The home of Jesus was the road along which he walked with His friends in search of new friends.'"[125]

The philosophy of the campus center is set forth on a plaque at the entrance.

> This Building erected by the sacrificial gifts of many alumni and friends of Princeton Theological Seminary is dedicated to the creation on this campus of a Christian community whose members drawn from diverse lands and churches shall serve in all the world the one church which is Christ's body.[126]

Speer Library was completed a few years later, shortly before the one hundred and fiftieth anniversary of the seminary in 1962, and Mackay personally shepherded the project through to completion. "Old Lenox," a neo-Gothic structure, had been erected in 1843 and was completely inadequate for modern research needs and for protecting the seminary's collection of books and manuscripts. The seminary's board of trustees had explored ways to preserve Old Lenox, but even relying on professional advice, no way could be found to integrate the older structure satisfactorily into the new building. At their meeting on January 28, 1952, the board of trustees determined to erect the library on the "general area occupied by the present library buildings. . . . [The] site was chosen partly upon the ground that it is the most central and adequate site available for the new building, and partly because the original Deed of Gift by Mr. Lenox linked this particular area very definitely to library purposes."[127] Dr. Metcalf, the librarian of Harvard University, served as a special consultant, and John G. Buchanan, a Pittsburgh lawyer, headed the special trustees' committee.[128] Vocal opponents tried to derail the project.[129]

On June 2, 1955, Eugene Carson Blake, stated clerk of the denomination, presided over a public meeting held at the campus center and attended by the mayor and the Princeton borough council. Mackay presented a forceful statement to persuade the council to approve the plans for the Robert E. Speer Library and to help the public understand the need for the new structure.[130] The council approved the plan, but criticism continued.

Mackay was skilled in debates involving public opinion. A "small but well-organized group of aesthetes" from the university community had charged that replacing the old building with a modern structure was "vandalism."[131] A *New York Times* editorial advanced the criticisms and identified "faculty members and graduate students at Princeton University" as opposing the change. The editorial went on to advocate preservation of landmarks, apparently without regard to the cost to be borne by the property owner, and advocated a commission to make decisions.[132]

The paper carried Mackay's rejoinder a few days later in which he minimized the opposition's strength, stressed the need to preserve and protect valuable books, and demonstrated the seminary's attempt to save the old structure. Mackay pointed out that only a small group opposed the new library and quoted from published material in the town's media contradicting any contrary impression. Mackay quoted distinguished colleagues at Princeton University that supported the project. Professor A. M. Friend, designer of the stained-glass windows of the university's Gothic chapel, had written, "It would be a crime, perhaps worse than vandalism, if the long history of a great library should be destroyed while any delay obstructs the erection of a fireproof structure to house this fundamental collection."[133] The director of the School of Architecture of Princeton University had written that the seminary trustees and administration had striven "valiantly" to save the building but could not within the resources available. In doing so the director corrected a misstatement by one of his own colleagues.

By New Year's Day, 1957, the new building made of Alabama limestone was nearly completed.[134] Mackay invited his friend Nathan Pusey, President of Harvard University, to present the dedication.[135] The words of the plaque at the main entrance express the spirit of Robert E. Speer and the objective of the library: "This Library which has been erected to the memory of a Christian statesman, scholar and saint, Robert Elliott Speer, a lover of books and of the Kingdom of Christ; is dedicated to the hope that within its walls the light of learning may illumine the life of piety, in the service of Jesus Christ the Truth."[136]

Expansion of the campus also occurred during Mackay's tenure due to demographic changes. At first married students lived on one floor of Hodge Hall. When the seminary acquired the Tennent Campus from the Hun School for graduate student housing, some married students could live in Tennent Hall. Because of wartime service, some students entering the seminary were older than in past eras, some were married, and others consulted Mackay about their plans for marriage because of limited housing and high costs. When Mackay retired, however, plans had been formed and land had been acquired for construction of an entirely new married student housing complex.[137]

Mackay's Small Groups and the Seminary Community

Mackay's own spirituality was aided and maintained in prayer and discussion groups in addition to his participation in large formal worship services and classroom work. In small groups he could speak his mind frankly with friends and colleagues. One prayer circle included John Mott. Mackay wrote,

> In the two decades before his death I was privileged to get to know Mott intimately. I was elected a member of a small prayer circle to which he belonged, a group of twelve friends who met once a year for a "quiet day" together, and who kept in touch with one another once a month by the circulation of "prayer notes." Another member of the circle was Robert E. Speer.[138]

In Princeton, Mackay formed a discussion group with colleagues from Princeton University and Princeton Seminary, which one of its members later described.

> In the early 1940s, he gathered together a discussion group that met monthly either at "Springdale" or at what is now known as "Lowrie House," the former residence of Walter Lowrie of Kierkegaard fame. In addition to Mackay and Lowrie, the group (which never adopted a name) included Robert R. Wicks, the first Dean of the University Chapel, "Jinks" Harbison of the university history department, "Ted" Greene of the philosophy department, George F. Thomas, the first professor of religion at the university, and from the seminary, Otto A. Piper, E. G. Homrighausen, Joseph Hromadka, and Hugh T. Kerr who, as the youngest member, was persuaded to accept the position of corresponding secretary.[139]

A third ongoing group that Mackay participated in came to be known as the "Young Theologians' Discussion Group," originally organized by John Mott. Mackay was invited to join the group in 1929 but could not do so at the time because of travel commitments.[140] It included Roland Bainton, Robert Calhoun, H. Richard Niebuhr, John Bennett, Henry Van Dusen, Reinhold Niebuhr, Douglas Steere, George F. Thomas, Angus Dun, Edwin E. Aubrey, Francis P. Miller, Georgia Harkness, Virginia Corwin, and Paul Tillich.[141] In 1945 the group produced a book titled *The Christian Answer*.[142] Mackay referred to his participation in this group when he reviewed the book for *Theology Today*.[143] This generation of Protestant leaders touched many movements from the 1920s to the 1960s.[144]

Thus, basic to Mackay's understanding and practice of Christian life and leadership was the collective aspect of Christian experience in which one received and enjoyed God's gift of community in a small society of fellow believers. Relationships formed in the intimate fellowship of small groups leavened the life of the seminary and expanded into larger social networks. Mackay emphasized aspects of community when as president of the American Association of Theological Schools from 1948 to 1950, he distinguished for the group a "community of Christians" from a "Christian Community":

> Christians within a university can be no more than a community of Christians. But Christians within a theological seminary, because of their commitment and profession, are or should be, a Christian community. Every relationship between seminary student and teacher, between teacher and teacher, between student and student, and between all of them together and God, should have sacramental significance. It is on the campus of a theological seminary, and in the relations between the members of the seminary community, more than anywhere else, that it is possible to restore and give contemporary meaning to Christian sanctity. A seminary community should be a holy community, the finest expression that human society has to offer of the family of God. To restore the Christian meaning of sanctity in worship, corporate and private, in the quality of personal life and relationships, and as a pattern group for the Christianization of the Church and society, is the supreme task of the theological seminary. Sanctity in this sense is also the indispensable condition for the fulfillment of those other tasks, theological and vocational, which we more commonly associate with theological education.[145]

Colleagues testified to the living experience of Christian community at Princeton. During Mackay's tenure the unseen, spiritual world was seen and experienced by the members of the community, and Homrighausen remarked at the close of Mackay's career, "The secret of this 'togetherness' has been the peculiar leadership of Dr. Mackay who has always pointed to our unity in the *koinonia* of Jesus Christ in which the integrity of each individual is respected and appreciated."[146] Dr. Gehman remarked,

> The spirit of the design of our Seminary has been carried out to the fullest extent under the Mackay regime, and in this respect there has been developed a more pronounced feeling of fellowship or community. . . . The spirit of a Christian Community, which has been fostered by Dr. Mackay, binds the dissimilar elements together without introducing a dull uniformity.[147]

Mackay himself would acknowledge that this "being together" in the New Testament sense was a gift of God and not merely the result of pastoral skill or desire for friendship.[148]

Mackay, like Henry Van Dusen of Union, Luther Weigle and Liston Pope of Yale, Ernest Colwell of Chicago and Claremont, and Lynn Harold Hough

Dr. and Mrs. Mackay, before their retirement in 1959, look through roses toward the garden where they held receptions for students and faculty in the spring. (*Presbyterian Life*)

of Drew, was a member of a generation of strong leaders in the field of theological education.[149] On retirement friends and colleagues honored Mackay in a symposium titled *The Ecumenical Era in Church and Society*. A special issue of *Theology Today* was dedicated to him, and an issue of the *Princeton Seminary Bulletin* reflected esteem and appreciation from his colleagues.[150] Finally, his longtime friend Ray Anderson of Chicago published a verse summing up his tenure:

> So here's to our Jock, from auld Inverness,
> When he came to Prince-ton, he found quite a mess.
> For his deeds existential and dreams ecumenical
> The church will hold him in her heart—reverential.[151]

When John and Jane Mackay drove their black Oldsmobile out of the driveway of Springdale for the last time, they once again left to begin a new life. This time it was in Washington, DC.

Chapter 11

Let the Church Be the Church (1936–1959)

"That all the kingdoms of the earth may know"
(Isa. 37:20 KJV)

A Presbyterian colleague wrote that Mackay's influence, leadership, and contributions lay in several areas: social and political thought and action, missions, and the ecumenical church.[1] The present chapter focuses primarily on the social and political dimensions of Mackay's work and thought and his application of the gospel to these areas. Chapter 12 directs attention principally to his contributions in the evangelistic, missionary, and unitive aspects of the Church. Mackay used the presidency of Princeton Seminary as one platform that enhanced his influence. As he worked on what has been called the great unsolved problem of Protestant theology, the Church, his perspective expanded. The Church became a central theme of his writings and lectures after 1936. As a public intellectual and churchman, he addressed the theme in many different venues: as a leader in the Oxford Conference on Church, Community, and State; in the Federal Council of Churches through its preaching mission, its studies of the state of the Church, and its work on religious freedom; and in his membership on the Committee for a Just and Durable Peace. During the war years and afterwards, led by Mackay and several others, the Protestant theological conception of the Church deepened as institutional organizations expanded and consolidated. As a leader in the movement towards united Protestantism, Mackay served as a draftsman for major conciliar and denominational documents. He applied gospel principles to the social and political problems of McCarthyism and the recognition of Communist China.

His personal interest in Spain and the Hispanic world made Mackay sensitive to the religious dimension of the Spanish Civil War. In North America when the Roman Catholic hierarchy advanced controversial social ideas, the Protestant reaction challenged the Roman Catholic understanding of the relationship of church to the state, just as the Protestant missionary movement challenged those ideas in Latin America. Polarization and parallel development of Protestant churches and the Roman Catholic Church in both North and South America continued, based on competing conceptions of the nature of religious liberty, and led to tensions especially in three areas and issues: Protestant missionary expansion in Latin America, communism, and the relationship of church and state. The dialectic between the two movements continued until the early 1960s when Vatican Council II radically renewed the theological landscape.

Oxford Conference, 1937: Ecumenical Church— Metaphor or Reality?

Mackay prepared to lead a study group at the Oxford Conference during his first year as president of Princeton Seminary. The General Assembly of the Presbyterian Church appointed him a delegate to the Life and Work Conference at Oxford, England, and to the Faith and Order Conference that followed at Edinburgh, Scotland.[2] The shadow of Hitler's religious persecution of Christian churches was falling over Germany as the Conference was being prepared. Charles S. Macfarland, the General Secretary of the Federal Council of Churches, who had been close to the German ecclesiastical scene for over thirty-five years, completed a book in December 1933 titled *The New Church and the New Germany*. It grew from his evaluations made in Germany during October and November 1933. By June of 1937, however, circumstances changed radically. Pastors had been beaten and arrested. A new form of Communion service had been introduced, and a new baptismal formula had been developed to fit in with the "blood and earth formula."[3] Macfarland sent a scathing letter to Chancellor Hitler that compared him to King Herod and charged, "You have violated every assurance that you made to me."[4] The Nazi regime banned German delegates from attending the Oxford Conference.

The official title of the meeting at Oxford was the Conference on Church, Community, and State. The term *community* was the closest English equivalent for the German word *Volk* (or "people"), which was central to the thinking of Nazi Germany. Retired president of Princeton Seminary J. Ross Stevenson described the Oxford Conference as "a tournament of scholars." "Inevitably so," he added, "for how is it possible to consider the totalitarian state except as a challenge to the Christian doctrine of man?"[5] Responding to the threats of German Nazism and Russian Communism, J. H. Oldham led three years of preparation for the Conference. The only volume of his project that the delegates received in advance of the Conference, however, was titled *The Church and Its Function in Society*, by Oldham and Visser 't Hooft.[6] When the Conference concluded, it had three tangible accomplishments: the message to the churches drafted by William Temple, the decision to approve a plan for the World Council of Churches, and the adoption of resolutions that included a message to the German churches. Important intangible accomplishments were the advancement of an inchoate understanding of the ecumenical church among the participants and a discussion of the concept of "middle axioms" for the social teaching and guidance of the church.

Mackay was invited to prepare the initial memorandum for section 5 of the Conference (the "Section on the Universal Church and the World of Nations"), which dealt with international affairs. The assignment came at a particularly hectic time for Mackay, who had recently completed extensive national travel and speaking on behalf of the National Preaching Mission for the Federal Council of Churches. As the new President of Princeton Seminary, then an institution with multiple problems, Mackay worked hard preparing his inaugural address for delivery on February 2, 1937. As a result of the combined pressures, Mackay's submission to Oldham of this initial draft for the Oxford Conference was delayed until early February.[7] By mid-March a revised draft copy prepared by Fenn, Paton, and Oldham and Mackay's draft were sent to him at Princeton for review. Little remained of the "actual phraseology" of Mackay's draft, and Oldham explained that "the thought poured from vessel to vessel was purified."[8] When Mackay recognized only a few initial sentences in the returned draft, he bristled at the thought of the "intellectual autocracy" that had edited his report so aggressively, but on reflection he understood the purpose of the changes and attempted to weave them into his own final draft.[9]

When Mackay circulated the final draft report to his friend Van Dusen and others for review, A. L. Warnshuis raised concerns about the concept of an ecumenical church, which he considered to be merely a metaphor, and "the place and function of the Church in relation to the state and community."[10] His comments exemplify the difficulty of the reception of the ecumenical concept at that time. The Conference's treatment of war and pacifism also arose during the preparation period, a subject on which Visser 't Hooft was preparing a paper. Mackay's attitudes toward the inevitability of war were closer to those of Oldham and Visser 't Hooft than to some American scholars who were more optimistic about the prospect of peace. Mackay was prepared to have the two subjects woven together into one report, but he believed some people in the United States who did not share the same view of the international situation might object. For these reasons he felt it far better that the two reports be handled separately, as they ultimately were.[11]

Mackay travelled to Oxford with his son, Duncan, who had recently graduated from high school. They crossed the Atlantic on the *Berengaria* and stayed at Oxford at the Eastgate Hotel, originally a seventeenth-century coaching inn. When Archbishop Cosmo Lang spoke on the opening evening at the Sheldonian, a circular assembly hall designed by Sir Christopher Wren, Mackay sat next to his friends William Paton of London, secretary of the International Missionary Council and editor of *International Review of Missions*, and Henry Pit Van Dusen, dean of Union Seminary, New York.[12] The first days of the Conference had been organized as addresses for the delegates, and the next days were dedicated to thought and constructive talk. During this second phase the group broke out into sections to deal with the five themes of the Conference.

Distinguished scholars led the Oxford Conference. The section on church and state was led by Dr. Max Huber, a former member of the International Court of Justice. Members of the free churches were well satisfied with the conclusions and the recognition of the degree of freedom needed within the state for the Church to flourish. The section on church and economic problems offered clear analysis and outlined alternatives and offered principles by which Christians could make practical decisions. J. H. Oldham first set forth the principles and usage of so-called "middle axioms," forms of ethical guidance made by the church that stopped short of being particular statements of policy. To Oldham these represented an early stage of grappling with the problem of Christian social thought in the context of church unity.[13]

The section on international affairs, whose official title was the Universal Church and the World of Nations, was led by Mackay. It had a very broad and distinguished membership, including John R. Mott; William Temple, Archbishop of York; Archbishop Germanos; Dr. Adolf Keller; Lord Lothian; John Foster Dulles; and Joseph Oldham.[14] As noted, Mackay's younger friend Visser 't Hooft, secretary of the World Student Christian Federation, headed a subsection on war.[15] Henry Smith Leiper, a section member, provides a glimpse of the section and its discussions in his book *World Chaos or World Christianity*.[16] Mackay and Visser 't Hooft chaired the drafting committee. Mackay presented the report to the full conference on July 19, after which more discussion ensued, and the report was again revised.[17] Mackay believed that the term "ecumenical" had been reborn at this conference.[18]

Unlike the Stockholm Conference of 1925 that had emphasized the role of the individual Christian, the Oxford Conference emphasized the role of the Church. Mackay provided the unofficial slogan for the Conference, which many believed to be the most significant crystallization of thought to emerge from it: "Let the Church be the Church."[19] The term and its explanation appear in Mackay's draft prepared for Commission Five. The sentiment and phrasing were adopted by the Conference when Archbishop William Temple's committee drafted the "message from the Oxford Conference to the Christian Churches" in the following words: "The first duty of the church, and its greatest service to the world, is that it be in very deed the church—confessing the true faith, committed to the fulfillment of the will of Christ, its only Lord, and united in him in a fellowship of love and service."[20]

In his original formulation of the thought, Mackay had written,

Let the Church be the Church. Let the Church know herself, whose she is and what she is. Discerning clearly her own status as the community of Grace, the organ of God's redemptive purpose for mankind, she must by a process of the most merciless self-scrutiny, become what God intended her to be. Nothing less than that, nor yet anything more than that. In penitence and in humility must the Church rediscover the meaning and implications of that word that comes to her from the earlier ages of her own history, "to be to the Eternal Goodness what his own hand is to a man." This involves a revivified sense of God as the real living God, the "god of the whole earth," over against a God who is no more than a dialectical process or a member of a polytheistic pluralism. This means concretely that the Church recognize herself to be the Church of Christ, the organ of God's purpose in Him. It must be her ceaseless concern to rid herself from all subjugation to a prevailing culture, an economic system, a social type, or a political order. Let the Church live; over against all these let the Church stand.[21]

This expression, "Let the Church be the Church," responded to the Protestant need to probe the "deeper question,"[22] a corporate understanding of the meaning of the Holy Catholic Church, the *Una Sancta*, in the Apostles' Creed. At the Conference the phrase meant "Let the Church be what it was called to be: the community of the new age, the spearhead of the Kingdom of God, the voice and the instrument of the Lord, who is King, Priest and Prophet."[23] Avery Dulles, who had also travelled to Europe that summer on the *Berengaria* with his father, John Foster Dulles, a conference participant, later observed that the expression "Let the Church be the Church" uses two meanings of the term *Church* in the same sentence. Let the sociological church be the theological church.[24]

The climax of the delegates' worship together occurred in the final service at St. Mary's Church. On July 25 the Archbishop of Canterbury broke with tradition by inviting "all baptized members of Christian churches, 'whate'er their name or sign,' . . . to receive communion."[25]

When the Conference ended, Mackay's task, and that of other North Americans, was to bring this metaphysical idea—so incompatible with empiricism—back to North America and to present Christianity to the public in a way that the modern world would understand. The new conception involved the development of a conscious awareness in church members of the universal Church's own organic and supernatural state and for Christianity to come to life as a living movement. Since the ecumenical movement conceived Christianity in a way that was unfamiliar to Christians of that time, one concrete method that Mackay used to communicate the idea was to embody the ecumenical ideal within the faculty, students, curriculum, and community of Princeton Seminary. The difficulty of the task was clear. One commentator noted that "in American Protestantism the church hardly exists even as an idea."[26] The ideas of Oxford did not travel well to the United States.[27] Some correctly believed that if the intentions of the Conference were to be carried out, they would be revolutionary.[28]

Mackay wrote his impressions of Oxford and Edinburgh in several articles, describing in greater detail the ecumenical concept and providing the outline of an agenda for concerted action. On the eve of World War II, he believed that "the essential oneness of the church as the Body of Christ must be gratefully acknowledged and visibly expressed, or one by one the churches will die."[29] The path ahead included the development of a deepening sense of God's world purpose in Christ within the churches, a self-examination within each Christian tradition to refine what is true and to remove what is false and obsolescent, the development of ecumenical theology to highlight revealed Christian insights of each tradition, and the development of a true church consciousness among all Christians. Interpreting the significance of the Oxford Conference to the Princeton Seminary community, he identified the task of the Christian church in the late 1930s:

> The intellectual task of the Christian Church in our time moves within two foci. One is the fact—the terrifying fact—of world disintegration. The second focus is the fact, the inspiring fact, of world unity in Christ. In the center of chaos in the secular order stands the Beloved Community, the Church of the Living God, the one great hope under God for mankind at such a time as this.[30]

Mackay sought to inspire each North American Christian to be conscious and aware of belonging

> to an abiding spiritual society that shall endure through all temporal change, even should the ecclesiastical system be shattered to pieces, to an inde-

structible community which contains the hope and promise of a new world, [and which] is to overcome all hostile circumstances, and amid the disintegration of society around him to maintain inviolate his faith in the coming of the Kingdom of God, whose servant the Church *is*, whose servants the churches should be. Let the churches know, therefore, that the Church is and that their supreme task is to *be* the Church. By being the Church and not something else shall they fulfill their God-given function.[31]

To accomplish this, spiritual renewal was needed.

Church leaders also aspired to organizational union, which was an extremely elusive goal to achieve. In 1938, in the aftermath of the Oxford Conference, Mackay served as a Presbyterian member of a joint committee attempting to work out unity with the Episcopal Church, and he preached at a service in which the two communions worshiped together in Cleveland, Ohio. He called on each to "know what we owe to other communions."[32] The move towards union continued until September 1946 when the Episcopal triennial convention unexpectedly killed these "Proposals Looking Toward Organic Union" by referring the matter to the Lambeth Council and seeking a redraft of the document.[33] The Episcopalians, under "high church influence," rejected the idea of common Communion in each other's churches and mutual recognition of ordination.[34] One Presbyterian said of the reunion attempt, "I felt like a man who had been invited to dinner and had the door slammed in my face."[35]

Federal Council of Churches

During the late 1930s and early 1940s Mackay took an active role in the Federal Council of Churches. By 1938 the organization represented twenty-three denominations having a total membership of 24,000,000. Before coming to Princeton Seminary as president, Mackay had agreed to give six weeks in the fall of 1936 to the National Preaching Mission, which had been originally suggested by Hugh T. Kerr of Pittsburgh and organized by the Federal Council.[36] The mission was a deliberate cooperative attempt to bring new energy to the American religious scene. Anticipating the mission, President Stevenson thought "its possibilities of good are incalculable,"[37] and that the mission was in accord with Princeton's ideals, past and present. Mackay's path of sermons and addresses took him from coast to coast, from Seattle to New York. A member of the audience at Billings, Montana, traveled over six hundred miles to hear the address. Later, Mackay spoke in New York.[38] When the National Preaching Mission ended, Mackay continued his efforts on behalf of the Federal Council by taking on the chairmanship of the University Christian Mission.[39]

Another important task came to Mackay in the spring of 1938 when Samuel Cavert asked him to head the Committee on the State of the Church for the Federal Council. Mackay's task was "to give a sense of direction to Protestant thinking. . . . Evangelistic and ecumenical notes . . . [would be] central in any report on the state of the church."[40] Mackay was familiar with the task, having served as a member of the committee that produced the insightful report for 1936.[41] In 1938 Mackay signed the Report on the State of the Church on behalf of the committee and presented it at the meeting in Buffalo. The Report set forth Christian commitment in the strongest possible terms, referring to the Messiah as making a "totalitarian claim upon human personality." It was proper for "Christians to respond without reservation to the imperious 'Follow Me' of the God-man."[42] In the document Mackay expanded for an American audience his thoughts derived from work at Oxford on what it meant for the churches to be the Church.[43] Other members of the Committee on the State of the Church in 1938 included John C. Bennett, Angus Dun, H. Richard Niebuhr, Charles P. Taft, and Ernest Trice Thompson.

Early in June 1937, before the Oxford Conference, Mackay had spoken on the ecumenical theme at the General Assembly of the Presbyterian Church in Columbus, Ohio. In his talk on the "Universal Church and the World of Nations," he traced the universal church as the fruit of the last one hundred years of missionary effort, noting that it was more appropriate to speak of the church as ecumenical than as international. Ecumenical signified a movement from the center radiating to the circumference. The international system was one of existing national groups seeking a basis of cooperation.[44] Penitence first was necessary: to take responsibility and repent for instances when the church could have acted for peace after World War I. Second, Mackay described the "part of the Church's responsibility toward the world of nations to create a new international order." The church had unique qualifications to do this based on its greater insight compared to sociologists and politicians who do not accept revelation. The church produces the character needed for a true international order. And the church is the organ of God's redemptive purpose. He wrote, "Society is most influenced by the Church when the Church is not thinking primarily of influencing civilization but in being true to its own nature." The fellowship of the Church should offer "a representation and anticipation of the Kingdom of God." Mackay refined these ideas about the duty of the church in the international order in later writings, such as his contribution discussed in the following section.

Mackay's creative thought about the Church arose from his active immersion in the Church's affairs. To produce sound theology a theologian must be securely based relationally within the Church, as the body of Christ, and Mackay reflected on, wrote about, organized, and exhorted members of the Church. During World War II Mackay and others began to see the Church in its institutional forms as a force in the world. In an important essay in 1941 he discussed the Church "not as this or that Christian group, even should any one of the existing churches make exclusive claim to be *the* Church, but rather as the organized, corporate expression of all groups. In a word, Church, in this discussion, will really be the synonym of Christianity in its institutional aspect."[45] Mackay extended his thought and experience at Oxford to speak of the Church in this way, describing its influence to be felt on a world scale. He described the details of a threefold role that it exercised: prophetic, regenerative, and communal. At the same time that Mackay was describing the Church that was taking shape and emerging, he was actively encouraging church members to a conscious understanding of the developments that were occurring.[46] From this normative theological conception of the Church, he challenged the flesh-and-blood members to meet the standard and gaged its adequacy.

The Churches and the Peace

During World War II the churches became part of a movement to guide and influence public opinion and to create an atmosphere in which the United States would assume responsibility to play an active role in a new world order. The U.S. Senate ratified the United Nations Charter to make this world order possible. Through speaking, preaching, and committee work, Cavert, Mackay, Dulles, and other leaders of the Federal Council of Churches played an active role in public-opinion formation in preparing the United States for peace and for the international structure that emerged after World War II.[47]

In December 1941, Samuel Cavert wrote Mackay, sending him a copy of an article that John Foster Dulles, a New York lawyer, had written before the war that was one of the "clearest and most thoughtful analyses of the existing world crisis that [he had] yet seen."[48] Mackay believed that Dulles's role at that time "showed his very, very basic concern . . . not merely to win a war, but to see that the country would be worthy of its tradition and also worthy of the role which it would have to play in international affairs."[49] Dulles, who had been greatly impressed by the fellowship that existed among delegates at the Oxford Conference, became interested in what the church could contribute to the world. The work of the Presbyterian Church and the Federal

Council of Churches played an influential role in establishing the world order that followed the war.

In its biennial meeting in December 1940, the Federal Council of Churches created a Commission to Study the Bases of a Just and Durable Peace, whose purpose was long-term planning, and one task of which was "to clarify the mind of our churches regarding the moral, political and economic foundations of an enduring peace."[50] The Delaware Conference was convened in March 1942 in furtherance of that task. Princeton University professor Theodore Greene was the chairman of section 1 on "The Relation of the Church to a Just and Durable Peace," and John Mackay was the *rapporteur* for that section. This Conference, held at Ohio Wesleyan University, had 377 appointed delegates, spoke only for itself in its message, and was referred to as "intellectually . . . the most distinguished American church gathering . . . in 30 years."[51] The section 1 conclusions in the Conference message had a distinctively ecumenical emphasis, referred to the world mission of the church, and articulated spiritual foundations as prerequisites for the church's ability to impact public questions.[52] The following month Mackay acted as moderator of the "Princeton Conference," a regional meeting of clergy and lay leaders of local churches in eastern Pennsylvania, New Jersey, and southern New York based on the study theme the "Christian Contribution to a Just and Durable Peace."

The Federal Council Commission on which Mackay served considered moral principles and attempted to formulate the political bases of a just and durable peace involving "agencies having the duty and the power to promote and safeguard the general welfare of all peoples."[53] John Foster Dulles chaired the group, which produced a booklet titled *A Righteous Faith for a Just and Durable Peace.*[54] The title of Mackay's chapter reflected a realistically modest appraisal of the churches' responsibility: "The churches do not, however, have a primary responsibility to devise the details of world order. But they must proclaim the enduring moral principles by which human plans are constantly to be tested."[55]

By February 1943 the Commission adopted a "Statement of Political Propositions," known as the "Six Pillars of Peace," which was developed mainly by Dulles and was hailed as a foundation for the postwar world. The ideas flowed from the Delaware Conference. These propositions represent the "middle axioms" or social guidance that Oldham wrote about at the Oxford Conference.[56] During four days in July 1943, a roundtable of sixty-one Christian leaders was held at Princeton, to disseminate these ideas and enlist a broader base of support. A paper titled "A Christian Message on World Order" from the roundtable found that "the basic social problem of world order is that of achieving moral and spiritual community."[57] The underlying premise was that "there is a moral order which is fundamental and eternal if mankind is to escape chaos and recurrent war, [and] social and political institutions must be brought into conformity with moral order." Dulles brought the work of the Federal Council to the attention of national political leadership. By October 26, 1943, the Senate began debate on post-war policy, and Dulles sent a letter on the just and durable peace to Senator Tom Connally asking for a resolution favoring collaboration along the lines of Six Pillars of Peace.[58]

Mackay and others in the Federal Council took an active role in the formation of public opinion during the war to prepare the country for the peace. Preaching in West-Park Church in New York in July 1943 Mackay declared the basic problem was to combine righteousness with mercy, so that the Axis nations could once again rejoin the world community conscious of God's compassion.[59] On World Order Sunday, in early November 1944, he preached a sermon on the theme "The Churches and the World Order." Later that month when the Federal Council met for its biennial meeting in Pittsburgh, the peace process was again the theme. Dulles spoke in support of the Dumbarton Oaks proposals, which did in modified form later serve as a framework for negotiations for the UN Charter. But although he supported the Dumbarton Oaks proposal, Dulles believed, "The greatest obstacle to world order is the lack of any universal moral judgment about national conduct." There was a need to safeguard peace through public opinion based on "world-accepted definitions of right and wrong conduct."[60]

The following year Dulles continued to guide public opinion through writing and public policy through diplomacy to generate support for the United Nations organization.[61] He reported to the Federal Council of Churches that the Charter signed at San Francisco, where he acted as chief consultant to the U.S. delegation, was "one which fulfills our hopes even beyond our expectations. . . . To a very large extent the specific recommendations made by our church groups have been given effect. . . . The charter was substantially rewritten to make the organization one which would promote justice and human welfare."[62]

Mackay also played a role in peace issues at the denominational level. The 154th Presbyterian General Assembly had formed a committee believing "the principles of the Christian religion must be made the foundation of national policy and of all social life in the establishment of a righteous peace."[63] The Committee on a Righteous Peace submitted its report to the General Assembly in 1943. Mackay along with Rev. Henry Sloane Coffin, Rev. J. Harvey Cotton, Rev. Hugh Thomson Kerr, and Dr. Robert E. Speer served on the committee. The report found the church in the deepest sense was "one in its faith and fellowship. . . . It is the earnest of a social order in which the will to peace will prevail. Today both the Church and the world are reaping rich harvests from the labor of the past."[64]

In addition to his work on committees and commissions, Mackay played a public, pastoral role as well. Contributing to the intellectual climate of the war era, he published a series of essays in the *New York Times Magazine* interpreting the signs of the times in light of Christian beliefs.[65] For specifically Christian audiences he contributed other articles,[66] sermons,[67] and a prayer.[68] One work, published in *Social Progress*, forcefully addressed his fellow Presbyterians and rallied them to the task ahead:[69] The Presbyterian Church constitution recognizes that God delegates to the state, in certain circumstances, the right to use force. Our part in the struggle now raging must be regarded as a titanic police measure. The unity of the Church must be preserved. The Church must gird itself to respond to increasing demands. Preaching must rediscover the redemptive depths of the Gospel and of the Bible as a whole. The Church, by all the means in its power, should set in high relief the principles of God's moral government of the world.

While the Protestant peace efforts were developing and expanding, Pope Pius XII and the Roman Catholic Church were formulating a plan of peace for the end of World War II. Pope Pius's task, however, was more complicated because he was acting both as a head of state and as head of the Roman Catholic Church, combining a spiritual and temporal task.[70] Acting at the political level President Roosevelt had assured Pope Pius in 1943 that the "neutral status of the Vatican City as well as of the Papal domain throughout Italy will be respected."[71] A public theological debate about the status of the Roman Church in world affairs developed as 1,600 Protestant clergy, including Mackay, signed a statement opposing religious representation in councils of state, meaning that a representative of the Vatican should not participate in World War II peace talks.[72] The Protestant churches would not have a spokesman at the peace conference, nor a corresponding juridical status to protect churches, land, and buildings owned by their denominations. The Rev. Fulton J. Sheen reacted to this declaration by suggesting that the era of the anti-Christ was approaching.[73] Mackay's friend, Methodist Bishop Bromley Oxnam, President of the Federal Council of Churches, framed the church-state issue sharply in the spring of 1946 when he called "upon the Roman Catholic Church to be a church and not to attempt to be a state and a church."[74]

The political influence of the Papal States had been in decline since the mid-nineteenth century when the Papal States had opposed Garibaldi's efforts to unify Italy. In 1870 Pope Pius XI lost his temporal powers when the

Italian state annexed Rome, making it the capital of Italy. A policy of papal self-imprisonment followed until February 1929, when the Lateran Treaty between Italy and the Vatican established an independent Vatican city-state, a local symbol with a universal claim. That treaty addressed three areas: a political agreement, a financial agreement, and a concordat governing in detail how the relations of church and state would be regulated in Italy.[75] A decade later a concordat favorable to the Vatican was also signed with Franco of Spain; it allowed the Vatican to keep the power it gained in the selection of bishops under both the Spanish monarchy and the republic.[76] In the 1930s the Vatican had its own foreign relations, currency, and subjects.

To act both as a church and a state, however, presented significant moral and theological contradictions and ambiguities for the Roman Catholic Church that were becoming clear to theologians like Don Luigi Sturzo in the 1930s. An important precept of moral theology is to avoid cooperating with or facilitating evil, and Sturzo raised the question of whether dealing with fascist governments could be considered licit under this precept.[77] The content of the government gave qualitative value to its form. He noted the corrupting effect and confusion created for some Roman Catholic writers of moral theology because of political relations between the Vatican and certain governments. While Sturzo did not draw conclusions or apply these principles to Vatican policies of the time, he did focus on the moral risks and complexities for a church-state to deal with fascism on a secular, political level.[78] These ambiguities are important to bear in mind in light of religious tensions that followed the war and flowed from different conceptions of the essence of Christ's Church.

Religious Liberty—The Spanish Civil War

Mackay believed that the Protestant Reformation had not been a schism *from* the Church but one *within* the Church. Having lived and worked in Europe and Latin America, he brought with him to the United States his direct knowledge of the practice and working theology of the Roman Catholic Church as a transnational entity. During World War II and for nearly twenty years afterwards, the growing ecumenical, pan-Protestant movement for world Christianity challenged the influence of the Roman Catholic Church and its hierarchy. The two perspectives on the Church contradicted each other, and the issue of religious freedom dramatically precipitated differences. The dialectic was sharpened in North America, as competing views were voiced by theologians, commentators, and partisans. As a public intellectual and advocate of the truth he discerned, Mackay explained and defended the Protestant heritage and advocated the deepening spiritual life of congregations.[79] As a philosopher he did not shy away from principled public debate to demonstrate that the Roman Catholic hierarchy of the time had a "false view of the church and the relationship between church and state."[80] Although attacked personally, he debated fearlessly. Though partisan writers characterized the theological debate as anti-Catholic rather than anticlerical, without the debate, it is unlikely that John Courtney Murray and others would have moved to revolutionize and transform Roman Catholic thinking on religious freedom as they did.

Mackay's authority in the 1950s as a public intellectual on world affairs derived from his travels and his writings on Spain and Latin America. Mackay, a recognized expert, was a member of the British Royal Institute of International Affairs between 1930 and 1937 when he resigned with the expectation of becoming an American citizen. The Institute had approached Mackay to participate in preparing the first objective political, economic, and cultural survey of South America for general readers. He contributed a thoughtful paper on the APRA political party of Peru as part of the "outer group" of authorities and experts. The book was published by Oxford University Press in October 1937.[81]

Having roots that go back more than a century, the Spanish Civil War is a complicated subject, but on that topic Mackay and the Roman Catholic hierarchy had directly opposite points of view. Jacques Maritain, a philosopher and a future French ambassador to the Vatican, realized that "adherence to General Franco had become throughout the world the criterion of Catholic Orthodoxy."[82] Mackay, recalling his studies in Spain during an era of liberalism, lamented the fall of the Spanish republic and actively supported its cause. While based in New York as a secretary of the Board of Foreign Missions, Mackay maintained contact with individuals and groups keenly attentive to developments in Spain and Latin America. In 1933 an association was formed called the Friends of Spain to "manifest spiritual understanding" and take an interest in the life of the new Spanish republic. Mackay was the chairman and his good friend Guy Inman acted as the secretary. The group sponsored Dr. Juan Orts Gonzalez, a Spanish evangelical and formerly a prominent member of the Franciscan Order, to take up residence in Madrid in April 1933.[83] At a rally sponsored by the Medical Bureau of the American Friends of Democracy, Mackay shared the podium with André Malraux, the French journalist and author of *L'Éspoir*, and Louis Fischer, the correspondent. An ambulance, the Benjamin Franklin, was given to the Spanish Consul.[84]

In North America Mackay drew attention to the religious element involved in the civil war and attributed the immediate anticlericalism to a backlash against the words and actions of the Archbishop of Toledo.[85]

> There was nothing fratricidal, no spirit of class, no anti-religious feeling, no anti-clerical feeling when the Spanish people voted for democracy. . . . But when within a few days after the election the hierarch of Spain, the Archbishop of Toledo, called upon the people to repudiate the Spanish democracy they had just won, that was too much. Trouble began. There was no anti-religious movement until a constitutional limitation was put on democracy by certain ecclesiastical authorities. And so I say that where anti-religious feeling appears today in Spain it is the result of the conflict.[86]

Mackay was referring to the pastoral letter of Pedro Cardinal Segura, Archbishop of Toledo, published May 7, 1931, which focused on threats of anarchy.[87] Another expert, Professor Salvador de Madariaga, shared this perspective on the religious element, suggesting that if the Cardinal had been more measured in his tone, resentment might not have taken hold in the Constituent Assembly.[88] A month after the New York rally the German Luftwaffe squadron the Condor Legion bombarded Guernica in April 1937, and Mackay was one of seventy-six signers of a statement titled "The Crime of Guernica."[89]

In early 1937, however, U.S. foreign policy implicitly tilted toward Franco through the Neutrality Act, which extended America's neutrality policy to civil wars, and in the denial of passports to those traveling to Spain.[90] These policies coincided with Roosevelt's domestic political interest in aligning himself with the Vatican's position on Spain prior to the American elections of 1938 and 1940.

Ecclesiastical Rivalry in North America— Heritage of Freedom

The Roman Catholic hierarchy had observed the fragmentations of Protestantism during the period between the wars and responded with attempts to enhance its own political and social interest in North America during the troubled period. In 1930, Francis X. Talbot, former editor of the Jesuit magazine *America*, had written that "the old Protestant culture is about at the end of its rope." He asked in the New York *Globe*, "Why can't we make the United States Catholic in legislation, Catholic in justice, aims and ideals? . . .

Now is the time to organize and strike hard to put the Catholic idea before all."[91] During the Spanish Civil War, Jacques Maritain articulated the challenge to the identity of the Roman Catholic polity. In the "great spiritual drama from which the Church is suffering . . . we must find out . . . whether a *political* conception of religion or an *evangelical* conception of religion is to prevail."[92] In the United States, Roman Catholicism was making assertions of social policy and theology in its capacities as both a church and a state. During the mid-1940s the Roman Catholic effort in North America to advance controversial social-policy principles and to distort the record and history of Protestantism began to meet Protestant resistance. This policy of social division at a time when the United States was recovering from its efforts in World War II and facing the challenge of communism threatened the existing American way of life.

World War II slowed but did not stop the ecumenical Protestant world-church movement. At the international level one Roman Catholic response to this development was to attempt to restrict Protestant missionary activities in Latin America. The legitimacy of the Protestant mission movement in that region became a subject of the North American public debate on religious liberty. Attacks by American Catholics against Protestant missions in Latin America had existed during the 1930s.[93] During the early 1940s the tension between Protestants and Catholics began to extend into American foreign policy. In the summer of 1942 articles appeared in a number of Roman Catholic periodicals seeking the withdrawal of Protestant missionaries from Latin America.[94] In a book published that summer, *New York Times* correspondent John W. White sharply attacked Protestant missionaries in Argentina.[95]

The "Victory and Peace Statement" issued in November 1942 made the Roman Catholic postwar strategy plain when the Roman Catholic archbishops and bishops charged at their annual meeting that Protestant missionaries were endangering Franklin Roosevelt's good neighbor policy in South America and that Protestant missions were the main stumbling block to friendly relations between the United States and South America. In their statement the bishops expressed "the hope that the mistakes of the past which were offensive to the dignity of our southern brothers, their culture and their religion, will not continue."[96] Thus, the Roman Catholic Church claimed a religious monopoly in regions where its strength was predominant, and it attempted to limit Protestant missionary influence in Latin America while taking advantage of Anglo-Saxon principles of religious liberty in North America, where the Roman Catholic Church was in a minority position.

Samuel Cavert, the general secretary of the Federal Council of Churches, asked Mackay to write an article of rebuttal to the "Victory and Peace Statement." Indeed, in early 1942 Mackay had begun to notice increased Roman Catholic influence at the State Department and had drawn this to Cavert's attention.[97] In the response he prepared Mackay noted that the Protestant tradition of freedom gave Roman Catholics and others their liberties in the United States. He submitted his paper, which was brief and to the point, to the Executive Committee of the Federal Council, which approved it.[98] A few weeks later at its biennial meeting, the Federal Council of Churches also approved Mackay's response. When the statement, titled "Our Heritage of Religious Freedom," was published in full in the *New York Times*,[99] it "came like a 'bomb,' unexpected and with power."[100] Reinhold Niebuhr then asked him for an article on the subject for *Christianity and Crisis*, and Mackay, who served on the magazine's editorial board, accepted. When the article was published the following May, it produced further furor.[101] The controversy continued when journalist John W. White, a nominal Protestant, collected and published the Roman Catholic charges in a book.[102] George P. Howard, a Methodist minister born in Argentina, vigorously rebutted the charges by compiling details of the dispute and documenting the opinions of Latin Americans themselves. A copy of Howard's book, with a foreword by Mackay, was sent to every member of Congress.[103]

In mid-January, shortly after the publication of "Our Heritage of Religious Freedom," a crucial meeting was arranged at the Faculty Club of Columbia University. Ernest Johnson of the Federal Council of Churches organized the dinner meeting for leaders of the Protestant movement and the Roman Catholic Church to discuss and explore why the two sides saw the issue of religious liberty so differently. Instead of preparing an agenda especially for the occasion, to begin discussion Johnson used an article from the *British Weekly* by a distinguished British Congregational leader, Nathaniel Micklem, President of Mansfield College, Oxford. The article was peaceful in tone but raised provocative issues by relying on references to specific circumstances. After a short time Johnson turned leadership of the meeting over to Mackay.[104]

The discussion probed what the two groups respectively meant by the term *religious liberty*. At one point, Gerald Walsh, SJ, the editor of *Thought*, remarked, "Religious liberty is a matter which the Roman Catholic Church deals with, not in terms of principle, but in terms of policy." For Mackay this was a "luminous remark." Writing years later Mackay recalled the statement. "What he meant to say was that the particular way in which the *principle* of religious liberty is applied depends upon existing circumstances. To all intents and purposes this important issue is determined in terms of *policy*, not principle."[105] At this meeting Mackay gained important insight into the nature of the conflicting viewpoints.

The "Heritage" statement also had dramatic effects on the religious scene, highlighting the contentious issue within several Protestant denominations. The Southern Presbyterian Assembly protested Catholic opposition to Protestant missionaries. Northern Presbyterians asked that freedom be expanded. The General Synod of the Reformed Church of America and the Baptist Church also protested.[106]

What had triggered the firestorm was this. Two cardinals had gone to the U.S. State Department with the message that only Roman Catholics should be sent as U.S. officials to Latin America, adding that the U.S. government should stop granting passports to Protestant missionaries going to Latin America.[107] By midsummer of 1943 doubt existed that the message behind the "Heritage of Religious Freedom" statement had gotten through to the State Department since passport facilities to certain young men were being declined. On behalf of several Protestant foreign mission boards, Mackay worked behind the scenes to resolve the issue. Acting as a liaison between the Federal Council's Dulles Commission and the State Department in connection with Latin American matters, Mackay arranged an interview with officials at the State Department in August 1943.[108] Representatives from the Presbyterian and Methodist mission boards joined him at the meeting. They came away from Washington satisfied with the assurances that the particular difficulties that had been discussed would be resolved within the next two months, and they were.

The difficulty, however, persisted in the form of delays rather than denial. The next year twenty mission board secretaries met Mr. Lane, Ambassador to Colombia, at the Office of the Passport Division of the State Department. A larger meeting was held two weeks later on May 26, 1944. The church representatives found that all applications had in fact experienced unreasonable delay.[109] Secretary of State Hull, however, publicly denied that passports to Protestant missionaries were being held back.[110] In November, Acting Secretary of State Stettinius issued a study of passports granted February, March, and April, 1944 (a period after Mackay's meeting with officials in Washington). It showed that during that short sample period passports had been issued without discrimination based on the religion of the applicant.[111]

This public debate over Latin American policy in fact opened a new era in missionary relations between some Roman Catholics and Protestants. Two prominent Catholic scholars, John J. Considine, MM, and Peter Masten Dunne, SJ, chairman of the History Department of the University of San Francisco, visited Latin America on fact-finding trips. After their visits both men published books detailing the spiritual needs of Latin America. Considine concluded that the shortage of priests there was so serious that forty thousand new priests in ministry would be needed to supply one priest for 2,000 souls. Dunne concluded that the Protestant missions had had good effects in Latin America.[112]

The political controversy over religious liberty for missionary activity expanded into an academic and philosophical debate. As Chairman of the Joint Committee on Religious Liberty of the Federal Council of Churches and the Foreign Missions Conference of North America, Mackay was at the focal point of the debate. The Joint Committee had been established in early 1942. Its functions were to survey the course of religious liberty during the Christian era; to survey contemporary situations in which liberty of worship, education, or missionary work was denied or curtailed; to analyze the problem of religious liberty as it would confront governments when the peace was made; and to formulate principles on which churches might unite to defend religious liberty.[113] For a meeting of the Joint Committee in May 1943 Mackay presented a paper on the nature and meaning of religious liberty that discussed different aspects of the topic: freedom to seek the truth, freedom to express religious truth, and freedom to propagate religious truth. Individual citizens and religious organizations were both subjects of religious liberty.[114] In the early spring 1944 the committee's "Statement on Religious Liberty" was adopted and distributed to political leaders. The work of the committee culminated in the publication of a comprehensive, six-hundred-page book titled *Religious Liberty: An Inquiry* (1945) by M. Searle Bates, Professor of History at Nanking University. Mackay wrote the foreword for the book.

Professor Bates's book quickly drew the attention of Roman Catholic theologians when John Courtney Murray, SJ, reviewed it in *Theological Studies*, the publication he edited.[115] Mackay responded to this review with a powerful essay of his own titled "As Regards Freedom of Religion," published in *Theology Today*. The essay framed the issue for debate. Mackay agreed with Murray that "among all the problems relating to a new world order, religious liberty occupies a unique position. The reason is, no other problem so directly and immediately faces an ultimate issue."[116] Religious freedom meant both the freedom to choose one's religion and the freedom to practice one's religion. As Mackay wrote, "The time has come when in the interests of all concerned, and having regard for the future of Christianity in the world, the basic claims of the Roman Catholic Church should be challenged upon Biblical, historical, and theological grounds."[117] He observed that the Church, "whatever we may regard it to be" has no "right to make the State an instrument of its will." Clericalism arose, he said, from attempts of ecclesiastical power to control secular power, and he quoted Salvador de Madariaga on the personal risks and difficulties in discussing clericalism.[118] Mackay's article closed with a quotation from William Penn: "We will oppose the Roman Catholic claims, but we will demand toleration for the Roman Catholic Church."[119] Mackay contributed further to the ongoing public theological debate when he published a long essay, "Protestantism," setting forth the claims of classic Protestantism.[120] Protestant Christianity was based on personal religion, which Mackay had eloquently described a few years earlier.[121]

The official Roman Catholic teaching on religious freedom at the time was clear, and Mackay described it correctly. Pope Leo XIII's encyclical *Immortale Dei* set forth the Roman Catholic doctrine of the relationship of church and state. In the encyclical, published November 1, 1885, Pope Leo XIII had written that "the Church, indeed, deems it *unlawful* to place the various forms of divine worship on the same footing as the true religion" (emphasis added).[122] The Roman Catholic Church interpreted that statement to mean that "in a genuinely Catholic State, public authority should not permit the introduction of new forms of religion; but when several denominations have already been established, the State may, and generally should, permit them all to exist and to function."[123] Thus, the church taught that religious freedom was only an accommodation to a preexisting condition if a variety of denominations are already present in a state. This is precisely the issue of a policy of accommodation, as Gerald Walsh had remarked. Clearly, the vigorous Roman Catholic opposition to Protestantism in Latin America and elsewhere was based on official social teaching.[124]

Mackay's own work had already drawn the attention of John Courtney Murray, SJ, who reviewed Mackay's book *A Preface to Christian Theology* in June 1941. The review illustrates the sharp theological differences between Protestant and Roman Catholic understandings of the Church at that time.[125] While acknowledging "considerable brilliance of style," Murray contested Mackay's statement that "the Ecumenical Church has arrived" and singled out Mackay's concept of "the *una sancta*, the one Holy Catholic Church," as "a tenuous abstraction." He quoted Père Georges-Yves Congar's words of 1937: "Catholics, protestants, orthodox, Anglicans have become *different men*. We have the same God but we are different men before him and cannot agree on the nature of the relation we have to him."[126] At the time it was completely unforeseen that within less than thirty years, denominational differences would be reduced and a spiritual unity across denominational lines between and among individual Christians based on personal Christian religion as described and advocated by Mackay would begin to take hold.

In March 1946 Mackay defended Protestantism from varied attacks. In March 1946 he called on Protestant clergy to come together in ecumenical unity to combat the trend of "militant Roman clericalism."[127] *Time Maga-*

zine quoted Mackay's disapproval both of conservative trends in the Roman Church that criticized "the traditionally independent policy of American Catholicism," and also the recent practice of "the official Catholic press in this country to attack, in a most unworthy way, the Protestant Reformation and its great leaders, particularly Martin Luther and John Calvin."[128]

At this time, too, the Roman Catholic Church advocated several divisive social policies, including public aid to parochial schools and continued U.S. government contact with the Vatican. Such policies led to a response. Following a series of conferences in 1947 an organization called Protestants and Others United for Separation of Church and State was formed, and a statement was adopted at the final conference in November 1947 setting forth a manifesto and the group's immediate objectives.[129] The leaders of the organization were prominent Protestants, and Mackay was elected a vice president. The group and individual leaders were immediately attacked by the *Tablet*, Mackay being termed a "pro Soviet sympathizer attested by support of Russian War Relief."[130]

When the issue of religious freedom was framed in part as the freedom to choose one's religion, John Courtney Murray experienced a period of "confusion," and then lashed out at Protestant philosophers and theologians.[131] One writer understated Murray's vilification and disparagement of Protestants as "rather disappointing": "He made verbal assaults on Protestant writers, employing the technique of guilt by association to condemn men and views. He carelessly generalized from the views of one or more writers to 'all Protestants.'"[132] In an ugly and mean-spirited attack Murray maligned the group organizing Protestants and Others United, linking Protestant ministers and Scottish Rite Masons, referring sarcastically to the "grave situation that alarms the Oxnams, Poteats, Morrisons, Newtons and Mackays,"[133] and later suggesting, "It is high time for Protestants to wake up—return to reality—see an analyst."[134] He closed his screed by comparing the Protestant challenge to the *Communist Manifesto* of Marx and Engels in 1848. The irony of this article is clear in retrospect, but vilification of Protestants as Communists continued in the 1950s.

The personal attacks against Mackay and other Protestants occurred in the theological debates in North America while events occurring abroad undermined the credibility of the attacks. Long-distance travel and transcontinental communications were becoming common, and after World War II the United States was less insulated from events overseas. Roman Catholics in North America could no longer easily dismiss journalistic accounts of Roman Catholic practices in Spain and Colombia.[135] North American Catholic assurances of religious tolerance were also contradicted from the right by conservative Roman prelate Cardinal Alfredo Ottaviani.[136] One Protestant deftly proposed a test to build confidence between Protestants and Roman Catholics: "Nothing would so clear the air as a repudiation of the religious liberty clause in the Spanish concordat by the Vatican."[137]

Mackay focused attention on the precise religious situation in Spain as a representative example of the Roman Catholic social teaching on church and state, and his view of Spain was supported by news reports.[138] In 1949 *Ecclesia*, a Roman Catholic publication, wrote, "The objective right to profess a false religion does not exist."[139] Though no longer the primate of Spain, Cardinal Segura remained active in 1952 as archbishop of Seville and issued a pastoral letter that denounced Protestantism and a campaign of "benevolence" to it.[140] The Roman Catholic Church in Spain was more nationalistic and less liberal than elsewhere in the world, including Latin America, and in 1951 the strongest forces supporting General Franco were the army and the Roman Catholic Church. At that time there were 184 Protestant chapels in Spain and 30,000 Protestants.[141] Protestant schools could not be established, and priests were assigned to the ministry of education, which controlled censorship.

Mackay's interest in liberal reform focused also on events in Colombia that at first were not widely known in North America. During a visit to Bogotá in 1946 Mackay met for two hours with liberal reform leader Jorge Eliécer Gaitán. Mackay believed that Gaitán was a person who "admired Christ but failed to see His true significance." Gaitán told Mackay that "no figure is worth more study for an aspiring leader of the people than that of Christ; His technique of appealing to the multitudes was beyond the power of any other known demagogue."[142] As he left his law office in the center of Bogotá for lunch in April 1948, two years later, Gaitán was assassinated for the liberal causes he advocated. The assassination set off riots in which over two thousand people were killed, and the incident became known as the *bogotazo*.[143] His rival, the demagogue Laureano Gómez, temporarily went into hiding and emerged June 25, 1949. The political violence that began in 1948 peaked in 1953 and ebbed only after 1957.

The period of rule of Laureano Gómez in Colombia from 1950 to 1953 marked a time of Protestant persecution. Gómez's political philosophy was influenced by Franco's rule in Spain, and it combined the military and *hispanidad* with uncontested Roman Catholic authority.[144] "With the support of the most belligerent sector of the clergy," Gómez fashioned "a fiercely militant church within the Christian Church."[145] Gómez chose Jesuit Félix Restrepo to assist in preparing a new constitution. Presbyterian missionary James E. Goff documented the religious persecutions in Colombia, and prepared a country-wide survey thanks to a special appropriation of the Presbyterian Board.[146]

Showing its solidarity with Christian believers in Latin America, the Presbyterian Church in North America brought these persecutions to public attention. In 1953 the *News Bulletin* of the Evangelical Confederation of Colombia documented persecution of evangelicals there. It reported that in the last five years, there had been "42 church buildings destroyed by fire and dynamite, 31 damaged, ten confiscated; 110 Protestant primary schools closed, 54 of them by government order, the rest by violence; 51 Protestant men, women & children killed; [and] $148,000 lost in buildings destroyed, damaged or confiscated." Ironically, the report showed that persecution strengthened the Protestant movement in Colombia: "Protestant church membership increased 51% from 7,908 in 1948 to 11,958 in 1953."[147] By 1956 the religious abuses had increased. Tad Szulc of *The New York Times* reported, "A methodical campaign openly directed by the Colombian Roman Catholic clergy and abetted by the government . . . aims at eradication of Protestantism in Colombia."[148] Ironically a 1956 letter from Gómez attacking the church delayed rather than accelerated the separation of the Roman Church from the new Colombian president.[149]

China Recognition

In addition to supporting progressive reforms in the Hispanic world, Mackay advocated U.S. diplomatic recognition of the new communist government of China in the 1950s for evangelistic and practical reasons. Some groups, however, falsely used this advocacy as evidence of communist sympathy. For Mackay, diplomatic recognition of the new regime in China was a means to enable the church to advance as a worldwide Christian fellowship in that country through communication, travel, and evangelism. Although Mackay's opponents used this support to discredit him and charged that it signified communist sympathy, his approach reflected the British international law rule of state recognition that was also being followed by many other nations. A realist approach to diplomacy does not use diplomatic recognition as a reward to induce good behavior in other countries.[150]

In May 1949 the Chinese revolution was nearing its final stage as the People's Liberation Army marched into Shanghai, and on October 1, 1949, the People's Republic of China was announced at Peking. The communist consolidation of power was completed later in May 1950.[151] Although some British politicians, like Lord Salisbury, wished to remain close to U.S. policy, in response to Mao's proclamation the British government announced de jure recognition of China on January 6, 1950.[152] Diplomatic recognition was based on several factors, including Britain's interpretation of international law, the practical need to protect British financial interests in China, the favorable support of the British ambassador in China, and unanimous support of British diplomats in the Far East meeting in Singapore. China accepted the offer of recognition a few days later.[153] Diplomatic recognition also was extended by Ceylon, India, Denmark, and Israel at this time.

A few days after returning from a two-month trip to East Asia, Mackay addressed a meeting of missionary and church leaders in New York on Wednesday, January 4, 1950. In his account of his trip Mackay reported that "the Christian missionary movement is now beginning in a bigger way, for bigger stakes and on a global scale in a more diversified form."[154] Because of the reputation of the missionaries in China, Mackay did not anticipate a hostile governmental response as had occurred previously in Russia: "I think we will be obliged to recognize the new government. Otherwise we will be alienating the Chinese people who by their attitude repudiated the other regime."[155]

Mackay's viewpoint on diplomatic recognition was repeated in April when sixty-eight Protestant missionaries and missionary executives, speaking as individuals, called on U.S. government officials to recognize the People's Republic of China. Most of them had worked as missionaries for twenty years or more.[156] On August 28, 1950, Mackay explained and elaborated his views in a letter to the editor of the *New York Times*. His position rested on political precedent, China's internal developments, the need to woo China from any Russian influence, and the need to foster China's considerable Christian community.[157] Recognition may also have been a step to aid missionaries who were held in Communist Chinese prisons.[158]

As the head of the Presbyterian Board of Foreign Missions, Mackay spoke at a plenary session of the National Assembly of the United Council of Church Women meeting in Cincinnati on November 15. The council represented ten million churchgoers of seventy Protestant denominations. Mackay invited the gathering to pray for greater international understanding and for the nine-member Chinese Communist delegation to be "patiently heard to a finish on whatever matter they may raise."[159] Several years later in 1956 Mackay and others advocated resumption of contacts between the churches in China and the churches in the West, but a Methodist leader had reservations about the idea.[160] The U.S. State Department publicly declined to change its policy on recognition in 1958.[161] Despite the pragmatic views and advocacy by Mackay and others, diplomatic relations were not finally established between the People's Republic of China and the United States until January 1, 1979.[162]

Church and State

Ecclesiastical rivalry continued in the 1950s between the organized Protestant churches and the Roman Catholic Church. As the Protestant churches continued seeking spiritual and organizational unity, Mackay played an active role in the early years of the National Council of Churches. He served in the role of draftsman, giving voice to corporate Protestant aspirations that had not existed before that time. Samuel Cavert had sounded out Mackay's attitude towards such service before Henry Knox Sherrill, the president of the National Council and Presiding Bishop of the Episcopal Church, wrote Mackay telling him how pleased and grateful he was that Mackay would serve as chairman of the Denver Committee on Message.[163] The Protestant message of the council took on added importance because thirteen Roman Catholic bishops in November had issued a statement on secularism and schools.[164] J. Howard Pew, an active Presbyterian layman, thought the bishop's statement was "by far the best pronouncement written on the Christian ethic in modern time that [he] had seen."[165]

In December 1952 the National Council of Churches assembled in Denver, Colorado, with more than 1,800 delegates. Twenty-nine member churches representing 33,000,000 members were present. Bishop Sherrill noted in his opening address that the "council is dependent . . . upon the member churches. . . . The real uniting power is that we find in Jesus Christ our Lord and Savior. In that fact is the heart of our cooperative effort."[166] Sherrill went on to say that there were issues on which the churches must speak out; otherwise the debate would be left to others having a different perspective and motivation. The Council then adopted and issued a significant and comprehensive statement titled "Letter to the Christian People of America," which Mackay's committee had prepared.[167] Mackay noted the import of the statement. "It's never been done before because we were not sufficiently united. There never before was a corporate Protestant voice."[168] The "document received more publicity from the press of the nation than any document ever got out by united Protestantism in this country," Mackay wrote to Pew.[169] Calling on the churches to fight secularism, the Council letter noted that "as this nation was intended to be a religious nation, we should use all legitimate means to prevent it from becoming a secular state in the current sense of the term."[170] It went on to address issues of freedom of thought and human rights. To fulfill their redemptive role the churches must deepen their spiritual lives, widen the area of Christian responsibility within the churches, and increasingly manifest oneness in Christ.

The following year the National Council of Churches also issued a letter critical of the methods of a congressional committee investigating communism in education. In debate the letter was supported by Mackay, Oxnam, Sherrill, and Charles P. Taft.[171]

John R. Mott and Robert E. Speer had energetically inspired and encouraged the involvement of the laity in church affairs, and Mackay continued to work to increase the involvement of laypeople in the National Council of Churches. He encouraged J. Howard Pew to "become related to the Council in a constitutional way rather than as a member of a group having a tangential or supervisory relationship." Mackay believed, "By coming to meet other business men and representative churchmen, I feel he would come to have a totally different view of inter-church relations and ideals."[172] Mackay was Pew's guest at a dinner with a group of laymen in Princeton, and the caliber and spirit of the group made a deep impression on him. He considered "that the emergence of the laity in the life of the Christian Church today is one of the most significant events in the recent history of Christianity. It can also be one of the most creative things in restoring to Protestantism all the wealth of meaning that is enshrined in the Reformation phrase, 'the universal priesthood of believers.'"[173] Unfortunately, the relationship of the Lay Committee with the National Council became a stormy one.[174] By 1957, Mackay also expressed growing reservations about size, complexity, and costliness of the National Council of Churches.[175]

The Protestant-Catholic rivalry manifested itself in conflicting ideas about the nature of the Church and its relationship to the state in the context of the appointment of a U.S. ambassador to the Vatican. When President Truman entertained the idea of expanding diplomatic recognition to the Vatican, Mackay opposed it vigorously. In a meeting in Dobbs Ferry, New York, Mackay told a clergy and lay group that had formed a community council of churches that Truman's proposal of General Mark Clark as U.S. ambassador to the Vatican was "a maneuver for political advantage in the home scene rather than against Communism in Europe." He went on to note that communism grew best in lands where church and state are closely linked, such as Spain and Italy, where they "impose an authoritative conformity." Mackay strongly objected to having an ambassador to the Vatican "because it gives preferential status to one religious body." That is "dangerous" because of "the political-clerical nature" of the Roman church. Mackay considered the justification that the ambassador was assigned to "a state or civic body" was "ridiculous and absurd." The idea was a "futile act and a regrettable mistake." The circumstances would be different "if we had an established state church in America." Mackay continued to develop a positive theme titled

"Our Faith and Our Country," which showed the effect that "a Bible-centered and Christ-centered faith" has had on American institutions. He noted, however, the church, too, is fallible.[176] Twenty-six Protestant leaders urged Truman to withdraw Clark's name.[177]

Mackay's conception of the relationship between religion and government was more nuanced and less radical than the constitutional doctrine developed in the late 1940s by the United States Supreme Court under the leadership of Hugo Black.[178] Black's sweeping adoption of the metaphor "a wall of separation between Church and State"[179] as a rule of constitutional law had no historical foundation. By calling for neutrality between religion and irreligion, the line of jurisprudence eventually undermined the "utterly conventional assumption that there was a necessary and valuable moral connection between religion and government."[180] As one commentator noted, the rights of free speech and the press should have been sufficient to protect atheists without resorting to the establishment of religion clause of the Constitution.[181]

Mackay's thought assumed a necessary connection between religion and government, and his idea of religious freedom did not involve separation in the moral sense. Mackay's understanding of relations between church and state was influenced by the Free Church movement in Scotland, where in modern times the Presbyterian Church had been the established church. In 1843 Thomas Chalmers, Robert Murray M'Cheyne, and others had led a "disruption" that began the principle of spiritual freedom for the Church from the government. The old Scottish regime of Presbyterian nationalism had been undermined. Chalmers and others had insisted on the doctrine that the kingdom of the church and the kingdom of the state had separate domains.[182] In a godly commonwealth spiritual truth would animate the citizenry, whose ideal was based on individual subordination of self-interest to a divine purpose. Mackay believed with Calvin that the state was "God's vicegerent."[183]

Thus in the spirit of Thomas Chalmers, a free churchman, Mackay described the lay state as not

> by nature indifferent or hostile to religion. It appreciates the importance of religion in human society and recognizes the service which it has rendered to mankind. It is, at the same time, not controlled by any given religious organization, nor does it function in the interests of any particular church or religious group. . . . [Religion and government] are rather like two circles which intersect at one point. That point is the reverent awareness of God and of spiritual values. While, in the name of Caesar, a lay state demands, and has a right to demand, the "things that belong to Caesar," it equally recognizes the obligation of Caesar, as well as of the citizens whom he rules, to "render unto God the things which are God's."[184]

In a lay state Christian believers would permeate the society as salt and light. But the Church itself would enjoy spiritual independence.[185]

For Mackay a lay state was not a secularized state. In the early 1950s Mackay set forth his philosophy of the relations between church and state in two essays, "Church, State, and Freedom" and "Religion and Government: Their Separate Spheres and Reciprocal Responsibilities."[186] The latter address was delivered in Constitution Hall at the fourth National Conference of Protestants and Other Americans United for the Separation of Church and State. The meeting had been postponed because the organization had been focusing on the presidential initiative of a diplomat being sent to the Vatican. Mackay was the keynote speaker on April 24, 1952, and Thomas Sugrue, a Roman Catholic, gave the daytime speech. They both emphasized personal religion.[187] In his address, after rejecting the possibility of a clerical state and a totalitarian state, Mackay wrote about the church's prophetic function, exercised through preaching and social teachings—along the lines of middle axioms but not specific policy directives—to the church and its members or to the public:

> Religion within the lay state, or for that matter within the life of any state, has a prophetic mission to fulfill. It must ever stand for the inalienable rights of man which he possesses in virtue of his creation by God, and in view of God's government of the world. It must emphasize the fact that souls, that is, responsible persons, are ultimately more important than civilizations. It must ever bring to the attention of rulers, and also jurists, that the Ten Commandments are moral ultimates for the formation of human character and for the conduct of human affairs. It must proclaim that a divine moral order is a reality which has to be reckoned with in the affairs of state and the conduct of government.[188]

As an experienced educator Mackay clearly emphasized the significance of religion in education. In doing so he may have surprised some listeners by advocating released time for students from school for religious study:

> It is perfectly clear, however, that in some way or other the most adequate provision should be made within the public school system for the inculcation of the great spiritual principles of religion at some time and place not in the school's precincts, but within the regular schedule of a pupil's working day.[189]

Mackay continued to warn prophetically against the insidious effects of secular cultural absolutes a decade later:

> In some democratic countries, the State creates secular absolutes which little by little assume religious significance. In this way the supreme abso-

lute sponsored by a government and commended to all citizens becomes a "way of life," "freedom," "national security," "anti-Communism," or even "Secularism." In a very subtle but real way, God, Religion, and the Churches are given importance in the measure in which they serve the cause of the new Divinities.[190]

Letter to Presbyterians

As the 1950s began, the Roman Catholic hierarchy was firmly opposed to the Protestant ecumenical effort, viewing Protestantism as a "false Christianity,"[191] and on June 6, 1948, the Holy Office in Rome repeated that if matters of faith were to be discussed, all Catholics were forbidden to attend meetings with Protestants. Mackay perceived Cardinal Spellman of New York as "the abiding symbol of nascent Roman Clericalism in the United States."[192] In the United States the hierarchy took positions on a variety of social questions that were not acceptable to non-Catholics. These issues included policies on public schools, religious liberty, separation of church and state, mixed marriages between Catholics and non-Catholics, and film censorship.

The political atmosphere in the United States was tense in 1953. The Soviet Union had a Communist government, and in East Asia, where U.S. policy had not been strong, Communists took over the government of China.[193] The Roman Catholic hierarchy was dogmatic in its opposition to communism. Pope Pius XI had formally condemned atheistic communism in March 1937 in his encyclical, *Divini Redemptoris*, and on July 1, 1949, the Vatican's Holy Office excommunicated Catholics who professed communism.[194] This clerical opposition to communism also manifested itself in other ways. When grave diggers at Calvary Cemetery went on strike for a pay raise in 1949, Cardinal Spellman of New York called them Communists and used seminarians to dig graves. The wives of the diggers visited Spellman to clear their husbands' names and deny his charges. Cardinal Spellman gave Senator Joseph McCarthy public support at a Communion breakfast at the Hotel Astor in New York on April 4, 1953. He told the gathering, "Senator McCarthy has told us about the Communists and the Communist methods. I want to say that I'm not only against Communism—but I'm against the methods of Communists."[195] Spellman also enlisted papal support for McCarthy. Pope Pius XII gave his apostolic blessing to McCarthy's wedding at St. Matthews Cathedral. Spellman became associated with Roy Cohn and defended McCarthy to a European group in Belgium. According to Eisenhower's Attorney General,

165th General Assembly, Presbyterian Church at Minneapolis where Mackay was elected Moderator, 1953.

Herb Brownell, Eisenhower thought that Spellman and others were attempting to make McCarthy president.[196]

Evidence suggests that the idea for Senator McCarthy's use of anticommunism as a political campaign issue came from a Roman Catholic priest. At a dinner at the Colony Restaurant on January 7, 1950, Fr. Edmund Walsh, SJ, dean of Georgetown's Foreign Service School, "suggested that McCarthy raise the issue of Communist subversion in the United States."[197] Several weeks after the dinner with Walsh and others in Washington, McCarthy charged that 205 Communists had infiltrated the State Department. Walsh never denied that he suggested this campaign issue.

In this climate of anticommunism, Mackay was chosen as the new moderator of the Presbyterian Church at General Assembly in 1953. Mackay and John Watson Christie of Delaware were the only two nominees; both had withdrawn in favor of Dr. Morse the year before.[198] When the outgoing moderator, Hermann N. Morse, asked for nominations, Dr. William Hanzsche, a pastor in Trenton, New Jersey, nominated Mackay, and James M. Tunnell Jr., associate justice of the Delaware Supreme Court, nominated Christie. Eugene Blake, the Stated Clerk, announced the final vote of 553 to 308, and

Mackay was elected. Dr. Christie moved to make the vote unanimous, and Mackay was brought to the podium and received a standing ovation. Dr. Morse told Mackay, "I resign with a great deal of happiness and commit you to the mercies of your brethren."[199] Mackay chose Dr. Christie to be his vice moderator the next day. At age sixty-four Mackay assumed the church's highest office.[200]

Mackay's term as moderator was hectic, filled with travel, addresses, and sermons. Two of his key themes were spiritual unity and religious freedom. His addresses "Mission and Unity" and "A New Idolatry" were excerpted in *Presbyterian Life*.[201] (The latter address was a response to the May 1953 issue of *The American Mercury*, which named Mackay as a top collaborationist with the Communists.) During his term as moderator, he wrote the statement "The Reformed Faith and Social Concern and Action," which came before the General Assemblies of the Presbyterian Churches U.S. and U.S.A. for action.[202] He toured Argentina, giving the Carnahan Lectures at Union Seminary, Buenos Aires.[203] In October, along with moderators Dr. Frank W. Price (Presbyterian U.S.) and Dr. Samuel C. Weir (United Presbyterian), Mackay spoke in his individual capacity in favor of union of the denominations:

The Christian Church is the instrument for the redemptive will of Christ. The Church cannot be the end in itself. . . . Unity of body and head must be a fact. Unity must be a dynamic unity. So the whole answer to the question of unity between these three Churches must lie in whether it is Christ's will that we be united.[204]

At the end of his tenure Mackay gave a report to the church[205] and preached a moderatorial sermon, "God's Servant The Church" on the text Isa. 49:3.

That summer the religious dimension of McCarthyism flared into public consciousness when Joseph Matthews, a congressional committee aide, published an article, "Reds and Our Churches," in the July issue of *The American Mercury*. The opening sentence made the following inflammatory claim: "The largest single group supporting the Communist apparatus in the United States today is composed of Protestant Clergymen." It claimed the Communist Party had enlisted seven thousand Protestant clergymen for support and published the names of many, including the Rev. John A. Mackay, President of Princeton Theological Seminary.[206] The firestorm was immediate, and Matthews was forced to resign a few days later.[207]

Mackay himself vigorously defended his reputation in press releases:

Speaking personally, I repudiate the charge that I am "pro-Communist." I have never supported any cause which, on its own merits, was unworthy of support by an independent Christian citizen of this country who is sensitive to human situations. If, in any instance Communists, unknown to me and for their own reasons, were interested in the same cause, that does not invalidate the importance of the cause, nor does it make me responsible for any casual coincidence in my interests and theirs. My life and interest have been entirely open. I have been consistently concerned about human freedom. I am not ashamed of any document I ever signed or of any cause I ever sponsored, whether it was in the interests of Republican Spain, or in favor of Spanish refugees from Fascist tyranny, or to advocate the repeal of the McCarran Act.[208]

In addition, Mackay made a strong statement advocating social justice as a positive means of combating communism:

What is meant by being "anti-Communist" or "pro-Communist"? Do we really want to combat Communism? The only constructive way, if admittedly the harder and more sacrificial way, to deal with Communism, is to tackle the ills in society and the weaknesses in human nature upon which Communism breeds. Let a concerted effort be made everywhere throughout the world to solve the problems of poverty and work, of social justice and brotherhood, and to give people a dynamic faith. Let all who believe in democracy develop a glowing, positive, fighting spirit. It is not enough to let passion flame in an anti-Communist crusade. Fanatical anti-Communism can blind rational judgement and create the kind of eerie silence that haunts graveyards. It can, with fiery vituperation, scorch values and personalities which our culture needs. The effort to uproot Communistic weeds in the garden of our society can blight flowers and destroy plants which this nation requires for its beauty and health, and ultimately for its security. Evil can never be dealt with by such a purely negative approach.[209]

The efforts of an employee of a powerful governmental congressional committee to discredit Protestantism resembled the Peruvian government's many attempts to limit Protestant influence in Peru and eliminate Mackay's mission there in 1923. Although prominent clergymen had written articles calling for action against McCarthyism, collective institutional resistance to the attacks on Protestants came from the Presbyterian Church, led by its new moderator, John Mackay.[210]

The publication of "A Letter to Presbyterians" in November 1953 was Mackay's most significant historical legacy as moderator, and its influence extended beyond church circles to impact the broader culture. Its publication was a pivotal event, turning the country away from McCarthyism. When it came, the impact of the "Letter to Presbyterians" was anything but gentle. Anti-Protestant attitudes died hard, however. As late as 1958 the Roman Catholic press continued to attack Mackay and Oxnam falsely as pro-Communist.[211]

After Mackay wrote the text of the "Letter to Presbyterians" in the autumn of 1953, it was approved by the General Council, a recently enlarged body to perform the executive function between General Assemblies. The text of the letter has been republished, studied, and analyzed.[212] Historians have concluded the letter was "theologically sound . . . socially relevant . . . historically correct."[213]

The letter begins by acknowledging the threat of communism to the society and the need for vigilance but then notes matters of concern. The sense of immanent peril and suspicion being created allowed a "subtle but potent assault upon basic human rights" threatening "freedom of thought." It noted the tendency of some congressional inquiries to become inquisitions. Treason and dissent were being confused, and communism was approached in a purely negative way. The letter pointed to the need for a constructive program of action to prevent the void being filled by a fascist tyranny and elaborated on three principles that should guide the life and thought of fellow Presbyterians:

1. The church has a prophetic function to fulfill.
2. The majesty of truth must be preserved.
3. The controlling factor in history is God's sovereignty.

Mackay's approach to the role of the Church in society coincided with J. H. Oldham's idea of middle axioms, stopping short of policy pronouncements:

> While it is not the role of the Christian church to present blueprints for the organization of society and the conduct of government, the Church owes it to its own members and to men in general, to draw attention to violations of those spiritual bases of human relationship which have been established by God. It has the obligation also to proclaim those principles, and to instill that spirit, which are essential for social health, and which form the indispensable foundation of sound and stable policies in the affairs of state.[214]

A correspondent for *Le Monde* wrote a story noting the firmness of the Protestant position against McCarthyism and all forms of totalitarianism, and noted also that there was no reaction from Catholic dignitaries. Indeed Cardinal Spellman had come to the rescue recently of Senator McCarthy in Brussels.[215]

Some Protestants also took up the anti-Communist themes of Matthews's July article in *The American Mercury*. Daniel A. Poling, editor of the *Christian Herald* and former minister at the Marble Collegiate Church in New York, criticized Mackay's views without naming him directly from the pulpit.[216] The following April after the "Letter to Presbyterians" was published, Poling contributed an article for the *Saturday Evening Post*, which compared the letter to the text of the *Cominform Journal*. Van Dusen answered Poling in the following issue.[217] Edward A. Dowey refuted the textual analysis.[218] Dowey later noted that "it was really quite shocking to me that a well-known clergyman, founder of Christian Endeavor, would be such a rascal. This was the work of a charlatan."[219]

The publication of the letter itself was highly controversial. In December 1953, Eugene Blake responded to criticisms of the letter in an address to the national conference of home mission leaders at Buck Hill Falls, Pennsylvania. The two groups that "stand to benefit by the weakening of the Protestant free churches," he noted, were communist and fascist totalitarianism, and anti-Protestant religious forces that believed they had the full truth. Favorable responses to a General Council statement were supportive by a rate of four-to-one, including support from outside the church constituency.[220]

Mackay's influence during his term as moderator was extensive. In January 1954 he spoke at the National Presbyterian Church, and Justice William

United States President Dwight Eisenhower, Rev. John A. Mackay, Rev. Edward L. R. Elson after a special service at the National Presbyterian Church, Washington, DC, January 1954. (AP Images)

O. Douglas, who had arrived late for the meeting, came up afterwards and talked with Mackay. Among the topics they discussed was the recent U.S. Supreme Court *Nugent* opinion limiting the right of cross-examination for those claiming conscientious objector status from military service. The next day from his chambers Douglas sent Mackay a copy of the opinion of the court, adding in a note to Mackay, "I am mighty proud of the great work you are doing in the cause of civil liberty."[221]

After the publication of the "Letter to Presbyterians," other Protestants began to stand up against McCarthy, including Episcopal bishop James A. Pike, a former Roman Catholic, who attacked Spellman the following March for his political involvement. In April 1954 the issue was still a lively one. At a lecture delivered under the auspices of the Department of Religion of Columbia University, Mackay spoke on "New Frontiers in the Life of the Church": "I am not ashamed of any support I ever gave at the time when I gave it, nor yet of the spirit and reasons which led me to give it," he said after "careful review" of the charges against him.[222] Because some people were suggesting that his support for the Spanish republic made him a communist sympathizer, he provided his analysis of the Spanish Civil War:

> My deep interest in Republican Spain and my indebtedness to Spain's culture and love of her people made it a sacred privilege for me to help meet the medical and other needs of the Spanish refugees from Fascist tyranny. Some of these were fellow-Protestants known and dear to me. I know whereof I speak.
>
> Forty years of intimate contact with Spain and Spanish America give me some authority. The Spanish Republic was a democratically constituted regime. It was controlled by Liberals and not by Communists. The great democracies refused to supply the Republic with the arms it needed in its struggle against the Franco rebellion, which was incited by the Spanish religious hierarchy and promoted by Hitler and Mussolini.
>
> To these arms the Republic was entitled under international law. The fact that it did not receive them will be remembered as one of the darkest betrayals in modern history and one of the chief sources of subsequent complication in European and world politics.
>
> It should never be forgotten that the present revolutionary era was born before the influence of communism began to be felt in the world at large.[223]

To Europeans the rise of McCarthy in the United States seemed comparable to the rise of Hitler or Mussolini in Europe. Visser 't Hooft told American Protestant leaders that "irresponsibility in the United States, as indicated by McCarthyism looms as large in the Western-European mind as the threat of aggression from the East."[224] Agents of the Federal Bureau of Investigation gathered material about Mackay, including articles and references to him in the *Daily Worker*, an east-coast Communist Party newspaper, and other publications. J. Edgar Hoover, however, found their efforts incomplete, inaccurate, and potentially embarrassing to him as director. A formal investigation of Mackay was not carried out. Mackay had never specifically criticized the FBI.[225]

The letter remained a topic of discussion at the opening session of the next Presbyterian General Assembly held in Detroit in 1954. Mackay addressed the opening assembly, asking that "the majesty of truth and the authority of law be restored. No immunity should put a subtle premium on 'patriotic lying.'"[226] The Assembly elected a well-qualified successor as moderator, Dr. Ralph Waldo Lloyd, President of Maryville College, American Secretary of the World Presbyterian Alliance, and a force working to encourage Presbyterian merger.

The General Assembly validated both the right and responsibility of the Council to act for the General Assembly between meetings. The principle was approved unanimously by the commissioners. On the motion of a former moderator, Dr. Roy Ewing Vale, the 166th General Assembly adopted and proclaimed the "Letter to Presbyterians" as its own action. Dr. John Sutherland Bonnell eloquently spoke in support of the resolution. He summed up the controversy and personal attacks made on Mackay that were

> so venomous and vindictive that the average person here would find it difficult even to imagine. Through it all . . . he has remained a Christian gentleman. No man will ever be able to say that Dr. Mackay, either by word or pen, has ever impugned the integrity or patriotism of a brother minister of another denomination. . . . I believe that Dr. John Mackay is one of the most completely consecrated and dedicated servants of Jesus Christ in this generation.[227]

After a few moments he stopped, and the commissioners rose and applauded for more than a minute.

When Moderator Lloyd called for the vote on the resolution, there was a hearty roar of "ayes" and two "noes." Mackay responded, "You have quite overwhelmed me this afternoon. The heart has to speak in silence, because words cannot express my feelings. . . . Thank you."[228] Other tributes to Mackay came as well.[229]

Further Theological Debate

The public debate about theology, society, and communism did not end with Mackay's term as moderator. In February 1955 Mackay, using historical arguments, spoke out to contradict Richard M. Nixon's statement that the Roman Catholic Church was "one of the major bulwarks against communism and totalitarian ideas."[230] This statement prompted a response published in *La Civiltà Cattolica* that linked communism to Protestantism in Latin America.[231] Later in the year Mackay spoke at the quadrennial meeting of the Student Volunteer Movement, where he linked Christianity's success in fighting communism to the church's efforts to defeat racial segregation and prejudice everywhere.[232] In a sermon at Riverside Church in New York, Mackay prophesied the inevitable defeat of Marxism and the eventual triumph of Christianity based upon a contrast of the personal qualities of the two leaders, Jesus and Marx.[233]

After his term as moderator had ended, Mackay also continued his theological writings under the auspices of the Presbyterian Church. Pope Pius placed increased emphasis on the role of the Virgin Mary and dogmatically and infallibly defined the Assumption of Mary into heaven in November

1950.[234] Mackay found the essential "riddle" of Roman Catholicism to be that Jesus Christ, the Son of God, the Savior, "is both adored and ignored."[235] He expected that the Roman Catholic Church would soon define Mary's role as coredemptrix with Jesus Christ.[236] Pope Pius XII had called for the Roman Catholic Church to dedicate a year to the Virgin Mary, and the Presbyterian General Assembly in 1954 had requested a report to consider issues connected with the observance of the Marian year. Pope Pius composed a prayer, printed in the *New York Times*, to begin that year.[237] In due course Mackay authored the report and delivered it on behalf of the Permanent Commission on Inter-church Relations in 1955 at the next General Assembly meeting held in Los Angeles.

The report titled "The Marian Cult in Relation to the Lordship of Christ and the Unity of the Church"[238] illustrates Mackay's strongly Christ-centered understanding of the Christian religion: "Nothing is more distasteful than to subject to unfavorable analysis developments which occur in another Christian Communion. Only when such developments affect the very core of the Christian religion . . . of the perfect Saviourhood and the complete Lordship of Jesus Christ can such a course be justified."[239] The action of the assembly noted "with sorrow this major departure from the historic Christian faith."[240] This theological statement showed that a theology emphasizing that all graces come to human beings through Mary or that she is considered as coredemptrix with Christ would defeat ecumenical unity. The criticism of the Marian doctrine, which wrongly exalted the status of the Virgin Mary with relation to Christ's place, was unanimously voted by the 167th General Assembly in Los Angeles.

Mackay also continued to work for church unity through the denomination. In 1958 at the 170th General Assembly, known as the Uniting General Assembly, Mackay was a member of the committee of three that prepared the document "In Unity—For Mission."[241] As its first act the General Assembly adopted this message as its own. Mackay facilitated the reunion by successfully arguing in favor of incorporating part of the name of the smaller entity into the name of the new denomination, the United Presbyterian Church in the U.S.A. He believed the old name, Presbyterian Church in the U.S.A., which had been the name of the southern and northern denominations before the Civil War, could be reserved for the future reunion with the Southern Presbyterian Church.[242]

He was invited to appear on NBC television to discuss the "Big Issue" with Dean Sayre, the grandson of Woodrow Wilson; Glenn Archer, former Dean of Washburn Law School; and Congressman Eugene McCarthy. Themes of discussion were potential issues of divided loyalty and separation of church and state. To a critic, the debate proved to be rather tame. To a question put by journalist James Reston, Mackay replied that a Roman Catholic president would not be required to take a loyalty oath but would follow his conscience.[243] Mackay stressed the issue of persuasion over coercion.

In his role as a theological leader Mackay held fast to the principle of separation of church and state and at the same time spoke out against the dangers of a secularized culture. The debate continued several more years as others like Bishop James Pike were concerned that many did not fully understand the teaching of the Roman Church on the subject of political influence.[244] The Vatican newspaper, *L'Osservatore Romano*, also proclaimed the right of the church to a role in politics.[245] The resolution of this debate, whose terms Mackay had helped to frame, did not occur until December 1965 with the publication of the "Declaration on Religious Liberty" at the Second Vatican Council.

Chapter 12

The Ecumenical Church (1936–1959)

"There is one body and one Spirit." (Eph. 4:4)

Mackay's training, energy, and natural and spiritual gifts allowed him to fill significant leadership roles in four international ecclesiastical organizations, and his influence radiated beyond them into the broader culture. Since sound theology can only be created within the Church, his participation and leadership in these organizations directly affected the development of his creative thought and writings. His roles as President of the Presbyterian Board of Foreign Missions (Board) from 1945 to 1951, as a member of the Provisional and Central Committees of the World Council of Churches (WCC) from 1946 to 1954, as Chairman of the International Missionary Council (IMC) from 1947 to 1958, and as President of the World Alliance of Reformed Churches (WARC or Alliance) from 1954 to 1959 amplified his influence and authority.

In these positions Mackay worked from the bottom up to harmonize and coordinate developments within each organization to form an ecumenical church as a worldwide, living organism—a fellowship of the road that reflected the body of Christ and was God's instrument in the world. The roles he played were complementary and mutually reinforcing, not duplicative, since he simultaneously worked on different aspects of a single spiritual task. Building on the spiritual work of Speer and Mott, Mackay led the movement and the institutions by skills of personal persuasion and the logical soundness of his theology. He worked toward a structure capable of continuing to perform John Mott's lofty objective of "evangelization of the world in this generation."[1] Accordingly this chapter focuses on and discusses Mackay's contributions to the missionary and ecumenical aspects of the church. It concludes with a section briefly summing up certain of Mackay's key thoughts and ideas largely in his own words.

As a member of the Presbyterian Board of Foreign Missions, Mackay directed and influenced Presbyterian missionary efforts for more than twenty years. The Presbyterian Church polity was particularly suited to foster church expansion on all continents. Through its expanding polity Presbyterianism could contribute to the WCC, just as Mackay became convinced that the IMC could infuse a missionary dynamic into the WCC. On the other hand he was also conscious that overemphasis on the confessional element could splinter the joint missionary movement fostered by the IMC, and he never wished to absolutize a particular institutional structure. Occasionally official offices Mackay held formally linked groups together, such as his service as chairman of the Joint Committee of the IMC and WCC, in which he succeeded John Mott in 1949.[2] Mackay's thought, efforts, and strategy on the subject of the One Holy Catholic Church benefited from the complementary roles he played and the synergy of organizations having common purpose. His administrative strategy was coordinated to express an overall systematic approach to the development of understanding of the term *church universal*. In the course of developing creative theology to advance needed practical goals, his writings contained insights into eternal truths of the mysteries of Christ's Church, themes to be developed further by others. This chapter describes concrete efforts made within organizations to foster conscious awareness and self-understanding of the Ecumenical Church.

The Presbyterian Board of Foreign Missions

From its outset the theology of the Presbyterian Board of Foreign Missions was "churchcentric," meaning that missions were ecclesiastically controlled and directed based on the principle that "Christ gave His commission to the disciples *assembled* and already the nucleus of His Church."[3] Presbyterian foreign missions were not "entirely a matter of individual Christians hearing a call, being commissioned by Christ, empowered by the Holy Spirit, and thereafter . . . self-propelled missiles not obedient to church courts or subject to church discipline."[4] The Board began in 1862 when New York State granted a charter to the organization, and its offices were located in New York City.[5] It had been founded by the uncle of the grandfather of Mackay's friend, Walter Lowrie. The founder The Hon. Walter Lowrie served from 1837 to 1868 after he had retired from his position as U.S. senator from Pennsylvania.[6] Walter Lowrie's son, John C. Lowrie, led the organization until 1891. Later Robert E. Speer took his place. Speer was conscious of this connection with the founders, even referring to it as an "apostolic succession."[7] The Board was divided into the secretarial and financial departments. At the turn of the century, after growth stimulated by the Student Volunteer Movement, the secretarial department was reorganized into a home department, with a home secretary handling correspondence with home churches, and a foreign department, with foreign secretaries keeping contact with missionaries abroad. In 1923 two new departments were added, a candidate department and a medical department.

Under the Board's charter the members of the board of trustees were appointed by the General Assembly of the Presbyterian Church in the U.S.A. The secretaries worked under the supervision of the Board to administer the organization. As growth continued, the organization was again reorganized so that two secretaries, Speer and Arthur Judson Brown, had general supervision over the entire work of the Board. They worked well together, and when Brown retired in 1929, Speer became the senior secretary. Salaries carried a special provision that when cuts in pay had to be implemented, the secretaries shared the cuts, which reached 20 percent during the Depression. The Presbyterian Board of Foreign Missions was a formidable international enterprise long before global commercial enterprises claimed the name of multinational corporations in the 1960s.

Mackay had been appointed a secretary in the foreign department of the Board of Foreign Missions in 1932.[8] Although he resigned as secretary to become president of Princeton Seminary in 1936, Mackay's attention to foreign missions continued in a different capacity when he became a trustee in the class of 1937–1940, during Charles Erdman's tenure as the Board president. Mackay was reappointed for further three-year terms until retirement in the late 1950s. In 1937 he contributed to the celebration of the Board's centenary volume and to the celebration of the Board's centennial year.[9] His speech provided the theme for a *New York Times* editorial quoting Mackay's ideas on missions and the church and praising the contribution of missions to human society.[10] A month after his election Mackay took office as the president of the Board in December 1944. He was pleased to work with a loyal group of men and women on the Board, who had achieved a "marvelous unity."[11] In 1946 under his leadership the Board developed a postwar strategy for advance.[12]

Prior to election to its presidency Mackay played a leadership role on the Board. One basic principle the Board confronted in the late 1930s and early 1940s was the "Chosen" (Korean) question, namely, what was the correct missionary response to the Japanese government's "Spiritual Mobilization," or emperor worship, that Japan required in Korea?[13] The Japanese believed that the sun goddess Amaterasu Omikami was the ancestress of an unbroken chain of Japanese emperors. To enhance Japanese nationalistic sentiments, shrines to the sun goddess were being erected in all cities and towns in Korea. Teachers and students had to bow to them periodically to show patriotism regardless of whether the schools were operated by government, mission, or church. This was a key element of the theocratic and fascist system of Japanese fanaticism.[14] Trouble for the Presbyterian Korean mission began on January 20, 1936, when the Japanese removed Dr. George S. McCune and Velma L. Shook, principals of a boys' and girls' academy, from their positions after McCune refused to take students to the town shrine to bow. Members of the mission negotiated with the government unsuccessfully. The government required that the executive committee of the Korea mission sign a pledge not to discuss the shrine question at the annual mission meeting in Seoul in 1936, and police monitored the meeting to ensure it was followed. The pledge was also required in the next three annual meetings. At the eight-day annual meeting the mission followed the executive committee's recommendation and voted 69 to 16 to withdraw from secular education. The methods for implementing this withdrawal took time and raised questions, including the possible sale and transfer of the school property. Provisions were included that a timely protest of a withdrawal from any station would be referred to the mission for further consideration. Several protests were received, and delays occurred in closing schools in Seoul and other mission stations. In one case the founder of a boys' academy in Taiku refused to resign. The harmful influence of the Shinto religion had been reported in 1937 by a missionary in an article in the *Presbyterian*.[15]

As reports in the press appeared, church leaders felt the increased need to resolve the issue decisively.[16] To deal with increasingly complex questions, on September 23 and 24, 1940, the Mission Board held a special conference among the Board and executive staff and fifteen members of the mission who were home in the United States on furlough. On one hand the mission and its executive committee had had serious difficulties carrying out the emergency educational policy during the prior five-year period. The difficulties included Japanese government opposition and interference, the fact that a minority in the mission who opposed mission policy had been given rights to object, and the practical issue of financial costs of closure, including the accrued deficits. On the other hand were communication and administrative elements. Staffing changes had placed a series of five different secretaries in charge of the issue, causing a lack of consistency in carrying out the Board's wishes; there were communications problems; and in the field, missionaries held majority and minority positions on the issue. Mackay was selected to act as chairman of the Foreign Department Committee of the Board and of the special committee appointed to draft a report on the Chosen conferences.

Mackay's draft report was circulated to Board committee members. They debated its final form and discussed which elements of the dispute should be made public. One committee member, W. H. Foulkes, pastor of Old First, Newark, favored a broad disclosure, while Charles R. Erdman, president of the Board, counseled privacy on the issue. He confidentially expressed to Mackay that the Board secretaries had not implemented the Board's policy, and expressed disappointment with the mission's position as well. Erdman's preference for privacy caused another member to believe that Erdman was trying to save his friends from embarrassment.[17] Mackay's inclination in his first draft of the report was to lean toward full disclosure, but in the end he fell back to the position of furnishing full background in response to any questions raised about the report.

The final report alluded to administrative factors but did not set forth or discuss them directly. The Board had consistently objected to allowing its representatives to take part in ceremonies involving an acknowledgment of a spiritual authority higher than Jesus Christ. The Board's policy statement of 1938 was reaffirmed. Finally, the Presbyterian Board refused to criticize or call other Christian groups in Korea or the world "apostate" that did attend the shrine ceremonies. The final document was published in *The Presbyterian* in November 1940.[18]

The Christian mission enterprise also had extensive interests in China. By 1930 there were about three thousand American missionaries in China representing sixty missionary societies.[19] During the late 1920s and early 1930s Christian missions influenced the cultural life of China especially through the Christian colleges that touched the portion of the educated class not inclined to revolution.[20] Although in 1936 only about 13.5 percent of the students of higher education attended Christian colleges, these colleges were pacesetters in instruction and standards of living.[21] The social programs of the YMCA also played a significant role in social reform.

Often an effective way of communicating that Christ came to bring life and bring it abundantly was through Christianity in action. To that end the Presbyterian Mission Board encouraged educational, medical, and agricultural missions around the world. Many educational institutions and hospitals founded by missionaries remain in operation. Perhaps less well known, the agricultural missions were a strong element of the church's work, especially in China and India. John Reisner served as Dean at the College of Agriculture and Forestry in Nanking University, in China. In 1919 he recruited to the school faculty Lossing Buck, whom he had known from a China Study Group at Cornell University, and Buck stayed for twenty-five years, becoming a leading authority on Chinese agricultural economics. His book the *Chinese Farm Economy* was published by the University of Chicago Press. In his later years Reisner returned to the United States, founded Agricultural

Missions in New York and travelled worldwide. Missionary teachers like Sam Higginbottom brought principles of economics, social justice, and agriculture to India. He helped students understand the error of believing that increases of wealth come from labor alone. He showed them that capital, understood as God's own gift, can relieve mankind from degrading toil.[22]

Mission work in China, and particularly Nanking, was difficult and dangerous in the years immediately before World War II. When Japanese military aggression in Nanking cut off the diverse, Western-inspired programs for social welfare, individual missionaries led a humanitarian effort to aid the Chinese people. In November 1937 W. Plumer Mills, a Presbyterian missionary, first suggested the creation of the Nanking Safety Zone to offer sanctuary for civilians, and led by John Rabe, a German businessman, in due time the zone accommodated between 200,000 and 300,000 refugees. The safety committee declined to follow the advice of U.S. diplomats to flee and remained behind in Nanking.[23] Robert Wilson, son of Methodist missionaries, trained in Princeton and Harvard Medical School, had returned to Nanking in 1935 and then remained behind as the only surgeon there when the Japanese bombing began in August 1937. M. Searle Bates, who became chairman of the International Committee after 1939, witnessed many brutal crimes and testified at the International Military Tribunal of the Far East held from August 1946 to February 1947 to investigate war crimes.[24]

Mackay's thinking about the practical role of missionary work in Japan during World War II is reflected in his writings. As has been noted, Reinhold Niebuhr enlisted Mackay to serve on the advisory board of the newsletter *Christianity and Crisis*, and Mackay did so for several years. In the winter of 1941 Mackay was asked to prepare an editorial for the March newsletter on the subject of the mission situation in the Far East. At that time the Methodist Board action was to withdraw missionaries from Japan, Korea, and occupied China, but the Presbyterian Board declined to do so. Before leaving Princeton for other meetings, Mackay submitted his editorial titled "The Missionary Stake in Japan," in which he described the foundation of the position for nonwithdrawal. Mackay pointed out that the Jerusalem Conference had placed the missionary enterprise beyond the protection of their home governments (though children and mothers responsible for their care could be withdrawn) based on "the nonpolitical character of the Christian mission." The need to demonstrate that "there is a community superior to the community of nations" made this policy imperative. Mackay reviewed the proofs of the article, but Niebuhr realized the controversial nature of the issue he had selected when several editorial board members, who were Methodists, were unable to commit themselves to Mackay's editorial position. Due to his heavy workload, Mackay declined Niebuhr's offer to expand that editorial into an article for publication later that spring.[25]

The missionary movement did create a transnational fellowship during the war. Concerned about the likelihood of hostilities, 190 American missionaries in Japan sent a telegram to the Federal Council of Churches on February 16, 1941, as an attempt to explore possible ways to avert a war. Mackay and sixteen other missionary leaders, including Douglas Horton, Bishop James C. Baker, Roswell P. Barnes, Kenneth S. Latourette, Walter W. VanKirk, and A. Livingston Warnshuis, attended a meeting at Riverside, California, during Easter week 1941 on behalf of the FCC. The nine delegates from Japan included Toyohiko Kagawa and Tsumejiro Matsuyama, a Member of Parliament. They discussed the danger of war and problems of the Christian movement in Japan, including participation in ceremonies at Shinto shrines. The visit could not prevent war, but it strengthened the ties of fellowship among Christian leaders for the coming years.[26] On their knees, the Christians "pledged one another that, whatever happened in the international sphere, we Christians would remain united in Christ."[27]

After the war Mackay travelled widely on behalf of the Mission Board. In 1946 the Board asked John and Jane Mackay to return to Latin America for an evangelistic trip, a "brief period of intensive work." During the seventeen-week trip from June to October, they visited fourteen countries, and Mackay spoke two hundred times, 90 percent of the time in Spanish. The trip was entirely by air, and everywhere he found evidence of "the new Roman imperialism" which "brought home to . . . [him], in an overwhelming way, the importance of united evangelical action." The trip involved "traveling, preaching, lecturing, interviewing and dealing with knotty problems in the life of a mission or national church."[28] It is documented in his contributions to *Theology Today* and *The Presbyterian*.[29] Three years later on a trip to East Asia, discussed below, Mackay visited and encouraged Presbyterian mission activities in that region.

Mackay also addressed, concisely and practically, the theology of missions in a booklet produced by the Board of Foreign Missions:

> What is a theology of missions? It is simply clear thinking in terms of God and His redemptive will regarding the responsibility of Christians for the World in which they live. For theology, in simplest terms, is the understanding of life in all its phases and problems in the light of God and His purpose. . . .

Four basic realities are taken into account:

1. Man and his need
2. God and His purpose
3. Jesus Christ as the Divine Redeemer
4. The Christian church as the Divine community.[30]

Because he had taken on a commitment as chairman of the IMC, Mackay declined to serve as president of the Board of Foreign Missions after 1951 when he resigned after six years, continuing as a member of the mission Board until its reorganization. He played an important role in the denomination's transition to a Commission on Ecumenical Mission and Relations[31] when the expression "foreign mission" was dropped as obsolete, the name of the Board was changed, and the role became a "fraternal" one.[32]

With regard to the Presbyterian Board of Foreign Missions one final point must be made. The unfortunate title of an autobiography by a dedicated Board secretary tended to blur analytical clarity about sharp distinctions between political/economic colonialism and the missionary movement. Although contemporary, the two movements in fact had distinct motivations, purposes, results, and consequences. They were not intertwined or conflated. One movement was primarily spiritual; the other was material. One was motivated by gain; the other was motivated by self-giving. The flow of the subjects' resources went in opposite directions. In the case of economic colonialism, profits derived from raw materials generally flowed to the developed West. In the case of the missionary movement, human and financial capital left the West, planted a new religion outside the West, and in the process created hospitals, schools, and colleges benefiting the developing world. When the process of indigenization was completed, the scaffolding of the missionary enterprise was removed, and younger churches stood on their own as partners in the evangelistic calling.[33]

The extensive and successful social-improvement aspects of the Presbyterian Christian missionary movement reflect an example of disinterested foreign aid well before unilateral and multilateral governmental aid became an accepted instrument of foreign policy after World War II. For a variety of reasons, the aid distributed as a secondary aspect of the Christian missionary movement was delivered more effectively by and through Christian missions than political foreign aid delivered by governments, their agencies, or private secular groups.[34]

World Council of Churches

The conception for the World Council of Churches occurred in 1935 in the living room of President Stevenson's home, Springdale, at Princeton Theological Seminary. There on December 15, Stevenson hosted a meeting attended by William Temple, Archbishop of York; J. H. Oldham; William Paton; Henry Smith Leiper; Samuel McCrae Cavert; and others. A convinced Presbyterian, Stevenson mentioned to his guests that Princeton Seminary had graduated seven men who later became bishops in the Anglican Communion, and then he quipped, "And, I must add, about seven thousand Presbyter bishops!"[35] At the meeting William Temple suggested the creation of "an interdenominational, international council representing all the churches with committees to carry on various projects now forming the objectives of distinct world movements." It would be a "thoroughly official council . . . thoroughly coordinated ecumenical movement."[36] Mackay believed that his predecessor, Stevenson, would be remembered for this meeting as a decisive event.[37]

Institutionally, the WCC had a complicated constitutional form derived from the Oxford and Edinburgh Conferences. Members of the provisional committee were appointed equally from the Faith and Order Movement and the Life and Work Movement. At its February 1946 meeting, the Faith and Order Committee unanimously elected Mackay as a representative of the Committee of Fourteen to succeed Dr. Mudge, who had recently died, and who had in turn succeeded Dr. Stevenson. As a member of the Committee of Fourteen, Mackay was also a member of the Provisional Committee. Until the First Assembly when the WCC would come into actual existence, the Provisional Committee was responsible for its organization and had authority to elect a general secretary. Mackay had not expected the honor, but was pleased to accept membership on the committee.[38] The following month he was also named to the board of the Ecumenical Training Center, which the generosity of John D. Rockefeller had made possible.[39]

Consistent with his insights Mackay worked and spoke over the years in meetings of the council to maintain a religious movement toward authentic evangelical personal religion that was biblically based. As a member of the Provisional Committee, and later the Central Committee, Mackay was at the heart of the founding of the WCC, serving with the group that wrote the WCC constitution. He warned forcefully against an institutional emphasis developing within the movement. At the meeting of the Provisional Committee of the WCC, held in Pennsylvania in April 1947, Mackay "thought that it should be made clear that the World Council was not moving towards a Romanised Protestantism, having before its eyes the ideal of a single ecclesiastical unit, whose chief officers would ecclesiastically and theologically control the whole church structure."[40] In later years he emphasized this point, namely that the council was not to be a super church and that the Central Committee was not a "College of Cardinals."[41]

The opening ceremonies of the First Assembly of the WCC in 1948 were held in Amsterdam, Holland, coincident with a festive historical occasion when the beloved monarch, Wilhelmina, abdicated the throne in favor of her daughter, Juliana. Canals were illuminated, and the streets were decorated for that event. For the Council Assembly representatives of one-hundred-fifty churches (i.e., denominations) attended. "The most important thing about the Amsterdam Assembly was that it happened," Mackay noted. "Our unity was in Christ, who, amid all our diversity, had made us one in Himself."[42] The Council began with a procession and service at Amsterdam's Nieuwe Kerk where three thousand persons crowded to hear John R. Mott preach the sermon. That evening the Conference venue shifted to the Concert-Gebouw, where Mackay gave one of the opening addresses, tracing missionary efforts that contributed to the formation of the Council, and stressing that the church must not only be a worshiping church but also a missionary church.[43] The next day Mackay was a guest of HRH Princess-Regent Juliana and Prince Bernard at a luncheon given at the Royal Palace, Amsterdam.[44] At the plenary meeting of section 2, Chairman Mackay presented the report and led the discussion.[45] *Theology Today* had focused on the church and the ecumenical gathering in its four issues immediately before the Assembly, and in the fourth Mackay wrote an editorial interpreting its meaning and the goal of ecumenism—evangelical catholicity.[46] After the Assembly had ended, Mackay editorialized that "perhaps the most significant thing that the World Council of Churches did, was to commit itself to missionary activity as an essential aspect of the Church's life."[47]

As Van Dusen later noted, Mackay's forceful advocacy significantly influenced historical development in the Central Committee of the WCC, which met in Rolle, Switzerland, in August 1951.[48] There a draft paper, "The Calling of the Church to Mission and to Unity," reviewed the relationship of the IMC and the WCC, raising thorny practical and theological questions. A trend to convergence was evident. The IMC was called to evangelism, but it also realized the need and advantage of institutional unity for its work. The younger churches themselves had also formed councils whose existence implied the need for structural unity. The arrangement was also complicated because of inconsistent relationships of missionary societies to churches within various denominations.

At Rolle, the committee's draft document on the missionary and ecumenical calling of the church limited the term *ecumenical* to the pursuit of unity.[49] Mackay, as chairman of the Joint Committee of the IMC and WCC, challenged that usage, thereby shaping the meaning of the word *ecumenical*. In discussion Mackay explained the

John Mackay, Joseph Hromádka, and Jane Mackay in Amsterdam, August 1948, for the First Assembly of the World Council of Churches.

dual functions of the church and the . . . terms in which these dual functions can best be expressed. . . . The Church exists in order to expand and it will do so by the proclamation of the Gospel and all that is involved in this. The Church exists also in order to express Christ's desire for unity. . . . The difficult problem concerns terminology, especially in reference to the use of the word "ecumenical." . . . I suggest that we reserve the term "ecumenical" as the generic term including work for missions and for unity. . . . The basic concerns of all of us to occupy the inhabited earth for Christ and to achieve unity among the forces engaged in this effort are indissolubly connected. It is in reference to this total task that we must use the word "ecumenical." . . . The greatest encounter of our time is that between the ecumenical Church and the totalitarian state, the ecumenical Church being that which is not necessarily united in visible form but in which people have a commanding loyalty to the Lord.[50]

Mackay's approach to the definition is found in the final draft of the Rolle declaration produced by the special committee under its chairman, Lesslie Newbigin, and as such became authoritative for the movement: "We would especially draw attention to the recent confusion in the use of the word 'ecumenical.' It is important to insist that this word, which comes from the Greek word for the whole inhabited earth, is properly used to describe *everything that relates to the whole task of the whole Church to bring the Gospel to the whole world*."[51] The Rolle declaration was republished in *Theology Today*.[52]

World Council of Churches Central Committee meeting at Rolle, Switzerland, August 1951. (WCC photo archives)

Contributing also to discussions in the fifth meeting of the Central Committee, Mackay introduced discussion of the theme of hope at the meeting at Lucknow in the winter of 1952–53. The formulation of Christian hope, he suggested, must meet two criteria: "First, the formulation must be biblically central, and second, it must be ecumenically unifying."[53] During summer of 1954 Mackay's travels and duties as moderator of the Presbyterian Church took a heavy toll, and immediately after the World Alliance meeting at Princeton (which followed an IMC gathering at Staten Island) Mackay "simply caved in." "Two days after the sessions were over, I suffered from complete prostration," he wrote to Goodall explaining his absence from the Second Council Assembly at Evanston, Illinois.[54] A three-week respite in the Shenandoah Valley of Virginia restored his energy. He wrote Visser 't Hooft of his great disappointment in missing the Evanston Assembly: "I was simply like a boxer who had got a knockout blow and was literally dazed and useless for anything further."[55] Unfortunately, the Evanston Assembly was a disappointment to many. Pierre Maury, D. T. Niles, and Max Warren were critical of various aspects.[56] French pastor Marc Boegner was correct that "the conference suffered from the absence of theologians Barth, Brunner, Mackay, Niebuhr."[57]

In discussions the following year at the Central Committee meeting at Davos, Switzerland, Mackay emphasized the connection between individual spirituality and the nature of unity being sought. While agreeing substantially with General Secretary Visser 't Hooft's address, he recommended the following clarifications:

1) The unity sought was not a monolithic structure.
2) The group should "stress . . . what unity meant in the relation of Christ to the individual Christian soul . . . [we] look too disparagingly on expression of Christian mysticism. The life of the Churches would be enriched if we could communicate to ordinary church members the experience of Orthodox, Roman Catholic, and Evangelical Christians."[58]
3) The unity sought implied mutual recognition . . . [Real understanding did not exist unless] participation in Holy Communion came at the beginning and not as the consummation.[59]

He also proposed, and the Committee agreed, the reformulation of a related question, namely, "In what way can the unity experienced by individuals in communion with Jesus Christ contribute to the promotion of unity among the Churches in the World Council?"[60] Finally Mackay advocated that the division of studies include "a study of the Lordship of Christ over the individual."[61] The Committee authorized the division to undertake the biblical study proposed. Leaving Davos, Mackay was convinced, prophetically, that if Christian movements "are to be saved from becoming mere historical memories or venerable façades . . . their supreme concern must ever be to become effective organs of the redemptive Will of Christ."[62]

As a member of the Central Committee and friend and colleague of its authors, Mackay reviewed the history of the ecumenical movement that the World Council published in 1954, ensuring that it documented and properly presented the essential contribution of the missionary movement to world Christianity. Visser 't Hooft asked Mackay to review his contribution to the *History of the Ecumenical Movement*.[63] Bishop Stephen Charles Neill provided Mackay a chance to comment on the treatment in the book's epilogue on the separation between the "two essential components" of the ecumenical movement, and noted to Mackay the important contribution of the missionary movement to the ecumenical movement in Kenneth Scott Latourette's section of the history.[64]

International Missionary Council

Major historical shifts and changes occurred in the period Mackay led the Protestant missionary movement. These included the dismantling of the colonial empires, the end of missions in China, the growth of a sense of global human interdependence, the growth of the concept of "development," the crisis of faith in the West, and the growth of the ecumenical movement.[65] As a manager and theoretician of evangelization, he addressed these issues in various ways.

Following the disruption of world missions during World War II, the need to take stock was apparent, and a small meeting was organized for 1947 to be held at a small town on Lake Ontario, about thirty miles east of Toronto. At Whitby, looking back at the world war, the conference participants may have thought problems for the missionary movement were behind it, but ironically new and different problems lay just ahead. Nationalism stimulated the resurgence of some world religions, and in the developed West, historian Kenneth Latourette memorably observed, "The Occident was being inoculated with a mild form of Christianity in such fashion that it was in danger of becoming immune to the genuine Gospel and its sweeping demands."[66]

The Whitby Conference was distinguished by the reality of the fellowship, and the members were drawn closer to one another spiritually after the war than before it. Historian William Richey Hogg thought that it "will probably be best remembered for three things: its determination to make evangelism the heart and core of the missionary movement; its revelation of a new equality, a new oneness, between older and younger churches; and its demonstration of the high unity of the Protestant world Christian community."[67] One of the signs of this unity was the reentry of Germany into the missionary fellowship.[68] Mott, now eighty-two, who had retired five years before as chairman of the IMC, gave the opening address at Whitby. Mackay met his old friends John Baillie and Walter Freytag, who attended.

Delegates studied and reflected on "the Given Word" and on the communication of that Word centering on the Holy Spirit as "the Dynamic Word."[69] They spent a day together meditating on the inner power within the church and against the outside world. Mackay led sessions with messages on "The Holy Spirit in Proclamation" and reflections on the meaning of the word "frontier."[70] When delegates from "younger" and "older" churches independently wrote virtually identical recommendations, Mackay stood and noted the work of the Spirit in the group.[71] One delegate observed, "True fellowship is somewhat like a sound digestion. You *must not* feel that it is taking place. If you do, something is the matter with it."[72] Another observed, "At the close of another one of these services there were prayers in many languages coming freely from the hearts of those there made one. A man may speak fluently in several languages; but when his heart is open to God, he can pray only in the freedom of his mother tongue."[73] In October 1947 Mackay was appointed chairman of the IMC, succeeding Bishop James C. Baker, and he took office on January 1, 1948.

WCC-IMC Joint Mission—The Eastern Asia
Christian Conference, Bangkok, 1949

Although Mackay's career is often closely associated with Latin America, his missionary leadership in his middle years also extended to East Asia: "After thirty-five years of intimate contact with the Christian missionary movement in the West, I came at length to that part of the world where mankind lives in densest number, where religions of world renown have their ancient seats, and where some of the most world-shaking events in history are taking place."[74] Mackay's trip to East Asia from October 20 to December 18, 1949, was a milestone in organized Christian expansion and missions, and during the trip he nimbly dovetailed efforts on behalf of the several different organizations. As a member of the Joint Committee of the World Council of Churches and the International Missionary Council, Mackay expanded and strengthened both organizations in that region. As President of the Presbyterian Board of Foreign Missions, Mackay also preached to, visited, exhorted, and encouraged Presbyterian missionaries in Japan, Korea, Hong Kong, the Philippine Islands, and Thailand.

Mackay's dominant perception during the trip was of the church moving into a void and of the need to balance the concerns of the confessional church and the church universal. Writing in *Theology Today*, he developed three themes. The first was "the *Abysmal Void* which underlies all life and thought in those lands. The heart of East Asia is a great emptiness, an immense vacuum, an eerie chasm." Next he writes that "the *ubiquitous Communist* is the second reality determining the destiny of the Orient," and third, he writes that the "most important present-day reality in East Asia . . . is the *youthful Church*."[75] A portion of an address made immediately on return from Asia stressed the dilemma of Christian unity from a confessional point of view. The Presbyterian Alliance "'does not regard as its main objective to promote Presbyterianism in the world.' On the other hand we cannot encourage the Churches of the Reformed family to give up treasures which appear essential to them for the sake of this unity."[76]

Soon after arriving in Tokyo Mackay spoke to a group of about sixty faculty members and students at the Meiji Gakuin, a Christian College of Reformed and Presbyterian tradition. After lunch two teachers drove him to Toyohiko Kagawa's home, where seven other Princeton Seminary men were gathered in a little upper room. Mackay found Kagawa in very good health—not a grey hair—and working hard. He preached every night, dividing his month into three parts: ten days in villages, ten days in the city, and ten days in social service and the country. Last year he had spent 180 nights in the trains without sleep. In addition he served as president of the Cooperative and Farmers' Union. Kagawa reported to Mackay that 180,000 persons left decision cards last year.[77]

Kagawa explained the condition of the Christian movement in Japan and said that communism and Russia were a real menace. Communists, especially Chinese and Korean Communists, were very active, and he considered the situation likely to become very serious on the retirement of occupation forces. The centralizing aspects of communism made an appeal to people accustomed to regimentation. From a spiritual viewpoint Kagawa found a tremendous Brethren influence in Japan, leading to interest in Christianity and the Bible, but there was a detachment from any active expression of Christianity in evangelism's social effort. Kagawa wanted all the missionaries who could be sent to Japan, whatever their gifts. The Japanese people had no deep resentment towards occupation forces. They appreciated the treatment and gifts but were now becoming somewhat restive. The restrictions of the occupation were gradually being relaxed, and intensive censorship was abolished.

Kagawa added that there were about 20,000 unattached Christians who met together for Bible study but did not belong to the institutional church or have a church organization. One of this group was the president of the Imperial University. They were good and influential people, but they criticized the churches. Pentecostals were doing good work among the lower classes that the regular churches were not touching.

In Tokyo Mackay made fact-finding visits to General Douglas MacArthur and the emperor of Japan. An aide led Mackay into the general's office after a few minutes' wait, and MacArthur met Mackay very cordially. The office was spacious but simple. On the wall on either side of the general's desk were two paintings of sailing ships. A piece of sculpture stood in the corner, and the windows overlooked the wall of a neighboring building. MacArthur's face was striking: calm and philosophic looking, Mackay thought, but somewhat more oval than the face of his former philosophy professor at Aberdeen, J. B. Baillie. He smoked a pipe continuously, and his occasional smile was somewhat aloof and reflective.

Mackay explained his mission to Japan, Korea, and the Philippines as an attempt to get a sense of the Asian situation prior to attending the Bangkok Conference. The general first broke out into a monologue on the Japanese people, and then, passing on to communism, discussed his philosophy of the occupation and the significance of Japanese religions and Christianity.

Mackay thought MacArthur's observations about religion were astute. The Japanese, he believed, transferred obedience and adulation to those who showed they had the power to conquer, an attitude usual to a religion that gave or promised direct benefits. They had become disillusioned: a vacuum was produced when their own religion did not help them, and they were beaten in the war. So they were now extraordinarily open to being led religiously and politically, if they were rightly treated.

"The men who brought me back from Australia along a road of blood were a very religious army,"[78] MacArthur told Mackay as he began to explain his philosophy of the conquest of Japan. Services were held before going into battle, and the soldiers' conduct was exemplary in Japan after the victory. Their attitude of power was a consistently calm self-reliance without flaw. The soldiers laid aside their guns and moved unarmed among the people, and their attitude made a profound impression on the Japanese. If military might had been dangled before the Japanese people, the consequences might have been different. The religious attitude of the army continued during the occupation. Churches were erected before hospitals, for example, and the objective of the occupation was to give a practical expression of the Sermon on the Mount and the meaning of loving one's enemies. Since lives of more people had been risked in Japan than in any other victory in modern times, MacArthur felt responsible to use victory wisely and unpretentiously. He wanted to provide a pattern that might work its way around the world to address the contemporary confusion.

Then MacArthur turned to his philosophy of ideas. An idea is the most potent force there is, he said. Since military might is impotent to deal with ideas, it is important that the right ideas be let loose in the world. MacArthur believed that communism in its current expression was a form of nihilism, rejecting both God and ultimate values, and equally, the dignity and freedom of the human individual. On the other hand, Christianity is a religion of faith: an adherent lives by the humble way and is not directly rewarded. Since the other religions of the East are of the directly rewarding type, said MacArthur, it was difficult for the Japanese to understand or appreciate Christianity. Christian churches and Christian missions must be aware of all the factors in the current situation including the advantages of the unparalleled opportunity. Political pressures should not be used to achieve conversions. The people should be free and not coerced.

The success of MacArthur's policies depended on the total impression made before the Japanese people. He deprecated any attempt by pressure groups of any kind, whether religious, political, or economic. He felt that the Japanese must not be exploited. Mackay's final impression of General MacArthur was that he was a sincere Christian idealist who had a real affection for the Japanese people.[79]

Next, Mackay was driven to the extensive palace area in the center of Tokyo for an interview with the emperor of Japan. After being admitted by very plain and unimpressive guards, Mackay entered the large, dilapidated area inside the front gate. No one was visible. The palace had been burned not by bombing but by flames from buildings adjoining the palace area. The emperor now occupied a section of the original administration building.

Mackay was admitted to a large waiting room; then the official interpreter and chamberlain visited and briefed Mackay on the procedure for the interview. When 2:00 p.m. struck, he was taken to a small reception room. The emperor was slim, had a slight moustache, and was dressed in a business suit with soft collar and tie. He greeted Mackay cordially and nodded his head constantly when Mackay was talking or being interpreted. The emperor allowed his guest to take the initiative and asked occasional questions. They discussed several personalities and topics, such as Dr. Mott; Mrs. Uemura, who was giving a lesson on Christianity once a week to the empress and her daughters; Korea; the relations between the United States and Japan; and the Bangkok Conference.[80] The emperor expressed his hope that the Christian churches would do everything in their power to establish peaceful relations between the two countries. At the close of the interview he shook Mackay's hand for over half a minute; he then turned and left by one door, and Mackay left by another.

Korea was Mackay's next destination, and he spoke often there. In Seoul, he preached in the Yung Nak Church, a large refugee church organized by Pastor Han Kyung Chik, a Princeton Seminary graduate, class of 1929. It was the largest congregation in Seoul with some two thousand members. The church was packed, with hundreds sitting outside the building's open windows.[81] On November 1 Mackay gave three versions of his address "Why I Am a Christian," successively at the Severance Medical School, Chosen Christian University, and Crothe University. In the evening Mackay had a pleasant dinner with President and Mrs. Syngman Rhee.[82] The president was in Princeton University from 1908 to 1910, lived in Hodge Hall, and was a member of the Calvin Club. The American ambassador was also present at dinner.

On Sunday Mackay preached in a former Buddhist temple. Six dormitories were former brothels owned by Japanese army authorities. Then he preached at the First Presbyterian Church of Seoul. Several days later, through the courtesy of a lieutenant serving at the front line, Mackay visited the 38th parallel, which separated North and South Korea.[83]

Passing over Okinawa by plane, Mackay next flew to Hong Kong, where he stayed several days. He was driven around the territory and visited the remarkable Christian monastery for Buddhist priests desiring to learn about Christianity. The name of the Buddhist Mission Center, *Tao Fong Shan*, means "The Mountain of the Logos Wind." During this part of the trip Mackay was also working on his article "Basic Christianity."[84]

After leaving Hong Kong, Mackay traveled to the Philippine Islands, visiting Manila, Dumaguete, Negros, Iloilo, Panay, Tuguegara in Northern Luzon, and Laoag. He stayed with the Carsons of Silliman University.[85] From the primitive conditions in Northern Luzon, Mackay returned to Manila and traveled through Hong Kong, arriving in Bangkok for the Conference. There he lodged with a missionary family, the Horace Ryburns.

The central purpose of Mackay's Asian trip was to attend the Eastern Asia Christian Conference, which met at Wattana Wittaya Academy, Bangkok. Ninety delegates from sixteen countries in East Asia met under the joint auspices of the IMC and the WCC.[86] Mackay found the Academy "a very lovely place. [His] Presbyterian heart filled with pride. Ranson, Visser 't Hooft, Leung, Manikam were present."[87]

The Conference was opened by the Prince Regent of Siam, who was welcomed by Manikam in full Indian dress and rajah headgear. Unfortunately, Mackay had little opportunity for further fellowship at that time, because after the opening ceremony he was met by a journalist from the Associated Press who wanted a statement. An uninvited group was attempting to disrupt the Conference. Carl McIntire, pastor of the Bible Presbyterian Church of Collingswood, New Jersey, had followed Mackay to Siam to charge that the "conference leadership was supporting communism."[88] Mackay rapidly dictated a brief statement about McIntire's group that included this remark: "The members of the group, while paying lip service to the Bible and to Jesus Christ, stand for an unbiblical Christianity. They express concern over communism and carry on their work with a communistic technique. They live by a Jesuitical Ethic."[89]

Although the dissident group asked to be admitted to membership in the Conference, they were excluded and formed their own conference, as they had intended to do all along.[90] The next day, however, the Chinese delegates to the McIntire conference withdrew from it and began to carry on evangelistic work in local Chinese congregations. They gave their travel money back to McIntire, alleging that they had been brought to Bangkok on false pretences. Manikam was in touch with the Indian delegate who had the same opinion. A few days later Mackay learned other details of McIntire's disruptive strategy that had been foiled.[91]

The content of the Conference itself was of high caliber. In one of the highlights Paul Devanandan gave a brilliant address on "The Christian Message in Relation to the Cultural Heritage of Eastern Asia."[92] Visser 't Hooft remarked that "communism is a problem in some form in every Asiatic country, where a new collectivism can fasten easily upon peoples just emerging from an ancient collectivism."[93] A final resolution called on Christians to "distinguish between social revolution which seeks justice, and the totalitarian ideology which interprets and perverts it."[94] As a lasting accomplishment the Conference agreed that a joint secretary for East Asia should be appointed who would, if possible, also visit Australia and New Zealand. Rajah Manikam became the leader who took on that task.[95]

Mackay was called on to give the closing address of the Conference, "Call to Discipleship."[96] The Sunday after his address a group including Mackay, Newbigin, Voelkel, the Thai moderator, a young Thai pastor, and Bishop Cipriano Navarro assembled at the Ryburns's house for dinner. Newbigin made interesting observations about the Eastern religions. He told the group that in government institutions in India a central picture of Gandhi was displayed with Christ and Buddha on either side, and that Gandhi's death violated Hindu sentiment regarding karma and focused attention on the cross. Gandhi's favorite hymn was, "When I Survey the Wondrous Cross." Hinduism would be willing to adopt Christianity if Christianity would not make any absolute claim for truth. Buddhism had virtually disappeared in India.[97]

After the Conference ended and before returning to the United States, Mackay flew north to Chiang Mai, Thailand, with a missionary group of twenty-one persons. Years before it had taken missionaries six weeks to reach that outpost by water, but it now took only two hours and fifteen minutes by air. In Chiang Mai, Mackay and Voelkel visited the Prince Royal College founded by Harris McGilvery, and on an island in the river seven miles from Chiang Mai, they visited the leper asylum. Of the 450 patients, 420 were Christians. Mackay's flight home travelling west took several days. When he arrived in New York at 2:30 a.m. he was joyously met at the airport by his wife and his daughter Ruth.

Just a few days after returning to the United States, Mackay met with Chinese exiles to discuss their situation and made a speech in New York supporting political and diplomatic recognition for Communist China to head off a fanatical nationalism. This speech and its advocacy of face-to-face communication between leaders led Mackay into extended controversy, as was noted in chapter 11.[98]

The pace of travel did not diminish. Under the auspices of the IMC, John and Jane Mackay made a four-week trip to Europe during the summer of 1951 focusing on religious freedom. The purpose of the trip was "to obtain first-hand information regarding the status of Protestant minorities in France, Belgium, Italy, Portugal, and Spain."[99] In Paris Mackay had a stimulating three-hour conference with seven eminent Roman Catholic scholars to discover what those liberal Catholics were thinking about various issues:

I discussed the Virgin of Fatima with my Roman Catholic friends. I asked them how they interpreted the development of the Virgin Cult. It was their opinion that it represented the beatification of humanity, "through the grace of our Lord Jesus Christ." But how has it come about, that the Madonna should straightway assume divine prerogatives? How has it happened that the Christian Trinity appears now as the Roman Quaternity, that the new Catholic mysticism is Madonna-centered and not Christ-centered? I received no real answer. To all intents and purposes the Holy Virgin has become the incarnation of the Holy Ghost.[100]

Travellling on to Spain, Mackay found the theory of nationality linked the government and Roman Catholic religion, and limitations on the rights of Protestants: "In a word, contemporary Spain is an intellectual sepulcher. My indignation burned when I thought of the Spain I had known. Today the true Spain is either not at home or is inarticulate."[101]

IMC and WCC—Organizational Integration?
Let the Church Be the Mission.

During the decade 1948 to 1958 the World Council of Churches and the International Missionary Council acted in association side by side while a theological, organizational, and practical consensus emerged that the two organizations should become one. As Mott's successor as chairman of the joint committee of the two organizations, Mackay's role was crucial to resolving difficult organizational and theological questions connected with integration of the two structures. His own thinking about the theological rationale for a merger based on the nature of the church, and the formation of a strong consensus to bring about integration, developed progressively in writings and in conference venues. The aftermath of the integration is examined in chapter 13.

Some Christians believed that their mission to the world was a primary responsibility of the church, but that the effort to recover Christian unity was not. Others thought that the WCC was bound to be composed of ecclesiastical officials, thus ensuring a measure of paralysis when anything important came up for discussion. Still others feared that the missionary movement would lose its sense of openness and commitment if it became a part of the WCC. Substantial bodies of Christians opposed the World Council because of that danger. On the other hand, Norman Goodall, who became secretary of the IMC in 1944 "had long taken it for granted that the paths of the IMC and a World Council of Churches would necessarily converge."[102] In 1948 Goodall had developed the expression that the two bodies would act "in association with" each other.[103]

At the WCC meeting in Rolle of August 1951, Mackay was still thinking of the effort towards world missions based on two organizations: "The I.M.C. was created under the missionary purpose of carrying the Gospel to the whole world whereas the W.C.C. was formed to achieve unity among those who have accepted the Gospel; and the I.M.C. is composed . . . of constituent councils, whereas the W.C.C. is composed of member churches."[104]

In January 1952 in Toronto Mackay delivered an address titled "The Two Foci of the Ecumenical Movement," and he discussed the problem again in a memorandum for a meeting of advisors.[105] In spring 1952 he also articulated in brief and synthetic form the problem of the relations between the two bodies for an editorial in *Theology Today*. He stressed expediency in meeting a functional goal as opposed to following an organizational formality. The publication of this article shows that in mid-1952 Mackay saw the two structures continuing as two separate entities:

> As we face this adventure let us who love the unity of Christ's Church, and long to see it assume its world-wide missionary responsibility, disabuse our minds of a dangerous fallacy. In the spiritual order mere structural bigness need not necessarily engender greater prophetic insight, greater redemptive action, greater organizational efficiency, or greater human harmony. The two bodies which constitute the organizational foci of the Ecumenical Movement must grow together on the road of loyal devotion to the Church's mission. They must not be simply pieced together at an ecclesiastical table in the name of the Church's unity.[106]

At Willingen, Germany, in July 1952, the IMC took up the conference theme "The Missionary Obligation of the Church." A commission had prepared a report with that title for study at the Conference together with the Rolle declaration prepared by the WCC.[107] Conference participants gathered in the small ski-resort town not far from the university center of Marburg, living in small hotels, pensions, and the homes of townspeople. A new frame town hall was built to house the meeting. The Council of German Missionary Societies provided generous hospitality at the first major international church gathering in Germany in over a hundred years. Bishop Otto Dibelius, President of the Evangelical Church Council of Germany, preached on Sunday at a conference Communion service at the small Lutheran Church, the only church in the town. It was reported that at this service for the first time in German history the Lutheran Church opened Communion to any baptized Christian.

Before Willingen Mackay had publicized mission through an editorial in *Theology Today*, where he wrote that "the Christian Church has no true meaning, and is positively untrue to its nature, if it fails to move from theological understanding and ecclesiastical comity to dynamic missionary action."[108] At Willingen IMC Chairman Mackay spoke to the conference theme, the missionary obligation of the church, in an address titled "The Great Commission and the Church Today." He used New Testament images of the towel of foot washing, the yoke of disciplined service, and the road of action to interpret how the great commission of the "imperious Christ"—a dominical command and summary of the gospel—relates to the church. Passing by objections that the great commission was valid only in the apostolic era and challenges to its literary authenticity as a late addition to the biblical text, he noted that action is the essence of life and that men and women must fit into God's plan for true human fulfillment. The great commission was not "Christological unitarianism," but the Trinity is directly implicated in the commission since "discipleship . . . was to be followed and sealed by baptism, baptism in the name of the Father and the Son and of the Holy Ghost."[109] Mackay emphasized membership in the institutional church, whose members were harnessed by a yoke with fellow Christians: "Unattached Christians who balk at complete identification with the Christian Church can never be Christian in the fullest sense, nor attain full Christian stature."[110] Nations in their revolutionary yearning must also be addressed by Christ's messengers. Mindful of the communist revolution in China and regretful that missionaries had not given the Chinese Church a theology and doctrine of the missionary obligation, Mackay urgently wished to provide a "doctrine of the Church in the purpose of God . . . while still there is time."[111] Moreover, Mackay noted,

A truly apostolic Church can never be satisfied with merely sponsoring missionary interest or in giving birth to "missions." It must itself become the mission. Let the Church be the Mission. . . . When the Christian Church as a whole recovers a sense of missionary responsibility and is imbued throughout its ranks with missionary ardour, certain things will happen. Christian thought will become concerned not merely with a theology of missions, but with a theology of mission. The role of the missionary society and the meaning of missionary vocation will be re-thought. The spontaneous expansion of the Church will be regarded as the natural thing to hope for and promote.[112]

David J. du Plessis, a Pentecostal leader, visited the Willingen Conference, where Mackay warmly presented him to individuals at the gathering and introduced him to the ecumenical movement. Addressing du Plessis,

Mackay asked, "Come and tell us in two five-minute periods *why* and *how* the Pentecostals accomplished so much in so short a time."[113] Through the power of the Holy Spirit, du Plessis answered the first question, and through the old-fashioned method each-one-tell-one, the second.

Under Mackay's leadership the Willingen Conference grounded mission in the doctrine of God and provided a Trinitarian basis for mission through the Church. The theological term *missio Dei* appears not to have been used at the Conference. The work of the conference catalyzed change in the paradigm of missionary work from a concept of "missions" to "mission." This basic shift has been broadly accepted and received, but the issue of the nature of the Church within the missionary movement was an issue of continuing debate. Dutch theologian Johannes Christiaan Hoekendijk attacked the view of churchcentric missions. Du Plessis, in fact, recorded that one unnamed person at the Conference thought the church was too institutionalized and "that it would be a blessing if some of these institutions burned down."[114] Though the meeting reached no consensus on the controversy over views of missions, the final report of the Conference affirmed that mission is God's Mission and that mission is of the essence of the church.[115] By defining the church only through its missionary function, Hoekendijk's approach later produced an unbalanced effect that caused great difficulty to the ecumenical movement in the 1960s.

Mackay considered the legacy of the Willingen Conference would be to extend ideas about the church from its earlier formulations of being sound in doctrine and pure in worship. The church must not only give

> birth to missions in the traditional Christian sense. The Christian church will fulfill its missionary obligation only when all its members, corporately and individually, bear witness to Christ. To have crystallized this thought and made it explicit in many ways and with diverse acts, and with the unanimous approval of the members of the older and the younger Churches who were present, will constitute I believe, the abiding significance of Willingen, 1952.[116]

Six months after the Willingen Conference, when God's hand led Mackay to India for three gatherings, the turning point came in Mackay's thinking about the issue of integration of the WCC and the IMC. His first visit to India for a study conference, the WCC Lucknow Central Committee meeting, and a Joint Committee meeting was full of meaning for Mackay. As a college student in Aberdeen he had studied, considered, and prayed about his own possible calling to India as a missionary. William Carey had begun mission work there in 1793, and Henry Martyn labored there at the turn of the century. Alexander Duff, the Scottish Presbyterian, after whom Mackay named his son, arrived in Calcutta in 1830 for mission work, after being shipwrecked twice.

The Asia Study Conference chaired by Henry Van Dusen convened at Lucknow, India, December 27–30, 1952, with the annual meeting of the Central Committee of the WCC to follow. This was its first meeting in Asia and the most important meeting to that time; it recognized the place and role of Asian Christianity within the World Christian Movement. Mackay's experience at the Study Conference changed his thinking about the role of the younger churches and the relationship between the two institutions of the ecumenical movement. Van Dusen, Mackay's companion on the trip, marked this turning point in Mackay's thinking. He observed Mackay silently watching as one by one the Asian Christians rose to speak, motivated by "profound dedication to Christ and his world wide Church." Two parallel institutions were an "anachronism," they argued, an "anomaly" that should "be resolved by the union of the IMC and the WCC."[117] Through the extremely high caliber of the contributions of the Asian Christians, Mackay realized "they have reached full maturity."[118] Van Dusen watched as Mackay stood in the closing moments and declared "his conviction that the day had come when the two Councils should be joined and that immediate steps should be initiated to bring their union to pass."[119] Van Dusen believed Mackay left Lucknow confident that integration would come to pass. Later in the year Mackay enlisted his friend Kenneth Grubb to assist in advocating a closer relationship between the two bodies.[120]

The issue was taken up again at the Joint Committee and Central Committee meetings in Hungary in July, 1956. Van Dusen, Goodall, and others agreed on the need for a strong introduction of the issue, setting "forth in as able, impressive, and conclusive as possible manner the underlying reasons for integration at this time; and all are agreed in asking you to take responsibility for a first draft of this highly important basic document."[121] Mackay complied by preparing a document that focused on the theological, ecclesiastical, psychological, and conciliar questions connected with integration and presenting it at the Central Committee meeting in Galyatető, Hungary. He emphasized that the "'re-birth of the sense of mission in the churches' was one of the most significant facts of our time, and recalled the bearing on the present proposals of the discussions at Rolle and subsequently on 'Mission and Unity.'"[122] The Joint Committee's statement on integration is included with the Central Committee's report as appendix 16.[123] Visser 't Hooft concluded discussion by offering several steps by which the interests represented in the IMC could be brought into the life of the WCC, with full responsibility, without disturbing the basis of the WCC as a council of churches.[124]

Preparing the way for the IMC conference on the Gold Coast at Ghana, Mackay wrote an editorial in *Theology Today* further developing the thought. He wrote,

> Let the so-called Older and Younger Churches truly become "partners in obedience" and give fulfillment to the missionary obligation of the Church. For it can now be taken for granted that the Christian Church has a "missionary obligation" to fulfill and that this obligation can be fulfilled only in partnership. . . .[125]
>
> Only on the road of missionary obedience, and not on the mere road of historical research, ecclesiological theory, or theological formula can the unity of the Church of Christ be realized.[126]

Decisive action on integration of the IMC and the WCC occurred under Mackay's leadership at the IMC meeting in Ghana where Mackay gave the keynote address on December 28, 1957, and presided over the Assembly held in Legon Hall of University College where "thirty-six national councils of churches and fifty-three nations" were represented. His keynote address, "The Christian Mission at This Hour," skillfully tied together themes of the development of the missionary movement in the twentieth century, the challenge of the present moment and the mission of the Christian faith, the individual Christian, the Christian group (such as a missionary society), and the Christian church.[127] Using defined terms and clear categories, the address is a succinct example of Mackay's mature thought on the missionary nature of the church. Mackay, along with Lesslie Newbigin, has been credited as one of the founders of missional theology.[128]

Various articles weighing the merits of integration had been published and discussions of the subject had occurred,[129] and when the time came at the meeting for debate, Mackay handled it deftly and sensitively. Max Warren, an Anglican who opposed integration, became a spokesman for the German and Scandinavian members, who also opposed integration. Knowing Warren's views and wishing to allow those opposed to integration to have their say, Mackay told Warren to speak for as long as he wished. In turn Warren began his thirty-minute speech by saying that he would vote for integration because "things have gone far too far for the Assembly to draw back."[130] Since the officers of the IMC had unanimously supported integration, if it were not adopted, Warren believed they would all resign, damaging the council's ability to conduct ongoing business without the leadership. Ten-

Mackay with colleagues at the International Missionary Council meeting held in Ghana, 1957–58

sions relaxed as Warren expressed his views and philosophy. Those opposed to integration had their voices heard.

By an overwhelming vote of 58 to 7 the Assembly adopted, in principle, integration of the IMC and the WCC, but requested that the WCC postpone until 1961 the third General Assembly, which was originally scheduled for Ceylon in 1960. The delay was intended to give churches an opportunity to study the integration plan. Second, the Assembly acted to accept a gift of $4,000,000 from John D. Rockefeller Jr. and eight boards of foreign missions of churches in the United States to establish or expand theological education in the lands of the younger churches. Princeton Seminary was well represented by eight assembly delegates who were alumni. Mackay met Ghanaian Prime Minister Kwame Nkrumah, an influential advocate of the Pan-African movement and graduate of Lincoln Theological Seminary in Pennsylvania.[131] Following the IMC meeting, Mackay, the outgoing chairman, travelled to Nigeria to attend an All Africa Church Conference.[132]

World Alliance of Reformed Churches

Simultaneously with his activities in the WCC and the IMC, Mackay participated in what has been termed the confessional movement, working to orient, link, and coordinate the Presbyterian and Reformed church group with the ecumenical movement as a whole. This was a logical development because Mackay, like Karl Barth, believed that the path to unity moved through the institutional church and not "on any neutral ground above or outside the severed churches."[133] Emphasizing the common background of these denominations, Mackay brought energy to the formerly sedate World Presbyterian Alliance. As president of the Executive Committee of the World Alliance of Reformed Churches (Alliance), Mackay forcefully set the agenda for meetings, bringing churches of the Reformed confessional type together in spirit through the councils.

The origins of the movement to bring Reformed churches together may be traced back to the Rev. James McCosh, President of Princeton University, who proposed a gathering of Presbyterians in Philadelphia in 1870.[134] Mackay's active participation with the Alliance began in the early 1940s when he presented a paper at the Western section of the Alliance meeting at Atlantic City, NJ, in 1942.[135] In early 1946 William B. Pugh, then stated clerk of the Presbyterian Church in the U.S.A., traveled to Britain and Europe to address the Eastern section of Presbyterian Churches, carrying a message of solidarity to the Europeans from Mackay. Pugh quoted Mackay as telling him, "Oh, Bill, when you are over there, please impress upon those Scots friends of mine how much we need the solidarity of the Presbyterian and Reformed Churches to make our greatest contribution to the World Council."[136]

Mackay began to energize the confessional movement and the Alliance through his writings and speeches. His essay "The Contribution of the Reformed Churches to Christian Doctrine" stressed six characteristics of these contributions: emphasis on doctrine itself, on truth, on divine sovereignty as an organizing principle of theology, on knowledge of God through biblical revelation, on doctrinal emphasis not for its own sake but rather for godliness, and on the ability to revise church creeds to meet new heresies and new developments.[137] Later, themes of unity and Reformed doctrine were blended together in a paper titled "Ecumenical Presbyterianism," in which Mackay stressed that the "purpose of the Alliance is not to promote Presbyterianism as an end in itself, but to make our great tradition serve the redemptive purposes of God in and through the Church Universal."[138] His goal was not a resurgence of denominationalism but a fulfillment of the redemptive designs of the Head of the Church.

When the Sixteenth General Council of the World Alliance convened for the first time on the European continent at Geneva in August 1948, shortly before the Amsterdam Assembly of the WCC, Mackay's speech articulated and identified two major trends: the "centripetal trend" toward "greater understanding, unity, and co-operation among non-Roman Catholic churches" and the trend toward formation of "ecumenical denominations or confessional blocks."[139]

During the next several years Mackay reflected on, spoke about, and advanced the delicate balance of ecumenical and confessional forces that finally culminated in a statement of guiding principles. WARC board members were strongly interested in the World Council. Minutes of the Executive Committee meeting at Westminster College, Cambridge, England, in July 1949 show that "there was unanimity of thought among the members present. . . . It was felt that while we want to be true to our Reformed and Presbyterian convictions, we are glad to be in the larger body of the World Council of Churches. We want to take our full part in the building of the 'Una Sancta.'"[140] The committee also discussed the relation of the Alliance to the younger churches. As a member who had direct knowledge and experience of being a missionary, Mackay warned of a potential danger: "If a certain trend in the confessional missionary Movement develops, it will break the Ecumenical Movement. It would tend to crystallize for the future the ecclesiastical traditions of the past. That would be a tragedy."[141]

Mackay's efforts were central to the expansion of the World Alliance to Latin America when the Inter-American Evangelical Conference was held in Buenos Aires in late July 1949. Mackay gave the inaugural address to six thousand Protestants.[142] Within this larger conference, Mackay was elected president of an assembly as a step toward formation of the Presbyterian Federation of Latin America.[143]

The WARC Executive Committee did not meet every year due to financial considerations, but a meeting was scheduled at Basle, August 13–15, 1951, following the WCC Central Committee meeting in Rolle, near Geneva. One of Mackay's concerns at Basle was to steadily advance the Alliance toward dialogue that had been in prior years somewhat static and ingrown. The meeting at Basle grappled with how to clarify the role of the Alliance in relation to the ecumenical movement. The Alliance's historian, Marcel Pradervand, noted that "Mackay played a decisive role in defining this relationship. He had prepared a draft statement which, with minor corrections, was unanimously adopted by the Executive Committee and became the historic 'Basle Statement' on 'The World Presbyterian Alliance in the Present Ecumenical Situation.'"[144] Leaders of the WCC also appreciated this statement because, in the words of Pradervand, "it clarified the position of the Alliance in the new situation created by the founding of the WCC."[145]

The Basle Statement presented the denominational balance through a paradox:

It is the true nature of Presbyterianism never to be merely an end in itself, but to serve the Church Universal of Jesus Christ, the Church which is His Body. . . .

There are Presbyterians today who are both more Presbyterian and less Presbyterian than ever before. They are more Presbyterian because they believe that in their religious heritage there are treasures of thought and life which are important for the Church Universal. They are less Presbyterian than ever before because they recognize that what God has said and done through the medium of other Christian Communions is also needed to enrich the Church Universal. They believe, therefore, that it is the highest glory of the Reformed tradition to maintain the vision and viewpoint of the Church Universal, seeking continually its welfare and unity, in accordance with the mind of Jesus Christ, the Head of the Church, and through the power of the Holy Spirit who indwells the Church.[146]

While meeting in Switzerland, Mackay had invited the World Alliance to hold its next council meeting at Princeton Theological Seminary, and, when the Seventeenth General Council of WARC did meet at Princeton in 1954, its representation was much broader than at prior WARC councils, which could not be characterized as worldwide. The gathering had representation from four African churches and from the churches of Australia and New Zealand. Six Asian churches and six churches from Latin America and the Caribbean also sent delegates. For the first time there were women delegates. Edgar F. Romig and Professor Joseph Hromádka chaired the Council because the president, Dr. E. J. Hagan of Edinburgh, was unable to attend. W. A. Visser 't Hooft and Eugene C. Blake were also present. Mackay delivered the opening address, "The Witness of the Reformed Churches in the World Today," on the theme of the Council. In the address he sensitively balanced and developed a series of potentially competing theological and ecclesiological points, emphasizing the sovereign rule of God in the affairs of men, the instrumental role of the Christian and the Christian Church, while cautioning the organization against becoming "an ecclesiastical power bloc." Exhorting commitment to the Church Universal while placing the "local in the sphere of the ecumenical," he stressed a "Biblically grounded, Christ-centered, and dynamic" theology and a church validated "by its missionary action."[147]

Mackay was elected president of the Executive Committee "to help the Alliance become a world-wide organization."[148] At the time he became president of the World Alliance in 1954, he was also a member of the Standing Committee of the WCC and the IMC. His use of these separate offices brought the ecclesiastical organizations into closer cooperation institutionally and theologically. Mackay's addresses and writings cross-pollinated these organizations with consistent but complementary, nuanced theological ideas and challenges.

Its meeting at Princeton gave the Alliance new importance and visibility. The message at Princeton was that church unity must become tangible and incarnational; spiritual unity was not enough. Unwillingness to practice intercommunion was seen as an impediment to unity.[149] The printed program included a greeting from President Eisenhower.[150]As an institutional advance Mackay initiated a resolution at a business session authorizing the Executive Committee of the Alliance to consider the best ways and means of furthering consultations that balanced ecumenical and confessional concerns, and the taking of any action.[151]

Mackay's leadership of the Alliance catalyzed closer relations with the International Congregational Council (ICC). Leaders of the World Alliance and the ICC had enjoyed a cooperative attitude for years, but during Mackay's tenure in the World Alliance, their relationship began to move progressively closer. The next year when Dr. S. Maurice Watts, Moderator of the ICC, read the Proceedings of the Princeton General Council of 1954—and especially Mackay's "great speech"—he realized that there was little difference between the Christian witness of each council. Leaders encouraged and facilitated the ICC to enter a constructive dialogue and theological studies with the objective of enjoying fuller unity.[152] These discussions bore fruit fifteen years later when a merger of the two councils occurred in 1970.

The meeting at Princeton received wide publicity and had other accomplishments as well. Actions were taken seeking religious freedom for Protestants in Colombia, criticizing the Greek Orthodox Church for restricting the Evangelical Church of Greece, and emphasizing that "it is God's will that every church of Christ should be allowed freedom by state and church"; declaring Communion open to any baptized person who loves and confesses Jesus Christ as Lord and Savior; declaring the church cannot withdraw from the world but also should not link itself with any particular political, social, or economic system; passing by one vote a nonbinding statement of attitude in favor of the ordination of women to ministry; calling for loyalty "to the Government of the nation in which you live." The Alliance had a strong base representing forty million Christians in forty-two nations and sixty-six denominations.[153]

Mackay wrote a message to the members of the World Alliance in January 1955 called a "Letter to the Reformed Family of Churches." Less well known than his "Letter to Presbyterians" (1953) or the message of the General

Assembly of the National Council of Churches, "A Letter to the Christian People of America" (December 1952), of which drafting committee Mackay was the chair, this letter sought to heighten the consciousness of individual congregants. It drew attention to the diversified problems faced by coreligionists, including racial problems in South Africa and the United States, Communist countries, and Spain and Colombia.[154]

Mutual efforts were made to coordinate schedules and locations of leadership meetings of ecumenical organizations to facilitate attendance for members who had responsibilities to more than one organization. The Central Committee of the WCC met in Hungary in 1955, and shortly after that in August, the Executive Committee of the World Alliance met nearby in Prague. Mackay preached in the Bethlehem Chapel in Prague where Jan Hus had preached many years before and where no Protestant service had been held since 1620. About three thousand persons attended the service. At this Council meeting Mackay gave a statement titled "The Confessional Resurgence and the Ecumenical Movement with Special Reference to the Role and Development of the World Alliance of Reformed Churches."[155]

In his address Mackay emphasized a new confessionalism in which an individual Christian is grounded in a specific church tradition and explores its historic roots without absolutizing its own structure and while being enriched by the heritages of other denominations:

> Each Confession begins to explore its historic roots. It raises the question of its own essential character and witness, as well as the question of its peculiar contribution to the Church Universal. It is being realized that a Christian cannot belong to the Church in general, any more than he can belong to the human race in general or have a mere general relationship to his own country. A person becomes truly and richly human only through life in a family circle, a community and a nation. So too a Christian becomes introduced into the fullness of Christ through a specific Church tradition which he treats, however, not as an idolatrous expression of the one and only Church but as a providential instrument through which he was introduced to the Christian faith and nourished in the Christian life. The new Confessionalism is thus different from the old. There is no disposition on the part of Anglicans, Congregationalists, Baptists, Lutherans, Methodists or Presbyterians to absolutize their several confessional structures or loyalties. No single confession believes that it represents the one and only Church of Christ, the *Una Sancta*. Each does believe, however, that it enshrines in its heritage something that is authentically Christian. It is this something that it would make its specific contribution to the ecumenical treasure house of Christian faith and life.[156]

To enhance the stature of the confessional movement and to encourage the policy of enriching the ecumenical movement by outreach and exchange of information with other confessional bodies that were developing side by side, Mackay offered the following motion at the business meeting in Prague:

> The Executive Committee of the World Alliance of Reformed Churches expresses the hope that in the near future an informal gathering can be arranged between representatives of the several world confessional bodies in the Protestant family of Churches. The object of this meeting would be to provide an opportunity for the representatives of each Confession to interpret to their brethren of the other Confessions the nature, objectives and development of the group to which they belong.
>
> The Committee accordingly request the officers of the Alliance to consult with the officers of other confessions with a view to a small informal gathering being convened for the purpose above indicated.[157]

Mackay was able to bring about an informal conference of responsible representatives of the seven worldwide confessional groups in July 1957 when the Central Committee of the WCC met in New Haven. The WARC Executive Committee wished to do more, adopting a statement and topical agenda on confessionalism and authorizing and encouraging the president of the Alliance to pursue a similar meeting the following year in conjunction with the Central Committee of the WCC.[158]

When the Executive Committee developed a program for the WARC General Council to be held in São Paulo, Brazil, in summer 1959, Mackay suggested and the committee adopted the theme "The Servant Image of the Church." It was a theme Mackay had been reflecting on for several years. The Alliance could emphasize by this theme that the Church, composed of Christ's disciples, was to serve and not to triumph, in contrast with the triumphalistic attitude of the Roman Catholic Church in Latin America at that time.[159] A study booklet was prepared called *The Servant Lord and His Servant People*. Mackay promoted the Conference with an editorial in *Theology Today* presenting the image of the servant "as the essential image of the Christian religion."[160] The theological secretariat of the World Alliance also developed a series of studies on the theme.[161] At the opening service on July 27, 1959, at the first Independent Presbyterian Church of São Paulo, Mackay preached in Spanish. The opening address emphasizing God's sovereignty was titled "Let Us Remember God."[162]

The World Alliance meeting in São Paulo marked the first time that a world gathering of a particular Protestant tradition met in Latin America rather than in Europe or North America.[163] Although younger than northern hemisphere counterparts, the Presbyterian denominational churches of Brazil were strong. Their committed members facilitated the Council meeting, which coincided with the centennial celebration of the Presbyterian Church of Brazil. The President of Brazil, Juscelino Kubitschek, visited the Council. The meeting strengthened ties between the Reformed churches in Latin America and those churches of other continents. David Du Plessis attended the Council as a Pentecostal fraternal delegate. When Mackay introduced him, he remarked on the significance of his presence: "This is the first confessional body that has extended recognition to the Pentecostal Movement as a sound Christian body."[164] When the Council admitted two more Asian churches to the fellowship, the total membership of the Alliance rose to seventy-eight. At Mackay's retirement from the World Alliance in 1959, Eugene Carson Blake paid tribute to Mackay's service: "John Mackay has influenced the whole Church by its leadership in thought and activity more than any other man of his time."[165]

Compendium of Elements of Mackay's Thought

This section presents a brief compendium of twelve core concepts important to Mackay's work: (1) the centrality of Jesus Christ, (2) the definition of a "true person," (3) revelation, (4) biblical authority, (5) Christian religious experience, (6) the church, (7) evangelical catholicity, (8) the church as a social force, (9) confessionalism, (10) the contribution of the Reformed churches to the ecumenical movement, (11) the relationship of church and state, and (12) theology of government. The following summary is merely an abbreviated introduction and is no substitute for Mackay's own nuanced and complete treatments and elaborations of these and many other subjects in his prolific writings. As an evangelist and author he communicated philosophical and metaphysical ideas about theological reality in language understandable by ordinary people, and he articulated his convictions with passion and clarity as a servant of Christ in response to circumstances, great and small, that he met on the road of his life.

Jesus Christ

Mackay's thought is christocentric beginning with Jesus Christ, "the most illuminating and transforming fact of human experience, and . . . the true key to the philosophic interpretation of the world."[166] Jesus Christ is both the pattern and the power of living.

> In the historical life of Jesus Christ . . . [are] the essential features that provide man, whatever his country, his culture, or his time, with the true *pattern* for living. . . . When man takes God seriously, God supplies him with the needed *power* to live in accordance with the divine pattern for human life, so that his life becomes vibrant with the life of God.[167]

The True Person

Mackay's metaphysic defines a *true person* with reference to God:

> What is a person? In its deepest Christian significance a person is one who responds to God. You become a person when you hear the Word of God and do it. A person takes to the road as a pilgrim not knowing whither he goes, but knowing that God knows. A true person, one who lives day by day by the Word of God, who listens for God's command and does God's will, fulfills the answer to that most basic of all questions: "What is the chief end of man?" "Man's chief end is to glorify God and to enjoy him forever."[168]

A sense of a person's sinfulness continues throughout one's life.

Revelation

The existence and character of God is known through God's revelation to man, a subject Mackay considered in philosophical terms when writing a thesis at Princeton Theological Seminary, "The Idea of Revelation," in 1915: "But in the 'fullness of time,' he wrote, ". . . there appeared a Person, Jesus of Nazareth, who was the Absolute Incarnation of the Invisible God, and in whom External and Internal Revelation were united and consummated."[169] God has spoken through the Bible, through the history of the Hebrew people, of his gracious purpose for mankind. He has spoken of redemptive unity with mankind, as a personal communication to all people.[170]

Biblical Authority

In his commentary on the Letter to the Ephesians, Mackay discussed biblical authority and maintained that in the Bible and only in the Bible are we brought face to face with God's self-disclosure of God's self and God's will. In light of some approaches to the Bible of the present time, Mackay's work warrants quotation at length:

> The Bible cannot be appreciated or understood by people who approach it with an air, and in the spirit, of pure objectivity. . . . The Bible demands that those who study it should become willing to adopt the basic attitude towards God and life which it challenges men to adopt. It demands especially that they submit to the sway of that central Figure, Jesus Christ, whom it presents. When men are willing to adopt a Biblical point of view, to put themselves in the perspective from which the Bible looks at all things and to identify themselves with the spiritual order of life which the Bible unveils, they understand the Bible, they see those spiritual realities about which the Bible speaks. If the unique self-disclosure of God and His will are to make any sense, if they are to make a true impression upon the student of the Biblical records, "eyes of faith" are needed.
>
> This is the method which the Bible itself proposes for validating the truth it proclaims. Obedience to God is the prerequisite for insight into God. Only when the spectator becomes a wayfarer upon the highway of God's purposes, only when he is willing to identify himself with God's great scheme of things as it is revealed in the Bible, is he capacitated to understand the Bible way of looking at things. In a word, when the detached observer of things Biblical becomes an actor in the Biblical drama, when he begins to think with the Bible and not simply about the Bible, when he follows the road signs that lead him to certain hills of vision, then and only then can he believe with all his heart that he has been listening to the Eternal. Then he will behold things that are veiled from scientific objectivity, he will follow in the footprints of the saints, he will become a citizen of the Commonwealth of God. For the Bible is validated, as every ultimate truth contained in the Bible is validated, by an inner witness in the human student of the Bible, the witness of the same Holy Spirit to whose special illumination the writers of the Bible owed their insight into God, His purposes and His works. We cannot get beyond that great, simple affirmation of Thomas à Kempis, that "the Bible is to be read with the same Spirit with which it was written."
>
> But then what becomes of "scientific objectivity"? What about the affirmation that no approach to truth is valid that is not made in "the antiseptic air of objectivity"? In this antiseptic sunlight, it is claimed, all germs die that make objective study difficult: germs of emotion, germs of prejudice, germs of commitment. The answer is that in that kind of approach to truth in which the very existence of the enquirer is at stake no such objectivity can exist. Where ultimate values are involved which must be chosen or

rejected, and when one's very life is staked upon their rejection or choice, the whole study is lifted far above and beyond "the antiseptic air of objectivity." When a man's very existence is involved in the particular value that he chooses or the ultimate decision which he makes, there simply is no such thing as absolute objectivity. Vital choices and decisions are made not upon objective, but upon very subjective grounds. When a man's all is at stake, he is obliged to think "existentially." In the realm of personal relations and of ultimate spiritual attitudes existential thinking is the only true and adequate form of thinking. A terrible and inescapable choice confronts every person who would explore the meaning of Biblical truth.[171]

Christian Religious Experience

Mackay developed ways of discussing religious experience as the heritage of the followers of Jesus Christ that were appropriate to hearers in both South and North America. In Latin America Mackay contrasted the vitality and authenticity of the spiritual life of the Spanish mystics to the deadness of the teaching of the institutional church in that region. He presented a thinker like Unamuno as the authentic heir to the classical mystics. In North America Mackay did not overlook the religious experience of Anglo-Saxons like Rutherford or the Puritans: "Spaniards were *acting* mystics, the Puritans were *reacting* mystics."[172] Mackay wrote that Unamuno referred to the apostle Paul as "the mystic discoverer of Jesus."[173] Concurring with Unamuno, Paul, and others, Mackay stressed Pauline mysticism expressed in the New Testament phrase "in Christ": "The phrase 'in Christ' denotes the transcendental relationship to Christ,"[174] but not "absorption into a state of transcendental calm,"[175] he wrote. "To be 'in Christ' is therefore more than to be 'in the heavenlies'; it is to have one's status in the very life of God and to draw one's sustenance from God in Christ."[176] Mackay noted that the German scholar Deissmann pointed attention to the category and found the phrase "in Christ" or "in Christ Jesus" used 169 times in Paul's letters. Religious experience in this sense is available to all persons who seriously seek it.

Knowing and understanding goes beyond the emotional and spiritual to involve the rational. In a convocation address, Mackay discussed his understanding of "personal religion as the most basic expression of Christian faith and life." As distinguished from conventional religion, personal religion in a general sense "is a religion in which divine reality . . . exercises an overmastering influence upon life. It becomes the fountain-head of emotion, the master light of thought, the source of moral energy." Personal religion in the Christian sense is "acquaintance with oneself and with God. There is in it self-knowledge and the knowledge of God."[177]

The Church

Mackay's thought related the ideas of being "in Christ" with being "in the Church," the former being a wider category. He noted, however, that "the Church in this ultimate sense [is] a fellowship of men and women [that are] 'in Christ.'"[178] Using the best definition he knew, Mackay defined the *church* as essentially the "Community of Christ. . . . The church is the fellowship of those for whom Jesus Christ is Lord."[179] Elsewhere he wrote,

> The concept of the "gathered Church," the Church made up of members who are totally committed Christians and who give evidence by the quality of their witness that they are "Christ's men and women," is native to historic Calvinism. It constitutes an ideal toward which all Presbyterian Churches should strive. . . .[180]
>
> [T]rue humanity, as well as true unity, can be achieved only through union with the will of God, through loyalty to the inmost meaning of life itself. This is what it means to live in the dimension of the eternal. Common loyalty to God creates a "road fellowship" in the highest degree and sense, a crusading missionary comradeship . . . [of people who share a common concern and march together towards the same goal].[181]

Commenting on Paul's Letter to the Ephesians, Mackay notes,

> Thus the unity of the Church is not a question of practical Church politics or statesmanship. Those who have "been brought near, in the blood of Christ" (2:13), who have been "reconciled to God through the Cross" (2:16), who have "access in one Spirit to the Father" (2:18), who "are a dwelling place of God in the Spirit" (2:22), who form the "Church, which is His Body," constitute an ontological unity. That is to say, the Christian Church, as Paul expounds its meaning in the Ephesian Letter, *is* a unity, a collective personality.[182]

Mackay's thinking on the essence of Christ's Church linked together the doctrine of mission and the doctrine of unity. His developing thought expressed itself in several epigrammatic mileposts from "Let the Church be the Church," in 1937, to "Let the Church be the Mission," in 1952. He linked the two concepts, mission and unity, in the usage of the term *ecumenical* at a meeting in Rolle in 1951. With others he related mission and unity through purpose by applying the terms in practice in the message to all congregations by the Uniting General Assembly: "In Unity—For Mission," in 1958.[183]

Evangelical Catholicity

For the Church to be "in very deed" the Church, Mackay believed it had four spiritual functions to fulfill: its worshiping, prophetic, redemptive, and unitive functions,[184] and of its tasks he says, "Evangelism is the supreme task of the Church."[185] Indeed, the Church, as a new society, expresses itself in evangelical catholicity:

> Evangelical catholicity is that worldwide expression of the Christian religion which is centered in Jesus Christ and the Gospel and not in any particular organizational or institutional structure of Church life. It recovers for our time the meaning of that adage of the early Christian Church, "Where Christ is, there is the Church" (*ubi Christus, ibi ecclesia*). It is that form of Christian unity which, starting from utter allegiance to Jesus Christ on the part of Christian Churches and all that such allegiance involves, seeks to manifest the spirit of Christ in corporate life and relations; but it is not bound to any particular theory or expression of Church organization. Evangelical catholicity leads Christians, and Christian Churches which recognize their essential oneness in Jesus Christ their Lord, to manifest in the world a visible unity deeper and wider than anything that can be achieved by membership in a single unified Church structure.[186]

The Church as a Social Force

Mackay, Dulles, and others during World War II rallied the Church as a social force and as an element of defense against fascism. Later, Mackay successfully rallied the church domestically in the United States against the evils of McCarthyism. These instances of social action show that Mackay saw and applied the two commandments, to love God and to love one's neighbor, as belonging together. They should not be separated in such a way as to absolutize the one or the other.[187] The church's role is not to present blueprints of social action to society but to speak prophetically.[188]

Confessionalism

In general, members of the Church as *Una Sancta* are members of institutional churches. Mackay's thought placed confessionalism in the form of faith groups such as Lutheran, Episcopalian, Methodist, or Presbyterian, within the ecumenical church:

> Each Confession begins to explore its historic roots. It raises the question of its own essential character and witness, as well as the question of its peculiar contribution to the Church Universal. It is being realized that a Christian cannot belong to the Church in general, any more than he can belong to the human race in general or have a mere general relationship to his own country. A person becomes truly and richly human only through life in a family circle, a community and a nation. So too a Christian becomes introduced into the fullness of Christ through a specific Church tradition which he treats, however, not as an idolatrous expression of the one and only Church but as a providential instrument through which he was introduced to the Christian faith and nourished in the Christian life. The new Confessionalism is thus different from the old. There is no disposition on the part of Anglicans, Congregationalists, Baptists, Lutherans, Methodists or Presbyterians to absolutize their several confessional structures or loyalties. No single confession believes that it represents the one and only Church of Christ, the *Una Sancta*. Each does believe, however, that it enshrines in its heritage something that is authentically Christian. It is this something that it would make its specific contribution to the ecumenical treasure house of Christian faith and life.[189]

The Contribution of the Reformed Churches

Mackay listed the following six contributions of the Reformed Churches, his own faith group, to the *Una Sancta*:

[1] The Reformed Churches have borne perpetual witness to the importance of doctrine in the life and thought of the Church. They have taken seriously the Biblical precept that God should be loved with the *mind*. . . .

[2] Truth, in all its cosmic implications, is the supreme concern of Reformed Theology. . . .

[3] Reformed doctrine when true to its nature begins and ends with God. . . . True to the essential meaning of "theology," Reformed theology is a doctrine of God, begun and pursued in the light of God. . . . What is unique is that divine sovereignty is the centre and organizing principle of theology. . . .

[4] While in Reformed theology of the classical type nature, history, and the soul of man all provide glimmers of the truth about God, it is through revelation as found in Holy Scripture that God becomes known. . . .

[5] Both in Calvin, and in the classical expression of Reformed theology, it becomes clear that Christian doctrine is not for its own sake, but for the sake of goodness. What supremely interested Calvin was "the pure

doctrine of godliness," that doctrine which led men ⸺
in their character and to do the will of God in their c⸺
order to goodness." . . .

[6] In loyalty to the genius of the Reformed theology, the Chu.
should, from time to time, revise her confession or creed. This ⸺ church
should do in order to bring her subordinate standards into closer harmony
with the Word of God and that the Body of Christ, in the face of new heresies that may be spawned and new situations that may develop, may be
provided with more adequate instruments for thought and behaviour.[190]

The Relationship of Church and State

The lay state is not

by nature indifferent or hostile to religion. It appreciates the importance of religion in human society and recognizes the service which it
has rendered to mankind. It is, at the same time, not controlled by any
given religious organization, nor does it function in the interests of any
particular church or religious group. . . . They [religion and government]
are rather like two circles which intersect at one point. That point is the
reverent awareness of God and of spiritual values. While, in the name of
Caesar, a lay state demands, and has a right to demand, the "things that
belong to Caesar," it equally recognizes the obligation of Caesar, as well
as of the citizens whom he rules, to "render unto God the things which
are God's."[191]

Religion within the lay state, or for that matter within the life of any
state, has a prophetic mission to fulfill. It must ever stand for the inalien-
able rights of man which he possesses in virtue of his creation by God, and
in view of God's government of the world. It must emphasize the fact that
souls, that is, responsible persons, are ultimately more important than civilizations. It must ever bring to the attention of rulers, and also jurists, that
the Ten Commandments are moral ultimates for the formation of human
character and for the conduct of human affairs. It must proclaim that a
divine moral order is a reality which has to be reckoned with in the affairs
of state and the conduct of government.[192]

Theology of Government

[G]overnment as such represents a creation of God, . . . of God's Common
Grace. God designed government to serve the best interests of people, to
guarantee order and justice.

A government is true to the meaning of government and fulfils its destiny, when, in the words of John Calvin, "it seeks to maintain humanity among men." The supreme criterion by which a particular government must be judged is whether those in authority are concerned, and are successful in their concern, to make it possible for all citizens, whatever their background or status, to live a truly human existence, in the enjoyment of elemental rights and with the assurance of unprejudiced justice.

It is a further conviction that, independently of any given religious affiliation on the part of those who govern or those who are governed, the true meaning of the natural order, or, if you like to call it so, the secular order, is fulfilled, when rulers recognize the reality of God's absolute sovereignty over nations and civilizations. Such recognition does not involve, of course, that it be formally written into a country's constitution.[193]

Ecumenical Church—Unity of Spirit, Diversity of Treasures

The twelve concepts discussed above are integral facets to understanding the spiritual mystery of the ecumenical church. Mackay devoted much creative thought and energy to the great unsolved problem of Protestant theology—the nature of the Church—and it may be useful to summarize briefly several high points in the gradual development of his idea of the ecumenical church. Mackay's thought was grounded both in practical experience of ecclesiastical and missionary life and in biblical revelation, system, and logic. Mackay succeeded John R. Mott in the chairmanship of the strategic Joint Committee of the WCC and IMC, and in the course of forming a reasoned decision to meld together the two councils, Mackay expounded universal principles, truths, and attributes of the *Una Sancta* of the Nicene Creed. This area of his work culminated in the publication of three books addressing the Church from three different perspectives.

As a boy in Scotland he entered the Church through the narrow gate of the Free Presbyterian Church and moved on to a missionary vocation in the Free Church of Scotland. In the course of world travels promoting missions, he became familiar with the unique gifts of Free Presbyterian, Baptist, American Presbyterian, Plymouth Brethren, Methodist, Quaker, and Episcopalian Churches.[194] Through his reading and study Mackay became acquainted with a Greek term newly used by a German philosopher, Count Keyserling, whose book *The World in the Making* perceived an inchoate globalization of culture that Keyserling referred to as "*ecumenic culture, a universal human culture*."[195] Mackay adopted the term *ecumenical* and used it in a political and sociological sense at a mission conference in Atlantic City, New Jersey, in January 1928.[196] The next year he added a religious dimension to the term in 1929 when he wrote, "The consciousness that secularism is the chief foe of Christianity is without doubt one of the potent factors tending towards Christian ecumenicalism with its ideal of a united Christendom."[197] The term and concept were further impressed on him when Mackay met Count Keyserling, who was lecturing in Montevideo in 1929. From that time until the spring of 1937 Mackay used the term to refer to "a devoted follower of Christ who belonged to no Church in particular, a Christian who transcended all the Churches as they then existed"[198]

In preparing for the Oxford Conference of 1937 he realized that a new global reality had been brought into being by the Christian gospel, namely, the church universal or, as he later called it the ecumenical church.[199] The experience at Oxford gave Mackay and others a vision that humankind was united by the love of God and that ecumenicity must be the goal of all our efforts.[200] To accomplish this vision, the ecumenical church must strive to (1) deepen the sense of God's purpose within churchgoers, (2) cleanse each separate Christian tradition into redemptive purity, (3) generate an ecumenical theology based on the different Christian traditions and relate ecumenical truth to contemporary life and thought, and (4) deepen and widen a true consciousness of the *Una Sancta*.[201]

During the years of the Second World War, Mackay saw the Church, the body of Christ, as a world force in its spiritual essence and institutional substance. An essay in 1941 discussed the church "not as this or that Christian group, even should any one of the existing churches make exclusive claim to be *the* Church, but rather as the organized, corporate expression of all groups. In a word, Church, in this discussion, will really be the synonym of Christianity in its institutional aspect."[202] He discussed the church and the secular order in *A Preface to Christian Theology*.[203] While his friend Dulles wished to use the Church in the realm of international relations to develop a peace after World War II, Mackay qualified his understanding of the Church's role when he wrote, "The churches do not, however, have a primary responsibility to devise the details of world order. But they must proclaim the enduring moral principles by which human plans are constantly to be tested."[204] In an essay in 1946, he sketched out what he meant by the "ecumenical goal," namely, "nothing less than the fulfillment by the Christian Church of its total task, on a world front, in the spirit of Christian unity."[205]

By 1949 Mackay's thinking about the nature of the Church had developed further when he wrote in the *Christian Century*,

It has grown upon me personally over the intervening years that the Christian church, in order to be truly the church, must be a missionary as well as a worshipping church. . . . The Christian church is worthy of the name it bears only when it emerges from the sanctuary where God is worshipped in order to express its devotion to God and its corporate understanding of his will in missionary action. The church can never be an end in itself, however perfectly it may formulate its faith, establish its order and conduct its worship. The church to be truly the church must be everlastingly an instrument of God's saving will, fulfilling his missionary designs in human history.[206]

Three years later he elaborated theologically:

A true "Ecumenical Movement" must have at the heart of it the dynamic expression of a pre-existing unity in Christ, which being missionary in character, strives to express itself throughout the entire *oikoumene*, that is, both in the world of Church relations and in the secular order.[207]

His thoughts on the Church crystallized between 1948 and August 1954, the period between the first and second Assemblies of the World Council of Churches, the period when the Lucknow and Willingen Conferences were held. His commentary and exposition of the book of Ephesians, *God's Order*, was published in 1953; the printed version of his Croall Lectures at the University of Edinburgh, in 1948. Here he interpreted God's purpose for the church, and his selection of a title for the book is illuminating. After a long consultation in 1946, the study commission in Cambridge asked Visser 't Hooft to seek a change in the wording for the subject of the First Assembly of the World Council. They wished to have the subject changed from "The Order of God and the Present Disorder of Man" to "Man's Disorder and God's Design."

The English-speaking commission members believed very strongly that the German translation of the title was more satisfactory than the English version because they thought the words "The Order of God" had no clear meaning in English and suggested something too fixed and static. The change in wording was not intended as a change in subject. They also thought that the term *design* suggested a purpose to be fulfilled in the future and an existing reality having a pattern that corresponded to what was originally intended in the use of "the order of God."[208] Mackay believed strongly that the Assembly theme had been needlessly changed. He was determined to use and reinforce the word "order" in the title of his commentary to convey a theological idea by consciously linking the title to the theme of the Amsterdam Assembly.[209] Mackay understood the Church as "God's Order" and had earlier referred to the body of Christ as "the spiritual correlate of the order of nature."[210]

In 1951 at Rolle Mackay guided the understanding of the word *ecumenical* so that the understanding of unity included mission. At Willingen the concept of church-centered mission was retained, and Mackay's address included the challenge "Let the Church be the Mission." Thus, the "great adventure that lies ahead of the Church of Christ in our time is to infuse into the Ecumenical Movement all that is involved in the Great Commission, 'Make disciples of all nations' and all that is involved in the words of our Lord's great prayer, 'that they all may be one.'"[211] This unitive mission function is sourced in the Trinity.[212] The workload of the Joint Committee may have underlined for Mackay organizational efficiencies that integration, if properly managed, could bring about. In its six meetings the committee understood more deeply the relations of the IMC and WCC. Mackay's Report of the Joint Committee at König-stein in 1954 recommended a permanent secretary for the committee and a proposed constitution.[213] Integration was approved in Ghana four years later. Two final books on the Church that distilled his mature thought and experience were published in the 1960s after his retirement. They were *The Presbyterian Way of Life* and *Ecumenics: The Science of the Church Universal.*

From its theological origins largely outside North America, the development of the ecumenical principle reached an important stage within North America when North American clergy formally embarked on the ecumenical movement at the Oberlin Conference in September 1957. More than a thousand persons contributed to the preparations and more than four hundred churchmen were involved in a study and discussion on the topic "The Nature of the Unity We Seek."[214] It appeared that the movement was poised for further advances, but surprising reversals lay ahead.

Chapter 13

Washington Years and Retirement (1959–1983)

"Faithful servant" (Matt. 25:21 KJV)

*W*hen the Mackays arrived from Princeton at their new apartment in the Washington, DC, suburb of Chevy Chase, Maryland, they began a new phase of their life together. During the first years of retirement the momentum of John's academic career continued as he completed two important books, toured the world lecturing, and addressed students as an adjunct professor at American University. He also remained an active Presbyterian. But the era of the 1960s and 1970s was turbulent, and Mackay prophetically analyzed the strengths, weaknesses, and direction of the Christian movement as portions of it reversed, reconfigured, and realigned themselves. Continuing to carry on the tradition of Princeton, Mackay spoke out, expressing ideas and insights or disagreeing with certain trends with both passion and courtesy.

A multitude of elements swirled in the maelstrom of worldwide social and cultural change. In North America new technology began to transform an industrially based society into an information-based one; new technology weakened social relationships. Television undermined a sense of authentic community, and the role models it presented altered society. The feminist movement in North America changed social and economic relationships as women sought new ways to express themselves and contribute to American life. In racial relations the process of integration gave way to more active desegregation efforts by the federal government. Foreign relations with the Soviet Union created generalized anxiety over the role of nuclear weapons. The war in Southeast Asia tore American society into fragments. In the developing world, expectations for economic progress sharply accelerated.

A Copernican revolution in reverse shifted the landscape in theology, especially within Protestant denominations engaged in the conciliar movement, as social action frequently became separated from the first commandment, to love God. Meanwhile the Second Vatican Council began a renewal and transformation of Roman Catholicism. Mackay's writings and addresses responded to the ebb and flow of radical theological and ethical changes. Widespread affluence and pervasive secularism made many North Americans less receptive to the spiritual message of the Church, which in the words of some observers became a cultural captive.

World Evangelistic Travel

To give incoming President James I. McCord a start at Princeton Seminary without being under the shadow of his predecessor, Mackay moved in June of 1959 from Princeton and settled in Chevy Chase not far from the campus of American University. Heavy travel commitments soon followed as Mackay attended a meeting of the Committee on the Theological Education Fund of the IMC held in mid-July 1959 in Compiégne, France. At this meeting in the outskirts of Paris a suggestion was made to him that he should write the book that became *Ecumenics*. After leaving France and spending a strenuous and busy few weeks in Brazil with the World Alliance, he returned to his new home and to his wife who had been settling into new surroundings.[1] Between November 1959 and March 1960 Mackay reduced his activities in order to write *The Presbyterian Way of Life*, which was long overdue to the publisher.

In *The Presbyterian Way of Life*,[2] Mackay discussed the denominational aspect, the history, organization, and theology of his own faith tradition. Each historic denomination had treasures of insight to offer the ecumenical Church. The book may be interpreted as showing that through its history, through elements of theology, and in its membership, a denomination offers a tributary flowing into and enriching the worldwide Church. As Mackay earlier developed the paradoxical idea of being both more Presbyterian and less Presbyterian in light of the ecumenical Church, he incorporated the tributary idea of the confessional denominational movement into his concept of the ecumenical church. In keeping with the unitive intention of the ecumenical movement, Mackay explicitly subordinated the institutional details of church polity to inchoate unity of a Universal Church.

A few years later in 1964 with the publication of his textbook *Ecumenics*, Mackay brought together in one volume his thoughts on the ecumenical church, based in part on the course he had taught at Princeton Seminary from 1937 to 1959. The book differed from previous volumes on the subject because it presented ecumenics broadly as the "Science of the Church Universal, conceived as a World Missionary Community: Its nature, its functions, its relations and its strategy."[3] To Mackay the field deserved the status of a science because the Church has a role in the purposes of God. As such it is "a study of what it means for the church to be in very deed the church, or what the church is called to do in light of its true nature."[4] The study centered on the Church's four functions: its worshiping, prophetic, redemptive, and unitive functions.

In September 1960 the Mackays set off on a strenuous but happy lecture tour that included the Joseph Cook Lectureship which Mackay had been unable to accept in the 1930s.[5] The full journey lasted from September 21, 1960, to March 25, 1961. Traveling eastward around the world, the Mackays journeyed first to Europe to fulfil personal commitments and made an important stop in Scotland. On October 13, 1960, Mackay delivered a lecture at the Act of United Thanksgiving and Witness held in Usher Hall, Edinburgh, in connection with the Fourth Centenary of the Scottish Reformation, where he spoke on the influence of John Witherspoon and Scottish Presbyterianism on the mission and unity of the church in the world.[6] The Moderator of the General Assembly of the Church of Scotland, Principal John H. S. Burleigh, presided. A. M. Renwick, Mackay's successor at the Colegio Anglo-Peruano, now called the San Andrés School, also participated. During the visit to Scotland the Mackays dined with Queen Elizabeth II and Prince Philip at Holyrood Castle. From Scotland Mackay left to present three lectures in Ireland before commencing the Cook lectureship.[7]

The Joseph Cook lecture tour lasted from October 19 to March 12, 1961. Along the way the Mackays stopped at Athens, Greece; Beirut, Lebanon; Cairo, Egypt; Karachi, Pakistan; Lahore, West Pakistan; and India, where they traveled for five-and-a-half weeks, stopping at Delhi, Poona, Kohlapur, Allahabad, Lucknow, and Calcutta. Because of her husband's sudden illness in India, Jane Mackay addressed the waiting group of one thousand persons. During the trip Mrs. Mackay spoke and consulted about the participation of women in the life and work of the church. The lecture tour was interrupted briefly from December 31 to January 3, 1961, when Mackay attended the SCM Conference of India, Ceylon, and Pakistan, which met in Lahore. Resuming the tour the Mackays travelled to Rangoon, Burma, then to Bangkok, where they stayed with their old friend Horace Ryburn. Then they left for the final leg of the trip to Djakarta, Indonesia; Manila, Philippines; Hong Kong, and Tokyo, Japan, finally sailing back to San Francisco.

Latin America—"We Must Make Christians"

From 1961 to 1964 Mackay continued his connection with the academic world as adjunct professor of Hispanic thought at American University in

Washington, DC, and Mackay's interest and travel to Latin America continued vigorously. He attended the Second Latin American Evangelical Conference held in Lima, July 29 to August 6, 1961, the latest in a series of conferences that began when the Committee on Cooperation in Latin America had organized the Panama Conference of 1916, the Montevideo Conference of 1925, and the Havana Conference of 1929. The Buenos Aires Conference of 1949, unlike the previous ones, had been organized by the Latin American councils of churches, rather than by mission executives. The Lima Conference of 1961 thus became the second indigenous conference in this tradition. The Assembly of 220 delegates and visitors represented thirty-four denominations and came from all the Latin American countries except Panama, Nicaragua, and Haiti.[8]

The Lima Conference revealed the strengths and weaknesses of the Protestant churches in Latin America, but improved coordination among the churches of different countries still lay in the future. Part of the disorganization was attributed again to Carl McIntire and the activities of his two organizations, the American Council of Christian Churches and the International Council of Christian Churches. Just as he had done earlier in Buenos Aires, Bangkok, and Mexico City, McIntire attempted to sow confusion, setting up a meeting across the street from the established meeting. McIntire made false accusations both through paid advertisements in city newspapers and from a public platform, claiming that the organizers of the Conference were pro-Communist. As a result of the false allegations John Mackay, José Miguez Bonino, and Thomas J. Liggett were taken into police custody for questioning.

Having maintained contacts with his original mission field, when Mackay arrived at the police station, he asked one of the officers, "Would you mind telling the Minister of Education that I am here?" Then, referring to McIntire, he suggested to the official, "Instead of investigating me, you should check on that man." Soon the police were making inquiries into McIntire's statements and challenging him: "You prove these charges, or leave the country tomorrow!" The confusion was soon corrected when McIntire left the country the next day![9] One paper "published a front-page story about Dr. Mackay and his significant contribution to Peruvian education."[10] For the next few days the Lima papers made much of the *Pleitos Entre Protestantes*, disputes among Protestants.[11] Mackay realized that McIntire wanted nothing better than a confrontation, which Mackay declined to give him. "The Lord will have to deal with him," Mackay said later.[12]

Mackay continued to exert an evangelistic personal influence over individuals he met, and during this visit in 1961 Mackay spent time with a student from Mackay's old school, the Colegio San Andrés. A fifteen-year-old reporter, Moisés Chávez, had read Mackay's *The Meaning of Life* and followed Mackay to the places where he preached or spoke, finally interviewing him at his hotel. In return Mackay asked Moisés to lead him down by bus to the expanding shantytowns of Lima "so that his heart might beat in sympathy with the victims of so much poverty and degradation." From the United States Mackay wrote a letter of encouragement to the boy, which concluded, "May God bless you in your studies and may you have a sense of his sovereign presence in your daily life, for the Christian vocation to which you are called."[13] Much later, the lad became a member of the faculty at Latin American Biblical Seminary in San José, Costa Rica.

On his return to the United States, Mackay addressed the annual fall study conference of the Committee on Cooperation in Latin America, now a unit of the National Council of Churches' Division of Foreign Missions. At the conference he noted the difference between the usage of the words "evangelical" and *evangélicos* in North and South America. In North America the term was applied to a conservative wing of Protestantism. In Latin America the term was attached to Protestantism as a whole. Mackay interpreted the period in church history saying, "This is when 'foreign mission' becomes the 'world mission of the church.'"[14] Later, the addresses that he gave at the conference were rewritten and expanded into a monograph, *The Latin American Churches and the Ecumenical Movement*.[15]

Mackay continued to acquaint North America with its southern neighbors by publishing articles on Latin American religion and culture. In April 1961, shortly after the Bay of Pigs invasion, Mackay contributed an article to *Presbyterian Life* interpreting the Cuban revolution of 1959.[16] He wrote that the Cuban revolution, like the Mexican one in 1910, was volcanic in nature and deeply rooted in the soul of the masses; agrarian reform followed, and religious freedom continued. He noted that a "Social Creed" was adopted by the Cuban Council of Churches at a meeting November 28–30, 1960. Shortly after it was issued, however, Cuban Protestants were cut off from contact with Cubans in the United States: diplomatic relations were cut off, an embargo was imposed, and Americans were not permitted to visit Cuba. Then came the U.S. invasion at the Bay of Pigs. Fidel Castro, a pure Spaniard, had a passionate sense of honor. In a teaching moment directed to North American Christians, Mackay drew attention to a personal slight to Castro by the U.S. government during a trip to the United States. In fact the failed Bay of Pigs invasion made Castro more popular in Cuba, strengthened the revolution, and led Castro to seek closer relations with the Soviet Union. As in the Mexican Revolution of the 1920s and 1930s, the Roman Catholic Church was targeted as 131 Roman Catholic clergy were expelled in 1961 and others were imprisoned.[17] Like his friend *New York Times* correspondent Herbert Matthews, Mackay analyzed this revolution in terms of distinctly Cuban social change. He did not focus on political aspects or personal pathologies of the leader, but later noted in print that the revolution had turned communist due to "special circumstances."[18]

In October of 1963 Mackay made his fifth visit to Cuba in thirty-five years. He went as guest lecturer to attend an institute of the Presbytery of Cuba on "The Nature and Mission of the Church in Cuba Today." Mackay spoke at the public sessions in the evening when Protestants of other denominations joined the Presbyterian delegates, who numbered about 150. The trip afforded an opportunity to reenter the public debate, this time with an article in the *Christian Century* describing his experience of the religious and political situation. He was sharply critical of U.S. policy of blockading Cuba as "morally reprehensible, pragmatically futile and politically disastrous."[19] This triggered a vigorous reader response, many supporting his position, but many, particularly Cuban exiles, in disagreement.[20] A few months later Mackay reiterated and elaborated his position in a second article, stating that other experts agreed with his position, explaining more broadly the theme of revolution and social change in Latin America, and urging the United States to avoid the polarization that had existed with Communist China.[21] Correct on theological grounds, Mackay's analysis tended to focus on broad cultural and social factors. Among the exiles were nominal Catholics, and the United States' relationship with Cuba persisted as a difficulty for American foreign policy.

Mackay published two more articles in the *Christian Century* in 1965 following a major trip to Latin America the prior year. These articles are noteworthy both for the content of Mackay's thought and analysis and for the substantive description of events and experiences during the trip. The nine-week lecture journey in 1964 to six Latin American countries was made under the auspices of the South American Federation of YMCA's.[22] There he found a new mood in the church, and he renewed "contacts with members and staffs of the associations, with church leaders and church people, with university students and professors, with government officials and with members of the press."[23] He gave the Unamuno centennial lecture in São Paulo. The president of the university, however, was absent because a military group had just arrived to interview him. Mackay noted the need for creative approaches to social and cultural unrest in Brazil. Meanwhile he recognized and described a different situation in Peru and Chile, where two Roman Catholic laymen, Eduardo Frei Montalva and Fernando Belaúnde Terry, were aware of and addressing the social problems. Mackay warned of the growing influence of Marxism on the campuses and universities.[24]

Mackay also found a new mood in the church and believed that the YMCA had a fine opportunity to present the Christian faith to both Catholics and Protestants. He noted that Pentecostalism had been a transforming force in Chile for fifty years, and he described a new day that had arrived in Protestant-Catholic relations in Latin America. On the trip he spoke frequently. In São Paulo Dominican friars invited him to visit their monastery and address the faculty and students of the theological seminary about the gospel. In Rio de Janeiro Mackay and other Protestants discussed with Benedictine fathers the place of Mary in the Christian religion. In Caracas, Venezuela, José Cardinal Quintero warmly welcomed Mackay and presented him a book that the Cardinal had inscribed. It contained Quintero's address delivered at the 1963 session of the Vatican Council II, in which he proposed that the Roman Catholic Church express responsibility for the separation at the time of the Reformation.[25]

In Chile a few weeks later dramatic examples of spiritual ecumenism occurred. Mackay participated in a public dialogue on the ecumenical movement with Fr. Juan Ochagaria, dean of the faculty of theology at the Catholic University of Chile. He had been a former student of Gustave A. Weigel, SJ, the ecumenical pioneer and professor at Woodstock College. A questioner asked, "Sir, what do you consider to be the main problem of your church today?" Ochagaria answered, "We Catholics must make Christians." Mackay commended his friend for speaking frankly and added, "We Protestants too must make Christians."[26] Mackay met Raúl Cardinal Silva Henríquez. Cardinal Silva had recently talked with Protestant mission leaders in the United States, thanking them for what Protestantism had contributed to the life of Latin America and the inspiration that it had given the Roman Catholic Church.

During Mackay's final visit to Peru during this trip in 1964, the minister of education, Francisco Miró Quesada, presented Mackay the *Palmas Magisteriales*, a civic honor and the highest award of the government for educational services to Peru. A second tribute at the school followed three years later when San Andrés celebrated its fifty-year jubilee in 1967. To honor the first promotion, or graduation, of 1923, the school's alumni group, known as the "Old Boys' Association" of the Colegio, prepared another celebration along the lines of the earlier one, but were disappointed that the founder was not able to participate. Mackay's friend Dr. Luis Alberto Sánchez, an authority on Latin American literature, former rector of San Marcos University, and a

John Mackay talks to the Peruvian Minister of Education, Francisco Miró Quesada, and others, after Mackay was awarded the *Palmas Magisteriales* for educational services to Peru, Lima, 1964.

successful politician, began the formal academic session of the celebration with an address in the assembly hall of the Colegio that focused on Mackay's contributions to the social life of Peru.[27]

Mackay's two articles in the *Christian Century* in November of 1965 discussed social changes and Latin America's new revolutionary mood. Mackay emphasized that "in the Latin American mind the term 'revolution' enjoys a certain sanctity," and ironically "Brazil's new military dictatorship speaks of itself as the fruit of a 'national revolution' and is opposed to 'counterrevolutionaries.'"[28] In discussing the meaning of the term "revolution," Mackay related the issues of social justice to the revolutionary mood and noted that the Mexican Revolution "brought the brown race into power for the first time since the fall of the Aztec and Incan empires. Because of special circumstances the latest Cuban revolution, that of 1959, turned communist."[29] The article went on to describe how different leaders were dealing with the challenges of change. The second article concentrated on the new mood in the churches.[30]

In a major step of ecumenical cooperation in North America, the Catholic Inter-American Cooperation Program (CICOP) invited Mackay to address a meeting. He was deeply moved when he rose to speak to the audience in Boston in 1967 at the age of seventy-seven. Founded in 1963 with offices in Washington, CICOP was sponsored by the Latin American Bureau of the U.S. Catholic Conference. Mackay's ecumenical approach at the occasion included the thought that "the Protestant advent in Latin America gave expression to yearnings and experiences and ideas which were present centuries earlier in the Spanish reformers and mystics, and in missionary personalities such as Bartolomé de las Casas."[31] In a sense this speech reflected the fulfillment of

John Mackay in Lima, 1964, meets some of the school's "Old Boys" as alumni of the Colegio are known.

the trend toward a more personal religion that he had discussed and advocated almost thirty-five years earlier in his book *The Other Spanish Christ*.[32]

Reversals in North America

Mackay's generation bequeathed to its successors a sound church and agenda, and much had been accomplished. Eugene Carson Blake, who followed Mackay as a Presbyterian leader and held the office of stated clerk, paid tribute to Mackay and his accomplishments: "If the United Presbyterian Church is stronger, more mature in its faith, more ecumenical in its vision, more respected in the nation, and more influential in the world family of Churches, it is in no small measure due to John Mackay."[33]

As Mackay and his contemporaries retired, however, members of the younger generation were eager to fill leadership roles in the church. Some were referred to as members of a "new breed"[34] and others aimed "to win control of the church from the Old Guard."[35] Very soon, however, these younger leaders and the church faced many difficult and complicated challenges. With the benefit of historical hindsight, an examination may be made of the new directions taken and of their consequences. These directions and emphases had antecedents in the "social gospel" initiatives of the early part of the twentieth century in America, in which Walter Rauschenbusch reinterpreted Christianity's basic doctrine of the atonement from being a personal and individual act of God to being a collective, social act. The growth of this nonpersonal Christianity had many aspects as it developed in America during the twentieth century.[36] There is no limit to the wrongs that can be added to Rauschenbusch's original list of six: "religious bigotry, the combination of graft and political power, the corruption of justice, mob spirit and mob action, militarism, class contempt,"[37] the latter of which included economic injustice. Making the atonement a social abstraction had placed a false utopianism into American religious thought and led to confusion about the theological idea of the kingdom of God, which in fact humanity can only announce but cannot create.[38]

The concept of secularism was an element in the new directions advocated by younger leaders in the 1960s. Sometimes two different meanings of the term *secularism* overlapped in popular usage, and the usages were gradually confused and blended together in the common mind. Arend van Leeuwen, under the auspices of the Missionary Council of the Netherlands Reformed Church, wrote an influential, though largely retrospective book, *Christianity in World History*, which discussed the term *secularization* and the process.[39] As derived from the Latin *seculum*, the word connoted a "new age of history," the Christian age. On the other hand, in New Testament terms the expression "secularization" suggested, as it did in Rom. 12:2, "being conformed to this world," implying a movement away from religious faith. Some liberal Christians, confusing secularization as a process and secularism as a philosophy, used a confused rationale of secularism for incorporating world-centered tendencies into the church. The sociological advancement of secularization theory, however, was "essentially mistaken."[40] A proponent of secular analysis years later acknowledged a category error in linking modernism with secularization rather than with diversity.[41]

These secularist tendencies produced a *reductio ad absurdum* within the church as so-called new atheists appeared within it. The news media propagated a paradoxically titled academic trend, "the death of God," which released blasphemous, defiant, and toxic elements into the culture.[42] It is no coincidence that this theme coincided with the turbulence, absurdity, and political existentialism of the late 1960s.[43]

Within this climate of thought the younger generation of religious leaders advocated several specific new directions and approaches. This group emphasized political activism, civil disobedience, pastoral managerial authority, and the subordination of the role of the elders to the role of the pastor. First, some leaders appeared to favor use of churches as instruments for political advocacy and activism in much the way that a labor union is active. The influence of political organizer Saul Alinsky on the new breed implied the subordination of the church to new political groupings to bring about social change known as the "people's organizations." The churches could be used to supply members and support to the new political groups that aimed at salvation on earth.[44]

Within the Presbyterian Church Eugene Carson Blake shifted the existing pattern of church leadership away from a bottoms-up style to a top-down, managerial leadership style emphasizing institutionalization rather than collegiality and consultation. Mackay had recognized this tendency earlier and, using his customary forthright method of communication within the church, wrote to Blake in 1958 to question Blake's understanding of his office as stated clerk of the Presbyterian Church: he was in fact the number-two officer of the church, not number one.[45] This exchange had little effect on Blake's style; as one correspondent wrote to a journal, he acted as a "ruler" of the church rather than as its servant.[46] The hierarchical trend was also encouraged, and many congregations redrafted their church property deeds after a U.S. Supreme Court opinion found a "hierarchical" government in the Presbyterian Church.[47] This decision surprised some church historians who had emphasized the democratic congregational decision-making process accompanied by a court structure to settle disputes. As a sense of hierarchical institutionalism increased, the theological sense of sin diminished within the church.

Another example of institutional managerial approaches within the church was Eugene Blake's dramatic use of a top-down attempt at church unity. The so called "Blake-Pike Proposal" for unity made in San Francisco in 1960 put other church leaders from other denominations in a difficult position since they had not been consulted in advance. Mackay did not hesitate to criticize sharply the initiative that he believed, in effect, made the pursuit of structural unity a church idol.[48]

Civil disobedience was also a technique of the new breed. But civil disobedience by individuals who relied on their religious institutional affiliations for authority and publicity had negative, long-term cultural consequences by reinforcing a false concept of salvation through political action while supplying youth with lawbreakers as role models. Such role models sharply delayed or disrupted the normal maturation process of susceptible students. Civil disobedience by church officials in America undermined the idea of law as a culturally unifying factor and advanced a sense of legal positivism in the culture as it undermined the rule of law and respect for governmental authority. It detracted from the church's spiritual goals. Eugene Carson Blake, John C. Bennett, and William Sloane Coffin acted out their civil disobedience in different fashions. Some members of the public may have been confused whether these actions were those of private citizens or of the church through an official. Civil disobedience in a stable constitutional democracy frequently brought them publicity with little actual risk of real punishment as would have occurred in most other countries. Mackay's friend John C. Bennett protested by chaining himself to a fence. William Sloane Coffin, the chaplain at Yale, avoided the legal consequences of civil disobedience when his attorney, former U.S. Supreme Court justice Goldberg, called the Justice Department and learned that Coffin would not be retried on federal charges.[49]

Disobedience of canon law coincided with disobedience of civil law and to a lack of church discipline. An eminent cleric of the Episcopal Church performed improper ordinations.[50] Divorce and remarriage became accepted among ordained clergy.[51] Coffin's view that "rules at best are signposts, never hitching posts"[52] tended to antinomianism and contributed to a sense of relativity and lawlessness. One mother of a student directly attributed her daughter's pregnancy to Coffin's influence.[53]

Finally, there was a reversal of initiative and momentum. Many Protestant clergy became fascinated by the spectacle of the Second Vatican Council and the renewal under way in the Roman Catholic Church. Protestant observers of the council seemed not to heed Karl Barth's caution that the problem posed by the Vatican Council was repentance and renewal of the non-Roman churches assembled at the World Council of Churches.[54]

Against the Fashion: Mackay's Message in Retirement

Mackay, who said that he "would rather burn out than rust out," continued to speak, preach, and write, attempting to counterbalance the mainline church's dominant fashion during his retirement by analyzing and commenting on these new currents. One place that he attempted to perpetuate by new vocabulary the spiritual emphasis on personal religion within the church was at his participation in the inauguration of the new president of Princeton Seminary. James I. McCord had insisted his predecessor give the charge to him as the fourth president. When Mackay did so on March 29, 1960, he referred in passing to his own inaugural address twenty-three years before, but he now discerned the need for leadership in a new direction. The need he spoke of was "to reinterpret and to rehabilitate the concept of Christian Piety. . . . The time has come to stress in church and in culture the reality of new being, ontological change, the meaning of sainthood in contemporary terms, and what it means to be 'God's men and women' today."[55] Although now a negative term, *piety* denoted the "timeless reality of man's intimate relationship to God and his devoted obedience to God. . . . To be truly pious means to be . . . an individual who has experienced the reality of spiritual change and gives expression to it in daily living."[56] Mackay provided several reasons piety was needed: to unify the ecumenical church, to challenge existentialism, and to provide an alternative to psychoanalysis as a solution of "the problem of man's inner life." The emphasis on reinterpreting piety was a way to provide the culture with a continued emphasis on individual religious devotion and conversion, and Mackay's statements proved theologically prophetic.[57]

A second clear example of Mackay's persistent efforts to keep the message of the church in balance occurred in an address that he gave at a memorial service for James Reeb. A Princeton Seminary graduate, Reeb was working at All Souls Church in Washington when Mackay met and spoke with him for what proved to be the final time. Mackay had addressed a men's group at the church, and his former student drove him home afterwards. As they said goodbye, they agreed to meet again for fellowship and conversation, but before they could do so, Reeb was dead. The young clergyman, who felt deep anguish and empathy for the plight of blacks, heeded a call for assistance in Alabama from Martin Luther King Jr. and was tragically killed by a blow to the side of his head from a heavy stick as he walked down a street in Selma, Alabama.

Mackay called the address "the most delicate assignment ever given [to him]."[58] Reeb, who had died to help his fellow humans, had become a virtual agnostic. Preaching for him became a sharing of his personal struggle. Mackay, in nuanced and highly sensitive fashion, described the tragic situation. He drew attention to a distortion in the application of the two great commandments found in Matt. 22:37–39, to love God and to love neighbor:

> Here is the irony, the tragic irony. This beloved, sincere and courageous man came to ignore and brush aside the commandment to love God, which is both the Christian pivot of human obligation and the inspiration of creative concern for others. The love of one's neighbor, which is the Second Commandment, became for him a substitute for the First Commandment, which is "to love God, with all one's heart, soul, strength and mind"—and in the light and strength of that devotion—"to love one's neighbor as one's self." James Reeb made concern for others the one ultimate source, norm and objective of human behaviour. These two commandments, however, belong together. When they are separated in such a way that either one becomes the sole absolute, or a substitute for the other, tragedy ensues.[59]

In the 1960s and 1970s as theological fashion decisively shifted, Mackay steadily and directly challenged the secularist philosophy but received no response. He asked rhetorically, "Upon what do you base the assumption, scientific or philosophical, that what I allege to have been a lifetime experience of the reality of God and his directive guidance has been pure illusion?"[60]

He was equally direct about the cultural emphasis on secularism:

> We have reached a moment in the history of classical Protestantism when the idea must be crusadingly challenged, that to be relevant to the problems of the secular order, a man must abstain from any claim to have a personal relationship with Deity as his Light and his Companion in struggle. . . . The reality of God's presence in day-by-day living, as well as in mission, must be experienced and proclaimed more than is now being done in the mainline Protestant churches. Otherwise, despite the New Secularism which many churches patronize, and the organizational oneness which they pursue, tragedy confronts us, unless a dimension now being lost or disdained is restored to status. In such a case, purely secular forces could temporarily prevail and provide leadership in seeking a solution of the problem of man and society.[61]

Mackay did not lose an opportunity to refer to the cultural situation at a ceremonial occasion when Karl Barth's first trip to the United States was timed to allow his participation in the Princeton Seminary sesquicentennial celebration. Mackay, Barth's English teacher of 1930, introduced him before his first lecture. In his introduction Mackay noted that "today stands in constant danger of succumbing to the current cultural situation, and in its institutional trend runs the peril of becoming God's patron instead of his servant."[62]

Through devotional writing Mackay also tried to counterbalance the secularist social trends. In 1964 he published a devotional book, *His Life and Our Life*, composed of two series of devotional articles that had appeared in *Presbyterian Life* as "Great Rhythms in the Life of Christ" and "When God Is Our Strength."[63] In contrast to the liberalizing tendencies within the churches, in this work Mackay called for more discipline. He encouraged limitations on the broadening church by urging a contemporary equivalent for the Scottish Presbyterian practice of "fencing the tables," namely, limiting reception of Communion to sincere believers through the use of Communion tokens for those who were members and who would follow Paul's injunction "Let a man examine himself, and so eat of the bread and drink of the cup" (1 Cor. 11:28 RSV).[64]

Mackay continued to emphasize the need for conversion to combat religious nominalism. On May 30, 1971, he preached the baccalaureate service for Princeton Seminary on the text "'What is that to you? Follow me!'" (John 21:22 RSV). Age had not dulled Mackay's evangelistic passion nor his discernment of the needs of the times. His sermon emphasized the need "to become a new being, to experience *conversion*, spiritual change." Aiming at the dominant spiritual temptations of the time, he warned of the "deification of feeling" and "theologization of Christ, that is the substitution of ideas about Christ for the reality of Christ." He warned that "today in our country and in other countries Mammonism is a more serious threat than Communism," and that "unity must be for mission and not mission for unity."[65]

He was direct but polite in defending historic Christianity against some contemporary theologians. Mentioning Bishop John A. T. Robinson, and Paul Tillich, who had both raised the question of deity in contemporary discussion, Mackay presented his own testimony of the historical Christian faith with a description and example of the personal guidance of God in his own life.[66]

In the mid-1930s, before assuming the duties of the presidency of Princeton Seminary, Mackay had participated in the Federal Council's preaching mission. In his retirement years he actively supported a similar enterprise, the "Key Bridge" initiative, which sought a stronger evangelical witness and unity in American life. The group, made up of individuals from nine major denominations, was a nonorganizational, evangelical coalition to advance cooperative efforts reminiscent of the Federal Council preaching mission of the mid-1930s. The meeting held December 2–3, 1967, included Carl Henry, Leighton Ford, John Mackay, and Rufus Jones.[67] The initiative also included a young evangelical leader named Peter C. Moore, an Episcopalian and founder of FOCUS.

Recognizing new conditions affecting church-and-state relations, Mackay called for revision in the goals of the organization Protestants and Others United (POAU). At the end of September 1965 he sent Glenn Archer an outline of an address containing ideas for updating the POAU manifesto. Archer responded favorably. The themes that Mackay identified were the Supreme Court decision regarding prayers in public schools, the emergence of a new American nationalism, the manifestation of government concern for human welfare, the new policy and mood of the Roman Catholic Church, the new mood in American Protestantism, and changes in the mood of secular America. He identified and singled out questions and issues that challenged the currently existing analysis of the church-state relationship: First, what attitude should be adopted to the question of church and state as cooperating partners in the context of administration of antipoverty programs? Would the churches become subservient to the state because of money and benefits they receive from the state, or would the state be subservient to the churches due to their voting power? The second issue involved the Vatican as a political entity to be recognized by an ambassador, and the third, the need for a distinction between the imposition of religion in public schools and the recognition accorded to the study of religion as a cultural reality.

"This involves the difference between the recognition of the reality of God in a classroom course," Mackay argued, "and the official worship of God by the school community." Fourth, Mackay felt there should be a critique of the spirit and style in which controversial discussion should be carried on. Finally, he called for a basic review of the meaning of church and state and of the relationship between them and the concern that "Christian churches become merely welfare organizations."[68]

Unfortunately, these major reappraisals had to be left for others. Mackay realized that he was no longer able to maintain his former pace. The intense period of travel, lecturing, and writing suddenly took its toll in February 1966, and Mackay, then age seventy-six, suffered "from physical and nervous exhaustion." He became aware that his health now limited his creativity to formulate a new and adequate statement for this organization.[69]

In retirement, Mackay also spoke out prophetically on public social issues, including God's righteousness and the moral law applied to American culture, materialism, the Vietnam War, and the civil rights movement. Drawing on his biblical philosophy of history he pointed to the idea that God could use even atheistic nations to exercise God's judgment: "A political power, ideologically godless could be used by God to exercise judgment upon any nation which while professing to live 'under God,' does not take God or his moral order seriously."[70] On another occasion he made the same point by a biblical reference to Jer. 43:10, when God refers to king Nebuchadnezzar as "my servant."[71] On the threat of materialism, borrowing an image for avarice from John Milton, he warned that "today in our country and in other countries Mammonism is a more serious threat than Communism."[72] Drawing on his international experience and his knowledge of foreign affairs, he urged a reappraisal of U.S. foreign policy and expressed his personal opposition to the Vietnam War through a letter to the *New York Times*.[73] In another address Mackay made clear his strong support for the civil rights movement.[74]

The relation of religion and culture was a popular academic topic. Some sociologists focused on the weakening of Protestant ideas and influence in American culture, the waning of the so-called Protestant establishment, and the identification of an American civil religion.[75] A sociological commentary published in 1964 used an acronym for white Anglo-Saxon Protestant, WASP, which became a caricature and blurred the distinction between a theological definition of Protestantism and a sociological one.[76] American Protestantism was examined from the angle of social leadership, highlighting a social superiority that manifested itself in some Protestant circles. Mackay, whose life and message forcefully challenged religious nominalism, was never part of a sociological segment that claimed or assumed superior social status.

As a theologian, his last book, *Christian Reality & Appearance* (1969), distinguished between authentic religious Protestantism and nominal or idolatrous substitutes and is one of his best books.[77] An excerpt published in *Christianity Today* criticized the trend towards institutional oneness while disregarding missionary or spiritual purpose.[78] The final chapter, which contrasts Christian obedience and the idol of ethicism, raises a theme still requiring attention in American political and commercial culture.[79] But an informal realignment toward spiritual unity had begun to take hold among Christians. Mackay's friend Marcel Pradervand observed in 1970 that "separations are no more essentially between churches but between Christians in each church."[80] Here Pradervand recognized a de facto spiritual ecumenism that was taking shape within the Christian movement despite the efforts of some leaders to focus on merely institutional or theological objectives.

The Confession of 1967

Three final subjects from Mackay's retirement years require attention: Mackay's attitude toward the Confession of 1967, his associations with the charismatic movement within the Presbyterian Church, and the reversal of ecumenical initiatives.

Adoption of the Confession of 1967 was a tipping point for the Presbyterian Church. Although the Westminster Confession was the basis of the merger of two churches in 1958, it appeared that leaders anticipated a confessional revision following the merger, and Mackay was one of the original nine men appointed by the first United General Assembly to serve on the Committee on a Brief Contemporary Statement of Faith.[81] He realized the direction the committee was taking, and not wishing to associate himself with it, Mackay retired from the committee in 1962, letting it be known that other commitments requiring world travel would interfere with his work on the project.[82] Nonetheless, he continued to correspond with committee members and attempted to influence the direction of the work.

In 1965 Mackay published an article titled "Commendation and Concern," which directly raised issues concerning the draft of the confession that was being circulated at that time.[83] Having exhorted seminary graduates in June 1958, "Ponder deeply before you take any stand that would dismember the Body of Christ,"[84] Mackay followed the principle himself when he shed light diplomatically on the weaknesses in the proposed document.

Should the document not rather be called a statement, since it was not actually "a compendium, a synthesis, a distillation of essential Christianity as interpreted by the church"?[85] asked Mackay. He also raised the issue of the Bible being much more than a "*'normative'* witness to Christ." He maintained that the Bible "is, itself, the supreme *source* from which we draw truth that is authentically Christian."[86] He believed it was "desirable that a Presbyterian confessional statement give more status to the Bible and greater attention to the fact and dimension of Revelation."[87]

Issues raised in "Commendation and Concern," including reconciliation, evangelism, and ethical issues connected with the new morality, suggested that liberalism was making its way into the heart of the church. In his article Mackay took seriously the concept of "reconciliation," although he would have preferred the theme of "redemption" for the confession. He noted, however, that full justice should be done to the meaning of the term *reconciliation* if it were to be used: "If alienation is to be transcended, both the divided parties must accept one another in a bond of mutual affection, understanding and trust."[88] In addition Mackay believed that a more direct definition of *evangelism* was needed in the context of a discussion of reconciliation: "It involves inviting men at an appropriate moment to commit themselves to God, and thereupon, through the Holy Spirit, join the Community of Christ for the service of mankind."[89] The secularized and politically based understanding of reconciliation in the document did not take the logical step that the true reconcilers are evangelists and that authentic reconciliation requires evangelism and involves repentance. Next, pointing out that "other grave issues in contemporary society also clamor for the church's attention," Mackay delicately directed attention to the document's deficit in not addressing the sexual revolution. Mackay raised the question in theological terms as "the type of relationship between men and women which is essential for true humanity, the New Morality and man's descent into Subhumanity, the place of commitment and discipline in the achievement of true manhood and true womanhood."[90] Finally, Mackay believed that the document failed "to do justice to subjectivity in the God-man relationship"[91] and give more status to "realities which cross the boundaries of Protestantism, Roman Catholicism and Eastern Orthodoxy . . . Christian conversion to God and Christian communion with God."[92]

Because of the draft's weak stand on the authority of Scripture, a group called Presbyterians United for Biblical Confession (PUBC) was organized and held a meeting of more than five hundred ministers and laypersons in Chicago in late November 1965. Mackay attended and noted that a confession properly so-called must convey "changeless truth in changing times in contemporary speech." He received applause when he said that "the Bible has greater literary and theological dimensions than is attributed to it in the proposed Confession."[93] He also pointed to the draft's weakness on the human response to God.

Mackay went on to add that he thought "the proposed Confession [was] right when it speaks out on issues of peace, poverty, and race."[94] Others, however, found weaknesses in the social and political teachings of the final document as it encouraged nations to cooperate toward peace "even at risk to national security."[95] In this light some asked whether public officials such as Dean Rusk, U.S. Secretary of State from 1961 to 1969, would have to resign office because if they followed their churches' teaching, they would not fulfill their constitutional duty of preserving the defense of the nation?

Mackay had evaluated the committee's composition and posture realistically and realized the inability of traditional theology to influence the outcome of debate and discussion. Rather than be a divisive force, however, he tried to influence the deliberations without stimulating disunity or division. After retiring from the committee, Mackay's role was that of a mediator between the denominational leadership and the constituency expressing its biblical concerns. His speech in Chicago in November of 1965 sought to bring the PUBC and the drafting committee closer together.[96] In 1967 Mackay also spoke at a breakfast at the 179th General Assembly to the Presbyterians United for Biblical Confession.[97] Edward Dowey and others on the committee preparing the confession wrongly believed that the literalistic inerrancy view of Scripture was the same as the Westminster Confession view of Scripture.[98] In the end the Confession of 1967 did not take a firm enough stand on the authority of Scripture and placed too much emphasis on reason. Soon after the adoption of the confession the church lost fifteen percent of its membership. The theology of the confession sowed the seeds for years of divisiveness and numerical decline within the Presbyterian Church.[99]

Charismatic Presbyterians

In retirement Mackay had become an elder statesman, and younger churchmen often sought his aid and counsel. Over the years he had taught and preached on the person and work of the Holy Spirit.[100] Since he was known for having sympathetic contacts with individual Pentecostals, such as David du Plessis, and with the Pentecostal movement itself,[101] several clergy sought out Mackay when they were caught up by controversy connected with the issue. In 1967 special committees were investigating two Presbyterian ministers, George C. "Brick" Bradford and Robert C. Whitaker, because of their charismatic experiences. The disagreements in their congregations and presbyteries could lead to their departures. In spring 1967 Mackay, then seventy-eight, wrote back to Whitaker saying they could "count on my concern and support."[102]

Mackay was scheduled to attend a Hispanic American Institute at Austin Seminary in Texas in October, and Bradford brought together twenty-two persons interested in the charismatic issue.[103] At the meeting in Austin, October 10–12, 1967, Mackay encouraged the Presbyterian charismatic ministers to bring about renewal within their denomination, not abandon it. He cautioned against absolutizing tongue speaking and urged them to reflect theologically about their experience in Reformed theological terms. The role of J. Rodman Williams, Professor of Systematic Theology at Austin, was important. Unlike Mackay, he had an experience of "speaking in tongues."[104] According to Whitaker, Mackay urged the ministers to follow a twofold approach: "Follow the rules of the *Book of Order* and appeal your case to the next judicatory. Take it all the way to the General Assembly. I will work behind the scenes to see to it that you get justice." He added that it was "terribly important that a committee be established at the General Assembly level to study the whole matter."[105]

On November 22 Mackay met with Stated Clerk William P. Thompson and discussed the possibility of a special committee being appointed by the General Assembly to study the work of the Holy Spirit. By this time the Presbytery of Phoenix had expelled Whitaker from his pulpit at a Phoenix church. When the General Assembly met in May, that action had precipitated four overtures calling for study of the Holy Spirit and spiritual gifts. The General Assembly created a "Special Committee on Glossolalia and Other Charismatic Gifts" to report the following year. The next day Whitaker, who had appealed to freedom of conscience, learned that the Permanent Judicial Commission had vindicated his complaints against the presbytery and synod. John Coventry Smith, Mackay's former colleague at the Board of Foreign Missions, was elected moderator. Together with Smith and Thompson, Mackay discussed potential members of the committee. Thompson felt that the neo-Pentecostals should not be evaluated only by outsiders. A very capable committee was formed representing diversified occupations. Its membership included Bruce Metzger, a biblical scholar; Charles H. Meisgeier, a psychology professor; and Thomas David Parham, a navy chaplain. A preliminary report was submitted in 1969, but the General Assembly granted an extension because the scope of the inquiry was expanded.

When the report was issued in 1970, it was groundbreaking in its thorough consideration of the subject matter, and it later served as a model for reports produced by other denominations.[106]

Shifting International Ecumenical Priorities

Reversals in leadership priorities were not limited to North American Protestantism but were also evident at the international level of the ecumenical
movement. Many of the founders of the World Council of Churches (WCC)
and the ecumenical movement, including Mackay, had come of age and served
within the Free Church tradition or on the mission field. Their ardent spirituality had been formed within the Student Christian Movement. Some members of the generation that inherited the work were powerfully influenced by
different ideas and trends in the social ether of some educational institutions
where they studied. As early as the mid-1950s the training grounds for new
leadership were experiencing spiritual erosion. Lesslie Newbigin received an
angry reaction from the faculty after a sermon he preached in 1954 at the chapel of Union Theological Seminary. The reaction caused him to observe that
the "seminary was in danger of succumbing to a sort of a-historical Gnosti-
cism."[107] The atmosphere where English clergy were educated was no better
a few years later. John Robinson wrote, "I believe I am not alone in finding a
theological college the most difficult rather than the easiest of places in which
to pray."[108] The social and spiritual consequences of spiritual erosion within
some educational institutions were clear to one visitor. Having returned to
North America after a long absence, in the fall of 1979 Bishop K. H. Ting
told Richard Shaull his first reaction: "Moral decadence . . . Decadence is the
inability of one generation to pass on to the next generation the vision and
convictions by which it has lived."[109]

Mackay and the International Missionary Council (IMC) leadership delib-
erated carefully over the theology and prudence of merging and integrating
the WCC and the IMC. In December of 1951, a year before the Lucknow
meetings, Mackay wrote to Ranson expressing reservations about the idea
of merger and setting forth his thoughts on prerequisites for a change in the
associative relationship of the two bodies, including ideas of decentraliza-
tion of the WCC to more effectively reach the "grass roots."[110] As discussed
previously, after the Lucknow meetings in the winter of 1952–1953, Mackay
recognized that members of the younger churches outside the West were
increasingly mature, should take an equal role in the WCC, and should be full
partners sharing the work of finishing the task of evangelization. Theological bases for this understanding rested on the growing understanding of the
missionary nature of God's church. Practical and logistical considerations
supported the decision based on the duplication of meetings, activities, and
resources and the enormous time demands made on some of the leaders.
Furthermore, the success of the missionary movement on six continents and

the planting of congregations around the world allowed the "scaffolding" of the missionary movement to be withdrawn.[111] The benefits of airplane travel and international telephonic communications had made the world smaller. After nearly a decade of careful and prayerful deliberations, at the IMC Ghana Assembly the vote in favor of integration produced an overwhelming majority.

In official minutes, the leadership explicitly documented the purpose of integration, namely, to place the missionary movement at the heart of the WCC. "The purpose of Integration is the putting of the missionary obligation of the church right in the centre of the Ecumenical Movement, so that in all their common thinking and action together in the World Council of Churches the member churches may be constantly aware of the missionary dimension of such thought and action."[112] This goal of incorporating the theology of missions into the central nature of the church structure resulted in a major shift of mission strategy and understanding of the church. After the Willingen Conference, missions had ceased to be understood geographically. Many recognized that the directness of missions did not exist after Ghana as it had before.

Unfortunately, a variety of factors, including organizational structure, secular theological initiatives, and the manner of exercising authority itself, prevented the integration of the ecumenical structures from turning out as its leaders had hoped and expected in 1959. First, the smaller IMC did not blend well bureaucratically into the much larger WCC. Other groups within the WCC, such as its Division of Inter-Church Aid, competed with it. Instead of energizing the static WCC with the missionary ideal, the former IMC was buried under bureaucratic weight. Newbigin himself took some responsibility for his failure to recruit appropriate younger churchmen to Geneva to take up the task of evangelism.[113]

Second, contradictory theological trends overrode implementation of the explicit terms of integration, putting the missionary purpose at the heart of the WCC. Instead of following the letter and spirit of the written terms for integration, the new generation, many with little or no missionary experience, fostered a radical secular theology that undermined and attacked the role and status of institutional churches.[114] A confused understanding of secularism and an underappreciation of the consequences of non-Christ-centered diversity took hold. The leaders of some Protestant churches looked to the world for their agenda.[115] Universal salvation, long considered a heresy, was presented by the WCC.[116] Passivity took the place of evangelism.[117] Some evangelicals criticized the "liberal agenda and frequently unprincipled methodology of the World Council of Churches."[118]

By the mid-1960s, a dominant radical theology expounded that "secularization was the fruit of the gospel."[119] The WCC called a conference at Geneva in July 1966, the World Conference on Church and Society, which has been considered a climactic event.[120] Whereas prior controversial or innovative conferences such as Jerusalem, Oxford, Willingen, and Ghana had closed with a message of strong acceptable consensus, the message and its management of the Geneva Conference created confusion and dissention within the church and were subjected to serious criticism by Paul Ramsey of Princeton University.[121] Speakers at the Conference, such as Richard Shaull, called for "radical theological reorientation." Shaull believed that "a contextual theology and ethic offer creative possibilities."[122] In retrospect it is clear that the long-term effect of such positions was to undermine the legitimacy and credibility of the WCC.

Despite the establishment of the guiding principle of integration—that mission was to be rooted in the WCC—during the leadership of Eugene Carson Blake, General Secretary of the WCC from 1966 to 1974, evangelism was not emphasized, and the WCC moved toward the oxymoron of "secular ecumenism" and political action.[123] Principled guidance had been bequeathed to these leaders, but the principles were implemented ineffectively.

During initial retirement years Mackay traveled extensively on the Cook lectureship and focused on ecclesiastical developments in Latin America, but church members and journalists naturally asked for his opinion and comments on the direction of the ecumenical movement. In an issue-oriented, nonpartisan fashion, by editorials, magazine contributions, and book excerpts, Mackay focused readers' attention on balanced spiritual ecumenism and warned against empty institutionalism, which itself was producing Christian nominalism.[124] He advocated moving beyond doctrine, structure, and ecclesial relations to "explore afresh the rich treasures of devotional literature which the Christian traditions have in common."[125] And he continued to advocate the functional idea that "Church is the instrument of God's glory."[126] An article titled "What the Ecumenical Movement Can Learn from Conservative Evangelicals"[127] stressed the need for biblical study, conversion, and better literature. He used the Billy Graham Association's *Decision Magazine* as a good example. Mackay warned against the idea that belonging to the church became a substitute for belonging to Christ. At a low point of the WCC, Mackay contributed his final article on the subject, an important statement of his ecumenical theology, "The Ecumenical Movement—Whence? And Whither?"[128]

Elsewhere, theological reaction began to gather as the radical message of the WCC brought John R. W. Stott, an Anglican pastor in London, to address the international gathering. In an impassioned debate at the WCC's Fourth Assembly at Uppsala in 1968, Stott spoke out: "The Lord Jesus Christ wept over the city which had rejected him. I do not see this Assembly weeping similar tears."[129] Several years later the upside-down theology of the church seeking direction from the world was challenged by the Lausanne Covenant: "The Church must be in the world (Jn. 17:15); the world must not be in the Church."[130]

Protestant leaders of Mackay's generation balanced the church's social and spiritual aspects and avoided worldly steps that could split the church. Joseph Oldham developed the concept of middle axioms at the Oxford Conference to supply intermediate forms of ethical guidance, and Archbishop Temple also opposed the church's commitment to any particular policy.[131] Mackay's "Letter to Presbyterians" provided a powerful emphasis and perspective on eternal truths. In the 1960s Princeton University ethicist Paul Ramsey suggested that the Second Vatican Council provided a helpful model to the World Council for the preparation of guidance of social thought. The WCC did not follow this moderate path, however. In a notorious example of political action by the WCC, a donation of $85,000 was made to the cause of Robert Mugabe and Joshua Nkomo in Zimbabwe. Some Western Christians had become "armchair guerrillas, vicarious doers of violence."[132] The ecumenical movement had survived the First and Second World Wars, but its new direction was drying it up from within. In North America the Vietnam War precipitated the end of a major stage of ecumenism.[133]

Certainly more subtle internal reasons, called by one writer "unavowed motives," contributed to the lack of success of the ecumenical movement of the 1960s and 1970s. Biblical scholar C. H. Dodd, a forty-year veteran of the ecumenical movement, noted in 1949 that the ground of ecumenical debate suddenly shifted when theologians were in sight of some real agreement. He suspected "unavowed motives" that needed to be explored, first in the area of confessional or denominational loyalty and second, where theologians' separate religious traditions are implicated in social and political traditions. Dodd found less respectable unavowed motives—perhaps pride of worldly place and selfish ambition—too obvious to write about and suggested they were a matter "for privacy or the confessional."[134] It may seem to the laity that the ecumenical movement has stopped because leaders no longer take an interest. Perhaps further realignment will be impelled by Christianity's increasingly close contacts with other world religions.[135] Some church members may look at some leaders and think, "It sounds as though you love the _____ Church more than you love Jesus Christ!"

Signs of the Times

Mackay, a strategic thinker, discerned long-term trends and their consequences. In the 1960s, at the end of his life, he did not hesitate through writings and speeches to attempt to rebalance skewed priorities that he saw developing. He continued to stress a relationally based message of Christianity involving conversion and did not focus solely on social and political issues. At the same time he did not act divisively and chose to resign from the committee developing the Confession of 1967 and to use his authority to avoid a split in the Presbyterian Church. Soon thereafter the new direction of mainline churches caused financial donations to decrease and to accelerate realignment of members to other churches. Congregants of biblical and evangelical persuasion, who in an earlier era would have made the mainline church their home, moved to new venues and established themselves there.[136]

A pithy statement in the late 1960s exemplifies Mackay's prophetic vision and discernment when he wrote, "The future of the Church could be with a reformed Catholicism and a matured Pentecostalism."[137] This prophetic thought was prompted as Mackay observed a reversal as the Protestant ecumenical movement began to emphasize formalism, institutionalism, and structure—the historic attributes of the Roman Catholic Church—while the leadership of the Roman Catholic Church began to emphasize sacred Scripture and conversion. He noted changes specifically in Latin America, as the Roman Catholic Church developed a new realism that included awareness that the Bible in the vernacular must be given a place in the life of the people. This change was also driven by "resurgent evangelicalism."[138] *Unitatis Redintegratio* (Decree on Ecumenism), November 21, 1964, allowed Catholics to come together with non-Catholics in common prayer, where permitted (sect. 2). Mackay also noted the important speech that Pope Paul VI gave at the General Assembly of the United Nations on October 5, 1965, in which, among other points, he referred to the need for conversion.[139]

The direction of Roman Catholicism was further clarified in 1980 when Pope John Paul II decisively guided the Roman Catholic Church away from political action by ordering priests worldwide to cease political activity. Speaking of Massachusetts representative Father Robert F. Drinan, Pope John Paul II said, "Politics is the responsibility of laymen and a priest should be a priest."[140]

The change continued after Mackay's death when in the 1990s certain important doctrines developed by Mackay and the Protestant ecumenical movement crossed ecclesiastical boundaries and appeared in Roman Catholic doctrine. The encyclical *Redemptoris Missio*, on the permanent validity of the church's missionary mandate, December 7, 1990, taught that "*the Church is missionary by her very nature*" (para. 62). Pope John Paul II's encyclical, *Ut Unum Sint*, "On Commitment to Ecumenism," May 25, 1995, reaffirmed "*irrevocably* to following the path of the ecumenical venture" (para. 3). It spoke of "exchange of gifts between the Churches" (sect. 57); "reciprocal fraternal influence" and "enrichment" (sect. 87); "conversion to the will of the Father" (sect. 82); noting that "Full unity will come about when all share in the fullness of the means of salvation entrusted by Christ to his Church" (sect. 86).

Mackay's reference to the future of Pentecostalism was expanded in a second statement emphasizing the vitality and life of the charismatic movement. He said, "If it is a choice between the uncouth life of the Pentecostals and the Aesthetic death of the older churches, I for one choose uncouth life."[141] Mackay saw the nature of the emerging church movement and by this statement clearly took sides with the authentic life to be found in that movement. Glimpsing "tragic reversals" ahead in what some later called the cultural captivity of the mainline church in North America, he cast his destiny with life. The trends he discerned in 1967 continued for the next thirty years as the Pentecostal movement came to number 600 million.[142] In the southern hemisphere where Mackay himself had sown the seeds of change more than seventy-five years earlier, the newer Pentecostal churches were having great impact.

From this examination of history and with the aid of hindsight, several conclusions can be reached and several principles can be derived regarding successful ecumenical leadership. First, leadership in God's Order is more complex than leadership in the commercial or even most governmental arenas because of the multiplicity of spiritual and worldly dimensions that must be simultaneously understood and considered. The dynamic aspect of God's Order as a movement must never be neglected. Leaders must not emphasize structures at the expense of the spiritual reality of the Church. Institutional overcentralization can prevent God's purpose from being done at the regional or local levels, and theatrical ecumenism does not work without careful grounding and preparation. In fact, it may falsely raise expectations of success and lead to disappointment and cynicism.

Second, at best, the leader is a teacher and a shepherd skilled at inspiring others with a vision, persuading others with knowledge and logic, and mentoring them by example. This requires natural abilities of public speaking, logical thought, and personal diplomatic skills of compatibility with all personality types. Moreover, leadership is a gift involving special spiritual qualities and an authentic divine vocation. Church authority is not about control or secular professionalism. Potential leaders, having humility and avoiding vain ambition, should allow themselves to be raised up to leadership positions rather than jockey for position within the Church in a self-seeking political fashion. This is not passivity but altruism and recognition of the primacy of God's interest in preference to individual self-interest. Spiritual authority of a church leader who holds office in this fashion is enhanced. When entering a position within the Church the holder should perform its duties in the spirit of service as though it were a lifetime appointment. Because actions within the Church have generational impact, important decisions must be principled rather than expedient, governed by accepted standards and logic rather than personal experiences, opinion, or private judgment, and should be taken only with strong consensual support, reflected by a large supermajority if a vote is taken. The pew cannot rise higher than the pulpit. Leaders must remember that continuous evangelism by all churches everywhere is a necessity for vigorous spiritual life of a community, large or small, or of a nation. The Church must pray for its leaders, and the leaders must ask God for devout humility and spiritual gifts to perform their tasks well and faithfully.

Third, if leaders of the Church in social teachings move beyond formulations of middle axioms to provide guidance through direct issue advocacy, such message must be carefully balanced with the Church's evangelistic message so that both are heard equally in the culture. If churches through their leadership engage in issue advocacy, the guidance must be theologically correct, competently crafted, properly motivated, not substantially divisive, and rightly implemented. Advocacy by individual leaders should be clearly distinguished from corporate church advocacy. Extreme care, even skepticism, is required if a teaching departs from the ancient triple test of ecumenical authenticity: "What has been believed everywhere, always, and by all."

Fourth, God's Order means order. Its fruit is peace, not disorder and confusion. Discipline must exist within the Church. This involves, in part, leadership by example, through the personal self-discipline of leaders who first of all must make efforts to sanctify themselves. The Bible teaches that church leaders are held to a higher standard than the general membership, (though all should aspire to high standards) and high personal, intellectual, and ethical standards and discipline are needed to maintain the integrity of the Church.

Return to New Jersey

Mackay and his wife returned to New Jersey in 1969 to reside in a retirement community, Meadow Lakes, located near Princeton in Hightstown,

Jane and John Mackay in retirement at their home in Hightstown, New Jersey, June 1978.

New Jersey. They enjoyed the companionship of the residents there, including several Presbyterian friends of longstanding: Harold Willis Dodds, former president of Princeton University; and Henry Smith Leiper. In his final years, Mackay assumed a pastoral role as residents came to him to discuss concerns and problems. Mackay attempted to begin to write his memoirs, but other matters took priority. Mackay's longtime friend Henry Van Dusen had moved to Princeton, but when Mackay learned of his suicide in 1975, he was greatly saddened.[143]

Mackay found the period of his later years theologically confusing, but he told a young man that these were exciting times to be a Christian and there were many challenges ahead. Prophetically, he noted the significance of tragic irony. Mackay, as an experienced observer of international relations, detected one final tragic and ironic reversal. Liberalizing trends were occurring in Latin America while United States culture began to take on some of the ethical and moral attributes that Mackay had preached and taught against in Latin America:

> There have begun to appear in the life of this nation certain ominous traits, psychological and sociological, political and religious, that have been native to the Hispanic tradition and have had fateful consequences in Latin American lands. Signs increase in the United States of America that we are headed for a tragic era.[144]

As signs of a tragic era he would have been saddened but not surprised if he had lived to witness the fragmentation of the American family and the fire-bombing of an evangelical pastor's home.[145]

The end of the Student Christian Movement was a sign that the former era was passing away, and observers recognized influences that had depleted its energy, including denominational campus ministries.[146] Confirming Mackay's status as a major spiritual leader, *The Christian Century* published a list of the ten books that had shaped Mackay's life.[147]

Mackay died at 4:00 a.m. on June 9, 1983. Before he slipped away his daughter, Isobel, who was at his bedside, read him Psalm 121 and Psalm 23. Mackay spoke no final words. Isobel listened as he sighed three times, then his spirit flew out and was gone, and he lay quiet. Isobel wept as she drove home but knew he had gone to be with his Lord. At 9:00 a.m. that morning the General Assembly met and voted to reunite with the Southern Presbyterian Church. It would have pleased Mackay, who had worked many years for the reunion of Northern and Southern Presbyterian Churches. He was laid to rest in Princeton Cemetery a few yards away from the plots of his seminary predecessor J. Ross Stevenson and colleagues Charles R. Erdman and Frederick Loetscher.

The hand of God had led Mackay on the road of life. As a youth he asked God for spiritual gifts, and they were granted him in abundance. Loyal to biblical authority and the guidance of the Holy Spirit, he lived life for others, founding a school and bringing a Presbyterian theological seminary to preeminence. Preaching a high doctrine of Christ that made for solidarity, he opened Latin America as a recognized mission field, successfully challenging the religious monopoly claimed by the Roman Catholic Church. Later, based in North America, he defended the heritage of religious freedom while working to slow the advance of secularism in the culture. As a churchman, a leader, and a spokesman of the Protestant conciliar movement, Mackay shaped an enduring understanding of spiritual ecumenism, supported by institutional structures, that embraced both the unity and the missionary nature of the one holy catholic and apostolic church. Faithful to the word of Christ and His call, in his preaching he summoned all people to personal Christian commitment and encouraged them to find their own places in God's Order as living stones of the temple of God, the body of Christ.

Notes

INTRODUCTION

1. John A. Mackay, *Ecumenics* (Englewood Cliffs, NJ: Prentice-Hall, 1964), 159.
2. John A. Mackay, "Ecumenical Presbyterianism," *Presbyterian World* 20, no. 2 (June 1950): 52–53.
3. Ibid., 53.
4. John A. Mackay, "A Theological Foreword to Ecumenical Gatherings," *Theology Today* 5, no. 2 (July 1948): 149.
5. "Te totum applica ad textum: rem totam applica ad te." J. A. Bengel (N^M T^M G^M Manuale, 1734, praefatio), quoted in D. Eberhard Nestle, *Novum Testamentum Graece et Latine* (Stuttgart: Württembergische Bibelanstalt, 1906).

CHAPTER 1: BOYHOOD

1. "Nation Greets Mission Societies," *New York Times*, April 22, 1900, 2.
2. "President in the City," *New York Times*, April 22, 1900, 2.
3. *Ecumenical Missionary Conference, New York, 1900*, vol. 1 (New York: American Tract Society, 1900), 476–84.
4. "Mission Workers Enthusiastic," *New York Times*, April 24, 1900, 5.
5. Abstract of the speech in ibid; Speer's address in full in *Ecumenical Missionary Conference,* 74–78.
6. *Ecumenical Missionary Conference,* 95–108.
7. Arthur Judson Brown, *Memoirs of a Centenarian* (New York: World Horizons, 1957), 35. On Harrison see William C. Ringenberg, "Benjamin Harrison: The Religious Thought and Practice of a Presbyterian President," *Journal of Presbyterian History* 64, no. 3 (Fall 1986): 175–89.
8. See "Culloden" in David Daiches, *Bonnie Prince Charlie* (1973; repr., New York: Penguin, 2002), 193–219; on the activity of the troops of George Mackay, 3rd Baron Reay, see Daiches, 205.
9. Charles R. L. Fletcher, *Gustavus Adolphus and the Struggle of Protestantism for Existence* (New York: G. P. Putnam's Sons, 1923), 113.
10. Angus Mackay, *The Book of Mackay* (Edinburgh: Norman Macleod, 1906); and *Oxford Dictionary of National Biography*, ed. H. C. G. Matthew and Brian Harrison, vol. 35 (New York: Oxford University Press, 2004), 510–13. David Daiches, *Bonnie Prince Charlie* (1973; repr., New York: Penguin, 2002), 12.

11. John A. Mackay, "'Trumpeter of the Lord,'" review of *John Knox's History of the Reformation in Scotland* by William Croft Dickinson and *John Knox in Controversy* by Hugh Watt, *New York Times Book Review*, March 11, 1951, 7.

12. John A. Mackay, "The Problem of Freedom within the Church," review of *Light in the North: The Story of the Scottish Covenanters*, by J. D. Douglas, *Christianity Today*, April 23, 1965, 33.

13. James Lachlan Macleod, *The Second Disruption* (East Linton: Tuckwell Press, 2000).

14. John A. Mackay, *Christian Reality & Appearance* (Richmond, VA: John Knox Press, 1969), 83–84.

15. John A. Mackay, "A Representative American of the Sixties: James Joseph Reeb," *Princeton Seminary Bulletin* 60, no. 1 (October 1966): 35.

16. John A. Mackay, *Heritage and Destiny* (New York: Macmillan Co., 1943), 12–13.

17. Regarding Communion season, see John A. Mackay, *The Presbyterian Way of Life* (Englewood Cliffs, NJ: Prentice-Hall, 1960), 162–64; see also 132, 156.

18. John A. Mackay, *God's Order* (New York: Macmillan Co., 1953), 6–8. References appear in other writings. In John A. Mackay, "What Jesus Means to Me?" *World's Youth* 6, no. 4 (1931): 56, he put it slightly differently: "A voice from somewhere said to me. 'You too will preach.' Such a thought had never once entered my mind before. I can recollect how I began to tremble. After the service I could speak to no one: I had to be alone." See also Mackay's speech in Chicago under the auspices of the YMCA on October 20, 1929: "The Secularization of God," *Finding and Sharing God* (New York: Association Press, 1929), 71–72. The address called for a new understanding of the "cosmic significance of Jesus." John A. Mackay's "When Truth Is a Belt" (*Princeton Seminary Bulletin* 59, no. 1 [November, 1965]: 6–7) restates the experience in terms similar to those in Mackay, *God's Order*.

19. John A. Mackay, "The Gospel and Our Generation," in *The Christian Message for the World Today* (New York: Round Table Press, 1934), 99.

20. John A. Mackay, *A Preface to Christian Theology* (London: Nisbet & Co., 1942), 97.

21. Mackay, *Christian Reality*, 84.

22. John A. Mackay, "Let Us Remember," *Princeton Seminary Bulletin* 65, no. 1 (July 1972): 27.

23. "John A. Mackay: Influences on My Life," interview by Gerald W. Gillette, *Journal of Presbyterian History* 56, no. 1 (Spring 1978): 23.

24. Mackay, "What Jesus Means to Me?" 56.

25. "Let the Church Be the Church," interview of John A. Mackay conducted on September 25, 1974, by George M. Booker (*Presbyterian Layman* 7, no. 9 [November–December 1974]: 8).

26. Adolf Deissmann, *Paul: A Study in Social and Religious History*, trans. William E. Wilson (1912; New York: Harper & Bros., 1957), 144. See also idem, *The Religion of Jesus and the Faith of Paul*, trans. William E. Wilson (London: Hodder & Stoughton, 1923), 195–96.

27. Mackay, *God's Order*, 97–98.

28. Mackay occasionally quoted Robert Burns's poetry but not Burns's satirical poem "The Holy Fair," which reveals Burns's "blind spot." Burns viewed the Communion season from the point of view of a scoffer, an onlooker rather than a participant in the eucharistic meal. See Leigh Eric Schmidt, *Holy Fairs* (Princeton, NJ: Princeton University Press, 1989), 172–79.

29. John A. Mackay, "Personal Religion," *Princeton Seminary Bulletin* 37, no. 1 (December 1943): 3–10.

30. Ibid., 8.

31. John A. Mackay, *Our World Mission* (New York: The Board of Foreign Missions of the Presbyterian Church in the U.S.A., 1934), 21–22.

32. John A. Mackay, Diary, November 15, 1908, Mackay Archive.

33. Luis Alberto Sánchez, "Juan A. Mackay y la Educación Peruana," *Leader* 48, no. 46 (December 1973): 69. Sánchez goes on: "Mackay con su aire angelical, con su hablar suave, con su mirar penetrante, con su lentitud para responder, no porque le faltaran palabras sino porque no quería que le sobraran que es cosa diferente, bastante distinta." [Mackay, with his angelical air, his soft voice, his penetrating gaze, with his slow response, not because he did not have the words but because he did not want to go too far, which is another thing, very much another thing.]

34. Webster E. Browning to John A. Mackay, July 8, 1919, Mackay Collection.

35. Mackay, "Personal Religion," 4–5.

36. Matt. 11:12. In Augustinian terms, "Our hearts are restless till they find rest in Thee" (*The Confessions of St. Augustine Bishop of Hippo*, bk. 1, chap. 1, sec. 1).

37. Mackay, "What Jesus Means to Me?" 56.

38. John Alexander Mackay, "The Communion of Saints in Our Time," *Crozer Quarterly* 16, no. 4 (October, 1939): 255.

39. "Distinguished Churchman's Inspiring Address," *Inverness Courier*, July 1, 1955; "'The World Expects Much of Scotsmen,'" *Press and Journal* (Inverness), July 1, 1955.

40. Professor Emeritus William John Watson, MA (Aber.), BA (Oxon.), LLD (Aber.), DLitt (Celt.), Hon. FEIS ("A Great Highland Scholar: Death of Professor W. J. Watson," *Inverness Courier*, March 12, 1948).

41. John Baillie, introduction to John A. Mackay, *A Preface to Christian Theology* (London: Nisbet & Co., 1942). John A. Mackay, "John Baillie, A Lyrical Tribute and Appraisal," *Scottish Journal of Theology* 9, no. 3 (1956): 225–26.

42. John A. Mackay to Robert E. Speer, October 28, 1930, Mackay Collection. On Cook see Steven R. Pointer, "Joseph Cook—Apologetics and Science," *Journal of Presbyterian History* 63, no. 3 (Fall 1985): 299–308.

CHAPTER 2: SCOTTISH EDUCATION

1. Josef L. Hromádka, *Thoughts of a Czech Pastor* (London: SCM Press, 1970), 20.

2. Ibid., 19.

3. Ibid., 20.

4. John A. Mackay, Diary, Sabbath, October 24, 1911, Mackay Archive.

5. Mackay, Diary, Evening, February 1, 1908, Mackay Archive.

6. Mackay, Diary, Evening, February 2, 1908, Mackay Archive.

7. Ibid., Mackay Archive.

8. Mackay, Diary, Evening, February 4, 1908, Mackay Archive.

9. Mackay, Diary, Evening, February 5, 1908, Mackay Archive.

10. Mackay, Diary, Midday, February 6, 1908, Mackay Archive.

11. Mackay, Diary, Evening, February 6, 1908, Mackay Archive.

12. Mackay, Diary, Evening, February 10, 1908, Mackay Archive.

13. Ibid.

14. Mackay, Diary, Evening, February 11, 1908, Mackay Archive.

15. Mackay, Diary, Evening, February 12, 1908, Mackay Archive.

16. Mackay, Diary, Midday, February 13, 1908, Mackay Archive.

17. Mackay, Diary, Evening, February 13, 1908, Mackay Archive.

18. Ibid.

19. Mackay, Diary, Evening, February 14, 1908, Mackay Archive.
20. Ibid.
21. Mackay, Diary, Evening, February 15, 1908, Mackay Archive.
22. Ibid.
23. Mackay, Diary, Midday, February 16, 1908, Mackay Archive.
24. Mackay, Diary, Evening, February 16, 1908, Mackay Archive.
25. Ibid.
26. Mackay, Diary, Morning, February 17, 1908, Mackay Archive.
27. Mackay, Diary, Evening, February 18, 1908, Mackay Archive.
28. Mackay, Diary, Evening, February 19, 1908, Mackay Archive.
29. Mackay, Diary, Evening, February 20, 1908, Mackay Archive.
30. Mackay, Diary, Midday, February 21, 1908, Mackay Archive.
31. Mackay, Diary, Evening, February 22, 1908, Mackay Archive.
32. Ibid.
33. Mackay, Diary, Morning, February 23, 1908, Mackay Archive.
34. Ibid.
35. Mackay, Diary, Evening, February 23, 1908, Mackay Archive.
36. Mackay, Diary, Evening, February 26, 1908, Mackay Archive.
37. Mackay, Diary, Evening, February 28, 1908, Mackay Archive.
38. Mackay, Diary, Evening, February 29, 1908, Mackay Archive.
39. Mackay, Diary, Midday, March 1, 1908, Mackay Archive.
40. Mackay, Diary, Midday, March 4, 1908, Mackay Archive.
41. Mackay, Diary, Evening, March 4, 1908, Mackay Archive.
42. Mackay, Diary, Evening, March 5, 1908, Mackay Archive.
43. Mackay, Diary, Morning, March 6, 1908, Mackay Archive.
44. Mackay, Diary, Evening, March 6, 1908, Mackay Archive.
45. Mackay, Diary, Evening, March 7, 1908, Mackay Archive.
46. Mackay, Diary, Morning, March 8, 1908, Mackay Archive.
47. Mackay, Diary, Evening, March 8, 1908, Mackay Archive.
48. Mackay, Diary, Midday, March 9, 1908, Mackay Archive.
49. Mackay, Diary, Morning, March 10, 1908, Mackay Archive.
50. Mackay, Diary, Evening, March 10, 1908, Mackay Archive.
51. Mackay, Diary, Evening, March 11, 1908, Mackay Archive.
52. Mackay, Diary, Morning, March 13, 1908, Mackay Archive.
53. Mackay, Diary, Evening, March 13, 1908, Mackay Archive.
54. Mackay, Diary, Evening, March 14, 1908, Mackay Archive.
55. Mackay, Diary, Evening, March 15, 1908, Mackay Archive.
56. Mackay, Diary, Morning, March 19, 1908, Mackay Archive.
57. Mackay, Diary, Morning, March 20, 1908, Mackay Archive.
58. Mackay, Diary, Evening, March 20, 1908, Mackay Archive.
59. Mackay, Diary, Sabbath Evening, October 18, 1908, Mackay Archive.
60. Mackay, Diary, Sabbath Evening, November 1, 1908, Mackay Archive. On Nicoll, see T. H. Darlow, *William Robertson Nicoll, Life and Letters* (London: Hodder & Stoughton, 1925).
61. Mackay, Diary, Sabbath Evening, November 8, 1908, Mackay Archive.
62. Ibid.
63. Mackay, Diary, Morning, Monday, October 26, 1908, Mackay Archive.
64. Mackay, Diary, Sabbath Evening, November 29, 1908, Mackay Archive.

65. Mackay, Diary, Evening, February 11, 1909, Mackay Archive.

66. Mackay, Diary, Evening, Sabbath, February 14, 1909, Mackay Archive.

67. Mackay, Diary, Evening, Sabbath, February 21, 1909, Mackay Archive.

68. Mackay, Diary, Monday, March 22, 1909, Mackay Archive.

69. Mackay, Diary, Monday, March 29, 1909, Mackay Archive.

70. Mackay, Diary, Morning, May 3, 1909, Mackay Archive.

71. Mackay, Diary, Evening, May 10, 1909, Mackay Archive.

72. Mackay, Diary, Evening, June 11, 1909, Mackay Archive.

73. Mackay, Diary, Evening, June 22, 1909, Mackay Archive.

74. Mackay, Diary, January 27, 1910, Mackay Archive.

75. See John A. Mackay, "Religious Concern and Christian Commitment," *Princeton Seminary Bulletin* 50, no. 3 (February 1957): 10.

76. John A. Mackay, interview by Gerald W. Gillette for the Presbyterian Historical Society, February 1, 1974, 5–6.

77. Mackay, Diary, Monday, Dec. 20 and Tuesday, Dec. 21, 1909, Mackay Archive.

78. Mackay, Diary, February 3, 1910, Mackay Archive. Robert E. Speer, "Missions and the Native Churches," in *Christianity and the Nations* (New York: Fleming H. Revell Co., 1910), 113–73.

79. John A. Mackay, introduction, *A Man Sent from God: A Biography of Robert E. Speer*, by W. Reginald Wheeler (Westwood, NJ: Fleming H. Revell Co., 1956), 9.

80. Mackay, Diary, Sabbath, April 24, 1910, Mackay Archive.

81. Mackay, Diary, May 19, 1910, Mackay Archive.

82. Mackay, Diary, May 30, 1910, Mackay Archive.

83. W. H. T. Gairdner, *Echoes from Edinburgh, 1910* (New York: Fleming H. Revell Co., 1910), 134, 179.

84. Mackay, Diary, October 4, 1910, Mackay Archive.

85. "Professor J. R. Mackay, D.D." *The Monthly Record of the Free Church of Scotland*, August 1939, 209–11. Mackay, Gillette interview, February 1, 1974, 15.

86. Mackay, Diary, January 20, 1911, [*sic*] extended entry referring to this subsequent event, Mackay Archive.

87. Ibid.

88. Mackay interview by Gillette, 18. See also Mackay, Diary, September 28, 1913, Mackay Archive.

89. Mackay, Diary, Sabbath, November 12, 1911, Mackay Archive.

90. Mackay, Diary, September 28, 1913, Mackay Archive.

91. Mackay, Diary, presentation at a devotional Sabbath morning meeting, December 1907, on the verse Ps. 73:25, Mackay Archive.

92. Mackay, Diary, February 18, 1908, Mackay Archive.

93. Mackay, Diary, May 16, 1909, Mackay Archive.

94. Mackay interview by Gillette, 9–10. See also Mackay, Diary, March 1, 4, 8, 1908, Mackay Archive.

95. Mackay, Diary, Sabbath, September 28, 1913, Mackay Archive.

96. Ibid.

CHAPTER 3: STUDENT DAYS AT PRINCETON

1. Members of the Princeton Seminary faculty published a volume in commemoration of the one-hundredth anniversary of the founding of the seminary titled *Biblical and Theological Studies* (New York: Scribner's Sons, 1912). It represented a sample of seminary scholarship of the time.

2. For an account of Warfield see Hugh Thomson Kerr, "Warfield: The Person Behind the Theology," *Princeton Seminary Bulletin*, n.s., 25, no. 1 (2004): 80–93; David N. Livingstone and Mark A. Noll, "B. B. Warfield (1821–1921): A Biblical Inerrantist as Evolutionist," *Journal of Presbyterian History* 80, no. 3 (Fall 2002): 153–71; Francis L. Patton, "Benjamin Breckinridge Warfield," *Princeton Theological Review* 19 (July 1921): 369–91.

3. William McElwee Miller, *My Persian Pilgrimage* (Pasadena, CA: William Carey Library, 1989), 18.

4. For an account of Patton see Hugh T. Kerr, "Patton of Princeton: A Profile," *Princeton Seminary Bulletin*, n.s., 9, no. 1 (1988): 50–70; William L. McEwan, "Dr. Francis L. Patton," *Princeton Seminary Bulletin* 27, no. 1 (June 1933): 3–9; "The Resignation of President Patton," *Princeton Seminary Bulletin* 7, no. 1 (May 1913): 5–6; Paul Kemeny, "President Francis Landey Patton, Princeton University, and Faculty Ferment," *Journal of Presbyterian History* 69, no. 2 (Summer 1991): 111–21.

5. Cullen I. K. Story, "J. Gresham Machen: Apologist and Exegete," *Princeton Seminary Bulletin*, n.s., 2, no. 2 (1979): 91–103. George Marsden, "Understanding J. Gresham Machen," *Princeton Seminary Bulletin*, n.s., 11, no. 1 (1990): 46–60.

6. Mackay, Diary, September 28, 1913, Mackay Archive.

7. Mackay, Diary, October 5, 1913, Mackay Archive.

8. Ibid.

9. Ibid.

10. Mackay, Diary, October 12, 1913, Mackay Archive.

11. Ibid.

12. The conference, followed by abstracts of addresses, is noted in "The Fall Conference," *Princeton Seminary Bulletin* 7, no. 3 (November 1913): 9–19.

13. Mackay, Diary, October 19, 1913, Mackay Archive.

14. Ibid.

15. Henry Wilkinson Bragdon, *Woodrow Wilson, The Academic Years* (Cambridge, MA: Belknap Press of Harvard University Press, 1967), 407.

16. John A. Mackay, interview by Gerald W. Gillette for the Presbyterian Historical Society, March 15, 1974, 19–20.

17. For an abstract of the talk see "Sir William Ramsay," *Princeton Seminary Bulletin* 7, no. 3 (November 1913): 7–8.

18. Mackay, Diary, October 26, 1913, Mackay Archive.

19. Mackay, Diary, November 2, 1913, Mackay Archive.

20. Ibid.

21. Mackay, Diary, November 16, 1913, Mackay Archive.

22. Mackay, Diary, November 23, 1913, Mackay Archive.

23. Ibid.

24. Mackay, Diary, December 7, 1913, Mackay Archive.

25. Ibid.

26. Ibid.

27. "The Student Volunteer Convention," *Princeton Seminary Bulletin* 8, no. 1 (May 1914), 11.

28. Robert F. Horton, "The Student Volunteer Convention in Kansas City," *Student World* 7, no. 1 (January 1914): 17–18.

29. Mackay, Diary, October 25, 1914, Mackay Archvie.

30. Ibid.

31. Ibid.

32. Ibid.

33. "President Stevenson and Professor Smith," *Princeton Seminary Bulletin* 8, no. 3 (November 1914): 1. Stevenson's inaugural address, "Theological Education in the Light of Present Day Demands" is summarized in *Princeton Seminary Bulletin* 9, no. 3 (November 1915): 6–9, and appears in the *Princeton Theological Review* 14 (1916): 82–95.

34. Mackay, Diary, October 25, 1914, Mackay Archive.

35. Mackay, Diary, December 6, 1914, Mackay Archive.

36. John A. Mackay, "When Truth Is a Belt," *Princeton Seminary Bulletin* 59, no. 1 (November 1965): 6.

37. Mackay, Diary, December 6, 1914, Mackay Archive.

38. Ibid.

39. Mackay interview by Gillette, 5.

40. Mackay, "When Truth Is a Belt," 8; and idem, "Life's Chief Discoveries," *Christianity Today*, January 2, 1970, 4; Paul L. Lehmann, "Also among the Prophets," *Theology Today* 16, no. 3 (October 1959): 354.

41. Mackay recalled the sermon on Ps. 31:15 fifty years later in a commencement speech. Mackay, "When Truth Is a Belt," 5.

42. Mackay was awarded the Gelston-Winthrop Fellowship in Didactic and Polemic Theology, "Fellowships and Prizes," *Princeton Seminary Bulletin* 8, no. 4 (May 1915): 4.

43. Mackay interview by Gillette, 25–26.

44. Ibid., 23.

CHAPTER 4: FINAL PREPARATIONS

1. Jowett served in New York from April 1911 to 1918, when he was called to Westminster Chapel, London, where he remained until his death. See John H. Jowett, *The Best of John Henry Jowett*, ed. and intro. by Gerald Kennedy (New York: Harper & Bros., 1948), xiii; and Arthur Porritt, *John Henry Jowett* (London: Hodder & Stoughton, 1924), 135.

2. Mackay's "Diary and Notes of Tour to South America May–August 1915" (hereinafter "Diary 1915"), Mackay Archive, which he kept during the trip, is the source for his "Report of Tour of Missionary Investigation in South America (May–September 1915) Presented to the Foreign Missions Committee of the Free Church of Scotland" and for details in this chapter. Mackay Collection.

3. John Ritchie was born in 1878 in Kilmarnock, Scotland, and quit school at age eleven. In 1893 Ritchie attended a temperance meeting with a friend, and a question he heard there stuck in his mind: "What shall it profit a man, if he shall gain the whole world, and lose his own soul?" (Mark 8:36). When Ritchie arrived in 1902 at Harley College, London, also known as Harley House Bible Institute, A. Stuart McNairn was a senior there. Ritchie was originally a Presbyterian, and his spiritual formation was also influenced by D. J. Finlay, a preacher in Glasgow. Like Finlay, Ritchie appears to have been cautious and skeptical of the emotional side of life and religion. Prior to Ritchie's mission to Lima, three Protestant missionaries, forerunners of Mackay and Ritchie, had sailed for Peru on April 15, 1893: J. H. Jarrett, R. A. Stark, and F. Peters.

4. Mackay, Diary 1915, June 5, Mackay Archive; and John A. Mackay, "First Impressions of Peru," a letter written July 19, 1915, Mackay Collection.

5. José Pardo was inaugurated president of Peru in August 1915.

6. Mackay, Diary 1915, June 8, Mackay Archive.

7. Mackay, Diary 1915, June 5, Mackay Archive.

8. Mackay, Diary 1915, June 17, Mackay Archive. The pity he felt was rooted in an incident he described. The leading doctor of Arequipa amputated the broken leg of a young Englishman, with nurse Pritchard, a Protestant, attending. This infuriated the hospital nurses. After the procedure when the doctor and Nurse Pritchard left the patient, the young man's leg was wrapped warmly with bandages and hot water bottles, and covered with blankets. An hour later the doctor returned and was amazed to find the leg exposed to the cold with only a sheet over it. In less than one day the patient died.

9. Mackay, Diary 1915, July 24, Mackay Archive.

10. John A. Mackay, "Leaves from the Diary of a Missionary Tour to South America," *The Instructor*, January 1917, 59.

11. Ibid., 60. After returning to England, Newell's widow influenced Annie Soper to become a missionary in Peru.

12. John A. Mackay, "Leaves from the Diary of a Missionary Tour to South America," *The Instructor*, February 1917, 75–76.

13. Mackay, Diary 1915, July 4, Mackay Archive.

14. Mackay, Diary 1915, July 27, Mackay Archive.

15. David Trumbull (1819–1889). See Robert E. Speer, "Study Five: 'David Trumbull, the Friend of Chile,'" in *Studies of Missionary Leadership* (Philadelphia: Westminster Press, 1914), 181–234; Florence E. Smith, "Some Significant Aspects of the History of the Chile Mission," in W. Reginald Wheeler et al., *Modern Missions in Chile and Brazil* (Philadelphia: Westminster Press, 1926), 132–51; Irven Paul, *A Yankee Reformer in Chile: The Life & Works of David Trumbull* (South Pasadena, CA: William Carey Library, 1973); H. McKennie Goodpasture, "David Trumbull: Missionary Journalist and Liberty in Chile 1845–1889," *Journal of Presbyterian History* 56, no. 2 (Summer 1978): 149–65.

16. See Jean Baptiste August Kessler, Jr., "The Pentecostal Division and the Later Development of Methodism in Chile," in *A Study of the Older Protestant Missions and Churches in Peru and Chile* (Goes: Oosterbaan & Le Cointre, 1967), 116–33; W. C. Hoover, "Pentecost in Chile," *World Dominion* 10, no. 2 (April 1932): 155–61.

17. The Instituto Ingles, the only Protestant school for boys in Santiago, was founded in Copiapo in 1874 and was relocated to Santiago in 1877. For twenty years Browning served as its head and made it a force in the life of Chile. See Robert E. Speer, "A Sunday in Santiago," in Wheeler et al., *Modern Missions*.

18. The Battle of Coronel occurred November 1, 1914. The German Pacific squadron under Admiral Graf von Spee wiped out two cruisers and seventeen hundred men of the British Navy.

19. Mackay, Diary 1915, August 22, Mackay Archive. Eduardo Monteverde, "Latin-American Students and Religion," *Student World* 9, no. 4 (October 1916): 121–32.

20. John A. Mackay, "War Unselfishness, and the Leadership of Jesus Christ, Being an Address Delivered in Buenos Aires at the Y.M.C.A. 4:45 p.m., Sunday, August 29, 1915," Mackay Archive.

21. Mackay, Diary 1915, September 16, Mackay Archive.

22. Ibid.

23. Ibid.

24. "Report of Tour of Missionary Investigation in South America" (May–September 1915), Mackay Collection.

25. Elsewhere Mackay wrote that the word *disinterestedness* did not exist in the Spanish vocabulary. "The South American Mission Farewell Meeting in Edinburgh," *Monthly Record of the Free Church of Scotland*, November 1916, 159.

26. "Report of Tour of Missionary Investigation in South America" (May–September 1915), Mackay Collection. A Latin American intellectual, Dr. Deustua, discerned that the study of Scripture was a moralizing force in Protestant nations (John A. Mackay, "Religious Currents in the Intellectual Life of Peru," *Biblical Review*, vol. 6 [1921]: 202).

27. "Report of Tour of Missionary Investigation in South America" (May–September 1915), Mackay Collection.

28. Ibid.

29. John A. Mackay to Alexander Stewart, November 6, 1917, Mackay Collection.

30. John A. Mackay, "Adventures in the Mind of Latin America," in *Students and the Future of Christian Missions*, ed. Gordon Poteat (New York: Student Volunteer Movement for Christian Missions, 1928), 169.

31. John A. Mackay, introduction to *The Oppression of Protestants in Spain*, by Jacques Delpech (Boston: Beacon Press, 1953), 9. Years later Mackay described Don Francisco's influence in a letter: "The man referred to is Don Francisco Giner de los Ríos. In the early seventies of the last century, Giner arrived in Madrid from Andalusia to fill the chair of law in the National University. From the very beginning he introduced a new note into Spanish education, establishing the closest personal contact with his students. In the summer they took long hikes into the country and in the winter they went skiing on the Guadarrama range. For about fifty years Don Francisco, as he was lovingly called, carried on his work with succeeding generations of Spanish youth. Sooner or later he would ask every one of his students, 'Well, and what do you propose doing with your life?'

"The new sense of vocation which he introduced into the cream of Spanish students has produced one of the most marvelous results of modern times. The Minister of Justice in the new Spanish republic is a nephew and old pupil of Don Francisco. He is himself a very eminent man and three years ago he delivered a course of lectures in Columbia University, New York" (John A. Mackay to Francis Henson, July 23, 1931, Mackay Collection).

32. John A. Mackay, interview by Gerald W. Gillette for the Presbyterian Historical Society, October 21, 1975, 2.

33. See, for example, Ciro Alegria, *Broad and Alien Is the World* (New York: Farrar & Rinehart, 1941).

34. J. A. Mackay, "The Communion of Saints in Our Time," *Crozer Quarterly* 16, no. 4 (October 1939): 255.

35. Mackay, *The Oppression*, 11.

36. Ibid.

37. Mackay interview by Gillette, 2.

38. Margaret Thomas Rudd, *The Lone Heretic* (Austin: University of Texas Press, 1963), 282.

39. John A. Mackay, *The Other Spanish Christ* (New York: Macmillan Co., 1932), 154.

40. J. A. Mackay, "Miguel de Unamuno" in *Christianity and the Existentialists*, ed. Carl Michalson (New York: Charles Scribner's Sons, 1956), 45.

41. Mackay interview by Gillette, 9.

42. Ibid.

43. Rudd, *Lone Heretic*, 95.

44. Mackay interview by Gillette, 10. See also Mackay, *The Oppression*, 9.

45. Juan A. Mackay, "El Cristo de los Místicos Españoles," *La Nueva Democracia* (December 1929), 17; Mackay, *Other Spanish Christ*, 154–55.

46. John A. Mackay, "Unamuno, Miguel de," in *Twentieth Century Encyclopedia of Religious Knowledge*, vol. 2, ed. Lefferts A. Loetscher (Grand Rapids: Baker, 1955), 1129–30; idem, foreword to *Poems by Miguel de Unamuno*, trans. Eleanor L. Turnbull (Baltimore: Johns Hopkins Press, 1952), vii–ix; idem, "Miguel de Unamuno," 43–58.

47. Mackay, *Other Spanish Christ*, 154.

48. John A. Mackay, "A Christmas Vacation in Old Castille" [1915], Mackay Archive.

49. Mackay interview by Gillette, 6.

50. Mackay, "El Cristo," 17.

51. Mackay, *Other Spanish Christ*, 9.

52. John A. Mackay, "Two American Civilizations and Their Implications for Reformed Theology," *Presbyterian Register* 18, no. 3 (March 1943): 92.

53. See Saint Teresa of Avila, *The Life of Teresa of Jesus: The Autobiography of St. Teresa of Avila*, trans. and ed. E. Allison Peers (Garden City, NY: Image Books, 1960), 128. On the subject see also E. W. Trueman Dicken, *The Crucible of Love* (New York: Sheed & Ward, 1963), 477. A comparison, analysis, or classification of Mackay's spiritual experience in Teresian terms as a unity with God or as the fourth water poses unanswerable questions. The importance of the event was its effect on his life.

54. J. H. Oldham to Miss Ruth Rouse, May 25, 1949, copy, Mackay Collection.

55. John F. Piper Jr., *Robert E. Speer, Prophet of the American Church* (Louisville, KY: Geneva Press, 2000), 209.

56. Gonzalo Báez-Camargo, "The Place of Latin America in the Ecumenical Movement," *Ecumenical Review* 1, no. 3 (Spring 1949): 311.

57. John H. Sinclair and Arturo Piedra Solano, "The Dawn of Ecumenism in Latin America: Robert E. Speer, Presbyterians, and the Panama Conference of 1916," *Journal of Presbyterian History* 77, no. 1 (Spring 1999): 4.

58. S. G. Inman, letter to the editor, *New York Times*, October 25, 1915, 8.

59. "Quit Mission Body over War on Pope," *New York Times*, October 27, 1915, 1.

60. See, for example, "Panama Conference Splits Episcopalians," *New York Times Magazine*, November 7, 1915, 11; "Opposes Panama Congress," *New York Times*, November 18, 1915, 4; "Rev. Dr. Manning Defends His Course," *New York Times*, December 3, 1915, 7; "Episcopal Parties Warned to Be Cool," *New York Times*, December 12, 1915, sect. 3, 3; "Deplore Prejudice in Episcopal Groups," *New York Times*, December 13, 1915, 9; "Cite Morgan Will in Panama Dispute," *New York Times*, December 31, 1915, 4; "Dr. Manning Assails Panama Conference," *New York Times*, June 26, 1916, 20; William T. Manning, "The Protestant Episcopal Church and Christian Unity," *Constructive Quarterly* 3 (March to December 1915): 679–96.

61. "Cite Morgan Will," 4.

62. "There is a suspicion that the invitation of the Panama spider was not meant to catch the Roman fly, but merely to hypnotize the Anglican fly" ("Assails 'Panama Spider,'" *New York Times*, January 4, 1916, 5).

63. On the conversations see John A. Dick, *The Malines Conversations Revisited* (Leuven: Leuven University Press, 1989).

64. "Porras Overrides Bishop," *New York Times*, February 10, 1916, 4. Sixty years later a representative of the archbishop of Panama brought fraternal greetings and offered apologies for the affront given by the archbishop to the Evangelical conference in 1916. See John H. Sinclair and Arturo Piedra Solano, "The Dawn of Ecumenism in Latin America," *Journal of Presbyterian History* 77, no. 1 (Spring 1999): 11, n. 32.

65. "Christianity Dying in Latin America," *New York Times*, February 12, 1916, 6.

66. "Religious Clash Avoided," *New York Times*, February 14, 1916, 5.

67. "Religious Session Ends," *New York Times*, February 20, 1916, sect. 1, 10.

68. John Fox, "Christian Unity, Church Unity, and the Panama Congress," *Princeton Theological Review* 14 (1916): 577.

69. Ibid., 555–56.

70. Ibid., 556.

71. *Regional Conferences in Latin America* (New York: Missionary Education Movement, 1917), ix–x.

72. "The South American Mission," *The Monthly Record of the Free Church of Scotland*, November 1916, 158.

73. Ibid., 159. On Duff, see Alexander Duff, *Missions: The Chief End of the Christian Church* (Edinburgh: John Johnstone, 1839).

CHAPTER 5: EARNING THE RIGHT TO BE HEARD

1. John A. Mackay, "Portent and Promise in the Other America," *Princeton Seminary Bulletin* 47, no 3 (January 1954): 8. See also Jane Mackay, Notebook, November 6, 1916, Mackay Archive.

2. "Our South American Mission," *The Instructor: A Magazine for the Young People of the Free Church of Scotland*, ed. Alexander Stewart, April 1917, 100.

3. Samuel Guy Inman, *Christian Cooperation in Latin America* (New York: Committee on Cooperation, 1917), 61.

4. Why Spain did not experience a religious reformation in the sixteenth and seventeenth centuries and the significance of the Spanish Inquisition are beyond the scope of the present study, but see Henry Kamen, *The Spanish Inquisition: An Historical Revision* (London: Weidenfeld & Nicolson, 1997), 101–102; Henry Charles Lea, *The Inquisition in the Spanish Dependencies* (New York: Macmillan Co., 1922); George P. Howard, "Latin America Needs a Religious Revolution," in *Religious Liberty in Latin America?* (Philadelphia: Westminster Press, 1944), 100–113.

5. Jean Baptiste August Kessler Jr., *A Study of the Older Protestant Missions and Churches in Peru and Chile* (Goes: Oosterbaan & Le Cointre, 1967), 32–35.

6. Ibid., 228, n. 50.

7. Ibid., 230.

8. Ibid., 231–33.

9. John A. Mackay, "First Days in Lima," *Monthly Record of the Free Church of Scotland*, June 1917, 79.

10. John A. Mackay, "Spiritual Spring-Time in Latin America," *World Dominion* 7, no. 4 (October 1929): 415.

11. On the school's history, see John M. MacPherson, *At the Roots of a Nation* (Edinburgh: Knox Press, 1993); and W. M. Alexander, "Dr. John A. Mackay and the Anglo-Peruvian College," *Aberdeen University Review* 14 (1926–1927): 207–212.

12. Raúl Chanamé Orbe, "La relación de Mariátegui con John A. Mackay" [The "Relationship of Mariátegui to John A. Mackay], *Textos para la Acción* 3, no. 3 (January 1995): 43, quoted in *Anuario Mariateguiano* 6, no. 6 (1994).

13. Mackay, "First Days," 79.

14. John A. Mackay, "South American Mission," *Monthly Record of the Free Church of Scotland*, September 1917, 113. Kessler, *A Study of the Older Protestant Missions*, 92.

15. John A. Mackay, "Mr. Mackay's Report," *Monthly Record of the Free Church of Scotland*, June 1918, 95–96.

16. John A. Mackay to Alexander Stewart, August 27, 1917, Mackay Collection. About Stewart, see Anna Stewart, "Memoir of Alexander Stewart," in *Shoes for the Road*, by Alexander Stewart (London: Pickering & Inglis, Ltd., 1939), 9–16.

17. Alexander Stewart to John A. Mackay, November 27, 1917, Mackay Collection.

18. Report, August 15, 1917, Mackay Collection.

19. John A. Mackay, "Mr. Inman's Report," *Monthly Record of the Free Church of Scotland*, May 1918, 70.

20. A later translation used a different title for the book: Clorinda Matto de Turner, *Torn from the Nest*, trans. John H. R. Polt (New York: Oxford University Press, 1998). On Inman's trip and cooperation in Peru see Inman, *Christian Cooperation*, 60–72.

21. "Missionary News. A Letter from Mrs. Mackay, Lima," *The Instructor*, December 1917, 51. Mrs. J. A. Mackay, "Among the Indians," *The Instructor*, January 1918, 68–70.

22. John A. Mackay, "Protestant Work in Peru," *Monthly Record of the Free Church of Scotland*, January 1918, 6.

23. Ibid.

24. John A. Mackay to Alexander Stewart, November 6, 1917, Mackay Collection. Mackay was the first of several colleagues who took a degree at San Marcos, including Browning, Browne, Renwick, and Rycroft.

25. John A. Mackay, "Don Miguel de Unamuno: Su Personalidad, Obra e Influencia" [Don Miguel de Unamuno: His personality, work and influence]. In *La Revista Universitaria de la San Marcos de Lima*, year 8, vol. 2, no. 4 (1918): 404–31.

26. John A. Mackay, "El Valor Cultural del Estudio de la Literatura Inglesa," Breve desarollo de la Conferencia inaugural dada por el Dr. John A. Mackay en la Facultad de Letras, el sábado, 31 de agosto del pte año 1918. ["The cultural value of studying English literature," brief unfolding of the inaugural conference given by Dr. John A. Mackay in the Letters faculty on Saturday August 31, 1918]. Mackay Collection.

27. Orbe, "La relación de Mariátegui con John A. Mackay," 42–43.

28. "Missionary News. A Letter from Mrs. Mackay," *The Instructor* 11, no. 8 (May 1917): 123–24 and J. L. Mackay, "The Lima School," *The Instructor*, June 1917, 140–41.

29. Mackay, "Mr. Mackay's Report," 95–96.

30. John A. Mackay, "Progress in Lima," *Monthly Record of the Free Church of Scotland*, March 1918, 37.

31. Ibid.

32. Ibid.

33. Mackay, "First Days," 79–80.

34. Mackay, "Mackay's Report," 95–96.

35. John A. Mackay to Alexander Stewart, November 6, 1917, Mackay Collection.

36. Ibid.

37. Alexander Stewart to John A. Mackay, April 10, 1918, Mackay Collection.

38. Alexander Stewart to John A. Mackay, June 7, 1918, Mackay Collection.

39. John A. Mackay, "God Reigneth." May 30, 1918, Mackay Collection.

40. Ibid. On Browne's arrival see "Progress in Lima," *Monthly Record of the Free Church of Scotland*, July 1918, 107.

41. John A. Mackay, "'God Is Dead!'" *The Instructor*, November 1918, 27–28.

42. Grover A. Zinn, "The History of Meditation on Jesus' Seven Last Words," in *Echoes from Calvary Meditations on Franz Joseph Haydn's* The Seven Last Words of Christ, ed. Richard Young (Lanham, MD: Rowman & Littlefield, 2005), 183–92.

43. Mackay, "Mr. Mackay's Report," 95.

44. John A. Mackay, "A Journey to the Montaña," *Monthly Record of the Free Church of Scotland*, April 1919, 53–54.

45. Alexander Stewart to John A. Mackay, September 4, 1919, Mackay Collection.

46. Mackay, "Mr. Mackay's Report," 95.

47. Alexander Stewart to John A. Mackay, October 15, 1919, Mackay Collection.

48. J. Calvin Mackay to Alexander Stewart, May 25, 1920, Mackay Collection.

49. Ibid.

50. The following four paragraphs are based on a letter from John A. Mackay to Alexander Stewart, January 1, 1920, Mackay Collection. See also John A. Mackay to Webster E. Browning, January 5, 1920, Mackay Collection.

51. John A. Mackay to Alexander Stewart, March 18, 1920, Mackay Collection.

52. J. Calvin Mackay to Alexander Stewart, May 25, 1920, Mackay Collection. ". . . virtual Episcopal authority of a functional kind." John A. Mackay, *The Presbyterian Way of Life* (Englewood Cliffs, NJ: Prentice-Hall, 1960), 136.

53. John A. Mackay to Alexander Stewart [n.d. c. 1920], Mackay Collection.

54. Alexander Stewart to John A. Mackay, June 12, 1920, Mackay Collection. The deputation arrived in Lima July 22, 1920, and returned to Scotland September 21, 1920. See *Reports of the General Assembly of the Free Church of Scotland* (Edinburgh: Free Church of Scotland, 1921), 659–60.

55. J. Kennedy Cameron, *Peru and Its Free Church of Scotland Mission* (Inverness: Northern Counties Newspaper and Printing and Publishing Co., 1921).

56. John A. Mackay, "Report of Peruvian Mission for the Year Ending 31 December 1920," 1, Mackay Collection.

57. Ibid., 6.

58. J. Calvin Mackay to Alexander Stewart, May 25, 1920, Mackay Collection.

59. James Bryce, *South America* (New York: Macmillan Co., 1912), 583.

60. John A. Mackay, "Student Life in a South American University," *Student World* 13, no. 3 (1920): 89–97.

61. John A. Mackay, "Religious Currents in the Intellectual Life of Peru," *Biblical Review Quarterly* 6, no. 2 (April 1921): 192–211.

62. *Protervia* was a "joke name" that Mackay translated as the "scallywags." John A. Mackay, interview by Gerald W. Gillette for the Presbyterian Historical Society, October 21, 1975, 18.

63. See reference to the *Protervia* in John A. Mackay, *The Other Spanish Christ* (New York: Macmillan Co., 1932), 176.

64. Mackay, "Religious Currents," 192–211 at 204; and see Luis Alberto Sánchez, *Testimonio Personal: Memorias de un Peruano del Siglo XX* [Personal testimony: Memories of a twentieth-century Peruvian], vol. 1.

65. See, for example, J. A. Mackay, "El Valor Cultural del Estudio de la Literatura Inglesa" ["The cultural value of the study of English literature"] *Mercurio Peruano* 2, no. 11 (May 1919): 354–60; idem, "Wordsworth y la Escuela Laquista" ["Wordsworth and his literary school"] *Mercurio Peruano* 3, no.15 (September 1919):178–93.

66. J. A. Mackay, "Dos Apóstoles de la Democracia: Woodrow Wilson and Lloyd George" ["Two apostles of democracy: Woodrow Wilson and Lloyd George"], *Mercurio Peruano* 1, no. 5 (November 1918): 255–60; H. McKennie Goodpasture, "The Latin American Soul of John A. Mackay," *Journal of Presbyterian History* 48, no. 4 (Winter 1970): 270.

67. John A. Mackay to W.E. Browning, October 16, 1918; John A. Mackay to Mr. McColloch, September 18, 1918, Mackay Collection. Belaunde's Albert Shaw Lectures on Diplomatic History in 1930 were published as Víctor Andrés Belaúnde, *Bolivar and the Political Thought of the Spanish American Revolution* (Baltimore: Johns Hopkins Press, 1938). A versatile man, Dr. Belaúnde was chosen president of the U.N. General Assembly in 1959. He visited Mackay in Princeton.

68. Webster E. Browning to John A. Mackay, May 8, 1919, Mackay Collection.

69. Webster E. Browning to John A. Mackay, July 8, 1919, Mackay Collection.

70. Webster E. Browning to John A. Mackay, October 25, 1919, Mackay Collection.

71. John A. Mackay to Webster E. Browning, January 5, 1920, Mackay Collection.

72. John A. Mackay to Webster E. Browning, October 14, 1920, Mackay Collection.

73. Guy Inman witnessed the riot. Samuel Guy Inman, *South America Today, Social and Religious Movement as Observed on a Trip to the Southern Continent in 1921* (New York: Committee on Cooperation in Latin America 1921), 49.

74. John A. Mackay to Webster E. Browning, June 13, 1921, Mackay Collection.

75. Víctor Andrés Belaúnde, "The Alienation of the Latin-American Mind from Christianity," *Biblical Review* 8 (1923): 578–86.

76. John Ritchie, "The Rise and Growth of Evangelical Congregations in South America," *Biblical Review* 8 (1923): 76–90.

77. Hays P. Archerd to John A. Mackay, April 16, 1923. Mackay Collection. Princeton Seminary Library.

78. Luis Minaya, "Is Peru Turning Protestant?" in *The Peru Reader*, ed. Orin Starn, Carlos Iván Degregori, and Robin Kirk (Durham, NC: Duke University Press, 1995), 471–76 at 473.

79. Juan A. Mackay, *La Profesión de Hombre* (Lima: Sanmarti y Ca.—Impresores, 1921). Published also in *Mercurio Peruano* 6, nos. 33, 34 (1921): 180–200.

80. *La Voz de Tarma* 9, no. 1199 (February 16, 1921), 1; vol. 9, no. 1201 (February 18, 1921), 1; vol. 9, no. 1203 (February 21, 1921), 1.

81. John A. Mackay, "Let Us Remember," *Princeton Seminary Bulletin* 65, no. 1 (July 1972): 27.

82. Copy of Memorandum from Henry H. King for John R. Mott, August 8, 1921, Mackay Collection.

83. John A. Mackay, "The Regeneration of Peru," *La Nueva Democracia*, July 1921.

84. Luis Alberto Sánchez, "John Mackay y la Educación Peruana" ["John Mackay and Peruvian education"], *Leader* 48, no. 46 (Lima: December 1973), 68.

85. John A. Mackay to Alexander Stewart, October 14, 1921, Mackay Collection.

86. John R. Mott to Alexander Stewart (copy), November 9, 1921, Mackay Collection.

87. John A. Mackay to Webster E. Browning, June 13, 1921, Mackay Collection.

88. *Reports of the General Assembly of the Free Church of Scotland* (Edinburgh: Free Church of Scotland, 1922), 858–59.

89. Mackay, *Other Spanish Christ*, 33–36.

90. J. Cameron Kennedy, *Peru and Its Free Church of Scotland Mission* (Inverness, Scotland: The Northern Counties Newspaper and Printing and Publishing, Ltd., 1921), 58–59. See "Annual Report of the Peruvian Mission" [1918], 6, Mackay Collection.

91. *Reports of the General Assembly* (1922), 858 and 862.

92. Juan A. Mackay, *Los Intelectuales y los Nuevos Tiempos* [The Intellectuals and the New Times], (address delivered in the theater at Cajamarca, Lima, 1923).

93. Ibid., 27, 29.

94. Alexander Stewart to Dr. John R. Mott (copy), February 20, 1922, Mackay Collection.

95. *Reports of the General Assembly* [1922], 859; *Quarterly Register* 12, no. 7 (August 1922): 522.

96. *Reports of the General Assembly* [1922], 855.

97. "The Lima Mission," *Monthly Record of the Free Church of Scotland*, November, 1922, 182. The largest meeting was on September 26, 1922, in Hope Street Church, Glasgow. Mackay's address is summarized in the *Monthly Record of the Free Church of Scotland*, November, 1922, 183.

98. Dr. John A. Mackay, "Methods of Deepening Missionary Interest in the Congregational Life of the Church," *Monthly Record of the Free Church of Scotland*, November 1922, 181–82. The address was delivered on October 19, 1922.

99. "W. Stanley Rycroft, Latin America Missiologist," interviewed by John H. Sinclair, *Journal of Presbyterian History* 65, no. 2 (Summer 1987): 119.

100. M. Stanley Rycroft, *Memoirs of Life in Three Worlds* (Cranbury, NJ: privately printed, 1976), 33.

101. Agnes R. Fraser, *Donald Fraser of Livingstonia* (London: Hodder & Stoughton, 1934), 245.

102. *Reports of the General Assembly of the Free Church of Scotland* [1923], 1056, 1061.

CHAPTER 6: EVANGELIST TO STUDENTS

1. John A. Mackay, *That Other America* (New York: Friendship Press, 1935), 127–28.

2. Ibid. About de la Torre, see Robert J. Alexander, "Victor Raúl Haya de la Torre and 'Indo-America,'" in *Prophets of the Revolution: Profiles of Latin American Leaders* (New York: Macmillan Co., 1962), 75–108.

3. V. R. Browne to John A. Mackay, August 8, 1922, Mackay Collection.

4. "Dr. John A. Mackay's Report," in *Reports of the General Assembly of the Free Church of Scotland* (1923), 1063.

5. Ibid., 1062–63. On church and state see also John A. Mackay, "Church and State in Peru II: The Conflict Deepens," *Monthly Record of the Free Church of Scotland*, January 1921, 5–6.

6. John A. Mackay to Leonard T. Skeggs, April 21, 1924, Mackay Collection.

7. Mackay, *Other America*, 105.

8. John A. Mackay, "Intelectuales de panteón," *Claridad: Organo de la Juventud Libre del Peru*" 1, no. 1 (May 1923).

9. Mackay profiled de la Torre's intellectual growth in John A. Mackay, *The Other Spanish Christ* (New York: Macmillan Co., 1932), 193–98. He discussed the Apra Movement in Mackay, *Other America*, 102–16. J. A. Mackay, "Students and Social Reform," *Scots Observer*, April 16, 1927, 13. Mackay and Haya corresponded often while Haya was in exile and afterwards. Also see *Worlds Youth* 6, no. 4 (1931): 57; Mackay also contrasted the backgrounds of Peron and de la Torre: "Peron was influenced by a group of fascistically minded Catholic clergy; Haya de la Torre was influenced by reading the Bible and by evangelical friends." *Theology Today* 3, no. 4, (January 1947): 431.

10. See Jeffrey Klaiber, SJ, *The Catholic Church in Peru, 1821–1985* (Washington, DC: Catholic University of America Press, 1992), 20–23 at 23.

11. In North America *The Nation* reprinted a detailed story about this incident that appeared in the *Monthly Record of the Free Church*. "The Story of Haya de la Torre," *The*

Nation 118, no. 3066 (April 9, 1924): 406–407 and correspondence from de la Torre at 408–409. Editorials also appeared: "Mighty Outreach of Courage" and "A Leader of Latin Youth," *Christian Century* 41, no. 19 (May 8, 1924): 587–88.

12. James C. Carey, *Peru and the United States: 1900–1962* (Notre Dame, IN: University of Notre Dame Press, 1964), 8.

13. John A. Mackay to Alexander Stewart, July 17, 1923, Mackay Collection.

14. John A. Mackay to Leonard T. Skeggs, April 21, 1924, Mackay Collection.

15. John A. Mackay to Alexander Stewart, September 13, 1923, Mackay Collection.

16. Rycroft, *Memoirs*, 50. Rycroft's memoir recounts the incident from the school's viewpoint, 50–52.

17. Ibid., 51.

18. John A. Mackay to J. Calvin Mackay, November 17, 1923, Mackay Collection.

19. John A. Mackay to Webster E. Browning, November 28, 1923, Mackay Collection.

20. J. C. Mackay to John A. Mackay, November 29, 1923, Mackay Collection.

21. John A. Mackay to Webster E. Browning, November 28, 1923, Mackay Collection.

22. John A. Mackay to Samuel Guy Inman, November 17, 1923, Mackay Collection.

23. John A. Mackay to John P. Trant, October 20, 1923, Mackay Collection.

24. John A. Mackay to John P. Trant, October 23, 1923, Mackay Collection.

25. John A. Mackay to Sr. Pedro Rada y Gamio, November 2, 1923, Mackay Collection.

26. John A. Mackay to Samuel Guy Inman, November 17, 1923, Mackay Collection.

27. Ibid.

28. John A. Mackay to Alexander Stewart, December 27, 1923, Mackay Collection.

29. John A. Mackay to Samuel Guy Inman, November 17, 1923, Mackay Collection.

30. John A. Mackay to G. T. Babcock, May 7, 1924, Mackay Collection.

31. Rycroft, *Memoirs*, 52.

32. Samuel Barrenechea Raygada to John A. Mackay, August 12, 1924, Mackay Collection.

33. John A. Mackay to Lord Herbert Hervey, April 7, 1924, and August 19, 1924, Mackay Collection.

34. John A. Mackay to W. R. T. Sinclair, July 31, 1924, Mackay Collection. The matter was resolved in the late 1920s. Mackay wrote separately on the subject; see John A. Mackay, "South America's Pacific Problem," *Student World* 21, no. 1 (January 1928): 78–81.

35. John A. Mackay to J. H. MacLean, July 24, 1924, Mackay Collection.

36. John A. Mackay to Samuel Guy Inman, February 14, 1924, Mackay Collection.

37. John A. Mackay to A. M. Ross, May 26, 1924, Mackay Collection.

38. John A. Mackay to W. R. Mackay, August 12, 1924, Mackay Collection.

39. John A. Mackay to Emmanuel Galland, June 9, 1925, Mackay Collection.

40. John A. Mackay to Alexander Stewart, September 13, 1923, Mackay Collection.

41. Ibid. The Superintendent had the functional authority of a bishop. John A. Mackay, *The Presbyterian Way of Life* (Englewood Cliffs, NJ: Prentice-Hall, 1960), 136. That Mackay was being undermined is clearly suggested in a letter from Mackay to Convener Cameron after his resignation when Mackay wrote, "Indirect information . . . has been the cause in the past of several bitter episodes in the life of the Free Church Peruvian Mission" (John A. Mackay to Kenneth Cameron, August 15, 1925, Mackay Collection).

42. John A. Mackay to Alexander Stewart, September 13, 1923, Mackay Collection.

43. Ibid.

44. John A. Mackay to J. Calvin Mackay, February 19, 1924, Mackay Collection.

45. Jean Baptiste August Kessler Jr., *A Study of the Older Protestant Missions and Churches in Peru and Chile* (Goes: Oosterbaan & Le Cointre, 1967), 148–49.

46. John A. Mackay to J. Calvin Mackay, August 7, 1924, Mackay Collection.

47. John A. Mackay to Alexander Stewart, December 3, 1923, Mackay Collection.

48. Mackay, *Other Spanish Christ*, 242. Description is based on one found in Phyllis Thompson's *Dawn Beyond the Andes* (London: Regions Beyond Missionary Union, 1955).

49. John A. Mackay, "Report of Peruvian Mission for the Year Ending December 31, 1920," 3, Mackay Collection. *Reports of the General Assembly of the Free Church of Scotland* (Edinburgh: Free Church of Scotland, 1921), 669.

50. Stewart advised Mackay that Miss Soper made a good impression at the General Assembly meeting. Alexander Stewart to John A. Mackay, June 13, 1921, Mackay Collection.

51. John A. Mackay to Alexander Stewart, July 17, 1923; John A. Mackay to Miss R. Gould, September 13, 1923; John A. Mackay to A. Soper, September 13, 1923; John A. Mackay to Alexander Stewart, September 13, 1923, Mackay Collection.

52. A. Soper to John A. Mackay, May 13, 1925, Mackay Collection.

53. John A. Mackay to A. Soper, June 16, 1925, Mackay Collection.

54. Thompson, *Dawn*, 114; Kessler, *A Study*, 150–51. As Kessler has noted, theological differences accounted for the varying degrees of success between the Evangelical Union of South America and the Christian Missionary Alliance, on the one hand, and the Free Church of Scotland, on the other. The former were principally composed of Baptists and Plymouth Brethren who regarded the church as composed of believers. Based on Calvinistic principles, the Free Church believed that, having been handed down from the apostles, the form of the church was an essential feature, and it did not adopt Roland Allen's missionary methods. See Roland Allen, *Missionary Methods: St. Paul's or Ours* (London: Robert Scott, 1912).

55. Kessler, *A Study*, 151–52, 155.

56. Charles Ewald to John A. Mackay, April 17, 1918, Mackay Collection.

57. Kenneth Scott Latourette, *World Service* (New York: Association Press, 1957), 224; John A. Mackay to Charles Ewald, August 28, 1919, Mackay Collection. The signers included Dr. Antonio Sagarna, the Argentine minister to Peru; and Dr. Augusto Durand, president of the Liberal Party in congress.

58. *El Amigo de Clero*, September 1, 1919, 276. Cited in Klaiber, *The Catholic Church*, 95, n. 92.

59. J. C. Field to John A. Mackay, May 19, 1924, Mackay Collection.

60. John A. Mackay to G. I. Babcock, August 27, 1924, Mackay Collection.

61. John A. Mackay to Charles Ewald, June 25, 1924, Mackay Collection.

62. John A. Mackay to J. C. Field, May 19, 1924, Mackay Collection.

63. John A. Mackay to Leonard Paulson, May 28, 1924, Mackay Collection.

64. John A. Mackay to Charles Ewald, June 25, 1924, Mackay Collection.

65. John A. Mackay to Hays P. Archerd, July 9, 1924, Mackay Collection. After leaving Lima, Monzó attended the World's Student Christian Federation meeting in High Leigh, England, in August 1924. Julio Navarro Monzó, "What I Learned at High Leigh," *Student World* 17, no. 4 (October 1924): 177–79; idem, "Need for the Social Gospel in South America," *Student World* 17, no. 2 (April 1924): 57–62.

66. John Ritchie to John A. Mackay, July 5, 1924, Mackay Collection.

67. John A. Mackay to John Ritchie, July 8, 1924, Mackay Collection. Mackay provides extended analysis of Monzó's works and ideas in Mackay, *Other Spanish Christ*, 213–30.

Monzó's ideas are found in English in Julio Navarro Monzó, *The Religious Problem in Latin American Culture*, intro. Charles J. Ewald and trans. Webster E. Browning (Montevideo: Continental Committee of the YMCA, 1925).

68. Leonard Paulson to John A. Mackay, August 22, 1924, Mackay Collection.

69. John A. Mackay to G. I. Babcock, July 11, 1925, Mackay Collection.

70. Samuel Guy Inman to John A. Mackay, September 12, 1924, Mackay Collection.

71. John A. Mackay to Samuel Guy Inman, October 2, 1924, Mackay Collection.

72. Yves Congar, *Divided Christendom* (London: G. Bles, Centenary Press, 1939), 120.

73. John Ritchie, "The Rise and Growth of Evangelical Congregations in South America," *Biblical Review* 8 (1923): 76–90 at 77–78. Hays P. Archerd to John A. Mackay, April 16, 1923, Mackay Collection.

74. Digest of the speech is found in *The Standard* (Buenos Aires), Sunday, March 29, 1925, 5.

75. Ibid.

76. John A. Mackay to John P. Trant, October 20, 1923, 2, Mackay Collection.

77. John A. Mackay to Samuel Guy Inman, June 30, 1924, and August 7, 1924, Mackay Collection.

78. John A. Mackay to Samuel Guy Inman, January 16, 1925, Mackay Collection.

79. Samuel Guy Inman, "Imperialistic America," *Atlantic Monthly*, July 1924, 107–16.

80. Samuel Guy Inman to John A. Mackay, September 12, 1924, Mackay Collection.

81. Emmanuel Galland to David R. Porter, July 6, 1925, copy, Mackay Collection.

82. Emmanuel Galland to David R. Porter, page 2 attachment, copy July 6, 1925, Mackay Collection.

83. Notes written on letter from Charles Ewald to John A. Mackay, November 26, 1924, Mackay Collection.

84. From John Mackay, "Report on the Montevideo Congress," Mackay Collection.

85. W. R. Wheeler et al., *Modern Missions in Chile and Brazil* (Philadelphia: Westminster Press, 1926), 399–400.

86. Ibid., 400.

87. "The Report of Commission Eleven on Special Religious Problems in South America," in *Christian Work in South America: Official Report on the Congress of Christian Work in South America at Montevideo, Uruguay, April, 1925*, ed. Robert E. Speer, Samuel G. Inman, and Frank K. Sanders (New York: Fleming H. Revell Co., 1925), 2:293–377. (The published volumes of the Congress are hereafter referred to as *Christian Work in South America*).

88. *Christian Work in South America*, 2:306.

89. Ibid., 2:349.

90. Ibid., 2:358–59.

91. Ibid., 2:369–70.

92. Ibid., 2:293–377.

93. Ibid., 1:139.

94. Ibid., 1:260–64.

95. Ibid., 1:327–28.

96. Ibid., 2:456.

97. Ibid., 2:230–32.

98. Ibid., 1:219–20.

99. Ibid., 1:491–92.

100. Ibid., 1:486.

101. Ibid., 1:491.

102. Charles Ewald to his colleagues, April 25, 1925, Mackay Collection.

103. The Continental Committee's fraternal delegates were H. P. Coates, Florencio Ochotorena, Eduardo Monteverde of Uruguay, Abeledo of Argentina (who did not attend), Pascual Venturino of Chile, Santos of Brazil, Ewing, Galland, and Ewald. Karl Fries and G. I. Babcock represented the World's Committee and the National Council of the United States.

104. *Christian Work in South America* 1:138.

105. Mackay, *Other Spanish Christ*, 81.

106. Titled *Congreso sobre Obra Cristiana en Sud América: Realizado en Montevideo: 29 de Marzo—8 de Abril* [Congress on Christian Work in South America held in Montevideo March 29–April 8] (El Comité de Cooperación en la América Latina, 1926). Instead of writing the Spanish Report of the Congress, Mackay hoped to be able to produce "a good number of articles some of which could serve Association purposes" (John A. Mackay to Charles Ewald, June 2, 1925, Mackay Collection).

107. Mackay, *Other Spanish Christ*, 80–81.

108. John A. Mackay to Samuel Guy Inman, April 12, 1926, Mackay Collection.

109. Samuel Guy Inman to John A. Mackay, December 7, 1925, Mackay Collection.

110. See Samuel Guy Inman, *Ventures in Inter-American Friendship* (New York: Missionary Education Movement of the United States and Canada, 1925), 133–34.

111. Samuel Guy Inman to John A. Mackay, December 7, 1925, Mackay Collection.

112. Inman, *Ventures*, 63; *Christian Work in South America* 1:341, 342, 343.

113. Mackay, *Other Spanish Christ*, 244. Mackay also quoted Morris's two mottoes: "He educates best who loves most" and "The most valuable treasures of a country are its children," at 245.

114. The quotation is found in Mackay, *Other America*, 139. On Morris's work, see also E. F. Every, *South American Memories of Thirty Years* (London: SPCK, 1933), 21–33; idem, *Twenty-Five Years in South America* (London: SPCK, 1929), 204.

115. John A. Mackay to Charles Ewald, June 2, 1925, Mackay Collection.

116. Robert E. Speer to John A. Mackay, July 29, 1925, Mackay Collection.

117. Jarrett had arrived in Peru, by way of the United States, in 1894 after training at Harley College in England. Kessler, *A Study*, 157, 160–62.

118. Inman, *Ventures*, 78–79.

119. John A. Mackay to Charles Ewald, June 2, 1925, Mackay Collection.

120. John A. Mackay to Robert E. Speer, August 27, 1925, Mackay Collection.

121. John A. Mackay to Webster E. Browning, August 18, 1925; John A. Mackay to G. I. Babcock, September 26, 1925, Mackay Collection.

122. John A. Mackay to Charles Ewald, June 2, 1925, Mackay Collection.

123. John A. Mackay to Webster E. Browning, August 18, 1925, Mackay Collection. The lecture was reported in *El Comercio* (Lima), October 12, 1925. Sundar Singh, a Christian, had a dramatic conversion experience. See Friedrich Heiler, *The Gospel of Sadhu Sundar Singh*, abridged and trans. Olive Wyon (New York: Oxford University Press, 1927), 41–45.

124. John A. Mackay to Samuel Guy Inman, April 12, 1926, Mackay Collection.

125. John A. Mackay to Samuel Guy Inman, April 12, 1926; also referred to in John A. Mackay, "An Introduction to Christian Work among South American Students," *International Review of Missions* 17, no. 2 (1928): 288–89; idem, "Adventures of the Mind in Latin America," in *Students and the Future of Christian Missions*, ed. Gordon Poteat (New York: Student Volunteer Movement for Foreign Missions, 1928), 169–70.

126. "Chocano, Peru's Poet Laureate, Shoots Elmore, Lima Writer, in Literary Dispute," *New York Times*, November 1, 1925.

127. Ibid.; "Poet Tells of Slaying," *New York Times*, November 5, 1925, 8; "Peru's Poe Gets Three Years for Killing American Writer," *New York Times*, June 23, 1926, 27. The incident is mentioned in Luis Alberto Sánchez, "John Mackay y la Educaión Peruana" [John Mackay and the Peruvian Education], *Leader* 48, no. 46 (Lima, December 1973), 66–67.

128. "Ex-Poet Laureate of Peru Is Slain," *New York Times*, December 14, 1934, 18. The assassination of Elmore is described in Mackay, *Other Spanish Christ*, 176–77.

129. John A. Mackay to Kenneth Cameron, August 15, 1925, Mackay Collection.

130. John A. Mackay to Eugene MacCornack, June 15, 1926, Mackay Collection.

131. "American Minister Made Mayor in Peru," *New York Times*, November 27, 1925, 8.

132. Eugene MacCornack to John A. Mackay, July 6, 1926, Mackay Collection.

133. Eugene MacCornack to John A. Mackay, February 21, 1927, Mackay Collection.

134. "Peru Frees Leguia's Son; He Goes to Chile by Air," *New York Times*, August 15, 1933, 9.

135. John A. Mackay to Kenneth Cameron, January 24, 1925 (covering letter), and January 16, 1925 (resignation letter), Mackay Collection.

136. The observation of Antonío Sagarna, who later served as a member of the Supreme Court of Argentina. See George P. Howard, *Religious Liberty in Latin America* (Philadelphia: Westminster Press, 1944), 150.

137. Stanley Rycroft to John A. Mackay, February 26, 1926, Mackay Collection.

138. Kenneth Cameron to John A. Mackay, March 5, 1925, Mackay Collection.

139. John A. Mackay to Kenneth Cameron, May 25, 1925, Mackay Collection.

140. W. Sinclair to John A. Mackay, April 20, 1925, Mackay Collection.

141. Alexander Stewart to John A. Mackay, March 27, 1925, Mackay Collection.

142. John A. Mackay to Kenneth Cameron, October 31, 1925, Mackay Collection.

143. Kenneth Cameron to John A. Mackay, December 16, 1925, Mackay Collection.

144. John A. Mackay to Kenneth Cameron, February 19, 1926, Mackay Collection.

145. John A. Mackay to Kenneth Cameron, April 26, 1926, Mackay Collection.

146. Ibid.

CHAPTER 7: THE YMCA IN MONTEVIDEO

1. John A. Mackay to Charles Ewald, June 25, 1924, Mackay Collection.

2. Charles Ewald to John A. Mackay, May 21, 1924, Mackay Collection.

3. Charles Ewald to John A. Mackay, October 7, 1924, letter 2, Mackay Collection.

4. John A. Mackay to Charles Ewald, November 17, 1924, Mackay Collection.

5. On the religious background of Uruguay see Russell H. Fitzgibbon, "The Political Impact on Religious Development in Uruguay," *Church History* 22 (1953): 21–32.

6. John A. Mackay to Samuel Guy Inman, April 12, 1926, Mackay Collection.

7. John A. Mackay to Dr. E. A. MacCornack, June 15, 1926, Mackay Collection.

8. Kenneth Scott Latourette, *World Service* (New York: Association Press, 1957), 30.

9. Ibid., 23.

10. Ibid., 26.

11. Ibid., 25.

12. John A. Mackay to Charles Ewald, November 22, 1926, Mackay Collection.

13. John A. Mackay, "The Y.M.C.A. in Roman Catholic Lands," October 3, 1924, Mackay Collection.

14. John Mackay, "The Association and the Right Use of Sunday," October 1924, Mackay Collection. As a Princeton Seminary student Mackay had written an exercise for Prof. Greene's class, "The Sanctification of the Lord's Day." On the Fourth Commandment he had studied the church fathers and James Augustus Hessey's Bampton Lectures (Augustus Hessey, *Sunday. Its Origin, History, and Present Obligation* [London: John Murray, 1860]). The issue remains important today. See Alexis McCrossen, *Holy Day, Holiday: The American Sunday* (Ithaca, NY: Cornell University Press, 2000).

15. Latourette, *World Service*, 209.

16. Ibid.

17. John A. Mackay to A. M. Renwick, June 2, 1926, and John A. Mackay to Samuel Guy Inman, April 12, 1926, Mackay Collection.

18. John A. Mackay to Charles Ewald, May 21, 1926, Mackay Collection. The *conferencia* was published: Juan A. Mackay "¿ Existe Relación entre La Asociación Cristiana de Jovenes y la Religión?" [Is There a Relationship between the Young Men's Christian Association and Religion?] (Montevideo: 1927).

19. John A. Mackay, "Administrative Report for 1926," 7, Mackay Collection.

20. John A. Mackay, "Administrative Report for 1926," 8, Mackay Collection.

21. John A. Mackay to Donald Fraser, October 11, 1927, Mackay Collection.

22. John A. Mackay "The Passing of Pan-Americanism," *Christian Century* 44, no. 20 (May 19, 1927): 618–19; idem, "La Desaparición del Panamericanismo y Qué Viene Después," *La Nueva Democracia* 8, no. 8 (August, 1927), 3–5; and see "Pan-Americanism Dead—J. A. Mackay," *Fortnightly News Service*, December 1927, published by the Bureau of Information, National Council, YMCA. For background see Frank Tannenbaum, *Mexico: The Struggle for Peace and Bread* (New York: Alfred A. Knopf, 1950), 268–78, 276 (Mexico); Samuel Flagg Bemis, *The Latin-American Policy of the United States* (New York: Norton, 1943), 210–13 (Nicaragua); 217–18 (Mexico).

23. Mackay, "The Passing of Pan-Americanism," 619.

24. John A. Mackay, "South America's Pacific Problem," *Student World* 21, no. 1 (January 1928): 78–81. The dispute is detailed in William Jefferson Dennis, *Tacna and Arica* (1931; repr., [Hamden, Conn.]:Archon Books, 1967).

25. John A. Mackay, "A Visit to the Buenos Aires Association," June 10, 1926, 2, Mackay Collection.

26. Ibid., 4.

27. Ibid., 5.

28. Mackay, "A Visit to the Buenos Aires Association," June 10, 1926.

29. Ibid.

30. The Reformed Church of Geneva began the first Reformed mission in Latin America on an island in Rio Bay in the mid-sixteenth century. See G. Báez-Camargo, "The Earliest Protestant Missionary Venture in Latin America," *Church History* 21 (1952): 135–45.

31. Sources include John A. Mackay, "Notes of a Visit to Rio de Janeiro—July 1 to 22, 1926," Mackay Collection; idem, "Diary of First Visit to Brazil—1926" (hereinafter referred to as "Brazil Diary"), Mackay Archive; John A. Mackay to Charles Ewald, July 22, 1926; and John A. Mackay, "Administrative Report for 1926," March 31, 1927, Mackay Collection.

32. Mackay, Brazil Diary, July 27, Mackay Archive.

33. Mackay, Brazil Diary, August 10, Mackay Archive.

34. Mackay, Brazil Diary, August 12, Mackay Archive.

35. Mackay, Brazil Diary, July 17, Mackay Archive.

36. Mackay, Brazil Diary, July 4, Mackay Archive.

37. John A. Mackay, Brazil Diary, July 20, July 11, Mackay Archive. See also Hugh C. Tucker, *The Bible in Brazil, Colporter Experiences* (New York: Fleming H. Revell Co., 1902), H. C. Tucker, "Influence of the Printed Page," *Missionary Review of the World* 58, no. 10 (October 1935): 482–84.

38. John A. Mackay to Charles Ewald, June 29, 1926, Mackay Collection.

39. John A. Mackay to Charles Ewald, July 22, 1926, Mackay Collection.

40. John A. Mackay to Charles Ewald, July 22, 1926, Mackay Collection.

41. John A. Mackay to Charles Ewald, July 22, 1926, Mackay Collection.

42. John A. Mackay, Brazil Diary, July 17, Mackay Archive.

43. John A. Mackay to Charles Ewald, July 22, 1926, Mackay Collection.

44. Ibid.

45. "He comes to us as One unknown, without a name, as of old by the lake-side, He came to those men who knew Him not. He speaks to us the same word: 'Follow thou me!' [John 21:22 KJV] and sets us to the tasks which He has to fulfil for our time. He commands. And to those who obey Him, whether they be wise or simple, He will reveal Himself in the toils, the conflicts, the sufferings which they shall pass through in His fellowship, and, as an ineffable mystery, they shall learn in their own experience Who He is" (Albert Schweitzer, *The Quest of the Historical Jesus*, 2d English ed., trans. W. Montgomery [London: A. & C. Black, 1926], 401).

46. John A. Mackay to Charles Ewald, July 22, 1926, 4, Mackay Collection.

47. Ibid., 5–6.

48. Ibid.

49. John A. Mackay, Brazil Diary, August 3, Mackay Archive.

50. John A. Mackay, "Administrative Report for 1926," March 31, 1927, 5, Mackay Collection.

51. John A. Mackay, "Adventures of the Mind in Latin America," in *Students and the Future of Christian Missions*, ed. Gordon Poteat (New York: Student Volunteer Movement for Foreign Missions, 1928), Tenth Quadrennial Conference, Detroit, Michigan, December 28, 1927, to January 1, 1928, 167–72; the convention is described in *Christian Century* 45, no. 2 (January 12, 1928): 54–55. John Coventry Smith, a future Presbyterian ecumenical leader heard Mackay at the 1928 Student Volunteer Conference (see John Coventry Smith, *From Colonialism to World Community* [Philadelphia: Geneva Press, 1982], 17).

52. John A. Mackay, "Contemporary Life and Thought in South America in Their Relation to Evangelical Christianity," in *The Foreign Missions Conference of North America 1928*, ed. Leslie B. Moss (New York: Foreign Missions Conference of North America, 1928), 135–42, at 140–41.

53. John A. Mackay, "Annual Report for the Year 1928 with Projects of 1929 and the Immediate Future," 2, Mackay Collection.

54. See D. S. Cairns, "The Christian Message, A Comparison of Thought in 1910 and 1928," *International Review of Missions* 18 (1929): 325–26; W. Freytag, "Changes in the Patterns of Western Missions," *International Review of Missions* 47 (1958): 163.

55. See, for example, Floyd E. Hamilton and Thomas Cochrane, *Basic Principles in Educational and Medical Mission Work* (London: World Dominion Press, 1928); Benjamin H. Hunnicutt and William Watkins Reid, *The Story of Agricultural Missions* (New York: Missionary Education Movement of the United States and Canada, 1931).

56. John A. Mackay, "A Tribute to Walter Freytag," in *Basileia: Tribute to Walter Freytag*, ed. Jan Hermelink and Hans Jochen Margull (Stuttgart: Evang. Missionsverlag GMBH, 1959),

13–14; on Freytag's life see also *International Review of Missions* 49 (1960): 80–82. Also see "William Temple Passes," *Theology Today* 1, no. 4 (1945): 537.

57. Samuel Guy Inman to John A. Mackay et al., November 29, 1927, Mackay Collection.

58. John A. Mackay, "Diary of a Visit to Egypt," 1928, Mackay Archive.

59. Ibid.

60. Tomas Shivute, *The Theology of Mission and Evangelism* (Helsinki: Finnish Society for Missiology and Ecumenics, 1980), 46; *The Jerusalem Meeting of the International Missionary Council* (New York: International Missionary Council, 1928), 1:345–48; William Richey Hogg, *Ecumenical Foundations* (New York: Harper & Bros., 1952), 242–43.

61. *The Jerusalem Meeting*, 1:301–302. Hocking's lecture on April 2, 1928, was titled "The Psychology and Conditions of the Growth of Religious Faith." He went on to suggest the establishment of "spiritual communities" for members of different faiths where they could live and study together. ("Proposes Centres for All Religions," *New York Times*, April 3, 1928, 3). The editors of *The New York Times* took up this idea and suggested that the first such community should be located in Jerusalem (Editorial, *New York Times*, April 4, 1928, 25).

62. "240 Missionaries Meet in Jerusalem," *New York Times*, March 25, 1928, 30.

63. "Jerusalem Greets Missionary Host," *New York Times*, March 24, 1928, 36.

64. "240 Missionaries Meet," 30. For a brief appreciation of Dr. Schlunk, who was born in India of missionary parents and held British nationality by right of birth in India, see "Martin Schlunk," *International Review of Missions* 47 (1958): 356–57.

65. Howard A. Bridgman, "As Missionaries View Their Growing World," *New York Times*, May 6, 1928, sec. 10, 14.

66. "240 Missionaries Meet," 30.

67. "Church Unity Pleas Made in Jerusalem," *New York Times*, March 26, 1928, 5.

68. "Social Injustice Laid to Christians," *New York Times*, March 28, 1928, 5. Tawney's writings later influenced a generation of senior Chinese leaders who revised the Chinese economy. See Lamin Sanneh, *Disciples of All Nations* (New York: Oxford University Press, 2008), 265.

69. "Social Injustice," 5.

70. Basil Mathews, *Roads to the City of God* (Garden City, NY: Doubleday, Doran & Co., 1928), 42.

71. "Tell of Missions in Many Countries," *New York Times*, March 29, 1928, 18.

72. Ibid.

73. "Education Debated by Missionaries," *New York Times*, March 30, 1928, 8.

74. Mathews, *Roads*, 34.

75. Ibid., 32.

76. Ibid., 33. On Hinduism and Christianity, see E. Stanley Jones, "Gandhi and the Christian Faith," in *Mahatma Gandhi: An Interpretation* (NY: Abingdon-Cokesbury Press, 1948), 51–77.

77. John A. Mackay, "The Power of Evangelism in South America" in *The Jerusalem Meeting*, 8:90–93. "Italy's Prince Has Part at Jerusalem," *New York Times*, April 2, 1928, 7.

78. John A. Mackay, "The Meaning to Latin America," *Missionary Review of the World* 51 (1928): 435; idem, "Annual Report for the Year 1928," 4–5.

79. F. A. Iremonger, *William Temple* (London: Oxford University Press, 1948), 396–97.

80. "Christian Message Sent from Holy City," *New York Times*, April 6, 1928, 5.

81. "Jerusalem Council Observes Good Friday," *New York Times*, April 7, 1928, 2.

82. Associated Press, "Racial Prejudice Decried," *New York Times*, April 8, 1928, 22.

83. *Jerusalem Meeting*, 1:402–407.

84. "Mission Council Hailed as Success," *New York Times*, April 9, 1928, 21.

85. W. Freytag, "Changes in the Patterns of Western Missions," *International Review of Missions* 47 (1958), 163.

86. John A. Mackay, "Christianity and Other Religions," in *Protestant Thought in the Twentieth Century*, ed. Arnold S. Nash (New York: Macmillan Co., 1951), 279.

87. "Mission Council Hailed," 21; Arthur J. Brown, letter to the editor, *New York Times*, April 17, 1928, 28. The works Brown cited in his letter included "49,426 schools of all grades, from kindergartens to universities; 858 hospitals, and 1,636 dispensaries treating 5,000,000 patients annually, churches in non-Christian lands with 6,540,830 baptized communicants and numerous adherents, 361 orphanages, 104 leper asylums, 47 homes for untainted children of lepers, 32 schools for the blind and the deaf and dumb, and a variety of other philanthropic and social institutions." He continued, "When one considers that the Roman Catholic Church also has a very large and prosperous missionary work, it becomes clear that modern missions have become a vast and varied enterprise."

88. "World Churchmen at Mosque of Omar," *New York Times*, April 4, 1928, 26.

89. "Moslems Close Shops in Jerusalem Protest," *New York Times*, April 22, 1928, 31. Samuel M. Zwemer, a missionary to the Muslim world, retired as professor of missions at Princeton Seminary in 1937. See John A. Mackay, "Dr. Samuel M. Zwemer, In Memoriam," *Princeton Seminary Bulletin* 46, no. 2 (October 1952): 25. Also see Samuel M. Zwemer, "The Allah of Islam and the God of Jesus Christ," *Theology Today* 3, no. 1 (April 1946): 64–77.

90. John Mott to John A. Mackay, April 11, 1928, Mackay Collection.

91. John Mott to John A. Mackay, May 25, 1928, Mackay Collection.

92. John Mott to John A. Mackay, July 18, 1928, Mackay Collection.

93. A. L. Warnshius to John A. Mackay, July 7, 1928, Mackay Collection.

94. John A. Mackay, "The Evangelistic Duty of Christianity" in *The Christian Life and Message in Relation to Non-Christian Systems of Thought and Life* (New York: International Missionary Council, 1928): 383–97.

95. Ibid., 383–84.

96. Ibid., 393–94.

97. Cairns, "The Christian Message," 330.

98. Ibid.

99. Ibid., 331.

100. Robert E. Speer, *The Finality of Jesus Christ* (New York: Fleming H. Revell Co., 1933), 315–20.

101. Robert E. Speer, "Jerusalem and Edinburgh," *Student World* 21, no. 4 (October 1928): 369.

102. Basil Mathews, *John R. Mott: World Citizen* (New York: Harper & Bros., 1934), 127.

103. "Many conditions made such a meeting desirable. The widespread criticism of Western civilization and the rising tide of nationalism in all lands have thrown doubt upon the worth of Christianity, engendered pride in the perpetuation of indigenous cultures and gone far to rehabilitate old faiths which had been pretty severely handled by the progress of modern science, philosophy and history but are now rallying their strength. Throughout Asia things that are Western have suffered a heavy slump. It is necessary to defend ideas and institutions that are associated with the West from attack; if felt to be true or good" (Luther A. Weigle, quoted in "Tells of Mission Parley," *New York Times*, May 14, 1928, 23).

104. Archibald G. Baker, "Jesus Christ as Interpreted by the Missionary Enterprise," *Journal of Religion* 9, no. 1 (January 1929): 6.

105. John A. Mackay to J. J. "Josh" Osuna, dean of the College of Education, University of Puerto Rico, May 25, 1928, Mackay Collection.

106. Mackay, "Annual Report for the Year 1928."

107. Ibid., 13.

108. Robert E. Speer to John A. Mackay, June 5, 1928. Collection of Presbyterian Historical Society, Philadelphia.

109. John A. Mackay to Robert E. Speer, September 10, 1928. Collection of Presbyterian Historical Society, Philadelphia.

110. Robert E. Speer to Charles R. Erdman and Eben B. Cobb, Memo, August 8, 1928. Collection of Presbyterian Historical Society, Philadelphia.

111. John A. Mackay to Robert E. Speer, October 17, 1928. Collection of Presbyterian Historical Society, Philadelphia.

112. John A. Mackay to Robert E. Speer, June 9, 1928, Mackay Collection.

113. John A. Mackay to the Rev. Bishop Robert Paddock, November 23, 1928, Mackay Collection. Mackay had notified Ewald that he planned to join the Presbyterian Board of Foreign Missions. See John A. Mackay to Charles Ewald, September 20, 1928, Mackay Collection.

114. John A. Mackay to Robert E. Speer, November 29, 1928, Mackay Collection.

115. John A. Mackay to the Rev. Bishop Robert Paddock, November 23, 1928, Mackay Collection.

116. J. Ross Stevenson to John A. Mackay, October 17, 1928, Mackay Collection.

117. John A. Mackay to J. Ross Stevenson, November 19, 1928, Mackay Collection.

118. James S. Kelso to John Mackay, June 19, 1926; John A. Mackay to James S. Kelso, September 4, 1926; Robert E. Speer to John A. Mackay, July 14, 1926; John A. Mackay to Robert E. Speer, December 31, 1926, Mackay Collection.

119. John A. Mackay to James S. Kelso, September 4, 1926, Mackay Collection.

120. Religious persecution had begun in July 1926. Pope Pius XI issued an encyclical, *Iniquis Afflictisque* (On the Persecution of the Church in Mexico), November 18, 1926. Priests martyred during 1927 include St. Cristóbal Magallanes Jara (1869–1927), St. Agustín Caloca Cortés (1898–1927), and Bl. Miguel Pro (1891–1927).

121. Mackay, "Annual Report for the Year 1928."

122. Administrative Secretary for Latin America to Guy C. Tetirick, July 23, 1928, Mackay Collection.

123. John A. Mackay, "Life's Chief Discoveries," *Christianity Today* 14, no. 7 (January 2, 1970): 4.

124. Mackay, "Annual Report for the Year 1928," 4. This valuable report contains perceptive analysis of the awakening of religious interest in Latin America and of the Roman Catholic reaction to it which included a new type of evangelism, sermons accompanied by no ritual act whatsoever. The tour is also described in *Boletín Nacional, De las Asociaciones Cristianas de Jóvenes de la República Mexicana* (The Organ of the National Committee) 1, no. 3 (August 1928).

125. John A. Mackay, "First Impressions of Mexico," Mackay Collection.

126. Samuel Guy Inman, "Young Churches in Old Lands," *International Review of Missions* 19 (1930): 113.

127. Mr. W. C. Taylor to John A. Mackay, copy, Sept. 27, 1928, Mackay Collection. William Wallace, dean of the Evangelical Missionaries in Mexico, regretted missing the mission in Mexico City. Will Wallace to John A. Mackay, October 11, 1928, Mackay Collection.

128. Will Wallace to John Mackay, October 11, 1928, Mackay Collection. Mackay replied to Wallace the next month that he had reversed his decision since "the Board could not guarantee indefinitely that I should devote an annual period of direct service to Latin America" (John A. Mackay to Dr. William Wallace, November 12, 1928, Mackay Collection).

129. John A. Mackay, "A Latin Leader Discovers Christ," *Christian Century* 45, no. 31 (July 19, 1928): 901–904. Dr. Ricardo Rojas was the president of the University of Buenos Aires.

130. José M. Rua, "A Student Camp in South America," *Student World* 6, no. 2 (April 1913): 67–70. The article describes Piriapolis.

131. John A. Mackay, "The Ecumenical Spirit and the Recognition of Christ," *International Review of Missions* 18, no. 2 (1929): 332–45; idem, "A Decade of Student Life in South America," *Student World* 22, no. 2 (1929): 146–54.

132. Juan A. Mackay, "La Juventud Estudiantil" [Young students] (Montevideo, Uruguay: 1929). For an account of the Hispanic American Evangelical Congress, see Samuel Guy Inman, *Evangelicals at Havana* (New York: Committee on Cooperation in Latin America, 1929). Professor Báez-Camargo was the president of the Congress.

CHAPTER 8: THE CHRISTIAN MESSAGE, FURLOUGH, AND TRAVELS

1. John A. Mackay to Samuel Guy Inman, August 1, 1929, Mackay Collection. On this attempt, see John A. Mackay to Jay C. Field, July 30, 1929; John A. Mackay to Count Hermann Keyserling, July 31, 1929; and John A. Mackay to Charles Ewald, August 2, 1929, Mackay Collection. Mackay later referred to him as "that strange German philosopher, Count Hermann Keyserling" (John A. Mackay, *The Presbyterian Way of Life* [Englewood Cliffs, NJ: Prentice-Hall, 1960], 188).

2. John A. Mackay to Samuel Guy Inman, August 1, 1929, Mackay Collection; Count Hermann Keyserling, "The Animal Ideal in America," *Harpers Magazine*, August 1929, 265–76; idem, *South American Meditations*, trans. Therese Duerr (London: Jonathan Cape, 1932); "W. Stanley Rycroft, Latin America Missiologist," *American Presbyterians* 65, no. 2 (Summer 1987): 128.

3. John A. Mackay, *Ecumenics* (Englewood Cliffs, NJ: Prentice-Hall, 1964), 143; idem, *A Preface to Christian Theology* (London: Nisbet & Co., 1942), 152.

4. Mackay, *Ecumenics*, 26. Count Hermann Keyserling, *The World in the Making* (New York: Harcourt, Brace & Co., 1927). The title in Spanish is *El Mundo que Nace* (The World That Is Being Born).

5. John A. Mackay, "Reflections on the Christian Message in the Present World Drama," *Student World* 23, no. 3 (July 1930): 221.

6. John A. Mackay to Robert E. Speer, October 16, 1929, Mackay Collection. Before landing in Peru, Mackay wrote to Ewald describing in detail his experiences in Argentina and Chile (John A. Mackay to Charles Ewald, September 9, 1929, Mackay Collection.

7. Regarding Rojas see John A. Mackay, "A Latin Leader Discovers Christ," *Christian Century* 45, no. 31 (July 19, 1928): 901–904.

8. Irene Sheppard to John A. Mackay, August 15, 1929 and October 14, 1929; and Memo, "Building Committee to Wheeler," August 13, 1929, Mackay Collection.

9. John M. MacPherson, *At the Roots of a Nation* (Edinburgh: Knox Press, 1993), 61–63, 185–86.

10. Ibid., 188.

11. John A. Mackay to Robert E. Speer, August 1, 1929, Mackay Collection.

12. R. E. Diffendorfer, Corresponding Secretary, to Bishop George A. Miller, Buenos Aires, copy, July 30, 1929; R. E. Diffendorfer to Honorable Henry L. Stimson, copy, August 2, 1929, Mackay Collection.

13. John A. Mackay to Robert E. Speer, August 1, 1929, Mackay Collection.

14. Samuel Guy Inman to John A. Mackay, Cablegram, September 12, 1929, Mackay Collection.

15. John A. Mackay to Robert E. Speer, October 16, 1929, Mackay Collection. The encyclical *Rappresentanti in Terra* (On Christian Education), December 31, 1929, provided that mixed schools of Catholics and non-Catholics were forbidden for Catholic children though they could be tolerated on the approval of the ordinary (para. 79), also put pressure on the school.

16. MacPherson, *At the Roots*, 66.

17. Stanley Rycroft to John A. Mackay, May 2, 1930; Stanley Rycroft to John A. Mackay, November 28, 1928, Mackay Collection.

18. Stanley Rycroft to John A. Mackay, November 17, 1931, Mackay Collection.

19. Stanley Rycroft to John A. Mackay, January 23, 1931, Mackay Collection.

20. William Soper to John Mackay, May 5, 1931, Mackay Collection.

21. Ibid.

22. John Mackay, "God Is in Sight!" *World's Youth* 6, no. 3 (1930): 41–42, 45, 48. *The World's Youth* was a monthly published by the World's Committee of the YMCA in Geneva. See also Mackay's three essays "The Everlasting Quest," 16–21, "Finding God in Christ" 33–37, and "The Secularization of God," 69–73, in *Finding and Sharing God: Report of the Fifth Annual Conference in Chicago of the National Council of the Y.M.C.A.'s* (New York: Association Press, 1929).

23. John A. Mackay to Charles Bentinck, December 24, 1930, Mackay Collection.

24. Charles Ewald to John A. Mackay, November 23, 1929, Mackay Collection.

25. John A. Mackay, *The Other Spanish Christ* (New York: Macmillan Co., 1932), 155–56.

26. Ibid., 196–97.

27. Duncan Leitch to John A. Mackay, January 6, 1930, Mackay Collection.

28. F. Woolnough to John A. Mackay, January 2, 1930, Mackay Collection.

29. Lesslie Newbigin to John A. Mackay, July 3, 1958, Mackay Collection. The letter went on to add, "I can only pray now that God has called me to follow in your footsteps that I shall not be wholly unworthy to do so." Newbigin succeeded Mackay as chairman of the International Missionary Council. See also Lesslie Newbigin, review, "John A. Mackay, *God's Order*," *Theology Today* 10, no. 4 (1954): 563.

30. F. Woolnough to John A. Mackay, January 21, 1930, Mackay Collection.

31. James A. Dobson to John A. Mackay, January 10, 1930, Mackay Collection.

32. W. A. Visser 't Hooft to John A. Mackay, March 27, 1930, Mackay Collection.

33. W. W. Gethman to A. Abeledo, January 24, 1930; W. W. Gethman to John A. Mackay, January 8, 1930, Mackay Collection.

34. W. W. Gethman to John A. Mackay, March 20, 1930, Mackay Collection.

35. W. A. Visser 't Hooft comments, March 31, 1930, Mackay Collection.

36. John R. Mott to W. W. Gethman, copy, April 21, 1930, Mackay Collection.

37. John A. Mackay, "Reflections on the Christian Message in the Present World Drama," *Student World* 23, no. 3 (July 1930): 221–33; idem, *Reflections on the Mission and Message of the Young Men's Christian Association*, series A, no. 7, World Conferences Study Outlines (Geneva, Switzerland: World's Committee of Young Men's Christian Associations).

38. John A. Mackay to Tissington Tatlow, February 14, 1930, Mackay Collection.

39. Henry Lightbody to John A. Mackay, February 22, 1930; and Donald Fraser to John A. Mackay, January 3, 1930, and March 10, 1930, Mackay Collection.

40. J. C. Stodart to F. E. Hawes, March 10, 1930; see also Hubert W. Peet to John A. Mackay, November 13, 1929 and December 30, 1929, Mackay Collection.

41. J. Ross Stevenson to John A. Mackay, Cable, September 16, 1929; John A. Mackay to J. Ross Stevenson, October 15, 1929, Mackay Collection.

42. Helen Hill Miller to Mackay, February 16, 1930, Mackay Collection.

43. John A. Mackay to Helen Hill Miller, February 19, 1930, Mackay Collection.

44. John W. Langdale to Mackay, June 3, 1929; Mackay to Langdale, October 25, 1929, Mackay Collection.

45. John A. Mackay to W. R. T. Sinclair, Esq., December 5, 1930, Mackay Collection.

46. A. L. Warnshuis to John A. Mackay, September 9, 1931; John Mackay to A. L. Warnshuis, September 21, 1931, Mackay Collection.

47. Dr. John A. Mackay, "Die Arbeit des Christlichen Vereins Junger Männer in Süd-Amerika" [The work of the Young Men's Christian Association in South America], Aus einem Referat; gehalten in dem Bonner Freundeskreis der St.A.G., June 1930.

48. *Die Lehre vom Worte Gottes: Prolegomena zur christlichen Dogmatik* [The doctrine of the word of God: Prolegomena to church dogmatics] (1927), and *Die Theologie und die Kirche* [Theology and church] (1928).

49. Thomas F. Torrance, *Karl Barth, An Introduction to His Early Theology 1910–1931* (Edinburgh: T. & T. Clark, 2000), 18.

50. John A. Mackay to Robert E. Speer, May 11, 1930, Presbyterian Historical Society Archives, Philadelphia.

51. Charles Ewald to John A. Mackay, May 21, 1930, Mackay Collection.

52. See Eberhardt Busch, *Karl Barth* (Philadelphia: Fortress Press, 1976), 204. Mackay also put Barth in contact with J. H Oldham, who arranged to meet Barth during his trip to the UK to receive an honorary degree. See John A. Mackay to J. H. Oldham, Letter, Mackay Collection.

53. John A. Mackay to Julio Navarro Monzó, October 13, 1930 (trans. Isobel Mackay Metzger), Mackay Archive. Mackay also popularized new theological ideas (see Juan A. Mackay, "Nuevas Orientaciones Religiosas" [New directions in religion], *La Nueva Democracia* [Enero 1931], 8–9, 25). See also John A. Mackay, editorial, "Bonn 1930– and After: A Lyrical Tribute to Karl Barth," *Theology Today* 13, no. 3 (1956): 287–94.

54. Dr. J. Müller to John A. Mackay, January 7, 1930, Mackay Collection.

55. John A. Mackay, "The Message of Christ" and "Bible Studies," in *Presenting the Christian Message* (Geneva: World's Young Women's Christian Association, 1930), 7–11 and 12–35.

56. Mackay, "The Message," 7.

57. Catherine Mackinnon to John A. Mackay, June 30, 1930 and June 24, 1930, Mackay Collection.

58. On Brunner see chap. 10 below. On Thurneysen, see James D. Smart, "Eduard Thurneysen: Pastor-Theologian," *Theology Today* 16, no. 1 (April 1959): 74–89.

59. John A. Mackay to William Ewen, December 27, 1930, Mackay Collection.

60. Robert E. Speer to John A. Mackay, May 27, 1930, Mackay Collection.

61. Robert E. Speer to John A. Mackay, July 14, 1930, Mackay Collection.

62. John A. Mackay, "Life's Chief Discoveries," *Christianity Today* 14, no. 7 (January 2, 1970): 5.

63. John A. Mackay to Robert E. Speer, August 1, 1929, Mackay Collection.

64. W. A. Visser 't Hooft, *Memoirs* (Philadelphia: Westminster Press, 1973), 40. Regarding a message, *Student World* opined: "A collectivity cannot declare a message because a message is only a message when it is the utterance of organic life. . . . No matter how vital a message is it cannot survive being embalmed in a conference resolution. A vital message does not in fact exist except as it is uttered by flesh and blood individuals speaking out of their own dynamic insight into the meaning of life as God gives them insight." See F. P. M., Editorial "Manœuvre or Message," *Student World* 24, no. 2 (2d Quarter 1931): 99. See also V. 't H., Editorial, "After a Year of Message Study," *Student World* 24, no. 2 (2d Quarter 1931): 101–103.

65. Visser 't Hooft, *Memoirs*, 42. See also Maury's account of the meeting in "Deux Voyages," *Foi et Vie*, n.s., 32e (1931), 44–52; and his discussion of the message, Pierre Maury, "The Message of the Federation," *Student World* 24, no. 2 (2d Quarter 1931): 124–31.

66. Mackay, "Reflections," 221–33, at 223.

67. Ibid., 226.

68. Ibid., 228.

69. John A. Mackay to Robert E. Speer, September 6, 1930, Presbyterian Historical Society Archives, Philadelphia.

70. John A. Mackay to Navarro Monzó, October 13, 1930, Mackay Collection.

71. See Gerald P. Fogarty, *The Vatican and the American Hierarchy from 1870 to 1965* (Stuttgart: Anton Hiersemann, 1982), 230–36. The Mexican persecution was the setting for Graham Greene's novel *The Power and the Glory* (1946), first published in March 1940 under the title *The Labyrinthine Ways*.

72. *Iniquis Afflictisque* (On the Persecution of the Church in Mexico), November 18, 1926, encyclical of Pope Pius XI, sets forth the Vatican's reaction.

73. John A. Mackay, "First Impressions of Mexico," [n.d.], Mackay Collection.

74. John A. Mackay to W. A. Visser 't Hooft, October 6, 1930, Mackay Collection. The article referred to is Emil Brunner, "Secularism as a Problem for the Church," *International Review of Missions* 19 (October 1930): 495–511. Regarding contemporary understandings of secularism, see also H. Kraemer, "Christianity and Secularism," *International Review of Missions* 19 (1930): 195–208.

75. Brunner, "Secularism," 509.

76. John A. Mackay, "First Impressions of Mexico, [n.d.]," Mackay Collection. From Mexico Mackay circulated essay letters to certain friends: "First Impressions of Mexico, México, D.F.," "The Campaign Begins, México. November 26, 1930," and, later, "Our Secretarial Retreat, México, D.F., January 29, 1931," Mackay Collection.

77. John A. Mackay. "First Impressions of Mexico," Mackay Collection.

78. Ibid.

79. John A. Mackay to William Ewen, December 27, 1930, Mackay Collection.

80. John A. Mackay, "The Campaign Begins," Mackay Collection.

81. Ibid.

82. Ibid.

83. Ibid.

84. John A. Mackay to Robert E. Speer, February 11, 1931, Mackay Collection.

85. John A. Mackay, "Our Secretarial Retreat," January 29, 1931, Mackay Collection.

86. John A. Mackay to Robert E. Speer, February 11, 1931, and May 11, 1931, Mackay Collection.

87. John A. Mackay to F. W. Ramsey, April 1, 1931, Mackay Collection.

88. John A. Mackay to Frank V. Slack, May 11, 1931, Mackay Collection.

89. John A. Mackay to F. W. Ramsey, May 26, 1931, Mackay Collection.

90. "Important Actions of General Assembly," *Presbyterian Advance*, June 11, 1931, 28.

91. John A. Mackay, "The Basic Insight," in *Report of the Decennial Conference on Missionary Policies and Methods of the Board of Foreign Missions of the Presbyterian Church in the U.S.A.*, Lakeville, Connecticut, June 20–30, 1931 (New York: Board of Foreign Missions of the Presbyterian Church in the U.S.A., [n.d.]), 35–41, at 38.

92. John A. Mackay, "A Preface to the Christian Message," in *Commission I: The Christian Conception of Personality* (New York: Methodist Book Concern, n.d.), 15–26.

93. Miron A. Morrill, "Methodists Seek to State Beliefs," *Christian Century* 48, no. 28 (July 15, 1931): 931–32; Editorial "The Methodists at Delaware," *Christian Century* 48, no. 29 (July 22, 1931): 943–44.

94. Clarence Prouty Shedd et al., *History of the World's Alliance of Young Men's Christian Associations* (London: SPCK, 1955), 502. The platform included Dr. W. Russell Maltby, England; Dr. T. Z. Koo, China; Dr. Toyohiko Kagawa, Japan; Bishop E. M. Rodhe, Sweden; Professor Henry P. Van Dusen, U.S.A.; Dr. Erich Stange, Germany; Professor Reinhold Niebuhr, U.S.A.; Dr. Cheng Ching Yi, China; Dr. Rufus M. Jones, U.S.A.; Bishop W. F. McDowell, U.S.A.; and Dr. John R. Mott.

95. John Mackay, "Youth's Adventure with God," in *Youth's Adventure with God* (London: British YMCA Press, 1931), 111–15. Mackay's speech is quoted and excerpted in *The New York Times*, August 5, 1931, 40.

96. Mackay, "Youth's Adventure," 112.

97. John A. Mackay to Hermann Schlingensiepen, October 6, 1931, Mackay Collection; Resolution 5, in *Youth's Adventure with God*, 227–30.

98. John A. Mackay, "God's Springtime in Latin America," in *The Christian Mission in the World of Today*, ed. Raymond P. Currier (New York: Student Volunteer Movement for Foreign Missions, 1932), 51–59. Speer and Mott also addressed the gathering. See Robert E. Speer, "The Living Christ," in *Christian Mission*, 175–84; and John R. Mott, "The Future of Christian Missions," in *Christian Mission*, 111–24.

99. "Named Seminary Speaker," *New York Times*, November 15, 1931, sec. 2, 6; "The Mission Lectures," *Princeton Seminary Bulletin* 25, no. 3 (November 1931): 26.

100. Webster E. Browning to John A. Mackay, October 23, 1931, Mackay Collection.

101. George E. Bevans, "Mexico's Church as It Really Is," *Presbyterian Banner*, March 23, 1933, 10.

102. John A. Mackay to Robert E. Speer, April 28, 1932, and May 20, 1932, Mackay Collection.

CHAPTER 9: NORTH AMERICA AND THE MISSION BOARD

1. Adolf Keller, *Karl Barth and Christian Unity* (New York: Macmillan Co., 1933), 239–47.

2. John A. Mackay, "Christianity and Other Religions," in *Protestant Thought in the Twentieth Century*, ed. Arnold S. Nash (New York: Macmillan Co., 1951), 283.

3. John A. Mackay, "The Madras Series," *International Review of Missions* 29, no. 2 (1940): 391–94; and see John A. Mackay, "Looking toward Madras," *Christendom* 3, no. 4 (1943): 566–75.

4. H. Kraemer, *The Christian Message in a Non-Christian World* (New York: Harper & Bros., 1938). Published for the International Missionary Council.

5. Henry P. Van Dusen, "Missions at Madras," *Religion in Life* 8, no. 2 (Spring 1939): 163–75.

6. John A. Mackay to Robert E. Speer, December 17, 1931, Presbyterian Historical Society Archives, Philadelphia.

7. Robert E. Speer to John A. Mackay, February 8, 1932, Presbyterian Historical Society Archives, Philadelphia.

8. Robert E. Speer to John A. Mackay, April 16, 1932, Presbyterian Historical Society Archives, Philadelphia.

9. Robert E. Speer to John A. Mackay, June 10, 1932, Presbyterian Historical Society Archives, Philadelphia.

10. "Dr. Mackay, Secretary Foreign Missions," *Presbyterian Magazine*, May 1932, 260–61.

11. Stanton R. Wilson, "John A. Mackay: Studies of an Ecumenical Churchman" (ThM diss., Princeton Theological Seminary, 1958), 28.

12. John A. Mackay to Charles Ewald, December 9, 1931, Mackay Collection.

13. John A. Mackay to Charles Ewald, December 17, 1931, Mackay Collection. Charles Jefferson Ewald, *Memoirs of Charles Jefferson Ewald* (Cleveland: 1955), 24.

14. P. A. Conard to John A. Mackay, September 12, 1931; John A. Mackay to P. A. Conard, December 24, 1931, Mackay Collection. By 1938 it was recognized that the YMCA had been a successful spiritual agency in bringing men together but had not made outstanding contributions to Christian theology.

15. John A. Mackay, "Life's Chief Discoveries," *Christianity Today* 14, no. 7 (January 2, 1970): 5

16. Donald Richardson, "Re-Thinking Missions—A Laymen's Inquiry after One Hundred Years," *Union Seminary Review* 44, no. 2 (January 1933): 145.

17. The first of a number of such studies at this time analyzed the YMCA. It was an expensive study employing twelve men for two years at a cost of $230,000. Although Mackay was mentioned in one section of the report, the descriptive part did not include the work of Mackay or Navarro Monzó, in South America or Yui and Koo in China. See W. A. Visser 't Hooft, "Survey of the Y.M.C.A. and Y.W.C.A.," *International Review of Missions* 21 (1932): 443. The review refers to a long article by Mr. Z. F. Willis in *World's Youth* (April 1932).Visser 't Hooft was critical of the report.

18. "Is Modernism Ready?" *Christian Century* 49, no. 48 (November 30, 1932): 1463.

19. Archibald G. Baker, "Reactions to the *Laymen's Report*," *Journal of Religion* 13, no. 4 (October 1933): 398.

20. "Better Missionaries Urged by Mrs. Buck," *New York Times*, November 3, 1932, 19.

21. Editorial, " 'The Best or Nothing.' "*New York Times*, November 6, 1932, sec. 2, 1.

22. "Backs Lay Report on Missions Abroad," *New York Times*, November 19, 1932, 9.

23. Ibid.

24. Commission of Appraisal, *Re-Thinking Missions* (New York: Harper & Bros., 1932), 26.

25. Ibid., 58.

26. Ibid., 44.

27. "Foreign Missions Said to Need Unity," *New York Times*, November 20, 1932, 30.

28. Ibid.

29. Richardson, "Re-Thinking Missions," 160–61.

30. John R. Scotford, "Present Laymen's Mission Findings," *Christian Century* 49, no. 48 (November 30, 1932): 1479.

31. Laymen's Foreign Missions Inquiry, *The Proceedings of the Meeting of the Directors and Sponsors of the Laymen's Foreign Missions Inquiry and Representatives of Foreign Missions Boards* (New York: Laymen's Foreign Missions Inquiry, 1932).

32. Scotford, "Present Laymen's Mission Findings," 1478.

33. Visser 't Hooft, "Spineless Missions," *Student World* 26, no. 3 (1933): 271. As noted, the year before another report had been issued surveying the work of the YMCA and YWCA. Visser 't Hooft was convinced that the report was unreliable: the principles used in the survey were "symptomatic of a secularized Christianity which has been adapted to a fashionable sociological philosophy." W. A. Visser 't Hooft, "Survey of the Y.M.C.A. and Y.W.C.A," *International Review of Missions* 21 (1932): 441–43. The report was "strangely silent" about the work of Monzó, Mackay, Yui, and Koo.

34. John A. Mackay, "The Theology of the Laymen's Foreign Missions Inquiry," *International Review of Missions* 22, no. 2 (1933): 174–88.

35. Ibid., 177.

36. Ibid., 178.

37. Ibid., 184.

38. Ibid., 185.

39. Ibid.

40. Ibid., 186.

41. Ibid., 187–88.

42. Commission of Appraisal, *Re-Thinking Missions*, 109.

43. Quoted at Mackay, "Christianity and Other Religions," 295. In retrospect, historian Kenneth Scott Latourette pointed out the major changes in the world that the appraisers did not foresee (Kenneth Scott Latourette, "Re-Thinking Missions after Twenty-five Years," *International Review of Missions* 46 [1957]: 164–70).

44. Pearl S. Buck, "The Laymen's Mission Report," *Christian Century* 49, no. 47 (November 23, 1932): 1434.

45. Pearl S. Buck, *Is There a Case for Foreign Missions?* (New York: John Day Co., 1932); idem, "Is There a Case for Foreign Missions?" *Harper's Monthly Magazine*, January 1933, 143–55.

46. "She likened Christ to the Buddha, declared that Christ's historical reality was irrelevant, denied the necessity for any specific dogma, and located the truth of Christianity in 'the essence of men's highest dreams'" (Peter Conn, *Pearl S. Buck* (Cambridge: Cambridge University Press, 1996), 154 and notes, 116–18). Also see "Mrs. Buck Extols a Creedless Faith," *New York Times*, April 14, 1933, 17.

47. Editorial "Mrs. Pearl Buck" *Presbyterian Banner*, May 11, 1933.

48. Buck's biographer believed that psychological alienation from her own father led to Buck's criticisms of the missionary movement, and that Hocking and Buck had had a strong affinity to one another since their first meeting at Nanking. History's verdict on Hocking's philosophy was as unfavorable as Mackay's view of his theology. Hocking's most important and complete scholarly work, *The Meaning of God in Human Experience*, was published in 1912, before World War I, and later he was not able to resolve some questions it raised. The Gifford Lectures that he delivered in Scotland in 1938–1939 were never printed. His idealist philosophy did not last after World War II. Interestingly, Hocking and Buck found solace together for three years until Hocking's death in 1966. See Conn, *Pearl S. Buck*, 150, 350, 352;

and Bruce Kulick, *The Rise of American Philosophy* (New Haven, CT: Yale University Press, 1977), 495.

49. John A. Mackay, "Robert Elliot Speer: A Man of Yesterday Today," *Princeton Seminary Bulletin* 60, no. 3 (June 1967): 19.

50. J. Gresham Machen, *Modernism and the Board of Foreign Missions of the Presbyterian Church in the U.S.A,: Argument of J. Gresham Machen in Support of an Overture Introduced in the Presbytery of New Brunswick at Its Meeting on January 24, 1933, and Made the Order of the Day for the Meeting on April 11, 1933* (New York: Board of Foreign Missions, 1933). Machen's 110-page pamphlet supporting his arguments is reprinted in full with that title in *Modernism and Foreign Missions: Two Fundamentalist Protests*, edited with an introduction by Joel A. Carpenter (New York: Garland Pub., 1988).

51. Machen was quoted as saying, "No sensible person can have confidence in a board which does not welcome open discussion of its policy with those to whom it appeals for funds" ("Amplifies Charges on Missions Board," *New York Times*, April 15, 1933, 11).

52. See John F. Piper Jr., *Robert E. Speer* (Louisville, KY: Geneva Press, 2000), chap. 13; and James A. Patterson, "Robert E. Speer, J. Gresham Machen and the Presbyterian Board of Foreign Missions," *Journal of Presbyterian History* 64, no.1 (Spring 1986): 58–68.

53. Machen, *Modernism and the Board of Foreign Missions*, 52–54. "The Oxford Group Movement," *Presbyterian Banner*, January 12, 1933, 6–7. "A New Lay Priesthood," *Presbyterian Banner*, January 19, 1933, 6–7. "The Oxford Group Movement and the Theology of Crisis," *Presbyterian Banner*, January 26, 1933, 8–10.

54. Webster E. Browning to John A. Mackay, May 23, 1933, Presbyterian Historical Society Archives, Philadelphia.

55. John A. Mackay to Webster E. Browning, June 28, 1933, Presbyterian Historical Society Archives, Philadelphia.

56. John A. Mackay, "Adventures of the Mind in Latin America," in *Students and the Future of Christian Missions*, Report of the Tenth Quadrennial Convention of the Student Volunteer Movement for Foreign Missions, Detroit, Michigan, December 28, 1927, to January 1, 1928, ed. Gordon Poteat (New York: Student Volunteer Movement for Foreign Missions, 1928), 167–72. John A. Mackay, "God's Springtime in Latin America," in *The Christian Mission in the World of Today*, Report of the Eleventh Quadrennial Convention of the Student Volunteer Movement for Foreign Missions, Buffalo, New York, December 30, 1931, to January 3, 1932, ed. Raymond P. Currier (New York: Student Volunteer Movement for Foreign Missions, 1932), 51–59. Speer and Mott also addressed this gathering. John A. Mackay, "Our Christ," in *Students and the Christian World Mission*, Report of the Twelfth Quadrennial Convention of the Student Volunteer Movement for Foreign Missions, Indianapolis, Indiana, December 28, 1935 to January 1, 1936), ed. Jesse R. Wilson (New York: Student Volunteer Movement for Foreign Missions, 1936), 15–22. Also present were William Temple, Reinhold Niebuhr, Báez-Camargo, Kagawa, Mott, Speer, and Van Dusen.

57. Jill K. Gill, "The Decline of Real Ecumenism: Robert Bilheimer and the Vietnam War," *Journal of Presbyterian History* 81, no. 4 (Winter 2003): 243–44.

58. John A. Mackay, "Christian Realism: or Some Things That Are," and "Christian Idealism: or Some Things That Should Be," in *A Christian Crusade: Report of the Spiritual Emphasis Conference, New York City, National Council of the Y.M.C.A.'s of the U.S.A.* (New York: Association Press, 1934), 9–20 and 55–69; idem, "My God and My Neighbor," in *Finding the Will and Power of the Living God*, Report of the Annual Spiritual Emphasis Conference Held at Lake Mohonk Mountain House, Mohonk Lake, NY, October 15, 16, 1932, under the

Auspices of the Commission on Message and Purpose of the National Council of the Young Men's Christian Associations of the U.S.A. (New York: Association Press, 1932), 27–36; idem, "A Preface to the Christian Message," in *Commission I: The Christian Conception of Personality* (New York: Methodist Book Concern, n.d.), 15–26; and idem, "The Basic Insight," Presbyterian Decennial Conference on Mission Policies, Lakeville, Connecticut (New York: Board of Foreign Missions of the Presbyterian Church in the U.S.A., 1931), 35–41.

59. John A. Mackay, "Some New Trends in Latin America," *Missionary Review of the World* 55, no. 1 (January 1932): 17–20; idem, "The South American Crisis," *Missionary Review of the World* 57, no. 2 (February 1934): 77–80; idem, "The Crucial Issue in Latin America," *Missionary Review of the World* 58, no. 11 (November 1935): 527–29.

60. John A. Mackay, "The Gospel and Our Generation," in *The Christian Message for the World Today: A Joint Statement of the World-Wide Mission of the Christian Church*, ed. A. L. Warnshuis (New York: Round Table Press, 1934), 95–126.

61. Wilhelm Pauck, review, *The Christian Message for the World Today*, *Chicago Theological Seminary Register*, March 1934, 41.

62. J. Lloyd Mecham, *Church and State in Latin America* (Chapel Hill: University of North Carolina Press, 1934), 489.

63. Charles S. Macfarland, *Chaos in Mexico: The Conflict of Church and State* (New York: Harper & Bros., 1935), 223.

64. John A. Mackay, "Mexico Revisited: The Report of a Secretarial Visit to Mexico, New York, May 4, 1934," 3, Mackay Collection.

65. Ibid.

66. Norman Taylor, *God-Given Promises Meet Every Need* (Pasadena, CA: William Carey Library, 1981), 34.

67. Ibid., 101–6. See also *The Ninety-eighth Annual Report of the Board of Foreign Missions of the Presbyterian Church in the United States of America* (New York: Board of Foreign Missions, 1935), 70, and *The Ninety-seventh Annual Report of the Board of Foreign Missions of the Presbyterian Church in the United States of America* (New York: Board of Foreign Missions, 1934), 37.

68. Untitled Memo on Mexico Mission. Box 11 Missions. Mackay Collection.

69. *The Ninety-second Annual Report of the Board of Foreign Missions of the Presbyterian Church in the United States of America* (New York: Board of Foreign Missions, 1929), 177.

70. Pope Pius XI responded sharply to this development with the encyclical *Acerba Animi* (On Persecution of the Church in Mexico), September 29, 1932.

71. John A. Mackay to W. Reginald Wheeler, April 26, 1932, Mackay Collection.

72. John A. Mackay to Robert E. Speer, May 20, 1932, Mackay Collection.

73. Mackay, "Mexico Revisited," 11.

74. Ibid., 1–17. This difficult situation is recounted in Charles S. Macfarland, "Protestant Churches and Protestant Opinion in Mexico," in *Chaos in Mexico: The Conflict of Church and State* (New York: Harper & Bros., 1935), 212–57. Mackay reviewed this book for the *International Review of Missions*; see John A. Mackay, review, *International Review of Missions* 25 (1936): 136. Mackay thought Macfarland's book set the context for Kenneth Grubb's book on Mexico: G. Báez-Camargo and Kenneth G. Grubb, *Religion in the Republic of Mexico* (London: World Dominion Press, 1935). Regarding the relations between church and state in Mexico, see also Frank Tannenbaum, *Mexico: The Struggle for Peace and Bread* (New York: Alfred A. Knopf, 1950), 122–35; Chester Lloyd Jones, "Roots of the Mexican Church Con-

flict," *Foreign Affairs* 14, no. 1 (October 1935): 135–45; M. Searle Bates, *Religious Liberty: An Inquiry* (New York: International Missionary Council, 1945), 62–73; J. Lloyd Mecham, "Church and State Conflict in Mexico: 1875–1933," in *Church and State in Latin America* (Chapel Hill: University of North Carolina Press, 1934), 456–501; Kenneth G. Grubb, "Religion in Mexico," *International Review of Missions* 24 (1935): 524–30.

75. Gonzalo Báez-Camargo, "Recent Progress in Mexico," *Missionary Review of the World* 9 (1936):178.

76. Ibid., 179. Báez-Camargo also writes, "Benito Juárez, the great Indian president of Mexico, once expressed his hope that Protestantism should become an active force in liberating the Mexican Indians from the state of ignorance, superstition and vice in which they lie."

77. John A. Mackay, "Education and Religion in Mexico," *Missionary Review of the World* 57, no. 3 (March 1934): 133–34; idem, "Whither Mexico?" *Missionary Review of the World* 58, no. 9 (September 1935): 389–90.

78. John Alexander Mackay, "The Communion of Saints in Our Time," *Crozer Quarterly* 16, no. 4 (1939): 255.

79. John A. Mackay to Samuel Guy Inman, April 12, 1929, Mackay Collection.

80. Eloy Alfaro had been pulled from prison in Ecuador and killed in 1911.

81. Jane Mackay to Webster E. Browning, May 22, 1933, Presbyterian Historical Society Archives, Philadelphia.

82. Details of the visitation are found in John A. Mackay to Robert E. Speer, May 8, 1933, and Jane Mackay to Webster Browning Letter, May 22, 1933, Presbyterian Historical Society Archives, Philadelphia. "President Is Slain in Peru on Leaving Review of Troops," *New York Times*, May 1, 1933, 1; and "Peru Pays Tribute to Slain President," *New York Times*, May 3, 1933, 2; John A. Mackay, "Lima, Peru, Revisited," *Missionary Review of the World* 56, no. 9 (September 1933): 421–23; idem, "A Voice from a Peruvian Prison," *Missionary Review of the World* 56, no.12 (December 1933): 583–86.

83. Harry Kantor, *The Ideology and Program of the Peruvian Aprista Movement* (New York: Octagon Books, 1966), 64. See, for example, the forty-eight rules of the "Aprista Code of Action for Youth" (1934), in appendix C, 135–37. The code is cited with approval in John A. Mackay, *That Other America* (New York: Friendship Press, 1935), 114. In a book review of Kantor's book, Rycroft pointed out Mackay's influence on Haya (W. Stanley Rycroft, "Intellectual Renaissance in Latin America," *International Review of Missions* 43 [1954]: 221).

84. Mackay, *That Other America*, 105.

85. "A Resposta Cristã ao Secularismo" and "O Novo Reino" in *"O Cristo Vivo" Relatório Oficial da 11." Convenção Mundial de Escolas Dominicais, Rio de Janeiro, 25 a 31 de Julho de 1932*, Redator de Volume em Português, Rev. Galdino Moreira (Rio de Janeiro: Editado pelo Conselho Evangélico de Educação Religiosa do Brasil: 1932), 130–33 and 133–37. "The Christian Response to Secularism" and "The New Kingdom" in *The Living Christ: Official Report of the 11th World Sunday School Convention Rio de Janeiro from 25 to 31 July 1932*, Editor of Volume in Portuguese, Rev. Galdino Moreira (Rio de Janeiro: Edited by the Evangelical Council for Religious Education in Brazil, 1932). The first world conference ever held in Latin America.

86. John A. Mackay, "The Gospel on the Great Divide," *Women and Missions*, May, 1934, 39–41. See reference in Mackay, *That Other America*, 151.

87. Mackay, "The Gospel," 95–126. Mackay, "Christian Idealism: or Some Things That Should Be," and "Christian Realism: or Some Things That Are," in *A Christian Crusade*, 55–69 and 9–20.

88. *Our World Mission* (New York: The Board of Foreign Missions of the Presbyterian Church in the U.S.A., 1934).

89. Burnham Carter, "The Study of a Murder," *Yankee* 41, no. 10 (October 1977): 102–107, 204, 207, 208, 211–14, 217, 218; Herbert Hall Taylor, "Murder on the Campus," *American Detective*, April 1935, 48–53, 77–78, 80; Dayton Stoddart, "Intrigue Stalks Private School," *Los Angeles Examiner*, Sunday, June 10, 1951, sec. 3, 3; Piper, *Robert E. Speer,* 102–105.

90. John A. Mackay, *The Other Spanish Christ* (New York: Macmillan Co., 1932). The book was reprinted many times in English and Spanish and received wide attention in the British Isles, North America, and Latin America. Samuel Escobar, "The Search for a Missiological Christology in Latin America," in William A. Dyrness, ed., *Emerging Voices in Global Christian Theology* (Grand Rapids: Zondervan, 1994), 210–13.

91. Reinhold Niebuhr to John A. Mackay, January 23, [1932], Mackay Collection.

92. As Peers put it a "title is easier to remember than to understand" (E. Allison Peers, *Bulletin of Spanish Studies* (January 1933): 47).

93. Alexander Parker, "Spain's Catholic Awakening," *Blackfriars* 14, no. 155 (February 1933): 138.

94. Mackay, *Other Spanish Christ*, 101.

95. Ibid., 41.

96. Ibid., 102.

97. Ibid., 98–99.

98. Ibid., 122.

99. Ibid., 97.

100. Ibid., 126–27.

101. Ibid., 127.

102. Peers, 47.

103. Mackay, *Other Spanish Christ*, 262.

104. Ibid., xii.

105. Mackay's *That Other America* was reviewed in *Missionary Review of the World* 58 (1935): 447; José Ortega y Gasset, "Aquella Otra América," *El Heraldo de Antioquia* (Medellín, Colombia), January 22, 1936, also *La Nación* (Buenos Aires, n.d.) reprinted in *El Tiempo* (Bogotá, n.d.); Kenneth G. Grubb, *International Review of Missions* 24 (1935): 552–53; *Federal Council Bulletin*, September, 1935; *Missions*, November 1935; Charles S. Macfarland, *Reformed Church Messenger*, July 11, 1935.

106. Gasset, "Aquella Otra America."

107. Mackay, *Other America*, 22–24, 30–36.

108. Ibid., 195.

109. Ibid., 41.

110. Ibid., 23–24.

111. Ibid., 38.

112. Ibid., 39.

113. Ibid., 192.

114. Ibid., 201. The reference is to Bentinck. On Morrow's career in Mexico, see Harold Nicolson, *Dwight Morrow* (New York: Harcourt Brace, 1935), chaps. 15 and 16.

115. John A. Mackay, interview by Gerald W. Gillette for the Presbyterian Historical Society, November 18, 1975, 1.

116. Elena Mackay Reisner, conversation with the author, January 8, 2005.

CHAPTER 10: RETURN TO PRINCETON

1. Henry Snyder Gehman, "As President," *Princeton Seminary Bulletin* 52, no. 4 (May 1959): 5, 7.

2. "An Affirmation of One Hundred and Fifty Liberal Ministers," *The Presbyterian,* January 17, 1924, 6–9; Charles E. Quirk, "Origins of the Auburn Affirmation," *Journal of Presbyterian History* 53, no. 2 (Summer 1975), 120–42.

3. Ross Stevenson to John A. Mackay, June 30, 1925; John A. Mackay to Ross Stevenson, August 13, 1925, Mackay Collection.

4. J. Ross Stevenson to John A. Mackay, March 26, 1926, Mackay Collection.

5. John A. Mackay to J. Ross Stevenson, April 27, 1926, Mackay Collection.

6. J. Ross Stevenson to John A. Mackay, June 25, 1926, Mackay Collection.

7. John A. Mackay to J. Ross Stevenson, December 31, 1926, Mackay Collection. The same year Mackay declined to teach in the chair of systematic theology in Western (now Pittsburgh) Theological Seminary, of the Presbyterian Church U.S.A., Mackay Collection.

8. John A. Mackay to Stanley Rycroft, June 1, 1926, Mackay Collection.

9. "The Mission Lectures," *Princeton Seminary Bulletin* 25, no. 3 (November 1931): 26.

10. J. Ross Stevenson to John A. Mackay, June 25, 1926, Mackay Collection.

11. Arthur S. Link, ed., *The First Presbyterian Church of Princeton: Two Centuries of History* (Princeton, NJ: First Presbyterian Church, 1967), 94. Tertius van Dyke, *Henry van Dyke* (New York: Harper & Bros., 1935), 375.

12. J. Ross Stevenson to John A. Mackay, October 17, 1928, Mackay Collection.

13. John A. Mackay to J. Ross Stevenson, November 19, 1928 and October 15, 1929, Mackay Collection.

14. J. Ross Stevenson and Charles R. Erdman to Mackay, Telegram, September 16, 1929, Mackay Collection. A previous cable from Speer and Stevenson, August 3, 1929, reached him in Buenos Aires. Mackay declined the new offer by letter on October 15, 1929, Mackay Collection.

15. Edwin H. Rian, "Theological Conflicts of the 1920s and 1930s in the Presbyterian Church and on the Princeton Seminary Campus," *Princeton Seminary Bulletin*, n.s., 5, no. 3 (1984): 216–23; Bradley J. Longfield, *The Presbyterian Controversy* (New York: Oxford University Press, 1991); Lefferts A. Loetscher, *The Broadening Church* (Philadelphia: University of Pennsylvania Press, 1954); John W. Hart, "Princeton Theological Seminary: The Reorganization of 1929," *Journal of Presbyterian History* 58, no. 2 (1980): 124–40.

16. J. Gresham Machen, "Westminster Theological Seminary: Its Purpose and Plan," *The Presbyterian*, October 10, 1929, 8–9.

17. John A. Mackay to J. Ross Stevenson, draft letter, April 27, 1926. Text not included in final letter, Mackay Collection.

18. Edwin Rian, *Presbyterian Conflict* (Grand Rapids: Wm. B. Eerdmans Publishing Co., 1940), 198.

19. Norman V. Hope, review of *The History and Character of Calvinism*, by John T. McNeill, *Princeton Seminary Bulletin* 48, no. 2 (October 1954): 51.

20. Rian, "Theological Conflicts," 221–22. Earlier Rian had written of the secession from the point of view of Westminster in *Presbyterian Conflict*.

21. Gehman, "As President," 3.

22. See, for example, H. Richard Niebuhr, Wilhelm Pauck, and Francis P. Miller, eds., *The Church Against the World* (Chicago: Willett, Clark & Co., 1935); E. G. Homrighausen, *Christianity in America: A Crisis* (New York: Abingdon Press, 1936).

23. Niebuhr, Pauck, and Miller, *The Church*, 67.

24. Ibid., 84.

25. John A. Mackay, interview by Gerald W. Gillette for the Presbyterian Historical Society, October 21, 1975, 33.

26. Lewis Seymour Mudge, Secretary, "Minutes of the Special Committee on Next President of Princeton Seminary Assembled in Accordance with the Call of the Chair on March 30, 1936 in 514 Witherspoon Building, Philadelphia," Mackay Collection.

27. John A. Mackay, interview by Gerald W. Gillette for the Presbyterian Historical Society, November 18, 1975, 1.

28. Mackay, interview by Gillette, October 21, 1975, 33 and November 18, 1975, 1.

29. "Dr. Mackay Named to Seminary Post," *New York Times*, May 19, 1936, 26; "To Head Seminary," *New York Times*, June 6, 1936, 10.

30. "New Jersey Church Life," *Presbyterian Banner* 123, no. 1 (July 2, 1936): 16.

31. "Charge to the President" [Charge at Inauguration of Dr. John A. Mackay as President of Princeton Theological Seminary by Dr. Robert E. Speer in behalf of the Board of Trustees], *Princeton Seminary Bulletin* 31, no. 1 (April 1937): 2–6.

32. "Seminary Inducts Dr. John A. Mackay," *New York Times*, February 3, 1937, 21; John A. Mackay, "The Restoration of Theology," *Princeton Seminary Bulletin* 31, no. 1 (April 1937): 7–18.

33. Mackay, "The Restoration," 9.

34. Editorial, "A New Theological Leader," *New York Times*, February 4, 1937, 20.

35. L. H. Robbins, "Man-God or God-Man—A Crisis for Religion," *New York Times Magazine*, February 21, 1937, 12, 26.

36. Ibid., 26. The interview was also noted in an editorial in the *Presbyterian Banner* 123, no. 36 (March 4, 1937): 3–4. Mackay also saw "educational anarchy" in the United States and called for friendship to be "the supreme object of education" (see "Teachers Warned on 'Elite' Culture," *New York Times*, March 31, 1937), sec. 2, 1–2.

37. John A. Mackay, "Concerning Man and His Remaking," *Princeton Seminary Bulletin* 30, no. 3 (December 1936): 1–6.

38. John A. Mackay, "The Rôle of Princeton Seminary," *Princeton Seminary Bulletin* 31, no. 3 (November 1937): 1–2; and *The Presbyterian*, December 30, 1937, 19.

39. Mackay, "The Rôle of Princeton Seminary," 1.

40. "Princeton Honors Paul Van Zeeland," *New York Times*, June 23, 1937, 20.

41. The core were Andrew Blackwood, homiletics and preaching; John Kuizenga, apologetics; Donald Wheeler, speech; Edward Roberts, homiletics; Caspar Wister Hodge, theology; Frederick Loetscher, church history; Donald Mackenzie and Henry S. Gehman, Old Testament; William Park Armstrong, New Testament; and Samuel Zwemer, missions. Blackwood reminded students, including my father, "Don't address God, the creator of the universe, with your hands in your pockets the way you would talk to a dog."

42. John A. Mackay to Robert E. Speer, December 15, 1937, Speer Collection, Princeton Seminary Library.

43. An opponent of modernism, Brunner had lectured at Princeton in October 1928 on "The Quest for Truth, Revelation" and "The Crisis of Theology and the Theology of Crisis." "Lectures by Professor Brunner," *Princeton Seminary Bulletin* 22, no. 3 (November 1928): 10.

On Brunner's year at Princeton see also Frank Jehle, *Emil Brunner Theologe im 20. Jahrhundert* [Emil Brunner: Theologian in the 20th Century] (Zürich: Theologischer Verlag Zürich, 2006), 355–80.

44. See Hugh T. Kerr, "John A. Mackay: An Appreciation," in *The Ecumenical Era in Church and Society: A Symposium in Honor of John A. Mackay*, ed. Edward J. Jurji (New York: Macmillan Co., 1959), 9.

45. John A. Mackay to Robert E. Speer, October 15, 1937, Speer Collection, Princeton Seminary Library. And see Mackay to the Curriculum Committee, Memo, November 4, 1937, Mackay Collection. Mackay found Hodge's article a revelation and mused that "had these and other sentiments . . . been taken into account by many brethren in our Church in recent years, a great deal of unhappiness could have been avoided, and they would not have dared to accuse Princeton of any departure from the essential Reformed faith. It is clear that a later generation at Princeton interpreted subscription to the Confession in a different way from that in which Dr. Hodge understood it." See Charles Hodge, "Adoption of the Confession of Faith," *Biblical Repertory and Princeton Review* 30, no. 4 (1858): 688–92. An editorial in "Presbyterian Standards," *The Presbyterian* found this an adequate protection "against invasion by that which is not definitively and characteristically Calvinistic and Reformed" (*The Presbyterian*, December 2, 1937), 3. The oath and explanation is also printed in that issue "Presbyterian Standards," *The Presbyterian*, 4, 5.

46. Emil Brunner to John A. Mackay, October 23, 1937, Speer Collection, Princeton Seminary Library.

47. John A. Mackay to Robert E. Speer, October 31, 1938, Speer Collection, Princeton Seminary Library.

48. "Return to Theology," *Time*, October 3, 1938, 25–26. *Time*'s photograph of Brunner shows him as a smiling, dynamic young man.

49. John A. Mackay, "The Outlook," *Princeton Seminary Bulletin* 32, no. 3 (January 1939): 2.

50. John A. Mackay, "The One Hundred and Twenty-Seventh Commencement," *Princeton Seminary Bulletin* 33, no. 1 (July 1939): 2.

51. John A. Mackay, "The Outlook," *Princeton Seminary Bulletin* 32, no. 3 (January 1939): 2. Twenty-five years before, only 58 percent of students were members of the Presbyterian U.S.A. denomination. In 1929 54 percent were members, and in the 1938–1939 year 79 percent of the student body were members. This percentage was reduced when graduate students were included in the calculation: 89 percent of undergraduates and 96 percent of the senior class were Presbyterians.

52. John A. Mackay, "The Coming of Prof. Brunner to Princeton," *The Presbyterian*, February 17, 1938, 8; "Emil Brunner Comes to America," *Presbyterian Tribune*, May 26, 1938, 9–10; and it appeared in *Christianity Today* 9, no. 1 (October 1938): 36–38, included among "Reprints of Recent Significant Articles on Princeton."

53. "Articles on Prof. Brunner," *The Presbyterian*, May 5, 1938, 4; Donald Grey Barnhouse, "Some Questions for Professor Brunner," *The Presbyterian*, May 5, 1938, 8, 10–11; John A. Mackay, "Some Answers for Dr. Barnhouse," *The Presbyterian*, May 5, 1938, 9, 16.

54. "Dr. Brunner: Correspondence and Comments," *Christianity Today* 9, no. 3 (Spring 1939): 105–10. The debate included an anonymous postcard quoted in "Speaking the Truth about Princeton," *Christianity Today* 9, no. 2 (1938–1939): 55.

55. Cornelius Van Til, "Brunner Comes to Princeton," *Christianity Today* 9, no. 3 (Spring 1939): 38.

56. Emil Brunner to the Board of Trustees of Princeton Theological Seminary, February 9, 1939, Speer Collection, Princeton Seminary Library.

57. "Princeton Seminary Gains New Strength," *Christian Century* 54, no. 39 (September 29, 1937): 1189. He had also written *Christianity in America: A Crisis* (New York: Abingdon Press, 1936) reflecting his view of the Bible, and translated sermons of Karl Barth (*Come Holy Spirit Sermons by Karl Barth and Eduard Thurneysen,* trans. George W. Richards, Elmer G. Homrighausen, and Karl J. Ernst [New York: Round Table Press, 1933]).

58. E. G. Homrighausen, "Calm after Storm," *Christian Century* 56, no. 15 (April 12, 1939): 477–79. An article by Homrighausen, "Convictions!" was published in *The Presbyterian,* May 11, 1939, 8–9, setting forth his views of dialectical theology.

59. "The Present Status of Dr. Homrighausen," *Christianity Today* 9, no. 2 (Winter 1938–1939): 54. "The Homrighausen Case," *Christianity Today* 9, no. 3 (Spring 1939): 102–104. "The Policy of Princeton Seminary Again a Matter of Controversy," *Christianity Today* 9, no. 1 (October 1938): 1–3.

60. Otto Piper, a versatile scholar, wrote also on the Christian meaning of sex and money. His series of articles in February and March 1946 in the *Christian Century* on "What the Bible Means to Me" had wide impact. On Piper see *Princeton Seminary Bulletin,* n.s., 4, no. 1 (1983): 52–55; C. Clifton Black, "Remembering Otto Piper," *Princeton Seminary Bulletin,* n.s., 26, no. 3 (2005): 310–27; and Otto Piper, *God in History* (New York: Macmillan Co., 1939) [The Croall Lectures, New College, Edinburgh April 1936]; idem, "Theology in the Ecumenical Age," *Theology Today* 4, no. 1 (April 1947): 19–33; idem, "Vengeance and the Moral Order," *Theology Today* 5, no. 2 (July 1948): 221–34; idem, "The Depth of God," a review of Robinson's *The Death of God, Princeton Seminary Bulletin* 57, no. 1 (October 1963): 42–48.

61. "The outline of this course was as follows: (i) main trends in liberal theology before World War I; (ii) the beginnings of the theology of crisis: Kierkegaard, Dostoyevsky, Overbeck, the Blumhardts, L. Ragaz, H.Kutter; (iii) the meaning of the term "crisis," paradox, *hic et nunc,* dialectical method; (iv) theology of crisis and natural theology—the controversy between K. Barth, E. Brunner and F. Gogarten; and (v) from a theology of crisis to a theology of the Church" (Milan Opočenský, Introduction to Josef L. Hromádka, *The Field Is the World* [Prague: Christian Peace Conference, 1990], 18).

62. Milan Opočenský, "Profile of a Teacher of Theology," introduction to *The Field Is the World: Selected Writings from the Years 1918–1968,* by Josef L. Hromadka (Prague: Christian Peace Conference, 1990), 19.

63. Jan Milič Lochman, "Joseph Hromadka: Ecumenical Pilgrim," *Princeton Seminary Bulletin* 20, no. 1 (1999):43.

64. Ibid. A biographical sketch of Hromadka by Josef Smolik appears in *Ecumenical Pilgrims* (ed. Ion Bria and Dagmar Heller [Geneva: WCC Publications, 1995], 103–107). Also see Joseph L. Hromadka, *Theology between Yesterday and Tomorrow* [The Laidlaw Lectures at Knox College, Toronto, 1956] (Philadelphia: Westminster Press, 1957); idem, *Thoughts of a Czech Pastor,* trans. Monika and Benjamin Page (London: SCM Press Ltd., 1970); and idem, *Looking History in the Face,* trans. Margaret Pater (Madras: The Christian Literature Society, 1982). His chapters and articles include "Christ as Giver of Reconciliation," *The Student World* 22, no. 3 (July 1929): 298–311; Foreword to Amedeo Molnár, *Czechoslovak Protestantism Today* (Prague: Central Church Publishing House, 1954), 9–16; "The Witness of the Reformed Churches in the Present Ecumenical Situation," *Princeton Seminary Bulletin* 48, no. 3 (January 1955): 14–18; "Civilization's Doom and Resurrection," *Theology Today* 1, no.1 (April 1944): 18–33; "Jesus Christ and the Present Distress," *Theology Today* 2, no.

1 (April 1945): 19–33; "Changing Europe and the Christian Faith," *Theology Today* 3, no. 1 (April 1946): 18–31; "The Church of the Reformation Faces Today's Challenges," *Theology Today* 6, no. 4 (January 1950): 446–64; "Social and Cultural Factors in Our Divisions," *Theology Today* 9, no. 4 (January 1953): 467–71; "Our Responsibility in the Post-War World," in *Man's Disorder and God's Design,* vol. 4, *The Church and the International Disorder* (New York: Harper & Bros., 1948), 114–42.

65. Georges A. Barrois, "The Rise of Marian Theology," *Theology Today* 12, no. 4 (January 1956): 463–76; idem, "Road from Rome," *Theology Today* 5, no. 1 (April 1948): 49–57; idem, "Mysticism—What Is It?" *Theology Today* 4, no. 2 (July 1947): 190–202; idem, "The Growth and Manifestations of Roman Absolutism," *Theology Today* 6, no. 1 (April 1949): 64–76; idem, "The Assumption: A New Dogma," *Theology Today* 7, no. 4 (January 1951): 444–57; idem, "Reflections on Two French Bibles," *Theology Today* 15, no. 2 (July 1958): 211–16; idem, "On Spiritual Resources," *Princeton Seminary Bulletin* 51, no. 3 (January 1958): 24–25; and idem, ed., *Pathways of the Inner Life: An Anthology of Christian Spirituality* (Indianapolis: Bobbs-Merrill, 1956).

66. See Richard J. Oman, "Emile Cailliet: Christian Centurion," *Princeton Seminary Bulletin,* n.s., 5, no. 1 (1984): 33–37. Cailliet's works include Emile Cailliet, "The Reformed Tradition in the Life and Thought of France," *Theology Today* 1, no. 3 (October 1944): 349–60; idem, "The Christian Experience," *Theology Today* 2, no. 3 (October 1945): 320–41; idem, "The Mind's Gravitation Back to the Familiar," *Theology Today* 15, no. 1 (April 1958): 1–8; idem, *The Clue to Pascal,* Foreword by John Mackay (Philadelphia: Westminster Press, 1943); idem, *Pascal: Genius in the Light of Scripture* (Philadelphia: Westminster Press, 1945); idem, *The Dawn of Personality* (Indianapolis: Bobbs-Merrill, 1955); idem, *The Christian Approach to Culture* (Nashville: Abingdon-Cokesbury Press, 1953); Blaise Pascal, *Great Shorter Works of Pascal,* trans. and intro. Emile Cailliet and John C. Blankenagel (Philadelphia: Westminster Press, 1948); Blaise Pascal, *Short Life of Christ,* trans. and intro. Emile Cailliet and John C. Blankenagel (Philadelphia: Westminster Press, 1950).

67. Jurji's works include Edward J. Jurji, *The Christian Interpretation of Religion* (New York: Macmillan Co., 1952); idem, ed., *The Ecumenical Era in Church and Society* (New York: Macmillan Co., 1959); idem, *The Middle East: Its Religion and Culture* (Philadelphia: Westminster Press, 1956); idem, *The Great Religions of the Modern World* (Princeton, NJ: Princeton University Press, 1946); idem, "The Science of Religion: A Christian Interpretation," *Theology Today* 7, no. 2 (July 1950): 194–205; idem, "The Impact of Christianity upon the Middle East," *Theology Today* 8, no. 1 (April 1951): 55–69; and idem, "The Great Religions and International Affairs," *Theology Today* 12, no. 2 (July 1955): 168–79.

68. See William G. Bodamer, "Reminiscences of Dr. George S. Hendry," *Princeton Seminary Bulletin,* n.s., 15, no. 1 (1994): 44–45; Daniel L. Migliore, "George S. Hendry: A Tribute," *Princeton Seminary Bulletin,* n.s., 15, no. 1 (1994): 46–51; George S. Hendry, *God the Creator* (London: Hodder & Stoughton, 1937); idem, *The Gospel of the Incarnation* (Philadelphia: Westminster Press, 1958); idem, *The Holy Spirit in Christian Theology* (Philadelphia: Westminster Press, 1956); idem, *The Westminster Confession for Today* (Richmond: John Knox Press, 1960); idem, "The Dogmatic Form of Barth's Theology," *Theology Today* 13, no. 3 (October 1956): 300–314; idem, Review of Tillich's Systematic Theology, vol. 2, *Theology Today* 15, no.1 (April 1958): 78–83.

69. Bruce Manning Metzger, *Reminiscences of an Octogenarian* (Peabody, MA: Hendrickson, 1997), 207. James A. Brooks, "Bruce Metzger as Textual Critic," *Princeton Seminary Bulletin,* n.s., 15, no. 2 (1994): 156–64.

70. "Princeton Seminary Sets Fund Campaign," *New York Times*, May 30, 1937, sec. 6, 7.

71. John M. Templeton, personal correspondence with the author, October 1, 2002.

72. Harold W. Dodds to John A. Mackay, November 14, 1941, Mackay Collection. Harold W. Dodds, "An Important Step," *Princeton Alumni Weekly* 42, no. 25 (April 17, 1942): 6.

73. Ledger Wood to John A. Mackay, April 30, 1959; John A. Mackay to Professor Ledger Wood, May 4, 1959, Mackay Collection.

74. J. A. M., "The Princeton Institute of Theology," *Princeton Seminary Bulletin* 36, no. 1 (August 1942): 1.

75. John A. Mackay, "The President's Page," *Princeton Seminary Bulletin* 40, no. 3 (Winter 1946): 20.

76. Albert Einstein, "Science and Religion" in *Ideas and Opinions* (New York: Crown Books, 1954), 41–44 referred to in Thomas Torrance, "Einstein and God," *CTI Reflections* 1 (Spring 1998): 8.

77. Martin Niemöller, "The Church in Central Europe," *Princeton Seminary Bulletin* 44, no. 3 (Winter 1950–1951): 16–23; idem, "What Is the Church," *Princeton Seminary Bulletin* 40, no. 4 (Spring 1947): 10–16.

78. Billy Graham, "Evangelism as I See It," *Princeton Seminary Bulletin* 46, no. 4 (April 1953): 13–20; idem, *Just as I Am* (San Francisco: HarperSanFrancisco, 1997), 58. Also see "Differing Views on Billy Graham," *Life*, July 1, 1957, 92; "Mackay Hails Graham," *New York Times*, September 6, 1957, 24.

79. W. A. Visser 't Hooft, "The Integrity of the Church," *Princeton Seminary Bulletin* 52, no. 2 (October 1958): 3–7.

80. John Foster Dulles, "The Churches and the World Order," *Theology Today* 1, no. 3 (October 1944): 340–48; George F. Kennan, "World Problems in Christian Perspective," *Theology Today* 16, no. 2 (July 1959): 155–72.

81. E. H. R., "Editorial Notes," *Princeton Seminary Bulletin* 37, no. 1 (December 1943): 2; Henry Snyder Gehman, "As President," *Princeton Seminary Bulletin* 52, no. 4 (May 1959): 5.

82. J. A. M, "A New Status for Theological Education," *Princeton Seminary Bulletin* 38, no. 1 (June 1944): 1–3.

83. "Thus Speak the Deans and Presidents—A Symposium," *Crozer Quarterly* 18, no. 2 (April 1941): 105–106.

84. John A. Mackay, "Theology in Education," *Christian Century* 68, no. 17 (April 25, 1951): 521, 522.

85. Liberal Christianity does not treat the Scriptures as the word of God by failing to focus on the plain meaning of the text. See T. W. Manson, "The Failure of Liberalism to Interpret the Bible as the Word of God," in *The Interpretation of the Bible*, C. W. Dugmore, ed. (London: Society for Promoting Christian Knowledge, 1944), 92–107.

86. The phrase is Albert Schweitzer's (*The Quest of the Historical Jesus*, trans. W. Montgomery with a preface by F. C. Burkitt, 2nd Eng. ed. [London: A. & C. Black, 1926], 208).

87. John A. Mackay, "The Finality of Theological Education," in *Bulletin—American Association of Theological Schools,* vol. 19 (June 1950), 71–84.

88. Ibid., 79.

89. Ibid., 83.

90. John A. Mackay, *Christianity on the Frontier* (New York: Macmillan Co., 1950), 8.

91. John A. Mackay, *A Preface to Christian Theology* (London: Nisbet & Co., 1942); Robert Strong, review in *Westminster Theological Journal* (May 1941): 133–38; Nels F. S. Ferré, *Journal of Religion* 21, no. 2 (April 1941): 217–19; J. E. Newhall, *Harvard Divinity*

School Bulletin 38, no. 27 (April 22, 1941): 85–86; John Courtney Murray, *Thought* 16, no. 61 (June 1941): 396; Robert Hastings Nichols, *The Presbyterian Tribune*, August 1941, 16–17.

92. Mackay, *A Preface*, author's preface.

93. Henry Sloane Coffin, review, *Review of Religion* 6, no. 1 (November 1941): 85.

94. Nels F. S. Ferré, review, *Journal of Religion* 21, no. 2 (April 1941): 219.

95. Brevard S. Childs, *Biblical Theology in Crisis* (Philadelphia: Westminster Press, 1970), 16. Walter Lowrie dedicated his book *A Short Life of Kierkegaard* (Princeton, NJ: Princeton University Press, 1944) to Mackay, "a Kierkegaardian."

96. John A. Mackay, *Heritage and Destiny* (New York: Macmillan Co., 1943); Frank Fitt, review, *Princeton Seminary Bulletin* 37, no. 1 (December 1943): 45; Richard W. Gray, review, *Westminster Theological Journal* 6 (November 1943): 206–209; Henry P. Van Dusen, review, *Crozer Quarterly* 20, no. 4 (October 1943): 352; P. W. W., review, "A Defense of Man's Faith," *New York Times Book Review*, May 23, 1943, 24.

97. P. W. W., review, "A Defense of Man's Faith," 24.

98. Mackay, *Heritage*, 12.

99. Mackay, *Christianity on the Frontier*. George S. Gunn, review, *Scottish Journal of Theology* 5, no. 1 (1952): 87–89; George Thomas Peters, review, *Princeton Seminary Bulletin* 44, no. 4 (Spring 1951): 48; Frederick W. Dillistone, review, *Theology Today* 8 (1951), 255–56.

100. Mackay, *Christianity on the Frontier*, 8.

101. John A. Mackay, "Christianity and Other Religions," in *Protestant Thought in the Twentieth Century*, ed. Arnold S. Nash (New York: Macmillan Co., 1951), 275–96.

102. John A. Mackay to C. W. Ranson, December 22, 1950, Mackay Collection.

103. *Westminster Study Edition of the Holy Bible* (Philadelphia: Westminster Press, 1948), vii.

104. F. W. Dillistone, "Retrospective for Today," *Theology Today* 40, no. 4 (January 1984): 395. The preface and "God Has Spoken," in *Westminster Study Edition,* vii–ix, xv–xx. The essay "God Has Spoken" also appears in Mackay, *Christianity on the Frontier*, 13–21, and idem, *Theology Today* 3, no. 2 (1946): 145–50.

105. Dillistone, "Retrospective," 395. See also Leonard J. Trinterud, "Reading and Writing in the Scottish Tradition," *Theology Today* 16, no. 3 (October 1959): 358–59.

106. "Our Arms," *Theology Today* 1, no. 1 (April 1944), 11.

107. *Theology Today* vol. 4, nos. 3 and 4; and vol. 5, nos. 1 and 2.

108. John A. Mackay, "The End Is the Beginning," *Theology Today* 5, no. 4 (January 1949): 461–66.

109. "Concerning Church and Mission," *Theology Today* 9, no. 1 (April 1952): 7.

110. Hugh T. Kerr, "John A. Mackay," in *The Ecumenical Era in Church and Society*, ed. Edward J. Jurji (New York: Macmillan Co., 1959), 15.

111. During the moderatorial year Mackay traveled nationwide. See Lefferts A. Loetscher, "Princetoniana, The Moderator," *Princeton Seminary Bulletin* 47, no. 3 (January 1954): 28.

112. John A. Mackay, "Theological Triennium: For What?" *Princeton Seminary Bulletin* 52, no. 3 (1959): 5–14, at 10.

113. John A. Mackay, "Personal Religion," *Princeton Seminary Bulletin* 37, no. 1 (December 1943): 4.

114. W. Eugene March, "'Biblical Theology,' Authority and the Presbyterians," *Journal of Presbyterian History* 59, no. 2 (Summer 1981): 123.

115. John A. Mackay, "Basic Christianity," *Princeton Seminary Bulletin* 43, no. 3 (Winter 1950): 5–13. This evangelistic message includes Mackay's idea that the church is a "road fellowship."

116. John A. Mackay, "When Truth Is a Belt," *Princeton Seminary Bulletin* 59, no. 1 (November 1965): 8.

117. Quoted by Paul L. Lehmann, "Also among the Prophets," *Theology Today* 16, no. 3 (October 1959): 354.

118. J. A. M., "The Student Center," *Princeton Seminary Bulletin* 35, no. 1 (August 1941): 1–2.

119. J. A. M., "Between the Times," *Princeton Seminary Bulletin* 39, no. 2 (November 1945): 1–2.

120. "The One Hundred and Twenty-Sixth Commencement," *Princeton Seminary Bulletin* 32, no. 1 (June 1938): 2.

121. John A. Mackay to Norman Goodall, June 13, 1952, Mackay Collection.

122. Published as John A. Mackay, "The Beginning of a Community Adventure," *Princeton Seminary Bulletin"* 46, no. 3 (January 1953): 15.

123. Ibid., 16.

124. Ibid.

125. Ibid., 17.

126. John A. Mackay, "Let Us Remember," *Princeton Seminary Bulletin* 65, no. 1 (July 1972): 31.

127. "The President's Page," *Princeton Seminary Bulletin* 45, no. 4 (Spring 1952): 29. A newer library building, "New Lenox," also made way for Speer Library.

128. "The President's Page," *Princeton Seminary Bulletin* 46, no. 4 (April 1953): 22.

129. "Library Is Razed, Controversy Ends," *New York Times*, December 20, 1955, 34.

130. "The Seminary's Library Project—A Statement by the President of the Seminary," *Princeton Seminary Bulletin* 49, no. 2 (October 1955): 30–34.

131. "The President's Page," *Princeton Seminary Bulletin* 49, no. 3 (January 1956): 26.

132. Editorial, "Good-by to Old Lenox," *New York Times*, December 23, 1955, 16.

133. A. M. Friend, "Friend Emphasizes Safety of Books in Comment upon Lenox Library Issue," *Princeton Herald,* October 13, 1954, 4, quoted in Letter to the Editor from John A. Mackay, *New York Times*, December 29, 1955, 22.

134. John A. Mackay, "The President's Page," *Princeton Seminary Bulletin* 50, no. 3 (February 1957): 29–31.

135. Nathan M. Pusey, "Address," *Princeton Seminary Bulletin* 51, no. 3 (January 1958), 51–55. President Pusey himself took a strong interest in theological education and worked to revitalize Harvard Divinity School. See, for example, his 1953 address, "A Faith for These Times," in Nathan Pusey, *The Age of the Scholar* (Cambridge, MA: Belknap Press, 1963), 1–8.

136. Mackay, "Let Us Remember," 31. The twelve symbols on the library tower at the main entrance were arranged in two equal columns. Images in the left column from top to bottom represented The Creative Hand of God, Tablets of the Law, Triumphant Lamb, Four Evangelists, Holy Spirit, Church United. The right column from top to bottom represented the Sword and Keys, Celtic Cross, Light in the Darkness, Burning Bush, Open Bible, Dedicated Heart.

137. Owing to objections by Princeton residents living near the newly purchased tract, those plans were later changed by a new president.

138. John A. Mackay, "John R. Mott: Apostle of the Oecumenical Era," *International Review of Missions* 44, no. 3 (1955): 334.

139. Hugh T. Kerr, "The Seminary and the College: The First Twenty-Five Years," *Princeton Seminary Bulletin*, n.s., 6, no. 1 (1985): 121–22.

140. John R. Mott to John A. Mackay, December 9, 1929, Mackay Collection.

141. Mackay presented at least one paper at the group: John A. Mackay, "The Universal Element in Christianity: With Special Reference to the Christian Approach to the Jew" (February, 1938), Mackay Archive. Also see Wilhelm and Marion Pauck, *Paul Tillich: His Life & Thought* (New York: Harper & Row, 1976), 187.

142. Henry P. Van Dusen, ed., *The Christian Answer* (New York: Charles Scribner's Sons, 1945). A full list of the thirty-eight members between 1933 and 1945 is found on page xi.

143. John A. Mackay, Editorial, "What Is the Christian Answer?" *Theology Today* 3, no. 1 (April 1946): 3.

144. Dean K. Thompson, "A Pre-eminent Generation of Protestant Leaders," *Christian Century* 93, no. 1 (January 7–14, 1976): 13–17.

145. John A. Mackay, "The Finality of Theological Education," in *Bulletin—American Association,* 83–84. On the subject see also John A. Mackay, "Some Questions Regarding Theological Education: With Special Reference to Princeton Seminary," *Princeton Seminary Bulletin* 49, no. 3 (January 1956): 3–12, and Editorial, "Education in Theology," *Theology Today* 7, no. 2 (July 1950): 145–50.

146. E. G. Homrighausen, "The Mackay Era," *Theology Today* 16, no. 3 (October 1959): 374.

147. Henry Snyder Gehman, "As President," *Princeton Seminary Bulletin* 52, no. 4 (May 1959): 9.

148. "It is the participation God allows us by His mysterious 'being together' in the Trinity. . . . God shares His Trinitarian community with the Church, and in the Church, each person shares the community experience" (Carlo Maria Martini, Cardinal Archbishop of Milan, *Journeying with the Lord* [New York: Alba House, 1987], 18–19).

149. F. Thomas Trotter, "A Generation of Leaders," *Christian Century* 92, no. 15 (April 23, 1975): 404–405.

150. Henry P. Van Dusen, "Christian Missions and Christian Unity," *Theology Today* 16, no. 3 (October 1959): 319–28. Nels F. S. Ferré, "Dynamic Centralism in Theology," *Theology Today* 16, no. 3 (October 1959): 329–37. Alberto Rembao, "Hispanic Culture and Christian Faith," *Theology Today* 16, no. 3 (October 1959): 338–44. Paul L. Lehmann, "Also among the Prophets," *Theology Today* 16, no. 3 (October 1959): 345–55. Leonard J. Trinterud, "Reading and Writing in the Scottish Tradition," *Theology Today* 16, no. 3 (October 1959): 356–59. "A Thesaurus of Tributes," *Theology Today* 16, no. 3 (October 1959): 360–72. E. G. Homrighausen, "The Mackay Era," *Theology Today* 16, no. 3 (October 1959): 373–75. Henry Snyder Gehman, "As President," *Princeton Seminary Bulletin* 52, no. 4 (May 1959): 3–14. David L. Crawford, "As Teacher and Pastor," *Princeton Seminary Bulletin* 52, no. 4 (May 1959): 14–20. Peter K. Emmons, "As Churchman," *Princeton Seminary Bulletin* 52, no. 4 (May 1959): 20–21. Richard Shaull, "As Missionary Statesman," *Princeton Seminary Bulletin* 52, no. 4 (May 1959): 22–26. John T. Galloway, "As Author," *Princeton Seminary Bulletin* 52, no. 4 (May 1959): 26–29.

151. Ray Anderson, *Presbyterian Outlook* 141, no. 23 (June 8, 1959): 2.

CHAPTER 11: LET THE CHURCH BE THE CHURCH

1. Eugene C. Blake, "John Alexander Mackay: An Appreciation," *Reformed and Presbyterian World* 25, no. 6 (June 1959): 247.

2. Lewis S. Mudge to John A. Mackay, June 10, 1937. Lewis Mudge was the Stated Clerk of the Presbyterian Church.

3. "Thanks for Hitler in Church Ordered," *New York Times*, January 30, 1937, 2.

4. Charles S. Macfarland, "Text of the Macfarland Letter Denouncing Hitler," *New York Times*, June 9, 1937, 16. Office of Strategic Services Research and Analysis Branch, "The Nazi Master Plan: The Persecution of the Christian Churches," Installment no. 1, *Rutgers Journal of Law and Religion*, July 6, 1945, http://www.lawandreligion.com/nurinst1.shtml (accessed June 30, 2004). "How Hitler's Forces Planned to Destroy German Christianity," *New York Times*, January 13, 2002, Week in Review, 7.

5. Howard Chandler Robbins, "An Apostle of Unity," *Princeton Seminary Bulletin* 33, no. 4 (January 1940): 12.

6. Van Dusen considered Visser 't Hooft's contribution to this book a "masterpiece in miniature."

7. On the drafting process see J. H. Oldham to John A. Mackay, December 16, 1936; December 21, 1936; February 2, 1937; February 19, 1937; March 10, 1937; Eric Fenn to John A. Mackay, March 25, 1937; John A. Mackay to J. H. Oldham, December 30, 1936, and February 5, 1937, Mackay Collection.

8. J. H. Oldham to John A. Mackay, March 10, 1937, Mackay Collection.

9. John A. Mackay to J. H. Oldham, April 22, 1937, in reply to J. H. Oldham to John A. Mackay, April 9, 1937, Mackay Collection.

10. Warnshuis commented, "To speak of the world-wide body of Christians is to use metaphorical terms" (A. L. Warnshuis to John A. Mackay, April 15, 1937, Mackay Collection). Warnshuis also commented, "The Ecumenical Church is an idea that is not readily understood and may result in woolly thinking and illusory wishes. Its life is not and cannot be expressed in a visible organization. Its unity is not manifested in action. External authority cannot give it unity unless we join the Roman Church. The Bible is not a basis for unity because of differing interpretation. The only basis for unity is in freedom of thought, which recognizes the sovereignty of God and believes in Jesus Christ as redeemer and Lord. The Ecumenical Church is the body of Christians in all the world, and the assumption that we can agree on who are Christians, but the body is not a 'corpus'" (A. L. Warnshuis to Mackay, April 12, 1937, Mackay Collection).

The draft was circulated to William Adams Brown, Coffin, Cavert, Howard Chandler Robbins, F. Ernest Johnson, Latourette, and Leiper, and, in addition, Paul Tillich, Reinhold Niebuhr, Russell W. Bowie, Henry Atkinson, A. L. Warnshuis, Bishop G. Ashton Oldham, and Francis P. Miller. (H. P. Van Dusen to John A. Mackay, April 5, 1937, and John A. Mackay to H. P. Van Dusen, April 7, 1937, Mackay Collection.)

11. John A. Mackay to Eric Fenn, May 13, 1937, Mackay Collection. On the treatment of the theme of war, see J. H. Oldham to John A. Mackay, March 23, 1937; Mackay to Oldham, April 2, 1937; Oldham to Mackay, April 29, 1937, Mackay Collection. Also see J. H. Oldham, *The Oxford Conference (Official Report)* (New York: Willett, Clark & Co., 1937), 151–71.

12. Henry Smith Leiper, *World Chaos or World Christianity* (New York: Willett, Clark & Co., 1937), 22.

13. W. A. Visser 't Hooft and J. H. Oldham, *The Church and Its Function in Society* (Chicago: Willett, Clark & Co., 1937), 193–94. Oldham went on to write, "It is both the strength and the weakness of Christianity that it has no political program" (124); and "[Christians] may thus help to redeem the movement of which they are a part from some of the dangers and weaknesses inherent in all human undertakings" (225). See also Keith Clements, *Faith on the Frontier* (Edinburgh: T. & T. Clark, 1999), 327–28. At the First Assembly of the World Coun-

cil of Churches in 1948 Oldham contributed the important paper "A Responsible Society" (in *The Church and the Disorder of Society*, vol. 3, *Man's Disorder and God's Design* (New York: Harper & Bros., 1948), 120–54.

14. For membership and a sense of discussion in the section, see Leiper, *World*, 54–62.

15. Ibid., 52.

16. Ibid., 54–62.

17. Oldham, *Oxford Conference*, 151–71.

18. John A. Mackay, "The Ecumenical Road," *Christendom* 2, no. 4 (Autumn 1937): 535.

19. Oldham's biographer concluded the phrase captured "much of the essence of what happened in preparation for Oxford, at the gathering itself and its aftermath." See Keith Clements, *Faith on the Frontier, A Life of J. H. Oldham* (Edinburgh: T. & T. Clark; and Geneva: WCC Publications, 1999), 307. See also Visser 't Hooft's address, "Our Ecumenical Task in the Light of History" (1955), cited at John A. Mackay, *Ecumenics* (Englewood Cliffs, NJ: Prentice-Hall, 1964), 13. Mackay had used the expression in 1935 with narrower connotation (*That Other America* [New York: Friendship Press, 1935], 195).

20. Oldham, *Oxford Conference*, 45.

21. J. A. Mackay, *A Preface to Christian Theology* (London: Nisbet & Co., 1942), 171; see Mackay, *Ecumenics*, 5, for an abbreviated form.

22. D. M. Baillie, "The Deeper Question: What Is the Church?" *Christendom* 2, no. 4 (Autumn 1937): 544–47.

23. "Report of the General Secretary," [W. A. Visser 't Hooft], to the Tenth Meeting of the Central Committee of the W.C.C. at New Haven, Connecticut, July 30–August 7, 1957, *Minutes and Reports of the Tenth Meeting of the Central Committee of the World Council of Churches* (Geneva: World Council of Churches, 1957), 81.

24. Avery Dulles, SJ, *Models of the Church*, expanded ed. (Garden City, NY: Doubleday & Co., 1987), 123. Avery Dulles stayed in Paris while his father, John Foster Dulles, attended the conference. They returned together to the United States later that summer.

25. Leiper, *World Chaos*, 36. Associated Press, "Canterbury Shatters Tradition at Communion," *New York Times*, July 26, 1937, 9. An American Baptist did not receive Communion because he could not receive from one who had not been properly baptized. See William Adams Brown, *Toward a United Church* (New York: Charles Scribner's Sons, 1946), 97.

26. Charles Clayton Morrison, "Oxford, Edinburgh, and the American Mind," *Christendom* 2, no. 4 (Autumn 1937): 592.

27. Peter H. Hobbie, "'Bringing Oxford Home': American Presbyterian Perceptions of the Oxford Conference on Church, Community, and State," *Journal of Presbyterian History* 66, no. 1 (Spring 1988): 23–36.

28. Charles W. Hurd, "Religious History Written in Oxford," *New York Times*, July 25, 1937, sec. 4, 4.

29. John A. Mackay, "The Ecumenical Road," *Christendom* 2, no. 4 (1937): 535–38.

30. John A. Mackay, "The Church's Task in the Realm of Thought: Reflections on the Oxford Conference," *Princeton Seminary Bulletin* 31, no. 3 (November 1937): 4.

31. John A. Mackay et al., "The State of the Church" in Federal Council of the Churches of Christ in America, *Biennial Report, 1938* (New York: Federal Council of the Churches of Christ in America, 1938), 42.

32. "Two Communions Worship Together," *New York Times*, May 29, 1939, 8.

33. George E. DeMille, *The Episcopal Church Since 1900* (New York: Morehouse-Gorham Co., 1955), 135–63. The Presbyterian Church had called for action by proposal of a

specific program by the Episcopalians at the Episcopal General Convention in 1946 (Mackay, *Ecumenics*, 205).

34. A printers' strike prevented Walter Lowrie's book *Ministers of Christ* from being given to each minister in both churches during negotiations. Lowrie did a great deal of theological work towards church union, which years later provided support for unification in the Church of South India. See Walter Lowrie, *The Church and Its Organization in Primitive and Catholic Times: An Interpretation of Rudolph Sohm's Kirchenrecht* (New York: Longmans, Green, 1904); idem, *Problems of Church Unity* (New York: Longmans, Green and Co., 1924); and idem, *Ministers of Christ* (Louisville, KY: Cloister Press, 1946).

35. DeMille, *Episcopal Church*, 160.

36. Samuel McCrea Cavert, *The American Churches in the Ecumenical Movement 1900–1968* (New York: Association Press, 1968), 153–55. The preaching mission had educational and inspirational goals. John A. Hutchison, *We Are Not Divided* (New York: Round Table Press, 1941), 282–83. On Mackay's portion, see *Princeton Seminary Bulletin* 30, no. 3 (December 1936): 13.

37. See Stevenson's commencement address, "The Princeton Seminary Ideal of Theological Education in the New Day," *Princeton Seminary Bulletin* 30, no. 1 (June 1936): 6.

38. "Mission Is Opened by Youth Service," *New York Times*, December 7, 1936, 4.

39. John A. Hutchison, *We Are Not Divided* (New York: Round Table Press, 1941), 283.

40. Samuel Cavert to John A. Mackay, April 29, 1938, Mackay Collection.

41. John A. Mackay et al., "The State of the Church," in Federal Council of the Churches of Christ in America, *Biennial Report 1936* (New York, 1936), 41–48; Hutchison, *We Are Not Divided*, 98.

42. Mackay et al., "The State of the Church" (1938), 39.

43. Ibid., 37–45.

44. John A. Mackay, *The Universal Church and the World of Nations* (Philadelphia: Board of Christian Education of the Presbyterian Church in the U.S.A., 1937), A Seminar held June 2, 1937 at the 149th General Assembly, Columbus, Ohio.

45. John A. Mackay, "The Rôle of the Church as a World Force," in Jacques Maritain et al., *Religion and the Modern World* (Philadelphia: University of Pennsylvania Press, 1941), 137–49. Definition at 138–39.

46. Mackay also expressed these ideas and others in "The Adequacy of the Church Today," in *Corpus Unum*, Report of the North American Ecumenical Conference, University of Toronto, Toronto, Canada, June 3 to 5, 1941 (New York: Conference Committee, 1941), 28–38. Also in *Christendom* 6, no. 4 (Autumn 1941): 483–94.

47. Dennis L. Tarr, "The Presbyterian Church and the Founding of the United Nations," *Journal of Presbyterian History* 53, no. 1 (Spring 1975): 5.

48. Samuel M. Cavert to John A. Mackay, December 18, 1941, Mackay Collection; John Foster Dulles, "Peace without Platitudes," *Fortune Magazine*, January 1942, 42–43, 87, 88, 90.

49. Quoted in John M. Mulder, "The Moral World of John Foster Dulles: A Presbyterian Layman and International Affairs," *Journal of Presbyterian History* 49, no. 2 (Summer 1971): 167. Of his friendship with Dulles Mackay remarked, "looking at the matter objectively, there were two Dulleses—the Dulles that I knew in those contacts in church gatherings and the Dulles that emerged as Secretary of State" (177).

50. Quoted in Federal Council of the Churches of Christ in America, "The Relation of the Church to a Just and Durable Peace," in *A Message from the National Study Conference on The Churches and a Just and Durable Peace, Ohio Wesleyan University, Delaware, Ohio,*

March 3–5, 1942 (New York: Commission to Study the Bases of a Just and Durable Peace, [1942]), 6.

51. "American Malvern," *Time*, March 16, 1942, 44, 46–48. The Presbyterian delegates were the Rev. Ralph C. McAfee, Erie, Pennsylvania; President Harold W. Dodds of Princeton University; John Foster Dulles of New York City; Henry P. Van Dusen of Union Seminary; Wilbur LaRoe, Washington, DC; and John Mackay. See Dennis L. Tarr, "The Presbyterian Church and the Founding of the United Nations," *Journal of Presbyterian History* 53, no. 1 (Spring 1975): 5.

52. Federal Council, "The Relation of the Church," 15–18. On the work of the Conference, see also "The Churches and a Just and Durable Peace," *Christian Century* 59, no. 12 (March 25, 1942): 390–97. "The Church Is Not at War!" *Christian Century* (March 25, 1942): 375–77.

53. Federal Council of the Churches of Christ in America, *A Righteous Faith for a Just and Durable Peace* (New York: Commission to Study the Bases of a Just and Durable Peace, [1942]), 101.

54. "Faith and Future," *Time*, November 23, 1942, 104–106.

55. John A. Mackay, "The churches do not, however, have a primary responsibility to devise the details of world order. But they must proclaim the enduring moral principles by which human plans are constantly to be tested," in Federal Council, CCA, *A Righteous Faith*, 39–44.

56. "Under the Six Pillars, the Peace must provide or establish: 1. A political framework for a continuing collaboration of the United Nations and later of neutral and enemy nations; 2. International collaboration in economic and financial acts of national governments; 3. An organization to adapt the treaty structure of the world to changing underlying conditions; 4. International organizations to assure and to supervise the realization of autonomy for subject peoples; 5. Procedures for controlling military establishments everywhere; 6. In principle, and seek to achieve in practice, the right of individuals everywhere to religious and intellectual liberty" (cited in Thomas E. Dewey "'Six Pillars of Peace' Program of the Federal Council of Churches," *New York Times*, June 27, 1943, 18).

57. "A Christian Message on World Order," Mackay Collection.

58. John Foster Dulles to Tom Connally, October 22, 1943, Mackay Collection.

59. "Peace Seen as Big Test," *New York Times*, July 26, 1943, 10.

60. "Back Nations' Plan in Church Council," *New York Times*, November 29, 1944, 17.

61. John Foster Dulles, "Peace Is Precarious—Can We Keep It?" *New York Times*, August 18, 1945, sec. 6, 12, 34, 35; idem, "The General Assembly" *Foreign Affairs* 24, no. 1 (October 1945): 1–11.

62. John Foster Dulles, "Beyond Our Expectations," *Time*, July 2, 1945, 21. A paper titled "Dumbarton Oaks and San Francisco" by Henry R. Luce and others had appeared as a supplement to *Fortune*, May 1945. It analyzed the proposals and suggested improvements in the charter.

63. "The Report of the Committee on a Righteous Peace," Addressed to the 155th General Assembly (15 pages). Other lay members of the committee were Jasper Crane, Dr. William Mather Lewis, Walter E. Hope, and Thomas J. Watson, Mackay Collection.

64. Ibid., 8–9.

65. John Alexander Mackay, "The Titanic Twofold Challenge: Religion and Democracy Are Linked in the Dictators' Attack," *New York Times Magazine*, May 7, 1939, 1, 2, 17; idem, "Things That Cannot Be Shaken," *New York Times Magazine,* April 21, 1940, 3, 18; idem, "'ON EARTH PEACE'—A Christmas Meditation," *New York Times Magazine,* December 22, 1940, 3, 13; idem, "Needed: Great Faith to Match Great Faith." *New York Times*

Magazine, September 20, 1942, 3, 31; idem, "Ordeal by Fire: An Easter Message," *New York Times Magazine,* April 25, 1943, 5, 29.

66. John A. Mackay, "The Perils of Victory," *Social Progress* 36, no. 1 (September 1945): 1–2. It also appeared in *Christianity and Crisis* 5, no. 12 (July 9, 1945): 1.

67. John A. Mackay, "The Truth That Makes Men Free" (Universal Bible Sunday, 1939) for December 10, 1939, and in Spanish, "La Verdad que hace Libres a los Hombres"; "Yet Not Consumed" delivered on December 29, 1941 in the Second Presbyterian Church, Philadelphia, on the occasion of a special day of prayer called by the Presbytery of Philadelphia North, Mackay Collection.

68. "An International Prayer Meeting," *Christian Century* 59, no. 11 (March 18, 1942): 351.

69. John A. Mackay, "God and the Decisions of History," *Christianity and Crisis* 1, no. 21 (December 1, 1941): 2–5; idem, "The Church in This Land at War," *Social Progress* 32, no. 5 (January 1942): 1–3.

70. "Text of the Pope's Christmas Eve Address as Broadcast to the World," *New York Times,* December 25, 1943, 10.

71. Telegram from Roosevelt to Pope Pius, July 10, 1943. See Franklin Roosevelt, *Wartime Correspondence between President Roosevelt and Pope Pius XII* (New York: Macmillan Co., 1947), 93. The Pope replied to Franklin Roosevelt, July 19, 1943, that the Vatican should be recognized as a neutral state with respect to its properties, in a class with Switzerland, Portugal, and Spain (ibid., 95–97). Also see Nazareno Padellaro, *Portrait of Pius XII* (New York: E. P. Dutton, 1957), 203–204.

72. "Any Church 'Deal' on War Is Opposed," *New York Times,* February 10, 1945, 4; "Church & State," *Time,* February 19, 1945, 85. Ecumenicus [John A. Mackay], "The Papacy and the Nations," *Theology Today* 2, no. 1 (April 1945): 108–110. Cardinal Spellman saw this as "an insult to 25,000,000 fellow-Americans," *New York Times,* February 12, 1945, 21.

73. "Era of Anti-Christ Declared at Hand," *New York Times,* February 19, 1945.

74. "Protestants v. Catholics," *Time,* April 8, 1946, 69.

75. Gaetano Salvemini and George LaPiana, *What to Do with Italy* (New York: Duell, Sloan & Pearce, 1943), 244. See also D. A. Binchy, *Church and State in Fascist Italy* (London: Oxford University Press, 1941).

76. Thomas J. Hamilton, *Appeasement's Child: The Franco Regime in Spain* (New York: Alfred A. Knopf, 1943), 98.

77. Luigi Sturzo, "Politique et Théologie Morale" [Moral politics and theology], *Nouvelle Revue Théologique* 65, no. 8 (September–October 1938), 947–65, and Salvemini and LaPiana, *What to Do with Italy,* 95–99.

78. Luigi Sturzo, "The Ethics of Political Collaboration," in *Politics and Morality* (London: Burns, Oates & Washbourne, 1938), 79–94.

79. For example, John A. Mackay, "Our Future as Protestants," *Presbyterian Life* 4, no. 1 (January 6, 1951): 8–9, 30; summarized in "Strategy for Protestants," *Time,* January 8, 1951, 46–47.

80. Ecumenicus [John A. Mackay], "A Form of Apologetic That Harms the Church," *Theology Today* 2, no. 3 (October 1945): 384–86. John A. Mackay to Ilion T. Jones, January 26, 1945, Mackay Collection. John A. Mackay, introduction, "Spain's Quest for Freedom," in Jacques Delpech, *The Oppression of Protestants in Spain* (Boston: Beacon, 1955), 3–16.

81. Royal Institute of International Affairs, *The Republics of South America* (London: Oxford University Press, 1937); Heather J. Harvey to John A. Mackay, July 29, 1936, and Heather J.

Harvey to John A. Mackay, July 19, 1937, Mackay Collection. Mackay resigned from the Royal Institute of International Affairs in 1937 because he anticipated taking up American citizenship and therefore would no longer be eligible for membership (Ivison S. Macadam to John A. Mackay, July 2, 1937; July 12, 1937; and July 16, 1937; Letter, Viscount Astor to Institute members, October 15, 1936, Mackay Collection). Mackay became an American citizen in 1941.

82. Jean-Luc Barré, *Jacques & Raïssa Maritain* (Notre Dame, IN: University of Notre Dame Press, 2005), 331. The observation, made in December 19, 1937, continued to be accurate for years after it was written.

83. John A. Mackay, "The Friends of Spain," c. 1934, Mackay Collection.

84. "Hate of Clergy Laid to Spanish Hierarchy," *New York Times*, March 6, 1937, 6. Fisher's and Malraux's political views on communism differed markedly from those of Mackay.

85. On the religious element recognized at the time, see also Lawrence A. Fernsworth, "Back of the Spanish Rebellion," *Foreign Affairs* 15, no. 1 (October 1936): 87–101, an article that Inman drew to Mackay's attention. Polarization over Franco was exemplified in such articles as John Langdon-Davies, "The Case for the Government," *Atlantic Monthly*, March 1938, 403–408; and Ian D. Colvin, "The Case for Franco," *Atlantic Monthly*, March 1938, 397–402. By summer 1937, the Roman Church supported the Franco rebellion. See "Text of Pastoral Letter Signed by Spanish Prelates Justifying Franco Rebellion," *New York Times*, September 3, 1937, 4, 5; "Vatican declares the Franco rising 'legitimate,'" *New York Times*, September 3, 1937, 1.

86. "Hate of Clergy Laid to Spanish Hierarchy," *New York Times*, March 6, 1937, 6.

87. Gabriel Jackson, *The Spanish Republic and the Civil War 1931–1939* (Princeton, NJ: Princeton University Press, 1965), 31–32.

88. Claude Bowers, *My Mission to Spain* (New York: Simon & Schuster, 1954), 4–5.

89. See "The Crime of Guernica." There were seventy-six signers of the letter (see *Catholic Herald Citizen*, [Milwaukee], August 21, 1937, 1).

90. Cordell Hull, *Memoirs of Cordell Hull*, vol. 1 (New York: Macmillan Co., 1948), 505.

91. Quoted in "A Roman Attack on Bishop Oxnam," *The Churchman*, February 15, 1948, 6.

92. Emphasis in original. Barré, *Jacques & Raïssa Maritain,* 333.

93. Father Edwin Ryan, addressing a Catholic organization, said Protestant missionaries in Latin America were "preparing a generation of atheists. . . . The intense dislike for this country is largely the result of Protestant religious activities" ("Attacks Missions in Latin America," *New York Times*, April 8, 1931, 5). Another writer, however, disagreed, attributing any dislike to "the natural envy and fear which poor and weak people have for those better off and more powerful. It is constantly played on by Catholic leaders in order to discredit Protestant Missions" (Carlyle B. Haynes, letter to the editor, *New York Times*, April 15, 1931, 26).

94. "Religious Liberty or Monopoly," *Christian Century* 59, no. 30 (July 29, 1942): 925–26.

95. John W. White, *Argentina* (New York: Viking Press, 1942), 266–67.

96. The "Victory and Peace Statement" appeared in the *New York Times*, November 15, 1942, 52. Mackay recalled it later; see John A. Mackay, "Historical Perspectives of Protestantism," in *Integration of Man and Society in Latin America*, ed. Samuel Shapiro (Notre Dame, IN: Notre Dame University Press, 1967), 182–83. See also W. Stanley Rycroft, *Memoirs of Life in Three Worlds* (Cranbury, NJ: privately printed, 1976), 77.

97. John A. Mackay to Samuel Cavert, March 12, 1942, Mackay Collection.

98. John A. Mackay to Samuel Cavert, November 24, 1942, Mackay Collection.

99. "Our Heritage of Religious Freedom," *New York Times*, December 12, 1942, 12; published also in *Federal Council of Churches Bulletin* 26, no. 1 (January 1943): 9–10; "Churches Defend Religious Freedom," *Philadelphia Inquirer*, Saturday morning, December 12, 1942, 18.

100. Stanton R. Wilson, *John A. Mackay: Studies of an Ecumenical Churchman* (Th.M. thesis, Princeton Seminary, 1958), 99.

101. John A. Mackay, "Hierarchs, Missionaries, and Latin America," *Christianity and Crisis* 3, no. 7 (May 3, 1943): 2–5.

102. John W. White, *Good Neighbor Hurdle* (Milwaukee: Bruce Publishing Co., c. 1943).

103. John A. Mackay, Foreword to George P. Howard, *Religious Liberty in Latin America?* (Philadelphia: Westminster Press, 1944), vii–xiv.

104. [Micklem used the pen name "Ilico"], "Freedom of Religion," *British Weekly*, December 3, 1942. Those invited to the meeting at Columbia were Rev. R. P. Barnes, associate secretary, Federal Council of Churches; Father George B. Ford, adviser to Catholic students, Columbia University; John Mackay; Father W. Eugene Shiels of the staff of *America*; Dr. George N. Shuster, president, Hunter College; Father E. Harold Smith, pastor, St. Jerome's Church, the Bronx; Father Gerald Walsh, Fordham University; Dr. A. L. Warnshuis, International Missionary Council; and Dr. A. W. Wasson, Board of Missions and Church Extension, Methodist Church. F. Ernest Johnson to John A. Mackay, January 9, 1943, Mackay Collection. Ilico's article cited Alexander McLeish, "The Atlantic Charter Endangered," *World Dominion* 20, no. 6 (Nov/Dec. 1942): 351–54; and C. J. Cadoux, *Roman Catholicism and Freedom* (London: Independent Press, 1936).

105. John A. Mackay, "The Other Side of the 'Catholic Issue,'" *U.S. News & World Report*, July 4, 1960, 50.

106. For the Southern Presbyterian Church, see *New York Times*, June 2, 1943, 26; for the Northern Presbyterian Church, see *New York Times*, June 1, 1944, 13; for the Reformed Church, see *New York Times*, June 6, 1943, 35; and for the Baptist Church, see *New York Times*, May 18, 1944, 8.

107. Stanton R. Wilson, "John A. Mackay Studies of an Ecumenical Churchman" (ThM thesis, Princeton Seminary, 1958), 99.

108. R. B. Shipley to Joe J. Mickle, July 24, 1943 (copy); L. K. Anderson to John A. Mackay, July 29, 1943; John A. Mackay to Llewellyn K. Anderson, July 30, 1943 (copy); John A. Mackay to Francis B. Sayre, August 19, 1943 (copy); John A. Mackay to Mrs. R. B. Shipley, September 14, 1943 (copy); Samuel M. Hann to John A. Mackay, September 1, 1943; John A. Mackay to Samuel M. Hann, September 15, 1943 (copy), Mackay Collection. On Vatican political activities in Spain and Italy at the time, see Thomas Jefferson Hamilton, *Appeasement's Child, The Franco Regime in Spain* (New York: Alfred A. Knopf, 1943); and Salvemini and La Piana, *What to Do with Italy*.

109. "Executive Committee on Cooperation in Latin America Meeting, Held June 15, 1944," Mackay Collection. During the period January 1, 1944, to June 15, 1944, fourteen boards reported: 25 applications for passports, 21 granted, 4 refused. Canadians received 3 out of 3 applied for. All had experienced unreasonable delays.

110. "Religion Not Involved, Hull says," *New York Times*, May 27, 1944, 16.

111. "Missionaries Get Equal Treatment," *New York Times*, November 26, 1944, 28; Emory Ross, "Religious Liberty Is at Stake!" *Christian Century* 62, no. 1 (January 3, 1945): 12–13.

112. John J. Considine, MM, *Call for Forty Thousand* (New York: Longmans, Green & Co., 1946); Peter Masten Dunne, SJ, *A Padre Views South America* (Milwaukee: Bruce Pub-

lishing Co., 1945); John A. Mackay, "Historical Perspectives of Protestantism" in *Integration of Man and Society in Latin America*, ed. Samuel Shapiro (Notre Dame, IN: University of Notre Dame Press, 1968), 183.

113. The six members of the committee appointed by the FCC and the IMC were John A. Mackay, E. E. Fischer, N. J. Padelford, H. P. Van Dusen, A. L. Warnshuis, and A. W. Wasson. Staff representatives who served in a consultative capacity were L. S. Albright, R. P. Barnes, M. S. Bates, Inez M. Cavert, J. W. Decker, F. E. Johnson, and E. Ross (see O. Frederick Nolde, "Constitution and Work of the Joint Committee on Religious Liberty," July 5, 1944).

114. John A. Mackay, "The Concept of Religious Liberty," May 8, 1943, Mackay Collection. Mackay resigned the chairmanship and membership of the committee in October 1944. He was connected with fifty outside organizations at that time and had to limit his participation. John A. Mackay to L. S. Albright, copy, October 18, 1944, Mackay Collection. On early aspects of the movement for religious liberty and human rights see Henry Smith Leiper, "Religious Liberty in Russia Weighed," *New York Times*, June 12, 1943, 14; and John S. Nurser, *For All Peoples and All Nations—The Ecumenical Church and Human Rights* (Washington, DC: Georgetown University Press, 2005). Frederick Nolde, executive secretary of the Joint Committee, issued a pamphlet drawing attention to these issues (see "Churches in Drive for Human Rights," *New York Times*, November 25, 1944, 15).

115. John Courtney Murray, "Current Theology Freedom of Religion," *Theological Studies* 6, no. 1 (March 1945): 85–113.

116. John A. Mackay, "As Regards Freedom of Religion," *Theology Today* 2, no. 4 (January 1946): 429–35, and reprinted in idem, *Christianity on the Frontier* (New York: Macmillan Co., 1950), 143–52.

117. Mackay, "As Regards Freedom," in *Christianity on the Frontier*, 151.

118. Ibid., 152. Mackay then offered a definition. "Clericalism is the pursuit of political power by a religious hierarchy, carried on by secular methods and for purposes of social domination." On the persistence of religious clericalism, see Russell Shaw, *To Hunt, To Shoot, To Entertain: Clericalism and the Catholic Laity* (San Francisco: Ignatius Press, 1993); and Richard John Neuhaus, "Clerical Scandal and the Scandal of Clericalism," *First Things*, March, 2008, 57–60.

119. Mackay, "As Regards Freedom," in *Christianity on the Frontier*, 152.

120. John A. Mackay, "Protestantism," in *The Great Religions of the Modern World*, ed. Edward J. Jurji (Princeton, NJ: Princeton University Press, 1946), 337–70; republished in Mackay, *Christianity on the Frontier*, 97–142.

121. John A. Mackay, "Personal Religion," *Princeton Seminary Bulletin* 37, no. 1 (December 1943): 3–10. The address opened the academic year at Princeton Seminary on September 22, 1943.

122. Pope Leo XIII, *Immortale Dei* (On the Christian Constitution of States), November 1, 1885, para. 36. See also Zachary R. Calo, "'The Indispensable Basis of Democracy': American Catholicism, the Church-State Debate, and the Soul of American Liberalism, 1920–1929," *Virginia Law Review* 91, no. 4 (June 2005): 1046.

123. Three editions of the standard Roman Catholic book on church-state relations contain this interpretation: John A. Ryan and Moorhouse F. X. Millar, *The State and the Church* (New York: Macmillan Co., 1927), 60; John A. Ryan and Francis Boland, *Catholic Principles of Politics* (New York: Macmillan Co., 1940), 342; and John A. Ryan and Francis J. Boland, *Catholic Principles of Politics* (New York: Macmillan Co., 1952), 342. In light of the teaching, the clergy in Peru struggled to maintain a Catholic society even after the national constitutional amendment accommodating other faiths had been adopted.

124. Resistance to change was strong. About a decade later in 1955, Murray's own progressive work was silenced by censors in Rome. See Gerald P. Fogarty, *The Vatican and the American Hierarchy from 1870 to 1965* (Stuttgart: Anton Hiersemann, 1982), 381.

125. John Courtney Murray, *Thought* 16, no. 61 (June 1941): 396.

126. "At the end of a long time of separation deep differences of mentality divide us today, not so much as regards the solution of problems as the actual way of approaching them. . . . Catholics, Protestants, Orthodox, Anglicans—we have the same God, but we cannot agree about the nature of our relations with Him." Georges-Yves Congar, *Chrétiens Désunis* (Paris, 1937), 47; translated by M. A. Bousfield as *Divided Christendom* (London: Geoffrey Bles, 1939), 39. At the dash Congar's translator omits a clause that appears in the review quotation and the original text: "nous sommes devenues *des hommes différents* (roughly, "we evolved into *different men*") (italics in original).

127. "Protestants Urged to Work for Unity," *New York Times*, March 15, 1946, 6.

128. "Clericalism & Vilification," *Time*, March 25, 1946, 72. *Time* published a portion of Mackay's complete statement in which he wrote, "The Protestant Reformation was not a schism *from* the Church, it was a schism *in* the Church. Protestant Christians lay claim to the evangelical core of the whole Christian tradition, Biblical and Apostolic, patristic and medieval.

> "Two things fill me with concern with respect to present trends in our great sister communion, the Roman Catholic, in this country. The first is its increasing commitment to a Roman, as distinguished from the traditionally independent policy of American Catholicism. Such a policy has invariably produced in history the phenomenon called Clericalism, from which we have been providentially spared in the United States. Clericalism is the pursuit of power, especially political power, by a religious hierarchy, carried on by secular methods and for purposes of social domination.
>
> "My second concern goes deeper. It is the practice, lately initiated in the official Catholic press in this country to attack, in a most unworthy way, the Protestant Reformation and its great leaders, particularly Martin Luther and John Calvin. Here is an example of what I mean. In a recent number (February 3, 1946) of a leading Catholic journal, *Our Sunday Visitor: 'The Popular National Catholic Action Weekly,'* the following occurs: 'Calvin, in his *Commentary on Second Epistle of Peter*, wrote: "Among a hundred Evangelicals, scarcely one can be found who became an Evangelical for any other motive than to be able to abandon himself with greater freedom to all kinds of pleasures and lusts."' I have two remarks to make. First: these words do not occur in either the English or the Latin version of Calvin's *Commentary on Second Peter*. Second: John Calvin never wrote these words anywhere. I plead with distinguished Roman Catholic scholars that they frown upon and repudiate this kind of approach to the religious problem" (emphasis in original).

129. "Separation of Church and State: A Manifesto," *Review and Expositor* 45, no. 2 (April 1948): 143–54. The first elected officers were (1) President: Dr. Edwin McNeill Poteat, president, Colgate-Rochester Divinity School; (2) vice presidents: Bishop G. Bromley Oxnam, New York area of the Methodist Church; Charles Clayton Morrison, founder of the *Christian Century*; and Dr. John A. Mackay, president, Princeton Theological Seminary; (3) recording secretary: Joseph Martin Dawson, executive secretary, Baptist Joint Committee on Public Relations; and (4) treasurer: E. H. DeGroot Jr. On Bishop Oxnam's involvement, see Robert Moats Miller, *Bishop G. Bromley Oxnam* (Nashville: Abingdon Press, 1990), 405–406.

130. "Implacable Foes of Church Unite to Make Trouble," *The Tablet*, January 17, 1948, 1, 6; see later criticism in "The Real Mackay," *America*, December 1, 1951, 242.

131. Thomas T. Love, *John Courtney Murray: Contemporary Church-State Theory* (Garden City, NY: Doubleday & Co., 1965), 13–14. Love defines the period of Murray's "dissatisfaction and confusion" as 1942–1946.

132. Love, *John Courtney Murray*, 54. Love dates this interlude characterized by attacks against Protestants from December 1946 through March 1948.

133. John Courtney Murray, SJ, "Religious Liberty: The Concern of All," *America*, February 7, 1948, 513–16, at 514.

134. Ibid., 515.

135. In Peru constitutional rights of worship had been abridged by government decree in January 1945. John Ritchie, "Protestants Restricted," *Christian Century* 62, no. 5 (January 31, 1945): 154.

136. "Catholics & Tolerance," *Time*, August 3, 1953, 41. For a progressive Roman Catholic's view of Ottaviani, see Leon-Joseph Cardinal Suenens, *Memories and Hopes*, trans. Elena French (Dublin: Veritas, 1992), 75–78.

137. Roland H. Bainton, "Catholic-Protestant Relations in the United States," *The United Presbyterian*, October 25, 1954, 11. The 1953 concordat was replaced by four agreements in January 1979.

138. C. L. Sulzberger, "Spaniards' Church Outrivals Falange. Catholic Institutions Are More Important in Their Political and Cultural Impact," *New York Times*, February 8, 1951, 9; Sam Pope Brewer, "Spain Will Expel Protestant Aides," *New York Times*, Sunday, February 25, 1951, 21; "Spain Persecution of Protestants Worst in Many Years," *The Churchman*, April 1, 1952, 19.

139. Quoted in Sulzberger, "Spaniards' Church Outrivals Falange," 9.

140. Camille M. Cianfarra, "Spanish Cardinal Denounces 'Benevolence' to Protestants," *New York Times*, March 10, 1952, 1, 4; idem, "Protestant Cleric Is Beaten in Spain," *New York Times*, March 6, 1952, 8. General Franco tried to distance himself from the position of certain clerics; idem, "Franco to Ask the Vatican to Curb Cardinal's Criticism of His Regime," *New York Times*, May 5, 1952, 1, 7. Franco believed that Cardinal Segura was mad; see Raymond Carr and Juan Pablo Fusi Aizpurua, *Spain: Dictatorship to Democracy* (London: George Allen & Unwin, 1981), 152.

141. Sulzberger, "Spaniards' Church Outrivals Falange," 9. The figure "30,000" may be exaggerated. The next year the Spanish Government reported the figure of 20,000, of whom half were foreigners. See Cianfarra, "Spanish Cardinal Denounces," 4.

142. "Church Here Praised for Racial Harmony," *New York Times*, March 29, 1948, 15; John A. Mackay to the Reverend Alfonso Lloreda, Ibague, Colombia, June 25, 1948, Mackay Collection. "It seems perfectly clear that clericalism was more responsible for the trouble than the Communists," wrote Mackay.

143. John D. Martz, *Colombia: A Contemporary Political Survey* (Chapel Hill: University of North Carolina Press, 1962), 55–68.

144. Ibid., 87, 147–50.

145. Germán Arciniegas, *The State of Latin America* (New York: Alfred A. Knopf, 1952), 163.

146. Goff wrote Mackay, "The signed statements we are collecting indicate a campaign of persecution which surpasses anything we had previously imagined. There is unsurpassed cruelty and sadism in many cases. I have wept over several stories I have written up" (James E. Goff to John A. Mackay, December 30, 1951, Mackay Collection). See W. Stanley Rycroft, "The Persecution of Protestants in Colombia," *Presbyterian World* 22, no. 1 (March 1953):

2–9; "It Happened in Colombia," *The Churchman*, April 15, 1952, 7–8; "Colombia," *The Churchman*, May 1, 1952, 25.

147. "Words & Works," *Time*, October 5, 1953, 72.

148. Tad Szulc, "Religious Abuses Grow in Colombia," *New York Times*, March 24, 1956, 9.

149. Martz, *Colombia*, 220–21. Szulc, "Religious Abuses," 9; Tad Szulc, "Colombia Church Replies to Exile," *New York Times*, March 25, 1956, 34.

150. Mackay's view followed the English rule. See Ti-Chiang Chen, "The Declaratory or *De Facto* Doctrine," in *The International Law of Recognition* (New York: Frederick A. Praeger, 1951), 117–30.

151. John K. Fairbank, Edwin O. Reischauer, and Albert M. Craig, *East Asia: The Modern Transformation* (Boston: Houghton Mifflin Co., 1965), 862.

152. Raymond Daniell, "Britain Announces Her Recognition of Peiping Regime," *New York Times*, January 7, 1950, 1 and 4.

153. "Peiping Accepts Britain's Offer," *New York Times*, January 10, 1950, 32.

154. "Recognition Is Urged for Chinese Regime," *New York Times*, January 5, 1950, 8.

155. Ibid.

156. "Recognize Red China, Mission Leaders Ask," *New York Times*, April 29, 1950, 16. They included Rev. Dr. Earle H. Ballou, the Rev. Dr. Charles L. Boynton, the Rev. Dr. Leland S. Brubaker, the Rev. Dr. Frank T. Cartwright, the Rev. Dr. Rowland M. Cross, the Rev. Dr. John W. Decker, the Rev. Dr. Wynn C. Fairfield, the Rev. Theodore F. Romig, the Rev. Dr. Lloyd S. Ruland, the Rev. Dr. Luman J. Shafer, Mrs. Arthur M. Sherman, and the Rev. Dr. Everett M. Stowe.

157. John A. Mackay, letter to the editor, *New York Times*, August 28, 1950, 16. Excerpts are reprinted in "China—Dr. John Mackay Makes Plain His Stand," *Social Progress* 41, no. 5 (December 1950): 18–20.

158. John D. Hayes, interview, "I Saw Red China from the Inside," *U.S. News & World Report*, March 13, 1953, 26–39; Sara Perkins, "My Years behind Bamboo Bars," *Presbyterian Life*, February 15, 1963, 12–15, 36; and March 1, 1963, 19–20, 36–37.

159. "Church Women Hit Radio, TV Beer Ads," *New York Times*, November 16, 1950, 47. John A. Mackay, "It Is Springtime in East Asia," *Current Religious Thought* 10, no. 9 (November 1950): 28.

160. George Dugan, "A Church Mission to China Is Urged," *New York Times*, December 11, 1956, 9; idem, "Church Contacts with China Urged," *New York Times*, December 13, 1956, 4; "Mackay Asks Visit by Press to China," *New York Times*, January 21, 1957, 31; George Dugan, "Churchman Cool to Visiting China," *New York Times*, January 18, 1957, 7.

161. "Text of U.S. Policy Statement on Non-Recognition of Communist Regime in China," *New York Times*, August 10, 1958, 30.

162. Henry Kissinger, *Years of Upheaval* (Boston: Little, Brown & Co., 1982), 63.

163. Henry K. Sherrill to John Mackay, October 23, 1952; Mackay confirmed his acceptance of the mandate in a letter to the bishop, November 5, 1952, Mackay Collection.

164. "Text of Statement by Catholic Bishops on Secularism and Schools," *New York Times*, November 16, 1952, 80.

165. J. Howard Pew to John A. Mackay, December 4, 1952, Mackay Collection.

166. "The National Council: Cooperation Counts," *Presbyterian Life*, January 10, 1953, 20.

167. See "Text of National Council's Letter to Christian People of America," from the General Assembly of the National Council of the Churches of Christ in the U.S.A., *New York Times*, December 13, 1952, 17. For excerpts, see "The Churches Speak Out," *National Council Outlook* 3, no. 1 (January 1953): 14, 16. The letter was serialized in "A Letter to the Christian People of America," *Presbyterian Outlook*, January 19, 1953, 4; January 26, 1953, 7; February 2, 1953, 6–7; February 9, 1953, 7; and February 16, 1953, 6–7.

168. George Cornell, "Protestants Warn of Road to War," *Louisville Courier-Journal*, December 13, 1952, 1.

169. John A. Mackay to J. Howard Pew, December 18, 1952, Mackay Collection.

170. "A Letter," *Presbyterian Outlook*, January 26, 1953, 7.

171. Russell Porter, "Churchmen Assail Congress's 'Abuses' in School Red Hunt," *New York Times*, March 12, 1953, 1; "Text of Council's Statement," *New York Times*, March 12, 1953, 13. The Council represented thirty Protestant and Eastern Orthodox communions having about 35,000,000 members. See also Editorial, "A Stand for Freedom," *New York Times*, March 13, 1953, 26.

172. John A. Mackay to Samuel M. Cavert, January 11, 1951, Mackay Collection.

173. John A. Mackay to J. Howard Pew, April 14, 1952, Mackay Collection.

174. National Council of the Churches of Christ in the United States of America, National Lay Committee, *The Chairman's Final Report to the National Lay Committee: June 16, 1950–June 30, 1955* [J. Howard Pew, Chairman] (Philadelphia: 1955).

175. In John A. Mackay, "Thoughts on the National Council of the Churches of Christ in the U.S.A.," Paper submitted to Donald C. Bolles of the council too late for inclusion in *Outlook* (October 30, 1957), Mackay Collection, Mackay states "As one who was close to the old Federal Council and to the National Council in the first years after its founding, I am happy to offer a few reflections on the Council's life and witness.

> "I am quite clear that the organization of the National Council of Churches, integrating in its structure a number of hitherto separate organizations, was a wise and creative move. American Protestantism was given a potent, representative voice, while an effective instrument was forged for cooperative action. I rejoice in all that has been accomplished.
>
> "Nevertheless certain things concern me. One is the size, the complexity, and the costliness of the new structure. It gives me concern, moreover, lest the cost of carrying on the Council's work should make its leadership defer unduly to the particular opinions of those who contribute heavily to its ongoing program.
>
> "I am especially concerned that the voice of prophecy be not stifled or silenced. Careful study needs to be given to the [current] process which is . . . in my judgment unduly long and complex, before a vital issue which may be controversial in character can be discussed on the floor of the General Board. It would be tragic, and could be disastrous, if it became routine policy that grave but unpopular public issues, in which the churches and Protestant Christianity in general have a stake, should die or be shelved in one of the Council's many committees and so never reach a public forum."

176. "8-Church Group in Dobbs Ferry Hears Rome Envoy Idea Assailed," *The Herald Statesman* (Yonkers, NY), October 22, 1951, 1, 2.

177. "Protestant Heads in Plea to Truman," *New York Times*, October 30, 1951, 19. Among the signers were Mackay, Henry Sloane Coffin, Henry Pitney Van Dusen, Norman Vincent Peale, Robert J. McCracken, A. L. Kinsolving, Harry Emerson Fosdick, and Franklin Clark

Fry. For the story of Vatican diplomacy related to the issue of U.S. recognition, see Gerald P. Fogarty, *Vatican-American Relations 1940–1984* (Notre Dame, IN: University of Notre Dame Press, 1984). United States law was changed in 1983 to permit diplomatic relations with the Vatican (Pub. L. 98–164, Title I, §134, Nov. 22, 1983, 97 Stat. 1029. 22 U.S.C.A. 2656 note).

178. Black had a negative viewpoint toward the Roman Catholic Church. See Hugo Black Jr., *My Father* (New York: Random House, 1974), 104; Philip Hamburger, *Separation of Church and State* (Cambridge, MA: Harvard University Press, 2002): 422–34, 463. Two early court opinions were *Everson v. Board of Education*, 330 U.S. 1 (1947) and *People of State of Illinois ex rel. McCollum v. Board of Education of School Dist. No. 71, Champaign County, Illinois*, 333 U.S. 203 (1948).

179. *Everson v. Board of Education*, 15–16.

180. Hamburger, *Separation of Church and State,* 480.

181. Mark DeWolf Howe, *The Garden and the Wilderness: Religion and Government in American Constitutional History* (Chicago: University of Chicago Press, 1965), 157. Black categorized Secular Humanism (capitalized) as a religion, *Torcaso v. Watkins*, 367 U.S. 488 (1961), note 11. Chief Justice Rehnquist dissented against the line of jurisprudential development from the "wall theory" and called for it to be overturned, *Wallace v. Jaffree*, 472 U.S. 38 (1985), 91–114.

Black's historical theory of the application of the Bill of Rights to the states set forth in *Adamson v. People of State of California*, 332 U.S. 46 (1947), 68–123, was also challenged on historical grounds. Charles Fairman, "Does the Fourteenth Amendment Incorporate the Bill of Rights?" *Stanford Law Review* 2 (December 1949): 5–139. Justice Harlan found the "overwhelming historical evidence marshaled by Professor Fairman" conclusive, *Duncan v. Louisiana*, 391 U.S. 145 (1968), 194.

182. Stewart J. Brown, "The Ten Years' Conflict and the Disruption of 1843," in *Scotland in the Age of the Disruption*, ed. Stewart J. Brown and Michael Fry (Edinburgh: Edinburgh University Press, 1993), 12–13.

183. Mackay, *Ecumenics*, 259.

184. Mackay, "Religion and Government: Their Separate Spheres and Reciprocal Responsibilities," *Theology Today* 9, no. 2 (July 1952): 206–207 (an address delivered in Constitution Hall, Washington, DC, under the auspices of Protestants and Other Americans United for the Separation of Church and State).

185. Alexander Stewart and J. Kennedy Cameron, *The Free Church of Scotland 1843–1910* (Edinburgh and Glasgow: William Hodge & Co., 1910); Stewart J. Brown, *Thomas Chalmers and the Godly Commonwealth in Scotland* (Oxford: Oxford University Press, 1982).

186. John A. Mackay, "Church, State, and Freedom," *Theology Today* 8, no. 2 (July 1951): 218–33; and idem, "Religion and Government: Their Separate Spheres and Reciprocal Responsibilities," *Theology Today* 9, no. 2 (July 1952): 204–22.

187. Glenn L. Archer and Albert J. Menendez, *The Dream Lives On: The Story of Glenn L. Archer and Americans United* (Washington, DC: R. B. Luce, 1982), 117–18; Thomas Sugrue, *A Catholic Speaks His Mind on America's Religious Conflict* (New York: Harper & Bros., 1952). The spiritual commentary in Sugrue's book is eloquent. For Mackay's address, see Mackay, "Religion and Government," 204–22.

188. Mackay, "Religion and Government," 207.

189. Ibid., 211. Kenneth Dole, "POAU Leader Urges Time for Religion," *Washington Post*, April 23, 1952, B1. On "released time" see *Zorach v. Clauson*, 343 U.S. 306 (1952).

190. John A. Mackay, "Religion and Government in the World of Today," *Review and Expositor* 60, no. 3 (1963): 277–86, at 286.

191. Pope Pius XI, *Mortalium Animos* (On Religious Unity), January 6, 1928, point 8. But American federalism had an "affinity" with Presbyterianism. See Jeffry H. Morrison, *John Witherspoon and the Founding of the American Republic* (Notre Dame, IN: University of Notre Dame Press, 2005), note 78 at 177–78 and related text.

192. John A. Mackay, "The Cleric of Clericalism," review of *The Cardinal Spellman Story*, by Robert I. Gannon, SJ, *Christianity Today* 6, no. 20 (July 6, 1962): 42. On Spellman's attitude to film censorship see the opinion of Felix Frankfurter in *Joseph Burstyn, Inc. v. Wilson*, 343 U.S. 495 (1952), 507–40.

193. Herrymon Maurer, "The Tyrannous Decade," *Fortune*, February 1948, 113–19, 150, 152–54, 156–58. Frederick W. Marks, *Wind over Sand* (Athens: University of Georgia Press, 1988).

194. "'Catholics who profess, and particularly those who defend and spread, the materialistic and anti-Christian doctrine of the Communists, *ipso facto*, as apostates form the Catholic Faith, incur excommunication'" (quoted in Nazareno Padellaro, *Portrait of Pius XII* [New York: E. P. Dutton, 1957], 223). The historic distinction between communism and a communist, separating the individual from the movement, came in Pope John XXIII's *Pacem in Terris* (Peace on Earth), April 11, 1963. "One must never confuse error and the person who errs, not even when there is a question of error or inadequate knowledge of truth. . . . The person who errs is always and above all a human being and he retains in every case his dignity as a human person" (sec. 158); and "'Salvation and justice are not to be found in revolution, but in evolution through concord'" (sec. 162).

195. John Cooney, *The American Pope: The Life and Times of Francis Cardinal Spellman* (New York: Times Books, 1984), 219. Many Roman Catholic clergymen supported McCarthy. Notable exceptions were Fr. George Ford, chaplain at Columbia University, and Bishop Bernard J. Sheil, of Chicago.

196. Ibid., 229. Spellman's relationship with McCarthy is documented at 217–30. For the Roman Catholic Perspective see Donald F. Crosby, SJ, "Protestant-Catholic Tensions and the McCarthy Issue," in *God, Church, and Flag* (Chapel Hill: University of North Carolina Press, 1978), 118–46. For contrasting approaches to communism at this time see G. Bromley Oxnam, "How the Protestants Fight Communism," *Look*, October 11, 1949, 23–25; and Francis Cardinal Spellman's article, "The Pope's War on Communism," *Look*, May 24, 1949, 25–27. Oxnam wrote, "Communism does not grow in the soil of freedom and justice. It takes root in the soil of exploitation" (see G. Bromley Oxnam, "Impostures of Pretended Patriotism," *The Churchman*, March 15, 1948, 8).

197. Cooney, *American Pope,* 219–20; Crosby, *God, Church, and Flag*, 47–52. Crosby defends Edmund Walsh, who never publicly denied the story of the dinner at the Colony Restaurant. It is of interest that as a scholar of foreign relations in an article in the *Washington Star*, Fr. Walsh seemed to support the concept of a "preventative" war. See "E. A. Walsh, S.J. Finds Moral Reasons for 'Defensive' Attack," *The Churchman*, February 15, 1951, 26–27.

198. "Two Candidates Endorsed for Assembly Moderator," *Presbyterian Life*, May 16, 1953, 23. Christie, pastor of the Westminster Presbyterian Church, Wilmington, Delaware, a church with 1,800 members, had an impressive academic background and had taught church history.

199. "The Church Chooses a New Moderator," *Presbyterian Life*, June 13, 1953, 20; George Dugan, "Mackay Elected by Presbyterians," *New York Times*, May 29, 1953, 23.

200. Dugan, "Mackay Elected," 23.

201. "Heard at General Assembly," *Presbyterian Life*, June 27, 1953, 22–23. The statement "The New Idolatry" was also published in *Theology Today* 10, no. 3 (October 1953): 382–83,

and *Christianity and Crisis* 13, no. 12 (July 6, 1953): 93–95. See also George Dugan "Presby-terian Hits New Anti-Red Cult," *New York Times*, May 30, 1953, 16. At that time, according to the *New York Times*, May 30, 1953, the Presbyterian Church in the U.S.A. (Northern) had about 2,483,000 members; the Presbyterian Church in the U.S. (Southern), 702,000; and the United Presbyterian Church, 220,000, for a total of about 3,500,000.

202. "Mackay Named USA Moderator on First Minneapolis Ballot," *Presbyterian Outlook* 135, no. 23 (June 8, 1953): 3.

203. "Moderator Mackay Tours Argentina," *Presbyterian Life*, September 19, 1953, 20–21.

204. "Presbyterian Moderators Speak Out for Union," *Presbyterian Life*, October 31, 1953, 18. The three moderators are pictured together on the cover of *Presbyterian Outlook*, vol. 136, no. 20 (May 24, 1954).

205. John A. Mackay, "Report to the Church," *Presbyterian Life*, May 15, 1954, 11, 12, 34, 35.

206. J. B. Matthews, "Reds and Our Churches," *American Mercury*, July 1953, 3–14, at 11. *The American Mercury* had been founded by H. L. Mencken. About Matthews's unusual background, see *Time*, August 10, 1953, 67.

207. See account in Fred J. Cook, *The Nightmare Decade* (New York: Random House, 1971), 429–33. Senators John L. McClellan and Jackson, Symington, and Monroney pushed McCarthy in the Senate. Dr. John Sutherland Bonnell, Msgr. John A. O'Brien, and Rabbi Maurice N. Eisendrath sent Eisenhower a telegram that precipitated Matthews's departure.

208. "The World Church: News and Notes: Mackay vs Matthews," *Christianity and Crisis* 13, no. 14 (August 3, 1953): 110. See also "Cleric Repudiates Matthews Charge," *New York Times*, July 12, 1953, 29.

209. "The World Church: News and Notes," 111.

210. R. N., "Will We Resist Injustice?" *Christianity and Crisis* 13, no. 6 (April 13, 1953), 41–42; John C. Bennett, "The Protestant Clergy and Communism," *Christianity and Crisis* 13, no. 14 (August 3, 1953): 107–10; H. P. V. D., "Can the Churches Halt 'McCarthyism'?" *Christianity and Crisis* 13, no. 14 (August 3, 1953): 105–106; G. Bromley Oxnam, *I Protest* (New York: Harper & Bros., 1954).

211. "Take Good Look at 'Oxnam & Friends,'" *Catholic Sentinel* (Portland, Oregon), Feb-ruary 20, 1958, 7. The article noted that "The *Wanderer* in St. Paul took three issues starting June 16, 1955, to list his record of helping commie causes."

212. See, for example, John Alexander Mackay, "A Letter to Presbyterians," *Princeton Seminary Bulletin*, n.s., 5, no. 3 (November 1984): 197–202; published as "This Nation under God," *Presbyterian Life* 6, no. 22 (1953): 10–11; published as "Our Freedom under God," *Social Progress* 44 (May 1954): 3–23 (includes a study guide); *Social Progress* 56, no. 2 (November–December 1965): 5–10. See document and related story in George Dugan, "Pres-byterians Warn on Methods Used Here in Fight on Communism," *New York Times*, November 3, 1953, 1; the letter appeared on 20. An editorial in the *New York Times* called it a "profoundly anti-Communist document" and pointed to some traps in the struggle against communism (*New York Times*, November 4, 1953, 32). Also see Daniel L. Migliore, "'The Majesty of Truth': Meditation on 'A Letter to Presbyterians,' 1954," *Princeton Seminary Bulletin*, n.s., 6, no 2 (1985): 78–80; James H. Smylie, "Mackay and McCarthyism, 1953–1954," *Journal of Church and State* 6, no. 3 (Autumn 1964): 352–65; Rick Nutt, "For Truth and Liberty: Pres-byterians and McCarthyism," *Journal of Presbyterian History* 78, no. 1 (Spring 2000): 51–66; K. Stephen Parmelee, "The Presbyterian Letter against McCarthyism," *Journal of Presbyterian*

History 41, no. 4 (December 1963): 201–23. The letter's first five paragraphs dealing with procedural issues were added by Eugene Carson Blake.

213. Parmelee, "The Presbyterian Letter," 216.

214. Mackay, "A Letter to Presbyterians," 199. Social science also suggested the wisdom of avoiding specific policy pronouncements. See Robert K. Merton, "The Unanticipated Consequences of Purposive Social Action," *American Sociological Review* 1, no. 6 (December 1936): 894–904.

215. Henri Pierre, "L'Eglise Presbytérienne Americaine Diffuse un Manifest Contre le Maccarthysme et l'Anticommunisme Négatif" [The American Presbyterian Church publishes a manifesto against McCarthyism and negative anti-communism], *Le Monde*, November 6, 1953, 1, 2.

216. "Poling Gives Alert on Reds in Pulpit," *New York Times*, September 14, 1953, 22.

217. "Dr. Poling's Confused Jumble," *Presbyterian Outlook* 136, no. 21 (May 31, 1954): 8.

218. Edward A. Dowey Jr., "Poling and the Presbyterian Letter," *Christianity and Crisis* 14, no. 16 (October 4, 1954): 124–27.

219. Daniel L. Migliore, "A Conversation with Edward A. Dowey," *Princeton Seminary Bulletin*, n.s., 9, no. 2 (1988): 94.

220. "Two Forces Called Anti-Protestant," *New York Times*, December 16, 1953, 21; "The Stated Clerk's View," *Time*, December 28, 1953, 33.

221. William O. Douglas to Dr. Mackay, January 4, 1954, Mackay Collection. See *U.S.A. v. Nugent*, 346 U.S. 1 (1953) and note dissent by Frankfurter, Black, and Douglas. The court held that a conscientious objector had no right under the Fifth Amendment to confront witnesses against his claim of conscientious objection. The appellant was not permitted to see the FBI report or to see the names of persons interviewed by investigators. In his *Almanac of Liberty* Douglas designated October 21, the day the General Council adopted the "Letter to Presbyterians," as a commemoration day for the letter, which he referred to as "The Presbyterian Manifesto of 1953" (William O. Douglas, *An Almanac of Liberty* [Garden City, NY: Doubleday & Co., 1954], 116).

222. "Dr. Mackay Defies Slurs on Record," *New York Times*, April 2, 1954, 12.

223. Ibid.

224. William Benton, "Europe and Senator McCarthy," *The Fortnightly*, April 1954, 219.

225. M. A. Jones to Mr. Nichols, Office Memorandum, June 2, 1955; M. A. Jones to Mr. Nichols, Office Memorandum, June 16, 1955; J. Edgar Hoover to the Groenke Organization, Cincinnati, Ohio, July 15, 1960, letter and notes thereon. Copies of documents released by the Federal Bureau of Investigation to the author under the Freedom of Information/Privacy Acts. Private Collection.

226. George Dugan, "Church Head Hits 'Patriotic Lying,'" *New York Times*, May 21, 1954, 13. Poling made a strong reply to Mackay's address in Detroit. See "Mundt Endorses Work of Inquiries," *New York Times*, May 22, 1954, 6.

227. "The Presbyterian Letter: A Vote of Confidence," *Presbyterian Life*, June 12, 1954, 13.

228. Ibid. See also George Dugan, "Inquiry Criticism Upheld by Church," *New York Times*, May 25, 1954, 17.

229. Mackay received the citation for 1954 of *The Upper Room*, the world's most widely used devotional guide. The citation was presented at the annual dinner held at the National Press Club in Washington, DC, where Francis Sayre delivered the tribute (*The Upper Room*

20, no. 4 [September–October, 1954]). His address was later published in the *Congressional Record* (see "Address of Hon. Francis B. Sayre in Tribute to Dr. John A. Mackay," Extension of Remarks of Hon. Brooks Hays of Arkansas in the House of Representatives, *Congressional Record* (January 13, 1955), A143–A145.

230. "Nixon Rebutted on Catholicism," *New York Times*, February 16, 1955, 11.

231. P. Damboriena, "Protestantesimo e Comunismo nell'America Latina" [Protestantism and Communism in Latin America], *La Civiltà Cattolica* Anno 107° 1 (1956): 382–96.

232. Stanley Rowland Jr., "End Racial Bars, Church Is Urged," *New York Times*, December 31, 1955, 6.

233. The sermon, "Gateway to Wisdom," was based on Psalm 111:10, "The fear of the LORD is the beginning of wisdom" ("Minister Contrasts Brotherhood Views of Marx and Christ," *New York Times*, July 2, 1956, 22).

234. Pope Pius XII, Apostolic Constitution, *Munificentissimus Deus* (The Most Bountiful God), November 1, 1950.

235. John Mackay, review of *The Riddle of Roman Catholicism* by Jaroslav Pelikan, *Theology Today* 17, no. 3 (October 1960): 388.

236. Ibid. See also Mackay, Foreword to Giovanni Miegge, *The Virgin Mary: The Roman Catholic Marian Doctrine* (Philadelphia: Westminster Press, 1955), 7–8.

237. "Prayer to Virgin Composed by Pope," *New York Times*, November 22, 1953, 19.

238. John A. Mackay, "The Marian Cult in Relation to the Lordship of Christ and the Unity of the Church," *Presbyterian Life*, June 11, 1955, 17–18, 37; idem, "The Marian Cult," *Presbyterian World*, vol. 23, no. 4 (December 1955): 146–52.

239. "Criticism of Marian Dogma Voted," *Los Angeles Examiner*, Tuesday, May 24, 1955, sec. 1, 14.

240. Ibid.

241. "In Unity—For Mission," *Presbyterian Life*, July 1, 1958, 20–23. See Mackay, *Ecumenics*, 100–101. The Presbyterian Church in the U.S.A. merged with the smaller United Presbyterian Church of North America to become The United Presbyterian Church in the U.S.A.

242. John Coventry Smith, *From Colonialism to World Community* (Philadelphia: Geneva Press, 1982), 173.

243. "Must Presidents Be Protestant?" *Presbyterian Life*, July 15, 1958, 6–8, 30. Jack Gould, "TV: Politics and Religion," *New York Times*, June 2, 1958, 46, and "Catholic President Topic of 4 at Forum," June 2, 1958, 19. The program reached twenty million viewers.

244. James A. Pike, *A Roman Catholic in the White House* (Garden City, NY: Doubleday & Co., 1960), 131–32.

245. "Vatican Paper Proclaims Right of Church to Role in Politics," *New York Times*, May 18, 1960, 1, 31; *New York Times*, May 19, 1960, 32.

CHAPTER 12: THE ECUMENICAL CHURCH

1. John R. Mott, *The Evangelization of the World in This Generation* (New York: Student Volunteer Movement for Foreign Missions, 1900).

2. Henry P. Van Dusen, "Christian Missions and Christian Unity," *Theology Today* 16, no. 3 (October 1959): 323.

3. Andrew T. Roy, "Overseas Mission Policies—An Historical Overview," *Journal of Presbyterian History* 57, no. 3 (Fall 1979): 192.

4. Ibid., 191–92.

5. It was incorporated by a law of the state of New York, chapter 187, public laws of 1862. For a copy of the revised charter see *Report of the Board of Foreign Missions* (New York: Board of Foreign Missions, 1950), 133–34.

6. Water Lowrie, in "A Thesaurus of Tributes," *Theology Today* 16, no. 3 (October 1959): 361. On the early history see Marjorie Barnhart, "From Elisha Swift to Walter Lowrie: The Background of the Presbyterian Board of Foreign Missions," *American Presbyterians* 65, no. 2 (Summer 1987): 85–95.

7. John F. Piper Jr., *Robert E. Speer* (Louisville, KY: Geneva Press, 2000), 148.

8. "Dr. Mackay, Secretary Foreign Missions," *Presbyterian Magazine*, May 1932, 260–61.

9. John A. Mackay, "This Centennial Year," *Presbyterian Tribune*, January 21, 1937, 11, 14.

10. Editorial, "Missions," *New York Times*, October 31, 1937, sec. 4, 8.

11. "Accepts the Presidency of Presbyterian Missions," *New York Times*, December 22, 1944, "Board General Letter No. 88," The Board of Foreign Missions of the Presbyterian Church in the United States of America, February 1, 1945, 1, Mackay Collection.

12. Andrew T. Roy, "Overseas Mission Policies—An Historical Overview," *Journal of Presbyterian History* 57, no. 3 (Fall 1979), 214.

13. See Harry A. Rhodes and Archibald Campbell, eds., *History of the Korea Mission*, vol. 2, 1935–1959 (New York: Commission on Ecumenical Mission and Relations, 1964), 7–16. See also George Thompson Brown, *Mission to Korea* (New York: Board of World Missions, Presbyterian Church U.S., 1962), 148–65.

14. Otto D. Tolischus, "The God-Emperor: Key to a Nation," *New York Times Magazine*, August 18, 1945, sec. 6, 8, 32–33.

15. An Experienced Missionary, "Some Factors Not Hitherto Brought Out in The Japanese Shinto Shrine Problem," *The Presbyterian*, December 23, 1937, 8–10. The author was likely J. G. Holdcroft or T. S. Soltau. See also "The Korean Shrine Question, A Debate"; George S. McCune, "Thou Shalt Have No Other Gods before Me"; Horace H. Underwood, "Render Unto Caesar the Things That Are Caesar's," *Presbyterian Tribune*, January 20, 1938, 6–11; Charles R. Erdman, "The Shrine Question in Chosen," *Women and Missions* 13, no. 9 (December 1936): 305, 307.

16. Harold E. Fey, "Rise Again, Amaterasu," *Christian Century* 57, no. 33 (August 14, 1940): 998–1000; "The Emperor Who Plays God," *Christian Century* 57, no. 35 (August 28, 1940): 1049–51; "A Christianity with Many Gods?" *Christian Century* 57, no. 38 (September 18, 1940): 1142–44; "Mobilizing Japanese Religion," *Christian Century* 57, no. 41 (October 9, 1940): 1244–47; *China Weekly Review* (Shanghai), September 14, 1940, 53.

17. Charles R. Erdman to John Mackay, November 7, 1940; William Hiram Foulkes to Charles Erdman, November 9, 1940, and edited drafts of related reports, Mackay Collection.

18. John A. Mackay, "The Board of Foreign Missions and the Chosen Question," *The Presbyterian* 110, no. 47 (November 21, 1940): 3, 6.

19. John K. Fairbank, Edwin O. Reischauer, and Albert M. Craig, *East Asia: The Modern Transformation* (Boston: Houghton Mifflin Co., 1965), 704.

20. Ibid., 702–706.

21. Ibid., 702.

22. Peter Conn, *Pearl Buck* (Cambridge: Cambridge University Press, 1996), 68, 114 (regarding Lossing Buck); Sam Higginbottom, *Sam Higginbottom: Farmer* (New York: Charles Scribner's Sons, 1949), 77.

23. Hua-ling Hu, *American Goddess at the Rape of Nanking* (Carbondale: Southern Illinois University Press, 2000), 71, 75; Iris Chang, *The Rape of Nanking* (New York: BasicBooks, 1997), 106.

24. Hu, *American Goddess*, 83–84; *Far Eastern News*, March 12, 1940, Mackay Archive. Also see Robert F. Smylie, "John Leighton Stuart: A Missionary Diplomat in the Sino-Japanese Conflict, 1937–1941," *Journal of Presbyterian History* 53, no. 3 (Fall 1975): 256–76.

25. John Mackay, "The Missionary Stake in Japan," galley proof for *Christianity and Crisis*, Mackay Collection.

26. Samuel McCrea Cavert, *The American Churches in the Ecumenical Movement 1900–1968* (New York: Association Press, 1968), 173–74.

27. "The Pacific Coast Revisited," *The Presbyterian* 116, no. 18 (May 2, 1946): 3. Soichi Saito, "The Significance of the Japanese Christian Deputation," *Japan Christian Quarterly* 16, no. 3 (July 1941): 225–30; William Axling, "An Adventure in Christian Fellowship," *Japan Christian Quarterly* 16, no. 3 (July 1941): 231–34.

28. John A. Mackay to Dr. L. K. Anderson, July 23, 1946, Mackay Collection.

29. John A. Mackay, "A Theological Meditation on Latin America," *Theology Today* 3, no. 4 (January 1947): 429–39; John A. Mackay, "Latin America—Thirty Years After" in six parts: "1. Travel in the Air Age," *The Presbyterian* 116, no. 51 (December 19, 1946): 4–5; "2. Peoples and Politics," *The Presbyterian*, December 26, 1946, 6–7; "3. Ideas and Persons," *The Presbyterian*, January 4, 1947, 6–7; "4. A Changed Spiritual Atmosphere," *The Presbyterian*, January 11, 1947, 6–7; "5. The Roman Catholic Reaction," *The Presbyterian*, January 18, 1947, 6–7; "6. The Coming of Evangelical Christianity," *The Presbyterian*, January 25, 1947, 7–8; John A. Mackay, "Latin America To-day," *World Dominion* 25, no. 3 (May–June 1947): 155–62. He also reported on the trip in a sermon to young members of the First Spanish Church at 54 East 102d Street. See "'Liberators' Held 'Jailers' by Youth," *New York Times*, December 23, 1946, 15.

30. John A. Mackay, "The Theology of Missions," in Board of Foreign Missions of the Presbyterian Church in the United States of America, *This Is Our World Mission* (New York: Board of Foreign Missions, 1943), 17–22 at 17–18.

31. W. Stanley Rycroft, *The Ecumenical Witness of the United Presbyterian Church in the U.S.A.* (New York: Board of Christian Education of the United Presbyterian Church in the U.S.A., 1968), 177. See also Donald Black, *Merging Mission and Unity* (Philadelphia: Geneva Press, 1986), 45. For a summary of this revolution in missions see Karla Ann Koll, "Presbyterians, the United States, and Central America: Background of the 1980s Debate," *Journal of Presbyterian History* 78, no. 1 (Spring 2000): 89–92.

32. George Dugan, "Foreign Missions Ended by Church," *New York Times*, May 31, 1958, 8.

33. John Coventry Smith, *From Colonialism to World Community* (Philadelphia: Geneva Press, 1982), 144–45, 152. In 1951 Kenneth Grubb and Lesslie Newbigin noted that missions themselves had not had political motives. Some elements of the general public in mission lands may have perceived it that way, however. World Council of Churches, *Minutes and Reports of the Fourth Meeting of the Central Committee Rolle (Switzerland) August 4–11, 1951* (Geneva: World Council of Churches), 14–15. Also on the translatability of the gospel, see the work of Lamin Sanneh.

34. See William Easterly, *The White Man's Burden* (New York: Penguin Press, 2006); Amartya Sen, *Development as Freedom* (New York: Alfred A. Knopf, 1999); David Rieff, *A Bed for the Night: Humanitarianism in Crisis* (New York: Simon & Schuster, 2002). Also,

Amartya Sen, "To Build a Country, Build a Schoolhouse," *New York Times*, May 27, 2002, A13; Mary Anastasia O'Grady, "Why Latin Nations Are Poor," *Wall Street Journal*, November 25, 2005, A11.

35. Howard Chandler Robbins, "An Apostle of Unity," *Princeton Seminary Bulletin* 32, no. 4 (January 1940): 13.

36. W. A. Visser 't Hooft, *The Genesis and Formation of the World Council of Churches* (Geneva: World Council of Churches, 1982), 36.

37. John A. Mackay, "In Memoriam," *Princeton Seminary Bulletin* 33, no. 4 (January 1940): 2. On this meeting, see also Keith Clements, *Faith on the Frontier* (Edinburgh: T. & T. Clark, 1999), 336–37; F. A. Iremonger, *William Temple* (London: Oxford University Press, 1948), 380–81; and "Archbishop Strengthens Ecumenical Outlook," *Federal Council Bulletin* 19, no. 1 (January 1936): 9.

38. W. A. Visser 't Hooft to John A. Mackay, February 28, 1946; Floyd W. Tomkins to John A. Mackay, March 18, 1946; Leonard Hodgson to John A. Mackay, March 2, 1946; John A. Mackay to Leonard Hodgson, May 1, 1946, Mackay Collection.

39. W.A. Visser 't Hooft to John A. Mackay, March 28, 1946, Mackay Collection.

40. World Council of Churches, *Minutes and Reports of the Meeting of the Provisional Committee of the World Council of Churches, Buck Hill Falls, Penna., April 1947* (Geneva: World Council of Churches), 13–14.

41. John Alexander Mackay, *The Latin American Churches and the Ecumenical Movement* (New York: Committee on Cooperation in Latin America, 1963), 18–19.

42. John A. Mackay, "The Significance of the Amsterdam Assembly," *Princeton Seminary Bulletin* 42, no. 3 (Winter 1949): 7, 8. Russian Orthodox and Roman Catholic representatives did not attend.

43. John A. Mackay, "The Missionary Legacy to the Church Universal," *International Review of Missions* 37, no. 4 (1948): 369–74; George Dugan, "World Assembly of Churches Opens," *New York Times*, August 23, 1948, 1, 15.

44. Visser 't Hooft to John A. Mackay, July 26, 1948, Mackay Collection.

45. W. A. Visser 't Hooft, ed., *The First Assembly of the World Council of Churches* (New York: Harper & Bros., 1948), 70–73. Shortly after the World Council, Mackay also attended the meeting of the IMC at Oegstgeest, the Netherlands. There he spoke of the functional relationships of the IMC and the WCC. International Missionary Council, *Minutes of the Committee of the International Missionary Council, Oegstgeest, the Netherlands, September 7–10, 1948* (London: International Missionary Council, 1948), 25–26.

46. John A. Mackay, "A Theological Foreword to Ecumenical Gatherings," *Theology Today* 5, no. 2 (July 1948), 145–50.

47. John A. Mackay, "The End Is the Beginning," *Theology Today* 5, no. 4 (January 1949): 465.

48. Henry P. Van Dusen, "Christian Missions and Christian Unity," *Theology Today* 16, no. 3 (October 1959): 324–25.

49. In the discussion, one speaker used the two terms *missionary* and *ecumenical*. WCC, *Minutes . . . , Rolle*, 12.

50. Ibid., 13–14. Mackay made clear in response to a question by Bishop Bereczky that by this latter statement he did not mean to set up an anti-Communist front (ibid., 15).

51. Ibid., 65. "The Calling of the Church to Mission and to Unity," *Theology Today* 9, no. 1 (April 1952): 15. This episode is mentioned in John A. Mackay, *The Latin American Churches and the Ecumenical Movement* (New York: CCLA, 1963), 15–16, emphasis in

original. The quotation from Rolle appears also in Mackay, *Christian Reality & Appearance* (Richmond, VA: John Knox Press, 1969), 86; and idem, *Ecumenics* (Englewood Cliffs, NJ: Prentice-Hall, 1964), 14.

52. "The Calling of the Church to Mission and to Unity," *Theology Today* 9, no. 1 (April 1952): 13–19.

53. World Council of Churches, *Minutes and Reports of the Fifth Meeting of the Central Committee Lucknow (India), December 31, 1952–January 8,1953* (Geneva: World Council of Churches), 12–13.

54. John A. Mackay to Norman Goodall, September 28, 1954, Mackay Collection.

55. John A. Mackay to W. A. Visser 't Hooft, November 2, 1954, Mackay Collection.

56. Daniel T. Niles, *The Message and Its Messengers* (New York: Abingdon Press, 1966), 113, 63. Max Warren, "The Fusion of I.M.C. and W.C.C. at New Delhi: Retrospective Thoughts after a Decade and a Half," in *Zending op web Naar de Toekomst* (Uitgeversmaatschappij J.H. Kok—Kampen 1978), 193.

57. Marc Boegner, *The Long Road to Unity* (London: Collins, 1970), 235.

58. World Council of Churches, *Minutes and Reports of the Fourth Meeting of the Central Committee Davos (Grisons) Switzerland, August 2–8, 1955* (Geneva: World Council of Churches), 23.

59. Ibid. The three points are found at 22–23.

60. Ibid., 26.

61. Ibid., 31.

62. John A. Mackay, "Between the Politicians and the Atomic Scientists," *British Weekly*, August 25, 1955, 1–2, at 2.

63. Willem Adolf Visser 't Hooft, "The Genesis of the World Council of Churches," in *A History of the Ecumenical Movement 1517–1948*, 2nd ed., ed. Ruth Rouse and Stephen Charles Neill (London: SPCK, 1967), 697–724.

64. Rouse and Neill, eds., *History*, 730. See Kenneth Scott Latourette, "Ecumenical Bearings of the Missionary Movement and the International Missionary Council," in Rouse and Neill, eds., *History*, 353–402.

65. Lesslie Newbigin, "Mission to Six Continents," in *The Ecumenical Advance*, vol. 2, *A History of the Ecumenical Movement 1948–1968*, ed. Harold E. Fee (Philadelphia: Westminster Press, 1970), 173–76.

66. Kenneth Scott Latourette, *Tomorrow Is Here* (New York: Friendship Press, 1948), 43.

67. William Richey Hogg, *Ecumenical Foundations: A History of the International Missionary Council and Its Nineteenth-Century Background* (New York: Harper & Bros., 1952), 339.

68. Walter Freytag, "Germany Re-enters the Missionary Fellowship," *World Dominion* 26, no. 2 (March–April 1948): 87–90. See also Stewart W. Herman, *The Rebirth of the German Church*, intro. Martin Niemöller (New York: Harper & Bros., 1946); B. D. Gibson, "Orphaned Missions," *World Dominion* 27, no. 5 (September–October 1949): 281–84.

69. Latourette, *Tomorrow*, 66–67.

70. John A. Mackay, "The Holy Spirit in Proclamation," in *Renewal and Advance*, ed. Charles W. Ransom (London: International Missionary Council and Edinburgh House Press, 1948), 148–61; idem, "With Christ to the Frontier," in Ransom, ed., *Renewal*, 198–205. Also "The Holy Spirit in Proclamation," in John A. Mackay, *Christianity on the Frontier* (New York: Macmillan Co., 1950), 22–40.

71. Latourette, *Tomorrow*, 68.

72. G. Báez-Camargo, "In the Light of Whitby . . ." *World Dominion* 26, no. 4 (July–August 1948): 223 (emphasis in original).

73. Latourette, *Tomorrow*, 71–72.

74. John A. Mackay, "East Asia under God," *Theology Today* 6, no. 4 (January 1950): 429–38, at 430. Because an earlier article sent airmail had not arrived, Mackay used the journey itself as an editorial subject. The temporarily missing article was published in the following issue: John A. Mackay, "Jesus, Lord of Thought," *Theology Today* 7, no. 1 (April 1950): 3–8. See also a briefer version, John A. Mackay, "Communism and Christianity in East Asia," *Outreach* 4, no. 3 (March 1950): 75–76, 90. On the spiritual condition of the Far East see Walter Freytag, *Spiritual Revolution in the East* (London: Lutterworth Press, 1940).

75. Mackay, "East Asia," 430, 433, 435 (emphasis in original).

76. Marcel Pradervand, editorial, *Presbyterian World* 20, no. 2 (June 1950): 50.

77. The material in this section is derived from notes of Mackay's trip, "Journey to Asia in 1949," Mackay Archive. On Kagawa see Charles R. Erdman, "Toyohiko Kagawa: A Tribute," *Princeton Seminary Bulletin* 52, no. 2 (October 1958): 27–29; Yasuo C. Furuya, "Who Was Toyohiko Kagawa?" *Princeton Seminary Bulletin*, n.s., 23, no. 3 (2002): 301–12.

78. Mackay, "Journey to Asia," November 9, 1949. The MacArthur quotation is a quotation in the original notes.

79. Mackay referred to this interview in his address "Splendor in the Abyss," *Princeton Seminary Bulletin* 44, no. 3 (Winter 1950–1951): 5–15 at 8.

80. Tamaki Uemura, "A Japanese Story," in *World Faith in Action*, ed. Charles T. Leber (Indianapolis: Bobbs-Merrill, 1951), 238. Mrs. Uemura attended the Whitby Conference. See also William C. Kerr, *Japan Begins Again* (New York: Friendship Press, 1949), 120, 146. Mackay read Kerr's book during his visit to Japan.

81. See Harold Voelkel, "Han Kyung Chik," in *Open Door to Korea* (Grand Rapids: Zondervan Publishing House, 1958), 49–62.

82. See Harold Voelkel, "President Syngman Rhee's Own Story" in *Open Door*, 21–24.

83. A picture of Mackay in the pillbox appears in "Dr. Mackay Reports on Trip to East Asia," *Presbyterian Life* 3, no. 2 (January 21, 1950): 6.

84. John A. Mackay, "Basic Christianity," *Princeton Seminary Bulletin* 43, no. 3 (Winter 1950): 5–13.

85. Arthur L. Carson, *Silliman University 1901–1959* (New York: United Board of Christian Education in Asia, 1965).

86. *The Christian Prospect in Eastern Asia*, Papers and Minutes of the Eastern Asia Christian Conference, Bangkok, December 3–11, 1949 (New York: Friendship Press, 1950); P. D. Devanandan, "The Bangkok Conference of East Asia Leaders: An Impression," *International Review of Missions* 39 (1950), 146–52. "Church Conferences End with Religious Services," *Bangkok Post*, December 12, 1949, 1, 8. Cecil Northcott, "Christian Prospects in East Asia," *The Fortnightly*, January, 1951, 27–31.

87. Mackay, "Journey to Asia," December 3.

88. "Mission Parley Split on East Asian Reds," *New York Times*, December 4, 1949, 36.

89. Mackay, "Journey to Asia," December 3. The substance of the quotation is included in "Mission Parley."

90. "Church Group Is Barred," *New York Times*, December 5, 1949, 10; "Asian Religious Body Set," *New York Times*, December 7, 1949, 25. The new body was called the Conference of Christian Churches in Asia.

91. On December 9 Mackay lunched with Southern Baptist missionaries from China who told Carl Mackay the story of the McIntire group. Their intention had been to get a church and constituency. They intended to invite two speakers a night from Mackay's conference to their meetings and to have them speak on certain topics. Then they intended to tear them to pieces towards the end of the week. But the whole scheme collapsed because no church would admit McIntire's group. After the conference Mackay learned that McIntire was going to Australia. Blanchard, the moderator of the Australian Presbyterian Church, was much concerned (Mackay, "Journey to Asia," December 9, 12).

92. P. D. Devanandan, "The Christian Message in Relation to the Cultural Heritage of Eastern Asia," in *Christian Prospect in East Asia*, 71–77. The address was about India. Gandhi's concepts, *ahimsa*, *satyagraha* and *ramrajya*, could be fulfilled only through the power of Christianity.

93. "Reds Seen Limiting Church to Worship," *New York Times*, December 8, 1949, 18.

94. "Asia Churches See Red Fight as Basic," *New York Times*, December 12, 1949, 2.

95. His writings include Rajah B. Manikam, "A New Era in the World Mission of the Church," *Union Seminary Quarterly Review* 13, no. 1 (November 1957): 31–39; idem, ed., *Christianity and the Asian Revolution* (Madras, India: Diocesan Press, 1954).

96. John A. Mackay, "Call to Discipleship," in *Christian Prospect in East Asia*, 104–13; and idem, "Call to Discipleship," *Theology Today* 7, no. 2 (July 1950): 217–27. The address was based on the text "What is that to thee? Follow thou me!" John 21:22 (KJV).

97. Mackay, "Journey to Asia," December 11.

98. John A. Mackay, "Those Who Imprison Truth," *The Churchman*, June 1964, 9.

99. John A. Mackay, "A Pilgrimage to Latin Europe," also published as "Protestant Pilgrimage," *Presbyterian Life* 4, no. 23 (November 24, 1951): 8–11. See also John A. Mackay, "The Voice of Latin Europe to the Religious Thought of America," *Princeton Seminary Bulletin* 45, no. 3 (Winter 1951–1952): 5–13, delivered at the opening of the one hundred and fortieth session of the seminary, September 25, 1951. On the Spanish portion of the trip see Dr. J. Mackay, "Impressions d'Espagne," extracted in *L'Étoile du Matin*, 3e Année, N° 106–107, IV e Trimestre 1951- 1e Trimestre, 1952, 51–53.

100. John A. Mackay, "The Voice of Latin Europe to the Religious Thought of America," *Princeton Seminary Bulletin* 45, no. 3 (Winter 1951–1952), 12. The identity of these scholars is uncertain.

101. Ibid., 9.

102. Norman Goodall, *Second Fiddle* (London: SPCK, 1979), 101. His chief opponent, Max Warren, paid him a compliment. See Kenneth Slack, "Memoir," in *One Man's Testimony*, ed. Norman Goodall (London: SCM Press, 1985), x–xi.

103. Norman Goodall, "The International Missionary Council and The World Council of Churches, Their Present and Future Relationships," *International Review of Missions* 37 (January 1948): 92.

104. WCC, *Minutes . . . Rolle*, 40.

105. John A. Mackay to J. C. Hoekendijk, June 18, 1952, Mackay Collection.

106. John A. Mackay, editorial, "Ecumenical: the Word and the Concept," *Theology Today* 9, no. 1 (April 1952): 6.

107. Basic Documents. Paul L. Lehmann, ed., "The Missionary Obligation of the Church," *Theology Today* 9, no. 1 (April 1952): 20–38. An abridged version of the report submitted for study at Willingen, this preparatory report linked the missionary task to Christ's sovereignty in the secular world. "The Calling of the Church to Mission and to Unity," *Theology Today*

9, no. 1 (April 1952): 13–19. This is the Rolle Statement received by the Central Committee, August 1951.

108. John A. Mackay, Editorial, "Theology, Christ, and the Missionary Obligation," *Theology Today* 7, no. 4 (January 1951): 429.

109. John A. Mackay, "The Great Commission and the Church Today," in *Missions under the Cross*, ed. Norman Goodall (London: Edinburgh House Press, 1953), 137.

110. Ibid.

111. Ibid., 139.

112. Ibid., 141.

113. David J. du Plessis, *The Spirit Bade Me Go* (Oakland, CA: privately printed, 1963), 14.

114. Ibid.

115. On the new emphasis, see David J. Bosch, *Transforming Mission* (Maryknoll, NY: Orbis Books, 1991), 389–93; Paul Avis, *A Ministry Shaped by Mission* (London: T. & T. Clark, 2005), 4–14; and articles in a special issue of *International Review of Mission*, "*Missio Dei* Revisited Willingen 1952–2002," vol. 92, no. 367 (October 2003), particularly Tormod Engelsviken, "*Missio Dei*: The Understanding and Misunderstanding of a Theological Concept in European Churches and Missiology," 481–97; Wolfgang Günther, "The History and Significance of World Mission Conferences in the 20th Century," 528–30; and Jacques Matthey, "God's Mission Today: Summary and Conclusions," 579–80. Also see William H. Crane, editorial, "Dropping the S," *International Review of Mission* 58 (1969): 141–44; Johannes Blauw, *The Missionary Nature of the Church* (New York: McGraw-Hill, 1962).

116. John A. Mackay, "Willingen 1952," *Presbyterian Outlook* 134, no. 34 (August 25, 1952): 5–6 at 6; and published in *Outreach* 6, no. 11 (November 1952): 269–70.

117. Henry P. Van Dusen, "Christian Missions and Christian Unity," *Theology Today* 16, no. 3 (October 1959): 326.

118. John A. Mackay, Foreword to *Christ—The Hope of Asia*, Ecumenical Study Conference for East Asia Lucknow, India, December 27–30, 1952 (Madras: Christian Literature Society, 1953).

119. Van Dusen, "Christian Missions," 326. For a more detailed description of the trip and conference at Lucknow, see Henry P. Van Dusen to Friends, "Letter 2," January 9, 1953, Mackay Collection.

120. Congratulating Grubb on the honor of receiving a knighthood, Mackay also added, "I feel that nothing would give greater energy and purpose to the World Council, or greater status and opportunity to the Missionary Movement, than that missionary concern, and the dynamism of our missionary tradition should be right at the heart of the World Council. But this can only be done if we find a way to make the several Christian councils throughout the world a real part of the World Council, giving them some kind of effective representation" (John A. Mackay to Kenneth G. Grubb, September 29, 1953, Mackay Collection).

121. H. P. Van Dusen to John A. Mackay, May 18, 1956, Mackay Collection.

122. World Council of Churches, *Minutes and Reports of the Ninth Meeting of the Central Committee, Galyatetö, Hungary July 28–August 5, 1956* (Geneva: World Council of Churches), 39.

123. WCC, *Minutes . . . Galyatetö,* 110–11. Mackay had presented a Report of the Joint Committee to the WCC Executive Committee at Königstein in 1954. The Report appears as Appendix B, Minutes of the Meeting of the Executive Committee of the World Council of Churches, Königstein in Taunus, Germany, February 2–5, 1954. WCC Archives, Geneva.

124. Ibid., 39–40.

125. Editorial, "An Ecumenical Era Calls for Missionary Action," *Theology Today* 13, no. 2 (July 1956): 143.

126. Ibid., 144.

127. John A. Mackay, "The Christian Mission at This Hour," *Theology Today* 15, no. 1 (April 1958): 15–35 and *Princeton Seminary Bulletin* 51, no. 4 (May 1958): 3–18.

128. Darrell L. Guder, "From Mission and Theology to Missional Theology," *Princeton Seminary Bulletin,* n.s., 24, no. 1 (2003): 43.

129. Norman Goodall, "WCC and IMC Relationships: Some Underlying Issues," *Ecumenical Review* 9, no. 4 (July 1957): 395–401; idem, "'Evangelicals' and the WCC-IMC," *International Review of Missions* 47, no. 2 (April 1958): 210–15; "Concerning the Integration of the WCC and the IMC" [The joint committee statement authorized for use by the World Council of Churches Central Committee, July 1956], *Ecumenical Review* 9, no. 1 (October 1956): 56–58; Henry P. Van Dusen, "World Council and IMC—One or Two Organizations?" *National Council Outlook* 7, no. 2 (February 1957): 11–12, 24; Sir Kenneth Grubb, "I.M.C.-W.C.C. Relations: A Personal View," *International Review of Missions* 46, no. 2 (April 1957): 299–305; E. J. Bingle, "Ad Interim, 1954: A Comment," *International Review of Missions,* 43, no. 4 (October 1954): 443–50.

130. Max Warren, *Crowded Canvas* (London: Hodder & Stoughton, 1974), 159.

131. "Princetoniana," *Princeton Seminary Bulletin* 51, no. 4 (May 1958): 47; "Mackay Speaks to IMC on "Servant Image" Theme," *Presbyterian Outlook,* January 13, 1958, 3; "IMC Approves WCC Merger at Ghana Meeting, 58–7," *Presbyterian Outlook,* January 20, 1958, 3–4; M. S., "The Christian Mission at This Hour," *International Review of Missions* 47, no. 2 (April 1958): 137–42; Gwenyth Hubble, "The Ghana Assembly, A Report on Group Discussion," *International Review of Missions* 47, no. 2 (April 1958), 143–49; "The Ghana Assembly Resolutions on Integration with the WCC," *International Review of Missions* 47, no. 2 (April 1958), 150–52; IMC, *Minutes of the Assembly of the International Missionary Council, Ghana, December 28, 1957, to January 8, 1958* (London: International Missionary Council, 1958).

132. L. B. Greaves, "The All Africa Church Conference: Ibadan, Nigeria: 10th to 20th January, 1958," *International Review of Missions* 47, no. 3 (July 1958): 257–64.

133. Karl Barth, *The Church and the Churches* (Grand Rapids: W. B. Eerdmans Publishing Co., 1936), 78 and discussion, 77–82.

134. J. David Hoeveler Jr., "Evangelical Ecumenism: James McCosh and the Intellectual Origins of the World Alliance of Reformed Churches," *Journal of Presbyterian History* 55, no. 1 (Spring 1977): 36–56.

135. John A. Mackay, "Two American Civilizations and Their Implications for Reformed Theology," *Presbyterian Register,* March 1943, 90–96.

136. "Abroad with Dr. W. B. Pugh," *Presbyterian Register,* December 1946, 481.

137. John A. Mackay, "The Contribution of the Reformed Churches to Christian Doctrine," *Presbyterian Register,* August 1948, 610–13 reprinted from *Theology Today* 5, no. 1 (April 1948): 3–8, and found in Mackay, *Christianity on the Frontier* (1950), 86–93.

138. John A. Mackay, "Ecumenical Presbyterianism," *Presbyterian World* 20, no. 2 (June 1950): 52–56, at 53.

139. John A. Mackay, "The Reformed Churches and the Ecumenical Situation," in *Proceedings of the Sixteenth General Council of the Alliance of Reformed Churches Holding the Presbyterian System Held at Geneva, Switzerland, 1948,* ed. W. H. Hamilton (Edinburgh: Office of the Alliance, 1948), 110–12.

140. Marcel Pradervand, *A Century of Service* (Edinburgh: Saint Andrew Press, 1975), 179–80, Pradervand quotes minutes of the 1949 Executive Committee at 10.

141. Pradervand, *Century of Service*, 180; quote at 11.

142. "Evangelical Christianity in Latin America," *Presbyterian World* 19, no. 3 (September 1949): 131–32.

143. "Reunion of Presbyterian and Reformed Delegates Taking Part in the First Evangelical Conference of Latin America," *Presbyterian World* 19, no. 3 (September 1949): 132–34.

144. Pradervand, *Century of Service*, 183–84. Executive Committee of the World Presbyterian Alliance, "The World Presbyterian Alliance in the Present Ecumenical Situation" ["The Basle Statement"], *Presbyterian World* 21, no. 3 (September 1951): 98–102; John A. Mackay, "Reflections on the World Confessional Issue," *Reformed and Presbyterian World* 27, no. 1 (March 1962): 15–21.

145. Pradervand, *Century of Service*, 184.

146. Ibid. "The Basle Statement," *Presbyterian World* 21, no. 3 (September 1951): 99–100.

147. John A. Mackay, "The Witness of the Reformed Churches in the World Today," *Presbyterian World* 22, nos. 7–8 (September–December 1954), 291–302; John A. Mackay, "The Witness of the Reformed Churches in the World Today," *Theology Today* 11, no. 3 (October 1954): 373–84.

148. Pradervand, *Century of Service*, 195.

149. Theodore A. Gill, "Presbyterians at Princeton," *Christian Century* 71, no. 33 (August 18, 1954): 969.

150. "The Presbyterian Alliance: New Life and New Stature," *Presbyterian Life*, September 4, 1954, 18–22, *Princeton Seminary Bulletin* 48, no. 2 (October 1954): 31.

151. Pradervand, *Century of Service*, 194, quoting proceedings of the 17th General Council at 37.

152. Ibid., 216.

153. George Dugan, "Policy of 'Ghetto' Laid to Catholics," *New York Times*, August 1, 1954, 63 (Colombia: Greek Orthodox Church restricting the Evangelical Church of Greece); idem, "Communion Rites Besought for All," *New York Times*, August 3, 1954, 16 (Communion for all baptized); idem, "Place of Church in Society Defined," *New York Times*, August 4, 1954, 15 (church's place in society; attitude toward women's ordination; vote was 66–65 in favor); "Christian World Seen Near Chaos," *New York Times*, August 5, 1954, 21 (speech by Hromadka); "Obey God, Not Man, Church Unit Asks," *New York Times*, August 6, 1954, 17 (make decisions based on obedience to God not men, but "be loyal to the Government of the nation in which you live").

154. Pradervand, *Century of Service*, 196–97; John A. Mackay, "A Letter to the Reformed Family of Churches," *Presbyterian World* 23, no. 1 (March 1955): 1–4.

155. Pradervand, *Century of Service*, 202. Mackay's statement was published as John A. Mackay, "The Confessional Resurgence and the Ecumenical Movement," *Reformed and Presbyterian World* 24, no. 3 (September 1956): 104–11. On the confessional movement see Harold E. Fey, "Confessional Families and the Ecumenical Movement," in *The Ecumenical Advance*, vol. 2, *A History of the Ecumenical Movement 1948–1968*, ed. Harold E. Fey (Philadelphia: Westminster Press, 1970), 115–42.

156. Mackay, "The Confessional Resurgence," 106–107.

157. Pradervand, *Century of Service*, 202.

158. Ibid., 206–207.

159. Ibid., 208, 233.

160. John A. Mackay, "Christianity's Essential Image," *Theology Today* 16, no. 2 (July 1959): 143–48 at 143. See also Mackay's editorial on this theme: John A. Mackay, editorial, *Reformed and Presbyterian World* 25, no. 5 (March 1959): 193–95. Mackay had been struck by the need to emphasize the servant theme since the Central Committee meeting of the WCC at Davos. John A. Mackay, "Between the Politicians and the Atomic Scientists," *British Weekly*, August 25, 1955, 1–2. He used it as a theme for a convocation address, "The Form of a Servant, The Restoration of a Lost Image," *Princeton Seminary Bulletin* 51, no. 3 (January 1958): 3–12, and as a motif within his keynote address at the Ghana meeting of the IMC.

161. Lewis S. Mudge, "The Theological Work of the Alliance: 1957–1962," *Journal of Presbyterian History* 55, no. 1 (Spring 1977): 101–106; idem, "The Servant Lord and His Servant People," *Scottish Journal of Theology* 12, no. 2 (June 1959): 113–28; idem, "On Living with a Conference Theme," *Theology Today* 15, no. 3 (October 1958): 352–58.

162. Pradervand, *Century of Service*, 234; John A. Mackay, "Let Us Remember God," in *São Paulo Story, Proceedings of the Eighteenth General Council of the Alliance of the Reformed Churches throughout the World Holding the Presbyterian Order*, ed. Marcel Pradervand (Geneva: Alliance Offices, 1960), 166–75.

163. John A. Mackay, "A New Chapter in Church History," in *São Paulo Story*, 9–12.

164. Du Plessis, *Spirit Bade Me*, 19.

165. Eugene C. Blake, "John Alexander Mackay An Appreciation," in *Reformed and Presbyterian World* 25, no. 6 (June 1959): 245, quoted in Pradervand, *Century of Service*, 238–39.

166. John A. Mackay, "An Introduction to Christian Work among South American Students," *International Review of Missions* 17, no. 2 (1928): 289.

167. John A. Mackay, *His Life and Our Life* (Philadelphia: Westminster Press, 1964), 10.

168. John A. Mackay, "The Endless Journey Starts," *Theology Today* 5, no. 3 (October 1948): 317.

169. J. A. Mackay, "The Idea of Revelation," thesis, Princeton Seminary, 1915, 39.

170. See John A. Mackay, "God Has Spoken," *Theology Today* 3, no. 2 (July 1946): 145–50.

171. John A. Mackay, *God's Order* (New York: Macmillan Co., 1953), 4–6. In 1949, the World Council developed guiding principles for interpreting the Bible: "Guiding Principles for Interpretation of the Bible as Accepted by the Ecumenical Study Conference at Wadham College, Oxford, 1949," in *Biblical Authority for Today: A World Council of Churches Symposium on "The Biblical Authority for the Churches' Social and Political Message Today,"* ed. Alan Richardson and W. Schweitzer (Philadelphia: Westminster Press, 1951), 240–44. Centripetal forces of the next half century necessitated the reclaiming of the Bible for the church: *Reclaiming the Bible for the Church*, ed. Carl E. Braaten and Robert W. Jenson (Grand Rapids: Wm. B. Eerdmans Publishing Co., 1995).

172. John A. Mackay, "Two American Civilizations and Their Implications for Reformed Theology," *Presbyterian Register* 18, no. 3 (March 1943): 92.

173. John A. Mackay, *The Other Spanish Christ* (New York: Macmillan Co., 1932), 154.

174. Mackay, *God's Order*, 98.

175. Ibid., 97.

176. Ibid.

177. John A. Mackay, "Personal Religion," *Princeton Seminary Bulletin* 37, no. 1 (December 1943), 4, 5.

178. Mackay, *God's Order*, 98.

179. John A. Mackay, "Let Us Remember," *Princeton Seminary Bulletin* 65, no. 1 (July 1972): 28.

180. John A. Mackay, *The Presbyterian Way of Life* (Englewood Cliffs, NJ: Prentice-Hall, 1960), 121. These distinctions leave room to take into account both the concept of the anonymous Christian and the fact that within the institutional church both the wheat and the tears may grow together (Matt. 13:29–30).

181. John A. Mackay, *That Other America* (New York: Friendship Press, 1935), 36–37.

182. Mackay, *God's Order*, 71.

183. "In Unity—For Mission," The Message of the Uniting Assembly, *Presbyterian Life* 11, no. 13 (July 1, 1958): 20–23. Mackay, *Ecumenics* (Englewood Cliffs, NJ: Prentice-Hall, 1964), 20–23.

184. Mackay, *Ecumenics*, 106.

185. "God's Servant, The Church," Opening Sermon by Dr. John Alexander Mackay, Retiring Moderator, 165th General Assembly, before the 166th General Assembly, Prebyterian Church in the U.S.A., Detroit, May 20, 1954, Mackay Collection.

186. John A. Mackay, Editorial, "Ecumenical: The Word and the Concept," *Theology Today* 9, no. 1 (April 1952): 4. This term was used earlier. Friedrich Heiler, *Evangelische Katholizität* (München: Verlag Ernst Reinhardt, 1926); G. K. A. Bell, foreword to Friedrich Heiler, *The Spirit of Worship Its Forms and Manifestations in the Christian Churches*, trans. W. Montgomery (New York: George H. Doran Co., 1926), ix–xiii.

187. John A. Mackay, "A Representative American of the Sixties: James Joseph Reeb," *Princeton Seminary Bulletin* 60, no. 1 (October 1966): 37.

188. John Alexander Mackay, "A Letter to Presbyterians," *Princeton Seminary Bulletin*, n.s., 5, no. 3 (November 1984): 199.

189. John A. Mackay, "The Confessional Resurgence and the Ecumenical Movement," *Reformed and Presbyterian World* 24, no. 3 (September 1956): 106–107.

190. Mackay, "The Contribution of the Reformed Churches to Christian Doctrine," *Christianity on the Frontier*, 87–93.

191. John A. Mackay, "Religion and Government," *Theology Today* 9, no. 2 (July 1952): 206–207.

192. Ibid., 207.

193. John A. Mackay, "Religion and Government in the World of Today," *Review and Expositor* 60, no. 3 (1963): 277.

194. Mackay, "The Communion of Saints in Our Time," *Crozer Quarterly* 16, no. 4 (1939): 255.

195. Count Hermann Keyserling, *The World in the Making* (New York: Harcourt, Brace & Co., 1927), 160.

196. John A. Mackay, "Contemporary Life and Thought in South America in Their Relation to Evangelical Christianity," in *The Foreign Missions Conference of North America 1928*, ed. Leslie B. Moss (New York: Foreign Missions Conference of North America, 1928), 136–37.

197. John A. Mackay, "The Ecumenical Spirit and the Recognition of Christ," *International Review of Missions* 18, no. 2 (July 1929): 334.

198. Mackay, *Ecumenics*, 27.

199. Ibid.

200. John A. Mackay, "The Ecumenical Road," *Christendom* 2, no. 4 (Autumn 1937), 537.

201. Ibid., 537–38.

202. John A. Mackay, "The Rôle of the Church as a World Force," in *Religion and the Modern World*, ed. Jacques Maritain et al. (Philadelphia: University of Pennsylvania Press, 1941), 138–39.

203. John A. Mackay, "The Church and the Secular Order," in *A Preface to Christian Theology* (London: Nisbet & Co., 1942), 159–83.

204. John A. Mackay, "The churches do not, however, have a primary responsibility to devise the details of world order. But they must proclaim the enduring moral principles by which human plans are constantly to be tested," in Federal Council of the Churches of Christ in America, *A Righteous Faith for a Just and Durable Peace* (New York: Commission to Study the Bases of a Just and Durable Peace, [1942]), 39–44.

205. John A. Mackay, "The Ecumenical Goal," in *Toward World-Wide Christianity*, ed. O. Frederick Nolde (New York: Harper & Bros., 1946), 40–58 at 40.

206. John A. Mackay, "More Light on the Church," *Christian Century* 66, no. 30 (July 27, 1949): 889.

207. John A. Mackay, Editorial, "Ecumenical: The Word and the Concept," *Theology Today* 9, no. 1 (April 1952): 5.

208. W. A. Visser 't Hooft to John A. Mackay, August 23, 1946, Mackay Collection.

209. Mackay, *God's Order*, vii, viii.

210. The quotation in full reads, "They make it up who call Jesus Christ Saviour and Lord and in whom through Him is the life of God. Such form the Body of Christ, that community whose presence in the existing churches gives them the spiritual reality they possess, and which itself forms a new divine order, the spiritual correlate of the order of nature" (John A. Mackay, "The State of the Church: A Report," Federal Council of the Churches of Christ in America, *Biennial Report 1938* [New York: Federal Council of the Churches of Christ in America, 1938], 42).

211. Mackay, "Ecumenical," 6.

212. John A. Mackay, "The Christian Mission at This Hour," *Theology Today* 15, no. 1 (April 1958): 35; and *Princeton Seminary Bulletin* 51, no. 4 (May 1958), 3–18. For exegesis, see T. Evan Pollard, "'That They All May Be One' (John xvii. 21) and the Unity of the Church," *Expository Times* 70, no. 5 (February 1959): 149–50.

213. "Minutes of the Meeting of the Executive Committee of the World Council of Churches, Königstein im Taunus, Germany, February 2–5, 1954," 8 and Appendix B, Mackay Collection.

214. The *Christian Century* published a series of articles between February 1956 and October 1957 prepared for the Conference. Also see *The Nature of the Unity We Seek, Official Report of the North American Conference on Faith and Order, September 3–10, 1957, Oberlin, Ohio*, ed. Paul S. Minear (St. Louis: Bethany Press, 1958); and Avery Cardinal Dulles, "Saving Ecumenism from Itself," *First Things*, December 2007, 23–27.

CHAPTER 13: WASHINGTON YEARS AND RETIREMENT

1. "Princetoniana," *Princeton Seminary Bulletin* 53, no. 2 (October 1959): 49. The gathering at Compiègne was followed from July 20 to July 24 by a meeting of an administrative committee of the IMC at Oise, France. From France Mackay traveled to São Paulo, Brazil, where he met with the Executive Committee and attended the 18th General Council of the World Presbyterian Alliance, July 27–August 6. Then he traveled to Rio de Janeiro for the centennial celebration of Brazilian Presbyterianism.

2. John A. Mackay, *The Presbyterian Way of Life* (Englewood Cliffs, NJ: Prentice-Hall, 1960).

3. John A. Mackay, *Ecumenics* (Englewood Cliffs, NJ: Prentice-Hall, 1964), 27.

4. Charles W. Forman, Editorial, "The Definition of Ecumenics," *Theology Today* 22, no. 1 (April 1965), 3.

5. Steven R. Pointer, "Joseph Cook—Apologetics and Science," *Journal of Presbyterian History* 63, no. 3 (Fall 1985): 299–308.

6. John A. Mackay, "Witherspoon of Paisley and Princeton," *Theology Today* 18, no. 4 (January 1962): 473–81.

7. "Mackay on Lectureship," *Presbyterian Outlook* 142, no. 37 (October 17, 1960): 12.

8. Howard W. Yoder, "The Second Latin American Evangelical Conference," *International Review of Missions* 51, no. 1 (January 1962): 75–78 at 75, and Thomas J. Liggett, "Protestant Parley in Peru," *Christian Century* 78, no. 40 (October 4, 1961), 1166–68.

9. Elena Mackay Reisner, conversation with the author, September 20, 2005. The Rev. Sherwood Reisner, her husband, attended the Conference with Mackay.

10. Liggett, "Protestant Parley," 1167.

11. Some years later McIntire was deported from Kenya ("McIntire Deported," *Christian Century* 92, no. 27 [August 20–27, 1975]: 727).

12. On McIntire see Luis Cassels, "The Rightist Crisis in Our Churches," *Look Magazine*, April 24, 1962, 46. At that time *Look* had a circulation of seven million.

13. John M. MacPherson, *At the Roots of a Nation* (Edinburgh: Knox Press, 1993), 191–92.

14. "Mackay Stresses Role as Ecumenical-Evangelical," *Presbyterian Outlook*, November 27, 1961, 10.

15. John A. Mackay, *The Latin American Churches and the Ecumenical Movement* (New York: Committee on Cooperation in Latin America, Division of Foreign Missions, National Council of the Churches of Christ in the U.S.A., 1963).

16. John A. Mackay, "Cuba in Perspective," *Presbyterian Life*, July 15, 1961, 16–18, 31–32. Also reflected in "Assessing Castro," *Christianity Today* 5, no. 22 (July 31, 1961): 52; "Mackay Assesses Relations between U.S. and Cuba," *Presbyterian Outlook*, September 11, 1961, 6–7; E. G. Homrighausen, "Another Look at Cuba," *Theology Today* 18, no. 3 (October 1961): 348–50.

17. Mary Anastasia O'Grady, "Onward Christian Cubans," *Wall Street Journal*, May 7, 2007, A14. "Seeking All Cubans through the Elite," in *Cross and Sword*, ed. H. McKennie Goodpasture (Maryknoll, NY: Orbis Books, 1989), 211–13.

18. John A. Mackay, "Latin America and Revolution—I: The New Mood in Society and Culture," *Christian Century* 82, no. 46 (November 17, 1965): 1409. A sensitive psychologist, Raquel Betancourt believed in the abnormal psychology of Castro. See Georgie Anne Geyer, *Guerrilla Prince* (Boston: Little, Brown & Co., 1991), 232.

19. John A. Mackay, "Cuba Revisited," *Christian Century* 81, no. 7 (February 12, 1964), 203. See also H. McKennie Goodpasture, "The Latin American Soul of John A. Mackay," *Journal of Presbyterian History* 48, no. 4 (Winter 1970): 289–91.

20. "Readers' Response to Mackay on Cuba," *Christian Century* 81, no. 13 (March 25, 1964): 402–406; "Mackay on Cuba," *Christian Century* 81, no. 43 (October 21, 1964), 1308. Those who disagreed included Rafael Diaz-Balart, Castro's former brother-in-law, who had studied for a year at Princeton Seminary while Mackay was president.

21. John A. Mackay, "A Fresh Look at Cuba," *Christian Century* 81, no. 32 (August 5, 1964): 983–87.

22. Highlights of this trip are recounted in a two-part article: John A. Mackay, "Latin America and Revolution," pt. 1, " The New Mood in Society and Culture," *Christian Century* 82, no. 46 (November 17, 1965): 1409–12; and "Latin America and Revolution," pt. 2, "The New Mood in the Churches," *Christian Century* 82, no. 47 (November 24, 1965): 1439–43.

23. Mackay, "Latin America and Revolution," pt. 1, 1409.

24. Ibid., 1411–12.

25. See Henri Fesquet, *The Drama of Vatican II* (New York: Random House, 1967), 239–40. And see *Unitatis Redintegratio* (The Decree on Ecumenism), November 21, 1964.

26. Mackay, "Latin America and Revolution," pt. 2, 1441. John A. Mackay, "The Great Adventure," *Princeton Seminary Bulletin* 64, no. 2 (July 1971): 32.

27. Luis Alberto Sánchez, "Juan A. Mackay y la Educación Peruana" [John A. Mackay and Peruvian Education], *Leader* (Lima), December 1973, 63–70. On Mackay's friend, Luis Alberto Sánchez, see obituary of Luis Alberto Sánchez, *New York Times*, February 7, 1994, B8. Dr. N. A. R. MacKay, "Lima Revisited," *From the Frontiers*, A Quarterly Magazine Issued by Authority of the Free Church of Scotland Foreign Overseas and Jewish Missions' Board, March 1974, 3–8.

28. John A. Mackay, "Latin America and Revolution," pt. 1, 1409.

29. Ibid.

30. Mackay, "Latin America and Revolution," pt. 2, 1439–43.

31. John A. Mackay, "Historical Perspectives of Protestantism," in *Integration of Man and Society in Latin America*, ed. Samuel Shapiro (Notre Dame, IN: University of Notre Dame Press, 1967), 179.

32. John A. Mackay, *The Other Spanish Christ* (New York: Macmillan Co., 1932).

33. Eugene C. Blake, "John Alexander Mackay: An Appreciation," *Reformed and Presbyterian World* 25, no. 6 (June 1959): 245–46, quoted in Marcel Pradervand, *A Century of Service* (Edinburgh: Saint Andrew Press, 1975), 238–39.

34. "Bishop Moore: A Leader of the New Breed," *Newsweek* 65, no. 13 (March 29, 1965): 77.

35. Harvey G. Cox, "The 'New Breed' in American Churches: Sources of Social Activism in American Religion," *Daedalus* 96, no. 1 (Winter 1967): 135–50 at 149.

36. In a brilliant critique, W. A. Visser 't Hooft wrote in 1928, "America produced a type of religious thought which was largely its own" (*The Background of the Social Gospel in America* [Haarlem: H. D.Tjeenk Willink & Zoon, 1928], 186). Francis Landey Patton regarded the new Christianity as "a disease and its rapid spread as an epidemic" (*Fundamental Christianity* [New York: Macmillan, 1926], 174). Henry Sloane Coffin, the uncle of William Sloane Coffin, taught a more balanced social gospel. See Timothy A. Beach-Verhey, "The Social Gospel and Reconciliation: Henry Sloane Coffin at Madison Avenue Presbyterian Church," *Journal of Presbyterian History* 74, no. 3 (Fall 1996): 193–207. Reinhold Niebuhr criticized a social gospel that did not include attention to the mechanisms of social justice (*An Interpretation of Christian Ethics* [New York: Harper & Bros., 1935], 104). This emphasis eventually led to a political left bereft of authentic spirituality. See Mark Hulsether, *Building a Protestant Left* (Knoxville: University of Tennessee Press, 1999).

37. John C. Bennett, *The Radical Imperative* (Philadelphia: Westminster Press, 1975), 45.

38. In 1907 Walter Rauschenbusch published *Christianity and the Social Crisis* (New York: Macmillan Co., 1907), xxv, to "discharge a debt" he felt he owed to "the working people." His book attracted a great deal of attention and went through a number of printings between 1907 and 1910. Rauschenbusch admitted in the foreword to his later work, *A Theology for the Social Gospel* (New York: Macmillan Co., 1917), that he was "not a doctrinal theologian either by professional training or by personal habits of mind." In fact he feared that publication of the book would cause him to lose his position in a theological seminary.

39. Arend Th. van Leeuwen, *Christianity in World History: The Meeting of the Faiths of East and West* (London: Edinburgh House Press, 1964), 331–34, 441–42.

40. Peter L. Berger, "The Desecularization of the World: A Global Overview," in *The Desecularization of the World Resurgent Religion and World Politics*, ed. Peter L. Berger (Washington, DC: Ethics and Public Policy Center; Grand Rapids: Wm. B. Eerdmans Publishing Co., 1999), 2.

41. Peter Berger, author of *The Sacred Canopy* (Garden City, NY: Doubleday, 1967), is quoted in "In God's Name, A Special Report on Religion and Public Life," *The Economist*, November 3, 2007, 11.

42. On the movement, see John Warwick Montgomery, "A Philosophical-Theological Critique of the Death of God Movement," in *The Meaning of the Death of God*, ed. Bernard Murchland (New York: Random House, 1967), 25–69. Also see Ved Mehta, *The New Theologian* (New York: Harper & Row, 1966); Langdon Gilkey, *Naming the Whirlwind: The Renewal of God-Language* (Indianapolis: Bobbs-Merrill Co., 1969); George William Rutler, *Beyond Modernity* (San Francisco: Ignatius Press, 1987), 161–62.

43. The Easter issue featured a black cover with red lettering: "IS God Dead?" *Time*, April 8, 1966, 82–87. See Abbie Hoffman, *Revolution for the Hell of It* (New York: Dial Press, 1968). On the religious climate see Camille Paglia, "Cults and Cosmic Consciousness: Religious Vision in the American 1960s," *Arion*, 3rd series, 10, no. 3 (Winter 2003): 57–111.

44. Cox, "The 'New Breed,'" 138–39. Saul D. Alinsky, *Reveille for Radicals* (Chicago: University of Chicago Press, 1945), 219, 152; editorial, "Exploiting Urban Decay," *Christian Century* 81, no. 7 (February 12, 1964): 195–97; Nicholas von Hoffman, "Reorganization in the Casbah," *Social Progress* 52, no. 6 (April 1962): 33–44.

45. See Blake's response in Eugene Carson Blake to John A. Mackay, December 30, 1958, quoted in R. Douglas Brackenridge, *Eugene Carson Blake* (New York: Seabury Press, 1978), 60, 199.

46. J. Merion Kadyk, letter to the editor, *Presbyterian Outlook* 146, no. 3 (January 20, 1964): 2. On managerial control, see Cox, "The 'New Breed,'" 141; and Paul M. Harrison, *Authority and Power in the Free Church Tradition* (Princeton, NJ: Princeton University Press, 1959), cited in Cox, "The 'New Breed,'" 149. On control see also Laurie Goodstein, "Pentecostal and Charismatic Groups Growing," *New York Times*, October 6, 2006, A22.

47. *Presbyterian Church in the United States v. Mary Elizabeth Blue Hull, Memorial Presbyterian Church*, 393 U.S. 440 (1969). The opinion was written by Roman Catholic Justice William Brennan.

48. Mackay, *Ecumenics*, 205–207; John A. Mackay, *Christian Reality & Appearance* (Richmond, VA: John Knox Press, 1969), 81–89.

49. Glenn R. Bucher, "John Coleman Bennett: The Presbyterian Years," *Journal of Presbyterian History* 50, no. 1 (Spring 1972): 17. William Sloane Coffin Jr., *Once to Every Man* (New York: Atheneum, 1978), 285. *U.S. v. Spock*, 416 F.2d 165 (1st Cir. 1969). Warren's opinion, *U.S. v. O'Brien*, 391 U.S. 367 (1968), upheld a criminal prohibition against draft-card burning.

50. Philip Turner, "The Episcopalian Preference," *First Things*, November 2003, 29–30.

51. Coffin was married three times and divorced twice. Divorce is a tragedy for everyone, but particularly for ordained clergy. The requiem service for Bishop Pike at Grace Cathedral, San Francisco, on September 12, 1969, was the first for an Episcopal bishop that was attended by all three of the decedent's wives. William Stringfellow and Anthony Towne, *The Death and Life of Bishop Pike* (Garden City, NY: Doubleday, 1967), 201–2.

52. William Sloane Coffin Jr., *Credo* (Louisville, KY: Westminster John Knox Press, 2004), 22.

53. Warren Goldstein, *William Sloane Coffin, Jr.* (New Haven, CT: Yale University Press, 2004), 232–33.

54. Karl Barth, "Thoughts on the Second Vatican Council," *Ecumenical Review* 15, no. 4 (July 1963): 357–67, at 367.

55. John A. Mackay, "The Restoration of Piety: Charge to President James I. McCord," *Princeton Seminary Bulletin* 54, no. 1 (July 1960): 49–50. In his address the prior evening President Robert F. Goheen of Princeton University recognized Mackay's efforts when he noted, "There has been a widespread rehabilitation of theology" (Robert F. Goheen, "The Seminary and the University," *Princeton Seminary Bulletin* 54, no. 1 [July 1960]: 10).

56. Mackay, "The Restoration of Piety," 49.

57. Donald G. Bloesch, *The Crisis of Piety*, 2nd ed. (Colorado Springs: Helmers & Howard, 1988), xv, 12; editorial, "The Loss of Personal Religion," *Christianity Today* 12, no. 13 (March 29, 1968): 24–25.

58. John A. Mackay, "A Representative American of the Sixties: James Joseph Reeb," *Princeton Seminary Bulletin* 60, no. 1 (October 1966): 36.

59. Mackay, "A Representative American," 37. Also see Duncan Howlett, *No Greater Love: The James Reeb Story* (New York: Harper & Row, 1966). Justice Hugo Black occasionally attended services at All Souls.

60. John A. Mackay, "Life's Chief Discoveries," *Christianity Today* 14, no. 7 (January 2, 1970): 4.

61. Mackay, "A Representative American," 38.

62. James E. Andrews, "Karl Barth, A Close-up," *Presbyterian Life*, June 1, 1962, 17.

63. John A. Mackay, *His Life and Our Life* (Philadelphia: Westminster Press, 1964); Donald Macleod, review, *Princeton Seminary Bulletin* 58, no. 1 (October 1964): 68.

64. Mackay, *His Life and Our Life*, 36–37. Also, "no one should participate in this sacrament who is living in open or unconfessed sin, or leading a life that is unworthy of Christ. For that reason appropriate discipline must be exercised to exclude such a person from the privilege of sitting down at the Lord's table" (Mackay, *Presbyterian Way of Life,* 100).

65. See John A. Mackay, "The Great Adventure," *Princeton Seminary Bulletin* 64, no. 2 (July 1971): 31–38.

66. John A. Mackay, "When Truth Is a Belt," *Princeton Seminary Bulletin* 59, no. 1 (November 1965): 5. For Tillich's attitude toward the Bible, see Avery R. Dulles, SJ, "Paul Tillich and the Bible," *Theological Studies* 17, no. 3 (1956): 345–67.

67. "Key Bridge II," *Christianity Today* 12, no. 6 (December 22, 1967): 42. See also "Evangelical Advance at Key Bridge," *Christianity Today* 12, no. 2 (October 27, 1967): 25–26, 42–43; John A. Mackay, "Toward an Evangelical Renaissance," *Princeton Seminary Bulletin* 64, no. 3 (December 1971): 93.

68. John A. Mackay, "Perspective for the Restudy and Reappraisal of the POAU Manifesto," September 30, 1965; John A. Mackay to Glenn L. Archer, October 21, 1965, Mackay Collection.

69. John A. Mackay to C. Stanley Lowell, February 4, 1966, Mackay Collection.

70. Mackay, "When Truth Is a Belt," 12.

71. Mackay, "The Great Adventure," 37.

72. Ibid.

73. John A. Mackay, "Reappraisal Urged of U.S. Foreign Policy," letter to the editor, *New York Times*, November 14, 1965, 11. He joined others in a letter to the president urging the end of the Vietnam War (*Presbyterian Outlook*, January 18, 1965, 7). He had signed a letter ten years before also opposing a drift towards war (*The Churchman*, April 15, 1955, 6).

74. "As regards Christian Churchmen, I thank God for the recent marches to Selma and Montgomery and for the new concern over international policy, racial equality, social justice, and human welfare in general. May this be an indication, in both the secular and the religious order, that the Cult of the Uncommitted is being replaced by another" (Mackay, "When Truth Is a Belt," 10).

75. Martin Marty, "America's Real Religion: An Attitude," in *The New Shape of American Religion* (New York: Harper & Bros., 1959), 67–89; Robert N. Bellah, "Civil Religion in America," in *Religion in America*, ed. William G. McLoughlin and Robert N. Bellah (Boston: Houghton Mifflin Co., 1968).

76. E. Digby Baltzell, *The Protestant Establishment* (New York: Random House, 1964). An exaggerated sense of social activism among some U.S. clergy may have arisen from sociological factors in their own background, just as some liberal theology in Germany may have resulted from guilt over failing to speak out in time or to prevent World War II.

77. Mackay, *Christian Reality*; Robert H. Heinze, "John Mackay on Reality and Shadow," *Presbyterian Life* 23, no. 1 (January 1, 1970): 33. Marcel Pradervand, review, *Theology Today* 27, no. 2 (July 1970): 221–25; Stuart Barton Babbage, "Rare Reflective Wisdom," *Christianity Today* 14, no. 12 (March 13, 1970): 23; David Willis, *Princeton Seminary Bulletin* 62, no. 3 (Autumn 1969): 87–88. See also John A. Mackay, *Realidad e idolatría en el cristianismo contemporáneo* (Buenos Aires: Editorial Aurora, 1970), the 1953 Carnahan Lectures delivered at the Evangelical Faculty of Theology in Buenos Aires, Argentina.

78. John A. Mackay, "Ecumenicalism: Threat to Christian Unity?" *Christianity Today* 13, no. 24 (September 12, 1969): 11–12, excerpted from Mackay, *Christian Reality*, 85–89; Max Warren used the term "neurotic" to refer to this type of unity.

79. Mackay, *Christian Reality,* 90–108.

80. Marcel Pradervand, review of *Christian Reality & Appearance, Theology Today* 27, no. 1 (April 1970): 224.

81. Jack B. Rogers, "Biblical Authority and Confessional Change," *Journal of Presbyterian History* 59, no. 2 (Summer 1981): 153 n. 27.

82. Ibid., 153 n. 29. On the liberal confession and difficulties, see William R. Hutchison, ed., *American Protestant Thought: The Liberal Era* (New York: Harper & Row, 1968), 226; James H. Moorhead, "Redefining Confessionalism: American Presbyterians in the Twentieth Century," in *The Confessional Mosaic*, ed. Milton J Coalter, John M. Mulder, and Louis B. Weeks (Louisville, KY: Westminster/John Knox Press: 1990), 82–83; Jack Rogers, *Reading the Bible and the Confessions: The Presbyterian Way* (Louisville, KY: Geneva Press, 1999), 25–27. Some members as students did not grasp fully the message of the new Princeton.

83. John A. Mackay, "Commendation and Concern," *Presbyterian Outlook*, December 13, 1965, 5–7.

84. John A. Mackay, "Make Every Thought Christ's Captive," *Princeton Seminary Bulletin* 52, no. 2 (October 1958): 9.

85. Mackay, "Commendation and Concern," 5.

86. Ibid.

87. Ibid., 6.

88. Ibid. Regarding the full biblical meaning of the term *reconciliation* contrast ambiguity in the discussion quoted in Daniel L. Migliore, "A Conversation with Edward A. Dowey," *Princeton Seminary Bulletin*, n.s., 9, no. 2 (1988): 98–99, with Mackay's statement in Mackay, "Commendation and Concern," 6. On reconciliation see also Mackay, "When Truth Is a Belt," 11.

89. Mackay, "Commendation and Concern," 7.

90. Ibid.

91. Ibid., 6.

92. Ibid.

93. Frank Heinze, "PUBC Meets in Chicago to Discuss 'Confession'," *Presbyterian Life*, January 1, 1966, 26. The meeting included a session to consider possible revisions and to forward recommendations to the Special Committee of Fifteen. See "Chicago Meeting Set on Confession of 1967," *Presbyterian Life*, November 15, 1965, 29.

94. Heinze, "PUBC Meets," 26.

95. "The Confession of 1967," in *The Constitution of the Presbyterian Church (U.S.A.)*, Part 1, *Book of Confessions* (Louisville, KY: Office of the General Assembly, Presbyterian Church (U.S.A.), 2004), 9.45. For Paul Ramsey's comment, see Paul Ramsey, *Who Speaks for the Church?* (Nashville: Abingdon Press, 1967), 180–81, n. 35.

96. Heinze, "PUBC Meets," 26; Kenneth John Wilkinson Jr., "The Confession of 1967: Presbyterians and the Politics of Reconciliation," PhD diss. Northwestern University, 2001, 105; see also John Wilkinson, "Edward A. Dowey, Jr., and the Making of the Confession of 1967," *Journal of Presbyterian History* 82, no. 1 (Spring 2004): 5–22.

97. "179th General Assembly," *Presbyterian Life*, June 15, 1967, 16.

98. Rogers, *Reading the Bible and the Confessions*, 25. Edward Dowey had refused to take the teaching oath required of professors when he joined the staff of Princeton Seminary (see Daniel L. Migliore, "A Conversation with Edward A. Dowey," *Princeton Seminary Bulletin*, n.s., 9, no. 2 [1988]: 95).

99. John R. Fry, *The Trivialization of the United Presbyterian Church* (New York: Harper & Row, 1975). Dowey believed in 1987 that the confession was ahead of its time (see Migliore, "A Conversation," 102). Dowey told the PUBC, "The confession does not deny inspiration, it simply refuses to place it at its center" (John Wilkinson, "The Making of the Confession of 1967," *Church and Society* 92, no. 5 [May–June 2002]: 35). Also see "Reconciliation and Liberation—The Confession of 1967," *Journal of Presbyterian History* 61, no. 1 (Spring 1983); George S. Hendry, "The Bible in the Confession of 1967," *Princeton Seminary Bulletin* 60, no. 1 (October 1966): 21–24.

100. See, for example, John A. Mackay, "The Holy Spirit in Proclamation," in *Christianity on the Frontier* (New York: Macmillan Co., 1950), 22–40; idem, "Make Sure You Believe in the Holy Ghost," *Princeton Seminary Bulletin* 46, no. 2 (October 1952): 11–12; idem, "Be Aglow with the Spirit," *Princeton Seminary Bulletin* 48, no. 2 (October 1954): 15–16.

101. Mackay, "Portent and Promise in the Other America," *Princeton Seminary Bulletin* 47, no. 3 (January 1954): 13–14; and Mackay, *God's Order*, 180.

102. Robert R. Curlee and Mary Ruth Isaac-Curlee, "Bridging the Gap: John A. Mackay, Presbyterians and the Charismatic Movement," *Journal of Presbyterian History* 72, no. 3 (Fall 1994): 141–56, 143. For the perceived controversial nature of the movement in some circles see, for example, James N. Lapsley and John H. Simpson, "Speaking in Tongues," *Princeton Seminary Bulletin* 58, no. 2 (February 1965): 3–18.

103. The meeting was also noted in Russell Chandler, "Fanning the Charismatic Fire," *Christianity Today* 12, no. 4 (November 24, 1967): 39–40. Some of Mackay's observations at

this retreat were reproduced in the *Newsletter of the Charismatic Communion of Presbyterian Ministers*, no. 4, November 1967, 1–5.

104. John A. Mackay to Brick Bradford, February 7, 1970. In *Newsletter of the Charismatic Communion of Presbyterian Ministers*, May, 1970, pt. A, 3.

105. Curlee and Isaac-Curlee, "Bridging the Gap," 148.

106. *The Work of the Holy Spirit,* Report of the Special Committee on the Work of the Holy Spirit to the 182nd General Assembly of the United Presbyterian Church in the United States of America (New York: Office of the General Assembly, 1970).

107. Lesslie Newbigin, *Unfinished Agenda* (Edinburgh: Saint Andrew Press, 1993), 141.

108. John A. T. Robinson, *Honest to God* (Philadelphia: Westminster Press, 1963), 93. See also Walter James, "The Education of the Clergy," *The Fortnightly*, November 1954, 316–21.

109. Richard Shaull and Waldo Cesar, *Pentecostalism and the Future of the Christian Churches* (Grand Rapids: Wm. B. Eerdmans Publishing Co., 2000), 206; K. H. Ting, *No Longer Strangers: Selected Writings of Bishop K. H. Ting*, ed. Raymond L. Whitehead (Maryknoll, NY: Orbis Books, 1989), 14.

110. John A. Mackay to Charles Ranson, December 12, 1951, Mackay Collection.

111. The term *scaffolding* is Robert E. Speer's. Newbigin noted the unity of WCC and IMC was a necessary effort to relate church and mission but did not touch the parish at that time. Lesslie Newbigin, *A Word in Season* (Grand Rapids: Wm. B. Eerdmans Publishing Co., 1994), 145.

112. Harvey T. Hoekstra, *The World Council of Churches and the Demise of Evangelism* (Wheaton, IL: Tyndale House Publishers, 1979), 49 (quoting from the *Minutes of the Assembly of the IMC, Nov. 17–18, 1961, and the First Meeting of the CWME, WCC, Dec. 7–8, 1961 at New Delhi*).

113. Newbigin, *Unfinished Agenda*, 186ff.

114. Johannes Christiaan Hoekendijk, whose first challenge at Willingen had not been successful, had a radical, low ecclesiology. See Hoekstra, *World Council of Churches*, 20, 70.

115. "Hence it is the world that must be allowed to provide the agenda for the churches" (World Council of Churches, Department on Studies in Evangelism, Western European Working Group, *The Church for Others and the Church for the World* [Geneva: World Council of Churches, 1968], 20).

116. "The passion and Resurrection of Jesus Christ is the Exodus for all men. Now the whole of mankind is delivered from bondage and brought into covenant with God. By the raising up of the New Man, Christ Jesus, every man has been made a member of the new mankind" (World Council of Churches, Department on Studies in Evangelism, *Planning for Mission*, ed. Thomas Wieser [New York: United States Conference for the World Council of Churches, 1966], 54).

117. "We have nothing to say. . . . Our calling is to sit down alongside secular man and let him teach us. We cannot aspire to be more than a Christian presence in the midst of the non-Christian world" (World Council of Churches, *Planning for Mission,* 122, 220, cited in John R. W. Stott, *Our Guilty Silence* [London: Hodder & Stoughton, 1967], 33).

118. John Stott, *Evangelical Truth* (Downers Grove, IL: InterVarsity Press, 1999), 20.

119. Newbigin, *A Word in Season,* 139.

120. John C. Bennett, "The Geneva Conference of 1966 as a Climactic Event," *Ecumenical Review* 37, no. 1 (January 1985): 26–33, at 29.

121. Ramsey, *Who Speaks for the Church?*

122. Bennett wrote that Shaull's "speech was along lines similar to his chapter." See Richard Shaull, "Revolutionary Change in Theological Perspective," in *Christian Social Ethics in a Changing World*, ed. John C. Bennett (New York: Association Press, 1966), 23–43, at 33 and 43. Mackay was disappointed in the direction of his former student.

123. R. Douglas Brackenridge, *Eugene Carson Blake: Prophet with Portfolio* (New York: Seabury Press, 1978), 160–63; Hoekstra, *World Council of Churches*, 49–131.

124. John A. Mackay, "Ecumenicalism: Threat to Christian Unity?" *Christianity Today* 13, no. 24 (September 12, 1969): 11–12, excerpted from Mackay, *Christian Reality & Appearance* (Richmond, VA: John Knox Press, 1969), 85–89. Mackay, guest editorial, "The Contemporary Task," *Presbyterian Survey*, January 1961, inside front cover; Mackay, "Toward the Recovery of a Lost Perspective," *Presbyterian Outlook*, February 19, 1962, 5.

125. Mackay, "Toward the Recovery," 5.

126. Mackay, "Contemporary Task," inside front cover.

127. John A. Mackay, "What the Ecumenical Movement Can Learn from Conservative Evangelicals," *Christianity Today* 10, no. 17 (May 27, 1966): 17, 20–23. Others also documented the crisis. See Albert van den Heuvel, "Crisis in the Ecumenical Movement," *Christianity and Crisis* 26, no. 5 (April 4, 1966), 59–63.

128. Mackay, "The Ecumenical Movement—Whence? And Whither?" *Bulletin of the Department of Theology of the World Alliance of Reformed Churches* 8, no. 4 (Summer 1968): 1–8.

129. World Council of Churches, *The Uppsala Report 1968*, ed. Norman Goodall (Geneva: World Council of Churches, 1968), 26; Timothy Dudley-Smith, *John Stott: A Global Ministry* (Downers Grove, IL: InterVarsity Press, 2001), 126. Mackay commended the trend toward discussion of conversion (John A. Mackay, "World Council and Evangelical Renewal," *Christianity Today* 12, no. 23 [August 30, 1968]: 23).

130. James A. Scherer and Stephen B. Bevans, eds., *Basic Statements 1974–1991*, vol. 1, *New Directions in Mission and Evangelization* (Maryknoll, NY: Orbis Books, 1992), 258.

131. "It is of crucial importance that the Church acting corporately should not commit itself to any particular policy" (William Temple, *Christianity and Social Order* [New York: Penguin Books, 1942], 18). On the theme see also John C. Bennett, "The Involvement of the Church," in *Man's Disorder and God's Design*, vol. 3, *The Church and the Disorder of Society*, World Council of Churches (New York: Harper & Bros., 1948), 91–102. Also contrast with C. L. Patijn, "The Strategy of the Church," in *Man's Disorder*, 155–75.

132. Jean Caffey Lyles, "That $85,000 Grant," *Christian Century* 95, no. 29 (September 20, 1978): 844. The violent efforts at reform produced long-term tragedy, disease, and starvation in Zimbabwe. See Peter Godwin, "Zimbabwe's Bitter Harvest," *National Geographic*, August 2003, 112–13.

133. Jill K. Gill, "The Decline of Real Ecumenism: Robert Bilheimer and the Viet Nam War," *Journal of Presbyterian History* 81, no. 4 (Winter 2003): 242–63.

134. C. H. Dodd, "A Letter Concerning Unavowed Motives in Ecumenical Discussions," *Ecumenical Review* 2, no. 1 (Autumn 1949): 52–56, at 56.

135. See, in particular, Hendrik Kraemer, *World Cultures and World Religions* (London: Lutterworth Press, 1960); Samuel P. Huntington, *The Clash of Civilizations and the Remaking of World Order* (New York: Simon & Schuster, 1996); and Joseph Cardinal Ratzinger, *Truth and Tolerance* (San Francisco: Ignatius Press, 2004).

136. D. Michael Lindsay, *Faith in the Halls of Power: How Evangelicals Joined the American Elite* (New York: Oxford University Press, 2007).

137. Russell Chandler, "Fanning the Charismatic Fire," *Christianity Today* 12, no. 4 (November 24, 1967): 40. Mackay, *Christian Reality*, 89. For the same idea, see John A. Mackay, "Toward an Evangelical Renaissance," *Princeton Seminary Bulletin* 64, no. 3 (December 1971), 95; and idem, "Great Adventure," 35.

138. John A. Mackay, "Roman Catholicism in the Pangs of Rebirth," *Presbyterian Outlook* 145, no. 6 (February 11, 1963), 6–7.

139. Pope Paul VI quoted the words of Saint Paul: "'To put on the new man, which after God, is created in righteousness and the holiness of truth.' Eph. IV. 23." See "Text of Pope Paul's Speech at U.N. Appealing for an End to War and Offensive Arms," *New York Times International Edition*, October 6, 1965, 6. For a view of the speech in terms of religious liberty, see Robert E. Cushman, "The Pope, The Council, and Religious Liberty—A Magnificent Risk," in *Best Sermons*, Vol. 10, *1966–1968*, Protestant ed., ed. G. Paul Butler (New York: Trident Press, 1968), 143–48.

140. Associated Press, "Pope, Asked about Rep. Drinan, Says 'A Priest Should Be a Priest'" *New York Times*, May 13, 1980, B14; Michael Knight, "Drinan's Aides Say He Is Told to Quit Politics," *New York Times*, May 5, 1980, 16.

141. John L. Sherrill, *They Speak with Other Tongues* (New York: McGraw-Hill, 1964), 162, quoted in W. J. Hollenweger, *The Pentecostals: The Charismatic Movement in the Churches* (Minneapolis: Augsburg Publishing House, 1972), 6.

142. For example, David Martin, *Tongues of Fire: The Explosion of Protestantism in Latin America* (Oxford: Basil Blackwell, 1990); David Stoll, *Is Latin America Turning Protestant? The Politics of Evangelical Growth* (Berkeley: University of California Press, 1990); Philip Jenkins, *The Next Christendom* (New York: Oxford University Press: 2002); Allen Anderson, *Spreading Fires: The Missionary Nature of Early Pentecostalism* (London: SCM Press, 2007); Lamin Sanneh, *Disciples of All Nations: Pillars of World Christianity* (New York: Oxford University Press, 2008).

143. Kenneth A. Briggs, "Suicide Pact Preceded Deaths of Dr. Van Dusen and His Wife," *New York Times*, February 26, 1975, 1, 43.

144. John A. Mackay, "Life's Chief Discoveries," *Christianity Today* 14, no. 7 (January 2, 1970): 5.

145. Leah Ward Sears, "The 'Marriage Gap': A Case for Strengthening Marriage in the 21st Century," *New York University Law Review* 82, no. 5 (November 2007): 1243–64; James Davison Hunter, *Culture Wars* (New York: BasicBooks, 1991), 3–8.

146. Andrew T. Roy, "The Death of a Movement," *Christian Century* 93, no. 1 (January 7–14, 1976): 19–20.

147. The books listed were *Confessions*, by St. Augustine; *Pensées*, by Blaise Pascal; *Paradise Lost*, by John Milton; *Pilgrim's Progress*, by John Bunyan; *The Journal of John Woolman* and *Life of David Brainerd*, by Jonathan Edwards; *Memoir and Remains of Robert Murray McCheyne* and *The Tragic Sense of Life*, by Miguel de Unamuno; *The Invisible Christ*, by Ricardo Rojas; and *The Epistle to the Romans*, by Karl Barth. See "The Books That Shape Lives," *Christian Century* 93, no. 13 (April 14, 1976): 371.

Bibliography of John A. Mackay

The following is a selected bibliography of Mackay's published works in both English and other languages, and it includes some descriptive notes for the reader.

English Publications

I. Books

1932

The Other Spanish Christ. New York: Macmillan.

1935

That Other America. New York: Friendship Press.

1941

A Preface to Christian Theology. New York: Macmillan. Reprint, London: Nisbet & Co. Ltd, 1942.

1943

Heritage and Destiny. New York: Macmillan.

1950

Christianity on the Frontier. New York: Macmillan.

1953

God's Order: The Ephesian Letter and This Present Time. New York: Macmillan.

1960

The Presbyterian Way of Life. Englewood Cliffs, NJ: Prentice-Hall.

1964

Ecumenics: The Science of the Church Universal. Englewood Cliffs, NJ: Prentice-Hall.
His Life and Our Life: The Life of Christ and the Life in Christ. Philadelphia: Westminster Press.

1969

Christian Reality & Appearance. Richmond, VA: John Knox Press.

II. Ecclesiastical Statements and Pronouncements

1938

The State of the Church: A Report. New York: Federal Council of the Churches of Christ in America. Committee on the State of the Church. Reprinted in *Biennial Report 1938*, 37–45. New York: Federal Council of the Churches of Christ in America.

1942

Our Heritage of Religious Freedom, adopted by the Federal Council of the Churches in Biennial Session, December 11; also ratified concurrently by the Foreign Missions Conference and the Home Missions Council. New York: Federal Council of the Churches of Christ in America. Reprinted in *Federal Council of Churches Bulletin* 26, no. 1 (January 1943): 9–10.

1951

"The World Presbyterian Alliance in the Present Ecumenical Situation." *Presbyterian World* 21, no. 3 (September): 98–102. The "Basle Statement."

1952

"A Letter to the Christian People of America," by National Council of the Churches of Christ in the United States of America General Assembly. Reprinted in parts in *Presbyterian Outlook* 135, no. 3: 4; no. 4: 7; no. 5: 6–7; no. 6: 7; no. 7: 6–7; see also "Text of National Council's Letter to Christian People of America," from the General Assembly of the National Council of the Churches of Christ in the U.S.A., *New York Times*, December 13, 1952, 17.

1953

"A Letter to Presbyterians Concerning the Present Situation in Our Country and in the World," Philadelphia: Presbyterian Church in the U.S.A. General Council. Reprinted in *New York Times*, November 3, 20; *U.S. News & World Report*, November 13, 116–18; and "A Letter to Presbyterians." *Princeton Seminary Bulletin* 5, no. 3, n.s. (November 1984): 197–202.

1955

"A Letter to the Reformed Family of Churches." *Presbyterian World* 23, no. 1 (March): 1–4.

1958

"In Unity—For Mission. A Message to All Congregations from the Uniting General Assembly of the United Presbyterian Church in the United States of America," May 30. Philadelphia. Reprinted in *Presbyterian Life* 11, no. 13 (July 1): 20–23.

III. Articles, Editorials, Pamphlets, Sermons, and Contributions to Books and Reports

1917

"Leaves from the Diary of a Missionary Tour to South America: The City of the Incas." *The Instructor* (January): 59–60.

"Leaves from the Diary of a Missionary Tour to South America: In the Urco Valley." *The Instructor* (February): 75–76.
"First Days in Lima." *Monthly Record of the Free Church of Scotland* (June): 79–80.
"South American Mission." *Monthly Record of the Free Church of Scotland* (September): 113–14.

1918

"Missionary News: Progress in Lima." *Monthly Record of the Free Church of Scotland* (March): 37.
"Mr. Inman's Report." *Monthly Record of the Free Church of Scotland* (May): 70–71.
"Mr. Mackay's Report." *Monthly Record of the Free Church of Scotland* (June): 95– 96.
"God Is Dead!" *The Instructor* (November): 27–28.

1919

"New School Premises in Lima." *Monthly Record of the Free Church of Scotland* (January): 6.
"A Journey to the Montaña." *Monthly Record of the Free Church of Scotland* (April): 53–54.
"Missionary News: From South America." *The Instructor* (July): 152–53.
"Work in Peru." *Monthly Record of the Free Church of Scotland* (July): 110.

1920

"The Lima Calendar." *The Instructor* (May): 125–26.
"The Lima School." *The Instructor* (December): 40–41.
"Student Life in a South American University." *Student World* 13, no. 3: 89–97.

1921

"Church and State in Peru. II. The Conflict Deepens." *Monthly Record of the Free Church of Scotland* (January): 5–6.
"Religious Currents in the Intellectual Life of Peru." *Biblical Review Quarterly* 6, no. 2 (April): 192–211.

1922

"Methods of Deepening Missionary Interest in the Congregational Life of the Church." *Monthly Record of the Free Church of Scotland* (November): 181–82.

1924

"Student Renaissance in South America." *Student World* 17, no. 2 (April): 62–66.
"Who and What Are We? The Fundamental Ideals and Purposes of the Association Movement Need to Be Given New Vitality." *Association Forum* 10, no. 2 (October): 1, 2, 17, 18. Note: Rethinking the connotation of the term "Christianization."

1925

"Our Ideals." *The Standard* (Buenos Aires), March 29, 5. Note: Digest of an address on education presented in Montevideo, Uruguay.
"The Report of Commission Eleven on Special Religious Problems in South America." In *Christian Work in South America: Official Report on the Congress of Christian Work in South America at Montevideo, Uruguay, April, 1925*, edited by Robert E. Speer, Samuel G. Inman, and Frank K. Sanders, vol. 2, 293–377. New York: Fleming H. Revell Co.

1927

"Students and Social Reform." *Scots Observer*, April 16, 13.
"The Passing of Pan-Americanism." *Christian Century* 44, no. 20 (May 19): 618–19.

1928

[Anonymous], "Latin America," *International Review of Missions* 17, no. 1 (January): 64–66.
"South America's Pacific Problem." *Student World* 21, no. 1 (January): 78–81. Note: The problem relating to the ownership of Tacna and Arica, two provinces of the Pacific Coast.
"The Evangelistic Duty of Christianity." In *Report of The Jerusalem Meeting of the International Missionary Council, March 24 to April 8, 1928*, vol. 1, 383–97. New York: International Missionary Council.
"The Power of Evangelism: In South America." In *Report of The Jerusalem Meeting of the International Missionary Council, March 24 to April 8, 1928*, vol. 8, 90–93. New York: International Missionary Council.
"An Introduction to Christian Work among South American Students." *International Review of Missions* 17, no. 2 (April): 278–90.
"The Meaning to Latin America." *Missionary Review of the World* 51, no. 6 (June): 435. Note: The reference and context is to the meaning of the Jerusalem Conference of 1928.
"A Latin Leader Discovers Christ," *Christian Century* 45, no. 31 (July 19): 901–4. Note: Regarding Ricardo Rojas, president of the University of Buenos Aires.
"Adventures of the Mind in Latin America." In *Students and the Future of Christian Missions.* Report of the Tenth Quadrennial Convention of the Student Volunteer Movement for Foreign Missions, Detroit, Michigan, December 28, 1927, to January 1, 1928, edited by Gordon Poteat, 167–72. New York: Student Volunteer Movement for Foreign Missions.
"Contemporary Life and Thought in South America in Their Relation to Evangelical Christianity." In *The Foreign Missions Conference of North America 1928*, edited by Leslie B. Moss, 135–42. New York City: Foreign Missions Conference of North America.

1929

"Spiritual Spring-Time in Latin America." *World Dominion.* 7, no. 4 (October): 415–20, 422, 424.
"A Decade of Student Life in South America." *Student World* 22, no. 2: 146–54.
"The Ecumenical Spirit and the Recognition of Christ." *International Review of Missions* 18, no. 2: 332–45.
"The Everlasting Quest," "Finding God in Christ," and "The Secularization of God." In *Finding and Sharing God: Report of the Fifth Annual Conference in Chicago of the National Council of the Y.M.C.A.s*, 16–21, 33–37, 69–73. New York: Association Press.

1930

"God Is in Sight!" *World's Youth* 6, no. 3: 41–42, 45, 48.
"The Message of Christ" and "Bible Studies." In *Presenting the Christian Message*, 7–11, 12–35. Geneva: World's Young Women's Christian Association.
"Reflections on the Christian Message in the Present World Drama." *Student World* 23, no. 3: 221–33.

1931

"The Basic Insight." In *Report of the Decennial Conference on Missionary Policies and Methods of the Board of Foreign Missions of the Presbyterian Church in the U.S.A.* Held at

Lakeville, Connecticut, June 20–30, 35–41. New York: Board of Foreign Missions of the Presbyterian Church in the U.S.A.

"Youth's Adventure with God." In *Youth's Adventure with God: Being the Official Report of the Third World's Assembly of Y.M.C.A. Workers with Boys, the First World's Y.M.C.A. Assembly of Young Men, and the Twentieth World's Conference of the Y.M.C.A., July 27th– August 2nd, and August 4th– 9th, 1931,* 111–15. London: British Y.M.C.A. Press.

"A Preface to the Christian Message." In *Commission I: The Christian Conception of Personality.* New York: Methodist Book Concern, 15–26. Note: An address delivered to the conference as an introduction to the studies in Group II, "The Christian Message for the Modern World."

Reflections on the Mission and Message of the Young Men's Christian Association. Geneva: World's Committee of Young Men's Christian Associations.

"What Jesus Means to Me?" *World's Youth* 6, no. 4: 55–58.

1932

"God's Springtime in Latin America." In *The Christian Mission in the World of Today,* edited by Raymond P. Currier, 51–59. New York: Student Volunteer Movement for Foreign Missions. Note: Report of the Eleventh Quadrennial Convention of the Student Volunteer Movement for Foreign Missions, Buffalo, New York, December 30, 1931 to January 3, 1932.

"Some New Trends in Latin America." *Missionary Review of the World* 55 (January): 17–20.

"The Missionary Significance of the Last Ten Years: A Survey of Latin America." *International Review of Missions* 21, no. 3 (July): 307–8, "Social Movement"; 308–9, "Intellectual Renaissance"; 318–19, "Mexico"; 319, "Peru." Note: Mackay's insights and analysis are quoted in the referenced sections of the article.

"My God and My Neighbor." In *Finding the Will and Power of the Living God.* Report of the Annual Spiritual Emphasis Conference Held at Lake Mohonk Mountain House, Mohonk Lake, NY: October 15, 16, under the Auspices of the Commission on Message and Purpose of the National Council of the Young Men's Christian Associations of the U.S.A., 27–36. New York: Association Press.

1933

"The Oxford Group Movement." *Presbyterian Banner,* January 12, 6–7.

"A New Lay Priesthood." *Presbyterian Banner,* January 19, 6–7.

"The Oxford Group Movement and the Theology of Crisis." *Presbyterian Banner,* January 26, 8–10.

"How to Get at Grips with This Hour of Crisis." *Presbyterian Banner,* March 23, 6–7.

"The Theology of the Laymen's Foreign Missions Inquiry." *International Review of Missions* 22, no. 2 (April): 174–88.

"Lima, Peru, Revisited." *Missionary Review of the World* 56, no. 9 (September): 421–23.

"A Voice from a Peruvian Prison." *Missionary Review of the World* 56, no. 12 (December): 583–86. Note: The prisoner was Haya de la Torre.

1934

"The South American Crisis." *Missionary Review of the World* 57, no. 2 (February): 77–80.

"Education and Religion in Mexico: Some Projected Changes in the Mexican Constitution." *Missionary Review of the World* 57, no. 3 (March): 133–34.

"The Gospel on the Great Divide." *Women and Missions* (May): 39–41.

Our World Mission. New York: Board of Foreign Missions of the Presbyterian Church in the U.S.A. Note: Address delivered at the General Assembly of the Presbyterian Church in the U.S.A., Cleveland, Ohio, May 30, 1934.

"Christian Realism: or Some Things That Are" and "Christian Idealism: or Some Things That Should Be." In *A Christian Crusade: Report of the Spiritual Emphasis Conference, New York City National Council of the Y.M.C.A.s of the U.S.A.,* 9–20 and 55–69. New York: Association Press.

The Friends of Spain. New York: Friends of Spain.

"The Gospel and Our Generation." In *The Christian Message for the World Today,* edited by A. L. Warnshuis, 95–126. New York: Round Table Press.

1935

"Whither Mexico?" *Missionary Review of the World* 58, no. 9 (September): 389–90.

"The Crucial Issue in Latin America: A Meditation on the Present Missionary Situation." *Missionary Review of the World* 58 (November): 527–29.

"Foreword." In *Lupita: A Story of Mexico in Revolution,* by Alberto Rembao. New York: Friendship Press.

"The Unfulfilled Dream of Columbus." In *Biennial Book,* 84–93. New York: Board of National Missions.

1936

"Our Spiritual Limitations and Resources." Note: An Address delivered at the Foreign Missions Conference of North America, Asbury Park, New Jersey, January 8.

"Concerning Insight." *Social Progress* 28, no. 3 (December): 24–30. Note: A sermon reprinted from the *Presbyterian Banner,* August 27.

"Concerning Man and His Remaking." *Princeton Seminary Bulletin* 30, no. 3 (December): 1–6. Note: The first address at the autumn 1936 alumni conference at Princeton Seminary.

"Our Christ." In *Students and the Christian World Mission.* Report of the Twelfth Quadrennial Convention of the Student Volunteer Movement for Foreign Missions, edited by Jesse R. Wilson, 15–22. New York: Student Volunteer Movement for Foreign Missions.

1937

"Historical and Superhistorical Elements in Christianity." *Journal of Religion* 17, no. 1 (January): 1-8.

"The Restoration of Theology." *Princeton Seminary Bulletin* 31, no. 1 (April): 7–18; *Religion in Life* 6, no. 2 (Spring): 163–79. Note: Mackay's address delivered at his installation as president of Princeton Seminary on February 2.

The Universal Church and the World of Nations. Philadelphia: Board of Christian Education of the Presbyterian Church in the United States of America. Note: A seminar held June 2 at the 149th General Assembly, Columbus, Ohio.

"The Ecumenical Road." In "Toward a United Christendom: Impressions of Oxford and Edinburgh," *Christendom* 2, no. 4 (Autumn): 535–38.

"The Church's Task in the Realm of Thought: Reflections on the Oxford Conference." *Princeton Seminary Bulletin* 31, no. 3 (November): 3–9.

"The Rôle of Princeton Seminary." *Princeton Seminary Bulletin* 31, no. 3 (November): 1–2; Reprinted in *The Presbyterian* 107, no. 52 (December 30): 19.

1938

"The Coming of Prof. Brunner to Princeton." *The Presbyterian* 108, no. 7 (February 17): 8.

"Some Answers For Dr. Barnhouse." *The Presbyterian* 108, no. 18 (May 5): 9, 16.

"Looking toward Madras." *Christendom* 3, no. 4 (Autumn): 566–75.

1939

"The Outlook." *Princeton Seminary Bulletin* 32, no. 3 (January): 1–2.

"The Titanic Twofold Challenge, Religion and Democracy Are Linked in the Dictators' Attack." *New York Times Magazine*, sec. 7 (Sunday, May 7): 1, 2, 17.

"The One Hundred and Twenty–Seventh Commencement." *Princeton Seminary Bulletin* 33, no. 1 (July): 1–2.

"On the Road." *Christian Century* 56, no. 28 (July 12): 873–75. Note: An article in the periodical's series on "How My Mind Has Changed in This Decade."

"The Communion of Saints in Our Time." *Crozer Quarterly* 16, no. 4 (October): 251–59. Note: Commencement address delivered at Crozer Seminary in June.

"The Truth That Makes Men Free." New York: American Bible Society. Note: For Universal Bible Sunday, December 10.

1940

"In Memoriam." *Princeton Seminary Bulletin* 33, no. 4 (January): 1–3. Note: Address in memory of J. Ross Stevenson, president emeritus, Princeton Seminary.

"Things That Cannot Be Shaken." *New York Times Magazine,* sec. 7 (Sunday, April 21): 3, 18.

"The Madras Series." *International Review of Missions* 29, no. 3 (July): 391–94.

"Report of the President of the Seminary to the Board of Trustees." *Princeton Seminary Bulletin* 34, no. 1 (July): 24–32.

"The Board of Foreign Missions and the Chosen Question." *The Presbyterian* 110, no. 47 (November 21): 3, 6. The "Chosen Question" means the Korea question.

"'On Earth Peace'—A Christmas Meditation." *New York Times Magazine,* sec. 7 (Sunday, December 22): 3, 13.

1941

"God's New Order," *Christian Education* 24, no. 3 (February): 122–27. Note: Digest of an address delivered at a conference in Naperville, Illinois, on the theme "The Christian Community on the Campus."

"Heritage and Destiny." *Princeton Seminary Bulletin* 34, no. 4 (February): 4–9. Note: An address delivered at the opening of the academic year at Princeton Seminary 1940–1941.

"Principles of Policy." *Princeton Seminary Bulletin* 34, no. 4 (February): 1–3.

"The Adequacy of the Church Today." In *Corpus Unum, The Report of the North American Ecumenical Conference, University of Toronto, Toronto, Canada, June 3 to 5, 1941,* 28–38. New York: Conference Committee. Reprinted in *Christendom* 6, no. 4 (Autumn), 483–94.

"The Student Center." *Princeton Seminary Bulletin* 35, no. 1 (August): 1–2.

"Frontiers That Remain." *The Presbyterian* 111, no. 42 (October 16): 7–8.

"God and the Decisions of History." *Christianity and Crisis* 1, no. 21 (December 1): 2–5.

"Yet Not Consumed." Note: Sermon delivered on December 29 in the Second Presbyterian Church, Philadelphia, on the occasion of a special day of prayer called by the Presbytery of Philadelphia North.

"Introduction." In *The Cross above the Crescent: The Validity, Necessity and Urgency of Missions to Moslems*, by Samuel Marinus Zwemer. Grand Rapids: Zondervan.

"Introduction." In *This Christian Cause (A Letter to Great Britain from Switzerland)*, by Karl Barth. New York: Macmillan.

"The Rôle of the Church as a World Force." In *Religion and the Modern World*, by Jacques Maritain and others, 137–49. Philadelphia: University of Pennsylvania Press.

1942

"The Church in This Land at War." *Social Progress* 32, no. 5 (January): 1–3.

"An International Prayer Meeting." *Christian Century* 59, no. 11 (March 18): 351.

"The Emotion of the Real." *Christianity and Crisis* 2, no. 12 (July 13): 1–2.

"The Princeton Institute of Theology." *Princeton Seminary Bulletin* 36, no. 1 (August): 1–2.

"Needed: Great Faith to Match Great Faith." *New York Times Magazine,* sec. 7 (Sunday, September 20): 3, 31.

"The churches do not, however, have a primary responsibility to devise the details of world order. But they must proclaim the enduring moral principles by which human plans are constantly to be tested." In *A Righteous Faith for a Just and Durable Peace*, by John Foster Dulles et al., 39–44. New York: Federal Council of the Churches of Christ in America, Commission to Study the Bases of a Just and Durable Peace.

1943

"Two American Civilizations and Their Implications for Reformed Theology." *Presbyterian Register* 18, no. 3 (March): 90–96. Note: Robinson Crusoe, the British sailor, and Don Quixote, the knight, are emblematic of two civilizations.

"Ordeal by Fire: An Easter Message." *New York Times Magazine,* sec. 7 (Sunday, April 25): 5, 29.

"Hierarchs, Missionaries, and Latin America." *Christianity and Crisis* 3, no. 7 (May 3): 2–5. Reprinted as *Why Protestant Missions in Latin America?* New York: Committee on Cooperation in Latin America.

Wayfarer [Mackay pseudonym], "Thoughts from the Wayside." *The Presbyterian* 113, no. 37 (September 30): 5.

√ "Personal Religion." *Princeton Seminary Bulletin* 37, no. 1 (December): 3–10. Note: Address delivered at the opening of the academic year at Princeton Seminary, September 22.

"Foreword." In *The Clue to Pascal*, by Emile Cailliet, 9–12. Philadelphia: Westminster Press.

[John A. Mackay], "The Theology of Missions." In *This Is Our World Mission*, 17–22. New York: Board of Foreign Missions of the Presbyterian Church in the United States of America.

1944

"The Church in the World." *Theology Today* 1, no. 1 (April): 121–25.

"Editorial: Our Aims." *Theology Today* 1, no. 1 (April): 3–11.

"Editorial: The Present Number." *Theology Today* 1, no. 1 (April): 11–15. Note: Regarding the theme of the issue: "The Human Situation from the Perspective of the Divine."

"A New Status for Theological Education." *Princeton Seminary Bulletin* 38, no. 1 (June): 1–3.

Ecumenicus [Mackay pseudonym], "The Church in the World." *Theology Today* 1, no. 2 (July): 255–58.

"Editorial: The Burden of This Issue." *Theology Today* 1, no. 2 (July), 152–55. Note: Regarding the theme of the issue: "The Human Problem."

"Editorial: Let the Church Live on the Frontier." *Theology Today* 1, no. 2 (July): 145–293.

Ecumenicus [Mackay pseudonym], "The Church in the World." *Theology Today* 1, no. 3 (October): 395–99.

"Editorial: Concerning Protestant Christianity." *Theology Today* 1, no. 3 (October): 285–93.

"Editorial: This Third Number." *Theology Today* 1, no. 3 (October): 293–97. Note: Regarding the theme of the issue: "The Christian Interpretation of History."

"The World Council in the Post-War Decade, vi." *Christendom* 10, no. 1 (Winter): 25–27.

"Foreword." In *Religious Liberty in Latin America?* by George P. Howard, vii–xiv. Philadelphia: Westminster Press.

1945

"Editorial: The Next Steps." *Theology Today* 1, no. 4 (January): 427–32.

"Editorial: Number Four." *Theology Today* 1, no. 4 (January): 432–37. Note: Regarding the theme of the issue: "God and Religion."

"The End of the First Year." *Theology Today* 1, no. 4 (January): 437–38.

[Mackay], "William Temple Passes." *Theology Today*. 1, no. 4 (January): 537.

"The Task We Envisage." *Princeton Seminary Bulletin* 38, no. 4 (March): 1–3.

Ecumenicus [Mackay pseudonym], "The Church in the World." *Theology Today* 2, no. 1 (April): 105–12.

"Editorial: Concerning Christ and the Church." *Theology Today* 2, no. 1 (April): 10–16. Note: Regarding the theme of the issue: "Jesus Christ and the Christian Church."

"Editorial: The Times Call for Theology," *Theology Today* 2, no. 1 (April): 3–10.

Ecumenicus [Mackay pseudonym], "The Church in the World." *Theology Today* 2, no. 2 (July): 255–61.

"Editorial: Believing and Living." *Theology Today* 2, no. 2 (July): 151–57. Note: Regarding the theme of the issue: commentary on the motto of *Theology Today*, "The Life of Man in the Light of God."

"Editorial: The Peril of a Vacuum." *Theology Today* 2, no. 2 (July): 145–51.

"The Perils of Victory." *Christianity and Crisis* 5, no. 12 (July 9): 1–2. Also in *Social Progress* 36, no. 1 (September): 1–2.

"Broken Cisterns and the Eternal Spring." *Theology Today* 2, no. 3 (October), 300–301.

Ecumenicus [Mackay pseudonym], "The Church in the World." *Theology Today* 2, no. 3 (October): 384–87.

"Editorial: From the Threshold of Tomorrow." *Theology Today* 2, no. 3 (October): 287–94.

"Between the Times." *Princeton Seminary Bulletin* 39, no. 2 (November): 1–2.

"Foreword." In *Religious Liberty: An Inquiry*, by M. Searle Bates. New York: International Missionary Council.

"Introduction." In *Doom and Resurrection*, by Joseph L. Hromádka. Richmond, VA: Madrus House.

1946

"Editorial: As Regards Freedom of Religion." *Theology Today* 2, no. 4 (January): 429–35. Reprinted in *Christianity on the Frontier*, by John A. Mackay, 143–52. New York: Macmillan, 1950.

"The Biblical and Theological Basis for Unity." *Information Service, Federal Council of Churches of Christ in America*, 25 no. 7: 1. Note: Excerpts from Mackay's paper at the Washington Conference on Christian Unity, January 2–4.

"Editorial: What Is the Christian Answer?" *Theology Today* 3, no. 1 (April), 3–10.

"The Christian Approach to the Jew." *Church and the Jew*, 1 no. 2 (April–June, 1946): 3–8.

"The Pacific Coast Revisited." *The Presbyterian* 116, no. 18 (May 2): 3, 5.

"Editorial: God Has Spoken." *Theology Today* 3, no. 2 (July): 145–50.

"The President's Page." *Princeton Seminary Bulletin* 40, no. 3 (Winter): 19–20.

"Latin America—Thirty Years After" [first two of six parts]: "1. Travel in the Air Age." *The Presbyterian* 116, no. 51 (December 19): 4–5; "2. Peoples and Politics." *The Presbyterian* 116, no. 52 (December 26): 6–7.

"The Biblical and Theological Bases for the Ecumenical Goal." In *Toward World-Wide Christianity*, edited by O. Frederick Nolde, 40–58. New York and London: Harper & Bros.

"Protestantism." In *The Great Religions of the Modern World*, edited by Edward J. Jurji, 337–70. Princeton, NJ: Princeton University Press. Reprinted in *Christianity on the Frontier*, by John A. Mackay, 97–142. New York: Macmillan, 1950.

1947

"Editorial: A Theological Meditation on Latin America." *Theology Today* 3, no. 4 (January): 429–39.

"Latin America—Thirty Years After" [final four of six parts]: "3. Ideas and Persons." *The Presbyterian* 117, no. 1 (January 4): 6–7; "4. A Changed Spiritual Atmosphere." *The Presbyterian* 117, no. 2 (January 11): 6–7; "5. The Roman Catholic Reaction." *The Presbyterian* 117, no. 3 (January 18): 6–7; "6. The Coming of Evangelical Christianity." *The Presbyterian* 117, no. 4 (January 25): 7–8.

"Editorial: Crucial Alternatives." *Theology Today* 4, no. 1 (April): 3–11.

"Latin America Today." *World Dominion* 25, no. 3 (May–June): 155–62.

"Editorial: Thoughts on Truth and Unity." *Theology Today* 4, no. 2 (July): 161–68.

"A Footnote to Kingsley and Newman." *Theology Today* 4, no. 2 (July): 172–73.

"Tighten the Belt of Truth." *Princeton Seminary Bulletin* 41, no. 1 (Summer): 9–10. Note: Words of farewell to new graduates of class of 1947.

"Editorial: Fire or Fire." *Theology Today* 4, no. 3 (October): 303–9.

"Editorial: When the Church Is the Church." *Theology Today* 4, no. 3 (October): 310–15. Note: The first of four issues to be devoted to Christianity and the Church in the present situation. The theme of this issue is the "Fellowship of the Spirit."

"Bread." *Christianity and Crisis* 7, no. 21 (December 8): 1–2.

1948

"Editorial: Interpretations." *Theology Today* 4, no. 4 (January): 450–54. Note: The theme of this issue analyzes Roman Catholicism, Protestantism, the Christian Ministry, liberalism, ecumenical theology.

"Editorial: Mexican Musings." *Theology Today* 4, no. 4 (January): 445–50.

"Christ Summons His Church to Action." Note: An address at the meeting to organize a National Council of Presbyterian Men, Chicago, February 12, 1948.

"Editorial: The Contribution of the Reformed Churches to Christian Doctrine." *Theology Today* 5, no. 1 (April): 3–8. Reprinted in *Presbyterian Register* 18, no. 19 (August): 610–13; and in *Christianity on the Frontier*, by John A. Mackay, 86–93. New York: Macmillan, 1950.

"Editorial: A Theological Forward to Ecumenical Gatherings." *Theology Today* 5, no. 2 (July): 145–50.

"The Reformed Churches and the Ecumenical Situation." In *Proceedings of the Sixteenth General Council of the Alliance of Reformed Churches Holding the Presbyterian System Held at Geneva, Switzerland 1948*, edited by W. H. Hamilton, 110–12. Edinburgh: Office of the Alliance. Note: Address delivered Friday, August 13.

"Robert E. Speer: The Missionary Statesman." *Princeton Seminary Bulletin* 42, no. 1 (Summer): 10–13.

"The Endless Journey Starts." *Theology Today* 5, no. 3 (October): 316–17; and *Princeton Seminary Bulletin* 42, no. 1 (Summer): 25–27. Note: Address to the Princeton Seminary graduating class of 1948.

"The Missionary Legacy to the Church Universal." *International Review of Missions* 37, no. 4 (October): 369–74. Note: Address delivered in August at the First Assembly of the World Council of Churches, Amsterdam.

"At the Frontier." *Princeton Seminary Bulletin.* 41, no. 3 (Winter): 14–21. Note: Address delivered at the opening of the academic year on September 30.

"The Holy Spirit in Proclamation." In *Renewal and Advance*, edited by Charles W. Ransom, 148–61. London: International Missionary Council and Edinburgh House Press. Reprinted in *Christianity on the Frontier*, by John A. Mackay, 22–40. New York: Macmillan. Note: Address delivered at the International Mission Council at Whitby, Ontario, 1947.

"Preface" and "God Has Spoken," in *Westminster Study Edition, The Holy Bible*, vii–ix, xv–xx. Philadelphia: Westminster Press. "God Has Spoken" also in *Theology Today* 3, no. 2 (July), 145–50; and in *Christianity on the Frontier*, by John A. Mackay, 13–21, New York: Macmillan.

"With Christ to the Frontier." In *Renewal and Advance*, edited by Charles W. Ransom, 198–205. London: International Missionary Council and Edinburgh House Press. Note: Address delivered at the International Mission Council meeting at Whitby, Ontario, 1947.

1949

"Editorial: The End Is the Beginning." *Theology Today* 5, no. 4 (January): 461–66.

"When Man Wants to Be God." *Review and Expositor* 46, no. 1 (January): 3–12.

"Editorial: Five Years After." *Theology Today* 6, no. 1 (April): 3–5.

"Editorial: Truth Is a Banner." *Theology Today* 6, no. 2 (July): 145–50.

"More Light on the Church." *Christian Century* 66, no. 30 (July 27): 888–90. Note: An article in the periodical's series on "How My Mind Has Changed in the Last Decade."

"The Grace of Jesus Christ." *Theology Today* 6, no. 3 (October): 297–98. An echo of "Words of Farewell to the Graduating Class." *Princeton Seminary Bulletin* 43, no. 1 (Summer): 12–13. Note: Address delivered to graduates of 1949 on "The grace of our Lord Jesus Christ be with you."

"The Significance of the Amsterdam Assembly." *Princeton Seminary Bulletin* 42, no. 3 (Winter): 7–9. Note: Résumé of address given on September 28, 1948, at the opening of the academic year at Princeton Seminary.

1950

"Editorial: East Asia under God." *Theology Today* 6, no. 4 (January): 429–38.

"Communism and Christianity in East Asia." *Outreach* 4, no. 3 (March): 75–76, 90.

"Editorial: Jesus Lord of Thought." *Theology Today* 7, no. 1 (April): 3–8.

"Ecumenical Presbyterianism." *Presbyterian World* 20, no. 2 (June): 52–56.

"Editorial." *Presbyterian World* 20, no. 2 (June): 49–51. Note: Containing quotations from Mackay on "The Christian Situation in East Asia" at a gathering in New York.

"The Finality of Theological Education." *Bulletin—American Association of Theological Schools* 19 (June): 71–84.

"Editorial: Education in Theology." *Theology Today* 7, no. 2 (July): 145–50.

"Keep Moving Beyond." *Theology Today* 7, no. 3 (October): 299–300.

"Call to Discipleship." In *The Christian Prospect in Eastern Asia, Papers and Minutes of the Eastern Asia Christian Conference, Bangkok, December 3–11, 1949*, 104–13. New York: Friendship Press. Reprinted in *Theology Today* 7, no. 2 (July): 217–27. Note: The closing address delivered at the East Asian Christian Conference, December 11, 1949, on the text "What is that to thee? Follow thou me" (John 21:22 KJV).

"Basic Christianity." *Princeton Seminary Bulletin* 43, no. 3 (Winter): 5–13. Note: Address delivered on September 27, 1949, at the opening of the academic year at Princeton Seminary.

"Splendor in the Abyss." *Princeton Seminary Bulletin* 44, no. 3 (Winter): 5–15. Note: Address delivered on September 26, 1950, at the opening of the academic year at Princeton Seminary.

"Latin America Thirty Years After—The Roman Catholic Reaction." In *The Crisis Decade: A History of Foreign Missionary Work of the Presbyterian Church in the U.S.A. 1937–1947*, edited by W. Reginald Wheeler, 181–84. New York: Board of Foreign Missions of the Presbyterian Church in the U.S.A.

"Preface." *The Christian Message to Islam*, by J. Christy Wilson, 9–10. New York: Fleming H. Revell Co.

1951

"Editorial: Theology, Christ, and the Missionary Obligation." *Theology Today* 7, no. 4 (January): 429–36. Note: An editorial written to prepare journal readers for the IMC Willingen Conference and its theological purpose.

"Our Future as Protestants." *Presbyterian Life* 4, no. 1 (January 6): 8–9, 30; summarized in "Strategy for Protestants," *Time*, January 8, 46–47.

Book Review. " 'Trumpeter of the Lord.' " *John Knox's History of the Reformation in Scotland* by William Croft Dickinson and *John Knox in Controversy* by Hugh Watt, *New York Times Book Review* (Sunday, March 11): 7.

"Editorial: Other Frontiers Call." *Theology Today* 8, no. 1 (April): 3–5.

"Theology in Education." *Christian Century* 68, no. 17 (April 25): 521–23.

"Dr. Mackay Reports on Protestantism in Europe." *Presbyterian World* 21, no. 4 (June): 172.

"Church, State, and Freedom." *Theology Today* 8, no. 2 (July): 218–33; and *Presbyterian World* 21, no. 1 (March): 2–12.

"The President's Page: Cherish the Communion of Saints." *Princeton Seminary Bulletin* 45, no. 1 (Summer): 10–11. Note: Words of farewell to the graduating class of 1951.

Protestant Pilgrimage: A Report on Latin Europe [Philadelphia]. Also published as "Protestant Pilgrimage: A Report on Latin Europe." *Presbyterian Life* 4, no. 23 (November 24): 8–11.

"The Voice of Latin Europe to the Religious Thought of America." *Princeton Seminary Bulletin* 45, no. 3 (Winter): 5–13. Note: Address delivered on September 25, 1951, at the opening of the 140th session of Princeton Seminary.

"Christianity and Other Religions: The Recovery of the Gospels." In *Protestant Thought in the Twentieth Century*, edited by Arnold S. Nash, 273–96. New York: Macmillan.

1952

"Editorial: Ecumenical: The Word and the Concept." *Theology Today* 9, no. 1 (April): 1–6.

"John and Laura Swink. In Memoriam," *Princeton Seminary Bulletin* 45, no. 4 (Spring): 37. Note: Words spoken in Miller Chapel on February 21.

"Religion and Government." *Theology Today* 9, no. 2 (July): 204–22. Note: Address delivered in Constitution Hall, Washington, DC, under the auspices of Protestants and Other Americans United for the Separation of Church and State.

"Willingen 1952." *Presbyterian Outlook* 134, no. 34 (August 25): 5–6. Reprinted in *Outreach* 6, no. 11 (November): 269–70.

"Dr. Samuel M. Zwemer: In Memoriam." *Princeton Seminary Bulletin* 46, no. 2 (October): 25–27. Note: Delivered at First Presbyterian Church of New York City on April 4.

"Make Sure You Believe in the Holy Ghost: Words of Farewell to Class of 1952." *Princeton Seminary Bulletin* 46, no. 2 (October): 11–12.

"Christ's Kingdom—Man's Hope." In *Christ's Kingdom Is Man's Hope,* compiled by Archie R. Crouch in cooperation with the Publications Committee of the 16th Student Volunteer Movement Quadrennial Conference, 18–29. New York: Association Press.

"Foreword." In *Poems*, by Miguel de Unamuno, translated by Eleanor L. Turnbull, vii–ix. Baltimore: Johns Hopkins Press.

"Preface." In *Christ's Hope of the Kingdom*, by Alexander McLeish, iii–iv. London: World Dominion Press.

1953

"The Bible, Book of Destiny." *Princeton Seminary Bulletin* 46, no. 3 (January): 7–12. Note: Address delivered on September 30, 1952, at the opening of the academic year.

"Church Order: Its Meaning and Implications." *Theology Today* 9, no. 4 (January): 450–66. Reprinted as "The Fullness of Christ," in *God's Order.* New York: Macmillan. Note: The article was based on the Croall Lectures delivered in the University of Edinburgh, January 1948.

"Dedication of the Campus Center: The Beginning of a Community Adventure." *Princeton Seminary Bulletin* 46, no. 3 (January): 15–17. Note: Address delivered on October 14, 1952, at the service of dedication for the Campus Center.

"The Great Commission and the Church Today." In *Missions under the Cross*, edited by Norman Goodall, 129–41. London: Edinburgh House Press; distributed in the U.S.A. by Friendship Press, New York. Note: Address delivered in July 1952 at Willingen on the conference theme "The Missionary Obligation of the Church," at the enlarged meeting of the Committee of the International Missionary Council.

"The New Idolatry." *Christianity and Crisis* 13, no. 12 (July 6): 93–95; also *Theology Today* 10, no. 3 (October): 382–83. Note: Statement issued at a meeting of the General Assembly of the Presbyterian Church in Minneapolis in May 1953 after Mackay's election as moderator.

"Words of Farewell to the New Graduates." *Princeton Seminary Bulletin* 47, no. 2 (October): 12–13. Note: Address on the theme "Seek a Shepherd's Heart" at the close of the academic year 1952–1953.

"Foreword." In *Christ—The Hope of Asia.* Papers and Minutes of the Ecumenical Study Conference for East Asia, Lucknow, India, December 27–30. Madras: Christian Literature Society.

1954

"Editorial: Our Aims." *Theology Today* 10, no. 4 (January): 447–55.

"Portent and Promise in the Other America." *Princeton Seminary Bulletin* 47, no. 3 (January): 7–16. Note: Address delivered September 29, 1953, at the opening of the academic year.

"Report to the Church." *Presbyterian Life* 7, no. 10 (May 15): 11–12, 34–35.

"God's Servant, the Church." Opening sermon before the 166th General Assembly, Presbyterian Church in the U.S.A., Masonic Auditorium, Detroit, May 20. Note: Given by Mackay as retiring moderator of the 165th General Assembly.

"New Frontiers in the Life of the Church." *Theology Today* 11, no. 2 (July): 250–68. Note: Address delivered at Columbia University, New York, April 1, in connection with the Bicentennial Celebration of the founding of the university.

"Be Aglow with the Spirit: Words of Farewell to the New Graduates." *Princeton Seminary Bulletin* 48, no. 2 (October): 15–16. Note: To the graduates of the class of 1954 on Romans 12:11.

"The Witness of the Reformed Churches in the World Today." *Theology Today* 11, no. 3 (October): 373–84. Reprinted in *Presbyterian World* 22, nos. 7–8 (September–December): 291–302. Note: Opening address delivered at the Seventeenth General Council of the World Presbyterian Alliance in Princeton, New Jersey, July 27.

1955

"The Glory and Peril of the Local: A Footnote to Ecumenical Discussion." *Princeton Seminary Bulletin* 48, no. 3 (January): 5–13. Note: Address delivered in the fall of 1954 at the opening of the 143rd session of Princeton Seminary.

"Editorial: Christian Faith and the International Situation." *Theology Today* 12, no. 1 (April): 1–4.

"The Marian Cult in Relation to the Lordship of Christ and the Unity of the Church." *Presbyterian Life* 8, no. 12 (June 11): 17–18, 37. Reprinted as "The Marian Cult." *Presbyterian World* 23, no. 4 (December): 146–52.

"John R. Mott: Apostle of the Oecumenical Era." *International Review of Missions* 44, no. 3 (July): 331–38.

"Between the Politicians and the Atomic Scientists." *British Weekly* 136, no. 3589 (August 25): 1–2.

"The Seminary's Library Project—A Statement by the President of the Seminary." *Princeton Seminary Bulletin* 49, no. 2 (October): 30–34. Note: Statement at a public meeting on June 2, 1955, in the Campus Center addressing the Princeton Borough Council and community leaders regarding library construction.

"You, Too, Make Your Bundle of Sticks: Words of Farewell to the New Graduates." *Princeton Seminary Bulletin* 49, no. 2 (October): 3–5.

"Thy Peace, O Christ, and Not Another's." *Christianity and Crisis* 15, no. 21 (December 12): 161–62.

Letter to the Editor, *New York Times*, December 29, 22. Note: Letter regarding the Princeton Seminary library project.

"Foreword." In *The Virgin Mary: The Roman Catholic Marian Doctrine* by Giovanni Miegge. Translated by Waldo Smith. Philadelphia: Westminster Press.

"Introduction: Spain's Quest for Freedom." In *The Oppression of Protestants in Spain*, by Jacques Delpech. Translated by Tom and Dolores Johnson, with preface by Howard Schomer, 3–16. Boston: Beacon Press.

"Unamuno, Miguel de." In *Twentieth-Century Encyclopedia of Religious Knowledge*, vol. 2, 1129–130. Grand Rapids: Baker.

1956

"Some Questions regarding Theological Education: With Special Reference to Princeton Seminary." *Princeton Seminary Bulletin* 49, no. 3 (January): 3–12. Note: Address delivered September 27, 1955, at the opening of the academic year.

"Editorial: Christ Is Risen—For What?" *Theology Today* 13, no. 1 (April): 1–6.

"Editorial: An Ecumenical Era Calls for Missionary Action." *Theology Today* 13, no. 2 (July): 141–44.

"The Confessional Resurgence and the Ecumenical Movement." *Reformed and Presbyterian World* 24, no. 3 (September): 104–11. Note: Presents ideas and thoughts central to the deliberations of the Executive Committee of the Alliance at its meeting in Prague, August 1956.

"Editorial: Bonn 1930—and After: A Lyrical Tribute to Karl Barth." *Theology Today* 13, no. 3 (October): 287–94.

"Let Love Be Your Only Debt: Words of Farewell to the New Graduates by the President of the Seminary." *Princeton Seminary Bulletin* 50, no. 2 (October): 11–13.

"Introduction." In *A Man Sent from God: A Biography of Robert E. Speer*, by W. Reginald Wheeler, 9–11. Westwood, NJ: Fleming H. Revell Co.

"John Baillie: A Lyrical Tribute and Appraisal." *Scottish Journal of Theology* 9, no. 3: 225–35.

"Miguel de Unamuno." In *Christianity and the Existentialists*, edited by Carl Michalson, 43–58. New York: Charles Scribner's Sons.

1957

"Religious Concern and Christian Commitment." *Princeton Seminary Bulletin* 50, no. 3 (February): 3–14. Note: Address delivered on September 25, 1956, at the opening of the academic year.

"The Eternal Imperative in a World of Change." *Theology Today* 14, no. 1 (April): 89–105. Note: An address to a recent meeting of the National Council of Churches.

"Cultivate the Real Presence: Words of Farewell to the New Graduates by the President of the Seminary." *Princeton Seminary Bulletin* 51, no. 2 (October), 9–10.

"Editorial: The Lordship of Christ in the Soul." *Theology Today* 14, no. 3 (October): 309–14.

1958

"The Form of a Servant, the Restoration of a Lost Image." *Princeton Seminary Bulletin* 51, no. 3 (January): 3–12. Reprinted in *Princeton Seminary Bulletin* 10, no. 3, n. s. (1989): 182–92. Note: Address delivered September 24, 1957, at the opening of the academic year.

"The Christian Mission at This Hour." *Theology Today* 15, no. 1 (April): 15–35; *Princeton Seminary Bulletin* 51, no. 4 (May): 3–18. Note: An address delivered at the opening of the Ghana Assembly of the International Missionary Council, December 28, 1957.

"Make Every Thought Christ's Captive: Words of Farewell to the New Graduates by the President of the Seminary." *Princeton Seminary Bulletin* 52, no. 2 (October): 8–9.

"Commission on Ecumenical Mission and Relations: The United Presbyterian Church in the United States of America: An Interpretation." New York. Reprinted in W. Stanley Rycroft, *The Ecumenical Witness of the United Presbyterian Church in the U.S.A.* [Philadelphia]: Board of Christian Education of the United Presbyterian Church in the U.S.A., 1968, 267–70. Note: An explanation of the proposed name for the body resulting from the merger of two Boards of Foreign Missions and three agencies dealing with Ecumenical Relations.

Protestantism and the Modern World. New York: National Council of Churches.

1959

"Theological Triennium: For What?" *Princeton Seminary Bulletin* 52, no. 3 (January): 5–14. Note: Address delivered on September 30, 1958, at the opening of the academic year.

"Editorial." *Reformed and Presbyterian World* 25, no. 5 (March): 193–95. Note: About the form of a servant.

"Editorial: Christianity's Essential Image." *Theology Today* 16, no. 2 (July): 143–48. Note: Regarding the servant Lord and the servant people.
"Shepherds and Crusaders: The 1959 Commencement Address." *Western Watch* 10, no. 3 (September 15): 3–11. Note: Commencement address delivered at Western Theological Seminary, Pittsburgh, following approval of the consolidation of Western with Pittsburgh-Xenia by the General Assembly in Indianapolis, May 22.
"Keep Moving Beyond." *Theology Today* 16, no. 3 (October): 317–18.
"Let Us Commence Together: Words of Farewell to the New Graduates by the President of the Seminary." *Princeton Seminary Bulletin* 53, no. 2 (October): 9–12.
"A Tribute to Walter Freytag." In *Basileia, Tribute to Walter Freytag*, edited by Jan Hermelink and Hans Jochen Margull, 13–14. Stuttgart: Evang. Missionsverlag.

1960

"The Other Side of the 'Catholic Issue.'" *U.S. News & World Report*, July 4, 48–51.
"The Restoration of Piety: Charge to President James I. McCord." *Princeton Seminary Bulletin* 54, no. 1 (July): 48–51. Note: Delivered March 29, 1960, at Princeton University Chapel at the inauguration of James Iley McCord as president of Princeton Theological Seminary.
Book Review. *The Riddle of Roman Catholicism* by Jaroslav Pelican. In *Theology Today* 17, no. 3 (October): 386–89.
"Let Us Remember God." In *Sao Paulo Story, Proceedings of the Eighteenth General Council of the Alliance of the Reformed Churches throughout the World Holding the Presbyterian Order*, edited by Marcel Pradervand, 166–75. Geneva: Alliance Offices.
"A New Chapter in Church History." In *Sao Paulo Story, Proceedings of the Eighteenth General Council of the Alliance of the Reformed Churches throughout the World Holding the Presbyterian Order*, edited by Marcel Pradervand, 9–12. Geneva: Alliance Offices.

1961

"Cuba in Perspective." *Presbyterian Life* 14, no. 14 (July 15): 16–18, 31–32.

1962

"Witherspoon of Paisley and Princeton." *Theology Today* 18, no. 4 (January): 473–81. Note: Address delivered at the Act of United Thanksgiving and Witness held in Usher Hall, Edinburgh, on October 13, 1960, in connection with the Four Hundredth Anniversary of the Scottish Reformation.
"Reflections on the World Confessional Issue." *Reformed and Presbyterian World* 27, no. 1 (March): 15–21.
Book Review, "The Cleric of Clericalism." *The Cardinal Spellman Story*, by Robert I. Gannon, SJ, *Christianity Today* 6, no. 20 (July 6): 42.

1963

"Roman Catholicism in the Pangs of Rebirth." *Presbyterian Outlook* 45, no. 6 (February 11): 6–7.
"Editorial: Mystic Guerillas—A Challenge to the Church." *Presbyterian Outlook* 145, no. 35 (October 7): 8
"Archibald Alexander: Founding Father." In *Sons of the Prophets*, edited by Hugh T. Kerr, 3–21. Princeton, NJ: Princeton University Press.

The Latin American Churches and the Ecumenical Movement. New York: Committee on Cooperation in Latin America, Division of Foreign Missions, National Council of the Churches of Christ in the U.S.A.

"Religion and Government in the World of Today." *Review and Expositor* 60, no. 3: 277–86.

1964

"Which Way Ahead?" *Theology Today* 20, no. 4 (January): 541–43.

"Cuba Revisited." *Christian Century* 81, no. 7 (February 12): 203.

"Those Who Imprison Truth." *The Churchman* (June): 9–10.

"A Fresh Look at Cuba." *Christian Century* 81, no. 32 (August 5): 983–87.

"What Is Life?" *Theology Today* 21, no. 3 (October): 272–73. Reprinted as "Prologue," in *His Life and Our Life*, by John A. Mackey, 9–14. Philadelphia: Westminster Press, 1964.

"Charles Clayton Morrison at Ninety." *Christian Century* 81, no. 49 (December 2): 1487.

1965

"The Problem of Freedom within the Church." Review of *Light in the North: The Story of the Scottish Covenanters*, by J. D. Douglas, *Christianity Today* 9, no. 15 (April 23): 33.

"Reappraisal Urged of U.S. Foreign Policy." *New York Times*, Sunday, November 14, 11. Note: Letter to the editor expressing personal opposition to the war in Vietnam.

"Latin America and Revolution—I. The New Mood in Society and Culture." *Christian Century* 82, no. 46 (November 17): 1409–412.

"Latin America and Revolution—II. The New Mood in the Churches." *Christian Century* 82, no. 47 (November 24): 1439–443.

"When Truth Is a Belt." *Princeton Seminary Bulletin* 59, no. 1 (November): 4–14. Note: Commencement address delivered June 7, 1965, to the class of 1965 at the time of Mackay's 50th reunion from his own graduation from Princeton Seminary.

"Commendation and Concern." *Presbyterian Outlook* 147, no. 45 (December 13): 5–7.

The Spiritual Spectrum of Latin America. New York: Latin American Department, Division of Overseas Ministries, National Council of the Churches of Christ in the U.S.A.

1966

"What the Ecumenical Movement Can Learn from Conservative Evangelicals." *Christianity Today* 10, no. 17 (May 27): 17, 20–23.

"A Representative American of the Sixties: James Joseph Reeb." *Princeton Seminary Bulletin* 60, no. 1 (October): 33–39. Note: Principal address of Alumni Day, June 5.

1967

"The Two Dimensions of Christian Living: Part 1: 'Creative Communion with God.'" *Presbyterian Life* 20, no. 9 (May 1): 12–14, 38–39.

"The Two Dimensions of Christian Living: Part 2: 'Creative Concern for Men.'" *Presbyterian Life* 20, no. 10 (May 15): 10–11, 36–39.

"Robert Elliot Speer: A Man of Yesterday Today." *Princeton Seminary Bulletin* 60, no. 3 (June): 11–21. Note: Address delivered at a special meeting held during the General Assembly of the United Presbyterian Church U.S.A. in Portland, Oregon, May 17, to celebrate the centennial of the birth of Robert Elliot Speer.

"Historical Perspectives of Protestantism." In *Integration of Man and Society in Latin America*, edited by Samuel Shapiro, 170–90. Notre Dame, IN: University of Notre Dame Press.

1968

"The Ecumenical Movement—Whence? And Whither?" *Bulletin of the Department of Theology of the World Alliance of Reformed Churches* 8, no. 4 (Summer): 1–8.

1969

"Ecumenicalism: Threat to Christian Unity?" *Christianity Today* 13, no. 24 (September 12): 11–12.

1970

"Life's Chief Discoveries: Reminiscences of an Octogenarian." *Christianity Today* 14, no. 7 (January 2): 3–5.

1971

"Toward an Evangelical Renaissance." *Christianity Today* 16, no. 9 (February 4): 6–8. Reprinted in *Princeton Seminary Bulletin* 64, no. 3 (December): 93–95.

"The Great Adventure." *Princeton Seminary Bulletin* 64, no. 2 (July): 31–38. Note: Sermon delivered on May 30, 1971, at the baccalaureate service of the 159th commencement of Princeton Theological Seminary in the First Presbyterian Church in Princeton, New Jersey.

1972

"Thoughts on Christian Unity." *Christianity Today* 16, no. 14 (April 14): 10–12. Note: The article explains why the COCU approach falls short.

"Let Us Remember." *Princeton Seminary Bulletin* 65, no. 1 (July): 25–32. Note: Delivered on Alumni Day 1972 at the traditional memorial service.

1974

"Let the Church Be the Church." *Presbyterian Layman* 7, no. 9 (November–December): 8. Note: Interview conducted on September 25, 1974, by George M. Booker.

1976

"The Books That Shape Lives." *Christian Century* 93, no. 13 (April 14): 371.

1978

"Influences on My Life." *Journal of Presbyterian History* 56, no. 1 (Spring): 20–34. Note: Interview conducted by Gerald W. Gillette.

1979

"The Soul and Heart of Belief." in *Protestantism: A Concise Survey of Protestantism and Its Influence on American Religious and Social Traditions*, edited by Hugh T. Kerr, 21–31. Woodbury, NY: Barron's Educational Series. Note: An excerpt from his essay "Protestantism," in Jurji, *Great Religions of the Modern World*.

Spanish and Portuguese Publications

I. Books

1919

Don Miguel de Unamuno: Su Personalidad, Obra e Influencia. Lima: Casa Editora de Ernesto R. Villaran.

1927

Más Yo Os Digo. Buenos Aires: Editorial Mundo Nuevo; la Federación Sudamericana de Asociaciónes Cristianas de Jovenes.

1931

El Sentido de la Vida, Pláticas a la Juventud. Montevideo: Editorial Mundo Nuevo.

1946

O Sentido da Vida, 3.ª Edição. Tradução de João del Nero. São Paulo: Livraria Liberdade.

Prefacio a la Teologia Cristiana [Versión de G. Baez–Camargo]. México, D.F.: Casa Unida de Publicaciones.

1952

El Otro Cristo Español: un Estudio de la Historia Espiritual de España e Hispanoamérica [Versión de Gonzalo Báez–Camargo]. México, D.F.: Casa Unida de Publicaciones.

1959

A Ordem de Deus e a Desordem do Homen: A Epístola aos Efésios e a Época Atual [tradução revista por Theodomiro Emerique e Jorge Cesar Mota]. São Paulo: União Cristã de Estudantes do Brasil.

1964

El Orden de Dios y el Desorden del Hombre: la Epístola a los Efesios y este tiempo presente [translado al castellano por Alberto Rembao]. México, D.F.: Casa Unida de Publicaciones.

1970

El Sentido Presbiteriano de la Vida: lo que Significa Vivir y Adorar Como Presbiteriano. Pbro. Abel Clemente, traductor. Englewood Cliffs, NJ: Prentice-Hall.

Realidad e Idolatria en el Cristianismo Contemporaneo. Buenos Aires: Editorial y Libreris La Aurora SRL. Note: The 1953 Carnahan Lectures delivered at the Facultad Evangélica de Teología in Buenos Aires, Argentina.

II. Articles and Editorials

1918

"Dos Apóstoles de la Democracia, Woodrow Wilson y Lloyd George." *Mercurio Peruano* 1, no. 5 (May): 255–60.

1919

"El Valor Cultural del Estudio de la Literatura Inglesa." *Mercurio Peruano* 2, no. 11 (May): 354–60.
"Wordsworth y la Escuela Laquista." *Mercurio Peruano* 3, no. 15 (September): 178–93.

1920

"La Vida Estudiantil en una Universidad Americana." *Verbum* 14, no. 55, (August–September), [370]–378; traducido por D. Acosta, de *Student World.*

1921

La Profesión de Hombre. Lima: Biblioteca del Mercurio Peruano. Reprinted in *Mercurio Peruano* 2, nos. 33, 34 (March–April): 180–200.
"Renacimiento." *Nueva Democracia* 2, no. 7 (July):18–20, 31–32.

1923

"Intelectuales de Panteon." *Claridad: Organo de la Juventud Libre Del Peru* 1, no. 1 (May): 6–7.
Los Intelectuales y los Nuevos Tiempos, Conferencia Pronunciada por el Dr. Juan A. Mackay en el Teatro de Cajamarca. Lima: Libreria e Imprenta "El Inca."

1925

"Libertad Espiritual." *Nueva Democracia* 6, no. 4 (April): 29–30.
"In Memoriam." *Mercurio Peruano* 15, nos. 89–90 (November–December): 430–31.

1927

"Andanzas Por Chile." *El Triangulo* 7, nos. 44–45 (May–June): 4–7.
"La Religión en Relación con la Vida Contemporánea e Individual." *Nueva Democracia* 8, no. 6 (June): 20–21, 28–29.
"Los Nuevos Tiempos," *Alma Latina (Publicación mensual editada por la Liga Metodista de Jóvenes)* 1, no. 12 (June): 3–4.
"La Desaparición del Panamericanismo y Qué Viene Después." *Nueva Democracia* 8, no. 8 (August): 3–5.
"A los Alumnos del Colegio Anglo-Peruano." *Leader* 2, no. 9 (November–December): 2–3.
¿Existe Relación Entre La Asociación Cristiana de Jóvenes y la Religión? Montevideo.
La Filosofia del Triangulo Rojo. Montevideo.

1928

"Nuestra Religion." *El Heraldo de La Asociacion Cristiana de Jovenes* 1, no. 4, (July): 1, 4–5.
"Eureka." *Nueva Democracia* 9, no. 12 (December): 14, 16, 27, 30–31.

1929

"¿Quién es mi Prójimo?" *Nueva Democracia* 10, no. 8 (August): 5–6, 32.
"Después de cuatro años." *Leader* 4, no. 3 (September–October): 345–46.
"En Torno al Progreso." *Nueva Democracia* 10, no. 11 (November): 18, 30.
"El Cristo de los Místicos Españoles." *Nueva Democracia* 10, no. 12 (December): 16–17, 30.
La Juventud Estudiantil: Primeras Indicaciones que se Ofrecen sobre este Tema a los Delegados al Congreso Hispano–Americano de la Habana para su Examen y Discusión. Montevideo, Uruguay. Reprinted from *Heraldo Cristiano* (Havana).

1930

"Dios es Amore." *Nueva Democracia* 11, no. 12 (December): 9–10, 28.

A los Pies del Maestro. Montevideo: Editorial "Mundo Nuevo."

1931

"Nuevas Orientaciones Religiosas." *Nueva Democracia* 12, no. 1 (January): 8–9, 25.

"Iglesia y Juventud." *Nueva Democracia* 12, no. 2 (February): 14–15, 18–19.

1932

"A Resposta Cristã ao Secularismo" and "O Novo Reino" in *"O Cristo Vivo" Relatório Oficial da 11.ª Convenção Mundial de Escolas Dominicais, Rio de Janeiro, 25 a 31 de Julho de 1932.* Redator de Volume em Português, Rev. Galdino Moreira, 130–33 and 133–37. Rio de Janeiro: Editado pelo Conselho Evangélico de Educação Religiosa do Brasil.

1933

"Semblanzas Americanas, Victor Raúl Haya de la Torre." *Nueva Democracia* 14, no. 5 (May): 15–16.

1934

"Editorial: Pensando a lo Vertical." *Nueva Democracia* 15, no. 1 (January): 11, 32.

"Editorial: La Escala Mística de la Salud." *Nueva Democracia* 15, no. 2 (February): 11, 31–32.

"Editorial: Pensamientos del Monte." *Nueva Democracia* 15, no. 3 (March): 11, 32.

"Editorial: Yo Necesito Creer." *Nueva Democracia* 15, no. 4 (April): 11, 26.

"Editorial: La Religión y la Vida." *Nueva Democracia* 15, no. 6 (June): 11, 31.

"Editorial: Hacia la Restauración de la Reverencia." *Nueva Democracia* 15, no. 7 (July): 11, 30–32.

1935

"Cumbres y Cavernas Latinoamericanas." *Nueva Democracia* 16, no. 6 (June): 13–15.

"Cráteres que Humean." *Nueva Democracia* 16, no. 9 (September): 22–24.

1937

"Metafísica es Menos que Teología." *Nueva Democracia* 18, no. 9 (September): 17–18. Reprinted *Puerto Rico Evangelico* (September): 5–6, 9.

1939

A Verdade que Liberta os Homens. Vertido para o português pelo Rev. Prof. Antônio de Campos Gonçalves. Rio de Janeiro: Sociedade Bíblica Americana.

La Verdad que hace Libres a los Hombres. Traducido por José Marcial–Dorado. La Rio de Janeiro: Sociedad Bíblica Americana.

1942

"La Iglesia de Cristo en Llamas." *Heraldo Cristiano* (Havana) 10, no. 4 (July): 4, 24.

1944

"La Cultura y el Protestantismo." *Heraldo Cristiano* (Havana) 13, no. 10: 2–3; *Vanguardia Juvenil* 3, nos. 11, 12: 10–11, 16.

"La Realidad Suprema." *Boletin Centroamericano* 9, no. 94; 15.

1945

"El Crepusculo de la Cultura." *Puerto Rico Evangélico* 34, no. 22 (May 25): 16.
"Naturaleza y Función de la Biblia." *La Voz Menonita* 14, no. 4: 68–70; *El Faro* 60, no. 17: 1, 18–19.

1948

"La Cultura en la América Latina." *Nueva Democracia* 28, no. 1 (January): 18–21.

1950

"Cristianismo Básico." *El Predicador Evangélico*, 8, no. 29 (July–September): 13–21.
"La Restauracion de la Teologia." *Cuadernos Teológicos de el Predicador Evangélico*, no. 1, primer semestre, 6–14.

1951

"Talk on the 400th Centenary of San Marcos University–Lima." In *Anales de la Universidad* (Annals of the University), no. 6, 1088–091. Lima: Universidad Nacional Mayor de San Marcos.

1952

"Al Encuentro de la Verdad." *Nueva Democracia*, 32, no. 4 (October): 22–23.
"La Gracia en Función de Fuerza y Belleza." *El Evangelisto Cubano* 46, no. 6: 2.

1953

"La Esencia del Protestantismo." *Nueva Democracia* 33, no. 1 (January): 64–71.
"Sentido Ultimo de la Revelación." *Nueva Democracia* 33, no. 2 (April): 20–21.
"Uno u Otro Fuego." *Testimonium* 1, no. 2 (June): 5–11.
"La Restauracion de la Teologia." *Testimonium* 1, no. 4 (December): 16–25.
"La Función Divina de la Biblia." *Heraldo Cristiano* (Havana) 21, no. 4: 16.

1954

"La Iglesia y el Orden Social." *Nueva Democracia* 34, no. 1 (January): 18–21.
"Teoría de la Retrospección." *Nueva Democracia* 34, no. 2 (April): 14–15.
"La Nueva Idolatría." *Nueva Democracia* 34, no. 3 (July): 16–17.
"De la Iglesia Una y Vera." *Nueva Democracia* 34, no. 4 (October): 42–43.

1955

"Las Realidades Centrales de la Vida." *Nueva Democracia* 35, no. 2 (April): 14–17.

1957

"Libertad de Conciencia y Libertad Religiosa." *Nueva Democracia* 37, no. 4 (October): 3–7.

1958

"Presença e dor do Forasteiro." *Únitas* 20, no. 7 (July): 49–52.
"Definición de la Libertad Religiosa." *El Centinela* 62, no. 9: 4–5.

1963

"Alberto Rembao: Alma Ecumenica," *Nueva Democracia* [43, no. 1] (January): 26–29.

1984

"Letter De J. A. Mackay a José Carlos Mariátegui, Montevideo, 6 de marzo de 1929." In Mariátegui, José Carlos, *Correspondencia (1915–1930)*, vol. 2, 524. Lima: Empresa Editora Amauta.

Other Non-English Publications

1953

"Der Missionsbefehl und die christliche Kirche heute." *Deutsche Evangelische Weltmission Jahrbuch*, 3–12.

1954

"Le Témoignage Des Églises Réformées dans le Monde d'Aujourd'hui." *Les Cahiers Protestants* 38, no. 6 (November–December): 321–36.

1956

"Das Wiedererstarken der Konfessionen und die ökumenische Bewegung." *Ökumenische Rundschau* 5, no. 4 (December): 136–41.

1961

Shimobe no katachi [The suffering servant and other sermons. Japanese.]. Translated by Keiko Obara and Yoshiko Watari. Tokyo: Kyōbunkan.

Index

Britain
   diplomatic recognition of communist
      China by, 285–86
   Mackay's furlough trip (1930) to, 154,
      188–90
   YWCA in, 195
British and Foreign Bible Society, 74
British Royal Institute of International
   Affairs, 276, 429n81
Broadening Church, The (Loetscher), 247
Brown, Arthur Judson, 174, 305, 402n87
Browne, Vere Rochelle, 103, 106, 108, 110,
   119, 121, *123*
Brownell, Herbert, 291–92
Browning, Webster E.
   Argentina's educational system and, 77
   on Belaúnde and political situation in
      Peru, 111–12
   as colleague of Mackay generally, xvii
   Instituto Ingles and, 72, 77, 136,
      386n17
   Lancasterian system of education and,
      136
   on Mackay, 208
   Montevideo Congresses (1925) and,
      136–37, 139, 145
   photograph of, *72*
   Presbyterian Board of Foreign Missions
      and, 72, 218
Bruce, Robert, 5
Brude, King, 4
Brum, Baltasar, 111, 139
Brunner, Emil, 183, 191, 195, 201, 242–44,
   416–17n43
Bryan, William Jennings, 53
Bryce, James, Viscount Bryce, 110, 113
Bubonic plague, 62
Buchanan, John G., 258
Buck, John Lossing, 307
Buck, Pearl S., 213, 214, 217, 218, 410n46,
   410n48
Buddha, 172, 322, 410n46
Buddhism, 169, 172, 320, 322
Buenos Aires. *See* Argentina
Buenos Aires Conference (1949), 331, 352
Bultmann, Rudolf, 191, 249
Bunge, Carlos Octavio, 143
Bunyan, John, 6, 257, 461n147
Burleigh, John H. S., 351
Burma, 212
Burnet, Gilbert, Bishop of Salisbury, 5
Burns, Robert, 4, 380n28

Burrell, D. J., 50
Bustamante, 150

Cailliet, Emile, 246–47, *246*, 255
Caird, Edward, 37
Caird, Helen, 37
Cairns, David S., 20, 35, 37, 38, 175
Cajamarca Mission, 116–18, 128–31, 132
Calhoun, Robert, 260
Calles, Plutarco Elías, 179, 198–99, 220
"The Calling of the Church to Mission and
   to Unity" (WCC), 312–13
Caloca Cortés, St. Agustín, 403n120
Calvert, Samuel, xvii
Calvin, John, 39, 283, 344, 432n128
Camacho, Manuel, 94–95
Cameron, Rev. Prof. J. Kennedy, 109, 117,
   394n41
Cameron, Kenneth, 150–52
Cameron, Tom, 19–20, 103
Campbell, J. Y., 18
Carey, William, 34, 326
Caribbean, 168–69, 178, 179
Carlisle, Lord Bishop of (John William
   Diggle), 31
Carlyle, Thomas, 18
Castro, Fidel, 353
Catholic Inter-American Cooperation Pro-
   gram (CICOP), 356–57
Cavert, Inez M., 431n113
Cavert, Samuel McCrae, 270, 271, 278–79,
   287, 311
Chalmers, Thomas, 7, 289
"changing and changeless," xiii
Chaos in Mexico (Macfarland), 412n74
charismatic movement, 367–69, 374. *See
   also* Pentecostalism
Charles I, King of England, 5
Charles II, King of England, 5
Chávez, Moisés, 352–53
Chicago, 155, 188, 206, 208
Chik, Han Kyung, 320
Childs, Brevard, 252
Chile
   border dispute between Peru and, 129, 161
   Browning in, 72
   churches in, 72
   Instituto Ingles in, 77, 79–80, 136, 185,
      386n17
   Mackay's fact-finding trip to, 71–73
   Mackay's travels and lectures in, 125,
      126, 159, 182, 185, 223, 355

finances of, 150
founding of, 66
library at, 147
Mackay as speaker and professor at, xii,
60, 100, 109, 111, 113, 147–48
Mackay's departure from, 150
Mackay's doctorate degree from, 75, 100,
104–5, 111
Pardo as rector of, 66
physical education at, 147
Santiago. *See* Chile
Santos, Dr., 167, 397n103
Sayre, Francis, 300–301, 439–40n229
scaffolding, 370, 459n111
Schleiermacher, Friedrich Daniel Ernst, 191,
192
Schlunk, Martin, 170, 401n64
Schönburg-Waldenburg, Prince Günther
von, 194
schools. *See* education; *and specific schools
and universities*
Schulz, Sofia Maria, 64
Schweitzer, Albert, 166, 192–93, 203,
400n45
Scotland
Communion season in, 10–11, 14
Fourth Centenary of Scottish Reforma-
tion, 351
history of, 4–7
Mackay clan in, 5–6
Mackays' furlough trips to (1922 and
1929–30), xii, 118–20, 182–84, 188–89
Mackay's secondary education in, 16–18
Mackay's travel to, in 1960, 351
Mackay's youth in, 3–18
Reformation in, 6–7
See also University of Aberdeen
Scott, Mr., 62
Scott, Sir Walter, 5
Scottish Churches' Missionary Campaign,
119–20
secularism
Brunner on, 201
and ecumenism in 1960s, 370–71
Jerusalem Missionary Council (1928) on,
169, 171, 173, 174
Mackay on, 225, 290–91, 301, 345,
361–62
meanings of term, 358
mission theology and, 169
Roman Catholic Church on, 287
Secular Humanism and, 436n181

"The Secularization of God" (Mackay),
380n18
Segura, Pedro Cardinal, 277, 284, 433n140
separation of church and state. *See* state-
church relations
Sermon on the Mount, 180, 203, 319
Servant Lord and His Servant People, The,
335
Seventh-Day Adventists, 66–67, 68, 94–95,
186
Shaull, Richard, 369, 371, 459n122
Sheen, Bishop Fulton J., 274
Sheil, Bishop Bernard J., 437n195
Sherrill, Bishop Henry Knox, 287, 288
Shiels, Fr. W. Eugene, 430n104
Shintoism, 172
Shook, Velma L., 306
Shuster, George N., 430n104
Sibley, Mrs. Harper, 214
Silva Henríquez, Raúl Cardinal, 355
Simonds, E. J., 206
sin, 194, 195
Sinclair, Kate, *150*
Sinclair, Walter, 40, 53, 128–29, *150*, 151,
151
Six Pillars of Peace, 272–73, 427n56
Smith, Fr. E. Harold, 430n104
Smith, John Coventry, 368
SNTS. *See* Studiorum Novi Testament Soci-
etas (SNTS)
social activism, 341, 349, 358–61, 364, 372,
373, 456–57n74, 457n76
social gospel, 357–58, 454n36
Social Progress, 274
Soderblom, Archbishop Nathan, 135
Song of Songs, 15, 25
Soper, Anne, xvii, 131–33, *132*, 187,
386n11
Soper, William, 187
South Africa, 334
South America
Bryce on absence of religious foundation
for, 110, 113
Christian university needed in, 78,
79–80
corruption in politics of, 77
Edinburgh Mission Conference (1910)
and, 85–86, 88
education reform in, 110, 182
Free Church missions in, 40, 43, 50, 54,
57, 59–60
infidelity and immorality in, 77, 88